P9-ECL-598

MAGILL'S
SURVEY
OF
CINEMA

MAGILL'S
SURVEY
OF
CINEMA

English Language Films

FIRST SERIES
VOLUME 2
EAS-LON

Edited by

FRANK N. MAGILL

Associate Editors

PATRICIA KING HANSON

STEPHEN L. HANSON

SALEM PRESS
Englewood Cliffs, N.J.

LIBRARY OF CONGRESS CATALOG CARD NUMBER: 80-52131

Complete Set: ISBN 0-89356-225-4
Volume 2:   ISBN 0-89356-227-0

PRINTED IN THE UNITED STATES OF AMERICA

LIST OF TITLES IN VOLUME TWO

MAGILL'S
SURVEY
OF
CINEMA

EASTER PARADE

Released: 1948
Production: Arthur Freed for Metro-Goldwyn-Mayer
Direction: Charles Walters
Screenplay: Sidney Sheldon, Frances Goodrich, and Albert Hackett; based
    on a screen story by Frances Goodrich and Albert Hackett
Cinematography: Harry Stradling
Editing: Albert Akst
Music: Johnny Green and Roger Edens (AA)
Song: Irving Berlin
Running time: 103 minutes

      Principal characters:
      Hannah Brown .... Judy Garland
      Don Hewes .... Fred Astaire
      Nadine Hale .... Ann Miller
      Jonathan Harrow III (Johnny) .... Peter Lawford

If *Easter Parade* were not one of the brightest and most enjoyable musicals of the 1940's, it would still be memorable as the only film in which Judy Garland and Fred Astaire performed together. However, in addition to the happy pairing of two of the screen's finest entertainers, the film offers the music of Irving Berlin and the contributions of the talented members of M-G-M's top musical production unit. The result is a film of great style, energy, and humor which offers a wide variety of musical numbers and performing styles.

The plot of *Easter Parade* consists essentially of a backstage romance set in the days of vaudeville. Don Hewes (Fred Astaire) learns that his dancing partner, Nadine Hale (Ann Miller), intends to leave their act to star in a Broadway musical. He attempts to change her mind by singing the romantic ballad "It Only Happens When I Dance with You," but Nadine is adamant. Don leaves angrily and has dinner with his friend Jonathan Harrow III (Peter Lawford) at a small cafe where a floorshow is in progress. Hurt by Nadine's rejection, Don tells Johnny he could take any girl out of the show's chorus line and make her as successful as Nadine. The girl he chooses is Hannah Brown (Judy Garland), who at first takes Don's offer of a job as his dancing partner as a joke. Upon learning who he is, however, Hannah quits her job and reports to Don's rehearsal hall the next morning.

Don soon realizes that Hannah is ill-equipped to fill Nadine's shoes, but he persists in his attempts to pattern her style and personality after his former partner's. The resulting act is a fiasco. Stung by his failure and by Nadine's accusation that Hannah is only an unsuccessful copy of her, Don at last understands the mistake he has made. He changes their act to suit Hannah's talents and the two become a great success. By this time, however, romantic complications have arisen: Johnny has fallen in love with Hannah, and Hannah with Don. Don continues to regard her as no more than a dancing partner, however, and she interprets his rivalry with Nadine as love.

Don turns down an offer from the Ziegfeld Follies when he learns that Nadine is the show's star, but he and Hannah are soon offered a show of their own. Hannah finally confronts Don with her feelings for him. They kiss and Don realizes that he has been in love with Hannah all along. Their show opens and is a tremendous hit. Don performs a snappy, stylish dance solo, "Steppin' Out with My Baby," while Hannah watches with delight from the wings. The two then join forces, dressed in tramp costumes, for "A Couple of Swells," and the audience cheers its approval. Now that their personal and professional lives are in harmony, it seems that nothing can stand in their way.

Nothing, that is, except Nadine. To celebrate their opening, Don takes Hannah to see Nadine's show, and the applause which greets their entrance angers Nadine. She invites Don onstage to dance with her, and Hannah leaves in tears, convinced that he still loves Nadine. She returns to the café where they first met and tells her troubles to the bartender in the song "Better Luck Next Time." The next morning, Easter Sunday, Johnny, who realizes his own love for Hannah is hopeless, persuades her that she must go after Don if she loves him. So Hannah arrives at Don's apartment with flowers, candy, and an "Easter Bonnet" for him—a top hat with a rabbit inside. She sings "Easter Parade" to him and he presents her with an Easter Bonnet of her own. The two link arms and, with Don now singing to Hannah, they join the splendid Easter Parade on Fifth Avenue.

The central attraction in *Easter Parade* is certainly the performances of its two stars. The pairing of Astaire and Garland was the result of a fortunate accident rather than the foresight of studio executives. The film had originally been planned as a vehicle for Judy Garland and Gene Kelly, but Kelly broke an ankle during rehearsals and Astaire came out of a brief period of retirement to take his place. He and Garland had both appeared in *Ziegfeld Follies of 1946* (the same film in which Astaire and Kelly did their memorable "Babbitt and the Bromide" dance together), but they had not performed in any of the same scenes. With her lively manner and nervous intensity, Garland had always seemed a more natural match for Kelly, while Astaire's partners had generally been cool, graceful, and somewhat restrained.

In *Easter Parade*, however, the differences in their styles are perfectly suited to the conflict between Don and Hannah. Don's efforts to transform the warm, down-to-earth Hannah into an aloof, ethereal dancing partner meet with dismal failure. It is only when he recognizes Hannah's (and Garland's) natural humor and vibrancy that the act begins to work. The merging of Astaire's elegance and Garland's buoyancy results in the film's best-remembered number, the classic "We're a Couple of Swells." Dressed in tattered tramp costumes, the two indulge in a high-spirited romp while singing a comical, mocking song about the life of the very rich. This humorous spoof of refinement and social graces presents a perfect blending of the equally remarkable, though widely different, talents of these two legendary performers.

Easter Parade is one of the most truly "musical" of all musical films. From its opening song "Happy Easter" to the final choruses of "Easter Parade," the film is filled with songs and dances which serve to illustrate and enhance both its story line and the emotions of its characters. Songs such as "Drum Crazy" and "Steppin' Out with My Baby" provide Astaire with opportunities to display his graceful, innovative dance techniques, while "Better Luck Next Time" presents a showcase for Garland's touching, emotional vocal style. Ann Miller is also given a spectacular solo, the rousing "Shakin' the Blues Away," and even Peter Lawford has a chance to display his musical abilities in a duet with Garland, "A Fella with an Umbrella." Many of the songs in the film were written by Berlin during the period in which the story is set, lending a very genuine feeling to the film's atmosphere.

Easter Parade is a product of the musical unit at M-G-M which was headed by producer Arthur Freed. The Freed unit was composed of a number of the top Hollywood musical talents of the 1940's and 1950's and was responsible for such films as *Meet Me in St. Louis* (1944), *An American in Paris* (1951), and *The Band Wagon* (1953). *Easter Parade*'s credits include Cedric Gibbons as art director, Johnny Green as musical director, and Roger Edens as associate producer. The film had originally been planned for Vincente Minnelli, the unit's principal director, but marital problems between Minnelli and Judy Garland resulted in the film's reassignment to Charles Walters. Although Walters' direction lacks the precision and delicacy of touch which Minnelli might have brought to the film, his presence lends it an exuberance which makes *Easter Parade* an enduring favorite among Hollywood musicals.

Janet E. Lorenz

EASY RIDER

Released: 1969
Production: Peter Fonda for Columbia
Direction: Dennis Hopper
Screenplay: Peter Fonda, Dennis Hopper, and Terry Southern
Cinematography: Laszlo Kovacs
Editing: Donn Cambern
Running time: 94 minutes

Principal characters:
Wyatt (Captain America) .... Peter Fonda
Billy .... Dennis Hopper
George Hanson .... Jack Nicholson

Easy Rider was, in 1969, both a propaganda film and a phenomenon of popular culture. It was the first time that what had come to be called the "counterculture" was featured in a major motion picture, and the men who made the film were well aware of the fact. The viewpoint of *Easy Rider* is not, however, wholehearted endorsement of its two counterculture "heroes," as too many people supposed; its outlook is more subtle than that and makes the film more than a period piece.

Easy Rider is basically the creation of two men: Peter Fonda and Dennis Hopper. Together with Terry Southern, they wrote the screenplay; Fonda produced the film, Hopper directed it, and both played leading roles. The story is essentially that of a journey. Two men, Billy (Dennis Hopper) and Wyatt (Peter Fonda), who is also called Captain America, smuggle cocaine from Mexico to California. Then, with the huge amount of money they have made, they head east on their motorcycles, bound for New Orleans and the Mardi Gras.

On their journey they encounter a variety of people. At a small ranch where they stop to fix one of their motorcycles, they stay to eat a meal, and Wyatt proclaims that the rancher should be proud because "You do your own thing in your own time." At a commune they find some of the members bickering and others sowing seed on unplowed, sandy ground, but Wyatt says, as if pronouncing a benediction, "They're gonna make it." In a small town where they join a parade on their motorcycles and are jailed for parading without a permit, their scruffy appearance does not endear them to the police—Billy has especially long hair and a moustache.

Also in jail is George Hanson (Jack Nicholson), a liberal young lawyer whose alcoholic binges frequently land him there. Dissatisfied with his restricted life, George decides to go to New Orleans with Wyatt and Billy. The next day when the three go into a cafe, all the customers make ill-natured comments and the waitress refuses to wait on them. That night around a campfire (hotels and motels will not take them), George tells Wyatt and Billy that people are certain to resent anyone who is free. After they all go to sleep, they are attacked by some of the men from the cafe, and George is killed.

Wyatt and Billy next go on to New Orleans, where they pick up two prostitutes in a brothel and wander through the Mardi Gras celebration. Then, in a cemetery, all four take a hallucinogenic drug. We see their drug experience, represented in a long, purposely chaotic sequence of brief and often distorted glimpses of the characters and the cemetery. After they leave New Orleans and continue east, Wyatt says to Billy, "We blew it." Billy does not understand, and Wyatt does not explain. The next day on the highway, two men in a pickup truck pull alongside Billy and point a shotgun at him; when he replies with an obscene gesture, they shoot him. Wyatt goes for help, but the men shoot him also, and the last thing we see is his burning motocycle beside the road.

Not only in its story but also in its style, *Easy Rider* broke with many Hollywood conventions. Little time is spent giving the background of the characters or explanations of their actions. In addition, two devices are used alternately to speed up and slow down the pace of the film. Rather than using a dissolve between scenes (having one scene slowly disappear as the next slowly appears), the makers of *Easy Rider* show a few quick glimpses of the next scene just before the previous scene ends. For example, a night scene will be interrupted by a few momentary views of daylight shortly before a morning scene begins. In an extension of this device, there is one flashforward in the film. While they are in the brothel in New Orleans, Wyatt is looking at the pictures on the wall, and he suddenly sees, for only a moment, an image of his motorcycle burning beside the road. At that time neither he nor the audience knows what it means. The flash shots quicken the pace of the film, but at other times the pace is deliberately relaxed by sequences of the men riding their motorcycles to a background of rock music. Besides varying the pace, these interludes serve to break up the story into stanzas and to emphasize the continuity of the journey. In addition, the fact that the words of the songs frequently reinforce or comment on the action can be suggested by some of their titles: "The Pusher," "Born To Be Wild," and "It's Alright Ma (I'm Only Bleeding)."

Easy Rider is too often seen as a blatant attack on middle-class mores, but its depiction of values is neither so simple nor so onesided as that. The generation gap and the counterculture are perhaps overemphasized and over-discussed, but the fact remains that, especially in 1969, the hair, clothes, and motorcycles of the protagonists were certain to provoke a strong reaction in any viewer. The feelings expressed in the cafe scene were the feelings of many in the audience; many others uncritically admired Wyatt and Billy. The film itself tries to change the uncritical reaction of both groups. It tries, usually successfully, to make a viewer who at first automatically rejects Wyatt and Billy feel sympathy for them ninety minutes later, enough to be moved by their deaths and by the film as a whole. The film also tries, although less successfully, to make the uncritical admirer of the two "heroes" see that behind their rebellion is little but emptiness and greed.

After smuggling the cocaine, for example, the two men begin their journey with a flourish of freedom—Wyatt throws away his wristwatch—but on the sound track is "The Pusher," a song that is strongly and quite overtly against the pushers of such drugs. They stop at a gas station and take gas without paying, even though they have thousands of dollars. The last shot of the station shows a poor child looking out the window. At the commune, Billy and Wyatt find a group of people who are barely surviving, yet they give them nothing more than a short ride on their motorcycles. Finally, in a moment of introspection, Wyatt recognizes that they "blew it." Though the statement seems out of character and Billy does not understand it, we can see that they certainly did blow it, both by choosing to sell hard drugs and by what they did with their lives and money afterwards. Indeed, in this way *Easy Rider* is like a gangster film, in which the audience is expected to feel some sympathy or identification with the gangster without admiring him.

Easy Rider is a film of contrasts. The interludes of motorcycling to rock songs contrast with the episodes between; the way of life of Wyatt and Billy contrasts with that of all the people they meet; and the low-key and rather flat characterizations of Wyatt and Billy sets off the fully realized characterization of George Hanson. As a counterbalance to the emptiness of Peter Fonda's Wyatt and the vague restlessness and paranoia of Dennis Hopper's Billy, Jack Nicholson's portrayal of George is crucial to the film, and Nicholson more than meets the challenge. First seen in a jail cell as he awakens from an alcoholic binge, he immediately animates the screen. He then proceeds to create a memorable and moving portrayal of the young lawyer, the son of a powerful man, who finds himself stuck in a small town until the chance encounter with Wyatt and Billy pushes him into trying to escape. Whether explaining freedom or expounding on UFO's, he is articulate and engrossing.

The other actors are not so exceptional. Fonda and Hopper satisfactorily fill the emotionally limited roles they wrote for themselves, but some of the people in the cafe and jail scenes were chosen because they were "real" people rather than actors and looked "right." Unfortunately, they sound more like bad actors than like real people.

Though much of *Easy Rider*'s immense popularity when it was first released was due to its contemporary subject matter and music, it is much more than a topical film. It remains remarkable for its artful stanzaic structure, for the performance of Jack Nicholson, and for its theme of the use and abuse of freedom.

Timothy W. Johnson

ELMER GANTRY

Released: 1960
Production: Bernard Smith for United Artists
Direction: Richard Brooks
Screenplay: Richard Brooks (AA); based on the novel of the same name by Sinclair Lewis
Cinematography: John Alton
Editing: Marge Fowler
Art direction: Ed Carrere
Costume design: Dorothy Jeakins
Music: André Previn
Running time: 146 minutes

Principal characters:
Elmer Gantry .... Burt Lancaster (AA)
Sister Sharon Falconer .... Jean Simmons
Jim Lefferts .... Arthur Kennedy
Lulu Bains .... Shirley Jones (AA)
William L. Morgan .... Dean Jagger
Sister Rachel .... Patti Page
George Babbitt .... Edward Andrews

Who is Elmer Gantry? Is he a savior or a scoundrel, a charlatan or a saint? This grinning, likable man at times appears to be the incarnation of insincerity and deviousness, but in a conversation with the atheistic newspaperman, Jim Lefferts (Arthur Kennedy), Gantry (Burt Lancaster) confesses that he does believe in the Lord, and it follows that he sees goodness in his questionable preaching. Gantry tells Lefferts that it is good for people to get down on their knees and pray. Throughout his story, he is fond of wistfully exclaiming, "Love is the morning and the evening star." Is this poetic declaration merely a clever phrase the rogue uses to gain the affections of women, or is it something the man believes in even though the tone of his voice mocks the words? Although he treats revivalism as theater and is forever giving a performance as God's messenger, Gantry is in his way both theologian and spiritual seeker. Having been expelled from a religious seminary for yielding to the temptations of the flesh, he is a man finding his own way to express the struggles of the soul, a way which requires that he be both angel and devil.

As Gantry exists both to question and to validate divine will, the film of which he is the protagonist exists in light and shadow, its figures traveling in and out of darkness with a vibrancy accentuated by the gaudy colors utilized solely for expressive purposes. In the first scene, when Gantry, drunk on Christmas Eve, convinces the apathetic customers that they should give their money to charity, he is a figure emerging from a literal blackness and becoming charismatic not only through movement but because a glaring light illuminates him. Later, the hard light associated with Gantry dominates all of his scenes as an evangelist, while in other scenes he moves in and out of the deep black shadows which daringly fill many of the images. Sister Sharon (Jean Simmons) is characterized by the dazzling white of her costume in the revival scenes, identifying her as an innocent sent from heaven. The hell on earth, of which the house of prostitution in which Lulu Baines (Shirley Jones) lives is only the most direct manifestation, is often visualized in artificial blues, reds, and yellows which fill the walls of interiors when there is no realistic justification for them. *Elmer Gantry* is a film in which the period detail beautifully evokes the Midwest of the 1920's, but in which at the same time a visual abstractness deliriously separates the story from naturalistic representation, revealing its true subject to be the contradictions within the soul.

The feverishness with which the film portrays the struggle between heaven and hell is never more evident than in the climax of the burning tent, in which Sister Sharon perishes. Having been led into the sin of her relationship with Gantry, she now believes that she is redeemed, and she is reaffirmed in her faith that she carries a divine message. As if God has intervened to punish her for her pride, calling upon the fires of hell to consume her, an image is imposed in which the orange flames overwhelm the spiritual white of her garments.

Gantry is powerless to save Sharon. Throughout the story, his ambivalent intentions have reaped a whirlwind. He is perceived as being right in chastising Jim Lefferts, with whom he maintains a friendly relationship; but the logic which Lefferts represents, while that of a devil's advocate, at least has the merit of temporarily exposing the sham of Sister Sharon's righteousness, which may be self-delusion on her part but is cynically used by Gantry. In his relationship with women, Gantry is never an unjust seducer. His love for Sharon is genuine, and her response to him is natural and should not provoke in her a feeling of shame. Gantry's mistake is in leaving her trapped between her spiritual aspirations and her worldly desires.

Similarly, Gantry is unjust to Lulu Baines. However, he is not blamed for having seduced an innocent girl and driven her into prostitution, since it is implied that Lulu's background as the daughter of a minister is responsible for the course her life takes. Rather, Gantry's mistake in his treatment of Lulu, for which he suffers, is his failure to understand that her love for him is strong enough to demand renewed expression, even if this must take the negative form of blackmail. Gantry has a certain perceptiveness about life, and he makes clever use of it in his relationships with the other characters; but he is blind to his own power as a catalyst in bringing about a tragedy which the film ambiguously suggests might be the result either of social and historical forces or of the will of God.

Elmer Gantry is a film which has enjoyed popularity and critical success for both good and bad reasons. As an adaptation of a controversial novel, it was bound to receive attention, and the skillfulness of Richard Brooks's adaptation has won deserved praise. The explicit subject of the story is the hold revivalism has over a great section of America, but the naïveté of the followers of Gantry and Sister Sharon is not enough to arouse a sense of self-importance in a film. While the film may have won some merited awards because Brooks was considered courageous to have undertaken it, its style found an appreciative following among the more adventurous European critics, whose perceptions of American films have always shown enviable insight.

It is appropriate that Brooks would realize this film with a fervor not always found in his work. The unbridled religious hysteria which Gantry uses like an artist cries out for a visual excitement which Brooks has provided with the skill of a conjurer. The color photography of *Elmer Gantry* owes a great deal to John Alton, an artist in his own right, whose lighting reminds us that he had made a reputation in black and white and showed a similar feeling for color with his first opportunity in that medium (the ballet in *An American in Paris*, 1951); but Brooks shares the credit for having chosen Alton and for having inspired the cameraman by composing vivid images.

Brooks also is responsible for the cast, and the actors make a notable contribution not only in the vividness of their physical presences but in the intensity with which they play their roles. A nice balance is achieved in the casting. The men are all expected choices, but the casting of the female roles is rather startling. Burt Lancaster is no surprise as a dynamic and colorful Gantry, just as Arthur Kennedy is ideal to convey the skepticism of Lefferts. Similarly, Dean Jagger has had many roles of weak men similar to Sharon's pathetic manager, Bill Morgan, and Edward Andrews might have been born to play the hypocritical businessman, George Babbitt. On the other hand, Jean Simmons might have been thought too refined to play the fiery Sister Sharon, but the impression of breeding and intelligence which are part of her image contribute to making this performance one of her most striking. The lovely Patti Page, a stranger to cinema, was picked to play a singer in the revival troupe whom Gantry seduces, and she is effective because her naturalness and reticence provide contrast to the prevailing mood. Especially offbeat is the casting of Shirley Jones, who revels in her role as a prostitute. Previously, sweet and wholesome girls had been her specialty, and the characterization cleverly comments on this, as Lulu was once sweet and wholesome herself.

The film was Brooks's first independent venture after ten years as a contract director at M-G-M, and he flaunted the opportunity by insisting that the film be shot in the unfashionable aspect ratio of 1.33, demonstrating scorn for the 1.85 and CinemaScope ratios which had been insisted upon in his M-G-M films. Brooks has often spoken of the ludicrousness of many of his M-G-M projects, although he wrote the scripts for most of them; and superficially, *Elmer Gantry*, which represents his blossoming into an artist, would seem to justify his view that a studio director is a slave. In retrospect, however, interesting themes and stylistic beauties may be found in many of his M-G-M films, of which one, *The Last Hunt* (1956), is as fascinating as *Elmer Gantry*. On the other hand, none of his later films is realized in quite so striking a manner as this one, although his gifts have been intermittently evident in all of them. In the context of Brooks's career, *Elmer Gantry* does not demonstrate the virtues of greater freedom; it only shows the level of artistry of which Brooks is capable but which has so often mysteriously eluded him.

Blake Lucas

THE ENCHANTED COTTAGE

Released: 1945
Production: Harriet Parsons for RKO/Radio
Direction: John Cromwell
Screenplay: DeWitt Bodeen and Herman J. Mankiewicz; based on the play
of the same name by Sir Arthur Wing Pinero
Cinematography: Ted Tetzlaff
Editing: Joseph Noriega
Music: Roy Webb
Running time: 92 minutes

> *Principal characters:*
> Laura Pennington .... Dorothy McGuire
> Oliver Bradford .... Robert Young
> Major John Hillgrove .... Herbert Marshall
> Mrs. Minnett .... Mildred Natwick
> Beatrice Alexander .... Hillary Brooke
> Violet Price .... Spring Byington
> Frederick Price .... Richard Gaines

When Sir Arthur Wing Pinero wrote the play *The Enchanted Cottage* it was
with the idea of trying to raise the morale of the men who came out of World
War I as human derelicts, scarred and maimed for the rest of their lives. It
was first produced with success on the London stage in 1922, and the following
year William A. Brady presented it on Broadway with Katharine Cornell as
its ugly duckling heroine. In 1924, it was filmed by First National as a silent
motion picture costarring Richard Barthelmess and May McAvoy as the
lovers. In the first years of the talking film, RKO/Radio acquired the rights
to the play, and first there was talk about Helen Twelvetrees making a new
version, then Helen Mack, and later Ginger Rogers. Nothing came of remake
plans, however, until World War II, when Harriet Parsons, one of Hollywood's
few female producers, was placed under contract by RKO. As is customary
with new producers searching for a suitable story, she went through the
catalogue of properties that the studio owned. She was attracted by *The
Enchanted Cottage* and believed that with the world at war, the time was right
to refilm the story, bringing it up to date and setting it in New England rather
than in the English countryside, the setting of the original drama.

Parsons asked that DeWitt Bodeen, also under contract to RKO, be assigned to work with her on the project as screenwriter, and the film finally
went into production in 1944 under the direction of John Cromwell, who
brought in Herman J. Mankiewicz for a rewrite. David O. Selznick took a
personal interest in the project, lending his contract star, Dorothy McGuire,
to play the heroine. Cromwell very correctly knew that the only way to

present a fantasy romance was realistically. The people in *The Enchanted Cottage* are very human and real, and the audience is led to believe that a "miracle" could take place.

The cottage of the title is on the New England seacoast and consists of only one wing of an estate built by an Englishman. The rest of the house was destroyed by fire, but the wing survives, inhabited by a widow, Mrs. Minnett (Mildred Natwick), who once lived there with her husband, and now acts as a housekeeper, renting out the cottage to honeymooners as the original owner had been accustomed to do. The lovers who lived in the cottage were always supremely happy, for they realized their love in an atmosphere of sublime harmony and contentment.

In the nearby village lives a lonely girl, an ugly duckling named Laura Pennington (Dorothy McGuire), and when Mrs. Minnett engages her services as a helper, Laura welcomes the opportunity of living in an environment that harbors warmth and care. Oliver Bradford (Robert Young) has heard about the enchantment the cottage weaves for lovers, and he brings his bride-to-be, Beatrice Alexander (Hillary Brooke), to look over the dwelling as an ideal honeymoon site for them. Before they can marry, however, the country goes to war, and Oliver, who is in the Air Corps, is immediately called to duty.

He comes back to the cottage alone, sooner than expected, for he has been seriously injured in a plane crash. The seventh nerve on one side of his face has been severed, and there is no hope for his recovery or help for the unsightly twist that distorts his facial expression. He has sought the cottage as a retreat from the world. Laura, in her severe plainness and lack of any prettiness, is the only person to whom he can talk. A neighbor, Major John Hillgrove (Herbert Marshall), who is blind, visits them, and he senses what is quietly happening; they are falling in love. They get married; later, they come to Hillgrove one night to confess that they have stayed away from the world, even avoiding the sight of Mrs. Minnett, ever since they became man and wife. For on their honeymoon night, a "miracle" took place. Oliver looked upon Laura and found her lovely and desirable; she saw him as she had first seen him, handsome, straight, and unmarred.

Hillgrove tries to persuade them that the "miracle" is true. He tells them to treasure it, believe in it, and continue to remain apart from others. And so they do, until the world intrudes. Oliver's superficial parents, mother and stepfather, come to see them. Their new world falls in ruins when they realize that they are the same as they have always been; there is no "miracle," even though every time they look at each other they continue to see each other as desirable. It is only those who are unsighted, like the Major, who can see them as they see themselves. Mrs. Minnett explains the "miracle" by telling them that they have fallen in love, that a man and a woman in love have a gift of sight that is not granted to other people. She has watched them from the beginning, and on the day of their wedding she saw their love blaze up like kindling wood. She tells them to keep that love burning and they will never be anything to each other but fair and handsome. That is the charm; that is the only enchantment that the cottage holds, and it is of their own making.

Audiences were themselves caught up in the enchantment. Although scorned by some critics, *The Enchanted Cottage* became one of the best-liked films of 1945, and its popularity has never dwindled; it is still a favorite on retrospective programs and is consistently screened on television. It became one of the few romances mingling fact with fancy that were popular during the war, and grateful servicemen who had been wounded and scarred in conflict took time to write the studio, the producer, the stars, and even the writers, telling them how much they appreciated the film and how they hoped that the people at home would also see it and so understand its theme, a philosophy they themselves knew to be true.

Dorothy McGuire, who had been introduced to the movie world through her stage success *Claudia*, played the homely spinster, Laura, with remarkable delicacy and warmth. In all other productions of *The Enchanted Cottage*, for the stage and the silent screen, Laura had been misshapen, cursed with a crooked nose, buck teeth, and near-sighted vision. One shoulder was higher than the other, and she walked with a limp. McGuire was adamant about not playing Laura with those encumbrances. She insisted on playing the part with no makeup, her hair drab and lifeless, her clothes homemade, and badly fitted. She maintained that the real job of the production department was to make her ravishingly beautiful. It became the task of Eddie Stevenson, costume designer, to make two of everything she wore: one that fitted her perfectly and another that did not fit at all. The makeup department and hairdressers, often the bane of the director and cinematographer, were not to touch her. McGuire had her way, and she made Laura believably drab, a Cinderella who never deserted the hearth. Only in her eyes was there any sign of beauty; she thought herself plain, and so she became plain. The role of Oliver was Robert Young's own favorite of all the parts he played; in later years he even named the home he built in Southern California "The Enchanted Cottage." Mrs. Minnett was one of Mildred Natwick's first screen roles, and she was absolutely right for the part. The audience believed in her proudly defiant confession at the climax of the film when she says that were the man she once loved to rise from his grave and walk in at the moment, she would be fair to him, for they too had loved, and the enchantment held fast.

Herbert Marshall's cultivated tones and calm acceptance of a "miracle" in which he can believe because he is sightless, make that "miracle" all the more believable. It is Marshall, as Major Hillgrove, who provides the frame for the story. Being a musician, he has composed a tone poem for the piano called "The Enchanted Cottage," and his friends have gathered in his house to hear him play it. As he starts to play an introductory passage featuring the major theme, he narrates the story, and there is a flashback to its natural beginnings, with necessary exposition backgrounded by him over the piano tones.

The Enchanted Cottage is a delicate piece of work. It weaves a spell of enchantment over the audience so that they believe, they sympathize, and they hope that Laura and Oliver will know a love and happiness unmarred by ugliness. It dispenses with the moments of fantasy indulged in by the play and the silent film. There are no wraiths, no shadows of other lovers from other times crowding the scene. Words, pictures, and a score that enhances them make the charm come real. The remarkable thing is that audiences today, seeing the picture for the first time, are caught up in its spell. It simply provokes imagination by making its audience believe in it as possible—and it becomes real.

DeWitt Bodeen

THE EXORCIST

Released: 1973
Production: William Peter Blatty for Warner Bros.
Direction: William Friedkin
Screenplay: William Peter Blatty (AA); based on his novel of the same name
Cinematography: Owen Roizman and Billy Williams
Editing: Jordan Leondopoulos, Bud Smith, Evan Lottman, and Norman Gay
Sound: Robert Knudson and Chris Newman (AA)
Running time: 121 minutes

Principal characters:
Chris MacNeil .... Ellen Burstyn
Regan MacNeil .... Linda Blair
Father Damien Karras .... Jason Miller
Father Merrin .... Max von Sydow
Lieutenant Kinderman .... Lee J. Cobb
Burke Dennings .... Jack MacGowran

The 1970's was the decade of the blockbuster, as movies from *The Godfather* (1972) to *Star Wars* (1977) completely rewrote the definition of a financially successful film. Grosses of over $100,000,000 became, if not exactly commonplace, at least no longer unheard of. *The Exorcist*, released late in 1973, was one of the first cinematic blockbusters. However, whereas *The Godfather* attracted its audiences on the strength of the acting of Marlon Brando and Al Pacino and a richly textured plot involving organized crime—a traditional source of fascination for American moviegoers—and whereas *Star Wars* took advantage of its dazzling special effects and a resurgence of interest in science fiction, *The Exorcist* captured its audience's imagination with a bit of orthodox (albeit esoteric) Christian theology and a lot of pure horror. It concerned the exorcism of demonic spirits from the body of a possessed child.

Based on the hugely successful novel of the same name by William Peter Blatty, *The Exorcist* was in many ways presold; by the time the movie was released, five million copies of the novel had been sold. Blatty produced the film and wrote the screenplay, which followed the outline of his novel closely, and his friend William Friedkin directed. Aided by some gruesome special effects, these men, together with young actress Linda Blair, put together a horrific masterpiece. The film's fans may have been badly frightened or even physically nauseated by *The Exorcist*, but they certainly were not disappointed.

The film opens innocently enough at an archaeological dig in Iraq, supervised by Father Merrin (Max von Sydow), a scholarly Jesuit. The first hint that something unusual is afoot occurs with the discovery of a small, gargoylelike statuette. Suddenly, an eerie wind begins to blow, and dogs begin fighting among themselves. Although it will be a while before the precise nature of the ancient evil manifests itself, Blatty and Friedkin have made it clear in the film that a demonic force has been loosed upon the world.

The scene shifts to Washington, D.C., and the lives of actress Chris MacNeil (Ellen Burstyn) and her twelve-year-old daughter Regan (Linda Blair). A divorcée, Chris leads a relatively unglamorous life despite her acting profession, and Regan is a bright, attractive young girl. Chris's closest friend is her director, Burke Dennings (Jack MacGowran), and both are casually acquainted with a number of Jesuit priests from nearby Georgetown University, one of whom is Father Damien Karras (Jason Miller), a psychologist whose job it is to counsel his fellow priests who feel that they are losing their vocation. Ironically, Father Karras is himself in the midst of a crisis of faith. Exhausted from sharing the burdens of others, Karras will soon face an even more strenuous test: he will be called upon to confront the incarnation of the devil himself.

The demon enters the MacNeils' lives subtly at first. Soon, however, the mysterious noises in the attic and the inexplicable open windows give way to a more disturbing phenomenon. Regan begins to act strangely. At one of Chris's dinner parties, Regan enters in bedclothes, urinates on the floor in front of the guests, and tells Burke that he is going to die. Horrified, Chris confronts her daughter in her bedroom after everyone has left only to discover that Regan is as puzzled and terrified by her behavior as is Chris. The filmmakers also introduce in this scene the first of their special effects for horror: as Chris attempts to comfort Regan, the bed upon which they are lying is racked with violent convulsions.

Regan's spells and seizures grow more uncontrollable, and Chris seeks medical assistance. A variety of doctors offer a variety of diagnoses, but none is able to help, and Chris despairs of convincing the doctors of the extraordinary nature of Regan's affliction. The once-pretty girl is growing more physically repulsive every day, and spends much of the time tossing violently in her bed, screaming gutteral obscenities.

Finally, however, a group of physicians at a psychiatric clinic begin to grope towards an accurate assessment of Regan's problem. Her symptoms, they say, match those of persons in primitive cultures who are believed to have been possessed by demons, and they suggest that an exorcism be performed on Regan. Furious, Chris declines to involve "witch doctors" in her search for a cure for her daughter. Meanwhile, Regan's prediction about Burke comes true; he is found dead outside the MacNeil's house. The police say that he was thrown from an upstairs window by a person of great strength. The only one in the house, however, has been the bedridden Regan.

Although Blatty and Friedkin have constructed a film that has been, up to this point, nerve-racking, they now turn the screws even tighter. The manifestation of Regan's possession becomes so grotesque that the film is almost painful to watch. One of *The Exorcist*'s most horrifying scenes occurs immediately after the psychiatric diagnosis of demonic possession. A crucifix has mysteriously appeared under Regan's pillow, and the by now horribly disfigured child begins to masturbate violently with it. The scene concludes with Regan spinning her head around a full 360 degrees several times in rapid succession, grinning hellishly all the while. That part of the audience which has not long since shut its eyes or simply left the theater is invariably left gasping for breath.

The incident causes Chris to abandon her initial skepticism about the diagnosis of demonic possession, and she takes her problem to Father Karras, who, though inclined to doubt Regan's possession, nevertheless agrees to see the child-monster. His interest intensifies when he is approached by Lieutenant Kinderman (Lee J. Cobb), who has been placed in charge of the Burke Dennings homicide investigation. Stating that the murder had ritualistic overtones, Kinderman asks the priest to watch for any of his flock who might be capable, physically and psychologically, of committing the murder. It soon becomes clear, first to Chris, then to Father Karras, and finally to Lieutenant Kinderman, that it was indeed Regan who killed the director.

Visits to Regan's bedside gradually convince the skeptical Karras that the girl is inhabited by a genuine demon. He is unimpressed by the physical manifestations of the possession, although these are both remarkable and revolting: the Regan-demon can reduce the room temperature at will, and spews bilious green vomit all over Karras. What is left of the real Regan writes "HELP ME" in angry red welts on the child-monster's abdomen. Instead, he is persuaded by the extensive knowledge of Catholic theology displayed by the demon that is using Regan as its mouthpiece. Karras requests permission from his superiors to conduct an exorcism. They agree and bring in an older priest, their most experienced exorcist, to assist him. Of course, this turns out to be Father Merrin, the archaeologist who had inadvertently released the demon in the first place.

Ironically, the exorcism itself turns out to be almost an anticlimax. Blatty and Friedkin merely offer a reprise of the grisly special effects that they have displayed throughout the film. Temperatures drop, bodies levitate, and vomit and curses spew forth as the demon fights with the holy men for possession of Regan's body and soul. The demon ultimately loses, but he exacts a price— both priests die during the exorcism. Regan, however, is made whole again, and, mercifully, remembers nothing of her ordeal.

The Exorcist must surely be the only R-rated film in history to have been made with the full cooperation of the Roman Catholic Church. Blatty and Friedkin assure us that, at least regarding the exorcism sequences, everything in the film is based on fact. The theological authenticity of the film, however, is largely beside the point. The impact of *The Exorcist* lies in its hideously realistic special effects and in the acting of the principals in the cast.

Ellen Burstyn, Jason Miller, and Linda Blair all garnered Academy Award nominations for their work on the film. Burstyn's Chris MacNeil is more the worried mother than the glamorous movie queen; she grows convincingly haggard as her daughter's ordeal is prolonged. Miller's Father Karras is a study in craggy intensity; driven at first by his loss of faith, and then, once his faith in God is restored, by the undeniable reality of the existence of the Devil and by the necessity of destroying this evil, Karras never has a moment's peace until he gives his life to save Regan's at the film's climax.

The most remarkable of the film's performances, however, is that of Linda Blair as Regan. A hitherto unknown twelve-year-old girl whose appearance in *The Exorcist* marked her acting debut, Blair was not asked to do much real acting. With the exception of the beginning and end of the film, when Regan appears as a normal child, the makeup men and special effects people take over the development of the character. Still, Blair deserves a good deal of credit for having survived the acting experience intact.

William Friedkin took Blatty's novel-turned-screenplay, which won an Academy Award, and transferred it to the screen virtually intact; and the impact of the film is undeniable. Friedkin melded the story, the actors, and the special effects into what must be described as a disgusting masterpiece. This seeming contradiction may account for the film's mixed reception by the critics; newspaper accounts at the time of *The Exorcist*'s release invariably mentioned that people in the audience literally became physically ill during some scenes, although curiously, this seemed only to add to the film's mystique. Some critics were outraged and said so emphatically. Others liked the film, and Hollywood gave *The Exorcist* its stamp of approval with ten Academy Award nominations and two awards (Best Screenplay and Best Sound). The ultimate judgment regarding *The Exorcist*, however, was rendered by its audiences who flocked to see it by the millions. Controversial though it may have been, it remains one of the cinema's all-time box-office moneymakers. The film spawned a host of imitators, including a disastrous sequel, and lifted horror films out of the realm of the B-movie and into big-budget respectability; but none of *The Exorcist*'s successors equalled the original, either in popularity or quality.

Robert Mitchell

FAHRENHEIT 451

Released: 1966
Production: Lewis M. Allen for Anglo Enterprise/Vineyard Films; released
  by Universal
Direction: François Truffaut
Screenplay: François Truffaut and Jean-Louis Richard; based on the novel
  of the same name by Ray Bradbury
Cinematography: Nicolas Roeg
Editing: Thom Noble
Music: Bernard Herrmann
Running time: 112 minutes

> *Principal characters:*
> Montag .... Oskar Werner
> Linda/Clarisse .... Julie Christie
> The Captain .... Cyril Cusack
> The Book-woman .... Bee Duffell

Fahrenheit 451 represents an unusual combination of the ideas of an
American science fiction writer and the cinematic style of a French director.
The film, written and directed by François Truffaut, is an adaptation of Ray
Bradbury's novel of the same name. Its story concerns one man's awakening
and struggle for individual freedom in a future of chilling conformity.

The film's title refers to the temperature at which paper will burn, for that
is what the story's central character does for a living. Montag (Oskar Werner)
is a fireman, but his job is not to extinguish fires; it is to start them. The
society in which Montag lives is one where complete control is exercised over
the lives and, more significantly, the thoughts of its members. An important
part of this process is the destruction of all books, since books are expressions
of individual ideas. As the film opens, Montag is an unquestioning member
of that society, answering calls reporting hidden books in people's homes and
burning what he finds. His supervisor, the Captain (Cyril Cusack), commends
Montag for the excellent work he is doing, and informs him that he may soon
be promoted.

At home, Montag's wife, Linda (Julie Christie), spends her days tranquil-
ized, watching a giant television wallscreen. There is no real love or affection
between Montag and Linda; there is only a placid acceptance of their life
together. Strong emotions such as love and hate have been discouraged by
the society in its efforts to keep everyone on a level of continuous complacency.

Beneath the surface of this calm façade, however, there are elements of
rebellion. Montag meets a young woman, Clarisse (also played by Julie Christie), who lives nearby and who asks him if he ever reads the books he burns.

He is intrigued by her comments, and on his next book-burning mission he steals a copy of *David Copperfield* and begins reading it secretly at night. When Clarisse loses her teaching job because of suspicions that she is working against the society, she appeals to Montag for help; but he is unable to assist her. Montag is sent to the house of an old woman (Bee Duffell) who has a hidden library in her attic and who chooses to burn with her books rather than surrender. Her devotion arouses Montag's curiosity still further, although the Captain warns him that books cause nothing but unhappiness and that he must resist the temptation to read them. However, Montag becomes more and more fascinated by the world of literature he has discovered, much to his wife's distress.

The old woman had been part of a network of people who are resisting the society's insistence on conformity. Clarisse is also a member, but the discovery of the old woman's library signals the beginning of a series of raids, and she is forced to flee and go into hiding. Montag goes to Clarisse's now-deserted house and finds her in the basement, where she is searching for an incriminating list that had been left behind. Montag uses his skill at ferreting out hidden books to help her find it, and she tells him that she is going to the country to join the book people, a group of persons who live outside the city and commit books to memory.

Linda, who has tried to persuade Montag to destroy the books he has hidden, finally betrays him and turns his name in to the firemen. On Montag's next mission, he is sent to his own house, where the Captain supervises the gathering of the books Montag has hidden. When the Captain orders him to start the fire, Montag uses the flamethrower to burn the television screen and other symbols of his old life, finally turning the torch on the Captain himself. Now a hunted criminal, Montag escapes across the river into the country, where he follows the directions Clarisse had given him to the settlement of the book people. There, he finds men and women, Clarisse among them, memorizing and reciting their favorite books, in effect "becoming" them, so that the books will live on in them. Montag joins the villagers and sets about learning Edgar Allan Poe's *Tales of Mystery and Imagination*. In the final scene, the book people walk through the woods in the falling snow, reciting the books they have become and preserving them for a future time when freedom of thought will prevail.

The choice of Bradbury's book as a subject seems, at first, to be an unusual one for François Truffaut, who is best known for his films dealing with childhood and romantic love. A closer examination of his work, however, reveals a preoccupation with reading and books among many of the characters in his films, and a reverence for literature which makes Truffaut's interest in Bradbury's book-burning theme understandable. Indeed, the film's most powerful scene is the one in which Montag destroys the old woman's secret library. As the books are tossed over the bannister, the camera follows them in their fall to the floor, where they are shown in closeups as the fire begins to curl and burn their pages. (One of the works is a copy of *Cahiers du Cinema*, the French film magazine for which Trauffaut wrote before becoming a director.) Truffaut's own love of literature and what it represents is strongly felt throughout the film.

Truffaut's admiration for Alfred Hitchcock is also an influence on *Fahrenheit 451*. At the time the film was conceived, Truffaut was working on his interview/book on Hitchcock, and his intensive study of the director's style is reflected not only in this film but in several others made during the same period. His handling of the suspense scenes and Montag's escape is reminiscent of Hitchcock, and the film's score is by Bernard Herrmann, who composed the music for many of Hitchcock's films.

As Montag, Oskar Werner moves convincingly from a mental vacuum to confusion and finally to self-determination, creating a character of fundamental decency whose life is drastically altered by the awakening of his thoughts and feelings. The decision to cast Julie Christie as both Linda and Clarisse was a fortunate one, as it serves to delineate the differences between individual thought and blind acceptance. As Linda, Christie is vacant and childlike, a frightening example of mindless conformity. The character of Clarisse is less well-defined, although she is a refreshing contrast to the self-absorbed automatons who surround her. Cyril Cusack is excellent as the Captain. In his conversations with Montag, we feel that he, too, has been tempted by the same curiosity which overpowers Montag, but that fear of his own individuality, rather than a true belief in the society's laws, has caused him to reject his longings. Just as Clarisse and Linda are two sides of the same coin, so the Captain is the man Montag might have become.

One of the most disturbing aspects of *Fahrenheit 451* is how closely the future resembles our own time. This is not a bizarre, stylized future with rocketships and strange beings. The machine that Montag and his men use on their book-burning missions is like present-day fire engines. At the end of the day, Montag commutes to the suburbs on a monorail train, where his home is identical to the homes around it, a futuristic version of today's tract houses. And Linda's constant use of tranquilizers, as well as her compulsive viewing of the enormous television screen, is not far removed from conditions in our own society. The film's vision of the future is a terrifying one, and Truffaut is clearly saying that it is not intended as a fantasy. It is a warning.

Janet E. Lorenz

FANTASIA

Released: 1940
Production: Walt Disney for Walt Disney Productions; released by RKO/ Radio
Production supervision: Ben Sharpsteen
Story direction: Joe Grant and Dick Huemer
Animation direction: Samuel Armstrong ("Toccata and Fugue in D Minor"/ "The Nutcracker Suite"); Bill Roberts ("The Rite of Spring"); James Algar ("The Sorcerer's Apprentice"); Hamilton Luske, Jim Handley, and Ford Beebe ("Pastoral Symphony"); T. Hee and Norman Ferguson ("Dance of the Hours"); Wilfred Jackson ("Night on Bald Mountain"/ "Ave Maria")
Music direction: Edward H. Plumb
Running time: 120 minutes

Fantasia, Walt Disney's most ambitious undertaking of his career up to that time, had its inception as a Mickey Mouse cartoon. Mickey had been Disney's biggest star since his debut in Disney's first sound cartoon, *Steamboat Willie* (1928); however, a decade after its release the spotlight had been usurped by Donald Duck and Goofy, two Disney characters with more distinct personalities than the basically passive Mickey. Concerned about the flagging popularity of the character with which he had achieved his greatest success, Disney conceived of an exceptionally elaborate short film as a vehicle for Mickey Mouse—a cartoon animated to the music of Dukas' "The Sorcerer's Apprentice," with Mickey appearing in the title role.

Disney had produced animated films throughout the 1920's; most notable were the "Alice in Cartoonland" series, which portrayed the adventures of a live girl in cartoon settings. Thus, when sound was introduced to filmmaking, he was ready to take full creative advantage of its potential. Even as far back as *Steamboat Willie*, Disney had displayed a keen awareness of the possibilities of music in animation, and during the succeeding years, had based many individual gags and a few entire films on the humorous juxtaposition of music with the antics of his animated characters. Among the notable examples are *The Skeleton Dance* (1929), animated to Saint-Saens' "La Danse Macabre," and *The Band Concert* (1935), wherein Mickey and his orchestra are whisked into the sky by a cyclone during a performance. Disney, however, especially during the 1930's, was never satisfied simply to repeat himself. The addition of Technicolor, the production of the first feature-length animated film, *Snow White and the Seven Dwarfs* (1937), and the development of the multiplane camera to give a greater illusion of depth to his films were all hallmarks of Disney's continuing quest to surpass his own considerable achievements. With the multiplane camera, first used for filming parts of *Snow White and the*

Seven Dwarfs, now available, *The Sorcerer's Apprentice* promised to be no ordinary cartoon.

Apparently it was originally the idea of Leopold Stokowski, a longtime admirer of Disney who had been engaged to conduct the score for *The Sorcerer's Apprentice*, to expand the concept to include other pieces of classical music, thus presenting a feature-length "concert" film. Disney, intrigued by Stokowski's suggestion, began discussions with the conductor and other musical experts, including popular music commentator Deems Taylor. Taylor, known to millions of Americans because of his radio broadcasts with the New York Philharmonic, eventually appeared in the film as a sort of master of ceremonies. Thus *The Sorcerer's Apprentice* evolved into the working title, "Concert Feature," then ultimately *Fantasia*. The eight pieces of music selected for *Fantasia* and the animated concepts to accompany them were, in order of appearance: Bach's "Toccata and Fugue in D Minor," presenting abstract forms and colors to illustrate "absolute" music; Tchaikovsky's "The Nutcracker Suite," demonstrating a celebration of nature featuring fairies, dancing plants, and the like; Dukas' "The Sorcerer's Apprentice," depicting Mickey Mouse trying out the sorcerer's magic and losing control of the results; Stravinsky's "The Rite of Spring," presenting the creation of the world; Beethoven's "Pastoral Symphony," showing characters of Greek mythology in a comic and romantic romp; Ponchielli's "Dance of the Hours," featuring a ballet burlesque danced by ostriches, hippos, and crocodiles; and Mussorgsky's "Night on Bald Mountain" and Schubert's "Ave Maria," depicting a battle between the forces of evil and goodness.

Because *Fantasia* was so far beyond the scope of any previous animated film, and because the quality of the music was so vital to the entire concept, Disney had his engineers develop an exceptional sound system for the film. Christened "Fantasound," it involved the recording of nine separate sound tracks using thirty-three microphones. This elaborate process, a precursor of later stereophonic systems, also required the installation of special playback equipment in theaters. (The fact that Fantasound has been adaptable to modern multitrack sound systems has undoubtedly contributed to the film's continuing popularity.) Using the Fantasound system, Stokowski and the Philadelphia Orchestra recorded the film's score over a two-month period.

With the major musical segments completed, the project now assumed immense proportions as Disney's army of animators went to work on the film's animation. *Fantasia* was in production for over two years and ultimately cost more than $2,000,000, an unheard-of sum for an animated film, and all the more astonishing when it is remembered that *Fantasia* was essentially an experiment—perhaps the most expensive "experimental film" of all time. The result was a unique achievement, unquestionably one of Disney's major works and certainly his most controversial.

Critics generally acknowledge that *Fantasia* is far from an artistic triumph.

Just as the musical selections are wide-ranging in style and mood, so also do the film's segments vary in degrees of success, from the delightfully anthropomorphic low-comedy ballet set to "Dance of the Hours" to the heavy-handed, pseudoscientific treatment of "The Rite of Spring." And to those who regard Disney as merely an entertainer, the artistic pretensions of such pieces as the final "Night on Bald Mountain"/"Ave Maria" sequence seem absurdly overinflated. Although no one can deny the amazing inventiveness of the film, *Fantasia* often seems to be straining for effect; it is alternately dazzling and preposterous, occasionally missing the mark embarrassingly as in the boy-meets-girl byplay of the centaurs in the "Pastoral Symphony" sequence. However, even great artists have their limitations, and it does not diminish *Fantasia* as a work of film art to note that it displays both the best and the worst of its creator. The film works most consistently when Disney does not stray too far from the essentially unpretentious animation which holds entertainment value above any "artistic" considerations. "The Sorcerer's Apprentice" in particular is among Disney's finest work from any period, as is "Dance of the Hours." Although most of the other segments are wildly uneven, the sheer technical quality of the animation carries the film over many of its rough spots, and occasionally achieves remarkable images of lasting power and beauty. For example, no matter how overdone the entire sequence may have been, the sight of the demon rising above the land to the strains of "Night on Bald Mountain" is not easily forgotten.

Among the charges leveled at *Fantasia* by its contemporary critics was the complaint that the liberties taken with the music were too great, not only in the types of illustration chosen (indeed, some disagreed with the entire concept of illustrating music) but also in the restructuring of the music itself. Nearly every piece was altered in some way to meet animation demands or time restrictions. "The Nutcracker Suite," for instance, omitted the first two movements of the original and rearranged the others to fit Disney's concept of a "ballet of nature in six scenes." Stokowski's conducting of the various selections was also criticized. Neither Disney nor Stokowski, however, aimed to please the purists or the music critics, but rather the public. "It isn't highbrow to like good music," Disney declared, and it is apparent that his intention was to make classical music more accessible to the mass audience. This was honorable enough, but the introduction and the explanatory interludes, narrated by Deems Taylor, had the unfortunate effect of giving the film something of the feel of a music lesson; and this sense of "talking down" to a musically uneducated audience is one of the more annoying aspects of the film.

Despite Disney's good intentions, however, the public failed to respond to *Fantasia*. A number of reasons have been suggested: the radical change in Disney's style, which may have been perceived by the average filmgoer as more extreme than it really was, given the context of Disney's career; the war in Europe, which had a detrimental effect on the carefully planned release of the film when defense requirements prevented installation of the elaborate Fantasound equipment in more than a handful of theaters; and, as one critic astutely observed, "the general impression that the art was too short for the longhairs and too long for the short." The financial failure of *Fantasia* had major ramifications for the Disney studio, putting it in a weakened financial position that seriously hindered its resistance to unionization over the next few years. Time, however, has vindicated Disney for his artistic and financial gamble. Many years later, audiences have become less concerned about distinctions between high art and popular art, and more in tune with the overwhelming imagination which fuels the film. Today *Fantasia* looks better than ever, undoubtedly because of the lack of comparable quality in most modern animation, and the film has finally turned a profit. One thing, however, has become apparent with the passage of time, and that is that with *Fantasia*, Disney, like so many innovators, was simply ahead of his time; *Fantasia* stands today as a remarkable achievement, an important work from a major film artist.

Howard H. Prouty

FAR FROM THE MADDING CROWD

Released: 1967
Production: Joseph Janni for Metro-Goldwyn-Mayer
Direction: John Schlesinger
Screenplay: Frederic Raphael; based on the novel of the same name by
  Thomas Hardy
Cinematography: Nicholas Roeg
Editing: Malcolm Cooke
Art direction: Richard MacDonald
Costume design: Alan Barrett
Running time: 168 minutes

Principal characters:
Bathsheba Everdene	Julie Christie
Sergeant Troy	Terence Stamp
William Boldwood	Peter Finch
Gabriel Oak	Alan Bates
Liddy	Fiona Walker
Fanny Robin	Prunella Ransome

John Schlesinger, the director of *Far from the Madding Crowd*, came into prominence in the early 1960's. He had acted with the Oxford University Dramatic Society and had begun to make experimental films while still at University. Later work for BBC Television attracted attention, and in 1962, producer Joseph Janni asked Schlesinger to direct his first feature film, *A Kind of Loving* (1962). It was the beginning of a successful artistic if not always financial partnership.

During the early 1960's, a new breed of young directors was emerging, and they were making films with very contemporary themes: Tony Richardson's *A Taste of Honey* (1962), Joseph Losey's *The Servant* (1963), Lindsay Anderson's *This Sporting Life* (1963), and Karel Reisz's *Saturday Night and Sunday Morning* (1960). The films were a harsh reflection of Britain in the 1960's, mostly set against a working-class background. Schlesinger's contributions to this minor renaissance were *A Kind of Loving* (1962), *Billy Liar* (1963) and *Darling* (1965). *A Kind of Loving* and *Billy Liar* showed two very different aspects of Northern life, and *Darling* was a glossy story of a young model ruthlessly using people in order to achieve her ambitions. It was a very stylish film and made an international star out of Julie Christie.

Far from the Madding Crowd was a complete change for Schlesinger. Thomas Hardy's classic story of passion in England's West Country had been filmed before as a silent film made in 1915 and starring Henry Edwards and the American actress Florence Turner (known as The Vitagraph Girl). Although made in England, it was directed by an American, Larry Trimble, who was responsible for some excellent pre-World War I British features.

The leading roles in the second version were given to two actors with whom Schlesinger had worked before, Julie Christie (*Billy Liar* and *Darling*) and Alan Bates (*A Kind of Loving*). Alan Bates, one of Britain's most successful young actors, who works in films, theater, and television drama, and who can play both classical and modern parts with equal ease, plays farmer Gabriel Oak, who loves Bathsheba Everden and waits patiently for her to return this love. Julie Christie is Bathsheba, a strong-willed and passionate young woman who, at the beginning of the story, is not fully aware of the strong emotions she can arouse in men. Christie had to overcome a major drawback in portraying the character; she has a "modern" face, at odds with the severe mid-Victorian costumes. She is able, however, to express the anguish of a woman who falls in love with the wrong man.

As the film opens, Gabriel proposes marriage to Bathsheba, who, being quite vain, makes fun of him. Bathsheba has inherited her uncle's farm. Nearby lives a wealthy gentleman farmer called William Boldwood (Peter Finch), who is unmarried. His single status is the subject of much speculation, and it is rumored that he was jilted as a young man. Bathsheba impulsively and coquettishly sends a valentine card to Mr. Boldwood, but unfortunately he takes it seriously and subsequently becomes obsessed with Bathsheba, begging her to marry him. Finch conveys perfectly the anguish of a man passionately in love with a younger woman.

Bathsheba is surprised and upset by the effect of her valentine on Boldwood. She has by now fallen desparately in love with Sergeant Troy (Terence Stamp), a cavalry officer stationed nearby. Bathsheba's maid Fanny Robin (Prunella Ransome) is pregnant by him, but as Fanny has disappeared, Troy switches his attentions to Bathsheba. They marry secretly and return to live at Bathsheba's farm. Both Fanny and Troy's child die in childbirth, after she has sought shelter in the workhouse. With Fanny's death, Troy, who has married Bathsheba, realizes that Fanny was the only woman he had ever loved and treats Bathsheba cruelly, even though she was in no way responsible for Fanny's tragic end. Troy leaves and is presumed to be drowned.

Although Stamp certainly looks right for the part of Troy, his voice is flat and colorless. There is no reason why a soldier should speak with the perfect vowel sounds of a well-trained classical actor. His lines are delivered without expression, and they contrast badly with the assurance of Peter Finch and Alan Bates. Yet there is a beautifully shot sequence in which Troy demonstrates to Bathsheba his skill with a sword. They are quite alone, surrounded by the gentle green hills of Dorset. Watched by a mesmerized Bathsheba, Troy (in his scarlet uniform) shows off his considerable skill at swordsmanship, slicing the air with arrogant authority. At the end of the demonstration he cuts off a piece of her hair in an act of startling self-confidence.

Meanwhile, Boldwood makes Bathsheba promise to consider his proposal (although he must wait six years before Troy's death is legally established), and she is so broken-hearted by the events of the past few months that she agrees, if not to marry him, at least to marry no one else. With this promise Boldwood has to be satisfied. However, one night at a party Boldwood gives for her, Bathsheba yields to his protestations of love and says that after the time has passed she will marry him. As she is leaving, however, Troy enters and Bathsheba falls to the floor in a faint. Everyone is so concerned for her and surprised by Troy's appearance that they do not notice Boldwood as he takes a gun down from the wall and shoots Troy in the chest. Troy dies immediately. Boldwood is subsequently tried for murder and ultimately committed to an institution.

Gabriel, who has been functioning as the manager or bailiff of Bathsheba's farm, decides to leave her service. Late one night, however, she goes to his cottage and indicates to him, more by gesture than by word, that he is the only person left to her now and that she needs both his help and his love. Gabriel accepts her plea, marries her, and thus becomes the master of her farm.

In addition to the dramatic events affecting the lives of the characters, the film also stresses Hardy's obsession with nature. Overshadowing the personal tragedies are the violent effects of natural disasters on the lives of the community. A torrential thunderstorm threatens to destroy Bathsheba's hayricks; Gabriel's entire flock of young lambs is herded over a precipice by a dog; a straw stack catches fire and threatens to burn the Everdene Farm; and a rare sickness is discovered in a flock of sheep. All these natural catastrophes directly affect the protagonists, and each event signals a change in their lives.

The color cinematography of *Far from the Madding Crowd* done by Nicholas Roeg, one of Britain's most distinguished cinematographers, is exquisite. Shot on location in Dorset and the Victorian seaside town of Lyme Regis, the film is dominated by the beautiful unspoiled countryside of rural England. The film is lovingly accurate in its period detail; much credit for this goes to production designer Richard McDonald and costume designer Alan Barratt for their faithful re-creation of nineteenth century English rural life.

The selection of actors for the supporting roles is uniformly excellent; they all resemble farm workers in early photographs. Particularly worthy of mention are Freddy Jones as Cainy Ball, Fiona Walker as Bathsheba's maid Liddy, Denise Coffey as Soberness, and Harriet Harper as Temperance, who look exactly right in the period costumes. Schlesinger's direction of the supporting cast is extremely sympathetic, especially in the scenes of social gatherings (the harvest supper; Boldwood's party) where he captures the awkwardness of the occasions when farmworkers are expected to mix with the landowners. The screenplay was written by Frederic Raphael, another Schlesinger regular who was also extremely faithful to the literary style of Hardy—not an easy task when faced with transferring rustic accents to the screen. With the exception of Boldwood, all members of the cast speak their lines with varying degrees of West Country accents and it all works surprisingly well.

Unfortunately, *Far from the Madding Crowd* was not very successful at the box office, nor was it a critical success. Peter Finch was praised for his sensitive portrayal of the tragic William Boldwood, and the cinematography and design were singled out for praise by the critics; but the general reaction was unenthusiastic. Perhaps it was this negative response which made Schlesinger return to more contemporary themes in his next films. It would be unfortunate, however, if Schlesinger allowed the adverse criticism of *Far from the Madding Crowd* to prevent another attempt at a period film.

Elizabeth Leese

FAREWELL, MY LOVELY

Released: 1975
Production: George Pappas and Jerry Bruckheimer for Avco Embassy
Direction: Dick Richards
Screenplay: David Zelag Goodman; based on the novel of the same name by
   Raymond Chandler
Cinematography: John A. Alonzo
Editing: Walter Thompson and Joel Cox
Music: David Shire
Running time: 95 minutes

   Principal characters:
      Philip Marlowe .... Robert Mitchum
      Helen Grayle/Velma .... Charlotte Rampling
      Lieutenant Nulty .... John Ireland
      Mrs. Florian .... Sylvia Miles
      Moose Malloy .... Jack O'Halloran
      Mr. Grayle .... Jim Thompson
      Marriott .... John O'Leary
      Amthor .... Kate Murtagh

   In *Farewell, My Lovely*, director Dick Richards has successfully captured
the ambience of both the hard-boiled school of literature and the traditional
film noir. This 1975 film is the third adaptation of Raymond Chandler's famous
suspense novel. Coming after a B-budget adaptation with the series hero
"The Falcon" substituting for Philip Marlowe in Edward Dymytrk's brilliant
Murder, My Sweet (1944) thirty years earlier, *Farewell, My Lovely* might be
considered a remake. Fortunately, Dick Richards and screenwriter David
Zelag Goodman went to the original source material to develop their version.
What emerges is a successful interpretation of Chandler and a studied homage
to the era which produced this unique style of literature. In the film, Philip
Marlowe (Robert Mitchum), an aging Los Angeles private investigator, is
sought in connection with several murders. Meeting with the police, Marlowe
begins to tell the complex story of Moose Malloy and Velma. Answers to all
the police's questions are wound up in that story.
   As soon as Malloy (Jack O'Halloran) gets out of prison, he stumbles upon
Marlowe and hires the private eye to find his ex-girl friend, Velma. The search
then leads Marlowe from the murder of a black nightclub owner to the widow
of Velma's ex-boss. The trail dries up at Camarillo State Hospital with a
woman Marlowe believes to be Velma. She is not. Marlowe then gets another
unusual job: accompanying Marriott (John O'Leary), an effeminate patsy,
on a wild-goose chase to recover a stolen jade necklace. This assignment
seems much simpler, but it is not; Marriott is murdered and Marlowe is
framed for the crime. He talks his way out of the charge and tries to find

Marriott's killer on his own. Marlowe looks up Mr. Grayle (Jim Thompson), a collector of jade, hoping to get a lead. Escalating coincidences link Marriott with Mrs. Grayle (Charlotte Rampling). After flirting with Marlowe, Mrs. Grayle also employs him, this time to find out who killed her friend Marriott. As if the story were not complex enough, Amthor (Kate Murtagh), a big-time Los Angeles madame, kidnaps Marlowe. It seems that she, like the police, is looking for Moose Malloy; but her methods are much less genteel than theirs. She resorts to drugs, and Marlowe is left in a room with a corpse to sleep off the effects.

Marlowe is eventually propositioned by nearly every influential character in the film in order to find Moose. He eventually does, and he sets up a meeting with the real Velma through the widow of her ex-boss. The whole meeting smells of double-cross and Marlowe begins to put the pieces together. Through the course of his unconventional investigation, Marlowe begins to suspect that Malloy and Marriott have something in common. That something turns out to be Velma, now known as Mrs. Grayle. She has moved up the social ladder and has been trying to put Malloy out of the way in order to keep her past hidden. The death of several incidental characters is of little consequence to Velma as long as her past is not exposed. In a final shoot-out onboard an offshore gambling ship, Velma kills Malloy and Marlowe shoots her in the stomach. Nearly every element of the novel is incorporated into this film. The weak romantic interplay between Marlowe and Mrs. Grayle's stepdaughter which gave John Paxton's screenplay of *Murder, My Sweet* a positive reinforcement (a romance which was not in the original novel) is not present in this recent version. Marlowe is presented as a middle-aged investigator who, although not perfect, is able to make a living by going through other people's trash.

The use of prostitution, vice, and corruption which was only hinted at in the earlier films is developed with a vengeance in *Farewell, My Lovely*; much of this atmosphere can be credited to an interest in simulating the aura of the *film noir*. A strong feeling of homage is present not only in the period settings but also in the situations and relationships developed in *Farewell, My Lovely*. One of the key elements which contributes to this *film noir*-type attitude was the selection of Robert Mitchum to portray Philip Marlowe. Placed in context, it is easy to link Mitchum with the *film noir*, in that many of his early successes came in such films as *Out of the Past* (1947) and *Macao* (1952). However, by the time of *Farewell, My Lovely*, Mitchum had replaced his boyish charisma and hulking physique for a "hound-dogged" expression and world-weariness which more aptly suits the character of the *film noir*. There is also a sense of *déjà vu* present in John Ireland's portrayal of Lieutenant Nulty, whose early career consisted mostly of roles in B-budget *films noir*.

Although she does not give the same sense of having been there before,

Charlotte Rampling plays the *femme fatale* to the hilt. Her screen presence is reminiscent of both Lauren Bacall and Lizabeth Scott. The characterization of the fatal woman is central to the development of the *film noir*. There is a certain decadence which follows a situation in which a woman is able to offer sexual identity which transcends middle-class restrictions. Rampling as Velma/Helen Grayle oozes with a sexual magnetism, so that it is not difficult to see how she could so thoroughly captivate a character like Moose Malloy. This ability to manipulate people, to make them respond without a sense of control, is also central to the *film noir* attitude.

Seen after *Chinatown* (1974) and *The Long Goodbye* (1973), *Farewell, My Lovely* is easier to place in line with the more traditional *film noir* moods and tone. In Robert Altman's *The Long Goodbye*, one of the more complex Chandler novels was brought to the screen. The setting, however, was contemporary and the milieu was typically Altman. The characterizations and situations did little to point out the basic existentialism of the novel; rather, the entire film maintained a dreamlike quality which overemphasized the negativism of the plot. Roman Polanski's *Chinatown* was cosmetically a homage to the *film noir* in its period setting, stiff dialogue, and grotesque characters; yet for all its association with the past, the tone of *Chinatown* is basically modern, the situations elliptical, and the logic of the characters not so much chaotic as decadently perverse. Gittes, the private eye hero, has the sense of emotional control that somehow never took root in classic *films noir*. *Farewell, My Lovely* falls somewhere in between these two films. A definite homage to the *film noir* era, the film does not flaunt its period settings. Whatever flashiness was found in *Chinatown* or whatever esoteric narrative structure was used in *The Long Goodbye*, neither approaches the mood of the *film noir* as successfully as *Farewell, My Lovely*. In this film, the characters and drama do not seem contrived; and no matter how unlikely the events of the plot might become, a suspension of disbelief is maintained.

Carl F. Macek

A FAREWELL TO ARMS

Released: 1932
Production: Paramount
Direction: Frank Borzage
Screenplay: Benjamin Glazer and Oliver H. P. Garrett; based on the novel
  of the same name by Ernest Hemingway
Cinematography: Charles Lang (AA)
Editing: Otho Lovering
Sound: Harold C. Lewis (AA)
Running time: 78 minutes

> *Principal characters:*
> Frederic Henry .... Gary Cooper
> Catherine Barkley .... Helen Hayes
> Major Rinaldi .... Adolphe Menjou
> Helen Ferguson .... Mary Philips
> The Priest .... Jack La Rue

Romance amid the chaos of World War I is the major theme of Frank
Borzage's screen version of Ernest Hemingway's novel *A Farewell to Arms*.
Unlike the original novel, which was a powerful indictment of war and its
effects upon the participants, the film is highly idealized and chooses to make
a statement through its dramatization of a touching love story. Yet some of
Hemingway's hardboiled realism of detail and the ultimate tragedy of the
characters' love temper the film's idealism and create a powerful picture of
love and war.

The behind-the-lines romance of Frederic Henry (Gary Cooper) and Catherine Barkley (Helen Hayes) begins as a casual meeting during an air raid.
This encounter does little to preface the romantic involvement they soon
share. Frederic's friend Rinaldi (Adolphe Menjou) is also attracted to Catherine and experiences some jealousy when Frederic begins to get serious
about her. Later, as an ambulance driver, Frederic is wounded and sent to
recuperate in a hospital in which Catherine is working. Rinaldi becomes
aware that Frederic's fascination with the nurse is more than a mere wartime
romance of little consequence. Rinaldi is also quick to realize that something
tragic may come of their love affair. This sentiment is also echoed by Catherine's friend, Helen Ferguson (Mary Philips), who tells Catharine and Frederic that they will never marry. To her, love is merely an illusion; fighting and
dying are the only realities.

After Frederic returns to the front, Catherine leaves her post at the hospital
and sets up residence in a Swiss village near the Italian border. She is pregnant
and feels it is best to live alone in a small flat rather than face the authorities
and expose Frederic to almost certain punishment. The lovers write letters

which, for one reason or another, are never delivered. Worried that something may have happened to Catherine, Frederic deserts his post and returns to the hospital in an attempt to be reunited with her. Catherine is not there and his search for her is hampered by Ferguson, who hates Frederic for making her friend pregnant. His continued absence without leave causes Frederic to face charges of desertion if he is ever captured.

Rinaldi, meanwhile, finds his old friend and tells him that Catherine is in Switzerland. Frederic makes his way without delay to Switzerland by boat from Italy. There he finds that Catherine, because of complications of her pregnancy, is dying. He arrives too late to help either her or their child; the baby is stillborn and Catherine is beyond help. Her death comes almost at the moment of armistice. Frederic is heartbroken; the pain of this loss is too great to bear. He speaks to her as she dies, hoping against hope that she will live. He proclaims his love for her, a love that will transcend her death, and she dies in his arms.

As the first Hemingway novel to be turned into a film, A Farewell to Arms is distinguished on several levels. The most obvious element of this senti- mental film is the ensemble acting of Gary Cooper, Helen Hayes, and Adolphe Menjou. Helen Hayes brings her incredible screen presence to her portrayal of Catherine. As one of the most respected actresses of the Broadway stage, Hayes was much sought after by motion picture studios. It is a testament to her personal stature as an actress that she chose to make so few films. Her ability to convey a convincing romance between herself and the lanky Gary Cooper is remarkable; another actress of her diminutive size might have made the entire affair seem ludicrous. Menjou adds the perfect blend of sophistication and humor necessary to carry this unhappy tale of ill-fated lovers. Gary Cooper is the perfect Hemingway hero. Having spent a great deal of his early career portraying World War I soldiers, it was only a short step to the more pessimistic characters of Hemingway's writings.

Frank Borzage made a career out of directing some of the most romantic films of Hollywood. In addition to A Farewell to Arms, he made such mem- orable romantic films as History Is Made at Night (1937), Man's Castle (1934), and the bittersweet Moonrise (1948). In the manner of such directors as Douglas Sirk and John M. Stahl, Borzage is able to present touching romantic films without the cloying quality that so often accompanies such stories. He was a straightforward director whose early experience as a silent film director of B-budget Westerns and genre films taught him the techniques of filmmak- ing.

In addition to Borzage, A Farewell to Arms also boasts the talents of cinematographer Charles Lang, who received an Academy Award for his work in this film. The montage sequence of Frederic trying to return to Catherine is breathtaking. Likewise, Lang's prolonged take which begins, from Frederic's point of view, rolling into the hospital, going through winding corridors, and eventually ending with Catherine's face filling the lens as she and Frederic meet in a loving embrace, is magnificent. The images of destruction and horror brought about by the war are enhanced by subtle superimpositions and religious icons which lend an overriding sense of morality to the sequences.

A Farewell to Arms was a bold film which presented the situation of clandestine love with candor and simplicity. It was not exactly as vivid a description of war and its aftermath as was Hemingway's original novel, and yet the film was able to capture the irony of Hemingway's chaotic world. It is only because of the perseverance of Borzage that Catherine was allowed to die at the end of the film; an alternative version was shot in which she recovers and supposedly lives happily ever after with her adoring Frederic. The fact that Hemingway's ending was finally decided upon—something that was frowned upon by certain studio advisers as being unacceptable to a large portion of the viewing public—is the key which allows the unabashed romanticism of *A Farewell to Arms* to survive the pitfalls of most unrequited love stories.

Carl F. Macek

FIDDLER ON THE ROOF

Released: 1971
Production: Norman Jewison for United Artists
Direction: Norman Jewison
Screenplay: Joseph Stein; based on his stage adaptation of the writings of Sholom Aleichem
Cinematography: Oswald Morris (AA)
Editing: Antony Gibbs and Robert Lawrence
Choreography: Tom Abbott; based on the stage choreography of Jerome Robbins
Sound: Gordon K. McCallum and David Hildyard (AA)
Music: John Williams (AA)
Song: Sheldon Harnick and Jerry Bock
Running time: 180 minutes

Principal characters:

Tevye	Topol
Golde	Norma Crane
Yente	Molly Picon
Motel	Leonard Frey
Tzeitel	Rosalind Harris
Hodel	Michele Marsh
Chava	Neva Small
Perchik	Michael Glaser
Lazar Wolf	Paul Mann

In 1971, at the time of filming *Fiddler on the Roof*, the movie musical was experiencing a major decline. Recent attempts to re-create the successful musical comedies of the 1940's and 1950's, as in the cases of *Star!* (1968) and *Paint Your Wagon* (1969), had failed miserably. Yet *Fiddler on the Roof* was such an internationally successful stage show with an excellent script and libretto that a film version was perhaps inevitable.

The adaptation of a Broadway musical to the screen was a rather awesome task. In the case of *Fiddler on the Roof* it was necessary to integrate the theatricality of the play with the ingrained realism of the screen. Norman Jewison was the director chosen by Walter Mirisch and United Artists to translate the play into film. At that time, Jewison was known largely for his work in television on eight Judy Garland shows, and in film on two Doris Day comedies and a Tony Curtis vehicle. Just prior to being approached by Mirisch for *Fiddler on the Roof*, however, Jewison had received acclaim for his films *The Russians Are Coming, The Russians Are Coming* (1966) and *In the Heat of the Night*, the latter winning an Oscar for the year 1967. Jewison, perhaps inspired by the success of *Fiddler on the Roof*, would go on to do *Jesus Christ, Superstar* (1973).

Fiddler on the Roof deals with the life of Russian Jews at the time of the 1905 pogroms carried out by the Tsar. On a smaller scale, it is the story of the dairyman Tevye, struggling for survival and adapting to a new, often bewildering world. This irrevocable move towards change is exemplified in the manner of the courtships and subsequent marriages of Tevye's three oldest daughters, as they break from the tradition of matchmakers and prearranged marriages.

The movie opens with Tevye (Topol) contemplating the way of life in Anatevka. He speaks to God and directs many of his musings to the audience. This device, used continually throughout the film, allows the audience a closer identification with the character of Tevye, and was an ingenious way of adapting Tevye's numerous monologues to the screen. Next, Tevye introduces us to the villagers, all at work, who break into the song "Tradition." Tom Abbott, the film's choreographer, was faced with the challenge of making the dance sequences derive naturally from the action, and of allowing for a seemingly smooth-flowing return to that action. The dance sequences would need to contribute to and be a necessary, rather than a superfluous, part of the movie. This effect is successful with "Tradition," as the dance derives from the work each villager is doing and contributes to the feeling of a village celebration, of a hard-working people still able to appreciate life.

Tevye continues on his way to his home, where he is confronted by his practical, long-suffering wife Golde (Norma Crane) and by his five daughters, three of whom are at a marriageable age. Why all daughters, asks Tevye, with a glance towards heaven and a shrug of the shoulders. The family gathers for dinner and a Sabbath prayer. The happiness, stability, and devotion to tradition depicted thus far are soon, however, to be threatened.

The oldest daughter, Tzeitel (Rosalind Harris), has become secretly engaged to Motel (Leonard Frey), the poor tailor, and rebels against a prearranged marriage with the wealthy old butcher, Lazar Wolf (Paul Mann). Tzeitzel and Motel confront Tevye, who is, after all, a good man and a loving father. He tries to think his way out of the dilemma. As the audience is included in Tevye's ponderings, the camera draws away from the other characters, who remain frozen. This repeated device is another acknowledgment of the film's legitimate stage source.

Deciding in favor of his daughter's happiness, Tevye is faced with the problem of explaining matters to Golde. He does so with the marvelous abstract dream sequence, which is the film's only lapse into fantasy and theatricality. In it, Golde's long-dead grandmother advises marriage between Tzeitel and Motel, since the fact that Lazar Wolf had previously been married would bring bad luck to the couple.

Tevye is a man beset by troubles; and no sooner is this first problem solved than the next storm cloud appears in the form of the film's revolutionary element, Perchik (Michael Glaser). Brought into the family as a tutor for the girls, he soon becomes involved with Tevye's second daughter, Hodel (Michele Marsh). As they approach Tevye merely for his blessing, rather than for permission to marry, he becomes more and more angry and frustrated at this defiance of tradition. Not being narrow-minded, however, Tevye himself begins to wonder whether this new practice of marrying for love is perhaps not better than the old tradition of marrying a selected stranger whom one might learn to love. Returning home, he asks Golde, "Do You Love Me?" in one of the movie's most touching scenes.

Eventually, however, Tevye is unable to reconcile himself entirely to the new way of doing things. As the pogroms continue and the residents of Anatevka are faced with eviction by the Russians, another of Tevye's daughters, Chava (Neva Small), becomes involved with a Russian officer. Tevye cannot condone this break not only with tradition but with religion as well, and he turns his back on his daughter.

The film closes with a mass exodus of Jews from Anatevka, which the film was more successful in depicting than the stage version had been. The final song, "Anatevka," sung as the villagers all file out along the road, expresses nostalgia for times past as well as a determination to face the future.

In keeping with the world of Sholom Aleichem, upon whose writings *Fiddler on the Roof* is based, Jewison strove for authentic detail. To achieve this, filming was done in Yugoslavia rather than on a Hollywood set. Jewison took great care with every aspect of the production. In his search for a location, he wanted a place far removed from the twentieth century with a warm, earthy quality and real peasants in the background. Elements of three different towns were incorporated in order to get the feel of the different sides of Anatevka. Jewison was so concerned with authenticity that Tevye's house, barn, and cheese hut were constructed with materials dating from the turn of the century.

The title *Fiddler on the Roof* was originally inspired by a painting by Marc Chagall, and Jewison wanted the overall production to aspire to the particular quality reflected in Chagall's art. The village of Lekenik, which served as residential Anatevka, conveyed that quality, as did the work of the film's cinematographer, Oswald Morris, who was awarded an Oscar for his cinematography. The dream sequence, much expanded for the screen, reflected the special Chagall quality in its style, design, and color. All other scenes were filmed through a silk stocking, resulting in the muted colors of the landscapes and the warm brown earth tones so evident in the overall production. Other members of the production staff whose excellent work earned them Academy Awards were John Williams for his adaptation and treatment of the music, and Gordon K. McCallum and David Hildyard for sound.

The acting in *Fiddler on the Roof* was uniformly excellent, with a fine cast headed by the Israeli actor Topol in the monumental role of Tevye. Chosen over Zero Mostel, who had headed the Broadway cast and set the type for every Tevye that followed, Topol, who had starred in the London production, was considered potentially a better movie actor, possessing more warmth and dignity, together with a sensual quality no previous Tevye had possessed. It was a fine enough performance, endowed with wisdom, humor, and vigor, to earn Topol and Academy Award nomination for Best Actor, although he lost to Gene Hackman for *The French Connection*. Other outstanding performances were Norma Crane's exasperated but warm Golde; Leonard Frey's enormously endearing Motel, possessed of an inner strength unknown possibly even to him; Rosalind Harris' equally appealing Tzeitel; and the delightful Yente of the veteran actress Molly Picon.

An enormous popular success, *Fiddler on the Roof* was acclaimed, for the most part, by the critics, and was nominated for an Academy Award for Best Picture of 1971, losing to *The French Connection*. What adverse criticism the film did receive derived from problems directly related to the medium of film: complaints that the movie was more ethnic, detailed, and realistic, and larger and less stylized than the Broadway musical. These problems could not effectively be avoided, however, given the nature of the screen. They are, instead, assets. *Fiddler on the Roof* remains one of the strongest movie musicals of recent years.

Grace Anne Morsberger

FILM

Released: 1966
Production: Evergreen Theatre, Inc.
Direction: Alan Schneider
Screenplay: Samuel Beckett
Cinematography: Boris Kaufman
Editing: Sidney Meyers
Running time: 22 minutes

> *Principal character:*
> The man .... Buster Keaton

The work of all dramatists is divided between journalism and poetry. Samuel Beckett has always approached drama the way he has approached his novels and stories, as poetic exercise. His genius has been one of condensation and suggestion, evoking haunting responses from the simplest materials, like a man in a furnished room listening to a voice (*Eh, Joe?*) or to a tape recorder (*Krapp's Last Tape*). A few vaudeville turns are strung together in *Waiting for Godot* to become a harrowing cosmic joke. Often his stage pictures are still-lifes that take on ineffable overtones as a single element begins to move. In the plays, and even more so in the novels, he has passed from settings as recognizable as Ireland to no-man's-land and then to a void that may simply be a map of our collective consciousness. His dramas make metaphors of minimal elements—whispers, broken phrases, pratfalls, ashcans, mounds of earth, strings of memories. There may be less of the journalist and more of the poet in Beckett than in any major dramatist to date. In his own classic phrase, he does not write about something; he writes something.

In *Film*, his only produced screenplay to date, he and his director, Alan Schneider, the man most often associated with staging Beckett in the United States, have created a film whose power lies precisely in this: it does not mean what it says. In a literal sense, it says nothing at all; but, like any great poem, it means what it is.

A man (Buster Keaton) is in flight from the eyes of the world and from the camera, which pursues him while keeping to an angle that avoids showing his face. People on the street are annoyed when he jostles them. A woman in a vestibule does not see him at all. But when these characters look into the pursuing camera—look at "us"—they are horrified, their mouths agape.

In the sanctuary of his room the man curtains his window, covers his mirror, shades his bird and goldfish, puts out his cat and dog, tears up his photos, and finally dozes off in his rocker, apparently safe from scrutiny. But then the camera tracks slowly around to face him at last and wake him by the very intensity of its gaze. The man looks up—into his own face, staring down at him with a terrible, haunting impassivity, neither angry nor bitter, just there.

The man in the rocking chair covers his eyes and slumps in despair. The standing figure continues relentlessly staring.

Discovering Beckett for the first time, it is often easiest to explain what he is by what he is not. *Film* is only twenty-two minutes long, with one main character played by Keaton at the age of sixty-nine. There is no dialogue, no color, no music, no titles, no sound of any kind, and no glimpse of Keaton's face until those final, shattering seconds.

What we are offered is two states of perception. The first is Keaton's as he runs, loping through the street in a long cumbersome overcoat with a kerchief over his face, clambering up the stairs, sneaking up on a mirror from underneath it to cover it lest he glimpse himself; putting out the cat only to have the dog come in; putting out the dog only to have the cat reenter. He is clumsy, precise, obsessive, funny, and, in the end, agonized in horror and defeat, covering his eyes, knowing that he cannot avoid his own self-perception.

The second mode of seeing, of course, is the camera's as it pursues. It is unlikely that any major American film since *Lady in the Lake* (1946) has so pointedly and repeatedly called attention to itself as a photographed object. The looks of the people in the street and the old woman in the vestibule remind us of their pursuing presence—and prepare us for the terror that is coming. When Keaton stands staring down at himself in the rocking chair, the geography of the film is revealed. For then we see how the two kinds of perception make up the contours of a single consciousness—one mind—the halves of a psyche, looking out on the world and in on itself. By sundering the eye (camera) and the object (Keaton), Beckett has made *Film* into a model of consciousness.

Beckett is clear about his intentions. In the preface to the published version (Grove Press, 1969), he gives as his text Berkeley's theory that to be is to be perceived; to be alive is to suffer self-perception. There is no escape. *Film* is the picture of a mind, including that part of consciousness we may fear but never evade. It has the deeply disturbing impact of a horror film, almost a horror film for philosophers. The real horror is never monsters or outlandish creatures, not mutants or bogeymen to frighten children. The true horror is continuing to see ourselves clearly, without escape, as long as we live.

The production serves Beckett beautifully in every way. Boris Kaufman's lighting washes the man's room in a neutral white, a soft, limbo light that brings the grainy plaster of the walls slightly into relief, as if to emphasize their emptiness. It picks up the sparkle in every eye—fish's, parrot's, passerby's, and finally even Keaton's—so as to increase the intensity of its observation.

Each move is orchestrated by Alan Schneider with a lunatic precision and craftiness. Keaton is diabolically clever about avoiding being seen. And Keaton himself, viewed from behind, shambling with a mixture of grace and awkwardness, or viewed from in front with a face of monumental, stoic sadness, is beyond acting. He is the embodiment of Beckett's *Film*, the perfect expression of that mind we have entered, that mesh which holds us.

The winner of a Nobel Prize, Beckett is recognized today as one of the most important writers of the century and possibly the most enduring, influential dramatist of our time. In all his work, the questions of perception and consciousness are central. Indeed, that work can be seen as a continuing examination and re-creation of modern consciousness. It is all of a piece with this small, simple, twenty-two-minute film that is just what meets the eye, and just what cannot bear the scrutiny of that eye.

Ted Gershuny

FIRE OVER ENGLAND

Released: 1937
Production: Erich Pommer for Pendennis/London Films; released by United
  Artists
Direction: William K. Howard
Screenplay: Clemence Dane and Sergei Nolbandov; based on the novel of
  the same name by A. E. W. Mason
Cinematography: James Wong Howe
Editing: John Dennis
Costume design: Rene Hubert
Music: Richard Addinsell
Running time: 92 minutes

Principal characters:

Queen Elizabeth	Flora Robson
Michael Ingolby	Laurence Olivier
Cynthia	Vivien Leigh
The Earl of Leicester	Leslie Banks
Philip II	Raymond Massey
Lord Burleigh	Morton Selten
Spanish Ambassador	Henry Oscar
Don Pedro	Robert Newton
Hillary Vane	James Mason

With the coming of sound, the swashbuckler, a genre singularly identified
in the silent era with Douglas Fairbanks, was eclipsed for five years, perhaps
because of the awkwardness of the early sound equipment and the need to
minimize movement away from the hidden microphones. With the *Count of
Monte Cristo* (1934) and *Captain Blood* (1935), however, the swashbuckler
was reborn and became one of the more vital forms of film for the next two
decades. Aside from *The Scarlet Pimpernel* (1934), which has more talk than
action, the first English contribution to the genre was *Fire over England*
(1937), an Elizabethan epic loosely based on a novel by A. E. W. Mason,
best known as the author of *The Four Feathers*.

Although the main conflict is between Elizabeth and Philip II of Spain,
the film's hero is a fictional young naval officer, Michael Ingolby (Laurence
Olivier). As the story opens, the ship in which Ingolby and his father are
cruising off the Spanish coast is attacked by several of Philip's ships. The
father is captured, but the son swims ashore and is given shelter and protection
by a Spanish friend, Don Miguel, whose daughter is romantically inclined
towards the young Englishman. Meanwhile, Ingolby's father has been taken
prisoner and is burned at the stake by the Inquisition. His son vows revenge.

With the assistance of Don Miguel, Ingolby returns to England, where he is promptly summoned into the presence of the Queen (Flora Robson), who wishes to hear the latest report from Spain. Cynthia, her lady-in-waiting (Vivien Leigh), and Ingolby have been in love, and when she impetuously dashes into the Queen's presence to embrace her sweetheart, the Queen peremptorily orders her from the room. Matters of state must come first. Elizabeth then questions Ingolby about the situation in Spain and makes him feel absurd by revealing that she already is familiar with the information he has brought. But she needs to know more, especially about the Armada that Philip is rumored to be preparing, and she sends Ingolby back in disguise as a secret agent to ferret out intelligence about the strength and disposition of Philip's fleet and the identity of Englishmen suspected of being traitors in Spanish hire. In an interview with Philip (Raymond Massey), Ingolby ascertains the names of all but one of the traitors, but he is tripped up by his ignorance of the remaining one and is arrested until his own credentials can be proved or disproved. Before the Spanish can put him to torture, he manages to set part of the palace on fire, outfence the guards, and escape back to England.

Barely has he returned when the Armada sets sail. During the battle, Ingolby is given another chance to serve the Queen by commanding the fire ships that played a crucial role in destroying the Spanish fleet. He is rewarded with knighthood and the hand of Cynthia.

The merits of *Fire over England* transcend the plot. Produced by Erich Pommer, who had worked in Germany on *The Cabinet of Dr. Caligari* (1919), *Die Nibelungen* (1924), *Metropolis* (1926), and *The Blue Angel* (1930), and photographed by James Wong Howe, with a score by Richard Addinsell, *Fire over England* is a very handsomely mounted production. The script by Clemence Dane and Sergei Nolbandov has some moments of pseudo-Shakespearean eloquence, and the cast is outstanding. Most notable is Flora Robson as Queen Elizabeth, a role she would repeat three years later in *The Sea Hawk*. We have since become accustomed to seeing numerous actresses in the part (Bette Davis, Glenda Jackson, Jean Simmons, and Irene Worth in films, and Eva le Gallienne and Judith Anderson on television), but by 1937 Elizabeth had been portrayed on screen only by Sarah Bernhardt in a 1912 French production; and by Florence Eldridge, not very memorably, in *Mary of Scotland* (1936). Flora Robson creates a Queen who is at once imperious, gracious, witty, and romantic—a monarch fit to inspire the loyalty of her subjects. Nearly as impressive are Leslie Banks as the Earl of Leicester and Raymond Massey as a dour, crooked-mouthed Philip II.

Fire over England is also notable for the part it played in the careers and lives of Laurence Olivier and Vivien Leigh. Although Olivier had been in films since 1931, none of his previous pictures, with the exception of *As You Like It* (1936), was in any way notable. Likewise, Vivien Leigh had made only four trifling and forgotten films in 1935; *Fire over England* was her first part in a major production with an international release. Off the screen, the film was crucial in the lives of Olivier and Leigh, for it was during the fourteen weeks of filming, their first time acting together, that they became lovers; thus *Fire over England* contributed to the establishment of England's most celebrated twentieth century acting team. Unfortunately, they were paired in only two subsequent films, *Twenty-One Days* (1939) and *That Hamilton Woman* (1941).

Despite its production values and impressive performances, the film has a few disappointments. The scene in which Olivier weeps on learning of the execution of his father was jeered at by American audiences, who expected more toughness from their heroes, and it was finally deleted from American release prints. It is, in fact, a rather maudlin scene that not even Olivier could manage to make convincing. Although the rest of the production is opulent, the climactic episode of the Armada is a sharp disappointment. The battle is confined to a glimpse of a few obvious and unmanned miniature model ships coming through the fog, and the English Navy is confined to a small boat manned only by Olivier waving his torch. The one bit of excitement occurs when Olivier leaps onboard the mock-up of a galleon, flings a firebrand onto the gasoline-soaked deck, and then dives overboard (into a concealed net, as the piece of the galleon was on a field at Denham studios). During one take, the flames got out of control, Olivier had to leap overboard in earnest; in his haste, he slipped on the ship's rail and fell so heavily into the net that he appeared to have broken his neck. Fortunately, he was uninjured; but for the remaining takes he utilized a stand-in.

Although it is a British film made by Sir Alexander Korda's London Films, *Fire over England* was directed by an American, William K. Howard, whose earlier credits included *Sherlock Holmes* (1932) and *The Power and the Glory* (1933).

In England and the rest of Europe, *Fire over England* received both audience approval and critical acclaim. Lionel Collier wrote in the British fan magazine *Picturegoer*: "This picture stands head and shoulders above any historical drama yet made in this country and it has had few rivals from other countries. . . . As the young lovers Vivien Leigh and Laurence Olivier are exceedingly good." The *New Statesman* overcame its qualms about glorifying the past and predicted that audiences would find the film stirring. In France, it won the Gold Medal of the *Comité International pour la Diffusion Artistique et Littéraire pour le Cinéma*, but in the United States it fared less well, despite a premiere at Grauman's Chinese Theater. For some reason, Hitler became so fond of the film that he screened it repeatedly, according to British newsmen who visited him before the war—though historical parallels would have identified him with the terror of the Spanish Inquisition and Philip II's goal of conquest—a parallel that was in fact clearly made in the beginning of *The Sea Hawk* three years later.

Seen today, *Fire over England* holds up on the strength of its performances, a literate script, spectacular sets, and James Wong Howe's brilliant cinematography. It remains a memorable example of the romantic costume film that flourished in the 1930's.

Robert E. Morsberger

FIVE EASY PIECES

Released: 1970
Production: Bob Rafelson and Richard Wechsler for Columbia
Direction: Bob Rafelson
Screenplay: Adrien Joyce; based on a story by Bob Rafelson and Adrien Joyce
Cinematography: Laszlo Kovacs
Editing: Christopher Holmes and Gerald Sheppard
Running time: 98 minutes

Principal characters:

Robert Eroica Dupea	Jack Nicholson
Rayette Dipesto	Karen Black
Partita Dupea	Lois Smith
Catherine Van Ost	Susan Anspach
Elton	Billy "Green" Bush
Stoney	Fannie Flagg
Betty	Sally Ann Struthers
Nicholas Dupea	William Challee

On the surface, it may not seem that a feature such as *Five Easy Pieces* would have had a wide public appeal; it was both thoughtful and intelligent and had nothing to do with the youth problems of the 1960's. Instead, it was a comedy-drama of a mature man's search for his own identity, and the fact that it elicited a positive response from moviegoers is indicative of its realistic treatment of a psychological problem that many have faced, particularly during the troubled decade in which the film is set.

Five Easy Pieces tells the story of Robert Eroica Dupea (Jack Nicholson), formerly a brilliant concert pianist, who has now abandoned his old life-style, adopted a fake Southern accent, and taken a job as an oil-rigger in the Southern California oil fields. He has completely turned away from classical music and from his old friends and is living with a featherbrained woman named Rayette Dipesto (Karen Black); their best friends are his fellow worker, Elton (Billy "Green" Bush), and his wife Stoney (Fannie Flagg). Why Dupea is masquerading like this and seeking the company of people so far removed from his intellectual background remains something of a mystery. When he learns that Rayette is pregnant, he quits his job and abandons her, realizing that she is trying to trap him into marriage.

Dupea goes into Los Angeles and attends a recording session of his sister, Partita (Lois Smith), who, like him, is an accomplished pianist. It is evident now that he is no common oil laborer; he is the music-oriented and very brilliant son of a family of wealthy and eccentric musicians who has been unable to run from what he calls his "auspicious beginnings." Partita, however, informs him that their father has had a stroke which has paralyzed his vocal chords, and is now confined to his home in the state of Washington.

Dupea, meanwhile, cannot shake Rayette, so he takes her with him when he drives north to Washington to visit his dying father. On the way there is a brilliant interlude when they pick up a couple of female hitch-hikers, one of them a brassy lesbian who is thumbing her way to Alaska with her girl friend because they are obsessed with cleanliness and have heard that Alaska is ecologically clean. They go to a roadside restaurant, and, in the most memorable sequence of the film, Dupea deliberately quarrels with the waitress and the owner. This whole sequence is brilliantly executed, and although it is admittedly a deviation from the main story line, it, more than anything else, explains Dupea's psyche and sets the stage for his subsequent behavior when he reaches his father's home.

He realizes that Rayette is too offbeat to present to his family, so he deposits her in a nearby motel and goes on to his father's home by himself. He dines there with his father, who has been painfully stricken dumb, his sister, and Catherine Van Ost (Susan Anspach), a charming piano student who is visiting the family with her boyfriend. Dupea immediately recognizes in Catherine the kind of girl who is in every way right for him. He boldly woos her, and although she resists his advances at first, she is attracted, and they make love.

Rayette rebels at being installed in a motel, and appears on the scene as Dupea's sweetheart. The family is coolly amused by her brashness, and they invite her to stay with them. Dupea is furious with her, but helpless to control her behavior. Furthermore, he has a disappointing confrontation with his father, and when he asks Catherine to go away with him, she turns him down because he lacks stability. Dupea leaves, and Rayette, who sticks to him like a leech, accompanies him on the way back to Los Angeles. He realizes that she is the most exasperating female he has ever encountered, and at a truck stop he manages to ditch her and get a ride back to somewhere else with a compatible truck driver. He has left his car for her, but wants nothing more to do with her, for he is off on a new journey to find himself in a new way. The title *Five Easy Pieces* does not refer to the sexual conquests of the main character as many filmgoers believe, but to the name of an elementary book of music which all piano students know; once they have learned that quintet of "easy" pieces, they are ready to learn advanced compositions. In other words, once they have mastered the basics, they are ready for the real compositions. Likewise, Dupea, once he has found himself, may be ready to face life.

More than one critic has commented that, in style, the film is more French than it is Hollywood, more like Truffaut's *Shoot the Piano Player* (1960) or Eric Rohmer's *My Night at Maud's* (1969). Its screenplay by Adrien Joyce (from a story by Bob Rafelson and Adrien Joyce) is immaculately constructed, and although it won an Academy Award nomination, the Oscar went to the writers of *Patton* (1970). The film is neatly directed by Bob Rafelson, who had previously worked with Nicholson in a film the latter wrote, entitled *Head* (1968).

Jack Nicholson has acted in a series of "B" pictures from 1957 to 1969, and had a devoted following by the time he played the lawyer who takes to the road with Peter Fonda and Dennis Hopper in *Easy Rider* (1969). Nicholson has a kind of wry, provocative amusement in his eyes that makes him ideal for the casually inconoclastic characters he plays so well. His success has continued in all his subsequent films, including *Carnal Knowledge* (1971), *The Last Detail* (1973), *Chinatown* (1974), and, finally, the picture that brought him an Academy Award in 1975, *One Flew Over the Cuckoo's Nest*.

DeWitt Bodeen

FLAMING STAR

Released: 1960
Production: David Weisbart for Twentieth Century-Fox
Direction: Don Siegel
Screenplay: Clair Huffaker and Nunnally Johnson; based on the novel of the
  same name by Clair Huffaker
Cinematography: Charles G. Clarke
Editing: Hugh S. Fowler
Running time: 101 minutes

Principal characters:

Pacer Burton	Elvis Presley
Sam Burton	John McIntire
Clint Burton	Steve Forrest
Neddy Burton	Dolores Del Rio
Buffalo Horn	Rudolph Acosta
Will Howard	Douglas Dick
Roslyn Pierce	Barbara Eden
Two Moons	Perry Lopez

It is frequently argued that his two years in the army took all of the artistic fight out of Elvis Presley. Having changed the face of popular music more radically than anyone before or since, he entered the military a worthy successor to such rebellious heroes as Marlon Brando and James Dean, so the argument goes, and returned in 1960 tame and civilized, with his best work behind him. The truth is a bit more complicated. Presley's career undeniably went into eclipse in the early 1960's, but not without a whimper. Just as the music on his *Elvis Is Back* album can stand with anything he recorded in the 1950's, in *Flaming Star* Presley gave what must stand alongside his work in *Jailhouse Rock* (1957) as the best acting of his long, if erratic, film career; and both the album and the film were released in 1960, after he left the army. *Flaming Star* is noteworthy in another way as well: it marked the first (as well as best and last) attempt to market Elvis as an actor rather than as a singer. The effort failed, but on financial, not artistic, grounds.

As the film opens, we hear Elvis singing the title song over the credits; shortly thereafter comes "A Cane and a High Starched Collar," a song so undistinguished that Elvis' record company did not release it on an album until sixteen years later. From that point on, there are no more songs; instead of good songs, what we get is a good film.

Flaming Star finds Presley under the directional guidance of Don Siegel, one of the few directors of any personal distinction (Michael Curtiz, who directed *King Creole*, 1958, is another exception) to work with Elvis. By 1960, Siegel had one classic film already under his belt—the original *Invasion of the Body Snatchers* (1956); ahead lay a series of highly successful (and controversial) films with Clint Eastwood. Siegel's best work always has seemed to feature a lone, often antisocial protagonist, such as Neville Brand in *Riot in Cell Block 11* (1954), Mickey Rooney in *Baby Face Nelson* (1957), and Eastwood in *Escape from Alcatraz* (1979) and the "Dirty Harry" Callaghan films. In this respect, *Flaming Star* is certainly of a piece with the rest of Siegel's classics.

Flaming Star is a Western. It was not Presley's first Western—in *Love Me Tender*, his screen debut four years earlier, he played Clint Reno, a hotheaded young rancher in post-Civil War Texas. Pacer Burton, his role in *Flaming Star*, is also a hot-headed young rancher of the same time and place, but with a twist. His mother, Neddy (Dolores Del Rio), is a full-blooded Kiowa Indian, and Pacer's status as a half-breed—unable to accept completely or reject completely either side of his nature—creates the dramatic tension that shapes the film's narrative.

Pacer lives with his father, Sam Burton (John McIntire), his mother, Neddy, and his half-brother, Clint (Steve Forrest)—Sam's son by a previous marriage. The Burtons, as Siegel emphasizes repeatedly, are a close-knit family. Their first loyalties are always to one another. These loyalties are sometimes strained, however, by the Indian blood in the family. For although Sam and Clint are well liked by the surrounding ranchers and townsfolk, and Pacer is tolerated, the long history of mutual hostility between the Kiowas and the white settlers makes Neddy an outcast.

In the first scenes of *Flaming Star*, Siegel emphasizes the dichotomy between the Kiowas and the whites, and shows us that while Pacer is somehow a part of both worlds, he feels truly comfortable in neither. The white world is exemplified in a birthday party attended by Pacer, Sam, and Clint. There is laughter and singing, and the Burtons fit in easily with their friends, the Howards and the Pierces (although a reference to Neddy casts a momentary pall over the celebration). In a scene that follows shortly thereafter, however, we see the other side of Pacer's character. The Burtons are at home, on their ranch, when Pacer spots a lone Indian on horseback, several hundred yards away. Although he comes no closer and says not a word, Pacer turns to his family and says "The Kiowas have a new chief." When asked how he knew, Pacer cannot explain. He only knows that the Indian side of his nature permits him to interpret these obscure portents.

It soon becomes clear that circumstances will never permit the peaceful reconciliation of the two sides of Pacer's personality. The new leader of the Kiowas, Buffalo Horn (Rudolph Acosta), is a war chief, and the first of a series of raids he orders is directed at the Burtons' friends: the Kiowas attack and massacre the Howard family. Only Will Howard (Douglas Dick) survives. Wounded, he crawls out into the prairie, where he will reappear at a crucial point in the film.

The pressure is now on Sam and Clint Burton, who is by now engaged to Roslyn Pierce (Barbara Eden), to abandon Pacer and Neddy and join the whites in fighting the Indians. But Sam responds firmly. "This family will stick together," he says. "We'll resist whoever and whatever comes against us." A stormy confrontation with the Pierces ends when Clint shoots one of the clan for referring to his stepmother as a "Kiowa squaw." Typically, the hot-headed Pacer is dissatisfied with Clint's handling of the incident, swearing that the offender should have been killed.

This early indication that Pacer may be more Kiowa than white is reinforced when, with Sam and Clint gone, two men ride up to the Burton ranch asking for food. When they learn that Pacer and Neddy are Kiowas, their manner changes abruptly. They call Pacer "red boy," and demand sexual favors from Neddy. Pacer thrashes them and drives them off, but Siegel uses this incident to illustrate that his protagonist is inexorably being forced to deny or ignore the white half of his heritage.

The next day, Buffalo Horn returns to visit Pacer and Neddy. He demands that Pacer return to his people. "I don't know who's my people," Pacer replies, confused. "Maybe I ain't got any." Nonetheless, he and Neddy return with Buffalo Horn to the Kiowa camp to talk to the Indians and try to convince them to abandon their attacks against the white settlers. When a brave named Two Moons (Perry Lopez) asks Pacer contemptuously if the white man is treating him well, Pacer replies evenly "My father and my brother do." This is an important and revealing exchange. It indicates that while Pacer may be on the verge of rejecting the white half of his heritage, he is not ready to embrace the Indian half either. His family is of paramount importance.

The visit ends in a standoff. The Kiowas will not cease their depradations, and Pacer will not join them. On their way home, however, tragedy strikes. Neddy is ambushed by Will Howard, the survivor of the first Kiowa raid. A stunned Pacer kills Howard and takes his badly wounded mother home.

The white ranchers' reaction to the news of Neddy's injury further fuels the flames of Pacer's resentment. When he and Clint ride into town for help, the residents sneeringly suggest that they get a medicine man instead. The town doctor refuses to accompany them, and agrees to treat Neddy only when Pacer kidnaps his daughter. Neddy dies before they reach her, and Pacer is furious. "White men shot her and white men let her die," he hisses, vowing revenge. He takes Neddy's body to the Kiowa camp, where he intends to join Buffalo Horn and his warriors; but before leaving, he promises Sam and Clint that no harm will come to them.

This, however, is not to be. Just as a white man killed Pacer's Indian mother, a band of Kiowas ambush and kill his white father. Clint buries Sam next to Neddy's grave, and rides off seeking revenge of his own. He soon encounters the band led by Buffalo Horn and Pacer, and, after a long chase in which he is seriously wounded by a Kiowa arrow, Clint kills Buffalo Horn. Once again, fate (and the filmmakers) have given Pacer no easy way out. Betrayed by both sides, Pacer now abandons both sides and returns to his family—his brother Clint. "We're the only family we got left now," he cries, stricken.

The tragic denouement, now inevitable, soon follows. After seeing that Clint gets back into town safely, Pacer rides off to avenge his father's death. His parting words are "If it's gonna be like this the rest of my life, to hell with it."

The film's final scene is also one of its most powerful. Back in town, Clint wakes up and struggles to his feet as a voice announces "Rider comin' in. Looks like he's bad hurt." The rider is Pacer Burton, come back to deliver his own epitaph. "I've been killed already, I'm just stubborn about dying," he announces. "I saw the flaming star of death. I gotta last long enough to go into the hills and die. . . . You live for me." Thus only in death can Pacer embrace and unify the conflicting halves of his heritage. He will die like an Indian, but not before reaffirming his kinship to his white brother. It is a moving end to a strong film.

As in all of Don Siegel's films, the action in *Flaming Star* is tightly paced, as the director and his writers Clair Huffaker and Nunnally Johnson eliminate Pacer's options one by one. The cast works well together, with Steve Forrest and Dolores Del Rio turning in good performances as Clint and Neddy Burton, respectively. Even more affecting is John McIntire as Sam Burton; McIntire brings an unusual degree of melancholy warmth to his role.

But the best acting in the film is undeniably that of Elvis Presley. Though Pacer Burton exhibits many characteristics of the stock Elvis part—he specialized in playing hot-heads in the early part of his film career—Presley, doubtless with the help of Don Siegel, brings something extra to this role. Not only Pacer's anger but also his pain, his confusion, and, by the end of the film, his quiet resignation, come across as genuine. For the first time—and regrettably the last—in his career, Presley was an actor of subtlety.

Flaming Star was the second Presley film of 1960. The first was *GI Blues*, a tuneful if formulaic romp that was the top-grossing Elvis film up to that time. By comparison, *Flaming Star* was a financial flop. The film did not lose money, but Elvis fans had clearly expressed their preference; they wanted to see their hero in a singing role, and his manager, Colonel Tom Parker, quickly obliged, hustling Presley into *Blue Hawaii* (1961) and a succession of other profitable, if boring, ventures. It would be foolish, of course, to claim that Elvis Presley would have been another Marlon Brando; but the evidence in *Jailhouse Rock* and *Flaming Star* indicates that, with the proper directorial guidance, and given the proper roles, he might have become a very good actor indeed. Alas, this never happened.

Robert Mitchell

FLYING DOWN TO RIO

Released: 1933
Production: Merian C. Cooper for RKO/Radio
Direction: Thornton Freeland
Screenplay: Cyril Hume, H. W. Hanemann, and Erwin Gelsey; based on a
  play by Anne Caldwell, adapted from a story by Lou Brock
Cinematography: J. Roy Hunt
Editing: Jack Kitchin
Dance direction: Dave Gould
Music: Vincent Youmans, Edward Eliscu, and Gus Kahn
Running time: 89 minutes

> *Principal characters:*
> Belinha de Rezende .... Dolores Del Rio
> Roger Bond .... Gene Raymond
> Fred Ayres .... Fred Astaire
> Honey Hale .... Ginger Rogers
> Julio Rubeiro .... Raul Roulien
> Titia .... Blanche Friderici

In 1933, the overwhelming box-office success of Warner Bros. *42nd Street*
revived the dormant film musical and inspired other studios to rush musicals
into production. RKO's entry was *Flying Down to Rio*, a musical that combined exotic South American settings with the romantic theme of air travel.
Even before the cast or director were decided upon, the studio dispatched
a camera crew to Rio de Janeiro to film background scenes. Indeed, one of
the strengths of the film is the artful blending of this background footage with
the studio sets to establish the mood and look of the city. *Flying Down to
Rio* will always be remembered, however, for the first important screen appearance of Fred Astaire (earlier in 1933 he had appeared very briefly in
Dancing Lady), the spectacular aerial finale, and "The Carioca" in which
Fred Astaire and Ginger Rogers danced together for the first time in a film.

Astaire had been a star in vaudeville and on Broadway with his sister
Adele, but when she retired in 1932, he was forced to find a new career and
a new professional identity for himself. He was intrigued by the possibilities
of dance on film, but he wanted to be more than just a performer, and signed
a contract with RKO, where he was able to supervise and control the cho-
reographing, filming, cutting, and scoring of his own musical numbers. The
studio executives apparently were not quite sure what to do with Astaire,
however, since he did not fit any of the conventional ideas of a romantic
leading man; so they decided to cast him in a secondary role in *Flying Down
to Rio* as the leading man's wise-cracking friend. Together with Ginger Rogers
(a late addition to the cast), Astaire handles most of the comedy and hovers
watchfully on the edges as the stars, Dolores Del Rio and Gene Raymond,

work out their romantic problems. But despite the handicap of such inane lines as "Hold onto your hats, boys, here we go again," and a hackneyed role as the hero's comic sidekick, Astaire, with his casual charm and debonair unpretentiousness, made such a favorable impression that many critics singled him out as the best thing about the film.

Although Astaire and Rogers do dance together briefly, this is not really an Astaire-Rogers film. There is no real relationship between them; both perform in nonromantic roles intended to provide the comic elements then standard in a musical. Their dance to "The Carioca" is engaging and spritely but not overwhelming. It is, rather, a portent of things to come in their later films—the delightful air of shared fun and spontaneity became one of their trademarks.

With its romantic setting of Rio de Janeiro and the glamour and novelty of air travel, the film has an energy and vitality that the tepid love story cannot diminish. As the film opens, Roger Bond (Gene Raymond) and his band, the Yankee Clippers, are playing at a Miami hotel. Roger, always on the lookout for a pretty girl though it has frequently gotten him and the band in trouble, notices a beautiful Brazilian, Belinha de Rezende (Dolores Del Rio), at a table with her aunt and some American friends. Attracted by Roger's blonde good looks, Belinha encourages his obvious interest in her. After her aunt leaves, she easily gets Roger to dance with her despite the warnings of his long-suffering friend, Fred Ayres (Fred Astaire), that it might cost the band their jobs. But Belinha's aunt Titia (Blanche Friderici) thinks Roger is a gigolo, and the hotel manager fires him for associating with the guests. The next morning, however, Fred tells everyone in the band including the vocalist, Honey Hale (Ginger Rogers), that Roger's Brazilian friend Julio Rubeiro (Raul Roulien) has gotten them a job in Rio de Janeiro at the Hotel Atlantico and that they will be flying down to Rio immediately.

By a happy coincidence, the Hotel Atlantico is owned by Belinha's ailing father whom she is returning home to visit. Roger, an enthusiastic aviator, immediately offers to fly her to Rio himself. During the flight Roger's airplane develops engine trouble and they are forced to land on a deserted island beach where Roger breaks down Belinha's already crumbling defenses by playing "Orchids in the Moonlight" on the specially built piano in his airplane. They quarrel, however, when Belinha says she must honor the engagement arranged by her family to a Brazilian. Belinha sleeps in the airplane and Roger on the beach. The next morning she refuses to speak to him, but when she sees some black faces peering at her from the jungle, she runs to him for help. Roger is struck down, however, by a missile that turns out to be a golf ball. A black golfer with a cultured British accent then appears and informs them that they are on the beach of the Port-au-Prince golf club, not a deserted island as they had supposed. Belinha catches another plane to Rio de Janeiro, and Roger completes the trip alone.

In Rio, Fred and Roger learn that the Hotel Atlantico has been denied an entertainment permit for its opening. (Although they do not know it, the problem is caused by the machinations of three Greek gambling operators—seen as menacing shadows—who plan to take it over.) Roger also discovers that his friend Julio is the man to whom Belinha is engaged. Since the hotel cannot have a regular floor show, Roger decides to save Belinha's father from ruin by staging a spectacular air show with hundreds of chorus girls riding on the wings of a fleet of airplanes. After the successful show, Julio, who now realizes Belinha and Roger truly love each other, hurries her onboard an airplane so she and Roger can be married by the pilot without delay. He then gracefully parachutes out of the airplane and out of their lives. Significantly, the film ends with a shot of Fred and Honey happily toasting the show's success with champagne as they watch Julio float to earth.

The aerial extravaganza that climaxes the film is still spectacular if slightly ridiculous, a fact which does not detract from its entertaining qualities. (Indeed, Ken Russell paid affectionate homage to this sequence in his 1971 film *The Boyfriend*.) As the flight of planes appears over the horizon, Roger's band strikes up "Flying Down to Rio." As the airplanes get closer, we see that chorus girls are performing on the wings of each airplane. They perform a series of synchronized, rhythmic movements in unison, reminiscent of a Busby Berkeley pattern, waving their arms and kicking their legs in a series of limited but effective patterns. In one breathtaking sequence, a few of the girls perform aerial acrobatics suspended beneath one of the airplanes; one misses the trapeze and falls through space but in the next shot she lands safely on the wing of an airplane flying below her. In another sequence several of the girls' scanty costumes are blown off to reveal scantier costumes beneath, and the girls then parachute to earth. Even to those who know that the entire sequence was shot in a hangar with the planes suspended from wires, there is an element of terror that adds to the effect, and it is a memorable, fantastic, and sometimes funny sequence.

One of the film's other memorable moments occurs when Astaire and Rogers, in the middle of a large production number of "The Carioca," step onto a small stage formed by seven white pianos to do a brief version of the dance and to "show 'em a thing or three," as Rogers' character buoyantly expresses it. The basic step in the dance is a backward and forward tilt with forehead pressed to forehead and hip to hip with the hands clasped over the head. Each partner is supposed to do a complete turn while still touching each other's forehead. "The Carioca" later became a craze and was taught at dance studios. The Astaire and Rogers portion of the dance is almost tantalizingly brief and ends on an amusing note as they bump foreheads and stagger dazedly around the dance floor for a few moments.

Astaire's first solo dance number in films occurs when he tries to teach some steps to the motley group of chorus girls hired for the Hotel Atlantico's floor show. The band keeps playing a song with an insistent beat that distracts him (a reprise of "Music Makes Me"), and, unable to control his dancing proclivities, he keeps breaking into a tap dance. Finally he surrenders and launches into a blazing tap exhibition of intricate steps. Astaire also does a brief tango with Dolores Del Rio to "Orchids in the Moonlight" but seems rather subdued by her stateliness, and it is not an important number in the film. Astaire's only vocal number, "Flying Down to Rio," begins the exciting aerial sequence that climaxes the film. It is a breezy, catchy tune that Astaire invests with all of his inimitable style, spontaneity, and vitality.

Before *Flying Down to Rio*, Ginger Rogers had appeared in nearly twenty films but had not yet caught the public's imagination. Her best previous roles had been as predatory showgirls in *42nd Street* (1933) and *Gold Diggers of 1933* (1933), and it seemed that she might be in danger of being typecast in such roles. As the band's vocalist in *Flying Down to Rio* she appears in a semitransparent black gown to sing the infectious "Music Makes Me" in her saucy style; and her costume seems to match both her vocal style and the somewhat suggestive lyrics. Her fresh, natural quality contributes to the fun of the song.

More than forty years later, *Flying Down to Rio* is still as charming, fresh, and enjoyable as the year it was released, primarily because of the presence of Fred Astaire and Ginger Rogers and its spectacular aerial climax.

Julia Johnson

FOLLOW THE FLEET

Released: 1936
Production: Pandro S. Berman for RKO/Radio
Direction: Mark Sandrich
Screenplay: Dwight Taylor and Allan Scott; based on the play *Shore Leave*
  by Hubert Osborne
Cinematography: David Abel
Editing: Henry Berman
Dance direction: Hermes Pan
Songs: Irving Berlin
Running time: 110 minutes

>   *Principal characters:*
>   Bake Baker .... Fred Astaire
>   Sherry Martin .... Ginger Rogers
>   Bilge Smith .... Randolph Scott
>   Connie Martin .... Harriet Hilliard
>   Iris Manning .... Astrid Allwyn
>   Kitty .... Lucille Ball

In the series of musicals that Fred Astaire and Ginger Rogers made for RKO between 1933 and 1939, *Follow the Fleet* came after the elegant and glamorous *Top Hat* (1935) and was designed to present as much of a contrast as possible to it. This was done by casting Fred Astaire as a brash, gum-chewing sailor and Ginger Rogers as an entertainer in a dance hall in San Francisco.

In most of their films together Astaire and Rogers are strangers who meet accidentally. He immediately falls in love with her but she is distant and cool, if not openly antagonistic, and resists his attempts to ingratiate himself. Finally, persuaded by a romantic dance number, she yields. *Follow the Fleet* varies this pattern by having the two meet as old friends. Astaire plays Bake Baker, a former vaudeville performer who had joined the Navy when his partner, Sherry Martin (Ginger Rogers), refused to marry him, preferring to try to achieve success by herself. When Bake is granted shore leave in San Francisco, he decides to look up Sherry and renew their acquaintance. Although Sherry has told him she works in a "high-class place where all the money goes," when he goes with his shipmates to the Paradise Ballroom, a dime-a-dance hall, he discovers that she is a hostess there.

A further variation of the usual pattern lies in the initial reaction of the characters to each other. Sherry does not try to pretend indifference or conceal her joy when she sees Bake again. In fact, he has to wipe away a few of her tears. He, on the other hand, is more nonchalant and indifferent, although he confesses that he has missed her a little. She is sentimental and anxious to resume their old friendly relationship; he is brash, cool, and supremely self-confident.

There is also a secondary romantic story involving Sherry's sister Connie (Harriet Hilliard) and Bake's sailor friend Bilge (Randolph Scott) which tends to slow the pace of the film. Connie is, at first, a mousy schoolteacher, who comes to the Paradise Ballroom to see Sherry. Once she removes her glasses and puts on a glittery evening gown, however, she is beautiful enough to attract Bilge's attention. Because he does not want to get married, Bilge stops seeing Connie when she starts getting "serious." There are several quarrels and reconciliations between the two couples before they are happily brought together at the end. The major complication is the fact that Connie needs money to salvage and refurbish her father's ship for Bilge, because his dream is to be the captain of his own ship someday. To solve this problem, Bake and Sherry stage a show to raise the money.

In *Follow the Fleet* the musical numbers are not as well-integrated as those in some of the other films in the series, but this does not make them less enjoyable in themselves. They are magnificent set pieces that show off the versatility, range, and skillful teamwork of Astaire and Rogers. "We Saw the Sea" at once establishes the film's mood and the character of Bake. It is sung by Bake in his sailor's uniform with a chorus of sailors on a white battleship. After he sings the lyrics, the sailors pick him up and toss him about before letting him fall to the deck.

At the Paradise Ballroom, Sherry entertains the customers with the catchy song "Let Yourself Go," a jazzy tune intended to typify the big band/swing era of the 1930's. Later, Sherry and Bake dance to the song in a competition sponsored by the Paradise. Couples for the dance contest were recruited by dance director Hermes Pan from various ballrooms in Los Angeles, and the best were selected to compete against Bake and Sherry in the picture. Instead of invoking glamour and sophistication, the dance tries to create a contemporary, modern mood. There are shifts in the rhythm and tempo of the dance as Bake and Sherry try to outdo their competitors. In contrast to Rogers, Astaire uses his upper body a great deal, especially his arms, as the two sometimes balance on one foot, and at other times throw their whole bodies into a step. At one point Sherry leans back and Bake catches her and holds her just off the floor for a moment, a movement in keeping with the flashy, exhibitionistic effects appropriate to a dance contest. At the end they each drop to one knee, both arms outstretched, asking for and receiving the applause of the sailors at the Paradise. It is an exciting dance, and its mood and tone are perfectly matched to its place in the story.

In order to help Connie pay for salvaging her father's ship, Bake decides to put on a show in which he and Sherry will star. We see them rehearsing one number for the show, "I'm Putting All My Eggs in One Basket," which Bake first plays on the piano and then sings to Sherry. After he finishes, she sings a chorus to him, then he pulls her up onto the stage. The dance they do is a lighthearted comedy of errors, almost a parody of their inimitable timing and teamwork. "It was every old vaudeville trick in the world stuck into one number," dance director Pan has commented. Rogers, for example, with hunched shoulders and deep concentration, continues a step after Astaire has gone on to something else. When he stops, she bumps into him, sending him flying offstage. It happens again, but the next time Astaire steps cannily aside, letting Rogers' momentum carry *her* off the stage. At one point he stops her and starts her again in the right step. Another time, fists up like boxers, they mime a boxing match. Finally Astaire gives up in disgust, sits down, and begins reading a newspaper. As Rogers dances by alone, he suddenly springs up, catches her by the arms and whirls her around the stage. At the end, they cannot even take their bows together because they keep getting in each other's way.

The big dramatic and romantic duet of the film, "Let's Face the Music and Dance," has no relation to the rest of the story but is inserted as a number in the show being performed on the ship. It is a completely self-contained miniature drama with its own special resonance and meaning. The haunting song and the beautiful, elegant dance provide the glamour and sophistication so conspicuously lacking in the rest of the film. Indeed, it is the only time in the film Astaire appears in his trademark outfit—white tie and tails.

The curtain opens on a Monte Carlo gambling casino with Bake at the roulette table surrounded by beautiful women. He quickly loses all of his money and is deserted by the women. The curtain then closes and opens on a terrace overlooking the sea where we see Bake pointedly shunned by all the passersby. Alone now, he takes a pistol out of his pocket, looks around to be sure he is alone, and puts the gun to his temple. He is startled, however, by Sherry, who enters and stops at the edge of the railing surrounding the terrace, twisting a long scarf in her hands. When she steps up onto the railing as if preparing to leap, he runs over and stops her. Then, to let her know that he too is troubled, he shows her his gun and empty wallet before throwing them both away with exaggerated theatrical gestures. While she leans despondently against a pillar, he sings, "There may be trouble ahead, but while there's moonlight and music and love and romance, let's face the music and dance."

At first she tries to ignore the invitation, but as he dances in front of her, using his hands as well as his body to entice her into the dance, she allows herself to be caught up in the spell of the music. Every graceful movement, every gesture, is used to establish the mood of melancholy and romance in which this dance is steeped. Several times she stands away from him at arm's length as if in a reluctant parting, but he holds her by both hands, compelling her to return to him and to the dance. At one point they circle each other, turning first one shoulder then the other toward each other in a series of abrupt, dramatic movements. Both use their arms and hands a great deal to create beautiful, graceful patterns that become part of the flow of the dance as well as providing dramatic emphasis. Sherry's dress of metallic threads, weighted at the sleeves and the hem, winds and unwinds around her, itself becoming part of the dance. At the end, Bake and Sherry sink to their knees, slowly rise together, then exit bravely, their backs arched, one knee held high, their heads thrown back, personifications of gallantry and courage.

Despite the problems caused by the inclusion of the uninteresting romance between Bilge and Connie, *Follow the Fleet* shows Astaire and Rogers at their best with all the qualities audiences had now come to expect from them—spontaneity, freshness, charm, and exquisite dancing. Even in a sailor suit, Astaire is never less than graceful, and Rogers in her satin sailor costume has all of her usual charm.

Astaire has one solo, "I'd Rather Lead a Band," in which he sings and dances on board ship in his white sailor's uniform. The number is in three parts—Astaire dancing by himself, Astaire tapping out commands to a double line of sailors as he "reviews" them, and then, as they march in place to establish a "base rhythm," Astaire being stimulated by their beat to a new exhibition of dazzling tapping as the sailors march off, leaving him alone for the finale.

From ballet, tap, and ballroom dancing, Astaire created for himself what he calls an "outlaw style" that blends all three. In all of his solo dances and in the dances with Ginger Rogers one can see favorite elements of this "outlaw style" which he used to great effect. He especially liked sudden transitions from flowing movements to abrupt stops. The technique of abrupt stops, holding the pose for a moment before continuing with the next step, is used for dramatic emphasis and contrast in both "Let Yourself Go" and "I'd Rather Lead a Band." Astaire received no screen credit for either dance direction or choreography for this film, although he was largely responsible for them. He worked in close collaboration with Hermes Pan on the dances in *Follow the Fleet*, as he did in all of their other films together. Astaire was primarily responsible for the way in which the dances were filmed, in addition to their staging. In addition to the actual filming of the dances, Astaire also supervised the orchestration and editing of the numbers, so that he was totally in charge of all aspects of the dances. He disliked "reaction shots" (shots of people watching the dancers), and tried to maintain proper camera angles so that the dances were all filmed at eye level, thus giving the audience a perfect perspective; he did not use close-ups on head or feet.

Julia Johnson

FOR WHOM THE BELL TOLLS

Released: 1943
Production: Sam Wood for Paramount
Direction: Sam Wood
Screenplay: Dudley Nichols; based on the novel of the same name by Ernest
  Hemingway
Cinematography: Ray Rennahan
Editing: Sherman Todd
Production design: William Cameron Menzies
Music: Victor Young
Running time: 170 minutes

> *Principal characters:*
> Robert Jordan .... Gary Cooper
> Maria .... Ingrid Bergman
> Pablo .... Akim Tamiroff
> Agustin .... Arturo de Cordova
> El Sordo .... Joseph Calleia
> Pilar .... Katina Paxinou (AA)
> Karkov .... Konstantin Shayne

Many films have been adapted from Ernest Hemingway's stories and novels, such as *A Farewell to Arms* (1932 and 1957) and *The Old Man and the Sea* (1958). One of the most memorable of the Hemingway adaptations is *For Whom the Bell Tolls*, based on the author's brilliant 1940 novel of the same name. The film made its debut in July of 1943, after three years of prerelease publicity, second only to that of *Gone with the Wind* (1939). Since 1940 when Paramount bought Ernest Hemingway's controversial best-seller about an American university professor-turned-dynamiter on the side of the Loyalists in the Spanish Civil War, the studio faithfully kept the book's millions of readers informed of the film's production problems and progress. During the casting season, thirty thousand Hemingway fans mailed Paramount their selections for the various roles. In the end, the author's choices—Ingrid Bergman and Gary Cooper—won out, and it is difficult to imagine an improvement in either characterization.

The gripping story is set during the Spanish Civil War in 1937. Gary Cooper (who had previously starred in the film version of Hemingway's *A Farewell to Arms*) plays the rugged, unassuming Robert Jordan, a young Montana schoolteacher who goes to Spain to fight for democracy. During these brutal times, Jordan first dynamites tracks beneath a speeding railway train and then joins a brigand band of Spanish guerrilla fighters whose mission is to blow up a strategic bridge behind enemy lines. When Jordan goes into the rugged hills around La Granja and passes three days with the group in their cave hiding place, he meets Maria (Ingrid Bergman), a Spanish refugee girl with whom he falls in love. It is this love story that dominates the second half of the film until the end, when the ill-fated couple is tragically separated.

In outline, Dudley Nichols' screenplay is faithful—almost too faithful—to the slender plot that covers only four days in Jordan's foredoomed mission. Politically, however, the film maintains a safe middle-of-the-road position. For example, when Jordan is asked by his guerrilla companions why he fights for the Loyalists, he replies, "The Nazis and Fascists are just as much against democracy as they are against the Communists." That is the film's only political speech and its sole mention of Fascism by name. Franco's legions are called Nationalists; the assorted Loyalists are Republicans; and the introduction of a bungling French Communist commissar and a contrastingly practical emissary from Stalin splits ideological hairs to a point of ultimate confusion unless the viewer clearly recalls the corresponding passages in the book.

In general, it is perhaps most advisable to consider *For Whom the Bell Tolls* as a poignant, ill-starred romance depicted against a melodramatic background. Although the film leaves a great deal to be desired, director Sam Wood does manage to whip the action into a superb fury of excitement and suspense in his scenes of carnage, particularly in the climactic destruction of the bridge, and in the gallant, hopeless delaying action by El Sordo (Joseph Calleia) on a vulnerable mountaintop.

Fortunately, Paramount had the luck and enterprise to assemble a distinguished group of actors to play some of the most arresting characters to appear on the screen for some time. As the hero, Gary Cooper seems to embody the traditional yet romantic American male; he is courageous, tender, melancholy, taciturn, and forgivably gauche. A Hemingway prototype, Jordan is a man of action, and Cooper is excellent in this role. Ingrid Bergman, who was twenty-seven at the time of filming, is moving as Maria, whose father, the mayor, was murdered and who was herself raped by the enemy. Bergman's emotional range progresses from delicate to powerful. Her confession of the rape is an exquisitely calculated tearjerker, and her final farewell scene is shattering to watch; its intention and sources are so accurate that she seems to have really studied what a young woman might actually feel and look like in such a situation, nearly insane with grief and panic.

Joseph Calleia as El Sordo, the guerrilla chieftain, and Konstantin Shayne as Karkov, the Soviet journalist, are also well suited to their roles, but the film's highest acting accolades must go to Akim Tamiroff and Katina Paxinou. Tamiroff, a wonderful scene-stealer, plays Pablo, the peasant guerrilla leader who serves as a symbol of a man devastated by the fear of death. A onetime warrior who was responsible for terrible atrocities, Pablo has since become remorseful, and has taken to drink; he now opposes Jordan's mission to dynamite the bridge because such an action would force him to seek quarters elsewhere. Greece's leading actress, Katina Paxinou, with her beautiful aquiline features, is magnetic as Pilar, Pablo's indomitable woman. Possibly because she is the most fully realized character in the book, Pilar dominates the scenes in the guerrilla hideout in the mountains. Paxinou takes brilliant advantage of every facet of the character.

Cinematographer Ray Rennahan does exquisite justice to the High Sierras, with their mountain crags and hillside streams. Several hundred matte shots also add to the film's overall dramatic effects.

Although Dudley Nichols' screenplay follows close to the original Hemingway novel in parts, there are some major distortions and omissions. The film depicts the Spanish Civil War as a struggle between foreign powers as if there were no internal political struggles in Spain between Fascist and democratic factions. (In fact, Jordan says he joined the fighting as a protest against German and Italian forces using Spain's civil warfare as a testing ground for their own mechanized fighting units.)

At the time, the film's producers did not want to antagonize Franco and his sympathizers; in the film, therefore, the names necessarily had to be altered. In spite of studio officials' denials, Washington political columnist Drew Pearson and others continued to report various attempts by the Spanish government to block production of the Paramount film. One of Franco's agents in Washington made overtures to the State Department, and a representative in Hollywood approached Sam Wood on the subject. Yet, because only those directly involved with the production were permitted to see the film before its release, Wood was able to stall efficiently. Interestingly, Franco's objections were said not to have been based on the film itself, but on the advertising the picture would give the book, thus stimulating sales.

The political detachment of the film detracts from what could have been a more intense and better-motivated product. At the same time, the three-hour film (with no intermission) is overly long, and, in places, too talky. Nevertheless, *For Whom the Bell Tolls*, with its suspenseful action and depictions of love, death, terror, and passion, continues to generate excitement, and to this day holds up as solid entertainment.

Leslie Taubman

FOREIGN CORRESPONDENT

Released: 1940
Production: Walter Wanger for United Artists
Direction: Alfred Hitchcock
Screenplay: Charles Bennett and Joan Harrison, with dialogue by James Hilton and Robert Benchley; based on the autobiography *Personal History* by Vincent Sheean
Cinematography: Rudolph Maté
Editing: Otho Lovering
Running time: 119 minutes

Principal characters:
Johnny Jones (Huntley Haverstock) .... Joel McCrea
Carol Fisher .... Laraine Day
Stephen Fisher .... Herbert Marshall
Scott Ffolliott .... George Sanders
Van Meer .... Albert Basserman
Stebbins .... Robert Benchley

Foreign Correspondent, released in 1940, signified a major turning point in director Alfred Hitchcock's career. Although the film was his second to be made in the United States, it constituted his first experience with a Hollywood-type production. His first American film, based on Daphne du Maurier's *Rebecca*, so retained the style and appearance of the director's English works that it is difficult to think of it as having been made in Hollywood. Interestingly, this result was not due to any stylistic intention on Hitchcock's part but was instead a reflection of the subject matter and of the production values aimed for by producer David O. Selznick.

Selznick had brought Hitchcock to Hollywood in 1940 with an $800,000 contract to make four important pictures. When the first project, *Titanic*, based upon the story of the doomed luxury liner, had to be temporarily abandoned, the director was given *Rebecca*, a property which he had earlier attempted to purchase and produce in England. Hitchcock's second chance to make this film of the Maurier novel was, of course, a major success, earning the Oscar as Best Picture of 1940, but it also proved to Hitchcock that working for Selznick would be a mixed blessing. In England, the director's creativity had been restrained by small budgets; in Hollywood, however, he could afford to explore more fully the technical tricks of movie-making and experiment with projects that were not hampered by budgetary limitations. There were, however, limitations imposed by Hollywood that Hitchcock had rarely encountered in England, where he was in almost complete artistic control of his films. In the United States during the 1940's, however, it was the producer who controlled the creative direction of the project, and his intentions and wishes always superseded those of the director. When the producer was a man like David O. Selznick, control was imperious and complete. This was the situation with *Rebecca*, even though the film seems to be a reflection of the Hitchcock style.

Foreign Correspondent, Hitchcock's second American film, provided him with more artistic freedom than had *Rebecca* and at the same time afforded the director most of the assets available at a Hollywood studio. Hitchcock had discovered that some other producers were less likely to interfere in his films than was Selznick; thus he endeavored to make additional pictures on loan to other studios. *Foreign Correspondent*, loosely based upon journalist Vincent Sheean's autobiography, *Personal History*, the first of these additional films, was made for Walter Wanger and United Artists. Its budget of one-and-one-half million dollars, which represented the most money with which Hitchcock had ever worked, was principally spent on scenery consisting of a ten-acre Amsterdam public square, a large section of London, a Dutch countryside complete with windmill, and a large transatlantic airplane. These items were planned and constructed by an army of 558 carpenters and technicians. Additionally, fourteen screenwriters worked at various times on the screenplay, and more than 240,000 feet of film were shot and edited to 120 screen minutes. The film displays some of the finest visual design and cinematography evident in any of Hitchcock's productions, indicating that the director quickly learned the manner in which to make optimum use of a generous budget.

Unlike many of Hitchcock's other famous thrillers, *Foreign Correspondent* features no superstars. Gary Cooper, for example, refused the role of reporter Johnny Jones, and although Joel McCrea was eventually placed in the role and did a solid job, he simply lacked the box-office appeal of a major star such as Cary Grant or James Stewart. The problem was that the "thriller" was held in rather low esteem by 1940 Hollywood, and Hitchcock, who had not yet established himself as the master of suspense, was not able to recruit the big-name actors he desired.

Foreign Correspondent establishes a pattern of suspense and intrigue that would become a hallmark of many of Hitchcock's American thrillers. Johnny Jones (Joel McCrea) is a tough, hard-headed crime reporter who is reassigned by his editor to investigate the prospects of an outbreak of hostilities in Europe just prior to the beginning of World War II. He thus becomes a foreign correspondent, and temporarily changes his name to Huntley Haverstock. Arriving in Amsterdam, Jones meets Van Meer (Albert Basserman), a Dutch diplomat who has memorized a secret clause in an Allied treaty for his country. Traveling with the diplomat is the head of a pacifist group, Stephen Fisher (Herbert Marshall), and his daughter Carol (Laraine Day). Van Meer is to make a speech to the pacifist organization on the opportunities of averting war.

In one of the most memorable scenes of any Hitchcock film, Van Meer appears to be assassinated as he arrives to address the pacifists; the scene occurs in the Amsterdam public square filled with people carrying umbrellas in a pouring rain, and the murderer escapes in a chase beneath the umbrellas, the scene being presented through some excellent camerawork from above. An elaborate drainage system constructed beneath the set carried off the rainwater to maintain some degree of traction for McCrea and the other actors involved in the scene. The murderer is pursued by Johnny Jones into the Dutch countryside. At a windmill, the reporter discovers the real Van Meer, kidnaped by Nazis who have staged the assassination by murdering a double. The Nazis disappear with their captive while Jones is trying to convince the Dutch police that the diplomat is a prisoner inside the windmill.

Jones searches for Van Meer both in Holland and England with the aid of Carol Fisher, who is slowly falling in love with him. They discover that Carol's father, who has been masquerading as a pacifist, is in reality an agent for the Nazis and has been instrumental in kidnaping Van Meer and in trying to extract his secret information. Jones and Herbert Ffolliott (George Sanders), an English reporter, rescue the Dutch diplomat, but Fisher escapes with his daughter, who is now confused and disillusioned in her romance with Jones. As war is declared, the Fishers take a plane from England to America only to find that Jones and Ffolliott are also onboard, and as the reporters confront Fisher, the plane, mistaken by a German ship below for an English bomber, is shot down. The survivors attempt to stay afloat upon the wing of the plane while Fisher, realizing that he faces arrest in America, sacrifices his life to save the rest. An American ship approaches, frightening off the German one, and rescues the plane's passengers. Barred from telephoning their newspapers, Jones and Ffolliott pretend to make a personal call and then reiterate the story to the captain loud enough to be heard by Jones's editor on the other end of the line. As the film ends, Jones establishes himself as a top foreign correspondent and marries Carol.

Foreign Correspondent has achieved a well-deserved reputation as a masterpiece of suspense and intrigue, and was instrumental in upgrading the reputation of the thriller genre, being nominated for Academy Awards for Best Picture and Best Screenplay. The fact that the film won in neither category may be due to one significant fault in Hitchcock's effort: the film is overly long and drags in spots because of diversions in the story line incorporated to promote America's entry into World War II. The film attempts to merge two levels in an emotional appeal to the viewer. The first, that of the suspenseful cloak-and-dagger chase across Europe, is what Hitchcock does best; the second, however, is propaganda advocating an end to American isolation and an entry into World War II, and although Hitchcock manages a merger of these two themes more successfully than many other directors at the time, the intertwining causes the film to be less taut and more meandering than many of his later masterpieces.

The best reporter in *Foreign Correspondent* is, unquestionably, the camera. When the diplomat is assassinated, Hitchcock's camera is in the right place observing the fallen man's face; when a man is on the verge of dropping from a tower, the camera follows a hat making the plunge first; as the stricken airplane hurtles to the sea at the film's climax, the camera peers anxiously from the pilot's seat, indicating that it too has the reporter's gift of not revealing everything.

According to a number of sources, Hitchcock ordered several retakes of the wreck of the *Clipper* because it pleased him to see Joel McCrea and George Sanders floundering in the water, and when McCrea protested that the scene had ruined one of his suits, Hitchcock, who claims to dislike actors, sent him a new one the next day—made for a ten-year-old. In his role, however, McCrea proves both likable and capable. His interpretation of the reporter establishes the man as a credible citizen who, as the film ends, has the audience convinced that he will stride to one journalistic triumph after another. Laraine Day performs solidly in the role of Carol Fisher, her most ambitious part to that date, but Herbert Marshall appears somewhat miscast as the peace advocate who turns out to be a spy. Although he gives a good performance, he is too suave for his character and loses a little credibility. George Sanders, Albert Basserman, and Edward Ciannelli add much to the film, but it is Robert Benchley who carries off the acting honors in his portrayal of the broken-down American journalist Stebbins in London. He brought much of his own experience to the role and was specially chosen by Hitchcock, who enjoyed his brand of satiric humor. All of the scenes in which the humorist appeared were, at Hitchcock's request, written by Benchley himself.

In viewing the film as fundamentally a spy melodrama which places more emphasis on the pacing of the action than on where the action takes us, there are still awkward aspects. The meeting of the peace society contains prominently overdone elements; the crucial secret is, for the most part, meaningless, and the speeches are sometimes heavy-handed, particularly toward the end. Otherwise, the film moves swiftly, and although the plot is bare enough, Hitchcock, in the manner of a painter, loves details and loads his set with them without weighing down his action. He makes a character out of every extra; he likes to have a bland face or a sweet old lady personify evil, while the sinister fellow turns out to be the good guy all along. He sprinkles his scenes with people and mechanical devices which are not direct accessories to the plot so that the film conveys the realities of life, with dogs and casual passersby who are real and have nothing to do with any plot.

Above all, the film exemplifies Hitchcock's ability to use people, sound, and objects for the sole purpose of suspense. The use of objects, for example, is seen in *Foreign Correspondent* in the reversing windmill, the assassin's

camera and the disappearing car. Hitchcock knows where to set the micro-
phone and camera to catch the effect he has planned, and with all of the
devices of this complex art completely at his fingertips, his characters never
enter a deserted building or a dark alley without the viewer wondering if they
will ever come out alive.

In short, *Foreign Correspondent* provides an example of all the techniques
that make a film move in the lightest and fastest manner possible, utilizing
all of the qualities that are available through a large budget and the art of
Alfred Hitchcock. In fact, Hitchcock's only oversight in making *Foreign Correspondent* was in forgetting his invariable signature of personally appearing
in the film. Fortunately, with a generous Hollywood budget, he had the means
to reshoot a scene in a railway station in order to get himself into the picture.

Thomas A. Hanson

42nd STREET

Released: 1933
Production: Warner Bros.
Direction: Lloyd Bacon
Screenplay: Rian James and James Seymour; based on the novel of the same
  name by Bradford Ropes
Cinematography: Sol Polito
Editing: Thomas Pratt
Music direction: Busby Berkeley
Song: Harry Warren and Al Dubin
Running time: 85 minutes

Principal characters:

Julian Marsh	Warner Baxter
Dorothy Brock	Bebe Daniels
Peggy Sawyer	Ruby Keeler
Billy Lawler	Dick Powell
Pat Denning	George Brent
Anytime Annie	Ginger Rogers
Abner Dillon	Guy Kibbee
Lorraine Fleming	Una Merkel

In 1933, Warner Bros. released three important musicals which revitalized
the moribund film musical and renewed its popularity with the moviegoing
public. The films are notable for their vitality, their originality in presenting
musical numbers on film, and the emergence of a major new talent in the
world of the film musical—Busby Berkeley. The first of these, *42nd Street*,
is the quintessential backstage musical. The familiar story of putting on a
play, with the star breaking her ankle at the last minute and the young
unknown stepping in to save the show, has been done many times, but seldom
with such zest and verve.

Under Lloyd Bacon's skillful direction that catches all the bustle and excitement of the backstage atmosphere, a group of engaging performers made
their niche in film history secure—Ginger Rogers as a shrewd chorus girl;
Warner Baxter as the tyrannical director of the show; Bebe Daniels as the
unhappy star who breaks her ankle just before opening night, giving Ruby
Keeler (in her screen debut) her big chance; and the baby-faced, mellow-
voiced Dick Powell, whose screen presence seemed tailored to fit Warner
Bros. musicals. But the biggest star, and possibly the most talented, was
Busby Berkeley, the man behind the cameras who conceived, staged, and
directed the musical numbers.

Berkeley's main contribution to the film musical was the staging of dances
especially for the camera, using all the cinematic resources at his command.

He is famous for the moving camera (which roved through, around, under, and over his dancers rather than remaining fixed in one position), and is particularly known for the overhead shot, in which the camera peers down at the dancers as they form everchanging patterns. Using dancers as elements in an abstract design to create his effects rather than as individuals who perform dance routines is one of his trademarks.

The backstage story concerns a famous Broadway director, Julian Marsh (Warner Baxter), who is preparing his last Broadway show, *Pretty Lady*. He is tired, ill, and broke, having lost all of his money in the stock market crash of 1929, and he realizes that this is his last chance to recoup his fortunes and retire with a respectable income. He is harsh, demanding, and driven to extract the last drop of energy out of his cast. Pacing and smoking nervously, he tells the cast that it will mean working day and night for five weeks until the show opens.

The show is backed by Abner Dillon (Guy Kibbee), a rich "sugar daddy" who is in love with the show's leading lady, Dorothy Brock. Dorothy tries to be sweet and friendly to Abner while keeping him at a distance because she is in love with her former vaudeville partner, Pat Denning (George Brent).

At the first casting call for the chorus of *Pretty Lady*, the stage is filled with eager hopefuls. Among them are Lorraine Fleming (Una Merkel), who gets a job in the chorus because she knows the stage director, and Anytime Annie (Ginger Rogers), a blonde with a monocle, a Pekingese, and a fake English accent; she has earned her nickname because she "only said no once and then she didn't hear the question."

Among the chorus girls is a naïve newcomer, Peggy Sawyer (Ruby Keeler). Recognizing her inexperience, the other chorus girls first direct her to the men's room, and then to the dressing room of Billy Lawler (Dick Powell), "one of Broadway's better juveniles" and the show's leading man, only to find him half dressed. Billy befriends the embarrassed and bewildered Peggy and later persuades Marsh to put her in the show.

Some of the best moments in *42nd Street* (aside from the musical numbers) are the vignettes of backstage life. There are numerous scenes of rehearsals with Marsh shouting at the dancers to "give it something," and to "work faster, faster," capturing some of the agonizing, endless work of rehearsing and the confusion and disorganization behind the glamour of the theater.

The character of the director, Julian Marsh, is particularly intriguing because it has some depth. We know he is a desperately tired man who has staked everything on making *Pretty Lady* a big hit. When told he is considered the "greatest musical comedy director in America today," he responds cynically that "You can't cash a reputation at the bank." In every scene he is chain-smoking, haggard, and wild-eyed, with shirt sleeves rolled up and tie askew. He screams and commands; he does not cajole or persuade. To encourage a tired Billy, he sarcastically tells him that all he needs is two license plates to look like a Model T Ford; the rest of the cast receives similar verbal treatment. When he informs them that the five-week rehearsal period will be the toughest five weeks they have ever lived through, we believe him.

The chorus becomes an impersonal group of girls driven beyond the limits of endurance. (At one point the image is reinforced by the superimposition of multiple images of legs and faces.) When Peggy faints during a rehearsal, Marsh screams at Billy to remove her quickly so that the rest can get back to work ("This is a rehearsal, not a rescue."). Outside the stagedoor entrance she is befriended by Pat, who is waiting for Dorothy, hoping that she will be alone so that he can see her. But later Dorothy tells him that they should not meet at all until they can meet openly; so he leaves for Philadelphia to be on his own.

At the final rehearsal before the out-of-town opening, a weary Marsh tells the cast that the finale looks like an amateur night and then dismisses them to get some rest. His troubles, however, have just begun. After a quarrel with Dorothy, Abner announces that he will withdraw his backing of the show if she is in it. As soon as Marsh solves that problem, he learns that Dorothy has broken her ankle.

The stage is now set for some of the film's best-known scenes. A reluctant Marsh chooses Peggy (on the recommendation of Anytime Annie, who unaccountably gives up her own chance for stardom) to go on and save the show. She is rehearsed remorselessly by Marsh, who yells at her, shakes her, and works her until she collapses. He encourages her by telling her that the jobs of two hundred people depend on her and that the audience has to like her. In the film's most famous line he says, "You're going out a youngster, but you've got to come back a star." Peggy also receives encouragement from Dorothy, who visits the theater on crutches and urges the trembling young woman to "go out there and be so swell you'll make me hate you."

Despite her exhaustion and imminent nervous collapse, Peggy does go on and, naturally, saves the show. In the last scene of the film, Marsh lingers outside the theater, listening to the comments of departing theatergoers. He smiles wryly as he overhears such comments as "Marsh gets all the breaks," and "With a kid like Sawyer how can he miss?" As the film ends he sits down wearily on the fire escape.

Throughout the film we have felt the tension mount as all efforts are concentrated on preparing for the opening night of *Pretty Lady*. We have been shown the enormous amount of work and discipline demanded of the cast and we have been tantalized by snippets of songs and dances seen in rehearsals. But not until the dress rehearsal do we see a number performed in its entirety. Although it is a bright, catchy song, "You're Getting to Be a Habit with Me," it is merely sung in front of the stage curtain by Dorothy with five male dancers; it is not a full-scale production number.

The pent-up emotions and tensions are released in three Berkeley production numbers that are seen as part of the show-within-the-show and that
serve as an exhilarating climax to *42nd Street*. These numbers are a good
introduction to the flair that Berkeley brought to the film musical. They are
fresh, imaginative, and vigorous; and they display many of Berkeley's favorite
devices—overhead shots, the moving camera, dancers creating patterns, and
vignettes that tell short, dramatic stories.

In the number "Shuffle Off to Buffalo," a honeymooning couple walks
along a train platform, waving good-bye to their friends. As the train pulls
away, the Pullman car suddenly splits down the middle and opens up to reveal
a cross section of the whole length of the coach. The compartments are filled
with beautiful chorus girls in satin pajamas or nightgowns, singing and cracking jokes. Some of them are wearing curlers and cold cream as if to emphasize
bachelor fears about marriage. The honeymooners dance down the length
of the coach as the chorus girls sing sarcastically that "matrimony is baloney."
But despite the knowing glances of the chorus girls and the pointed jokes
about shy bridegrooms and eager brides, the humor is too innocent and naïve
to be offensive. The number ends with a startling contrast: an old black porter
falls asleep as he cleans the chorus girls' shoes. (Contrasts are a favorite
Berkeley device.)

The next number, "I'm Young and Healthy," is more typical of Berkeley's
work. Billy Lawler steps to the front of the stage and sings the lyrics to a
young and obviously very healthy blonde in a low-cut ermine-trimmed gown
and ermine muff. The angle shifts to an overhead shot of the two on a dark
circular revolving stage, ringed by prone chorus boys. A line of blondes in
brief costumes now encircle the glittering stage. Several overhead shots reveal
the chorus forming kaleidoscopic patterns. The scene ends with the camera
speeding down a tunnel formed by the open legs of the chorus girls to find
at the end a smiling Billy and his blonde partner.

The best number is the title song, "42nd Street," which uses short, interwoven vignettes to convey a dramatic impression and tell a story. It starts
simply, with Peggy Sawyer singing the lyrics in front of the curtain, which
then parts to reveal "naughty, bawdy" 42nd Street. Peggy jumps down from
what proves to be the top of a taxi as 42nd Street slowly fills with people.
The camera weaves in and out among the "big parade," showing us a barber
and his customer, midgets, a peddler with a pushcart full of fruit, automobiles,
an Indian chief, and finally a room where a girl is arguing with a man. They
quarrel, and she leaps from the window onto a ledge, and then to the street;
the man follows, catching her and stabbing her. It is only a glimpse, and the
camera does not linger as it turns to the street, now filled with dancing chorus
girls who turn to reveal the New York skyline. We then see Billy and Peggy
at the top of a skyscraper, waving to the audience before pulling down an
asbestos curtain. The moving camera, the cross section of people, and the

dramatic glimpses that build to a rousing climax are all Berkeley trademarks. The musical numbers in *42nd Street* are not as opulent or dazzling as those in later Berkeley films, but their comparative restraint and their vitality more than compensate for that.

The film musical was never quite the same after *42nd Street*. It confirmed the emergence of a major new talent—Busby Berkeley—and the emergence of the musical as a new art form. It was one of the top-grossing films of the year and is credited with rescuing Warner Bros. from bankruptcy.

Julia Johnson

FOUR FEATHERS

Released: 1939
Production: Alexander Korda for United Artists
Direction: Zoltan Korda
Screenplay: R. C. Sherriff, with additional dialogue by Lajor Biro and Arthur
   Wimperis; based on Oliver H. P. Garrett's adaptation of the novel *The
   Four Feathers* by A. E. W. Mason
Cinematography: George Perinal and Osmond Borradaile
Editing: William Hornbeck
Art direction: Vincent Korda
Running time: 130 minutes

> *Principal characters:*
> Harry Faversham ....John Clements
> John Durrance .... Ralph Richardson
> Ethne Burroughs .... June Duprez
> Lieutenant Arthur Willoughby .... Jack Allen
> General Burroughs .... C. Aubrey Smith
> Lieutenant Peter Burroughs .... Donald Gray

Alexander Korda's masterful period piece *Four Feathers* evolved film spectacle to a high art. It endures, unsurpassed, as an early classic of the epic
film genre. This 1939 cinematic re-creation of the popular 1901 adventure
novel transcended the 1915, 1921, and 1929 film versions as well as the 1955
remake, *Storm over the Nile*. Indeed, the location footage of the 1939 *Four
Feathers* was used for the latter and is still used today for its North African
scenes and its depictions of British military might in North Africa during the
1890's.

Decried as grandiose flag-waving, the film was a rare collaboration of the
famed Korda brothers: producer Alexander, director Zoltan, and art director
Vincent. Hungarian-born Anglophile Alexander, a romantic patriot, believed
heartily in the British Empire and its policies. He strove to serve his adopted
country by championing its era of invincible imperialism to war-worried audiences of 1939-1940. His younger brothers were also students of the period;
their synergism could only mean a film reveling in the far-flung outposts of
Victorian Britain. One of these, Sudanese Egypt, was the site of General
George Gordon's murder in 1885 at Khartoum, climaxing the triumph of
Mahdist power over British colonial forces there. The story of *Four Feathers*
is based on this pivotal event.

The year 1885 finds bookish Harry Faversham (John Clements) at home
in London celebrating his fifteenth birthday at a massive dining table among
bullish old gentlemen glorying in battles long past. Chief among them is his
father, whose attempts to browbeat a sense of the Faversham military legacy

into his one son only further intimidate the boy. Ten years later a uniformed Harry stands among his friends as an officer in the Royal North Surrey Regiment, half-heartedly committed to a life of soldiering in pursuit of the destiny to which he was born. Other than poetry, his only source of happiness is his engagement to Ethne Burroughs (June Duprez), the sister of one of his fellow officers and the daughter of the most vociferous member of his father's dinner table battalion.

Harry's impending marriage to Ethne is announced at her "coming-of-age" party, a lavish ball given by her father, white-haired General Burroughs (C. Aubrey Smith), at his resplendent estate. It is in these scenes that the meticulously researched production violates authenticity for art's sake. Advised by military authorities on the period of the blue color of officers' dress uniforms, Korda demanded that the numerous custom-made costumes be remade in brilliant red lest the gorgeous party appear instead to be an "officers' mess!" Handsome in his radiant red jacket, Ralph Richardson as John Durrance, the film's star though not its lead, professes his love to Harry's fiancée but concedes the winning of her hand to his regiment mate.

During the ball, orders are received to report to the Sudan to aid General Kitchener in revenging the death of Gordon. On the eve of his departure, a morose Harry resigns his commission, having accepted it only to please his father, who died a year earlier. Espousing pacifist principles, he explains to a dismayed Ethne the "futility of this idiotic Egyptian endeavor" and that he is at last "released from the life of an impostor." A messenger arrives bearing his three regiment mates' cards, each of which is attached to a white feather, the emblem of cowardice. Realizing that Ethne too is scornful of him, he symbollically adds her white feather fan to his lot.

The reality of his motives becomes clear to Harry when he discovers that he is indeed cloaking his cowardice in the guise of pacifism. To overcome his fears and to redeem himself to the four, he secretly sets out for Egypt alone. With the aid of a native doctor he effects the disguise of a Singli, a North African tribe whose members are branded on the forehead and relieved of their tongues. While only pretending to be speechless (the better to hide his British accent), he is truly transformed by the scar between his eyes, his dyed-red skin, and turban-wrapped head. Harry meets Kitchener's Anglo-Egyptian Army by joining the enslaved hordes which haul the troop-laden Nile boats by ropes across the river's massive cataracts. In one of the most magnificent scenes on film, the elegantly graceful feluccas scud backward with the force of the violent waters in defeat of the shackled men at rope's end on the shore, accompanied by an ominously beautiful male chorus of increasing volume.

Escaping detection, Harry infiltrates the fanatical followers of the Mahdi, the dervishes. Lieutenant John Durrance, meanwhile, stands watch for them; then, while climbing a rocky elevation to spot their position better, he loses his helmet. The blazing midday sun renders him unconscious, but only after he spies the advancing enemy on the distant horizon. The men under his command who are dispatched to find him bear him back to camp. Trying to regain his senses, Durrance orders that camp be struck in advance of the enemy. It is only in his tent, alone, that he realizes he has been blinded; none of the lighted matches he holds before his eyes will pierce the darkness. The authority and force with which he continues to command his company keeps the ghastly truth from them, and wisely so, for they are soon overwhelmed by the combined strength of the dervishes and the Fuzzy Wuzzies. Named for the wavy character of their hair, these nomadic Haden Dowa tribesmen are superbly represented on the screen by handsome, exotic blacks with aquiline features and outrageous coiffures. They are magnificently lighted and photographed, *en masse* and in profile.

Despite advance warning by a shouting scarface (Harry), Durrance's company is brutally defeated. The few who survive are taken prisoner, while Durrance is left for dead. Harry discovers the blind man and silently cares for him, leading him out of the desert and to safety on the banks of the Nile where, before abandoning him, he tucks the man's calling card and white feather into his jacket. The long trek of the speechless and sightless pair is composed of exhausting and moving scenes—Durrance ignorant of his bene-factor's identity and of the buzzards ceaselessly overhead; Faversham word-lessly hearing his friend babbling in delirium about the unreturned love for a girl named Ethne. There is no finer performance than Ralph Richardson's disciplined, dignified officer at once in command of, yet piteously succumbing to, the abject terror of blindness.

While Durrance recovers at home in the company of old friends, including Ethne, Harry encounters great danger in freeing Lieutenant Peter Burroughs (Donald Gray) and Lieutenant Arthur Willoughby (Jack Allen) from the Khalifa's prison camp. For his efforts he too is imprisoned as a British spy and flogged almost to death. In planning the liberation of all prisoners from the Omdurman hellhole, particularly those who have been there since Gor-don's defeat thirteen years earlier, he reveals his identity to the two astonished lieutenants. The escape is timed to coincide with the incipient battle between the Khalifa's Arab forces and Kitchener's badly outnumbered army. Harry's convicts, a ragtag horde, snatch victory from the enemy and raise the British flag over the mud huts of the Sudanese capital.

Ethne, meanwhile, has learned the whereabouts of Harry from the souvenir of Durrance's weeks with the mysterious Arab savior, which he carries in his pocket, his blindness preventing him from identifying the card and feather within the envelope. In Harry's long absence, Durrance hopes to marry Ethne, but his plans are dashed upon hearing the newspaper account of Kitchener's triumph at Omdurman with the help of the fearless descendant of the distinguished Faversham military lineage.

John Clements in the lead role performs his deeds of derring-do in earnest, though he is rather too effeminate in looks and manner to have made—credibly—the transition from sulking gentleman officer to raging daredevil. June Duprez of the Korda stock company possesses an exotic beauty better suited to the sands of the Sudan than a Victorian drawing room. As Ethne, she is upset much of the time and otherwise fails to elicit concern for her character. *Four Feathers'* real stars are the superb production values, including the awesome 3-strip Technicolor cinematography and the direction of Zoltan Korda. A protracted eight weeks of desert shooting, during which cast and crew stumbled over actual shells left behind by Kitchener, yielded scenes of such breathtaking grandeur that they steal the show from the performers.

The story, not entirely faithful to Mason's original, is an interesting study of the interplay of courage and cowardice. Underlying Harry's early timidity is the courage to resign from his regiment. Real nerve is shown as he undergoes the facial scarring by a red-hot iron. Durrance's bravery in blindness falters badly during a middesert suicide attempt from which Harry saves him. In a moving show of courageous nobility, Durrance writes a letter of lies to Ethne, releasing her from her promise to marry him. This he does upon learning that Harry is alive and indeed the hero of the Sudanese empire. Ethne herself bewails her cowardice toward Harry at the time he most needed her love. Her self-redemption is attempted by bravely consenting to marry a second man who needs her desperately.

Harry returns featherless to friends and family. As General Faversham, his forehead has sufficiently healed to permit his easy reentry into London society and Ethne's arms. His most glorious victory is won, however, as he claims a place beside his father-in-law as new commander of the dinner table battalion.

Four Feathers' most recent revival took place on the television screen in January, 1978, and starred Beau Bridges and Harry Andrews. Predictably, it joined the ranks of its predecessors in the shadow of Alexander Korda's *magnum opus.*

Nancy S. Kinney

FRANKENSTEIN

Released: 1931
Production: Carl Laemmle, Jr., for Universal
Direction: James Whale
Screenplay: Garrett Fort and Francis Faragoh; based on John Balderston's
   adaptation of the novel of the same name by Mary Wollstonecraft Shelley
Cinematography: Arthur Edeson
Editing: Clarence Kolster
Makeup: Jack Pierce
Running time: 71 minutes

Principal characters:
Dr. Henry Frankenstein .... Colin Clive
The Monster .... Boris Karloff
Elizabeth .... Mae Clarke
Victor ....John Boles
Dr. Waldman .... Edward Van Sloan
The Dwarf .... Dwight Frye

Carl Laemmle, Jr., the head of Universal—the studio that had produced such classic films as *The Hunchback of Notre Dame* (1939), with Lon Chaney, Sr., and the 1931 *Dracula*, starring Bela Lugosi—selected his new director, James Whale, to direct the screen version of Mary Shelley's classic novel, *Frankenstein*. British-born Whale had distinguished himself in the English theater, first as an actor and later as a director and producer. The screenplay for Universal's newest horror film was written by Garrett Fort and Francis Faragoh from a stage adaptation by John Balderston. The setting is a small windswept Bavarian village. Isolated from the village in an old abandoned mill is a laboratory where a scientist, Dr. Henry Frankenstein, conducts grisly experiments in his search for a way to create artificial life. Colin Clive, who played Captain Stanhope in the London stage production of *Journey's End* as well as the Hollywood film, was brought from England to play the role of Dr. Frankenstein.

As the film opens, Dr. Frankenstein, aided by a hunchbacked dwarf (Dwight Frye), is seen crouched near the edge of a cemetery watching the progress of a midnight funeral service. As soon as the mourners have left, the doctor and his assistant creep across the lonely moor to claim the object of their secret midnight excursion from its fresh grave. Next Dr. Frankenstein is shown stealing forth to cut down a corpse from the gallows, also to be cut up and used to assemble a new human form into which he hopes to inject the spark of life. To complete his gruesome work, the doctor needs a brain, so he sends the dwarf to a nearby medical school to steal one. In the gloom of the dissecting room, he inadvertently drops the glass bowl containing the brain he had been sent to procure. In order not to disappoint the doctor, however, he steals the brain of a criminal, a fact of which Dr. Frankenstein is never made aware.

Dedicated in his research to the point of obsession, Frankenstein shuts himself off from the outside world, working to the limit of his endurance. Alarmed over the doctor's complete disregard for his physical well-being, his fiancée, Elizabeth (Mae Clarke); his best friend, Victor (John Boles); and his old teacher, Dr. Waldman (Edward Van Sloan), descend on the mill where the experiments are taking place. The sequence that follows is a marvelous piece of theatrics. Frank Grove, Kenneth Strickfaden, and Raymond Lindsay get full credit for the creation and operation of the laboratory's electrical machinery. Here, within the horrified sight of his fiancée and friends, Dr. Frankenstein harnesses the awesome energy of a violent electrical storm which rages outside the old mill, jolting life into the inanimate monster strapped to the operating table.

Frankenstein's unholy creation is ably portrayed by Boris Karloff. Jack Pierce, Universal's head makeup expert, who worked on Dracula, was assigned the task of creating the monster. Pierce did research for more than three months before coming up with the final design. The application of the makeup for the role was an ordeal; nearly three and a half hours were required every morning to put it on, and nearly as long was required at night to remove it. Karloff struggled under the weight of sixty pounds of wardrobe accessories; the shoes alone weighed eighteen pounds apiece. Because the film was shot in midsummer, the heavy quilted suit often left him soaking wet. "Throughout the filming," he said, "I felt as if I was wearing a damp shroud, which no doubt added to the realism." Despite the physical handicaps that the makeup imposed, Karloff considered the role a challenge to his acting ability. Because the creature could utter only a few inarticulate cries, it was necessary for Karloff to act primarily with his eyes. He did not, however, yield to the temptation of melodrama by resorting to exaggerated gestures and expressions. This simplicity and restraint created a monster all the more frightening.

Following his "birth" in the laboratory, the monster is kept locked in the dungeon of the old mill, where he is tortured by the dwarf, whose mind is as twisted as his body. Tormented beyond endurance, the monster strangles the dwarf; afterwards, the concentrated effort of all concerned is needed to restrain him. While Dr. Frankenstein had been proud of his creation, he now knows he has reason to fear the creature, for it is no longer under his control. The full realization of the horror he has precipitated drives the doctor to the verge of a nervous breakdown. He returns to his estate to recover, after eliciting a promise from Dr. Waldman that he will destroy the monster while he is away. On the day that he and Elizabeth are to be married, the doctor is horrified to learn that the monster has strangled Dr. Waldman and escaped from the mill. Arthur Edeson's camera effectively follows Frankenstein's monstrous creation, his heavy-lidded, lizardlike eyes staring straight ahead, plodding like an automaton across the wild and sinister countryside. Karloff's superb performance arouses much more than spine-tingling fear. This alien creature with his terrible aloneness, his fear of fire, and his strange, pathetic cries, arouses compassion. The viewer knows that the creature must be destroyed but has empathy for his suffering.

After receiving the terrible news of Dr. Waldman's death, Dr. Frankenstein and Elizabeth return to the village, and the doctor joins the mob in their search for the creature. By this time, he has killed again, inadvertently drowning a little peasant girl, and the villagers, driven by fear and hate, have redoubled their efforts to hunt him down and destroy him. The doctor, however, becomes separated from the others and finds himself face to face with his hideous creation. The monster easily overcomes Frankenstein and carries him back to the mill, pursued by the villagers. Inside, Frankenstein regains consciousness and a struggle ensues. In the process, Frankenstein is hurled several stories to the ground and severely injured. The villagers, who by now have arrived, set fire to the mill. Amid the crackling of the flames, we hear the quavering, frightened cries of the dying monster. Following its destruction, a final scene shows Dr. Frankenstein recovered and in the process of marrying Elizabeth.

The studio was unsure how they should film the ending. In Shelley's novel and in previous stage presentations, Dr. Frankenstein dies; however, the studio felt that such an ending would leave the audience disappointed. Consequently, two endings were filmed, and, after a preview, the ending in which Dr. Frankenstein lives was decided upon. In another departure from the original text, the scene depicting the monster's murder of the little girl was deleted when the film was first released. The monster had been playing with the child on the bank of the river, watching her toss blossoms in the water. He had picked her up and thrown her in the water, expecting her to float as the blossoms did. Instead of a diabolical murder, therefore, the monster's act was an act of ignorance which, if it had appeared, would have aroused even more audience sympathy for the plight of the creature. Through the years, however, this scene has been reinserted, and the sympathetic interpretation of the monster has become popular.

Financially, *Frankenstein* was one of the most successful films of the 1931-1932 season, grossing more than $12,000,000 from an investment of $250,000. It set a pattern, even more so than *Dracula*, for Universal's subsequent treatment of the subject of horror. More significantly, however, it launched the career of Boris Karloff, whose portrayal of Frankenstein's monster catapulted him to international fame. In addition to his successes in subsequent Frankenstein films and over eighty other screen roles, Karloff also made extensive appearances on Broadway and on television; likewise, Colin Clive, who played the dedicated, inspired doctor with such believability and finesse, went on to appear in more than fifteen other films before his untimely death in 1937, and in *The Bride of Frankenstein* (1935) he again costarred with Boris Karloff.

The characters of Frankenstein and his monster have been portrayed on the screen many times since 1931. *Frankenstein*, in various forms, has proven to be saleable for almost fifty years. Such films as *Son of Frankenstein* (1939), *I Was a Teenage Frankenstein* (1957), and Mel Brooks's *Young Frankenstein* (1974) have all helped to enhance the popularity of the original story.

D. Gail Huskins

THE FRENCH CONNECTION

Released: 1971
Production: Philip D'Antoni for Twentieth Century-Fox (AA)
Direction: William Friedkin (AA)
Screenplay: Ernest Tidyman (AA); based on the book of the same name by
  Robin Moore
Cinematography: Owen Roizman
Editing: Jerry Greenberg (AA)
Stunt coordinator: Bill Hickman
Running time: 104 minutes

Principal characters:
Jimmy "Popeye" Doyle	Gene Hackman (AA)
Buddy Russo	Roy Scheider
Alain Charnier	Fernando Rey
Sal Boca	Tony LoBianco
Pierre Nicoli	Marcel Bozzuffi
Devereaux	Frederic De Pasquale
Mulderig	Bill Hickman
Lieutenant Simonson	Eddie Egan
Klein	Sonny Grosso
Weinstock	Harold Gary

The French Connection, which won several Academy Awards, including
Best Picture and Best Actor (Gene Hackman), is a fast-paced thriller which
immediately captures the audience and never lets go. The true-to-life story
depicts the biggest narcotics seizure of all time, the 1962 confiscation of 120
pounds of pure heroin, which constitutes enough "junk" to keep every addict
in the United States supplied for eight months.

Now an American crime classic, the film is the semidocumentary story of
the actual detectives Sonny Grosso and Eddie Egan, who had worked together
for nearly a decade, mostly in Harlem, on New York's special narcotics squad.
Having smashed the multimillion-dollar international dope smuggling ring,
Gross's and Egan's exploits were captured in a best-selling book by Robin
Moore and translated onto the screen by a talented production team headed
by William Friedkin, the director of such diverse films as *The Night They
Raided Minsky's* (1968), *The Boys in the Band* (1970), and *The Exorcist*
(1973).

While a few scenes were set in Washington, D.C., and Marseilles, France,
the gangster picture was filmed almost entirely on location in New York: in
Bedford-Stuyvesant, the Lower East Side, Times Square, and Grand Central
Station. In gritty street pictures, Owen Roizman's camera captures the seamy
side of New York: the garbage, the pollution, and the city's brutal winter.
Composer-conductor Don Ellis' moody score, with its effective use of the

trombone, adds to the atmosphere.

Following the murder of a French detective in Marseilles by a professional killer, Pierre Nicoli (Marcel Bozzuffi), the dope-related mugging in Brooklyn of Detective Buddy Russo (Roy Scheider), and the suspicious flashing of large sums of money in an Eastside club, "supercops" Russo and Jimmy "Popeye" Doyle (Gene Hackman) play a long shot. Following some alleged heroin dealers into Brooklyn, the two plainclothesmen establish surveillance on a shady-looking candy store owned by Sal Boca (Tony LoBianco). Later, they trail Sal to the Manhattan apartment of Jewish Mafioso Joel Weinstock (Harold Gary), known to be the chief financial backer of illicit narcotics importation into the United States. Following that, Russo and Doyle persuade their boss, Lieutenant Simonson (Eddie Egan), to put Federal authorities on the case.

Meanwhile, the debonair French businessman Alain Charnier (Fernando Rey) and his wife; a leading French television personality, Henri Devereaux (Frederic De Pasquale); and the assassin Nicoli have arrived in New York and are seen meeting with Weinstock and Boca. Following assorted chases and shootouts, con-games and gundowns, the enormous consignment of smuggled drugs is uncovered, ingeniously hidden in Devereaux's specially designed Lincoln. As the story unfolds, Boca is exposed as the smugglers' Brooklyn contact, while Devereaux is inveigled into shipping his dope-laden car to America. Charnier is (unbeknownst to his innocent wife) the kingpin of the vast operation, and Nicoli is discovered to be his kill-happy strongarm.

By far the most memorable scene is the exciting chase through Bensonhurst, Brooklyn. Brilliantly executed, it is almost too gripping to enjoy. Spotting Nicoli, Doyle begins the hot pursuit. The hit man mounts the elevated station and takes over a moving train. Doyle, on the ground below, quickly commandeers a passing car and follows the path of the train. Amidst the fender-crunching, train-clacking, tire-shrieking noise, Nicoli ignores all station stops, terrorizes the passengers, and kills a transit motorman and policeman. Still down below, Doyle keeps one eye on the traffic and the other on the train as he weaves in and out at top speed, careens around pedestrians and track supports, and forces other cars off the road. Jerry Greenberg's editing is taut, hard, and relentless. With constricted stomachs, the audience feels that they, too, are participants in the furiously paced chase. It is reminiscent of Steve McQueen's car chase sequence in *Bullitt* (1968), which was also produced by Philip D'Antoni, but directed by William Friedkin.

Tough, violent, and brutal, *The French Connection* is not without some grim humor. In one scene Nicoli and Charnier elegantly dine in high style, while, outside in the bitter cold, Doyle disgustedly eats rubbery pizza and drinks muddy coffee. At another time, Nicoli tears a piece of bread from the loaf clutched by a man he has just shot in the face.

A melodrama with authenticity, the film provides insight into the nature of the police and the mobsters. Equally cold-blooded and callous, there are no good guys and bad guys, characters all black and white; instead, they are black and deep gray. Obscene, ferocious, and unheroic, Roy Scheider and Gene Hackman are excellent. Spanish actor Fernando Rey, in his first major American film, is suave and cool as the French mastermind with the silver-handled umbrella. Marcel Bozzuffi, who played the homosexual killer in *Z* (1969), is equally malevolent as Nicoli. Real-life detectives Egan and Grosso served as technical advisers during production, and each has a role in the film. Egan portrays Lieutenant Simonson, head of the two-hundred-man New York narcotics squad. Simonson was the police officer who had been Egan's actual supervisor during the original investigation. Sonny Grosso also has a minor role as Klein.

Ending on an ironic note, the action-adventure concludes as the hard-nosed detectives are transferred out of narcotics and the criminals escape with light sentences—or none at all. One difference between real life and this film is that the French assassin killed by Egan in the movie is actually now serving an eleven- to twenty-two-year sentence in prison.

So financially successful was the film that it spawned a sequel, *French Connection, II*, in 1974. That picture was not as well received critically as the original, but it did very well at the box office. It again starred Hackman and Rey, although most of the other principals were played by actors who had not been in the original production.

Leslie Taubman

FROM HERE TO ETERNITY

Released: 1953
Production: Buddy Adler for Columbia (AA)
Direction: Fred Zinnemann (AA)
Screenplay: Daniel Taradash (AA); based on the novel of the same name by
  James Jones
Cinematography: Burnett Guffey (AA)
Editing: William A. Lyon (AA)
Art direction: Cary Odell
Sound: John P. Livadary and Columbia Studio Sound Department (AA)
Music: George Duning
Running time: 118 minutes

> *Principal characters:*
> Sergeant Milton Warden .... Burt Lancaster
> Robert E. Lee "Prew" Prewitt ..... Montgomery Clift
> Karen Holmes .... Deborah Kerr
> Angelo Maggio .... Frank Sinatra (AA)
> Alma (Lorene) .... Donna Reed (AA)
> Captain Dana Holmes .... Philip Ober
> Sergeant "Fatso" Judson .... Ernest Borgnine

James Jones's 1951 novel, *From Here to Eternity*, whose title was taken from a line ("damned from here to eternity") in Rudyard Kipling's poem "Gentlemen Rankers," is based on the author's own military experience and presents a scathing portrait of barracks' life in a peacetime United States Army company. In some respects it is hardly a novel at all, resembling a sort of literary Rorschach Test. When the novel appeared, every reader seemed to see something different in it and responded emotionally in diverse ways. Most agreed, however, that it embodied a tremendously vivid and exciting picture of men in mass groupings and added up to as powerful an expression of love and hate for the United States Army as had every been published. Written in sprawling and vigorous style, *From Here to Eternity* became a best seller and won the National Book Award. In so doing it came to the attention of Columbia's head, Harry Cohn, who eventually bought the rights to the novel from Jones for $82,000 and set out to get an acceptable film treatment written.

It was the feeling at Columbia that the explicit nature of the novel would have to be toned down to make it suitable for the screen. This attitude frustrated Jones greatly; his own treatment was rejected because it followed too closely the obscene and sadistic flourishes of the novel. A somewhat diluted version, written by Daniel Taradash, was finally accepted by the studio. Even in its new state, however, *From Here to Eternity* is a powerful story, and director Fred Zinnemann brought it to the screen with great skill and fidelity to the original source. In Zinnemann's refinement, however, there are touches of slick sentimentality that do not seem to come from the book; and many viewers have noted the absence of some of the novel's honest and rough-hewn vignettes that had to be shorn away during its transformation to the screen. Through its cold professional eye, though, Zinnemann's camera sees the persons of the drama more clearly and at the same time less bitterly than did Jones.

Following the selection of Zinnemann as director, the casting of the performers became a focal point of controversy among Cohn, Zinnemann, and Jones, as well as various other studio executives. Cohn recommended that the part of Robert E. Lee Prewitt, the young soldier who refuses to box for his company and is therefore persecuted, be given to Aldo Ray. Both Zinnemann and Jones had hoped that the part would be given to Montgomery Clift. Jones and Clift had become drinking companions and Clift had already worked for Zinnemann in the film *The Search* (1948). It was finally agreed that Clift would be given the role since he had a reputation for being well-equipped to interpret sensitive roles as demonstrated in such films as *A Place in the Sun* (1951) and *Red River* (1948). The part of Karen Holmes, the frustrated wife of Captain Dana Holmes, was originally given to Joan Crawford, but because of a disagreement over costume selection she quit, leaving the role open for English actress Deborah Kerr.

The remaining performers rounding out the cast were also excellent choices. The part of Sergeant Milton Warden went to Burt Lancaster who was perfectly suited to play the character of the solid career soldier who is aware of how to manipulate the system but is unwilling to do so merely for the sake of promotion. Frank Sinatra, who had to convince the studio heads that he could perform a nonsinging role, won the part of Angelo Maggio, the good-natured friend of Prewitt. In an uncharacteristic role, Donna Reed was cast as Alma (Lorene), the prostitute who befriends Prewitt.

On the wide screen and in stereophonic sound, *From Here to Eternity* draws the viewer into the world of the military. The film is more than noteworthy as being a significant example of a hardhitting and honest 1950's drama: a microscopic look at the undercurrents which ran through a peacetime military company stationed in Hawaii just before the attack on Pearl Harbor. The story line revolves around Private Prewitt, played in extraordinary depth by Montgomery Clift. The screenplay focuses more sharply than did the novel on Private Robert E. Lee "Prew" Prewitt, the "hardhead" who can soldier with any man, but who cannot play it smart because he is cursed with a piece of ultimate wisdom. As he puts it, "If a man don't go his own way, he's nothing." The character is essentially a loner who becomes further removed from the other men in the company because of his conscience. Transferred into Company G at Schofield Barracks in Hawaii, Prew is immediately informed by Captain Dana Holmes (Philip Ober) that he cannot go his own way. Captain Holmes, a boxing fanatic who wants his company to win the regiment championship, knows that Prew is a first-class middleweight, and insists that he box for his new outfit. Prew, who quit fighting after he blinded a friend with a "no more'n ordinary right cross," refuses. Furious, Holmes orders his noncommissioned officers—all of whom are on the boxing team—to give Prew "the treatment."

Prew endures this harassment for months on end. The sergeants trip him in bayonet drill and cheat him in rifle inspection, and for every fault they find, Prew has to pay with K. P., extra laps around the track under full pack, or hours of digging enormous holes in the ground so that the jeering noncoms can bury a single newspaper. His superiors even refuse his request to become the company bugler even though he is a polished musician (Clift spent a good deal of time learning to play the bugle so he could feel comfortable when the role called upon him to do so).

In addition to the story of Private Prewitt, there are other threads which are finely woven to fill in the picture of Army life between the world wars. There is the rowdy comedy of the soldiers' night out at the "New Congress Club" and the bittersweet story of Prew's love for a warm-hearted prostitute with visions of respectability. Although the novel bluntly called the girl a whore, the film manages to make the point merely by including her in some of the most accurately depicted brothel scenes in cinema. There is, by contrast, the fierce meeting of First Sergeant Warden (Burt Lancaster) and the captain's wife, Karen Holmes (Deborah Kerr), two people who think they know what they need and almost make life give it to them. Warden and Karen's love scene in the Hawaiian surf is one of the most famous moments in cinema history, and for some people the dominant romantic image of the film. Additionally, there are the stories of Private Maggio (Frank Sinatra), Prew's friend who is beaten to death in the stockade by "Fatso" Judson (Ernest Borgnine), the brutal captain of the guard, and of Prew's tragic revenge. The climax of the film is December 7, 1941, which, for all of its horror, finally ends this cycle of human misery. Fred Zinnemann, who fought tirelessly to hold the scenario as closely as possible to James Jones's original, deserves credit for molding the diverse lines of action at once large in scope, in power, and in passion, and also for conveying an intimacy of personal triumphs and tragedies. There is a clarity of purpose in his direction and a respect shown for the characters and the talented group of actors who portray them which effectively strengthens the story line.

The three male leads in the film turn in arguably the finest performances of their careers to that time. Burt Lancaster as the tough career military man is appropriately physical and obvious in his manner. He is the model of a man among men, absolutely convincing in his instinctive awareness of the subtle elaborate structure of force and honor on which a male society is based.

Sergeant Warden uses the military system to his advantage though he will not allow himself to bend to it and pull the right strings to become an officer, which would make his life easier. His love for Captain Holmes's wife is passionate and genuine. Their love affair eventually fails because of his refusal to make it easier on himself and succumb to the system. The film's big performance is given by Montgomery Clift. He does an ingenious job of acting a plain, slow-thinking individual who compares interestingly in scenes with Lancaster, who does everything with a glib, showy animal magnetism. Clift displays a marvelous capacity to contract his feelings into the tight little shell of Prew's personality. At the same time, he manages to convey that within this limited man there blazes a large spirit.

Frank Sinatra, in an Academy Award-winning performance, portrays Private Maggio like nothing he has ever done before. His face conveys the calm confidence of a man who is completely sure of what he is doing as he plays it straight from Little Italy. In certain scenes—performing duty in the mess hall, reacting to some foul piano playing—he shows a marvelous capacity for phrasing and a calm expression that is unique in Hollywood film.

Ernest Borgnine as Fatso, with his smiling villainy, is hard to forget. Deborah Kerr as Karen, playing a part far removed from the more refined roles for which she had been previously noted, brims with sensuality. As a woman married to the brutal military opportunist, she attempts to sieze a forbidden love, disregarding the consequences of such an act in the closed world of the military.

From Here to Eternity, under the care and direction of Fred Zinnemann, involves the viewer from beginning to conclusion, from the initial naïveté and innocence of Private Robert E. Lee Prewitt, on through the frustration and torment of the career soldiers and the women who become bruised casualties of this man's world. The performers convey that curious and captivating presence that director Zinnemann refers to as "behaving rather than acting," which he developed in such notable films as *The Search*, *The Men* (1950), and *The Member of the Wedding* (1953). Vienna-born Zinnemann, a former cameraman, uses the camera with easy familiarity and with a cool simplicity that seems surprised by nothing, but shows compassion for everything. The location cinematography took place at Schofield Barracks in Hawaii, which becomes a large, stark frame for some memorable scenes, such as the rite of taps for Private Maggio.

Great care and intent went into the making of *From Here to Eternity*. Zinnemann and Daniel Taradash share the credit for an outstanding script. Although the shift from one story to another is sometimes too abrupt, that is only a minor defect in a highly professional job of writing. Although this film is what Hollywood considers "a big picture" with slick production values, it is also something more. It attempts to tell a truth about life and the inviolability of the human spirit. It is not a total success but it does show powerfully that Americans care very much about a man's right to go his own way even though the times and the world may be contrary.

The public approved the effort and made *From Here to Eternity* a big box-office success for Columbia. The Motion Picture Academy followed suit by awarding the film seven Academy Awards, including Best Supporting Actor (Frank Sinatra), Best Supporting Actress (Donna Reed), and Best Picture. The New York Film Critics gave laurels to *From Here to Eternity* for Best Picture, Best Director, and Best Actor (Burt Lancaster). Montgomery Clift was nominated for Best Actor by the Motion Picture Academy, but the award went to William Holden that year for his performance in *Stalag 17*.

Jeffry Michael Jensen

FROM RUSSIA WITH LOVE

Released: 1964
Production: Harry Saltzman and Albert R. Broccoli for United Artists
Direction: Terence Young
Screenplay: Richard Maibaum; based on Johanna Harwood's adaptation of
the novel of the same name by Ian Fleming
Cinematography: Ted Moore
Editing: Peter Hunt
Running time: 118 minutes

> *Principal characters:*
> James Bond (007) ....Sean Connery
> Tatiana Romanova .... Daniela Bianchi
> Rosa Klebb .... Lotte Lenya
> Red Grant .... Robert Shaw
> "M" .... Bernard Lee
> Miss Moneypenny .... Lois Maxwell
> Kerim Bey .... Pedro Armendariz

During the mid-1960's, James Bond ranked just behind the Beatles among British contributions to American culture. Even President John F. Kennedy had expressed his admiration for the hero of Ian Fleming's popular spy novels; thus, when Bond made his screen debut in 1963 in Terence Young's adaptation of *Doctor No*, starring Sean Connery as agent 007, the character quickly established itself as one of the most enduring screen icons of the 1960's and 1970's. Audiences loved the film—particularly the outrageous villains, the exotic weapons, and other somewhat campy elements. Young and Connery took the hint: they made *Doctor No*'s successor, *From Russia with Love*, with tongue firmly in cheek.

From Russia with Love finds the superspy contending with an organization known as SPECTRE. (Special Executive for Counterintelligence, Terrorism, Revenge and Extortion; the specter of SPECTRE, incidentally, has been added to the film version of *From Russia with Love* by the writers. This organization, which appears in Fleming's *Thunderball* and *On Her Majesty's Secret Service*, never appears in the novel from which this film is adapted.) The organization's target is a Russian cryptographic device known as a Lektor, and most of the action takes place in the Balkans, from Istanbul to Trieste.

The film opens, however, on SPECTRE Island, where the evildoers are engaged in a continuous round of exotic combat training which uses live targets, including one poor fellow made up to look exactly like James Bond. He is garroted by Red Grant (Robert Shaw), SPECTRE's top assassin, who will soon get an opportunity to test his mettle against the real agent 007. The SPECTRE high command consists of Colonel Rosa Klebb (Lotte Lenya), recently defected from the Russian intelligence apparatus; an international chess grandmaster named Kronsteen; and Number 1, their mysterious leader, whose face is never seen, and who strokes a white kitten as he issues his deadly commands. Klebb is to implement Kronsteen's plan, which involves luring James Bond to Istanbul, allowing him to steal the Lektor, and then taking the Lektor from him. SPECTRE has a score to settle with Bond, who was responsible for the death of their operative, Doctor No. "Make his death a particularly unpleasant one," intones Number 1. The bait for SPECTRE's trap is Tatiana Romanova (Daniela Bianchi), a luscious young woman who serves as a minor functionary in the Soviet spy system. She has access to the Lektor, and she is unaware of Colonel Klebb's defection from the ranks. Thinking all the while that she is serving Mother Russia, Tatiana agrees to seduce Bond.

After this lengthy explication, Young permits Bond his initial appearance in the film. The scene has become a standard one: Bond is dallying with a voluptuous woman and just when they are about to get down to brass tacks, a buzzer goes off, summoning Bond to headquarters and the start of a new adventure. "M" (Bernard Lee), the head of British intelligence, outlines the situation to 007. They have received a message from a pretty young Russian cipher clerk in Istanbul. She claims to have fallen in love with James Bond, having seen his dossier and read of his exploits, and promises to deliver the Lektor to the British under the condition that Bond takes her with him back to England. The whole thing sounds suspicious, but the Lektor is of sufficient importance to the British government that the risk is deemed worthwhile. "Suppose that when she meets me in the flesh, I don't come up to expectations," asks Bond with a smile. "See that you do," "M" responds drily.

Before he is dispatched to Istanbul, Bond is given a secret weapon, an obligatory piece of exotic machinery that will, *deus ex machina*-style, snatch him from the jaws of certain death. In this film, it is an innocuous looking briefcase. It features a number of secret compartments, one of which contains a particularly nasty knife. If opened improperly, the briefcase will emit a blast of tear gas.

Briefcase in hand, Bond travels to Istanbul, where he joins forces with Kerim Bey (Pedro Armendariz), the head of the Turkish secret service and a fellow *bon vivant*. Bey is also skeptical of the validity of Tatiana's offer, but, like Bond, he suspects the Soviets, not SPECTRE, of setting the trap. The Russians unknowingly play into SPECTRE's hands as they choose this moment to mount several assassination attempts against both Bond and Bey. Ironically, Red Grant, the SPECTRE killer who has been shadowing 007, is forced to save Bond's life twice. It would not work to have him killed before he delivers the Lektor.

Meanwhile, Tatiana Romanova makes contact with Bond: he returns to his hotel suite to find her in his bed. He makes love to her—strictly in the line of duty, of course—and she is not disappointed. Neither is SPECTRE. As the couple begins to get amorous, Director Young pans away from their bed and into the next room, where, behind a two-way mirror, SPECTRE agents are filming the whole proceedings. Their Number 1 has ordered that Bond be disgraced as well as killed, and these films are part of the plan. None of this, however, is known to Tatiana, who soon actually falls in love with Bond.

With Bey's assistance, Bond and Tatiana make off with the Lektor and board a train for Trieste, one step ahead of the Russian KGB, but also one step behind Red Grant, who has monitored their every move. The lethal Grant kills first Bey and then the genuine British agent who was to meet Bond. Then, masquerading as the dead agent, Grant introduces himself to 007 as Captain Nash of the British secret service.

"Nash" is rather uncouth, calling Bond "old man" incessantly and ordering red wine with fish at dinner; Bond is nonetheless taken in by his deception. The SPECTRE assassin drugs Tatiana, and, back in their berth on the train, attacks and disarms the unsuspecting Bond. "You may know the right wines," Grant as "Nash" sneers when Bond regains consciousness, "but you're the one on your knees." Grant delights in explaining the intricate SPECTRE plot to Bond, including the part about the films of his tryst with Tatiana, which will form the basis of the staged murder of Tatiana and suicide of Bond designed to discredit 007 and the whole British secret service.

Bond asks for a last cigarette, thus bringing his exploding briefcase into play. The tear gas and the knife within it do their work, and Bond and Tatiana escape. They gain their hard-earned freedom after a few well-staged chase scenes. The first, patterned after the scene in Alfred Hitchcock's *North by Northwest* (1959), in which Cary Grant is pursued by a crop-dusting plane, ends with Bond shooting down a SPECTRE helicopter. The second occurs after Bond has commandeered a boat with which he lures what appears to be the entire SPECTRE navy onto a gigantic oil slick and then proceeds to ignite it.

SPECTRE makes one last attempt to steal the Lektor when Bond and Tatiana arrive in Venice. Disguised as a hotel chambermaid, Rosa Klebb enters their room and very nearly kills Bond with a venom-tipped blade protruding like a spur from the toe of her shoe. However, Bond is saved by Tatiana, who seizes a gun and shoots her former superior. The film ends with Bond and Tatiana drifting down one of Venice's famous canals, Bond slowly unraveling SPECTRE's pornographic film of them into the water, where it disappears from sight.

From Russia with Love represents the cinematic James Bond at his best. Terence Young, the director who initiated the series, and Sean Connery, the actor who first brought Bond to life, are at their best. Young paces the film expertly, and his delay in introducing Bond into the film, except for the opening tease involving a SPECTRE victim disguised as Bond, whets our anticipation nicely. He mixes the comedy, the romantic interludes, and the fast-paced action sequences with a sure hand.

Among the supporting cast, Bernard Lee as "M" and Lois Maxwell as Miss Moneypenny continue their roles as Bond's professional family, and similar to Connery, they seem made for their roles. A bleached blonde Robert Shaw is appropriately thuggish as Red Grant, SPECTRE's top assassin. Top acting honors among the villains, however, must go to Lotte Lenya for her portrayal of Colonel Rosa Klebb, a characterization of pure, venomous evil. Indeed, it is almost axiomatic that the only interesting women in Bond's world are villains; thus Daniela Bianchi as Tatiana Romanova is called upon to do little more than look lovely, a task which she accomplishes nicely.

Sean Connery, of course, is James Bond incarnate. He alone seems capable of projecting the wit, the romantic prowess, and the derring-do that made 007 a cinematic legend. The later Bond films starring George Lazenby and Roger Moore do not lack merit, and many of them are quite good; all feature their share of fine cinematography, stunning women, and even more stunning special effects. Perhaps therein lies the problem. Without Sean Connery to lend weight to the series' main character, the directors who succeeded Terence Young, who left after *Thunderball* (1965), the fourth Bond film, were forced to rely more and more on special effects, tricks, and gimmicks. The campy elements that Young and Connery used in moderation gradually became the entire *raison d'être* of the later Bond films. To purists, the early Bond films are the best, and *From Russia with Love* is one of the best of the early films.

Robert Mitchell

THE FRONT PAGE

Released: 1931
Production: Howard Hughes for United Artists
Direction: Lewis Milestone
Screenplay: Bartlett Cormack and Charles Lederer; based on the play of the
  same name by Ben Hecht and Charles MacArthur
Cinematography: Glen MacWilliams
Editing: W. Duncan Mansfield
Running time: 101 minutes

> *Principal characters:*
> Walter Burns .... Adolphe Menjou
> Hildy Johnson .... Pat O'Brien
> Peggy Grant .... Mary Brian
> Bensinger .... Edward Everett Horton
> Murphy .... Walter Catlett
> Earl Williams .... George E. Stone
> Sheriff Hartman .... Clarence Wilson

When Ben Hecht and Charles MacArthur wrote *The Front Page* in 1928, they used the basic premise that everyone is corrupt in one way or another, and, furthermore, that everyone enjoys it. The motley assortment of newspapermen and politicians who appear in the play are a cynical group who expend a great deal of energy in trying to outwit everyone else. They all are aware of who is playing games, and in many cases what the results will be; but the real fun will come in trying to be the first to acknowledge it publicly. The protagonists of *The Front Page*, scheming newspaper editor Walter Burns and his ace reporter Hildy Johnson, are the cleverest of the lot because they manage to outsmart the politicians as well as the other newspapermen. No other character in the play or film could possibly steal the show from these two cheerfully corrupt souls, who effortlessly manipulate everyone in the story.

The success of the Broadway production of *The Front Page*, directed by the legendary George S. Kaufman, was so great that it led to a proliferation of stories with newspapermen as protagonists both on stage and in the new "talkies." In most of these stories, the reporter, although he is working for a just cause, is pictured as a driven, almost inhuman individual; it is the female lead who begs him to "get out of the racket." Some of these stories chose to bypass the rich comedic vein unearthed by *The Front Page* to make more serious points. Paramount's *Gentlemen of the Press* (1929), for example, while containing most of the elements of *The Front Page*, is really more like a soap opera: editor Walter Huston's zeal for his job keeps him from his daughter's deathbed in one scene, and most of the people in the film remind him at one point or another that he is a heartless individual.

Hecht and MacArthur were very much a part of the Chicago of 1928 that they describe in the play; they could not have captured the nuances of the newspaper racket so skillfully had they not been, but it is obvious that, like the protagonists about whom they write, the authors feel a certain exhilaration for their characters and the unscrupulous schemes they perpetrate. Lewis Milestone directed this film version of *The Front Page*, and his dedication to the structure of film is evident in his attempts at staging. To avoid a slow, static rendition of a stage play, Milestone kept his camera on the move; he made sure that the audience realized that rooms have four walls (we never see four walls in a play); and he had the film cut quickly from shot to shot to give visual pace to the staccato dialogue, which had been a part of Kaufman's directorial technique for the play. Unfortunately, sound recording techniques in 1931 were not as sophisticated as they were later in the decade, and prints of *The Front Page* exhibited today have poor sound reproduction, forcing newer audiences to strain to hear the dialogue. Aside from that, however, *The Front Page* is a creditable effort to release the early talkie from its one-sct, stagebound qualities, and it succeeds quite well.

As the story begins, we learn that ace reporter Hildy Johnson (Pat O'Brien) is leaving the newspaper racket, much to the chagrin of his unscrupulous editor Walter Burns (Adolphe Menjou), who wants Hildy to cover the hanging of Earl Williams (George F. Stone), a poor clerk who went temporarily mad and shot a policeman. Hildy no longer wants any part of the business as he is engaged to be married to Peggy Grant (Mary Brian). The other reporters, staying in the Press Room of the Criminal Courts building to cover the hanging, deride Hildy goodnaturedly about quitting, but he remains adamant. He, Peggy, and her mother are leaving for New York to begin life anew, far away from Chicago and its crooked politicians, gangsters, and cheap reporters.

When Williams escapes by accident, Walter realizes that he has the conclusive proof of ineptitude in the local government, and by disclosing this information to the public, can force the ouster of Sheriff Hartman (Clarence Wilson). Hartman is only the political puppet of the Mayor, who desperately needs Williams' immediate recapture since an election is forthcoming. Convincing Hildy that he will help the newlyweds after the capture of Williams, Walter persuades the reporter to cover the story for him. Hildy and the other newspeople fail to realize that Williams, a timid individual by nature, has not even left the Criminal Courts building. The sheriff mounts a citywide manhunt, and the reporters follow every lead hoping for a scoop. Hildy, alone in the Press Room, is surprised by Williams' entrance; he persuades the harried fugitive to hide in the Press Room, concealing him inside a rolltop desk. Hildy then summons Walter, who plans to return Williams officially to the police, not only getting the scoop but embarrassing the police as well.

Other reporters nearly discover Earl in the desk, and Walter's sudden appearance makes the sheriff suspicious. The police circulate stories of William's maniacal attack on his guards, and issue orders to "shoot to kill." Thus, the sheriff is in no mood to entertain a messenger from the Governor who brings a reprieve for Williams. Hartman attempts to bribe the messenger and sends him away, but the slow-witted messenger returns just as Williams has been exposed, and Walter and Hildy arrested as accessories. This new evidence is what Walter needs to expose the corruption within the city's administration. During all the excitement, Hildy realizes that he is a newspaperman for life, and he and Walter contemplate further double-dealings.

Howard Hawks remade *The Front Page* for Columbia in 1940. Changing the character of Hildy Johnson from a man to a woman and making Walter Burns more suave made *His Girl Friday* (1940) sparkle; the male-female relationship gave additional bite to many of the play's original lines. Charles Lederer, who worked on *The Front Page*, did the screenplay for *His Girl Friday* as well, and the Hawks film, curiously, retains much of the play's original integrity. In 1976, Billy Wilder, himself a cynical journalist, screenwriter, and director, remade *The Front Page* under its original title, starring Jack Lemmon as Hildy Johnson and Walter Matthau as Walter Burns. Despite the teamwork of Lemmon and Matthau, the film was surprisingly flat, and it was generally felt that the material had already been given the definitive screen treatment.

Ed Hulse

FUNNY GIRL

Released: 1968
Production: Ray Stark for Columbia
Direction: William Wyler
Screenplay: Isobel Lennart; based on her musical play of the same name
  with music by Jule Styne and lyrics by Bob Merrill
Cinematography: Harry Stradling
Editing: Robert Swink, Maury Weintrobe, and William Sands
Costume design: Irene Sharaff
Music direction: Herbert Ross
Running time: 151 minutes

> *Principal characters:*
> Fanny Brice .... Barbra Streisand (AA)
> Nick Arnstein .... Omar Sharif
> Rose Brice .... Kay Medford
> Georgia James .... Anne Francis
> Florenz Ziegfeld .... Walter Pidgeon

When the $8.8 million film version of *Funny Girl* had its premiere on September 19, 1968, it succeeded in doing what every reporter, journalist, and columnist had predicted it would—it catapulted Barbra Streisand into superstardom. It also led to an Oscar for her performance as Best Actress of the Year, tying Katharine Hepburn for *The Lion in Winter*. This was only the second time that a tie had occurred in an acting category, the first having been the one between Wallace Beery for *The Champ* and Fredric March for *Dr. Jekyll and Mr. Hyde* in 1931.

Streisand, the ugly-duckling Jewish girl from Brooklyn, had already wooed recording and television fans, and had scored personal acting successes, with her Miss Marmelstein role in Broadway's *I Can Get It for You Wholesale*, and her stage impersonation of Fanny Brice in the Broadway hit version of *Funny Girl*. When the stage version of *Funny Girl* opened at the Winter Garden Theatre in New York City, on March 26, 1964, where it was to run for a total of 1,348 performances, Bette Davis attended the opening night performance and exclaimed afterwards, "The girl has star quality."

Indeed, Streisand's star quality is her greatest asset and her greatest liability. The motion picture version of *Funny Girl* was tailor-made for Streisand's unique personality; most viewers did not care that what remained of Fanny Brice's story was little more than a glossy Cinderella story. The other films which Streisand has made since *Funny Girl* have likewise been tailor-made for her, each capitalizing on her star quality with varying degrees of artistic success, although most have also been box-office blockbusters.

Funny Girl property rights belong to producer Ray Stark, who is married to Fanny Brice's daughter, Frances, by Nick Arnstein. He had Isobel Lennart fashion a script for the musical play, to which Jule Styne and Bob Merrill added music and lyrics, respectively. While the play takes liberty with the actual facts of Fanny Brice's life, it is an affectionate and nostalgic recalling of America's Broadway past and a vehicle perfectly suited to the comic talents of Barbra Streisand. Stark produced the stage version, Garson Kanin directed it, and Carol Haney staged the musical numbers. When preparing the project for the screen, additional changes were made to more carefully create a showcase for Streisand's motion picture debut.

Herbert Ross, who was a former dancer and choreographer and who had directed Streisand in *I Can Get It for You Wholesale*, was called in to stage the musical numbers in the screen version; this staging is certainly the most important ingredient in the film version. (Ross would later direct Streisand in *The Owl and the Pussycat*, 1970, and *Funny Lady*, 1975, and Anne Bancroft and Shirley Maclaine in *The Turning Point*, 1977. Curiously, veteran director William Wyler consented to direct the film, the first time in his illustrious career (*Wuthering Heights*, 1939, *The Little Foxes*, 1941, *Roman Holiday*, 1953, and *Ben-Hur*, 1959) that he ever tackled a musical. Although a number of songs from the stage version were cut, Styne and Merrill created three new songs for the film—"Roller Skate Rag," "The Swan," and "Funny Girl"—and two longtime standards, "I'd Rather Be Blue" by Fred Fisher and Billy Rose and "My Man" by Maurice Yvian, were added.

The script for *Funny Girl* covers the early years of Fanny Brice's career and her marriage to and divorce from Nick Arnstein. The film opens with Fanny (Barbra Streisand) seated in front of her dressing room mirror in the Ziegfeld Theatre; as she looks at her reflection, her first words are, "Hello, gorgeous!" From this point on, the audience is made aware that this is going to be Streisand's show and nobody else's. The scene next flashes back to the old days on Henry Street where she fails to get a job at Keeney's Oriental Palace because she does not look like the other girls. Not one to give up, Fanny talks her way into a roller-skating production number and wins the applause of the audience as she hams it up with her comic skating; she also wins the job. This is one of Streisand's best scenes, putting to use her excellent talent for comedy and mimicry without being concerned about her "image." Fanny further pleases the audience with her rendition of "I'd Rather Be Blue," prompting suave gambler Nick Arnstein (Omar Sharif) to visit her backstage where he helps her get a fifty-dollar raise.

Fanny Brice soon comes to the attention of Florenz Ziegfeld (Walter Pidgeon), who hires her to appear in a musical "bride" number. Fanny argues with Ziegfeld that she is not pretty enough for this song, but Ziegfeld insists. On opening night, still not convinced, Fanny plays the bride with a pillow under her gown for obvious comic effect. It is a scene which makes excellent use of Streisand's abilities as a comedienne, even though, in reality, Ziegfeld would never have tolerated a star of his show getting away with such blatant insubordination. Ziegfeld would also never have had nearly nude showgirls in his Follies, as is depicted in this film.

Nick attends opening night and then accompanies Fanny to her mother's saloon for the after-theater party. Fanny goes on to become a star of the first rank, Nick continues with his gambling and con-artist games, and their paths cross in courtship which leads to love. The film's intermission finds Fanny aboard a tugboat heading to board Nick's European-bound ocean liner and singing "Don't Rain on My Parade."

Their marriage leads Fanny and Nick to a Westchester Tudor mansion, a daughter named Frances, and then bankruptcy and prison for Nick, who gets involved in a phony bond-issue deal. A scene in which Fanny leaves the jail after seeing Nick and faces a throng of loud, pushy reporters, is one of the best in the film, and perhaps Streisand's best on screen. With very little dialogue, she conveys the hurt and love she feels for Nick and the realization that the marriage cannot work out. Eighteen months after going to jail, Nick appears in Fanny's dressing room and kisses her good-bye. This leads to the film's finale in which Fanny tearfully sings "My Man."

Funny Girl is a sumptuous production. Streisand is swathed in exaggerated period costumes designed by Irene Sharaff, and the first-rate technical aspects, as well as settings and cinematography, all aim at making Streisand look good; and she does. What is missing in the film, however, is more story, more characterization, and more directing expertise by William Wyler, whose scenes are underplayed in comparison to the flamboyant musical numbers directed by Herbert Ross. Likewise, the supporting players are so eclipsed by Barbra Streisand that their roles seem insignificant. Kay Medford has a few good moments as Fanny's mother, and Mae Questel is briefly and delightfully seen as the nosy neighbor. The role of Fanny's showgirl-friend is so cut in the final print that actress Anne Francis, who played the role, demanded that her name be omitted from the credits. Even amiable Walter Pidgeon is made short shrift of as Ziegfeld. It is this catering to Streisand that prevents *Funny Girl* from being a good musical biography; instead it is simply superficial glossy entertainment.

Ronald Bowers

A FUNNY THING HAPPENED ON THE WAY TO THE FORUM

Released: 1966
Production: Melvin Frank for United Artists
Direction: Richard Lester
Screenplay: Melvin Frank and Michael Pertwee; based on the musical comedy of the same name by Burt Shevelove, Larry Gelbart, and Stephen Sondheim
Cinematography: Nicolas Roeg
Editing: John Victor Smith
Costume design: Tony Walton
Music: Ken Thorne (AA)
Running time: 99 minutes

Principal characters:

Pseudolus	Zero Mostel
Lycus	Phil Silvers
Hysterium	Jack Gilford
Erronius	Buster Keaton
Hero	Michael Crawford
Philia	Annette Andre
Domina	Patricia Jessel
Senex	Michael Hordern
Miles	Leon Greene

The film version of *A Funny Thing Happened on the Way to the Forum* is in reality two movies existing under the cover of a title quite long enough to shelter several more: it is both a producer's movie and a director's movie, at once an adaptation of a Broadway hit and a zany film farce ressembling director Dick Lester's Beatles films, *A Hard Day's Night* (1964) and *Help!* (1965). Each part has its strengths, amounting at times to comic genius. When combined, however, they make a work which, while intermittently excellent, is not quite the masterpiece that the encounter between a brilliantly inventive director and first-rate material might have been expected to produce.

A Funny Thing Happened on the Way to the Forum first appeared as a play on Broadway in 1963. It was enormously successful, and Zero Mostel won a Tony for his portrayal of Pseudolus. Melvin Frank originally planned to direct the movie version himself, but finally hired Richard Lester instead. By all accounts the relationship was not a happy one: according to Lester, "we just violently argued from six weeks before shooting until the picture was out." Despite Frank's opposition, Lester managed to introduce a string of characteristic sight gags, a few engaging cameos such as Roy Kinnear's gladiator trainer, and elements of what he saw as the "brutality" of ancient Rome. He stacked the sets with fruit and vegetables which were then left to rot in the Spanish sun, ensuring that there was no shortage of flies. The flies became a motif in the film and were featured heavily in British animator Richard Williams' superb final credits, a series of cartoon friezes linked by a horde of flies, animated in both senses of the word.

The extent to which the producers disagreed over the movie is indicated by the fact that it was not premiered until more than a year after the completion of shooting; it was finally screened at New York's Cinemas 1 and 2 on October 16, 1966. Vincent Canby of the *New York Times* decided that it was a successfully funny film in the vaudeville tradition—"a motion-picture spectacle for old men of all ages." But *Time* magazine thought that Lester's "wham-bam camerantics" had "about the same effect on this picture as a dachshund puppy might have on a game of chess." Other reviewers found the pace too frenzied and the film too overloaded with single-take gags; Pauline Kael commented that "the viewing experience becomes like coitus interruptus going on forever."

Criticism of Lester for "tampering" with *A Funny Thing Happened on the Way to the Forum* is probably unfair: the Broadway original depended very much on a kind of vaudeville style and a farcical pace which belongs exclusively to the live theater. It quite simply could not be captured intact on film. Lester's solution was to aim for a style which might be described as cinema-farce: establishment of the rhythms through editing rather than leaving them to the pacing of the actors, and insertion of sight gags as an alternative to the mechanisms of stage farce, where the laughs come as a result of the audience's ability to watch the whole stage for an accumulation of complex, interlocking actions.

The story of *A Funny Thing Happened on the Way to the Forum*, which has nothing to do with the title, is similar to the Roman comedies of Plautus on which it is based; it is a highly complicated excuse for one-line jokes which are old but not exactly classical, farcical actions, and Stephen Sondheim's songs, only five of which survive in the film version. Reduced to its essentials, the story concerns a Roman slave, Pseudolus (Zero Mostel), who is left in charge of the household while his master and mistress, Senex (Michael Hordern) and Domina (Patricia Jessel), go off to visit the latter's mother (a Roman mother-in-law joke). The son of the house, Hero (Michael Crawford), has fallen in love with Philia (Annette Andre), a young virgin currently housed on a nonparticipatory basis in Lycus' (Phil Silvers) brothel across the street. Pseudolus agrees to fix things up for Hero in return for his freedom. Pseudolus's job is not made any easier by the arrival of Miles Gloriosus (Leon Greene), the outrageously vain soldier to whom Philia is bethrothed, and by the early return of Senex. He also rather literally runs into Erronius (Buster Keaton), an old man in search of his long-lost children who is running seven times around the seven hills of Rome as a result of a fake bit of soothsaying dreamed up by Lycus to get rid of him. This part was to be Buster Keaton's last screen appearance, and although he appears in almost all the publicity stills for the movie, he appears in very little of the actual footage; it is a sad swan song.

Confusions and mistaken identities reach their climax when Philia has to be impersonated by Senex's majordomo, Hysterium (Jack Gilford), to cover up an earlier scheme in which she had died of the plague. In the end, Philia and Miles turn out to be the long lost children of Erronius, and all ends happily. The plot is not intended to be taken seriously, and nobody does so. In both the stage original and the movie, it is used as a pretext, although not always for the same thing. The screenplay abounds in one-line gags. Pseudolus surveys a bottle of wine and inquires: "Was One a good year?" Miles enters the brothel declaring: "I want a sit-down orgy for forty." Pseudolus examines twin slave girls like a collector in an antique store and asks optimistically: "I don't suppose you'd break up the set?" Most of these one-liners rely on the time-honored device of anachronism, while Lester's direction adds the cinematic equivalent—a string of sight gags. A pigeon, dispatched across the alleyway by Hero with a message for his lady love inscribed on a wax tablet, is unable to carry the weight and flutters leadenly down to join its friends in the alley. A horse sits glumly in a steambath because Hero needs mare's sweat for an aphrodisiac potion he is gathering. The movie is more like a mosaic than anything else, and indeed the final shot of Buster Keaton dissolves into a pseudo-Roman mosaic—a frieze frame. Scenes are broken up into brief shots and divided off from each other by dissolves which bleach the screen to white in an indication of the blinding heat that is one of the film's motifs.

Lester has expressed his regret that the film did not adequately show off Zero Mostel, an actor whose comic appeal lies very much in the improbable combination of elephantine bulk and balletic grace: placed into the close-up which is the movie's favorite shot, Mostel sometimes seems merely to be mugging. In terms of performances, Lester is best served by the deftly idiosyncratic delivery of Michael Hordern's Senex, or by small cameo shots such as Roy Kinnear training gladiators with the tired persistence of a golf pro— the only difference being that, instead of golf balls, the gladiators practice their swings on live slaves.

Lester approaches the musical numbers in the same manner, and they achieve their rhythm through editing rather than choreography. Pseudolus's opening number, "Comedy Tonight," which is basically designed as an overture, is put together from brief shots of Mostel singing, and even briefer shots—some of them well under a second—of pratfalls and gags: a man falling off a roof, collisions in the street, a man painting stripes on a zebra. The film's prime romantic number, "Lovely," is first done in the manner of a pastiche of a commercial (a continued source of income for Lester), with Hero and Philia tripping happily through misty fields and soft-focus green woods; then the song is presented as a parody of this pastiche, with Mostel and Gilford in drag doing much the same routine. Lester applies to all the musical numbers the device he first used on "I Wanna Hold Your Hand" in *A Hard Day's Night*—animation-style jump cuts, so that a single line may be delivered in up to three locations and the whole thing then joined together in a piece of cinematic choreography which only comes into existence in the cutting room.

A Funny Thing Happened on the Way to the Forum is a movie one remembers for moments of delight rather than for sustained brilliance—moments such as an unexplained longshot of tiny figures dancing in silhouette along the top of an aqueduct, or Miles's triumphal entry into Rome, operatically intoning "Bring Me My Bride" from the back of his horse while his soldiers trip over their drums and have garbage dumped on them. It is a movie made up of sight gags and one-liners, a brave attempt at adapting the unadaptable whose main failing, perhaps, is that it tries a bit too hard.

Nick Roddick

FURY

Released: 1936
Production: Joseph L. Mankiewicz for Metro-Goldwyn-Mayer
Direction: Fritz Lang
Screenplay: Bartlett Cormack and Fritz Lang; based on a story by Norman Krasna
Cinematography: Joseph Ruttenberg
Editing: Frank Sullivan
Running time: 94 minutes

Principal characters:
Joe Wilson	Spencer Tracy
Katherine Grant	Sylvia Sidney
District Attorney	Walter Abel
Sheriff Hummel	Edward Ellis
Bugs Meyers	Walter Brennan
Tom Wilson	George Walcott
Charlie Wilson	Frank Albertson

Fury occupies a niche in film history as an important social document of its time and as a rather daring and ambitiously unique film which strongly influenced Hollywood moviemaking. Through its analytical portrayal of mob violence and individual lust for vengeance, *Fury* puts the human psyche under a magnifying glass to observe it in much the way a scientist might stick a pin through a fluttering specimen to hold it steady for the eye to see.

The darkness and cynicism of Director Fritz Lang's vision are strongly evident in this film, and these characteristics certainly reflect the influence of his roots. Lang was a successful filmmaker in Germany before fleeing the Nazis, first to France and then to Hollywood when M-G-M brought him over in the early 1930's. During the 1930's, hundreds of German filmmakers emigrated to Hollywood to continue their careers as directors, actors, and technicians. Though they were rapidly assimilated into American culture and Hollywood's studio system, they still contributed much that was unique to American filmmaking, both overtly and through their influence on others over the years. The two most notable and creative directors were Ernst Lubitsch and Fritz Lang. The former was the master of a style of sexual innuendo which came to be known in his comedies as the "Lubitsch touch"; and the latter, with his dark, depressing, sometimes apocalyptic vision, did much to inspire and set the tone for what came to be known as *film noir.* Lang's 1931 German film *M*, for example, is hailed as the first psychological crime thriller of its kind and the prototype for the American crime/detective films of the 1930's and 1940's. The haunting atmospheric qualities of these films—the dark, wet streets, the long shadows, the obscure corridors and alleys, the sense of tension and impending doom—all hail back to German Expressionism. In fact, *Fury*, which was Lang's first American film, fits the definition of Expressionism with remarkable precision: ". . . the external representation of man's inner world, particularly the elemental emotions of fear, hatred, love, and anxiety . . . the dual nature of man, the power of fate, and the fascination of monstrous or sub-human creatures. . . ."

In *Fury*, Lang's singularly stark vision of men and women as monsters is made most vivid through the use of grim stop-action close-ups of the voracious, contorted faces of a lynch mob. The scene is a pivotal one which takes place halfway through the film; later, the same material is treated more probingly and from different angles in a climactic courtroom scene in which the lynch mob is on trial for murder.

The film's story is that of Joe Wilson (Spencer Tracy), an ordinary, unpretentious "nice guy" who harbors honest middle-class aspirations and who becomes the innocent victim of an angry mob—strangers who have labeled him a kidnaper. The first few minutes of the film focus on Joe and his fiancée, Katherine (Sylvia Sidney), and on their dreams of happiness. Certain references are made which will have eventual significance—Joe's passion for salted peanuts, which he keeps in his coat pocket; his mispronunciation of the word "memento" and Katherine's correction of it; an engraved ring she gives to him; and his ripped coat, which she repairs with blue thread. Every scene and bit of minutiae is deliberate, laying the ironic groundwork for the coming tragedy.

A year passes (deftly presented in a two-minute transition through close-ups on the letters and pictures which Joe sends to Katherine), until finally Joe has saved enough money to rejoin his fiancée in the small Midwestern town where she now lives and to get married. As he travels across country he is stopped by a grizzled, gun-wielding deputy (Walter Brennan). A kidnaping has occurred, and the evidence is loaded against Joe. Again Lang uses an ominous close-up, this time of a telegram stating that traces of salted peanuts had been found in connection with the kidnaper. The news travels rapidly around town that the criminal has been captured, and we see a kind of insanity growing like wildfire as the townspeople trade gossip in the streets. The filmmaker's indictment is made in a sequence of exaggerated images of the malicious, blustery townspeople lustfully spreading the news: talkative ladies call each other on the telephone, groups of self-righteous men gather on the streets and in bars to moralize and condemn, city officials gloat over the good publicity their town is receiving for capturing the kidnaper. It is a clean-cut, overly tidy view of hypocrisy. In one shot, a brief fade-out is made from a pair of prattling women to a flock of strutting chickens. Another scene displaying Lang's slightly perverse sense of humor shows an eccentric German barber fantasizing about cutting throats.

The madness grows, and the mindless mob finally marches on the jailhouse and breaks down the door. When they cannot reach the keys to the prisoner's cell, they set fire to the building and stand back in a sort of holy, reverential silence to watch the holocaust. The glowing flames are reflected in the rapturous faces of the witnesses while the doomed man screams from the window of his cell. Three rapid, successive images show us the men's monstrous faces twisted with gleeful horror and fascination; a wide-eyed boy chomps on a hotdog while watching the spectacle, and a mother holds her baby up for a better look.

When it is discovered that Wilson was an innocent man and that what occurred amounts to murder, the townspeople become frightened and self-absolving. We see Joe's two brothers, enraged and grieving; then suddenly Joe's figure appears dark and forbidding in their doorway like a ghost. He has miraculously escaped the fire and no one else knows he is not dead. "All day I've been watching myself being burned alive," he says with a stony glare. "They like it!" He pulls down the shades and orders the lights doused. He has become a man of darkness, feeling nothing but hate and desire for revenge. "I am legally dead and they are legally murderers," he says, and he proceeds to lay out a plan to have the mob members tried, convicted, and executed. The tables have turned: Joe has now become the monster; he has undergone a Dr. Jekyll/Mr. Hyde transformation. Like that earlier horror story, *Fury* deals with the question of innate evil in man; only here it is presented in a societal rather than in a science fiction context. At the time the film was made, lynching was a real problem (the district attorney in the movie even gives a speech in which he gives the number of lynchings as 6,010 in "the last forty-nine years"), and for a movie to tackle a social issue with such forthrightness was uncommon in this era of escapist musicals and comedies. But for a man who saw and decried the Nazi terror, the implications of a mob banding together in madness against a single scapegoat, and of the debilitating hunger for revenge in a survivor, were profound. Lang takes this film further than other "lynch mob" movies, displaying an entire cycle of fury and despair in subjective, dramatic terms.

The courtroom scene is momentous. The editing is precise and taut as the tension builds. The intercutting between the in-court action and Joe's savoring of it via his radio in a dark, anonymous hotel room builds momentum. The clever district attorney allows the defendants to perjure themselves by providing one another with false alibis, and then presents the telling evidence— a film of the actual event taken by a newsman from a balcony. The twenty-two defendants are horrified as they watch themselves as savages. The idea of incriminating film footage being brought into a courtroom as evidence was unique at the time *Fury* was made, and Lang chose to use the device in spite of the fact that there was then no such judicial precedent. Indeed, he was probably the first to suggest it.

When proof is demanded that Wilson is really dead, Joe sends his half-melted ring to the judge along with an anonymous letter stating that the ring had been found in the charred rubble. In the climactic scene, Katherine, who does not yet know the truth, is to be the key witness for the prosecution. As she rides up the elevator with Joe's brother, she sees him put his hand into his coat pocket and bring out a couple of peanuts. She glances down and sees a rip which has been repaired with blue thread. When she enters the court-room, the district attorney asks if she is ready to take the stand. She falters but says "Yes." However, the judge himself takes the stand first to present the evidence he has recently received in the mail. As the district attorney reads the anonymous letter aloud he stumbles over the misspelled word "mementum," and Katherine glances up with a look of shock. Suddenly realizing the truth, she stares terrified and disbelieving at Joe's brother. He grips her hand pleadingly as she is called to the witness stand. In the middle of her shaky testimony one of the defendants leaps up screaming, "I'm guilty! We're all guilty!" and the trial is over.

Now the guilt has been transferred, and the brothers have trouble dealing with their own consciences. Joe becomes a haunted man. Katherine begs him to admit the truth and to leave his vengefulness behind. "I want to be happy again," she cries. But he is consumed by his own hate. "From now on I'm gonna do everything alone!" he screams. "I don't need any of you!" He wanders dark, deserted streets haunted by the twenty-two defendants. As he gazes in a shop window, reminiscent of the first scene of the film, twenty-two faces appear behind him reflected in the glass. As he walks down the street glancing fearfully behind, we hear the inexorable footsteps of the twenty-two pursuing him. He hears festive noises and voices coming from a bar and runs in to find the place deserted—only one man is mopping up. When the date on the calendar is ripped off, a page sticks and a bold-faced "22," framed ominously by the camera, leaps out at us. Joe runs home screaming for Katherine, and we next see him walking into the courtroom where the judge is about to pass sentence. "I came for my own sake," he tells the judge. It is not for the murderers, for they are still murderers. "They lynched what mattered to me . . . my liking people and having faith in them." He has been turned into a different person. Though many say that the ending of *Fury* is optimistic, it is so only to a certain extent. It is true that Joe escaped death and in the end was able to escape the evil within him, but he is scarred.

Lynn Woods

GASLIGHT

Released: 1944
Production: Arthur Hornblow, Jr., for Metro-Goldwyn-Mayer
Direction: George Cukor
Screenplay: John Van Druten, Walter Reisch, and John L. Balderston; based
  on the play of the same name by Patrick Hamilton
Cinematography: Joseph Ruttenberg
Editing: Ralph E. Winters
Art direction: Cedric Gibbons and William Ferrari (AA)
Interior decoration: Edwin B. Willis and Paul Huldschinsky (AA)
Running time: 114 minutes

Principal characters:
Paula Alquist .... Ingrid Bergman (AA)
Gregory Anton .... Charles Boyer
Brian Cameron .... Joseph Cotten
Nancy Oliver .... Angela Lansbury
Miss Thwaites ....Dame May Whitty
Elizabeth Tompkins .... Barbara Everest

  Gaslight is George Cukor's classic Victorian melodrama. Nominally a murder mystery, the plot is on the skimpy side, and the murder which opens the film is solved at the end, but the "whodunit" aspects of the plot are peripheral to Cukor's real concerns. *Gaslight* is a study in induced madness, and, paradoxically, the film sustains our interest because Cukor's direction intentionally subverts the traditional elements of mystery in the plot. Cukor unmasks the villain early on; and the tension in the film comes as a result of the audience watching helplessly as the villain very methodically sets about driving the heroine insane. *Gaslight* opens with a murder on a foggy night (in contrast to his interior shots, Cukor's exteriors are rather unimaginative, consisting primarily of swirling fog). The headline on a newspaper unfolds the story: "Thornton Square Strangler on Loose." The entire sequence spans less than two minutes, and provides the backdrop for the remainder of the film.
  Cukor next shifts the scene to Italy. It is a decade after the murder, and a young English voice student, Paula Alquist (Ingrid Bergman), is being courted by Gregory Anton (Charles Boyer), a French pianist. Although she is obviously in love with the man, she protests that she hardly knows him, and resolves to spend a week at Lake Como to think things over. On the train to Lake Como, Paula finds herself seated next to Miss Thwaites (Dame May Whitty), a garrulous Englishwoman addicted to murder mysteries. Elsewhere in the film, Cukor uses Miss Thwaites primarily for comic relief but here she serves as the link between the heretofore unexplained opening murder scene and the happy, if confused, Paula Alquist. The book Miss Thwaites is reading

on the train reminds her of a genuine murder that occurred in her neighborhood in London ten years earlier—the Thornton Square strangling. As the old woman prattles on about the murder, Paula grows increasingly agitated. Thus Cukor reveals that there is some sort of connection between Paula and Thornton Square, although the precise nature of this connection will not be clarified until later in the film.

As the train pulls to a stop at the lake, an arm is suddenly thrust through the open window of Paula's berth. Cukor quickly defuses the sinister implications of the incident; the arm belongs to Gregory Anton, who, unable to bear the idea of being separated from his beloved, has preceded Paula to her destination. She is happy enough to see him, and the jarring note is temporarily forgotten. It represents, however, Cukor's first hint that Gregory is not the perfect lover that Paula takes him to be. *Gaslight*'s story is written largely from Paula's point of view, which will grow increasingly distorted as Gregory's machinations progress. Cukor reveals this distortion to the audience by his choice of camera angles, lighting, and pacing, all of which will serve notice that, whatever Paula may believe, Gregory Anton is not be be trusted.

At Lake Como, Paula agrees to marry Gregory, who reveals to her that he has always wanted to live in London. By a curious coincidence, the dream house that he describes to Paula bears an uncanny resemblance to the one that Paula herself already owns, the house at 9 Thornton Square, which she inherited from her murdered aunt, the victim in the film's opening scene. Although she dreads living in this, of all houses, she accedes to Gregory's pleas: "I've found peace in loving you. You shall have your house in Thornton Square." With his two principals safely ensconsed in their new surroundings, Cukor devotes himself to the crux of his story—the persecution and near destruction of Paula Anton by her husband. Shortly after they set up residence, Gregory, pretending to be solicitous of Paula's health, gradually closes her off from the outside world. He is forever nagging her about her supposed memory lapses. One key sequence in the film illustrates both Gregory's technique and that of George Cukor in explicating it.

Immediately prior to one of their rare excursions outside their house—a trip to the Tower of London to see the Crown Jewels—Gregory gives Paula a brooch. With a condescending smile, he chides her for losing things, and makes a great show of putting it in her handbag. They visit the Tower, and upon returning home, Gregory asks to see the brooch. An incredulous and panicky Paula empties her bag, but to no avail. To her dismay, the brooch is nowhere to be found, and Gregory, having made his point, contents himself with only a mild reproof.

From the dialogue in this sequence, there is no evidence to support either Gregory or his wife on the question of the loss of the brooch. We never see Paula lose it, but she is off camera part of the time, and could have lost it then. Nevertheless, by the end of the scene, Cukor has made it clear that it is Gregory, not Paula, who is responsible for the brooch's being missing. He keeps the camera focused on Gregory's face longer than usual, and his lighting emphasizes his eyes, which glint strangely. By tilting the audience's sympathy in this fashion towards Paula, the director undercuts much of the script's suspense, but the removal of any doubt about Gregory's guilt permits Cukor and the audience to concentrate on the melodramatic irony implicit in the situation: whether Paula is losing her mind on her own or being driven insane by her husband becomes secondary to the simple fact that she is, indeed, going mad.

Not the least of Gregory's weapons in his effort to rob his wife of her sanity is the house at Thornton Square itself. More than a mere set, the house becomes, in Cukor's hands, a third character. 9 Thornton Square is a marvelous three-storied building, and Cukor uses each of the stories in his narrative. The first floor of the house belongs to Gregory. It is where he administers most of his admonitions to Paula about her failing mental health, and it is also where Paula is forced to deal with Nancy Oliver (Angela Lansbury), a cheeky young girl whom Gregory has hired as a maid. Nancy clearly has eyes for her employer and makes no effort to disguise her contempt for Paula. Although she is unaware of Gregory's plotting, she serves his purpose well, constantly keeping Paula in a state of agitation.

The bedrooms are on the second floor, but Paula finds no refuge in her room. Left alone every night since Gregory claims to have rented a flat elsewhere, to which he purportedly goes nightly to practice his piano, Paula is beset by flickering lights, the gaslights that give the film its title, and mysterious noises that seem to emanate from the third floor. Indeed, the third floor seems, inexplicably at first, to be the symbol of Paula's horrors because on the third floor, behind locked and boarded doors, are all of her dead aunt's furniture and other possessions, providing a constant reminder of Paula's childhood trauma.

Gregory, meanwhile, steps up his assaults on Paula's sanity. His admonitions are no longer gentle, and he begins to accuse her of theft as well as mere forgetfulness. He browbeats her in front of Nancy and forbids her to see any of her neighbors, including Miss Thwaites, the woman she had met on the train to Lake Como. Indeed, Paula leaves the house at Thornton Square only once after her visit to the Tower of London, and that turns out to be a disaster. When she insists upon attending a party, Gregory reluctantly agrees to let her go, but quickly reduces her to hysteria once they arrive, and the pair returns home immediately, where Gregory threatens to have his wife declared insane and institutionalized.

What remains to be revealed is the motive for Gregory's villainy. The mechanism for this revelation is Brian Cameron (Joseph Cotten) of Scotland Yard. Cameron, as it happens, had been a fan of Paula's aunt, and when he catches sight of Paula at the Tower during the Antons' fateful visit, he is intrigued by the resemblance between aunt and niece. He finds himself drawn to the Thornton Square neighborhood, where Miss Thwaites fills him in as best she can. His interest piqued still further, Cameron reopens the ten-year-old murder case, which occurred, we now learn, during an apparently unsuccessful attempt to steal the victim's jewelry. Cameron puts Gregory under surveillance, and the policeman assigned to the task reports that Gregory leaves home every night, walks around the block, and then climbs onto the roof of his own house, which he thereupon enters through a trapdoor. Cameron, meanwhile, learns that Gregory had also been an admirer of Paula's aunt, and a jewel thief as well.

Piecing the facts together, Cameron rushes to 9 Thornton Square. He arrives as Paula is being tormented by flickering lights and moaning noises; and, winning her confidence with the story of his affection for her aunt, he tells her his theory about all of her problems. Gregory, he says, murdered her aunt, and is currently spending his nights above Paula's bedroom methodically ransacking her aunt's possessions in search of her jewelry, as well as driving Paula mad from fear in the process. Paula hardly knows what to believe, but when Cameron, in searching Gregory's desk, discovers the long-missing brooch, she is convinced. Having revealed the ultimate solution to the mystery, Cukor brings *Gaslight* to a close. Brian Cameron arrests Gregory, ironically, just after he finds the jewels that have led him on his bizarre quest; and, in a deliciously vengeful scene, Paula declines her husband's pleas for help. She is insane, Paula taunts; how could she possibly help anyone? The film ends on a comic note as Miss Thwaites, the neighborhood busybody, walks in just as Cameron and Paula are discussing what promises to be the start of a long relationship.

Gaslight is a claustrophobic film, and Cukor makes this claustrophobia work for him rather than against him. The tension generated by the house at Thornton Square, and the increasingly suffocating relationship between the two principals, more than replace the potential plot tension which Cukor diffuses early by revealing that Gregory Anton is manipulating his wife.

None of this would have worked, however, without top actors in the starring roles. Charles Boyer, an Academy Award nominee, plays Gregory Anton as a suave sadist, nearly always under control and able to turn every situation to his advantage. In turn soothing and bullying, he is able to take the young and naïve Paula to the edge of insanity with consummate ease. Ingrid Bergman, who won an Academy Award for her portrayal of Paula, is outstanding. Her physical beauty makes Paula an attractive character from the outset, and her acting skill insures that none of the impact of her psychic disintegration is lost on the audience. In the film's minor roles, Joseph Cotten has little to do but act stalwart as Brian Cameron of Scotland Yard. More noteworthy is the acting debut of Angela Lansbury; a Cukor discovery, Lansbury plays the tarty young Nancy Oliver with the aplomb of a veteran actor; she earned an Academy Award nomination as Best Supporting Actress for her efforts.

Gaslight owes its success to George Cukor, and to the performances he elicited from his cast, particularly Charles Boyer, Ingrid Bergman, and Angela Lansbury. The film thus stands near the top of its genre, a classic of melo-drama.

Robert Mitchell

THE GAY DIVORCEE

Released: 1934
Production: Pandro S. Berman for RKO/Radio
Direction: Mark Sandrich
Screenplay: George Marion, Jr., Dorothy Yost, and Edward Kaufman; based
   on the play *The Gay Divorce* by Dwight Taylor
Cinematography: David Abel
Editing: William Hamilton
Dance direction: Dave Gould
Song: Herb Magidson and Con Conrad, "The Continental" (AA)
Running time: 107 minutes

> *Principal characters:*
> Guy Holden .... Fred Astaire
> Mimi Glossop .... Ginger Rogers
> Aunt Hortense .... Alice Brady
> Egbert Fitzgerald .... Edward Everett Horton
> Rodolfo Tonetti .... Erik Rhodes
> Waiter .... Eric Blore

In 1934, Fred Astaire and Ginger Rogers starred in *The Gay Divorcee*, beginning the series of classic musicals which they made for RKO. Both had appeared in secondary roles in *Flying Down to Rio* in 1933 and had danced briefly together in that film to "The Carioca." Accidentally cast opposite each other, they made an impact on the public strong enough for the studio to team them again in *The Gay Divorcee*, which firmly established their screen personalities and became the model for most of their films to follow. The use of the songs and dances to enhance or deepen moods or emotions, the accidental meeting of the two at which she is antagonized and he smitten, the spontaneity and freshness of the musical numbers, and the shaping of the films to the personalities and talents of the stars—these became trademarks of the Astaire-Rogers films.

The film is based on the *Gay Divorce*, a stage play in which Astaire had starred on Broadway and in London a few years earlier, but the censors insisted that the last word of the title be changed to *Divorcee*. In keeping with the customary procedure at the time, new songs were written for the film version; only one song from the original Cole Porter score was retained—"Night and Day." It was kept because it had been a big popular hit and had already achieved the status of a classic.

No one would claim that the story of *The Gay Divorcee* is very original, but Astaire and Rogers, in a triumph of style over content, transcend the somewhat preposterous coincidences underlying the plot to make their series of encounters into a fresh and meaningful romance.

The film opens in a Paris nightclub with Guy Holden (Fred Astaire), an American dancer, with his English friend, Egbert Fitzgerald (Edward Everett Horton), a fussy, bumbling lawyer, watching the floor show. The chorus girls sing "Don't Let It Bother You" as they do a dance with finger dolls. Later, Guy is forced to dance to the song in order to identify himself to the proprietor since neither he nor Egbert can find his wallet. Looking bored and unhappy, Guy reluctantly complies, at first merely going through the motions, but the tempo and beat of the music soon stimulate him in spite of himself into an intricate series of frenzied tap steps. He finally collapses disgustedly onto the floor just as the proprietor ostentatiously tears up the bill and Egbert finds his wallet.

Later, while waiting to clear customs in England, Guy comes to the aid of a pretty girl (Ginger Rogers) whose dress accidentally has been caught in a trunk locked by her flighty aunt. Unfortunately, he rips her dress while trying to free her, both embarrassing and annoying her. Ever gallant and already in love with her, he gives her his raincoat to hide the damage, but she leaves without telling him her name or where she lives. When the raincoat is later returned by a messenger without any indication of the girl's identity or whereabouts, Guy shakes off his disappointment and determines to find her "if it takes me from now on," expressing his determination by singing and then dancing "Needle in a Haystack."

This number establishes and defines Astaire's screen *persona*. Sitting on the couch in his silk dressing gown, he sings of his need to find his unknown love. As he continues the song, he walks to the window to look out, as if already beginning his search. His valet enters, and Astaire, still singing, debonairly tosses him his dressing gown, selects a tie, then goes to the fireplace and absentmindedly begins tapping the mantelpiece with his hand, lost in thought as he considers his strategy. Soon his feet have picked up the beat and then he is off, sailing over the couch, leaping onto a chair, clicking his heels together in midair. Not missing a step, he puts on his coat, leaps onto a chair where he catches the hat and cane thrown to him by his valet and strolls insouciantly out the door with a tip of his hat. Performed with great style and flair, these commonplace actions are incorporated into the ritual of the dance and seem to say that he can do anything, including finding his true love in a great city. Astaire liked to do getting-dressed-and-going-out routines, and here he gave the concept added meaning by using it to express feeling appropriate to both the character and the story.

He does find the girl but is able only to learn that her name is Mimi before she runs away once more. Then he does not see her again until he accompanies Egbert to Brightbourne, a fashionable seaside resort. When he unexpectedly sees her there, she immediately runs away, and he pursues her to a deserted beach pavilion bathed in moonlight. There he tells her of his longing for her by singing "Night and Day" with romantic intensity. The dance which then follows is a small drama in itself, portraying her reluctance, hesitation, increasing involvement, and eventual surrender to him. As the dance begins, she tries to leave, but he prevents her. Finally, as she turns to leave yet again, he catches her wrist, turning her toward him, and dances a few steps for her. She turns away once more, but the next time he catches her hand and pulls her toward him, she joins him in the dance. At one point she turns and walks away from him, as if making a final bid for freedom, and he pursues her. She seems to strike him, and he staggers back the length of the dance floor, but when he recovers his balance, he brings her back into the dance. At the end, another extraordinary moment occurs. As he lowers her gently onto a bench, she, half-reclining, gazes up at him, on her face an expression of rapt bemusement, and for a wordless moment the spell of the dance is prolonged.

The dances of Astaire and Rogers convey many different moods and feelings, but this great dance, portraying longing and desire, is one of their most intense and dramatic. Rogers was not yet the accomplished dancer she became later in the series, but that does not detract from the impact and the beauty of the dance. Unlike most of the later Astaire-Rogers dances, this one is shown from various angles, including a shot through some venetian blinds, devices with which Astaire would later almost entirely dispense. His favorite method of filming a dance number was to film it straight through, keeping the full length of the dancer in the camera frame and the flow of the dance intact. He liked the camera at eye level to keep the audience from being aware of it. Since film can present dance from the ideal perspective, the audience is thus able to follow intricate steps that would be lost on a theater stage.

Not yet sure that a musical could be filmed without a big production number for a climax, and perhaps uncertain of the ability of Astaire and Rogers to carry the film by themselves, the studio built a big production number around "The Continental," which won the first Academy Award for Best Song. A catchy tune, it is first sung by Rogers to Astaire as they watch the dancers from a balcony. Caught up in the song's insistent rhythm, they decide to join the dancers below, who gradually fall back, leaving them dancing alone in the middle of the floor. The two now proceed to do their own spirited version of the dance, dancing mischievously around each other with tilted, outstretched arms, seemingly unable to contain their high spirits. Rogers carries in one hand a long chiffon scarf which she uses for dramatic emphasis like a theatrical prop. The dance is another demonstration of the pair's almost perpetual spontaneity and freshness. The applause of the other dancers brings them back to reality, and they dash off the floor. Their exit is the signal for hordes of other dancers to enter and begin a protracted series of dance patterns and movements. The number was more than seventeen minutes long, a length unmatched then and for some time to come for a dance number. Not only does the piece contain many permutations of groupings and formations but variations in costumes and camera angles as well. In the midst of this madness Astaire and Rogers return for a brief interlude, which includes dancing up and down the steps before running up them and exiting through the revolving doors.

"The Continental" and one other number, "Let's Knock Knees" (in which Astaire and Rogers do not appear), are not really an integral part of the story but are set pieces to display formations of dancers or, in the case of "Let's Knock Knees," a novelty number for Edward Everett Horton, who plays Egbert Fitzgerald. Later in the series, big production numbers or novelty numbers unrelated to the plot or feelings of the characters would practically disappear.

The film ends exhilaratingly as Astaire dances Rogers around their hotel room to the strains of "The Continental"—over the sofa, over tables, up onto chairs—to express their delight in finally being together. At the end of this short dance, they stroll jauntily out the door, arm in arm, half dancing, half walking.

Although it is the music and the dancing which make the film so memorable, *The Gay Divorcee* is also impressive in its comic scenes. The comic plot revolves around the fact that, unknown to Guy, Mimi is getting a divorce from her wandering geologist husband and has hired Egbert as her lawyer. He advises her that the easiest way to get a divorce in England is for her to be found alone in a hotel room with a man, and Egbert promises to hire both the man (a professional corespondent) and the detectives who will find them. Thus the technical grounds for the divorce will be established. Complications ensue, however, when—after the "Night and Day" dance—Guy accidentally gives the proper password and Mimi mistakenly thinks he is the corespondent hired by Egbert. But with the help of an eccentric waiter at the hotel, all the plot complications are finally resolved.

The direction by Mark Sandrich and the script emphasize and give full value to the comic scenes. Imported from the stage production was Erik Rhodes as the effeminate Italian professional corespondent, Rodolfo Tonetti, whose slogan is "Your wife is safe with Tonetti. He prefers spaghetti." Although his role is a comic stereotype, he adds immeasurably to the droll and slightly ridiculous fun of the film as he continually garbles the password which he is to use to identify himself to Mimi: "Chance is the fool's name for fate." Edward Everett Horton as Astaire's bumbling lawyer friend, so inept that he forgets to arrange for the detectives who are essential to the divorce case, is an excellent foil for Astaire and for Alice Brady, who plays Mimi's twittering, flighty aunt Hortense to perfection. Eric Blore is also delightful as the waiter who has "an unnatural passion for rocks," a zeal which turns out to be extremely important in resolving the complications of the plot. Together with Astaire and Rogers, who also prove themselves to be fine light comedians, they give the film a mischievously amusing tone that seldom slackens.

The Gay Divorcee was a big box-office success (audiences often broke into applause at the end of the dance numbers), ensuring that there would be future Astaire-Rogers teamings. It also became the model for many of the scripts in the later films and firmly established the legendary style and charm of Astaire and Rogers.

Julia Johnson

GENTLEMAN'S AGREEMENT

Released: 1947
Production: Darryl F. Zanuck for Twentieth Century-Fox (AA)
Direction: Elia Kazan (AA)
Screenplay: Moss Hart; based on the novel of the same name by Laura Z. Hobson
Cinematography: Arthur Miller
Editing: Harmon Jones
Music: Alfred Newman
Running time: 118 minutes

> *Principal characters:*
> Phil Green .... Gregory Peck
> Kathy Lacey .... Dorothy McGuire
> Dave Goldman .... John Garfield
> Anne Dettrey .... Celeste Holm (AA)
> Mrs. Green .... Anne Revere
> Miss Wales ....June Havoc
> John Minify .... Albert Dekker
> Jane Lacey .... Jane Wyatt
> Tommy Green .... Dean Stockwell
> Professor Lieberman .... Sam Jaffe

In the 1930's and 1940's, Twentieth Century-Fox produced many socially conscious films, including *The Grapes of Wrath* (1940), *The Ox-Bow Incident* (1942), *The Snake Pit* (1948), and *Pinky* (1949). In 1947, Darryl F. Zanuck produced Moss Hart's adaptation of Laura Z. Hobson's best-selling novel *Gentleman's Agreement* as a major feature film which went on to win the Oscar as Best Picture of the Year. Although the film is somewhat dated and its initial impact is difficult to appreciate today, this social drama is generally acknowledged to be one of the first to attack openly prejudice against Jews, along with *Crossfire*, produced by RKO the same year.

Gregory Peck plays the protagonist, widower journalist Phil Green, a feature writer for *Smith's Weekly*, an important news magazine. At the suggestion of his liberal managing editor, John Minify (Albert Dekker), Green moves with his young son Tommy (Dean Stockwell) and mother (Anne Revere) from California to New York in order to work on a series of articles on anti-Semitism. In New York, he meets and falls in love with Minify's niece, Kathy Lacey (Dorothy McGuire), a beautiful, intelligent, and socially correct divorcée.

Green is unsure about his articles. He wants to approach the subject with an entirely new slant, but cannot come up with one which seems right. At first he wants to do the articles based on the experiences of his Jewish friend Dave Goldman (John Garfield), whom Green feels is similar to himself except that he is a Jew. However, when Goldman discusses what it is like to be a Jew, Green finally stumbles upon what he is sure will be the right angle to break the issue of anti-Semitism "wide open." Green decides to call his story "I Was a Jew for Six Weeks," and begins by telling the superintendent of his apartment building to add the name "Greenberg" to his mailbox. Although he never actually tells anyone that he is a Jew, he allows people to think that he is and to draw their own conclusions about him. When Kathy anxiously asks him whether or not he really is a Jew, Phil realizes with shock that even she is prejudiced.

In the course of his research, the journalist discovers prejudice in almost all aspects of his daily life. When Goldman cannot find a home for his family, Green learns that there is a sort of "Gentleman's Agreement" not to rent to Jews. He also learns that his Jewish secretary (June Havoc) is herself anti-Semitic—she has changed her name from Walorsky to Wales and refers to Jews as the "wrong ones"; and Tommy finds himself exposed to the cruelty of other children when he is taunted and called "dirty Jew" by his so-called school friends. Finally, feeling humiliated when he must leave a "restricted" New Hampshire hotel which abruptly cancels his reservations after learning that his name is "Greenberg" rather than "Green," Phil writes his series of articles. In the end, the series becomes a successful exposé which stuns many of his acquaintances. After reading the articles and thinking about her own views, Kathy finally overcomes her prejudices and rents her Connecticut cottage to Goldman and his family. Her act of courage touches Phil and they are reunited.

Gregory Peck is good, although a little stiff, as the crusading writer. Dorothy McGuire is also fine as his fiancée. Celeste Holm, who plays the vivacious, sophisticated Anne Dettrey, the open-minded fashion editor of *Smith's Weekly*, won an Oscar for Best Supporting Actress for her role. Sam Jaffe, who had only one scene in the film, is memorable as Professor Lieberman, the scientist who explains that Jews are practitioners of a particular religion and do not comprise a race. John Garfield, in a role which does not follow his usual "tough guy" screen image, gives a wonderfully underplayed performance as Dave Goldman. He is particularly moving when he speaks of his own children being barred from summer camp, or of the dying soldier whom a fellow GI called "Sheeney." In another scene he is arresting when he reacts to Kathy's description of the horror of an anti-Semitic party she attended by repeatedly asking, "But what did you *do*?"

Gentleman's Agreement was filmed in near-documentary style by cinematographer Arthur Miller. It was directed by the prolific Elia Kazan, who, in the manner of directors such as Sidney Lumet and Martin Ritt, is noted for his message pictures, usually photographed in black-and-white. He is also known for his concern for minority groups, as seen in such films as *Pinky*, which focused on Southern blacks, and *Panic in the Streets* (1950), which dealt with New Orleans Sicilians. Kazan won the Academy Award for Best Direction for *Gentleman's Agreement*.

Leslie Taubman

GENTLEMEN PREFER BLONDES

Released: 1953
Production: Sol C. Siegel for Twentieth Century-Fox
Direction: Howard Hawks
Screenplay: Charles Lederer; based on the musical comedy of the same name
   by Joseph Fields and Anita Loos
Cinematography: Harry J. Wild
Editing: Hugh S. Fowler
Choreography: Jack Cole
Music: Jule Styne and Leo Robin
Song: Hoagy Carmichael and Harold Adamson
Running time: 91 minutes

   Principal characters:
   Dorothy .... Jane Russell
   Lorelei Lee .... Marilyn Monroe
   Gus Esmond .... Tommy Noonan
   Sir Francis Beekman .... Charles Coburn
   Detective Malone .... Elliott Reid

Gentlemen Prefer Blondes, a brassy musical comedy, would be unexceptional were it not for the presence of Marilyn Monroe. Though some people have considered her to be an untalented product of publicity and others have maintained that she was a great actress who never had the serious roles or serious consideration she deserved, neither extreme is true. Monroe had a screen presence which overcame her technical limitations in acting and singing when she was given a role suited to her screen *persona*. With her husky, whispery voice, wide-eyed innocent stare, round baby face, and pouting mouth, Monroe was perfectly suited to the role of Lorelei Lee, a seemingly scatterbrained but not-so-dumb blonde dedicated to securing her future by marrying a millionaire.

Engaged to a young millionaire, Gus Esmond (Tommy Noonan), Lorelei takes a ship to France where Gus is to meet her later. To make sure that Lorelei does not get into trouble, Gus sends along her friend Dorothy (Jane Russell), and his father sends along a detective, Malone (Elliott Reid). During the crossing they meet a rich elderly Englishman, Sir Francis "Piggy" Beekman (Charles Coburn), whom Lorelei blackmails into giving her his wife's diamond tiara. Malone finds this out, and when the girls reach Paris, they discover that Gus has cancelled their hotel reservations and their credit. They have to get jobs as showgirls in Paris, but all ends happily when Gus and his father come over and meet Lorelei. The film ends with a double wedding: · Lorelei to Gus and Dorothy to Malone.

Lorelei originated in stories by screenwriter and author Anita Loos, who created the character when she was in love with editor and essayist H. L. Mencken. When she saw herself being neglected by him for a vacuous, un-intelligent blonde, Loos was hurt and bewildered and decided to sublimate her jealousy by writing a story about an empty-headed blonde flapper of the 1920's whom she called Lorelei. *Harper's Bazaar* accepted her story and asked for more adventures of Lorelei. Eventually the magazine pieces were col-lected in a book, *Gentlemen Prefer Blondes*, which made Loos both famous and wealthy. The book remained popular over the years, being adapted first as a play, later as a silent film, then as a Broadway musical, and finally as the Twentieth Century-Fox film with Marilyn Monroe as Lorelei.

By the time the book reached the screen, it had lost some of its sharp characterization and wit, but it is often amusing, especially when Lorelei is explaining her philosophy of life to her friend Dorothy. When Lorelei advises her to find a rich man to marry, Dorothy replies that some people simply do not care about money. Lorelei is amazed by this naïve attitude. If a girl has to spend all her time worrying about money, she asks Dorothy, how can she have time to be in love? Marriage is a serious business to Lorelei. She may not be an intellectual, but she does know that her beauty will not last forever, and she intends to provide for her future. As she explains to one of her admirers, "A kiss on the hand might feel very good, but a diamond tiara is forever."

Lorelei is a shrewd judge of men's characters. When the outraged father of the naïve young millionaire she intends to marry warns her she is not fooling him, she responds instantly that she is not trying to, but that she could if she wanted to. She explains to him, with a logic that leaves him speechless, that a "man being rich is like a girl being pretty. You might not marry her just because she's pretty, but my goodness, doesn't it help?" Sometimes Lorelei seems dumb and other times astute. As she explains to Gus's father, she can be smart when it is important, but most men do not like that.

The film gains immediate momentum from a vividly colorful and sparkling musical number, "Little Girls from Little Rock," which Dorothy and Lorelei, in red sequined gowns slit up to the thighs and with feathers in their hair, perform in front of violet sequined curtains in a nightclub. Halfway through the number the credits for the film appear, and when the credits end, Lorelei and Dorothy return to finish the song. The motions and gestures of the number are based on burlesque movements, as they are also in the film's other musical numbers, but the bumps and grinds were toned down for the movie censor.

The other eye-catching number, "Diamonds Are a Girl's Best Friend," is strikingly staged and photographed and is the film's highlight. It opens in a manner reminiscent of Busby Berkeley: girls in full pink gowns and men in white ties and tails dance around human candelabra, formed by girls in black costumes. The colors, deep red and bright pink, clash excitingly. In the midst of the swirling couples, the audience suddenly sees Lorelei, sitting with her back to the audience, in a bright pink satin sheath and long pink gloves. Diamonds sparkle from her wrists, her ears, her throat. Suddenly she turns, facing the camera, and the men offer her cardboard hearts which she spurns, trilling in an operatic voice, "No, no, no," before launching into the lyrics in her own husky, whispery voice. Marilyn Monroe's singing and dancing are surprisingly effective, although the dancing consists largely of a few modified, gyrations very much as those used in "Little Girls from Little Rock." Still, within the context of the number, it is sufficient, and Monroe as Lorelei, clasping strings of diamonds to her face and surrounded by men in formal black evening attire, presents a striking picture.

The other musical numbers are more routine, both musically and dramatically, although Monroe's "Bye-Bye Baby," which she croons wistfully to her millionaire boyfriend as she sets off for Europe, is musically and emotionally effective. "When Love Goes Wrong" is Lorelei and Dorothy's best duet, sung in a bar after they have been forced to leave their luxurious hotel suite. Gradually, as the denizens of the bar gather round, two little boys begin clapping and everyone joins in for the big finale.

"Anyone Here for Love?" is a misconceived idea for Jane Russell's solo musical number as Dorothy. More interested in sex than money, Dorothy thinks she has found a gold mine when she discovers that members of the American Olympic team are aboard the ocean liner. She is quickly disillusioned when she learns that the men spend their time working out in the ship's gymnasium and must be in bed by nine o'clock. As she strolls around the gym watching the men practicing handstands, somersaults, weight lifting, and wrestling, she wryly sings the lyrics. The men's calisthenics are as carefully choreographed as a dance, but the effect is flat and unsatisfying.

Beside Marilyn Monroe the other actors are rather flat and colorless. Tommy Noonan as Gus Esmond, Lorelei's ineffectual millionaire boyfriend who is dominated by his father, seems perfectly cast, but Elliott Reid as Detective Malone, assigned to gather evidence against Lorelei by the elder Esmond, is dull as Dorothy's love interest. Charles Coburn is better in the role of Sir Francis "Piggy" Beekman, but his performance is only a collection of his now-famous mannerisms. Even Jane Russell, the brightest star in the cast besides Monroe, is somewhat wooden, though genial.

Director Howard Hawks, whose credits include *Bringing Up Baby* (1938), *Red River* (1948), and *To Have and Have Not* (1944), is obviously out of his element in *Gentlemen Prefer Blondes*, but as a star vehicle for Marilyn Monroe the film succeeds admirably and was in the top ten at the box office in its year.

Julia Johnson

GIANT

Released: 1956
Production: George Stevens and Henry Ginsberg for Warner Bros.
Direction: George Stevens (AA)
Screenplay: Fred Guiol and Ivan Moffat; based on the novel of the same name by Edna Ferber
Cinematography: William C. Mellor
Editing: William Hornbeck, Philip W. Anderson, and Fred Bohanen
Music: Dmitri Tiomkin
Running time: 198 minutes

    Principal characters:
        Leslie Lynnton Benedict .... Elizabeth Taylor
        Bick Benedict .... Rock Hudson
        Jett Rink .... James Dean
        Luz Benedict (the older) .... Mercedes McCambridge
        Vashti Snythe .... Jane Withers
        Uncle Bawley Benedict .... Chill Wills
        Luz Benedict (the younger) .... Carroll Baker
        Jordan Benedict III .... Dennis Hopper
        Juana Benedict .... Elsa Cardenas
        Judy Benedict .... Fran Bennett

Giant belongs to the Hollywood era that saw the release of films such as *The Ten Commandments*, *Around the World in 80 Days*, *War and Peace*, and *The King and I* all in the same year. Emphasis was on spectacle, grandeur, extravagance, and length. Producer/director George Stevens, in keeping with the trend, ambitiously attempted to film a great American epic from Edna Ferber's sprawling best seller about a colorful, land-rich Texas family. The film's mixed critical reviews did not prevent its commercial success and kudos for individual performances and Stevens' overall work in the film. Some skeptical critics attributed the film's success to the last performance of James Dean, who became an object of adulation after his death in a fiery car crash. Dean portrayed Jett Rink, one of the three central characters in this saga that covers approximately twenty-five years of American, and especially Texan history.

Before Jett Rink is introduced, the two other central characters meet, fall in love, and set the stage for their future conflicts. The film opens with Texas cattle baron Bick Benedict, played with authority by Rock Hudson, being out of his element in Maryland, in the elegant, cultured society of the prominent Maryland surgeon, Dr. Horace Lynnton, whose prize stallion Bick has come to purchase. While visiting the Lynntons, he meets their lovely daughter Leslie (Elizabeth Taylor). Although Bick and Leslie sense an immediate attraction to each other, their totally dissimilar natures and backgrounds spark some spirited and lively scenes. Leslie Lynnton is the despair of her social-climbing mother because she has a sharp mind and a tongue to match. Mrs. Lynnton fears that Leslie, although she is engaged, may never marry the "right" husband. Bick is attracted to Leslie but is totally immersed in his ranch and completely convinced of the greatness of the Texas way of life. When Leslie tries to discuss certain controversial points of Texas history, such as how the large landowners obtained their vast holdings, Bick's response is hardly polite. Key areas of conflict are identified early in the film, even during this courtship stage, and foreshadow the power struggles and troubles to come.

These opening Maryland scenes are photographed in bright colors amid lush surroundings. There are shots of the green, rolling, fox-hunting country of Maryland, detailed close-ups of the lavish life style of the Lynntons, and lingering close-ups of the attractive Bick and Leslie as they fall in love. Stevens is painstaking in portraying small, sensitive details.

The scene now changes. Mr. and Mrs. Bick Benedict and the prize stallion, War Winds, are off to Texas to Bick's massive ranch, Reata, and to a bout of culture shock for the former Leslie Lynnton. Again, differences between Bick and Leslie are shown in Leslie's gracious greeting of a Mexican youth who has come to meet them at the train station. Bick tells her that she should not make such a fuss over a Mexican boy. They have their first quarrel as man and wife, but are reconciled on the drive to their home, which is a memorable visual experience. In contrast to the green, lush countryside of Leslie's Maryland home, Texas is introduced desolately as the speeding car kicks up the brown-gray dust for mile after mile of the vast, treeless ranch until the stark Gothic outline of the Big House emerges above the horizon.

Leslie is the outsider now. She must grapple with a new set of customs, beliefs, and people. First, there is Luz (Mercedes McCambridge), Bick's spinster older sister who finds it impossible to relinquish her tightly held rein on the Big House and on her younger brother. Luz is cordial to Leslie but treats her as a guest rather than as the new mistress of Reata. Other people whom Leslie meets are friends and neighboring ranchers. Leslie, who has spent her mature life engaging in adult conversations with men such as her father and other cultivated society folk, now is part of a completely different society. In Texas, the men talk only to other men about substantive matters. The women spend idle lives filled with shopping, endless coffee-klatching, and frivolous gossip. The prime example is Vashti (Jane Withers), the bulky awkward daughter of the neighboring ranch owner, who had hoped to land the dashing Bick and who marries one of her father's ranch hands out of spite.

Leslie's liberal instincts are stimulated by the plight of the Mexicans on the ranch and in the surrounding community. Her attempts to aid them only arouse Bick's anger, and this prejudice shown early in the film eventually will build to a climax in which Bick must come to terms with his own weaknesses and complacency.

The presence of the swaggering wrangler, Jett Rink (James Dean), adds a dimension of menace to the plot. The Benedicts of Reata are the "haves"; the insecure, upwardly striving, threatening Jett is a "have not." In his early scenes as a sullen ranch hand, he conveys an adulterous lust for Leslie, an arrogant hostility towards his employer Bick, and the hint of an unhealthy relationship with Luz. Jett's interference in Benedict affairs causes Luz, who is feeling spurned by her brother, to ride out in a fury on the stallion, War Winds. She suffers a fatal fall, and in a rage Bick runs Jett off the ranch. Luz, however, has willed Jett a seemingly worthless bit of land on the ranch and Jett will be heard from again. James Dean's performance, straight method acting, is photographed almost entirely in shadows. Together, Stevens and Dean have captured a sense of dramatic unity.

After Luz's death, a pattern of living emerges for Bick and Leslie. The slow pace is one method Stevens uses to reinforce his vision of reality. He wants to convey the feeling of twenty-five years slowly passing, of the adjustments and responses to change that his characters must make. Bick and Leslie become the parents of a son, Jordy (Dennis Hopper), and two daughters, Judy (Fran Bennett) and Luz (Carroll Baker), after her aunt. Now a new generation of Benedicts must deal with the conflicting values of their parents: Bick, who lives for the ranch and his traditions, and Leslie, still the liberal, fighting for causes and trying to impose some elegance and taste on the bleak Texas atmosphere.

Young Jordy, the pride and hope of his father, shows a marked distaste for the life of a rancher. In temperament, he takes after his mother, and, as he grows up, he longs to be a doctor. Jordy's twin sister Judy is a disappointment first to her mother for her tomboy ways, and, later, to her father for her growing attachment to an experimental farmer named Bob Dietz (Earl Holliman), whom she eventually marries. More arguments occur between Leslie and Bick as their preconceived expectations for the children do not take into account that they are individuals with individual needs and desires. Even Leslie becomes narrow-minded as she insists on molding her daughters into unsuitable, unwanted roles.

Part of the pattern of Texas living is the old cattle aristocracy making way for the new oil rich. In some of the most carefully crafted scenes in the film, Stevens shows Jett Rink's financial rise. Jett's character develops as Stevens portrays his enthusiasm in working his own piece of land. Jett at last has something that belongs to him, and he feverishly works his "worthless" land for oil harder than he ever worked for the Benedicts. At last, his gusher comes in, and a rapturous Jett is drenched by the black gold. His tie to the Benedicts, part resentment, part envy, and part desire to show off to Leslie,

prompts him to race over to the Big House where the Benedicts are entertaining. Smirking over his success, he becomes a bit too familiar with Leslie,
which causes Bick to strike him. Jett recovers quickly, delivers a sharp blow
in return, and then furiously rides off.

Jett's increasing wealth and power in the state are often discussed by the
other characters. Years later, still crude and insecure in spite of his wealth,
he is back on the scene trying to woo young Luz. He has planned a huge
party to celebrate the grand opening of one of his hotels. All Texas society,
new and old, feels obliged to attend, including the Benedicts, despite their
aversion to Jett. Dr. Jordan Benedict III and his Mexican wife Juana (Elsa
Cardenas) make the trip, as well as graying Bick and Leslie. The Bob Dietzes
and their young child are the only family members who do not attend the
great affair. Juana has made an appointment with the hotel's beauty parlor
under the name Mrs. Jordan Benedict. When she arrives, she is told that
Mexicans are not served. She calls Jordy, who demolishes the beauty parlor
in a rage and proceeds to the big banquet hall for a confrontation with Jett.
Jett is surrounded by bodyguards who hold Jordy down for Jett's attack in
front of a crowd of people which includes the other Benedicts. Bick, in spite
of his conflicting emotions, rises to defend his son, and he too is felled by
Jett.

Drunk and despondent over his failed attempt to impress Texas society,
Jett has a touching scene in which he makes a pathetic speech to the deserted
banquet hall. The speech is overheard by Luz, who earlier had defended Jett
in defiance of her parents. Now at last she realizes that in Jett's eyes she is
no more than a substitute for her mother.

After the disastrous banquet, Bick and Leslie drive Juana and her young
son back to the ranch. They stop at a roadside restaurant where once again
Juana is refused service. All the years of Bick's prejudice and conservatism
now intermingle with his sense of family pride and Leslie's liberal influence.
He engages in a wild brawl with the restaurant owner, amid the strains of the
film's popular ballad "The Yellow Rose of Texas." The film ends back at
Reata where Bick and Leslie compromise their old positions and look to their
two grandchildren, one half Mexican, the other a blond toddler, to bring
about needed changes and social justice.

A major criticism of *Giant* is that the film, like the Edna Ferber novel, has
no focus, that it has combined melodramatic themes of family conflict, the
alien outsider, and racial prejudice, without any true resolution. Another
criticism is that the disdain for the crass, bigoted, materialistic society on the
move is not balanced by a sensitive understanding of the individual motivations of the people in that society. These points may be valid, or only
partially so; but such deficiencies are redeemed by the strengths of George
Stevens' work. He is able to elicit more than competent performances from
Rock Hudson and Elizabeth Taylor, especially before they are required to

age. James Dean ended his career with a stunning characterization that received almost universal praise. Dean, Rock Hudson, and Mercedes Mc-
Cambridge received Best Actor and Best Supporting Actress nominations,
respectively. Other nominees from the film were Dmitri Tiomkin for the
scoring; William Hornbeck, Philip W. Anderson, and Fred Bohanen for film
editing; Ralph S. Hurst for art and set decoration; Moss Mabry and Marjorie
Best for costume design; and Fred Guiol and Ivan Moffat for the screenplay.

Despite its faulty plot, George Stevens is able to bring to this film a visual
sweep, careful attention to sound, and many striking small touches. Examples
of Stevens' sensitive direction include the shot of the drunken Jett walking
to the dais at his banquet, the beautifully framed long shot of the horse that
has just thrown Luz on her return to Reata, and the warm pillow-talk conversations between Bick and Leslie. For his efforts in delineating a sensitive
landscape of the human condition, Stevens the producer received an Academy
Award nomination for Best Picture and won the Best Director Award for
1956.

Maria Soule

GIGI

Released: 1958
Production: Arthur Freed for Metro-Goldwyn-Mayer (AA)
Direction: Vincente Minnelli (AA)
Screenplay: Alan Jay Lerner (AA); based on the novel of the same name by
  Colette
Cinematography: Joseph Ruttenberg (AA)
Editing: Adrienne Fazan (AA)
Art direction: William A. Horning and Preston Ames (AA)
Set decoration: Henry Grace and Keogh Gleason (AA)
Costume design: Cecil Beaton (AA)
Music direction: André Previn (AA)
Music: Frederick Loewe and Alan Jay Lerner
Song: Frederick Loewe and Alan Jay Lerner, "Gigi" (AA)
Running time: 116 minutes

> *Principal characters:*
> Gigi .... Leslie Caron
> Honoré Lachaille .... Maurice Chevalier
> Gaston Lachaille .... Louis Jourdan
> Madame Alvarez .... Hermione Gingold
> Aunt Alicia .... Isabel Jeans
> Liane d'Exelmans ....Eva Gabor

A stylish, elegant musical set in turn-of-the-century Paris, *Gigi* is based on the novelette by the French author Colette. The film depicts the coming of age of a young French girl, Gigi, and her development from a tomboy into a lovely young woman. Though Gigi is being educated to become a courtesan in a fashionable world of luxury, scandal, expensive mistresses, and lavish entertainments, the approach of director Vincente Minnelli and scriptwriter Alan J. Lerner is so light and delicate and the ending so appropriately romantic that the story never seems at all sordid or the atmosphere decadent.

Although the novelette had previously been filmed in France in 1950 and presented as a Broadway play in 1951, Lerner—with Minnelli's encouragement—based his adaptation almost entirely on the original work, delicately expanding it to enhance the tone of Colette's story. His only significant addition was the character of Honoré Lachaille, which was written especially for Maurice Chevalier. Barely hinted at in the novelette, the character was introduced by Colette herself for the French film, thereby justifying its inclusion in Lerner's script.

Rather than being a drama with songs inserted in it, *Gigi* is truly an integrated musical, with the songs so deftly interwoven into the story that they are perfect expressions of the characters' feelings and thoughts and often develop the plot. Indeed, they are so much a part of the story that they are not quite as impressive when removed from their context in the film. The unusual vocal style used in nearly all of the songs also serves to integrate them into the rest of the film. Parts of these songs are delivered in a recitative manner—a rhythmic, rhymed delivery halfway between singing and ordinary speaking. Instead of suddenly breaking into song, a character may subtly slip from normal speaking into recitative, and then into singing.

Many scenes were shot in Paris—in the Bois de Boulogne, at Maxim's famous restaurant and the Palais de Glace. Scenes were also shot using the interiors and exteriors of various residences. This location shooting and the fact that the leading performers are French adds immeasurably to the Parisian charm and feel of the film. Director Vincente Minnelli relied heavily on the drawings of the French caricaturist Sems (whose work appears under the credits) to guide his choice of costumes, settings, and even faces to establish a visual style appropriate to the period. This careful attention to the overall visual design of the film results in a most satisfying re-creation of period and place.

The film begins charmingly with a sequence in the Bois de Boulogne show-ing pretty women and elegant men in stylish carriages. Having established the atmosphere and mood of fashionable, turn-of-the-century Parisian society, the camera moves in closer to show an elderly, elegantly dressed man-about-town who turns to the camera and introduces himself as Honoré Lachaille, a "lover and a collector of antiques." As he gazes at a group of young girls playing nearby, his speech glides into the song "Thank Heaven for Little Girls." He interrupts the song to tell us that this is a story about a particular little girl, Gigi. The camera then follows Gigi (Leslie Caron) as she leaves the group of girls and runs home to the little upstairs apartment she shares with her grandmother, Madame Alvarez (Hermione Gingold).

Gigi is a tomboyish schoolgirl dressed in long black stockings, plaid suit, and sailor hat. We find that this is the day of the week she has lunch with her great-aunt Alicia (Isabel Jeans), who "never sets foot out of her apartment or her past." A great courtesan in her heyday, she is determined to train Gigi in the arts of pleasing a man in order that she too can become a successful courtesan. Gigi's lessons range from how to eat and how to pour coffee properly ("bad table manners have broken up more households than infi-delity") to how to choose cigars and evaluate the quality of jewels.

Gigi is bored and impatient with her lessons. Forbidden by her grandmother to accept invitations from children of her own age, she is also lonely and isolated. When she questions the need for some of Aunt Alicia's lessons, she is told that "love is a work of art and like art must be created." But Gigi is still not convinced. As she walks home after her lessons she vents her frus-tration in the song "I Don't Understand the Parisians," which expresses her inability to understand their preoccupation with love.

On her way home she meets Gaston Lachaille (Louis Jourdan), who is going to the Palais de Glace (an indoor ice-skating rink) to meet his mistress, Liane (Eva Gabor). Gaston is a rich and bored friend of the family who likes to visit Gigi and "Mamita," as he calls Madame Alvarez, to enjoy a cup of camomile tea. With them he is not bored and can relax. Mamita says of his visits, "It's always a pleasure to watch the rich enjoying the comforts of the poor." Gigi reluctantly agrees to accompany Gaston to the Palais, where he finds Liane skating with a handsome instructor of whom he is immediately jealous. When he asks Gigi's opinion of Liane, Gigi says bluntly that she is pretty but common and coarse. Gaston is at first taken aback by this directness but then decides it is refreshing and entertaining.

Later that evening when Gaston escorts Liane to Maxim's, he is bored and also suspicious and uneasy because of Liane's exuberant gaiety. In a musical interior monologue he tells himself that "she's so gay tonight" that "she's not thinking of me," and ends the evening by pouring a glass of champagne down the front of her dress.

The scenes at Maxim's are cleverly staged to emphasize the ostentatious display and gossipy throngs that made it such a popular place at which to be seen. As Gaston and Liane enter, the noise of the crowd stops for a moment, isolating the couple in silence; then, as they walk to their table, everyone turns to look at them and chants in unison the current gossip about them. As they are seated at their table, the natural sounds of the crowd resume. Each time another couple enters, the process is repeated.

The next morning Gaston confides his suspicions about Liane to his Uncle Honoré, unconsciously echoing Gigi's opinion of her as he sums up his relief that the affair is over: "The woman was common." Honoré persuades Gaston that to save face he must confront Liane and the skating instructor. Gaston does so, and gets rid of the lover by paying him to leave; he then informs Liane that their affair is over. Later, she tries to commit suicide—in "the usual way: insufficient poison," Aunt Alicia acidly remarks. Liane's attempted suicide is the talk of fashionable Paris, and the story appears in all the newspapers. The whole affair makes Gaston depressed and edgy, and he thinks of going to the country until it subsides. But Honoré warns him that his honor is at stake; rather than being despondent, he must act cheerful and high-spirited.

Gaston obediently embarks on a round of extravagant party-giving which bores him extremely. One evening, however, he comes to visit Mamita and Gigi and asks to be allowed to share their simple dinner; he spends the evening with them before leaving for Trouville, a fashionable seaside resort. Gigi has never seen the ocean and makes Gaston promise to take her and her grandmother with him if she beats him at cards. Indulgently, he allows her to win, although he knows she has cheated him; he even permits her to drink champagne over her grandmother's objections. Tipsy and in high spirits, all three dance and sing "The Night They Invented Champagne." Gigi is especially exuberant as she cavorts with a rose in her teeth and finally jumps into Gaston's lap.

Gaston keeps his promise and takes Gigi and Mamita to Trouville, where we see Gigi giggling, playing tennis, swimming, and riding a donkey along the beach with Gaston. Gigi's high spirits and natural behavior are contrasted with that of the other young women we see, all of whom are correctly dressed, reserved, and decorous.

Honoré is also visiting Trouville in pursuit of his usual quarry, women; but when he sees Mamita, he remembers his youthful love affair with her. The two had almost married, but Honoré, not wanting to become entangled permanently, had involved himself with another woman to offend Mamita. They reminisce in song about their youthful romance in "I Remember It Well," in which each recalls the past somewhat differently.

When Gigi and Mamita return from Trouville, Aunt Alicia, realizing the possibility of fixing Gaston's interest in Gigi, buys her a new wardrobe and intensifies her lessons, teaching her how to drink wine, how to enter and leave a room, and how to sit down gracefully. Later, when Gaston returns from a trip to Monte Carlo, Gigi models one of her new dresses for him; but instead of being pleased, he is upset and tells her she looks "like a giraffe with a goiter." He leaves angrily but soon returns with an offer to take her out for a drive. Mamita intervenes at this point, telling Gaston that Gigi cannot be seen with him lest she be compromised and her reputation ruined. Now angrier than ever, he leaves again and goes for a solitary walk. In a long soliloquy that leads into the title song, "Gigi," he finally realizes what his feelings toward Gigi really are. He begins his musings in an angry, frustrated mood in ordinary speech and then alternates between bitterness and pleasant memories as he slips into recitative and finally into song. The continual changes in the delivery and tempo reflect his alternating moods and effectively vary the soliloquy.

At the end of his musings, realizing what he wants, he goes back to Mamita and offers his usual business arrangement: he will provide lavishly for Gigi and she will become his mistress. This is entirely satisfactory to Mamita, but Gigi is upset, and especially so when Gaston confesses that he is in love with her. She is horrified that he would want to involve her in the sort of scandalous notoriety that would make her suffer, for she does not want that kind of life. But she finally accepts his offer because she would rather be miserable with him than without him.

We now see how Aunt Alicia's lessons benefit Gigi as, beautifully dressed in white satin, she is escorted to Maxim's by Gaston. Again, there is no sound as everyone turns to stare at Gigi and Gaston. After they are seated, the noise of the crowd resumes and Gigi selects his cigar for him, comments knowledgeably on another woman's pearls, deftly pours his coffee, and when he gives her an emerald bracelet, admires his taste.

Throughout the evening Gaston is obviously ill at ease, and his feelings are crystallized by Honoré's remarks when he comes over to compliment him on Gigi's looks after she has left to put on her bracelet. Gaston grows increasingly restive because of Honoré's fulsome and cynical comments, especially when Honoré remarks on Gigi's freshness and youth, saying "It's the sophisticated women who get boring so quickly. . . . But someone like Gigi can amuse you for months." When Gigi returns, Gaston abruptly seizes her by the hand and drags her, protesting and crying, out of Maxim's. Still not having given her a word of explanation, he leaves her with her grandmother and walks broodingly away, lost in thought.

As the music for the title song comes up on the sound track, Gaston paces back and forth past some of the picturesque settings of his earlier soliloquy. Both the music and the settings recall his earlier thoughts about Gigi. One pose, in which, deep in thought, he is silhouetted against a floodlit fountain, is visually striking and indicates his inner turmoil. At last he strides purposefully up the stairs of Mamita's apartment, a determined look on his face. Both Mamita and Gigi are startled and apprehensive when they see him, but all ends happily when he asks for Gigi's hand in marriage. The film ends on the same buoyant note on which it opened, with Honoré in the Bois de Boulogne. As we watch the strolling couples, one of them comes closer to the camera and we see that it is Gaston and Gigi.

The delightful performances in *Gigi* add charm and warmth to the elegant visual style and atmosphere of the film. Maurice Chevalier displays his relaxed charm and wit in the role of Honoré Lachaille, the rather detached philosopher and cynical commentator on the society of which he is so conspicuously a part. Leslie Caron as Gigi convincingly manages the transition from awkward tomboy to beautiful young woman, and Louis Jourdan as Gaston is appropriately handsome and charming. The supporting cast was especially well chosen. Hermione Gingold as Mamita perfectly blends practical common sense with a genuine concern for Gigi's future, and Isobel Jeans as Aunt Alicia is the consummate embodiment of the successful courtesan from another era who has never forgotten her past triumphs.

Gigi is a film in which almost every element is not only excellent but also fits perfectly with the others. In addition to the acting, other notable elements are the script by Alan Jay Lerner, the songs by Lerner and Frederick Loewe, the costumes by Cecil Beaton, and the cinematography of Joseph Ruttenberg. But perhaps the greatest credit should go to director Vincente Minnelli for uniting all these in a seamless whole.

Musicals, even very good ones, tend to emphasize the musical numbers at the expense of the story so that they become virtually independent of their setting. M-G-M demonstrated this in its compilations called *That's Entertainment* (1974) and *That's Entertainment, Part 2* (1976), which are largely a series of separate musical numbers from dozens of the studio's musicals. But

Gigi is a different kind of musical in that all the elements have the same general tone, and develop the characters while they advance the story.

The Motion Picture Academy recognized the overall excellence of *Gigi* with nine Oscars, including the one for Best Picture of the Year. Maurice Chevalier also received a Special Academy Award for his contributions to the world of entertainment for more than half a century.

Julia Johnson

GILDA

Released: 1946
Production: Virginia Van Upp for Columbia
Direction: Charles Vidor
Screenplay: Marion Parsonnet; based on a screen story by E. A. Ellington
Cinematography: Rudolph Maté
Editing: Charles Nelson
Running time: 110 minutes

> *Principal characters:*
> Gilda .... Rita Hayworth
> Johnny Farrell .... Glenn Ford
> Ballin Mundson .... George Macready
> Obregon .... Joseph Calleia
> Uncle Pio .... Steven Geray
> Casey .... Joe Sawyer

In 1946, Columbia president Harry Cohn was quoted as saying that Rita Hayworth was the fourth most valuable property in the business. Cohn, almost universally despised by the people who worked for him during his thirty-odd-year reign at Columbia, was nonetheless regarded as a reliable barometer of the motion picture industry, and if he said Rita Hayworth was the fourth most valuable star in Hollywood, then she *was*. And Cohn never let anyone forget that he was responsible for Hayworth's success.

Born Rita Cansino in 1919, the dark Latin beauty made her first motion picture appearance in 1926 in a ten-minute short subject produced by Vitagraph in Brooklyn, New York, and starring her family, The Dancing Cansinos. Rita's first feature film appearance was a dancing role filmed for Fox's 1935 *Dante's Inferno*, starring Spencer Tracy. She was given a Fox contract for her efforts and, in fact, two subsequent appearances (in *Under the Pampas Moon*, 1935, and *Charlie Chan in Egypt*, 1935) reached the screen before the official release of *Dante's Inferno*.

After appearing in minor roles at Fox and as an ingenue in numerous "B" Westerns for independent producers, Rita signed a contract with Columbia in 1937, where she was assigned to the Irving Briskin unit. Briskin, then making inexpensive program pictures, was charged with giving exposure to Columbia contract players, and toward this end, Rita did a series of memorable roles in largely unmemorable pictures such as *Girls Can Play* (1937), *Paid to Dance* (1937), and *Special Investigator* (1939). It was at Columbia that Rita's last name was changed from Cansino to Hayworth, and that she received the buildup and grooming necessary for stardom and obtainable at major studios. Her first major role at Columbia was the second female lead in Howard Hawks's *Only Angels Have Wings* (1939), and following favorable reaction to her performance, Rita was loaned to both M-G-M and Warner Bros. It was on loan to Twentieth Century-Fox, however, that Rita demonstrated her value as a star in the remake of *Blood and Sand* (1941), with Tyrone Power playing the Rudolph Valentino role. Hayworth, playing the fiery Dona Sol, gave a spectacular performance and returned to her home lot a star. She was immediately cast opposite Fred Astaire in *You'll Never Get Rich* (1941) and *You Were Never Lovelier* (1942). Loaned to Fox again for *My Gal Sal* (1942), and *Tales of Manhattan* (1942), Rita returned to Columbia in 1944 for two of her best pictures, *Cover Girl* (1944), starring Gene Kelly, and *Tonight and Every Night* (1944), with Janet Blair and Lee Bowman.

In 1945, Columbia decided to change Rita's image. Since her triumph in *Blood and Sand*, Cohn had cast her in big-budget musicals playing a warm, all-American girl. After a sultry pinup picture of Rita, clad in a nightgown and kneeling on a bed, had been distributed to millions of soldiers during the war, the decision was made to exploit Rita as a love goddess. Her long, luscious red hair, originally dyed for her role in *Blood and Sand*, and her voluptuous figure had been displayed in dozens of studio publicity stills, and Cohn decided to blend her appearance and fiery Latin image in a new film, *Gilda*. Although Cohn had envisioned the new potential here, not even he could have realized the effect that *Gilda* would have on Hayworth's career.

Gilda was one of the earliest postwar thrillers which, in predating what French critics would later describe as *film noir*, painted a darker side of life than Hollywood films had been accustomed to portray. Its story, heavily rewritten during production, was seamy and turgid, and director Charles Vidor, working closely with its stars, Hayworth and Glenn Ford, was able to deliver a film of smoldering sensuality.

Gilda begins with the narration of Johnny Farrell (Glenn Ford), a two-bit American gambler down on his luck in South America. While collecting his winnings from a crap game in a seedy section of Buenos Aires, Johnny is attacked by two thugs who attempt to rob him. He is saved by the timely intervention of Ballin Mundson (George Macready), a fashionable gentleman who frightens the would-be bandits off with a sword cane. Mundson introduces himself to Johnny as the owner of a luxurious gambling casino. Johnny is naturally suspicious of the stranger who invites him back to the casino, but he nevertheless goes. Mundson is looking for a man whom he can trust to assist in running the casino since he has other commitments which demand much of his time. Johnny finds himself curiously drawn to Ballin; they share many of the same attitudes and dislikes, and the young American accepts Mundson's proposal. The audience later learns that Ballin is the front man for a Nazi-backed cartel in Europe. In his new position at the casino, Johnny finds himself annoyed by the presence of Uncle Pio (Steven Geray), one of the casino's most philosophical employees.

Ballin returns to Buenos Aires after one of his mysterious trips with a new wife, Gilda (Rita Hayworth). When Johnny meets Gilda, he becomes aware of traits in her that he knows all too well, and while taking a dislike to her, he nonetheless respects her as Ballin's wife and assigns himself the task of watching her to make certain that she does not embarrass Ballin. A love-hate relationship soon develops between Gilda and Johnny, which is noted by Ballin. Ballin, however, soon finds himself in grave danger after killing one of his partners in crime; his cartel is exposed, and, refusing to give himself up, he flies his private plane into the sea, apparently comitting suicide.

Johnny marries Gilda, but not for love; he blames her for Ballin's suicide and is determined to see that she remains faithful to his memory. Gilda tortures herself over Johnny's hatred of her, and exhibits bizarre behavior, even attempting to make a spectacle of herself in the casino by doing an abortive striptease.

Ballin, having convinced everyone of his death, thereby averting a man-hunt, returns to the casino to kill his trusted friend and loving wife, who have both betrayed him. Crazed by passion, he almost succeeds with the murders until the intervention by Uncle Pio, who stabs Ballin with his own stiletto. At this point in the film, plot and characterizations change abruptly, and Johnny and Gilda, now free from Ballin forever, are portrayed as, at last, being able to pursue their own happiness together.

The perplexed critics who reviewed the film on its initial release were puzzled by the abrupt shift in Gilda's character and the muddled motivations of the others as well. They found the plot, with good justification, to be confusing and pointless; but the film is rich in suggestive dialogue and steamy love scenes between Hayworth and Ford. Despite its poor reviews, *Gilda* was a huge success with the public, grossing more than three million dollars. It changed Rita Hayworth's career dramatically; and she found herself in later years forced, in picture after picture, to live up to the image created for her in this film.

Ed Hulse

GIRL CRAZY

Released: 1943
Production: Arthur Freed for Metro-Goldwyn-Mayer
Direction: Norman Taurog
Screenplay: Fred F. Finklehoffe; based on the musical play and book of the same name by Guy Bolton and Jack McGowan
Cinematography: William Daniels and Robert Planck
Editing: Albert Akst
Choreography: Charles Walters
Music: George Gershwin and Ira Gershwin
Running time: 99 minutes

> *Principal characters:*
> Danny Churchill, Jr. .... Mickey Rooney
> Ginger Gray .... Judy Garland
> Bud Livermore .... Gil Stratton
> Henry Lathrop .... Robert E. Strickland

Girl Crazy is a Mickey Rooney/Judy Garland musical out of the "let's put on a show" mold. In several respects it is the best of the formula musicals which paired the two. The score by the Gershwins includes many of their classics. Norman Taurog, who replaced Busby Berkeley midway through the shooting, directed with more depth than Berkeley had in earlier Rooney/ Garland movies, with more sensitivity to the strengths of his leading players, and with less delight in creating "camp" musical numbers. Where Berkeley tended to stress the geometry of big production numbers with Rooney and Garland as figureheads who lead the band, Taurog set up simpler musical numbers which permitted greater subtleties.

In *Girl Crazy*, Rooney and Garland finally grow up, despite the best intentions of a formula which saw them as kids on stage in film after film. For Judy Garland especially, *Girl Crazy* marks a change in presentation, although the script sees her, once again, as a teenager. This time she is Ginger Gray, the daughter of a college president. The character Garland once described as "Dorothy Adorable," once given free rein in *Babes on Broadway* (1941), *Babes in Arms* (1939), or the Andy Hardy movies, has, however, grown more complex. Ginger Gray shows the contradictory and ironic charm of the later Garland characters, both vulnerable and quick to laugh at herself in a way that the roles as "Dorothy Adorable" hardly suggest.

The musical number which marks a transition point for this musical is "I Got Rhythm." It was the number which, according to several accounts, caused Berkeley to lose control of the movie. His idea for it involved very large ensembles with anonymous girls in fringe cracking whips and plenty of trick camera shots. Obviously this style buried the principal characters, who by this time were both important stars on the lot. Furthermore, the style reflected an approach to musicals that was becoming passé at M-G-M. Musicals such as those at which Berkeley excelled, which were collections of flashy production numbers only vaguely involving character development, were on their way out. M-G-M—especially the Freed production unit which handled big-budget musicals with big-name casts—was quickly adopting the style of the so-called "integrated" musical. In the integrated musicals, songs, dances, and plot all reflected and extended character development; each element deepened the understanding of the others. Berkeley films such as *Babes on Broadway* and *Babes in Arms* had used the "let's put on a show" format as an excuse for Garland, Rooney, and dozens of chorus people to concoct variety shows. They might do a melodramatic farce, a takeoff on Franklin D. Roosevelt, or a minstrel show—anything that might be performed on a stage. Meanwhile, offstage they were just kids who wanted to be onstage. Their roles were fleshed out just enough to allow the romantic subplot a conventional credibility. Berkeley followed this pattern in filming the "I Got Rhythm" sequence for *Girl Crazy*. But this time, there was enough disagreement with that concept among his coworkers to have Berkeley taken off the picture.

Although Taurog's direction and staging of the musical numbers reflected the beginnings of a new style in film musicals, the plot of *Girl Crazy* is altogether conventional. It involves reeducating a wayward youth in the simple values of a small-town, middle-class community. The young man, Danny Churchill, Jr. (Mickey Rooney), has lost sight of these values because he has too much money. The need to teach spoiled rich people what is truly valuable in life was a constant convention of Americana films made at M-G-M and other studios in that period. Also true to convention, Danny's means of education is a woman who has the integrity and proper sense of values he lacks, and who has faith that the man she loves will regain his appreciation of them.

Danny Churchill, Jr., is a college playboy who is sent to a boy's school in the West. There life is different for Danny, away from the comforts and influence his money has always supplied. No taxis meet him at the station; he walks. Once at the college, he is stricken at learning that he must rise daily at 6:00 A.M. Worse, he must suffer ignoble lessons in horseback riding. At first Danny's pride creates his problems, since he refuses to admit that he has anything to learn. Gradually, however, with the help of Ginger Gray (Judy Garland), his character improves. Danny's feelings for Ginger and for the school are completely changed for the better by the time a financial crisis hits the college. Money has run out, and the school is faced with closing. Ginger and Danny raise the money to save the school by staging a Western jamboree. Once again, Rooney and Garland "put on a show." The new school will be coeducational, and Danny and Ginger are classmates as the picture ends.

The filming of this variation on the familiar "let's put on a show" plot is what sets *Girl Crazy* apart from the earlier musicals. Not only are Rooney and Garland featured in virtually every scene, but they usually dominate the frame in Taurog's composition. The difference in style becomes glaringly apparent in the final production number, "I Got Rhythm," which Berkeley shot before leaving the picture. It is the only number which uses its main characters as solutions to geometry exercises. The numbers which Taurog shot are much less busy. Garland sings "Embraceable You," "But Not for Me." "Bidin' My Time," and other lesser-known Gershwin songs. Newcomer June Allyson appears in one specialty number at the film's beginning, and the popular band leader, Tommy Dorsey, plays in several numbers.

Leslie Donaldson

THE GO-BETWEEN

Released: 1971
Production: John Heyman and Norman Priggen for EMI Films and World Film Services; released by Metro-Goldwyn-Mayer
Direction: Joseph Losey
Screenplay: Harold Pinter; based on the novel of the same name by L.P. Hartley
Cinematography: Jerry Fisher
Editing: Reginald Beck
Running time: 116 minutes

> *Principal characters:*
> Marian Maudsley .... Julie Christie
> Leo Colston (younger) .... Dominic Guard
> Leo Colston (older) .... Michael Redgrave
> Ted Burgess .... Alan Bates
> Mrs. Maudsley .... Margaret Leighton
> Hugh Trimingham .... Edward Fox
> Marcus Maudsley .... Richard Gibson
> Mr. Maudsley .... Michael Gough

Joseph Losey, director of *The Servant* (1963), *Accident* (1967), and *Figures in the Landscape* (1970), has re-created excellently the atmosphere of lost innocence evoked in L. P. Hartley's novel *The Go-Between* in his film of the same name. He portrays a turn-of-the-century home resplendent in details such as heavy, dark wood furniture, stately rooms, and a sweeping staircase, and dwells on the rituals of the upper class from their formal promenade to dinner and pious morning prayer before breakfast to their unwritten code of class behavior in which one class does not mix with another except within closely defined limits. Although he was restricted to a one-million-dollar budget and an eight-week shooting schedule, his film won the Grand Prize at the Cannes Film Festival. Losey had collaborated with Harold Pinter in *The Servant* and *Accident*, and he again utilized this combination which seems to bring out his best work. Pinter's script has been criticized by some as being too obscure in dialogue and unclear in action, but his adaptation takes into consideration the viewpoint of a young boy who in his immaturity does not understand many of the reasons behind adult activities and therefore does not observe every event clearly. However, one confusing element is the way Pinter telescopes time, inserting scenes of the present-day Leo Colston returning to Brandham Hall, while dramatizing his past.

Losey establishes the primarily melancholy tone from the beginning, running the credits over a window drenched with rain while the haunting musical theme is played in the background. The audience is prepared to see a different world, metaphorically peeping into the window of the past, reminiscing with a man now sixty years old who had sojourned at Brandham Hall when he was twelve. Michael Redgrave as the old Leo Colston speaks the most famous line of the novel: "The past is a foreign country: they do things differently there."

The film flashes back to the summer of 1900 when Leo (Dominic Guard) first arrives at the Maudsley home, Brandham Hall. The servants take care of his luggage while his schoolfellow Marcus Maudsley (Richard Gibson) shows him around the mansion, situated near Norwich, England, on a two-hundred-acre park. Marcus laughs with condescension at Leo's awe of the mansion and estate, and delights in introducing his young guest to upper-class life, a much different world from Leo's modest middle-class upbringing. Here at the Hall, family and guests spend their time in various idle diversions: a lady is asleep in a hammock, shading her face from the sun with a frilly parasol; a gentleman reads aloud from a novel; and other guests play croquet on the vast lawn. These adults, most of them dressed in white, seem to Leo to be residents of paradise. Yet during a tour of the grounds Leo also discovers a poisonous nightshade plant, symbolic of the forbidden knowledge of good and evil within this paradise that Leo will be tempted to learn.

Leo finds that he does not fit into this idyllic society and that he must struggle to learn etiquette and discover an acceptable new role. At school, his wit and instinctive knowledge had stood him in good stead as a new student, because he had gained an enviable reputation as a magician. At the Hall, this reputation is ridiculed, forcing Leo to search for a new role. Marcus provides little support and denigrates his ignorance of common customs, while the adults tease him for wearing his heavy winter clothing instead of the appropriate light summer suit. Leo does not own another suit and lies about his mother's neglecting to pack his summer suit in his bags. As Mrs. Maudsley (Margaret Leighton) presses him to send home for it, Marian (Julie Christie), Marcus' older sister, intervenes and offers to buy him a set of summer clothing. Mrs. Maudsley offers a slight objection about her going alone into town, but Marian jokingly and insistently overrides her objections. The next evening Leo models his suit for the family and guests; it is Lincoln green, which Marian declares is the perfect color for Leo. Mrs. Maudsley questions her daughter about whether she has seen anyone in town, and Leo supports her denial, forgetting that she had spoken to someone during the hour she had asked him to amuse himself in the cathedral. Someone nicknames Leo Robin Hood, and the grateful boy develops an infatuation for his kind and generous Maid Marian. She encourages his heroine worship when she flirts with him during the bathing party in the river where the audience is introduced to the handsome and virile Ted Burgess (Alan Bates), a neighboring tenant farmer.

Marcus is suddenly taken ill, and Leo amuses himself by exploring the surrounding countryside, where he stumbles across Ted's farm. Succumbing to temptation, he slides down a haystack he finds in the barnyard but injures his knee on a cutting block half hidden in the hay. Ted hears him cry out and is angry with him for trespassing until he discovers that Leo is from the Hall. After Ted bandages his knee, Leo asks if he may do anything in return and is surprised when Ted asks him to take a note to Miss Marian—strictly a business message which Leo is to keep secret. Leo complies, in this way beginning his role as the "Postman" for Ted and Marian's trysts. Leo further plays out his role by taking part in a coy courtship between Marian and her upper-class suitor, Viscount Hugh Trimingham (Edward Fox), who christens Leo Mercury, the messenger of the gods. Leo finds that his place in adult society at the Hall is enhanced when he plays his new role, which elevates his status to one of tolerant acceptance. Leo innocently participates in the adults' games, having no comprehension of what is going on behind the superficial conversation and idle messages of the Hall, or of the meaning of the secret messages between Ted and Marian.

Leo is further accepted by the group when he participates in the annual cricket match between Brandham Hall and the village and catches Ted out in a lucky play to win the game for the Hall. He sings at the celebration after the match and is roundly applauded, reaffirming his acceptance. On the way back to the mansion, Marcus complains about the stink in the pavilion from the villagers and also tries to put Leo down as an inferior. They scuffle, and when Leo wins Marcus appeases him with a secret: Marian and Hugh are to be married. But Leo, meanwhile, discovers that Marian and Ted are in love when she inadvertently slips him an unsealed note, trying to hide it from Trimingham, who has interrupted the exchange. When Leo tries to explain to Marian why he should not carry notes any more, Marian is furious, accusing him of wanting money for simple errands. He is bewildered and upset at her outburst and snatches the letter from her, delivering it despite his reservations. He then demands that Ted explain "spooning," knowing that Ted and Marian engage in this activity and wanting them to share their knowledge with him. He threatens to stop delivering notes if this mysterious activity is not fully explained to him; but Ted is uncomfortable about discussing sex with Leo and becomes angry, frightening him away.

Leo then decides he must handle this moral dilemma himself since his mother will not send for him earlier than planned and Marian will continue her meetings with Ted. He accidentally reveals to Marcus that he knows where Marian goes in the afternoons; Marcus later reports this to his mother. He also tries to cast a spell over Ted and Marian, gathering a part of the nightshade to mix the potion (symbolically marking his taste of the knowledge of good and evil). He feels that this will force the couple to forget each other.

The next morning is Leo's birthday and the weather changes for the first time that summer from shimmering heat to thundering rain, signaling an ominous change in mood. Mrs. Maudsley catches Marian attempting to send Leo to the farm with a message and bullies Leo into revealing that he has not been delivering notes to Nanny Robson, Marian's former nurse, as she had maintained. Mrs. Maudsley does not pursue the subject very long, much to Leo's relief; but she suspects Marian's affair.

The birthday celebration begins in the late afternoon, but Marian does not appear to present her gift, a green bicycle, to Leo. Everyone comments on her absence until Mr. Maudsley sends a carriage for her at Nanny Robson's cottage. When the carriage returns empty and Nanny Robson sends a message that she has not seen Marian all afternoon, Mrs. Maudsley snaps that they will not wait for Marian, and, dragging Leo after her, she leads the way to Ted's farm in the pouring rain. They enter the barn and there find Ted and Marian making love. Leo is disillusioned with Marian because she is not the virtuous Maid Marian he had placed on a pedestal, and also because she has selfishly used him to continue her affair. This loss of his innocence affects Leo for the rest of his life, resulting in the fact that he never marries.

In a cinematic flash forward to Leo's present life fifty years later, he talks to the aged Marian, who lives in Nanny Robson's old cottage. Marian tells him that she married Trimingham and bore Ted's child, but was saved from overt abuse because she was Lady Trimingham. Ted had killed himself after the discovery of their affair, and her family was broken in the resulting disgrace. Marian asks Leo to be a go-between one more time, this time to talk with her grandson, who never visits her because he is ashamed to be a descendant of her illicit union. She begs Leo to tell her grandson how he had witnessed an affair full of love, perfectly harmless and devoid of evil. She hopes that Leo can convince her grandson that he should be happy to be descended from such a beautiful union. Although Leo realizes the extent of Marian's self-deception, the film leaves him as he approaches Brandham Hall, presumably to deliver Marian's lonely message.

Losey and Pinter have collaborated to create a subdued atmosphere charged with hidden passions in a society where sex is shameful and all feelings are hidden beneath a surface of gaiety and idle pleasure. Losey keeps the actors controlled and their performances understated and implied rather than frank and straightforward. In this way, their undisguised feelings burst out in shocking uncontrolled fury, as in Marian's outburst or Mrs. Maudsley's attack on Leo. Dominic Guard is wide-eyed and eager beside the aloof and enigmatic Julie Christie and the openhearted, honest Alan Bates. When this film was first planned in the 1950's, shortly after the novel was first published, Margaret Leighton was suggested to play the role of Marian. By the time the film was made, she was mature; and instead of Marian, she expertly plays the frenzied mother who must keep track of her daughter's purity and has high hopes for her upwardly mobile marriage to the Viscount.

The cinematography is excellent. The countryside adds to the mood of an

Eden on earth, while Ted's earthy barnyard full of animals and hay is lusty and his kitchen intimate and completely masculine in its stark simplicity. The costumes are historically accurate and yet reflect the characteristics of each personality: Leo is romantic and innocent in Lincoln green, while the stained Marian is dressed deceptively in off-white, a reflection of Leo's image of her. Ted is at home in rustic browns, in contrast to the Viscount in formal black. The past is fused with golden light until Leo's birthday, when the sunlight is snuffed out and darkness and rain rule. This same darkness pervades Leo and Marian's conversation in Nanny Robson's cottage, where the darkness of reality reigns and Leo's perceptions are stripped of imagination's golden aura. The drenching rain at the end of Leo's visit to Brandham Hall combines with the drenched window at the beginning of the film to encircle the story in melancholy.

There are several dimensions to Leo's role as a go-between. He is a messenger for the adults who see him only as an errand boy. He also travels the social ladder; he is a middle-class boy who moves between the wealthy and the working class, feeling comfortable in neither and attracted to both. He is inadvertently the middleman of courtship propriety between Marian and the Viscount, and he interferes in the improper sexual passion between Marian and Ted. Finally, Leo is the interpreter of the past for the audience, who sees the events only through his eyes. Leo resigns himself to his role when Marian asks him to be an intermediary, and once again he becomes the outsider observing groups who will never fully accept him, perpetually living out his identity as the lonely go-between.

Ruth L. Hirayama

THE GODFATHER

Released: 1972
Production: Albert S. Ruddy for Alfran Productions; released by Paramount (AA)
Direction: Francis Ford Coppola
Screenplay: Mario Puzo and Francis Ford Coppola (AA); based on the novel of the same name by Mario Puzo
Cinematography: Gordon Willis
Editing: William Reynolds and Peter Zinner
Music: Nino Rota
Makeup: Dick Smith and Philip Rhodes
Running time: 175 minutes

Principal characters:

Don Vito Corleone	Marlon Brando (AA)
Michael Corleone	Al Pacino
Sonny Corleone	James Caan
Clemenza	Richard Castellano
Tom Hagen	Robert Duvall
Kay Adams	Diane Keaton
Captain McClusky	Sterling Hayden
Jack Woltz	John Marley
Barzini	Richard Conte
Sollozzo	Al Lettieri
Tessio	Abe Vigoda
Fredo Corleone	John Cazale
Connie Corleone Rizzi	Talia Shire
Carlo Rizzi	Gianni Russo
Mamma Corleone	Morgana King
Johnny Fontane	Al Martino
Luca Brasi	Lenny Montana

A quintessential gangster film that elevates the longstanding popular genre to the highest level of art, *The Godfather* portrays a Mafia organization that is a malevolent extension of the ethics of capitalism and the free enterprise system. Its Sicilian-American "family" serves as a metaphor for corrupt big business and government. At one point in the film, the heads of the underworld sit around a large conference table as if they comprise a corporate board of directors. At another point, Michael Corleone (Al Pacino) says that his father, Don Vito (Marlon Brando), is "no different from any other powerful man." "You're being naïve," responds his Anglo-Saxon girl friend, Kay Adams (Diane Keaton), "Senators and Congressmen don't have people killed." "Who's being naïve now, Kay?" Michael replies.

Nearly three hours in length, and played without intermission, the massive epic costing $6,300,000 had a large ready-made audience since it was based on Mario Puzo's best-selling novel. Italian-American Puzo adapted his own work for the screen, keeping the action close to that of the book. His cowriter on the script, and the film's director, was another Italian-American, Francis Ford Coppola. Coppola had previously been responsible for the screenplays of *Reflections in a Golden Eye* (1967) and *Patton* (1970).

Reminiscent of Orson Welles's *Citizen Kane* (1941) and Luchino Visconti's *Rocco and His Brothers* (1961) and *The Damned* (1969), *The Godfather* is a powerful story tracing the history of a Mafia clan, showing how its members live, how they work, and how they die. Because they feared a negative image, the Italian-American Civil Rights League saw to it that Paramount hired a League member to assist on the production and insisted that the words "Mafia" and "Cosa Nostra" be removed from the script. We see the close-knit Corleone family as folksy people, with their wives, their babies, and their subculture, with its ritualistic funerals, baptisms, and weddings replete with "vino," the tarantella, mandolin music, and Sicilian folk songs. We also experience the flavor of Italian home life and witness the ethnic preoccupation with food, as pasta is prepared in the kitchen.

The patriarch of the clan is the Godfather himself, Don Vito Corleone. Ostensibly a gentle man, the aging Don is seen inhaling the fragrance of a rose, stroking a cat as it sits on his lap, and proudly dancing with his daughter at her wedding. A scene depicting the playful Don doting on his grandson in the garden is particularly charming, with its natural, seemingly improvised quality. The Don is only seemingly benign, however. Just as in the garden scene when the Don inserts a bit of orange rind into his mouth to scare and tease the child, the film shows that the Godfather is really a monster. He is a man made rich by corrupt unions and gambling houses and by wielding enormous power as he metes out favors and punishments, orders men to be murdered, and makes offers one "cannot refuse." Indeed, the Don is the chieftain of one of the five most ruthless families of the criminal underworld. Thus the film serves as a powerful metaphor for the separation between private and public lives.

A period piece set between 1945 and 1955 in New York City; New Jersey; and the Long Beach, Long Island, family compound, *The Godfather* begins with the wedding of the Don's daughter Connie (Talia Shire) to Carlo Rizzi (Gianni Russo). At this point, the family's cultural roots are revealed as are the principal characters and their relationships.

It is a custom for the father of the bride to grant favors to all who ask, and during the wedding reception, the Don attends to business: he sees to it that the assaulters of one supplicant's daughter receive proper "justice" and that his godson, the famous singing idol Johnny Fontane (Al Martino), receives a part in a Hollywood movie. Overseeing these activites is Tom Hagen (Robert Duvall), the Don's non-Italian adopted son and "consigliere" (adviser) whose law degree gives the dynasty a respectable façade and a veneer of class. At the wedding we are introduced also to the Godfather's three sons: Fredo (John Cazale), shy, vulnerable, and weak; Michael (Al Pacino), the Ivy League-educated, sensitive, and withdrawn marine captain and war hero; and Sonny (James Caan), the sexually athletic, hot-blooded extrovert.

When the rival "capo" Sollozzo (Al Lettieri) wants to introduce heroin dealings into the Mafia operations, Don Vito refuses—not for moral reasons, but because he does not want to jeopardize his relations with his political contacts. In the course of the ensuing bloody gang war for control of the entire Mafia empire, the Godfather is gunned down by two rival henchmen as he walks across a street; he is severely wounded but not killed. Taking over the reins is his volatile oldest son, Sonny; the big, boisterous, violent successor soon becomes a victim of his own unleashed passions, however. Following his assault on Carlo for beating his sister Connie, Sonny is ambushed with Carlo's help and killed at a highway toll bridge.

With Don Vito now retired, Michael, the youngest and favorite son, becomes the next chieftain. Though he originally wanted to have his own legitimate identity away from the Corleone "business," the murder attempt on his father and Sonny's assassination changes Michael's mind and plans. He becomes inextricably involved after he kills Sollozzo and McCluskey (Sterling Hayden), a corrupt police captain. After hiding out in a village in Sicily, and after the brutal killing of his young Italian wife, Apollonia, by a rival gang, Michael returns home as the hardened new Don.

No longer naïve, Michael is now shrewd, devious, and ruthless. Following his marriage to Kay Adams and the death of his father, Don Vito, Michael expands his family's operations into prostitution, narcotics, and legal Nevada gambling enterprises. In the end, he coldbloodedly orders Barzini (Richard Conte), a prime enemy and rival boss, to be murdered, and has his loyal hit man, Clemenza (Richard Castellano), assassinate the weak and treacherous Carlo Rizzi. Closing the door on his wife Kay, Michael, now a methodical murderer, also lies to her; in the film's final shot, he tells Kay that he is not responsible for the brutal death of his sister's husband Carlo. Michael then accepts the kiss of his ring from his followers.

A "blockbuster" of a film, with tremendous mass appeal, *The Godfather* was a critical and commercial success. Along with such movies as *Gone with the Wind* (1939), *The Sound of Music* (1965), and *Jaws* (1975), it became and has remained one of the all-time box-office favorites. Not only did the film have an excellent screenplay, extraordinary direction, and outstanding production values, it also had a brilliant cast.

Marlon Brando's portrayal of the Godfather is a genuine *tour de force*. Along with Dick Smith's unique makeup (Smith was also responsible for Cicily Tyson's makeup in *The Autobiography of Miss Jane Pittman* on television, as well as Dustin Hoffman's in *Little Big Man*, 1970), the forty-seven-year-old non-Italian Brando was transformed into a sixty-two-year-old Sicil-ian-American. With an elaborate mouthplate that extended his jowls to create a pugnacious bulldoglike jaw, dirty teeth, drooping eyelids, graying temples, and a pencil-thin moustache, Smith and Brando create the look of a paunchy (padded), slightly feeble, stiffly moving man, dressed in fedoras and overcoats or in his formal wear with its stand-up collar. With his harsh, guttural, rasping whisper, his slightly mumbling Italian accent, his mannerism of scratching his cheek with one finger, and his mirthless smile, Brando's characterization combines terror and tenderness as he moves from the demeanor of invinci-bility, to deterioration, to death in the idyllic garden. A performer of great control (although, as usual, he often forgot his lines and needed to rely on hidden cue cards), Brando is riveting. Although the part of the Don is not a particularly large one, the Godfather's presence dominates the picture; for his role, Brando won the Oscar for the Best Actor of 1972.

Ironically, Brando nearly failed to get the part. Numerous others were talked about for the role—Laurence Olivier, George C. Scott, Frank Sinatra, Lee J. Cobb, Carlo Ponti, and many others. Most important, however, Brando was considered a virtually "unbankable" star. His reputation for temperament on the set was noted in *Mutiny on the Bounty* (1962) and *One-Eyed Jacks* (1961), and though still a technically brilliant actor, he had not given a really satisfying performance in years. Some of his "clinkers" included *A Countess from Hong Kong* (1967) and *Candy* (1968).

Coppola wanted to use the star, however, and Brando himself was extremely eager for the role, so he tested for the part. At the audition, Brando used such props as a cup of expresso, an Italian stogie, and a plate of apples and cheese; he also put shoe polish under his eyes and stuffed wads of tissue paper in his cheeks. Brando was hired with a minimal salary, but he was given a percentage of the film's considerable profits. Brando's performance in *The Godfather* is so stunning that it revitalized his reputation and brought him back to eminence, allowing him to go on to other interesting parts in *Last Tango in Paris* (1973), *Superman* (1978), and Coppola's own *Apocalypse Now* (1979).

Interestingly, when Brando won the Academy Award, he sent an Apache Indian militant named Sasheen Little Feather to speak at the ceremonies on his behalf. Announcing through her that he was declining the Oscar as a protest against film and television treatment of the Indian, Brando once again made cinema news. His proclamation, and decline of the award, were greeted with "boos" at the televised ceremonies and scathing comments in the press.

The Italian-American actor Al Pacino, young and relatively unknown at the time (his only previous film was *The Panic in Needle Park*, 1971), is magnificent in the pivotal role of Michael Corleone. Originally, both Warren Beatty and Jack Nicholson were considered for the part, but the brooding, callow, and ferocious Pacino creates a multifaceted character of tremendous variety and depth. Michael convincingly moves from a nervous young G.I. to a menacing Mafia leader.

James Caan, who had starred previously in Coppola's *The Rain People* (1969), is effective as the high-spirited, ill-fated Sonny, whose explosively hot temper leads to his downfall. John Cazale, another Italian-American, is sympathetic as the timid, feckless, and slightly dim-witted Fredo; he is particularly amusing as he attempts to be a Las Vegas "stud" and particularly affecting as he sits next to his father's bullet-riddled body and helplessly wails. Robert Duvall (who, along with Brando, would star in Coppola's *Apocalypse Now*) is believable as Tom Hagen, the Don's counselor, valet, and advance man. Hagen makes it clear that he is totally unapologetic about who he is and about what he is doing.

Shot mostly at New York locations (Brooklyn, the Bronx, Manhattan, and Staten Island), *The Godfather* is beautifully photographed by Gordon Willis. The camera moves back and forth between light and dark scenes, as when we see the Godfather in the darkened, closed room with patterned shadows on the walls created by the shutters, and then are transported to the bright exterior light of the wedding. Thematically, the lighting reflects the dual nature of the family and of a man who is warm and generous and is also a murderer. Some interiors have the burnt-umber look of old photographs, and the outdoor tableaux of the garden party and the Sicilian interlude are bathed in warm sunlight. Unlike the visual style of most films of the period, *The Godfather* makes little use of jarring close-ups, fast cuts, or zoom shots.

Warren Clyner's art direction and Dean Tavoularis' production design are superb and accurate down to the smallest, well-researched details. The (post-World War II) period is excellently re-created with such details as the handbills and street posters of Dean Martin and Jerry Lewis, the old-time autos and taxis, the movie marquee announcing Ingrid Bergman and Bing Crosby in *The Bells of St. Mary's*, and the song "Have Yourself a Merry Little Christmas." The musical score is also outstanding. Written by Nino Rota, who also composed the music for Fellini's *La Strada* (1954), *8½* (1963), and *La Dolce Vita* (1959), as well as for *The Taming of the Shrew* (1967) and *Romeo and Juliet* (1966), *The Godfather*'s musical theme has since become a classic.

William Reynolds' and Peter Zinner's brazen editing is equally effective. With the score here by J. S. Bach, the camera cuts back and forth between Michael at the baptismal ceremony for his sister Connie's baby (where he literally becomes a godfather) and the bloody extermination of the rival families that Michael has arranged to take place. The scenes of violence make effective use of special effects and stunts. For example, Sonny's death scene, in which a 1941 Lincoln Continental wired with 110 explosive charges is blown up, cost $100,000 to film.

A richly textured and dramatic portrait of racketeers and the underworld,

The Godfather shows the viewer violence as a way of life. The violence is realistic and gory, graphically depicting a strangulation, a hoodlum's hand being pinned to the table with a knife, a machine-gunning, and a mass murder. In one chilling scene, the movie mogul, forced into signing the singer for his movie, slowly awakens to find the severed and bloody head of his prize stallion in his bed; the scene is accompanied by the man's horrified screams. Interestingly, there is little sex in the film.

More than merely a taut action melodrama, *The Godfather* is a compelling psychological character study of inner motivations and relationships, as well as a sociological study of a deplorable aspect of American society. Characters are not reduced to stereotypes, nor are they sentimentalized. We see that the family is made up of racists, liars, hypocrites, and killers. We may empathize with them to some degree, but we do not condone their life style.

It is the artistry of Francis Ford Coppola that pulls the enormous production together. Although as a director he had never had a hit film before this one (he had done the low-budget *You're a Big Boy Now*, 1966 and the big-budget flop *Finian's Rainbow*, 1968), Coppola manifests his overall unifying vision in *The Godfather*. Elaborate, haunting, frightening, and gripping, *The Godfather* is a towering achievement. The Academy Award-winning film was eventually sold to television for ten million dollars, and was followed by an equally magnificent sequel, *The Godfather, Part II* (1974).

Leslie Taubman

THE GODFATHER, PART II

Released: 1974
Production: Francis Ford Coppola for Paramount (AA)
Direction: Francis Ford Coppola
Screenplay: Francis Ford Coppola and Mario Puzo (AA); based on the novel
  The Godfather by Mario Puzo
Cinematography: Gordon Willis
Editing: Peter Zinner, Barry Malkin, and Richard Marks
Art direction: Dean Tavoularis and Angelo Graham (AA); set decoration,
  George R. Nelson (AA)
Costume design: Theadora Van Runkle
Music direction: Carmine Coppola
Music: Nino Rota, with additional music by Carmine Coppola (AA)
Running time: 200 minutes

Principal characters:
Michael Corleone .... Al Pacino
Tom Hagen .... Robert Duvall
Kay Corleone .... Diane Keaton
Vito Corleone .... Robert De Niro (AA)
Fredo Corleone .... John Cazale
Connie Corleone Rizzi .... Talia Shire
Hyman Roth .... Lee Strasberg
Mama Corleone .... Morgana King
Merle Johnson .... Troy Donahue
Tessio .... Abe Vigoda
Carlo .... Gianni Russo
FBI Man .... Harry Dean Stanton
Senator .... Roger Corman
Sonny Corleone .... James Caan
Frankie Pentangeli .... Michael Gazzo

Like a great nineteenth century novel that relates the progress of a family and society, *The Godfather, Part II* continues the saga of the Corleone family while exploring the nature of power in the United States. Spanning six decades and three generations, this personal and historical drama is not only a sequel to the monumental *The Godfather* (1972), but also serves as a prologue to that production. The film begins where *The Godfather* left off and follows the career of the youngest Corleone son, Michael (Al Pacino), in the mid-1950's, as he continues the reign established by his father, Don Vito. At the same time, the film is intercut with the background story of the youthful Don Vito (played by Marlon Brando in the original film). The story chronicles the rise and fall of the Italian-American empire; the making of a Mafia chief; the rise of Don Vito; and the prime and decline of Michael.

Whereas *The Godfather* begins with a wedding, *The Godfather, Part II* begins with a funeral. It is 1901 in Sicily. After the child Vito witnesses the murder of his family by the local Black Hand, the nine-year-old orphan is shipped off to the ghetto of New York's Little Italy; the Ellis Island immigration clerks name the boy Vito "Corleone," after the Sicilian village of his birth. At first a scrawny pox-ridden waif, young Vito grows up to be an honest laborer in a grocery store, but soon wanders into petty crime where he picks up the phrase, "I made him an offer he couldn't refuse." Following a return to Sicily to carry out his twenty-year-old vendetta, Vito attains a position of power, and he finally emerges as a Mafia leader with his own "family."

Just as Vito sheds his innocence and transforms from a delicate, sensitive youth into a ruthless Mafia operator, so, too, does his son Michael. In a 1940's flashback sequence set in the Corleone Long Island compound (a setting from *The Godfather*), we see the young Dartmouth-educated Michael reveal to all the second generation Corleones that he has enlisted in the Marines. When his brother Sonny (James Caan in a brief appearance repeating his role from the earlier film), curses him, saying the family is the only cause worth fighting for, the idealistic Michael disagrees. In the course of the film, however, the war-decorated, would-be professor of mathematics inherits Vito's empire and becomes the new Godfather. "If anything in this life is certain," says the now-ruthless Michael, "if history teaches us anything, it's that you can kill anyone."

Don Michael's enterprises consist of operations in Las Vegas, Miami, and Havana (the latter an aborted attempt to take over the rackets in Cuba before Castro's revolution), and three of his many enemies include his own brother Fredo (John Cazale), a Jewish crime czar, and a family informer. In the end, the merciless Michael has all three killed simultaneously. Ultimately, Michael himself is "destroyed," not by a rival gang or by a Senate investigation of criminal activities, but by himself. He becomes trapped by his own emptiness, a prisoner of his own paranoia.

Although both *The Godfather* and *The Godfater, Part II* are concerned with the themes of power and corruption, family loyalties, and revenge, *The Godfather* is dominated more by violence and suspense, while *The Godfather, Part II* is quieter, more solemn, more introspective, and more concerned with intense and difficult human emotions. Al Pacino is chilling as the soulless Don Michael who cares for nothing but power and whose only concern is the "business." An actor of enormous range and power, Pacino is almost, but not quite, pitiable as Michael—he is simply too repellent.

Robert De Niro gives an astonishingly controlled performance as the deceptively mild-mannered and soft-spoken Vito as he magnificently conveys the character's underlying iron will and moral corruptibility. Replacing Marlon Brando, the original Godfather, De Niro maintains the same whispery, gravelly voice, grimaces, and mannerisms. (Interestingly, De Niro was signed to play in *The Godfather* for the small part of Carlo Rizzi, the brother-in-law who sets Sonny up for the kill; when a larger part came along for the actor, however, in *The Gang That Couldn't Shoot Straight* [1971] Coppola released him.) Robert Duvall, with his understated strength, does well as Tom Hagen, the Corleone's adopted son and *consigliere*, as does John Cazale as Fredo, Michael's older but weakling brother, Mariana Hill as Fredo's slatternly wife, and Talia Shire (Coppola's sister) as Connie, the Corleone's spoiled sister. Diane Keaton is especially good as Michael's second wife Kay, the WASPish, New England woman who eventually leaves her husband. As she tells Michael bitterly of her so-called "miscarriage," "It was an abortion, Michael, just like our marriage is an abortion."

Other interesting casting in the film includes former teen idol Troy Donahue as Connie's sycophantic gigolo husband; producer-director Roger Corman (who gave Coppola his start in the film business) as a senator, and playwright Michael Gazzo (*Hatful of Rain*) as a *capo* informer. In his screen debut, although well into his seventies, Lee Strasberg, the Artistic Director of the Actors' Studio, is excellent as Hyman Roth, powerful syndicate boss; with his nervous cough, deceptive charm, and Talmudic façade, Strasberg does extremely well as the aging, ailing financial mastermind. "Michael, we are bigger than U.S. Steel," Roth says, as he and Michael embark on their uneasy alliance to seize control of Havana with Batista's cooperation.

The film's fifteen-million-dollar budget allowed for lavish production values. Dean Tavoularis' production design is exquisite; noteworthy scenes include the arrival of immigrants past the Statue of Liberty and the cattle-pen chaos of Ellis Island, the expertly detailed re-creation of the picturesque but teeming Little Italy at the turn of the century, the Festa of San Rocco, the Corleone estate parties, the whorish pre-Castro Havana of the eve of the revolution, and the Kefauver Committee hearings on criminal activities in the Senate Caucus Room. Theodora Van Runkle's costume designs, which span decades of changing styles, are also magnificent.

Cinematographer Gordon Willis continues the admirable work he did on *The Godfather*, here characterizing Vito's early life with soft, delicate, and warm pastels. The Sicily sequence is sun-bleached; the New York of 1900, with its sepia tones, resembles Jacob Riis's documentary-style photographs; the family fortress in Lake Tahoe is photographed in low-key lighting with many shadows; and Michael's world is revealed to us in dark, somber, mahogany tones.

Nino Roto and Carmine Coppola's music combines sensuality and terror; the score includes the familiar "Godfather" waltz theme, "Senza Mamma," "Napule Ve Salute," "Mr. Wonderful," and "Heart and Soul." The editing of Peter Zinner, Barry Malkin, and Richard Marks is fascinating as the film moves back and forth in time. The first time, for instance, that we move from present to past, from Michael to Vito, we see Michael putting his son (the boy who is playing with Don Vito in the garden when he dies in the earlier film) to bed, and Michael's face is at the left; then there is an elegant dissolve to Vito, whose face is at the right of the frame as we see him putting his son Fredo to bed. The film receives additional richness from the use of English subtitles for the spoken Sicilian dialects and the Italian and Spanish languages.

To be sure, *The Godfather, Part II* has a few minor flaws: twenty-two minutes longer than the original, the sequel runs a lengthy three hours and twenty minutes without intermission. One scene between Michael and Mama Corleone (Morgana King) tends to be too sentimental, and the fact that young Vito at Ellis Island has smallpox has no dramatic bearing on the story, since Vito does not seem to bear either literal or figurative scars from the disease.

Nominated for eleven Oscars and winner of six, *The Godfather, Part II* is considered by many to be the greatest gangster saga ever filmed. Dense with characters, locations, plots, subplots, and political, social, and psychological ideas, and replete with alliances, betrayals, renunciations, and ambushes, the exhilarating picture is romantic, violent, and tragic. It both enriches and expands the Corleone story and the American myth, for ultimately, the film deglamorizes violence as it shows a family in disintegration, corrupt senators and businessmen, and the connection between criminals and capitalists.

Francis Ford Coppola, who had total control over the filming of *The Godfather, Part II*, has created a masterpiece, a film that may rightly be called a triumphant chapter in screen history; one can no longer say a sequel is never as good as its predecessor. Coppola has made a film that is both art and popular entertainment, a work of the stature of *Birth of a Nation* (1915), *Gone with the Wind* (1939), and *Citizen Kane* (1941).

Leslie Taubman

GOING MY WAY

Released: 1944
Production: Leo McCarey for Paramount (AA)
Direction: Leo McCarey (AA)
Screenplay: Frank Butler and Frank Cavett (AA); based on a screen story by Leo McCarey (AA)
Cinematography: Lionel Lindon
Editing: Leroy Stone
Song: Johnny Burke and James Van Heusen, "Swing on a Star" (AA)
Running time: 130 minutes

> *Principal characters:*
> Father Chuck O'Malley .... Bing Crosby (AA)
> Father Fitzgibbon .... Barry Fitzgerald (AA)
> Father Timothy O'Dowd .... Frank McHugh
> Genevieve Linden .... Risë Stevens
> Carol James .... Jean Heather
> Ted Haines, Jr. .... James Brown
> Ted Haines, Sr. .... Gene Lockhart

Going My Way is a film that clearly embodies the essentially optimistic spirit that pervaded Hollywood films during the World War II years. The film is also typical of the work of its director Leo McCarey. Although McCarey received two Academy awards for direction—one for *Going My Way* and the other for his classic "screwball" comedy *The Awful Truth* (1937)—his films are generally regarded as being too sentimental for modern tastes. However, at the time of its release in 1944, *Going My Way* was well received by critics and was such a box-office hit that it spawned a sequel, *The Bells of St. Mary's* (1945). Like most of the films that McCarey directed, *Going My Way* is consistently romantic, idealistic, and centered not around epic events of Herculean endeavors, but around the attempts of rather average people to cope with the problems of daily living. McCarey was not a director with a strong visual style, but, as *Going My Way* reveals, he had a talent for showing the humor and poignancy in life. To a nation embroiled in the uncertainty of war, the optimism and good humor of this film provided a welcome escape from its fears.

As with the films of John Ford, *Going My Way* is a product of the Irish-American background of its director. The familiar stock figures of the Irish widow, the Irish cop, and the Irish priest are all included in the film, but these characters are not simply the creations of a screenwriter; they are based on types that were actually very common in the Irish immigrant ghettos of Eastern cities.

The film is concerned with the experiences of a young Irish-American priest, Father Chuck O'Malley, who is sent by his Bishop to a poor New York City parish to help an old Irish-born priest keep his church from impending financial disaster. This situation, it is implied, has been caused by the latter's increasing inability to perform his duties successfully. *Going My Way* focuses comfortably on this decidedly uncomfortable relationship.

Unlike many previous films dealing with priests as major characters, such as *San Francisco* (1936) and *Boys Town* (1938), *Going My Way* presents characters that contrast sharply with the usual movie priest, who was most often a figure of bland and boring piety, with an all-consuming interest in saving souls. The collective sameness of that Hollywood image of the Irish and Irish-American priesthood does not reflect the real diversity that was present in the Catholic clergy. Father O'Malley (Bing Crosby) and Father Fitzgibbon (Barry Fitzgerald) provide the basis of a classic confrontation between two distinct and conflicting personalities. After his abundant sports gear has preceded him, Father O'Malley appears for his initial meeting with Father Fitzgibbon in a rumpled St. Louis Browns sweatshirt. O'Malley receives a telephone call from an old school friend, Father Timmy O'Dowd (Frank McHugh), and literally climbs over Father Fitzgibbon so he can get to the phone to join Timmy in a yowling rendition of their school song. Father Fitzgibbon is immediately convinced that his new assistant should certainly not be *his* assistant, and should probably not even be a priest. O'Malley's continuing display of a curious blend of naïveté and shallow humor force the defensive Fitzgibbon to employ his last and only line of defense—a very sharp wit.

Father Fitzgibbon is more than a character tailored to capitalize on the droll physicality and staple Irish *persona* of actor Barry Fitzgerald. Father Fitzgibbon embodies the vulnerability, frustration, and fear of aging that concerned director McCarey; McCarey had confronted these issues more directly in an earlier film, *Make Way for Tomorrow* (1937). Fitzgibbon's strong ties to the traditions of his rural homeland and his resulting inability to accept those of the new one make him incapable of dealing with the problems of an urban American ghetto. Although he is well-intentioned, Father Fitzgibbon refuses to recognize the delinquency of the boys in his parish and can only spout trite formulas to a runaway girl in need of help. He finds his memories of the past more comforting than the realities of the present or his prospects for the future. After serving St. Dominic's for more than forty-five years, Fitzgibbon knows he is regarded as inept. Driven to distraction when Father O'Malley starts a boys' choir, he goes to the Bishop to ask that he be assigned a new assistant. Fitzgibbon returns from the Bishop aware that O'Malley has actually been in charge of St. Dominic's since his arrival. Humiliated, Fitzgibbon impulsively runs away, but he is returned by a local policeman who chides him for acting like a child. He is lovingly accepted back by the housekeeper, and by O'Malley.

The reconciliation that follows between O'Malley and Father Fitzgibbon is both the turning point in the film and its most touching scene. Its beauty lies in the fact that the communication between the two is accomplished primarily through gestures rather than dialogue. The ritual of drinking "a wee bit of the crature" together, and O'Malley's singing of "Too-raa-loo-ra," suggests that the two are reconciled not only as individuals but also as generations of Irishmen, immigrant on the one hand and American-born on the other. The drinking together, done at O'Malley's suggestion, reflects his sensitivity to Fitzgibbon's strong ties to old-country traditions.

The song links Fitzgibbon to Ireland and to his memories of a mother he has not seen in almost half a century. Within the scene, past and present are united, cultural bonds recognized, and emotional issues resolved. At the end of the scene, Fitzgibbon indulges in a perfectly timed bit of comic business that turns the sentimentality of the scene upside down with a gently mocking nudge. Balancing the poignant and the comic, this reconciliation scene exemplifies McCarey's direction at its best. Excellence of ensemble acting is the key to the success of *Going My Way*. O'Malley's singing of "Too-raa-loo-ra" also reveals how McCarey could use music as an important means of expressing a character's personality and his emotional response to the moment.

In the final scene of the film, as the parish celebrates the dedication of a new chapel, Father Fitzgibbon is reunited with his mother. He is a changed man whose capacity for life has been renewed by his contact with O'Malley. Although Fitzgibbon, on hearing the news that O'Malley has been assigned to another parish, exclaims that he does not know how he can go on without him, one is left with the feeling that Fitzgibbon is now capable of carrying on very well without O'Malley. O'Malley is replaced by the irrepressible Father Timmy O'Dowd, a condition which promises to make Father Fitzgibbon's life a demonstration of that old Irish saying that contention is better than loneliness.

Even though *Going My Way* cannot be acquitted of the charge of sentimentality, it emerges as a very personal expression of a filmmaker whose optimism and humanistic spirit affirms the potential goodness in man. *Going My Way* creates a world of music, laughter, tears, and cherished friendships in which the challenge of life is something as simple, and as vastly complex, as the challenge and responsibility of caring.

Gay Studlar

GOLDEN BOY

Released: 1939
Production: William Perlberg for Columbia
Direction: Rouben Mamoulian
Screenplay: Lewis Meltzer, Daniel Taradash, Sarah Y. Mason, and Victor
   Herman; based on the play of the same name by Clifford Odets
Cinematography: Nicholas Musuraca and Karl Freund
Editing: Otto Meyer
Music: Victor Young
Running time: 98 minutes

> *Principal characters:*
> Lorna Moon .... Barbara Stanwyck
> Tom Moody .... Adolphe Menjou
> Joe Bonaparte .... William Holden
> Eddie Fuseli .... Joseph Calleia
> Mr. Bonaparte .... Lee J. Cobb
> Siggie .... Sam Levene

When Columbia first announced its purchase of Clifford Odets' Group
Theatre play *Golden Boy*, it seemed a strange choice, because that studio
had never favored dramas of strong social significance. Odets was not hired
to adapt his own play for film; instead, four top writers carefully deleted the
play's social comment from the screenplay that was being prepared. Some
of the controversial characters were completely eliminated; the romance was
built up; and the hero's conflict was simplified. A happy ending was devised
as a substitute for the play's conclusion. All things considered, the screenwriters did a good job, for *Golden Boy* as a movie proved to be much stronger
entertainment than the play. Today the play is dated, but the movie is still
as pertinent as it was at the time of its initial release.

When the production was first announced in the trade magazines, it featured
an appealing painting of Jean Arthur, who was announced as its star. Producer
Harry Cohn was biding his time, hoping to borrow John Garfield from Warner
Bros. for the title role, but Jack Warner and Harry Cohn were feuding, so
Garfield could not be secured for the part. Things began to fall into place,
though, when Rouben Mamoulian was signed as director. Mamoulian was a
versatile man who could never be typed in any one kind of film. Whatever
the background of the story he was directing, its cinematic mood was always
beautifully sustained. He was faced with two strong dramatic story lines to
resolve: the romance between an unworldly youth and a sophisticated girl;
and the internal struggle of the boy who had to choose between fulfilling
himself artistically through his music, and the opportunity to achieve quick
success as a boxer. Mamoulian had one advantage in telling the story on the

screen that could never be realized in the theater: he could show the prizefight sequences realistically. In the theater these scenes had to take place offstage; in the film they are superbly done, and convey an electric charge of quick ringside excitement and suspense.

Mamoulian demonstrated superb taste in casting his picture. He was fortunate in being able to get Barbara Stanwyck for the heroine, Lorna Moon, the girl friend of the fight manager Tom Moody, who is perfectly played by Adolphe Menjou. Stanwyck had just finished her last scenes as the heroine in De Mille's *Union Pacific* (1939), and she came over to Columbia with almost no break from her Paramount duties. Lee J. Cobb had been in the original stage play in a minor part, but was cast by Mamoulian in the more important role of Mr. Bonaparte, the boy's father, who dreams of his son's becoming a great violinist and who strongly opposes his son's boxing career because of the threat it holds of injuring the boy's hands. Joseph Calleia was exactly right for the mobster, Eddie Fuseli, and Sam Levene, as the taxi driver Siggie, provided the humor the story needed.

The most difficult role to fill was that of the young hero, the golden boy himself, Joe Bonaparte. Sixty-five youthful actors were tested for the part, and Mamoulian, a perfectionist, found fault with all of them. He finally tested an unknown, a youth of twenty-one, who was under contract to Paramount but had done virtually nothing on the screen except a few appearances in such routine pictures as *Prison Farm* (1938) and *Million Dollar Legs* (1932). His name was William Holden, and Mamoulian detected something in his screen test that was just what he wanted to portray in the character of Joe Bonaparte. Harry Cohn opposed the casting, but Mamoulian went to bat for young Holden; so did Barbara Stanwyck. Grudgingly, Cohn agreed to Holden's playing the part, but when he made the deal to borrow the boy from Paramount, he insisted on buying half of his contract. Because Holden was only under stock contract at that time and Paramount was paying him fifty dollars a week, it meant that Columbia was getting him for a weekly twenty-five dollars.

Holden's performance is workmanlike, believable, often brilliant, and deserving of the stardom he subsequently gained. Joe Napoleon is a sensitive youth whose father has sacrificed much to make him an accomplished musician. The boy is dual-natured, for he has mastered the difficult violin and is on the threshold of a career as a virtuoso. Yet, in exercising at the gym, he has gained a reputation as an amateur boxer, and when an impecunious manager, Tom Moody, sees him fight in the ring, he envisions a winner and signs the boy to a contract, promising him a quick rise to fame and fortune. Moody, also aware of the boy's innocence concerning women, instructs his own mistress, Lorna Moon, to lure the boy and entice him to stay in the fight world rather than pursue his music. Lorna does as Moody wishes, but she falls in love with Joe, even as she is urging him to stay with his fighting career.

Joe introduces Lorna to his family. When she understands what Joe's life has been and comprehends his genuine love of music, she switches her loyalties to persuade him to give up his fighting career. A gangster, however takes over the boy's contract for betting purposes, causing Lorna to be so disillusioned and disgusted that she agrees to marry Moody.

In the big fight, Joe's opponent is a young black prizefighter. Joe knocks him out with such a punch that he breaks his own hand and kills the black boy. Joe, overwhelmed by this tragedy, throws away his gloves and all thoughts of a career in the ring. In a well-played scene, he goes to the black fighter's father, who is mourning his dead son. The father tells him tearfully that he does not blame Joe for his boy's death. He had never wanted his son to fight, and he is sorry that it had to be a boy of Joe's caliber who killed him.

Lorna breaks with Moody and his way of life and comes to Joe. They are reunited, with his father's blessing. This ending was generally applauded by film critics. Even the few who were disappointed did admit that the double suicide of the boy and the girl in the play had been meaningless and that the movie reconciliation was done with taste and tenderness and did not signify a "tacked-on" happy ending.

Golden Boy was one of Columbia's all-time best films, and the fact that it gained only one Academy Award nomination—to Victor Young for Original Score—should not be held against it. It was released in 1939, frequently cited as the greatest year for the talking film, and was in competition with *Gone with the Wind*; *The Wizard of Oz*; *Wuthering Heights*; *Mr. Smith Goes to Washington*; *Goodbye, Mr. Chips*, and other films that are still favorites among both moviegoers and moviemakers. *Golden Boy* remains well-liked, however, and gains new admirers whenever it is revived, for it is one of Mamoulian's finest contributions to the cinema.

DeWitt Bodeen

GONE WITH THE WIND

Released: 1939
Production: David O. Selznick for Selznick International; released by Metro-Goldwyn-Mayer (AA)
Direction: Victor Fleming (AA)
Screenplay: Sidney Howard (AA); based on the novel of the same name by Margaret Mitchell
Cinematography: Ernest Haller and Ray Rennahan (AA)
Editing: Hal C. Kern and James E. Newcom (AA)
Production design: William Cameron Menzies (AA Special Award)
Art direction: Lyle Wheeler (AA)
Special effects: Jack Cosgrove
Costume design: Walter Plunkett
Music: Max Steiner
Running time: 219 minutes

Principal characters:
Scarlett O'Hara	Vivien Leigh (AA)
Rhett Butler	Clark Gable
Ashley Wilkes	Leslie Howard
Melanie Hamilton	Olivia de Havilland
Mammy	Hattie McDaniel (AA)
Gerald O'Hara	Thomas Mitchell
Ellen O'Hara	Barbara O'Neil

Gone with the Wind is unique among motion pictures. From the time of its initial release until 1980—forty-one years later—it was and is the most popular and profitable (in terms of uninflated dollars) film ever made. Margaret Mitchell's first and only published novel was a literary phenomenon. Shortly after its appearance in May of 1936, it became an unprecedented best seller, and it continues to enjoy impressive sales.

In July of 1936, independent producer David O. Selznick paid $50,000 for the screen rights to *Gone with the Wind*, the highest price paid to an unknown author for a first novel up to that time. The initial problem was to adapt the 1,037-page book to the screen. Selznick considered playwright and screenwriter Sidney Howard "a great constructionist" and hired him to write the script. Selznick believed strongly that "in connection with adaptations of books, the trick is to give the *illusion* of photographing a book. The only omissions from a successful work that are justified are omissions necessitated by length, censorship, or other practical considerations." To photograph the novel literally would, of course, have yielded a film that ran seven or eight hours or more; thus artful pruning, telescoping, and rearrangement of the story and characters were mandatory.

Gone with the Wind is set in the Old South, moves through the Civil War, and then on to the Reconstruction period. Its heroine, Scarlett O'Hara, who, as the book begins, lives on the plantation called Tara, loves idealistic and sensitive Ashley Wilkes of nearby Twelve Oaks. The young, high-tempered Scarlett spitefully accepts the impetuous proposal of Charles Hamilton, upset that his sister, shy and sedate Melanie, is going to marry Ashley. When Charles dies of pneumonia after going off to war and Atlanta is seized by the Northerners, Scarlett is poverty stricken. She is forced to struggle for her family and also for the aristocratic Ashley, who has not been trained to work with his hands. Yet, Scarlett is determined to keep Tara: she does manual labor, marries her sister's fiancé Frank Kennedy for his money, and, after his death in a Ku Klux Klan raid while avenging Scarlett's honor, marries Rhett Butler, the black sheep of a good family, a blockade runner and an unscrupulous profiteer. Scarlett has had a child by each of her husbands, but Bonnie, her child by Rhett, is killed in a riding accident. Because of Scarlett's lasting love for Ashley, Rhett finally deserts her, but she realizes at last, after the death of Melanie and the indifference of Ashley, that Rhett, similar in spirit to her, was her real love.

Before and during the filming of *Gone with the Wind*, various writers had a hand in working on the script. After Sidney Howard completed his draft, Oliver H. P. Garrett, Ben Hecht, Jo Swerling, John Van Druten, F. Scott Fitzgerald, John Balderston, and others worked from a few days to several weeks on the constantly changing script. Finally, Selznick went back to what was basically Howard's version, but he personally kept modifying it, even during shooting.

Remarkably, Margaret Mitchell's book remained relatively intact, or, more precisely, gave the illusion of remaining the same during its transfer to film. However, Scarlett's first two children were eliminated; Rhett's candid confessions of his blockade activities were minimized; the book's Belle Watling character was cleaned up; love scenes, particularly the so-called "Orchard Love Scene" or "paddock scene," were toned down; any mention of the Ku Klux Klan was dropped; Rhett's contempt for Ashley was not depicted; nor was the book's implication that Rhett began living with Belle Watling after Scarlett vowed to have no more children even remotely suggested in the film. Also, of course, some characters were dropped or fused and many scenes and events eliminated.

Because of complications in the areas of casting, screen adaptation, and distribution contracts, Selznick was unable to begin actual shooting with the principals until January, 1939, although the burning of the warehouse district in Atlanta was filmed on the night of December 10, 1938. Only four actors were ever considered for the role of Rhett Butler: Clark Gable, Gary Cooper, Errol Flynn, and Ronald Colman. Gable was under contract to M-G-M, and Coleman was mentioned only in the early weeks. Flynn was a relatively strong contender as far back as December, 1936. Warner Bros. had both Flynn and Bette Davis under exclusive contract, and for a while it looked as though Warners and Selznick were going to work out a package deal for Davis and Flynn that would also include Olivia de Havilland as Melanie, but the negotiations and interest bogged down. Gary Cooper was under contract to Samuel Goldwyn at the time, and discussions seemed to be getting nowhere. Besides, the public was almost unanimous in its choice of Clark Gable. Selznick finally worked out an arrangement to get Gable and partial backing from M-G-M in exchange for distribution rights and fifty percent of the profits. Since Margaret Mitchell wrote the bulk of *Gone with the Wind* between 1926 and 1929, the apocryphal story about her having Gable in mind for Rhett while she was writing the novel has no validity. Gable was an obscure stage actor in the late 1920's and did not start to come into his own in films until 1931 and 1932.

Whereas there was relative agreement on the ideal actor to portray Rhett Butler, there were considerable differences of opinion regarding the choice for Scarlett O'Hara. Incredibly, casting the part of Scarlett fascinated the world. Thirty-one women were actually screen tested—including a good many unknowns and amateurs—from September, 1936, until December, 1938. Among the better-known personalities tested were Tallulah Bankhead, Susan Hayward, Paulette Goddard, Anita Louise, Frances Dee, Lana Turner, Diana Barrymore, Jean Arthur, Joan Bennett, and a dark-horse contender, a British actress named Vivien Leigh. Selznick had always favored finding a relative newcomer for the role, someone fresh who would not be identified with previous performances. Other well-known actresses who were high in the running at one time or another, but who for various reasons did not test, include Margaret Sullavan, Miriam Hopkins, Joan Crawford, Norma Shearer, Loretta Young, and Katharine Hepburn. In November, 1938, Selznick stated in a memo that Hepburn has "yet to demonstrate that she possesses the sex qualities which are probably the most important of all the many requisites of Scarlett." At one point Paulette Goddard was about to be signed for the part, but she could not produce a license proving that she and Charlie Chaplin were married. Selznick was afraid of negative public opinion, since she and Chaplin had been living together for quite some time. By December 12, 1938, the choice had narrowed down to Paulette Goddard, Jean Arthur, Joan Bennett, and Vivien Leigh; shortly thereafter Vivien Leigh signed a contract to play the role.

For the part of Ashley, Leslie Howard had been considered early, but Selznick's main concern was that he was considerably older than the young man in his twenties depicted in the novel. Melvyn Douglas gave what Selznick described as "the first intelligent reading of Ashley we've had, but I think he's entirely wrong in type." Regarding Ray Milland, Selznick stated that he was "very definitely a sensitive actor, possessing the enormous attractiveness and at the same time the weakness that are the requirements of Ashley." Before signing Leslie Howard for the role, Selznick had also considered Robert Young, Douglas Fairbanks, Jr., Jeffrey Lynn, and Lew Ayres.

Olivia de Havilland became the first choice for the role of Melanie with other possibilities being Janet Gaynor, Dorothy Jordan, Andrea Leeds, and Julie Haydon. Although Warner Bros. was initially unwilling to loan her to Selznick, they finally relented in late 1938. Interestingly, neither Gable nor Howard wanted to be in the film, and only after much coaxing, persuading, and money did they relent. Gable felt he could never live up to the public's advance expectations of the role, and he was not drawn to the character or the period. Leslie Howard had no desire to play yet another weak and sensitive soul and did not even bother to read the novel.

Principal cinematography began on January 26, 1939, under George Cukor's direction. Immediately there were problems. Within two-and-a-half weeks Cukor was off the picture. The exact circumstances behind his exit are not totally clear. Selznick was quoted in 1947 as saying: "We couldn't see eye to eye on anything. I felt that while Cukor was simply unbeatable in directing intimate scenes of the Scarlett O'Hara story, he lacked the big feel, the scope, the breadth of the production." Speculation in the industry at the time centered about M-G-M being dissatisfied with the speed at which the scenes were being photographed, Cukor objecting to revisions of Sidney Howard's script, changes in the dialogue by Selznick being delivered on the set continuously, and Clark Gable's unhappiness over Cukor's supposed preoccupation and fastidiousness with the characters portrayed by Leigh and de Havilland.

The day following Cukor's exit, Victor Fleming, a good friend of Gable, was taken off the completion of *The Wizard of Oz* (1939) at M-G-M and signed to direct *Gone with the Wind*. Fleming was the antithesis of Cukor, and the leading ladies were unhappy. There were tensions and disagreements throughout the production. At one point Fleming collapsed and veteran Sam Wood replaced him. When Fleming returned, Selznick kept both directors—in addition to second unit directors—shooting different scenes concurrently. This was possible due to William Cameron Menzies' carefully detailed production design. Finally, following five months of arduous and complicated filming, the picture was finished.

After several more months of editing, effects cinematography, some retakes, and scoring, *Gone with the Wind* had its world premiere in Atlanta, Georgia, on December 15, 1939. Its success was even greater than anyone had anticipated. In addition to being voted the Best Picture of 1939 by the Academy of Motion Picture Arts and Sciences, *Gone with the Wind* was the unprecedented recipient of nine other Oscars, including Best Actress, Best Director, Best Screenplay, and the Irving G. Thalberg Memorial Award for consistent excellence of production, which went to the producer David O. Selznick. Selznick, without question, was the dominant force behind *Gone with the Wind*. He was involved in every single detail of the film, and in every sense of the word it is primarily his film—not a committee film, not a director's film, and not a star's film, but a spectacular example of a creative producer's work.

When finally shown in Europe after World War II, *Gone with the Wind* had a tremendous impact since it represented for the French a story about surviving a defeat, and Japan has been particularly addicted to the picture over the years. Extraordinarily successul full-scale theatrical reissues in America in 1947, 1954, 1961, and 1967 followed. For the 1967 run it was blown up optically to "the splendor of 70mm wide screen and full stereophonic sound." The splendor was dubious; *Gone with the Wind* is at its best in the format originally photographed and shown, and that format was retained for its network television debut on NBC in November, 1976, where it promptly drew the largest audience of any program shown on one network in television's history. In 1977, from a list of more than one thousand entries, *Gone with the Wind* was voted by members of the American Film Institute the greatest film made in the United States, with *Citizen Kane* (1941) and *Casablanca* (1942) placing second and third in the poll.

Whether or not it is "the greatest" film, *Gone with the Wind* is certainly the most enduring and endearing. Very few motion pictures have been able continuously to captivate the mass audience in theaters and on television over the decades. The film represents the high-water mark and quintessence of the big super-attraction of Hollywood's golden age. The mosaic is composed of an "epic" narrative, varied and rounded characters enduring overwhelming obstacles, family crises, unrequited and idealized love stories, war, turmoil, nostalgia, and Technicolor.

Many people are still extremely drawn to the essentially soap opera aspects of some of the material. This is particularly true of events which take place during the last quarter of the film, where, because of the need to telescope drastically a great many chapters of the book, tragedy and climax seem to pour forth without relief—Scarlett's miscarriage, Bonnie's death, Melanie's death, and Rhett's abandonment of Scarlett. Although Selznick's production is characteristically meticulous, some of the settings are highly romanticized and have, in many instances, a picture postcard quality, particularly the settings for Twelve Oaks.

The remarkable and enduring performance of Viven Leigh makes every scene in which she appears come alive, bringing dimension and magnetism to the role of Scarlett, along with beauty, tenacity, fire, humor, intelligence, and, above all, great charm. Gable, despite his fears, superimposes his disarming screen presence and personality on the novelist's Rhett Butler for a colorful and believable blend. Leslie Howard's Ashley is exactly right, albeit he is too old for the character; and Olivia de Havilland's performance underlines, perhaps a shade too much, the inherent sweet and altruistic characteristics of Melanie.

There is much in terms of characterization with which audiences can or wish to identify. Scarlett is both self-centered and realistic. She can stand on her own; she is resourceful, aggressive, passionate, and realizes too late that she has loved the wrong man far too long. Rhett is the personification of the free spirit who flouts public opinion, knows what he wants, and goes after it. He is a man's man and a lover: shrewd, realistic, and earthy, but also capable of tenderness, compassion, and tears.

To further dissect and analyze the myriad ingredients that have made *Gone with the Wind* the most popular film over the decades would be useless. It is sufficient to state that it has that rare quality of still being able to capture the imagination of a great many people. That is more than we can expect and more than we receive from most films.

Rudy Behlmer

GOODBYE COLUMBUS

Released: 1969
Production: Stanley R. Jaffe for Paramount
Direction: Larry Peerce
Screenplay: Arnold Schulman; based on the novella of the same name by
  Philip Roth
Cinematography: Gerald Hirschfeld
Editing: Ralph Rosenblum
Running time: 105 minutes

Principal characters:
Neil Klugman .... Richard Benjamin
Brenda Patimkin .... Ali MacGraw
Mr. Patimkin .... Jack Klugman
Mrs. Patimkin .... Nan Martin
Ron Patimkin .... Michael Meyers

Philip Roth's award-winning 1959 novella, *Goodbye, Columbus*, is a bittersweet tale of a summer romance between a sensitive young man and a
pampered, wealthy, sexually aware girl. Both partners are Jewish, and, in
the uncertain, hyperactive world of Philip Roth's America, both hold onto
each other for a kind of security. While Neil Klugman (Richard Benjamin)
believes in poetry, honest sex, and sincere *angst*, Brenda Patimkin (Ali
MacGraw) devotes her attention to sex, platitudes, and the comfort of her
father's enormous home in Westchester. It all fails in the end: Neil learns that
Brenda does not have much going for her despite her lithe body, and he will,
one assumes, value the balmy summer experience for what it was worth. The
novella is about values clashing amid a dissipated ethnic tradition of the late
1950's. The film translation of Roth's story has been updated to 1969 by
director Larry Peerce.

The sun is out every day at the country club where Neil and Brenda first
meet; the summer greenery of the richly endowed home of Mr. Patimkin
(Jack Klugman) shimmers with inviting warmth; there is no intrusion by a
war in Vietnam or civil disturbances. All is quiet and peaceful; and while
everybody else eats lots of fruit and fried chicken at the Patimkin house, Neil
and Brenda meet, slip away, and make love in various places. MacGraw does
a fine job of convincing one that spoiled late adolescents who attend Radcliffe
are not meant to be cherished by spiritually aware young men such as Neil,
who, more than anything else, seek sex and love and meaning in a reasonably
sterile suburban world. The film does a relatively good job of conveying the
substance of Neil's and Brenda's awkward relationship. The camera records
Richard Benjamin's various facial expressions, which transparently reflect his
feelings: his throat pulses with aroused desire when he first encounters the

beautiful Brenda in the pool at the country club. He mumbles when he just does not know what to say to this creature who so excites him.

Neil's world is portrayed in an overly stereotyped way; it includes a protective Jewish family whose mutterings about jobs and girls and chicken soup become tedious and distracting. However, the dialogue between Neil and his assorted relatives, although occasionally strained and ridden with clichés, does point out just how different Neil is from Brenda. He has attended a city college in New Jersey and served an unheroic term as a private in the army; his current vocation places him in a library in the city. He has to deal with his aunt and uncle, as well as with his status-conscious cousin who sits around the country club pool, her skin peeling away like red paint while she tries to read *War and Peace*. Neil comes from a different world, but he is, the audience is reminded, a boy with promise.

Brenda knows a life of overabundance, living in a suburban mansion, wearing fur coats, and enjoying frequent buying trips to Bloomingdale's. Her family's wealth, which comes from her father's plumbing supply business, has transformed the family. The elder son, Ron (Michael Meyers), is a nice guy, a dumb former jock who spent his glory years on Ohio State's basketball court; the youngest daughter is her father's pet, and is extremely spoiled. The mother spends most of her time wrapped up in mudpacks, tissue paper, and eyeshadow.

All of these characters are literally thrown together for the audience. The director's intent was to filter all of this subject matter through Neil's expanding perspective. Although the real strength of Roth's story lies in Neil's first-person narration, the film changes the structure. The audience is shown everything, and it is occasionally hard to determine just what Neil is seeing and feeling. There are, for example, several scenes when Neil is not present, moments when the camera focuses on Brenda and her father at the lavish wedding of Brenda's brother. It is, to be sure, a tender moment between father and daughter; both realize, perhaps for the first time, that they know very little about each other. The father wants his daughter to be the princess she believes she is, but the scene's sadness revolves around his real ignorance of her life (in this case, the furtive and passionate relationship between Neil and Brenda).

At the same time, however, the film succeeds in its attempt to introduce some marvelous characters caught up in the materialism of American life. In the case of the Patimkin family, abundance leads to a sense of fear that their recently acquired wealth will crumble. Mr. Patimkin yearns for everything to remain the same. He sweats and grimaces over his son's fate (always, it seems, to be employed as a lackey at the plumbing supply store), his wife's fears about her daughter's marital prospects with an unpromising boy like Neil, and his own ability to preserve and protect his pampered flock.

When *Goodbye Columbus* strays from Neil's point of view, therefore, the audience is presented with a portrait of the upper middle class and, specifically, the descendants of poorer people from New York's Lower East Side. This is certainly what Roth intended his readers to see while judging the perceptions of Neil as he makes his way through the country clubs, the ostentatious wedding, and the mind of a materialistic girl. In the short span of one summer, Neil Klugman is introduced to a dream girl who in the end is as vacuous and selfish as the head librarian at Neil's reference desk at the library. Even as the librarian, his small eyes screwed up with dislike and fear of a small black child who wants to look at the "big pictures" in a book of Paul Gaugin's paintings in the library's art collection, Brenda Patimkin is fearful of real and honest values. Although one may wish to dismiss the deftly placed clichés in the script as attempts to inject a few laughs at the expense of the Patimkin family and everything it represents, *Goodbye Columbus* is a well-played critique of romance, love, and sexual attitudes shaped by the harsher dictates of a material culture.

Lawrence J. Rudner

GOODBYE, MR. CHIPS

Released: 1939
Production: Victor Saville for Metro-Goldwyn-Mayer British Studios
Direction: Sam Wood
Screenplay: R. C. Sherriff, Claudine West, and Eric Maschwitz; based on the
  novel of the same name by James Hilton
Cinematography: Freddie A. Young
Editing: Charles Frend
Running time: 110 minutes

> *Principal characters:*
> Mr. Chips .... Robert Donat (AA)
> Katherine Ellis .... Greer Garson
> John Colley/Peter Colley I/Peter Colley II/
> Peter Colley III .... Terry Kilburn
> Peter Colley (younger) .... John Mills
> Max Staefel .... Paul Henreid
> Flora .... Judith Furse

To American audiences, the impact of the film *Goodbye, Mr. Chips* may
be lessened by ignorance of the social importance of the complex British
public school system. This first major screen chronicle of the venerable tradition illuminates the narrow, ordered existence of boys and schoolmasters
during a time when such private, elitist education was revered and fashionable. James Hilton drew upon his experience with senior master of classics,
William H. Balgarnie, of the Leys School, Cambridge, for his story of the
priggish young pedagogue who becomes a beloved old gentleman at the
Brookfield School over a sixty-three-year period. (Balgarnie died at age
eighty-two in Wales in 1951.)

Victor Saville's sentimental film re-created Hilton's setting at Repton
School, founded in 1557. During summer holiday, students and faculty returned to the school to assist in the filmmaking, volunteering their time and
hard work as a public service. The money paid for the use of the school was
donated to the Repton scholarship fund at Oxford University. The exquisite
Anglican Gothic architecture provided the suitably intimidating atmosphere
in which to set a nervous young classics scholar beginning his career as schoolmaster to a pack of boisterous lower-school boys.

Unfortunately, the tale unfolds as a flashback. We glimpse the doddering
eccentric Mr. Chipping (Robert Donat) too soon and guess the outcome of
the story when his stuffy younger self is first introduced. The well-worn device
of the old man nodding off in front of the fire while reminiscing takes us back
in time to see the youthful Mr. Chipping about to board the train for his first
trip to Brookfield. The story and no doubt the boys age him quickly, easing

the stiffness and reserve with which Mr. Chipping first comports himself. The Academy of Motion Picture Arts and Sciences found Donat's portrayal of this transition so skillful that he was awarded the Oscar for Best Actor of 1939.

The humiliating bedlam which ensues during his first day in class does not shake Mr. Chipping's resolve to become headmaster of Brookfield. His humorless teaching methods and disregard for cricket matches earn him the respect but not the admiration of his pupils. His austerity is tempered by earnest but failed attempts at camaraderie. We are fully sympathetic to the deeply drawn character so caught up in the proprieties of life that his feeble efforts at amiability come to nothing. He is crushed to learn that the housemastership which was his due has gone to another not in possession of "his gift for getting work out of the boys."

The dismayed Mr. Chipping is cajoled by an associate, Max Staefel (Paul von Hernreid, later Paul Henreid), into accompanying him on a walking tour of the Tyrol. Chipping characteristically resists such self-indulgence during the summer holiday but in the end relents. As a result—in the only artificially contrived turn of the story—he meets spunky Katherine Ellis (Greer Garson) on a lofty peak during one of his solitary climbing tours. In her first screen appearance, Garson is arrestingly pretty if not rather too perfect looking for just having scaled a mountain. Her beauty and the mountain air bring Mr. Chipping out of himself, and the two get along very well.

That evening at the chalet, in the company of Max, Katherine, and her companion Flora (Judith Furse), shyness again consumes Chipping, and he retires to pass the evening on the balcony of his room. He later hears Katherine on the adjoining balcony rhapsodizing to Flora about the delightfully old-fashioned Mr. Chipping whom she fears she will never see again. A series of mishaps prevent their reunion until they meet by chance on the Danube boat as it docks in Vienna.

It requires of Katherine much restrained and ladylike humoring to penetrate Chipping's hard shell. With the aid of Viennese waltzes she succeeds, and the two whirl away the loveliest evening of their lives, with Flora and Max conveniently off dancing together themselves. Bidding good-bye at the train the next morning, Katherine kisses Chipping farewell, thus sealing their fate; such a kiss means she must marry him now, shouts a breathless Chipping to the departing coach. Max catches up with the wide-eyed schoolmaster, reassuring him that Katherine and Flora have been planning the details of the wedding for weeks now.

In the Brookfield teachers' common room, the faculty is amused to read the newspaper account of Chipping's marriage, but they are subsequently astounded to be confronted by the beauty of his new wife. Katherine thoroughly charms them with her warmth but startles them by affectionately calling her husband Chips. As Mrs. Chips, she also captivates the boys, particularly at the Sunday afternoon teas she initiates for them in the Chips's parlor. Quite in spite of himself, Mr. Chips is soon able to banter with his young charges and even joke in Latin during class. The long-sought house-mastership soon comes his way with only the goal of headmaster remaining. After a brief year together, Katherine dies in childbirth, as does her infant. Aghast, Chips presides at class that day in one of the most moving scenes in film.

The passage of time is cleverly implied by bits of conversation about news events exchanged by an unending procession of boys. Much older, for we have traversed Victorian, Edwardian, and Georgian history, Chips has become an eccentric, white-haired gentleman who has continued to cast off his stuffy ways in tribute to Katherine. Now a beloved relic, the boys will not permit him to retire, in spite of the commands of the new headmaster who is bent on modernization. Contrary to Katherine's conviction, Mr. Chips has not become headmaster, a reality to which he has peacefully resigned himself.

Five years later, a biscuit box to which each boy has contributed without coercion is presented to Chips in commemoration of his well deserved retirement. However, the demands of World War I soon deplete the Brookfield faculty, and Chips is called out of retirement to head the school. With a portrait of Katherine tucked under his arm, he at last enters the headmaster's office. Age has not taken its toll on the genial man's mind or mettle. He canes a lesson in respect into a badly misinformed young man with as much well-intentioned vigor as he had ever mustered. And while bombs drop about the school, he calmly hears the pupils' Latin recitations in a classroom shrouded in blackout curtains. It is a sad day in chapel when Chips reads Brookfield's war losses, particularly the death of Peter Colley (Terry Kilburn), whose father and grandfather Chips had fondly taught and caned and whose wife and son he looked after in the lieutenant's absence.

Now that the war is over, Chips passes his retirement days occasionally serving tea and buns to former students. He is visited one evening by a young man whom he instantly recognizes as yet another Colley (John Mills), the son of the slain elder Colley. The recurrence of four Colley progeny throughout the film serves to unify the story and evoke the tradition of continuing family and school ties. In Chips's last sleep, little Peter Colley, III bids "Goodbye, Mr. Chips" amid a dreamy succession of passing boys of all ages and from all eras, each of whom Chips claims as one of his own.

Directed by Sam Wood, who has many college pictures to his credit, including the Mickey Rooney features, the film explores the unchanging nature of youth. At times the boys' chaotic misbehavior is too lengthy in contrast to the somewhat sentimental scenes involving Mr. and Mrs. Chipping. Greer Garson was on the screen too briefly; she lent the slow-paced, nostalgic story a sorely missed radiance.

Goodbye, Mr. Chips provided great revenue for M-G-M British. In addition to the Best Actor Award, it received several other Academy nominations despite the stiff competition of *Gone with the Wind*. An excellent study of traditional English school life spanning the years from 1870 to 1933, the film was successfully remade as a musical in 1969 starring Petula Clark and Peter O'Toole. The latter version proved its timeless appeal to American and British audiences and its innate ability to bring tears to the eyes of audiences even today.

Nancy S. Kinney

THE GRADUATE

Released: 1967
Production: Lawrence Turman for Embassy Pictures
Direction: Mike Nichols (AA)
Screenplay: Calder Willingham and Buck Henry; based on the novel of the same name by Charles Webb
Cinematography: Robert Surtees
Editing: Sam O'Steen
Running time: 105 minutes

Principal characters:
Benjamin Braddock .... Dustin Hoffman
Mrs. Robinson .... Anne Bancroft
Elaine Robinson .... Katharine Ross
Mr. Braddock .... William Daniels
Mrs. Braddock .... Elizabeth Wilson

The Graduate is one of the most important films of the late 1960's. Through it, Hollywood discovered that the "misunderstood youth" of years past, from the Holden Caulfields to the James Deans, were no longer teenagers. Alienation had gone to college, and for much of the next decade, those who made films about youth in America concerned themselves with the problems and priorities of men and women between the ages of twenty and thirty. This is not to suggest that *The Graduate* was simply another kind of exploitation movie. Although critics were by no means unanimous, the film and its principals were widely acclaimed. Director Mike Nichols was hailed as a major new talent in American film; Anne Bancroft was justifiably lauded for her portrayal of the neurotic seductress, Mrs. Robinson; and, perhaps most importantly, Dustin Hoffman's illustrious film career was launched by his stunning performance as Benjamin Braddock—the graduate of the film's title.

Benjamin Braddock (Dustin Hoffman) is an upper-middle-class young man from Southern California who has just graduated from an Eastern college, and is not yet ready to face adult life, which he regards as a game with rules that do no make much sense. The film opens with a close-up of Benjamin's impassive face (Nichols uses these close-ups continually throughout the first part of the film); his blank expression mirrors his feeling of emptiness while Paul Simon and Art Garfunkel's "The Sounds of Silence" plays on the sound track, reinforcing the impression of Benjamin's alienation from his surroundings.

This alienation carries over into Benjamin's family life. His parents (William Daniels and Elizabeth Wilson) have arranged a welcome home party for him, inviting all of their own friends rather than his. Their intentions are not malign; they simply want to show off a son of whom they are justifiably proud, but Benjamin wants no part of the occasion. He is worried about his future, and wants to be alone with his thoughts. With his parents insisting that he put in an appearance, however, Benjamin runs the gauntlet of inane small talk, including one guest's now-famous remark that the future lies in "plastic."

Unable to tolerate any more, Benjamin retires from the party to his bedroom, where he is followed by Mrs. Robinson (Anne Bancroft), the wife of his father's business partner. Although Benjamin would rather be alone, Mrs. Robinson insists that he take her home, and he reluctantly agrees to do so. Just as reluctantly, he complies with her request that he accompany her inside the house, have a drink, and remain with her until her husband returns. Mrs. Robinson's conversation grows increasingly intimate, which thoroughly flusters Benjamin, and she plays on his confusion. Alternately seductive and maternally imperious, she lures him up to her daughter's bedroom, where she begins to disrobe. Significantly, we see Mrs. Robinson's nudity reflected in the glass which covers her daughter's picture, foreshadowing the role that the two women will play in the film. Benjamin is terrified, but Mrs. Robinson remains calm, offering herself to him, now or at any later time. Benjamin rushes down the stairs, only to meet Mr. Robinson (Murray Hamilton), who, while Benjamin literally whimpers in terror, proceeds to administer a fatherly chat. His advice is that Benjamin should sow a few wild oats.

The scene shifts to the Braddock house on the occasion of Benjamin's twenty-first birthday. As usual, his parents have thrown a party for him, again inviting only their own friends, and Benjamin is called upon to perform for them—in this case, to model his new scuba gear. Completely dressed in it, he moves ponderously through the crowd to the pool, where he jumps in and sinks gratefully to the bottom in peace. Nichols reinforces the adsurdity of the scene by shooting it entirely from Benjamin's perspective—through the goggles of his diving suit.

Time passes, and Mrs. Robinson's offer of seduction begins to look more attractive to Benjamin. At once eager and apologetic, he calls her, and she agrees to meet him in the bar at the Taft Hotel. Under her patient prodding, Benjamin agrees to get a room, thoroughly embarrassing himself in the process since he is certain that the desk clerk knows what he is about to do. In the room, Mrs. Robinson is calm and almost businesslike, which further aggravates Benjamin's case of nerves. He bangs his head against the wall in frustration, and decides to end the affair before it begins. Mrs. Robinson defeats this resolve by accusing him of being a virgin. Outraged, he defends his virility by consummating the liaison.

The summer passes with Benjamin spending most of his time diving into his parents' pool or into bed with Mrs. Robinson. Nichols shoots this sequence in a series of montages that begin and end with the now-familiar close-up of Benjamin's blank stare against a white background—alternately a pillow in the Taft Hotel and an inflatable rubber raft in his parents' pool. The effect is intentionally disorienting, and suggests that both pursuits are as empty of meaning as the expression on Benjamin's face, while the sound track under-lines this impression with a reprise of "The Sounds of Silence."

Thus far in the film, Benjamin has never really talked to anyone. He has merely been spoken to; and he has responded in as perfunctory a way as possible. His intimacy with Mrs. Robinson has never gone beyond the phys-ical, as evidenced by the fact that he never calls her by her first name, which indeed is never learned throughout the film. Now, however, he feels a need for communication, and his attempts to initiate a conversation with the more carnally inclined Mrs. Robinson result in some of the film's funniest moments. Once the conversation starts, however, it focuses on the Robinsons' marriage and their daughter Elaine (Katharine Ross). This sets the stage for the second, more serious part of the film.

Although Mrs. Robinson is adamantly opposed to Benjamin's dating Elaine, and although Benjamin is also unenthusiastic about the prospect of such an encounter, he finally gives in to the matchmaking pressure from his parents and Mr. Robinson, and agrees to take Elaine out one time. As the evening begins, Benjamin is deliberately offensive, driving recklessly and taking Elaine to a tawdry strip joint. Humiliated, Elaine runs away in tears, while Benjamin, realizing he is fond of the girl, pursues her, calms her down, and kisses her. In a conversation in which he shows genuine feeling for the first time in the film, he explains that he has been confused and worried about his future. Without naming Mrs. Robinson, he tells Elaine of an unsatisfactory relationship that he has been having with an older woman. She seems to sympathize, and they spend the rest of the evening happily, their affection for each other grows, and Elaine agrees to see Benjamin the next day.

When Benjamin arrives at the Robinsons' house the next day, however, a furious Mrs. Robinson meets him before he can get out of his car and threatens to reveal their affair if he continues to show any interest in Elaine. Benjamin rushes into the house and attempts to talk to Elaine, with Mrs. Robinson in hot pursuit. Elaine, seeing them together, realizes that her mother is the older woman with whom Benjamin is having an affair, and refuses to speak to him. Up to this point, the film's emphasis has been on humor; however, when Benjamin finds his true love, the film shifts gears perceptibly. Nichols aban-dons most of his broad satiric swipes at suburbia and the scene shifts from Los Angeles to Berkeley, where Elaine has gone back to school. In short, the film, though it never ceases to be funny, becomes more earnest in its later scenes.

Benjamin follows Elaine to Berkeley, tracks her around campus, and finally confronts her with his presence, only to discover that she has a buttoned-down, pipe-smoking fiancé named Carl Smith. Although Elaine is uneasy in Benjamin's presence, she is not sufficiently angry to order him away. Confused by her feelings for Benjamin, Elaine appears one day in his room and demands an explanation for his actions with her mother. He tells Elaine that he loves her. In their conversation it is divulged that Mrs. Robinson has told her daughter that Benjamin raped her; reluctantly, however, she believes him when he tells her the true story. As the days pass, although Elaine declines to commit herself to marriage with Benjamin she seems to be moving in that direction.

Matters soon come to a head in the Robinson family, however. Mr. Robinson is divorcing his wife, and Elaine, without Benjamin's knowledge, has left school to marry Carl Smith. When he finds out that she is gone, he embarks on a frantic Berkeley to Los Angeles to Berkeley to Santa Barbara drive to find her. His car runs out of gas a few blocks from the church where the wedding is in progress. Running into the church, Benjamin finds the ceremony just completed. Torn between Benjamin on the one hand and her parents and new husband on the other, Elaine finally chooses Benjamin, and the couple fight their way through the crowd in the church, with Benjamin swinging a large cross, in a bit of heavy-handed symbolism, to clear the path and then to bar the door once they are outside. Benjamin and Elaine run to a conveniently departing bus, where they rush to the back amid puzzled looks from their fellow passengers. The pair is strangely silent at this climactic moment, and the film ends much as it began—with "The Sounds of Silence" on the sound track, and a close-up of Benjamin staring wordlessly ahead. This time, however, he is grinning broadly.

Much of the effectiveness of the film lies in the masterful work of the principal actors, all three of whom won Academy Award nominations for their work. Katharine Ross as Elaine brings dimension to a role that could easily have been played as just another "girl next door" stereotype. Anne Bancroft is outstanding as the predatory Mrs. Robinson, who, of the three major characters in the film, is the least sympathetic. Bancroft, however, conveys not only her character's bored cynicism and self-loathing, but her wit as well. Despite her calm expression, the twinkle in her eye when she first encounters Benjamin in the bar of the Taft Hotel indicates that she finds Benjamin's discomfiture as amusing as the audience does. The best acting in the film, however, is the work of Dustin Hoffman. Benjamin is the only character that is required to change during the course of the film. A very passive young man until he meets and falls in love with Elaine, he erupts into a frenzy of activity during the second half of the film. Whether he is squirming with embarrassment at one of his parents' parties or frantically swinging the cross at Elaine's wedding, Hoffman is utterly convincing. His performance is the cohesive element that bonds the two parts of the film and keeps it coherent; it captured the imagination of a generation, and propelled Hoffman to instant stardom in his first screen role.

For all its success, however, *The Graduate* is not a perfect film. Mike Nichols goes for some too-easy laughs at the expense of the plastic Los Angeles suburbanites; and, more importantly, he changes the tone of the film too abruptly when the scene shifts from Los Angeles to Berkeley. His mistakes are ones born of enthusiasm, however, and can be excused. Although *The Graduate* failed to win the Academy Award for Best Picture, Nichols did win the Award for Best Director.

The Graduate was a seminal film in that some of Nichols' innovations, such as the focus on the new, older youth culture, and the use of pop/rock music on the sound track as commentary on the action, were so successful that they have now become commonplace. *The Graduate* is truly a landmark in American cinema.

Robert Mitchell

GRAND HOTEL

Released: 1932
Production: Irving Thalberg for Metro-Goldwyn-Mayer (AA)
Direction: Edmund Goulding
Screenplay: William A. Drake; based on the novel and play *Menschen im Hotel* by Vicki Baum
Cinematography: William Daniels
Editing: Blanche Sewell
Running time: 115 minutes

Principal characters:
Grusinskaya .... Greta Garbo
Baron Felix von Geigern .... John Barrymore
Flaemmchen .... Joan Crawford
Preysing .... Wallace Beery
Otto Kringelein .... Lionel Barrymore
Dr. Otternschlag .... Lewis Stone
Senf .... Jean Hersholt

Grand Hotel was the precursor of many films in which characters from all walks of life are thrown together by chance in the same hostelry, airplane, oceanliner, storm-swept island, or other location removed from the rest of civilization. The so-called disaster film of the 1970's can trace much of its origins to this film. Like many of its successors in the multistory, multicharacter genre, *Grand Hotel* was adapted from a best-selling novel. Vicki Baum's book, and later play, *Menschen im Hotel*, was a familiar story to audiences when it was brought to the screen in 1932. In order to bring an immediate and fresh impact to the screen, director Edmund Goulding opened the film with shots of a vast switchboard and busy operators which set the tone and pace for *Grand Hotel*. The feeling of fast-moving and varied action was further reinforced by the magnificent setting of a multileveled lobby which resembled a towering beehive. For the next two hours, the audience sees a constant intermingling of characters and stories which were foreshadowed in the opening shots.

The characters are quickly introduced to enable the audience to become immediately enmeshed in the individual stories. Greta Garbo plays Grusinskaya, an *émigré* ballerina for whom everything since the fall of St. Petersburg seems "threadbare" and lonely until she meets Baron Felix von Geigern (John Barrymore), who brings her out of her cocoon. The Baron is really an erstwhile aristocrat-turned-jewel thief who goes about his career of crime with a heart of gold that will not stoop to petty maliciousness. At one point he steals a wallet belonging to Otto Kringelein (Lionel Barrymore), but when he hears the old man bemoaning his loss, the Baron somehow "finds" the lost billfold. Kringelein is the meek and musty bookkeeper whose life has been spent working with figures and eking out an existence. Early in the film it is revealed that he is going to die, and it is his impending death that brings him to a plush suite in the hotel where he has decided to live what is left of his life the way the "other half" does. Wallace Beery plays Preysing, an overbearing industrialist who is on the verge of bankruptcy but who cashed out on his humanity years ago. Joan Crawford plays Flaemmchen, his stenographer of questionable repute, who at last finds a friend and protector in the dying Kringelein. These are the main characters around whom the film revolves but there is also the added equivalent of the Greek chorus in the person of the world-weary Dr. Otternschlag, wonderfully enacted by Lewis Stone. It is his famous line that is the epithet of the hotel: "people coming, people going—always coming and going—and nothing ever happens."

In some ways, that remark is an accurate observation reflecting not only the subplots within the main story line but also the main plot itself; yet in other ways, it is a statement that seems to deny the throbbing life within the hotel. First, it is true that there is tremendous hustle and bustle; but although much emotion is expended in the scenes, the characters—with the possible exception of Kringelein—do not often strike a responsive chord of truth in the audience. There are interesting and sometimes enchanting incidents, but for the most part they are nothing more than the inconsequential business of vain, unlikable people.

As the Baron, Barrymore does an exceptional job of creating a charming and engaging larcenist and lifting him out of the ranks of what is essentially an ordinary leading-man role; but played by someone of less stature and skill, the Baron could have come across as silly. The character of the ballerina Grusinskaya borders on the absurd, and again, it is only because of Garbo's performance that she does not become grotesquely comical; Garbo instills her with a sprinkling of humor that saves the characterization. Wallace Beery makes the swaggering businessman Preysing appropriately mean and despicable; yet, because we are not shown any redeeming quality in the character's makeup, he is easy to dismiss as completely unreal and, therefore, not truly threatening. As his secretary and doxy, Joan Crawford plays a woman whose brash exterior only hides an insecure personality.

It is Lionel Barrymore's portrait of Kringelein, however, that gives an essentially superficial movie an element of depth and sensitivity. His interpretation of the abject and querulous clerk who blossoms amid the luxurious surroundings and companionship of the huge hotel is magnificent. He displays the complex mixture of comedy and tragedy abiding in everyone; and when he and Crawford board a train together for Paris and whatever new adventures they can find together, the audience wishes the best for them. Lionel Barrymore won more acclaim for this role than any other; he was so convincing that in his last scene the tears Crawford shed—not called for in the script—

were the actress' natural reaction to his moving performance.

For its time, *Grand Hotel* is technically impressive. From the sweeping opening shots of the switchboard and the expansive marble-floored lobby to the intimate close-ups in the private rooms, the film is rich in texture and tone. Interestingly, *Grand Hotel* won the Academy Award for Best Picture, but received no other awards or nominations. The fact that neither actors, director, nor technical staff were acknowledged for their contributions to what was considered a landmark picture caused considerable commotion. In fact, this was the only such case in the more than fifty-year history of the Motion Picture Academy.

Because the film contained such a large number of prominent actors, the press was eager to play up what they termed "the Battle of the Stars" during production. One such instance involved John Barrymore, who was purportedly unbearably demanding when it came to such things as lighting. According to Hollis Alpert, author of *The Barrymores*, however, Barrymore only gave a witty response to the lighting director's question about how he wished to appear: "I'm a fifty-year-old man and I want you to make me look like Jackie Cooper's grandson." (Cooper, of course, at the time, was merely a child.) Most authoritative sources agree that, in reality, all the stars involved in *Grand Hotel* made an extra effort to accommodate one another, despite publicity to the contrary.

Grand Hotel was an attempt by M-G-M to attract a larger profit at the box office by putting more established stars in a single film. This practice was to go in and out of fashion in the following decades. One other film which attempted to do the same thing was M-G-M's own remake of *Grand Hotel* entitled *Weekend at the Waldorf* (1945), which boasted such top box-office attractions as Lana Turner and Van Johnson, but it was unable to equal the impact of the original version.

Juliette Friedgen

THE GRAPES OF WRATH

Released: 1940
Production: Darryl F. Zanuck for Twentieth Century-Fox
Direction: John Ford (AA)
Screenplay: Nunnally Johnson; based on the novel of the same name by John
  Steinbeck
Cinematography: Gregg Toland
Editing: Robert Simpson
Running time: 128 minutes

Principal characters:

Tom Joad	Henry Fonda
Ma Joad	Jane Darwell (AA)
Pa Joad	Russell Simpson
Grandpa Joad	Charley Grapewin
Rosasharn	Dorris Bowdon
Casy	John Carradine
Muley	John Qualen

The Grapes of Wrath, based on John Steinbeck's widely read novel about
the plight of migrant workers during the Great Depression, is director John
Ford's most famous work. It bears the characteristic stamp of many of his
classic films; it is the story of a hapless society told with strong visual narrative
technique. In this case, the microcosm of migrant workers is represented by
a single family, the Joads from Oklahoma.

The film opens with the view of a small figure walking down the road
against an expansive Oklahoma landscape. It is Tom Joad (Henry Fonda),
recently paroled from prison. He is returning after four years to the home
of his family, who are tenant farmers. Things have changed during his absence.
The dust bowl conditions, combined with the advent of mechanized farming,
have caused their ruthless landlords to force the Joads, as well as hundreds
of their neighbors, off their lands. Tom rejoins his family just as they are
preparing to leave for California, where handbills have proclaimed that there
is plenty of work harvesting fruits and vegetables. The Joads—Tom, Ma (Jane
Darwell), Pa (Russell Simpson), Grandma and Grandpa (Charley Grapewin),
Uncle John, Tom's sister Rosasharn (Dorris Bowdon) and her new husband,
and other brothers and sisters—set off in an overloaded, dilapidated truck
for the "promised land" of California.

The trip itself takes its toll on the family: the elder Joads, first Grandpa,
then Grandma, die en route, and pregnant Rosasharn's husband deserts her.
Moreover, once in California, they find that the working conditions there in
no way compare with the glowing accounts of the handbills. Thousands of
migrants like the Joads have answered the call, and jobs are scarce. All are

forced to live in squalid transient camps and work for starvation wages, when indeed any work is to be had. Eventually, the Joads find jobs on a ranch where some of the workers are on strike and are attempting to organize a union. During an altercation between the striking workers and a band of deputies, Casy (John Carradine), a friend of the Joads who traveled west with them, is killed. In retaliation, Tom kills one of the officers. The family flees, ending up at a clean, democratically run government camp. Contrasted with all the other places they have stayed, this camp seems almost like paradise. However, as a fugitive who has broken parole, Tom realizes the inevitable. He must leave the family and strike out on his own. In one famous scene, he bids farewell to Ma, promising to fight for social justice. As the film ends, the family continues its ever-moving search for work.

As with any film adaptation of a popular literary work, one of the first questions raised is that of the film's fidelity to its source. From the first, *The Grapes of Wrath* was praised for its faithfulness to Steinbeck's book. Indeed, despite the careful pruning of curse words from the dialogue and the compression necessary to reduce a six-hundred-page novel to standard feature length, Steinbeck's characters and events come to life on the screen with remarkable vitality. Nunnally Johnson's screenplay, which has retained Steinbeck's themes concerning human dignity and the fundamental importance of the family, along with the performances of an outstanding cast, constitute the major achievement of the film. The screenplay, however, does deemphasize some of Steinbeck's material. The angry political message of the novel, as well as its religious satire, are considerably muted on the screen. In addition, by means of a single omission and transposition the screenplay has fundamentally altered the structure of the novel and the artistic vision of its author. This was accomplished by deleting in its entirety Steinbeck's controversial ending involving the death of Rosasharn's infant and by reversing the order of two major episodes in the novel: the government camp sequence and the strike sequence in which Tom kills Casy's assassin. By concluding with the comparatively upbeat government camp episodes, the film tends to imply an optimism—not present in the novel—about the power of the American government to solve the deplorable socioeconomic problems illustrated by the odyssey of the Joads. This faith in democracy is also implicit in Ma Joad's final speech in the film: "We're the people that live! We'll go on forever because we're the people!"

The acting by the major players in *The Grapes of Wrath* is superb. Henry Fonda's portrayal of Tom Joad, who angrily insists on decency and human dignity, is one of the memorable achievements of his career. Jane Darwell's performance as the courageous Ma Joad, who struggles to preserve the family unity as the key to its survival, is sensitive and compassionate—among the strongest in the film. One of her most effective scenes is that which takes place in the predawn darkness while the family prepares for their journey

West. Ma is seen sorting through a small box of mementos. In this wordless solo scene the actress conveys a sense of the human dimensions of the past now irretrievably lost as the family leaves the farm, never to return. Charley Grapewin is effective as Grandpa Joad, who first bubbles with enthusiasm at the prospect of being able to pick grapes in California, but later balks at leaving home. Clutching a fistful of soil, he cries, "It's my dirt—no good, but it's mine!" The testimony of Muley (John Qualen) to the land—"We were born on it, and we got killed on it, died on it; even if it's no good, it's still ours"—is delivered with such skill that it becomes one of the most poignant moments in the film.

The success of the film is also due to its remarkable visual impact. Gregg Toland's evocative black-and-white cinematography gives the film an epic quality reminiscent of the great photographic record of rural America during the Depression sponsored by the United States Farm Security Administration. His strikingly photographed landscapes give graphic expression to the involvement Steinbeck's characters have with the land, and the documentary quality of the visual images succinctly underscores the hopeless conditions of the migrant workers. Productive collaboration between the photographer and the director has resulted in many images that linger in the memory: the inexorable progress of the house-demolishing tractors in Oklahoma; the journey west along Highway 66 with its montage of signs ("We fix flats," "Water 15¢ gal.," "Last chance for gas and water"); the nighttime reflection of the three riders in the truck's windshield through which can be seen the passing desert; and the subjective camera record of the arrival of the Joads at the first migrant camp as it tracks through the campground crowded with jobless, hungry people.

The Grapes of Wrath was a popular and critical success when it was first released. Both Jane Darwell and John Ford won Academy Awards for their contributions. Although it lost the Academy Award for Best Picture to Hitchcock's *Rebecca*, the film was named the outstanding film of 1940 by many other groups, including the New York Film Critics. It is historically important as one of the first Hollywood films to portray honestly and realistically one of the least admirable aspects of American society. Although the implications of the film's ending may seem too simplistic for modern audiences, *The Grapes of Wrath* remains a powerful dramatization in personal terms of a major socioeconomic problem, the rumblings of which were beginning to be heard in the 1930's.

David Bahnemann

THE GREAT DICTATOR

Released: 1940
Production: Charles Chaplin for United Artists
Direction: Charles Chaplin
Screenplay: Charles Chaplin
Cinematography: Karl Struss and Rollie Totheroh
Editing: Willard Nico
Music: Meredith Willson
Running time: 127 minutes

Principal characters:
Adenoid Hynkel/Dictator of Tomania/
A Jewish Barber .... Charles Chaplin
Hannah .... Paulette Goddard
Benzini Napaloni/
Dictator of Bacteria .... Jack Oakie
Schultz .... Reginald Gardiner
Garbitsch .... Henry Daniell
Herring .... Billy Gilbert

Five years had passed between Charles Chaplin's *Modern Times* (1936) and *The Great Dictator.* Chaplin was the last holdout against the talking film; *Modern Times* was essentially silent, dependent on his genius for pantomime, except for a comic song made up of rhyming pig-Latin lyrics. Thus, *The Great Dictator* marks Chaplin's talking film debut. In it, the dialogue is as important as the masterful pantomime, for Chaplin had something to say, and he felt that he had to say it in words. Although the dialogue is funny throughout the film, the six-minute speech which he delivers near the end of the film is definitely an example of the misuse of dialogue, for it is didactic and misfires completely in a picture that is already too long. Nevertheless, *The Great Dictator* is a great tragicomedy and one of the best creative films Chaplin ever made.

Chaplin plays a dual role: a Jewish barber and a dictator. In World War I the barber had suffered an injury that affected his mind. He has regained his sanity twenty years later and has returned to his shop in the Jewish ghetto of a great city in Tomania. He is unaware that while he has been away, a dictator named Hynkel has risen to power. Hynkel, a persecutor of Jews, has built up a strong police force. The irony of the situation is that the little Jewish barber and the great dictator Hynkel are look-alikes. Almost immediately the little barber becomes a victim of the police when he attempts to resist them. He is beaten and incarcerated, and then escapes and flees to a bordering country.

Meanwhile, however, he finds himself attracted to a pretty little laundress named Hannah (Paulette Goddard), whom he defends against Nazi oppression. The ghetto people realize that Hynkel must be destroyed, and there is a very funny sequence in which four of them meet to eat puddings containing coins to determine by lot which of them shall become a martyr and slay the dictator.

Hynkel, completely mad, delivers a wild, senseless speech that is a conglomeration of German, Yiddish, and pig-Latin. Later, when he is alone, he performs a solo ballet with a huge balloon representing the world. He bounces it protectively, leaping and pirouetting to catch it once more in his embrace, then he twirls it lovingly. Accidentally, in his fervor, he breaks it and is reduced to childish tears; his world is shattered.

The border country where the barber and Hannah have sought refuge is one that Hynkel has recently annexed, and the inhabitants mistake the barber for Hynkel himself. He finds himself pushed forward upon a speaker's platform, where he is expected to address the crowd. He chooses, rather than an inflammatory, screaming speech, to make an impassioned plea for reason and mercy. The crowd is moved and applauds him, and it is on this note of triumph that the picture ends.

Chaplin is wistful and moving as the small, persecuted barber, much as he had always been as the beloved little tramp. But it is as Hynkel that he enjoys his greatest triumph. Satire and ridicule have always been the sharpest weapons against wrong, and Chaplin portrays Hynkel with all the genius of his comic skill. Hynkel becomes an insane fool who can inspire only derisive laughter in any thinking person. Yet Hitler, of whom Hynkel is obviously a portrait, could not be laughed into nonexistence. *The Great Dictator* was released on the eve of World War II; one could still laugh then at Chaplin's satiric portrait of the Nazi dictator. All too soon, however, a war that embraced the world was raging, and there were times when it seemed that the mad power that bloomed even in mythical Tomania was hardly a funny thing since the satire struck too close to home.

Some of the wildest humor in the picture comes in the sequence in which Hynkel is visited by Napaloni, the dictator of Bacteria, with which Tomania has formed an alliance. Jack Oakie plays Napaloni as a wonderful caricature of Mussolini, and if making fun of one dictator is funny, deriding two is twice as hilarious.

At Academy Award time *The Great Dictator* was nominated for Best Picture, and Chaplin received nominations as Best Actor and Best Writer of an Original Story; Jack Oakie was nominated for Best Supporting Actor of the Year; and Meredith Willson's original score gained a nomination as well. But there were no Oscars awarded to *The Great Dictator*. When the awards were made in February of 1941, the world was seething with news of Hitler's newest devastations abroad, and America was very soon to be drawn into the conflict. As World War II raged, Chaplin wisely withdrew *The Great Dictator* from circulation, and it did not reappear until after the war, when the Allies had won and Hitler and Mussolini were dead. The full bittersweet power of Chaplin's tragicomedy could draw a smile again. Hitler could be an object of mirth. *The Great Dictator* was not shown in Rome until 1961, long after Mussolini's empire had fallen and there was a whole new generation of Italians who had not lived under Fascist rule. Then *The Great Dictator* became the reigning hit of the movie season in Rome, and the Romans thought Jack Oakie the funniest man they had ever seen. They literally rolled in the aisles and jumped up and down with glee at his interpretation of Napaloni, Dictator of Bacteria.

Chaplin chose an excellent cast to support him. Paulette Goddard had been Chaplin's leading lady in *Modern Times* and his wife from 1933 to 1942, and Hitler's two aides, Goebbels and Göring, are effectively parodied by Henry Daniell as Minister of Propaganda Garbitsch (Goebbels) and Billy Gilbert as Minister of War Herring (Göring). There is also an amusing impersonation by Reginald Gardiner as a high-ranking Tomanian named Schultz.

By 1940, Chaplin had become a world figure, dominating film comedy with his superb gift of pantomime. Internationally known and loved, his gift for laughter transcended language barriers; thus, it is not difficult to understand how he went on making silent films when nobody else bothered with them. Warner Bros.' *The Jazz Singer* first initiated the "talkie" in 1927, and by 1929, there remained only three great holdouts against the talking film. Two of them, Lon Chaney and Greto Garbo, appeared in talkies in 1930, but Charles Chaplin did not relent until 1940, when *The Great Dictator* was released. In 1928, the very year after *The Jazz Singer*, he released *The Circus*; it was the first year of the Academy Awards, and the silent film still made nearly a clean sweep at the awards. Along with Emil Jannings and Richard Barthelmess, Chaplin was nominated as Best Actor for his performance in *The Circus*. Even though Jannings won the Oscar, a special award was given to Charles Chaplin "for versatility and genius in writing, acting, directing and producing *The Circus*."

One of his best and most poignant features, *City Lights*, came out in 1931. It was a moving silent picture, gaining no attention from the Academy voters, but becoming one of his best-liked and biggest moneymaking films. He did not release another comedy until 1936 when *Modern Times* appeared. Again, the Academy gave him no recognition. As the one successful silent star, he was an oddity, and possibly could not have been considered as competition for Paul Muni, Gary Cooper, Walter Huston, William Powell, and Spencer Tracy, the five nominees in 1936 for Best Actor. But in 1940, with the release of his first all-talking feature, *The Great Dictator*, the Academy took notice again of Chaplin's genius, rewarding him with five nominations. In 1947, Chaplin's most impudent black comedy, *Monsieur Verdoux*, received an Academy nomination for Best Original Screenplay.

In subsequent years right wing forces came to the fore, especially in the film industry. *Limelight*, released in 1952 (the year Chaplin left the United States), was not allowed to play in the Los Angeles area mainly because of the protests of the American Legion. When *Limelight* was finally presented in Hollywood in 1972, it received an Oscar for Best Original Score. That was the year after the Academy, in 1971, gave Chaplin a Special Honorary Oscar, which he accepted in person on Awards night. It was his last important public appearance; and the ovation given him by the audience proved that he was regarded as one of the screen's few authentic geniuses.

DeWitt Bodeen

THE GREAT ESCAPE

Released: 1963
Production: John Sturges for United Artists
Direction: John Sturges
Screenplay: James Clavell and W. R. Burnett; based on a book of the same
  name by Paul Brickhill
Cinematography: Daniel L. Fapp
Editing: Ferris Webster
Music: Elmer Bernstein
Running time: 168 minutes

> *Principal characters:*
> Hilts .... Steve McQueen
> Hendley .... James Garner
> Bartlett .... Richard Attenborough
> Velinski .... Charles Bronson
> Blythe .... Donald Pleasence
> Sedgwick .... James Coburn

The Great Escape details the true story of the largest mass escape of POW's
during World War II. Utilizing an all-star cast and a running time which
approaches three hours, director John Sturges creates a compelling tribute
to the human spirit. The film is rather complex and can be broken down into
three distinct parts: the elaborate preparations leading to the escape; the
escape itself; and the eventual recapture of most of the prisoners.

The prison camp in the story is populated by the most notorious trouble-
makers encountered by the Germans in their various camps all over Europe.
The Germans, having isolated the most volatile elements among their cap-
tives, intend to scrutinize them intently. Bartlett (Richard Attenborough),
the British officer who is the leader of the escape committee, is able to recruit
experts for every phase of the well-planned mass exodus. He uses master
tailors to create civilian clothes; visas and identity cards are forged by cal-
ligraphers and artists; mine workers dig the escape tunnels. There is a sense
of harmony in their efforts.

The only discouraging voice is that of Hilts (Steve McQueen), a captured
American flyer, who is a loner and would prefer to escape on his own. After
several attempts and as many terms in solitary confinement, he manages to
get out, only to be captured and returned. At this point Bartlett realizes his
need for Hilts, since he is the only prisoner who knows exactly how far it is
to the forest and what lies immediately beyond. Persuaded finally to work
for the group, Hilts assists in the escape plans. The escape is partially successful, with more than two-thirds of the planned escapees making it out of
the tunnel before their escape is detected.

From this point the film breaks its unified focus to concentrate on the various routes taken by the more significant prisoners. The ingenuity of the individuals to make good their escape is punctuated by scenes of the Gestapo capturing or killing other escapees. Bartlett is recaptured, and, in a move of savage revenge, he and a large number of other prisoners are trucked to an isolated spot and machine-gunned. Hilts, who manages to commandeer a motorcycle, gives the Germans a wild race for the Swiss border, but he fails in a final attempt to breach the fence that separates him from neutrality and freedom. Returned to the POW camp, he is once again placed in solitary confinement as the names of those escapees killed by the Germans are read to the assembled prisoners.

What is unique about *The Great Escape* is the sense of camaraderie expressed through various characters in the film. There is a feeling of community enveloping the prison camp which is not found in such films as *The Bridge on the River Kwai* (1957), *Stalag 17* (1953), or *King Rat* (1965). Each of these other films concentrates on one aspect of men in prison. *The Bridge on the River Kwai* dealt with the obsessions of a man trying to maintain his sanity in a world of total chaos. *Stalag 17* was more optimistic, showing how individuals can survive in an environment of pain and suffering. *King Rat* utilized a similar theme, but, rather than showing the humor in the situation, it concentrates on unscrupulous characters who take advantage of human misery. This lack of harmony found in most POW films is avoided in *The Great Escape*. There is no concern with finding the traitor selling information to the captors for extra rations of food, there are no exploiters, and there is no real concern about poor living conditions. Rather, the focus of the film drives home a single goal: escape.

The selection of the cast is important in the success of *The Great Escape*. Steve McQueen's portrayal of Hilts functions as an extention of the loner *persona* of the 1950's and is thus somewhat of an anachronism in the film's 1940's setting. James Garner as the "scavenger" is perfectly suited to the role of the wheeler-dealer, and Richard Attenborough is flawless as Bartlett, the organizer of the escape. The secondary characters also seem perfectly suited for their roles.

James Clavell, one of the screenwriters for *The Great Escape*, later wrote another prisoner-of-war film, *King Rat* in which he concentrated on the darker side of the human condition. There are glimpses of this bleak outlook in the conclusion of *The Great Escape* in which most of the cast is either killed or recaptured; however, *The Great Escape* was made during the period of epic length motion pictures, and director John Sturges preferred to concentrate on entertainment rather than on stark realism to carry the dramatic story line.

There is a sense of the humor and joy of life in *The Great Escape* that transcends the ramifications of the escape. Based on a true situation and embellished with Hollywood's characteristic flair, the film functions both as a document of World War II and as a proclamation through its characters' of ingenuity and irrepressible instinct for survival.

Carl F. Macek

GREAT EXPECTATIONS

Released: 1947
Production: Ronald Neame for Cineguild; released by Universal-International
Direction: David Lean
Screenplay: David Lean, Ronald Neame, Anthony Havelock-Allan, Kay Walsh, and Cecil McGivern; based on the novel of the same name by Charles Dickens
Cinematography: Guy Green (AA)
Editing: Jack Harris
Art direction: John Bryan (AA)
Set decoration: Wilfred Shingleton (AA)
Running time: 118 minutes

Principal characters:
Pip (older)	John Mills
Estella (older)	Valerie Hobson
Pip (younger)	Anthony Wager
Estella (younger)	Jean Simmons
Joe Gargery	Bernard Miles
Jaggers	Francis L. Sullivan
Magwitch	Finlay Currie
Miss Havisham	Martita Hunt
Herbert Pocket	Alec Guinness
Wemmick	Ivor Barnard
Mrs. Joe	Freda Jackson
Biddy	Eileen Erskine
Bentley Drummle	Torin Thatcher
The Aged Parent	O. B. Clarence

Charles Dickens' novel had been filmed twice in the silent days and once as a talkie (by Universal in 1934) before David Lean and cinematographer-turned-producer Ronald Neame collaborated on the 1946 British version. On the world market, the British cinema until the end of World War II was known almost exclusively for this kind of expensively produced film with a literary flavor, although the prewar success of Hitchcock's thrillers should have alerted distributors to the possibility that less expensive British films could also be profitably exported. It was not until after the successful United States release of the modestly budgeted Ealing comedies and crime pictures in the late 1940's that giant combines such as the Rank Organisation risked exporting British films without the benefit of lavish production values and the cachet of Shakespeare, Dickens, and Bernard Shaw. (Even Ealing had flirted briefly with elaborate all-star vehicles such as *Dead of Night*, 1946, and a Dickens adaptation, *Nicholas Nickleby*, 1947.) This is not to suggest that films like

Olivier's *Henry V* (1945) and *Great Expectations* were somehow less "cinematic" than inexpensive films written directly for the screen like Ealing's *The Blue Lamp* (1950) and *Passport to Pimlico* (1948), but it should be noted that Olivier and Lean were working within a tradition that would occupy a less dominant position in the British film industry in years to come.

With this as background, it is tempting to regard *Great Expectations* and Lean's other Dickens film of the period, *Oliver Twist* (1948), as representing the high-water mark of the British "literary" cinema. Lean's beginnings as an editor helped him to a mastery of the language of montage unequaled by any British director save Hitchcock (a mastery he has never lost even when confronted by the demands of the wide screen in such later epics as *The Bridge on the River Kwai*, 1957; *Lawrence of Arabia*, 1962; and *Dr. Zhivago*, 1966); and throughout his career he has been a fine, much underrated director of actors as well. (In this respect, he is as much Olivier's equal as he is Hitchcock's.)

The Dickens films, shot in black and white for the old narrow screen (the first and still the best of all screen shapes) and based faithfully on works by the most stagestruck and naturally dramatic of great novelists, might more accurately be called translations rather than adaptations. In the case of *Great Expectations*, Lean, Neame, and their fellow scriptwriters (including the actress Kay Walsh, who had performed in Lean's *In Which We Serve*, 1942; and *This Happy Breed*, 1947) seem to have approached their task in the spirit of someone cutting a long play like *Hamlet* (which takes about four hours to perform as Shakespeare wrote it) for presentation at normal length. The skeleton of the work has been altered very little, but the viewer familiar with the book may regret the absence of minor characters and secondary incidents whose existence the rest of the audience does not even suspect.

Philip Pirrip (Anthony Wager)—called Pip for short—is a young orphan who lives with his sister (Freda Jackson) and her husband, Joe Gargery (Bernard Miles), a blacksmith, in an isolated village on the Thames estuary between London and the coast. Two things happen to Pip in his childhood that have a profound effect on the course of his future life: he meets an escaped convict, Magwitch (Finlay Currie), for whom he steals some food from his sister's cupboard; and he receives a summons from a rich eccentric, Miss Havisham (Martita Hunt), to visit and play with her ward, Estella (Jean Simmons). Years ago, Miss Havisham had been jilted on her wedding day as she was dressing for church. She has lived ever since amid the wreckage of the never-eaten bridal feast, never taking off her white gown and never seeing the light of day through the tightly drawn blinds of her mansion, Satis (meaning a sufficiency—of grief perhaps?) House. She has been rearing Estella to be the instrument of her revenge upon the whole male sex, and she sees with grim satisfaction that Pip has been instantly smitten by the girl. Estella, for her part, never loses an opportunity to remind Pip of his inferior social status, waking in the boy a burning desire to become a real gentleman. At first, though, there seems no likelihood of his ever rising above the mechanics' class occupied by the goodhearted Joe, to whom he is finally apprenticed at the age of fourteen. At about the same time, Miss Havisham sends Estella abroad to complete her education as a lady, and for the next few years Pip has no contact with Satis House except for a yearly visit to Miss Havisham on his birthday, when she gives him a gold sovereign.

When Pip is twenty (at which point John Mills takes over for young Wager), he is visited at the forge by Miss Havisham's attorney, a Londoner named Jaggers (Francis L. Sullivan, who later made a memorable Bumble in *Oliver Twist*). To Pip's delighted surprise, Jaggers tells him that he has "great expectations" from a mysterious benefactor whose name he is not at liberty to mention, although Pip naturally assumes that Jaggers is speaking of Miss Havisham. Pip is to leave for London at once, where Jaggers will superintend his training in the ways of the great world where Pip will henceforth make his home. In London, to further strengthen Pip's conviction that Miss Havisham is his benefactor, Jaggers places him in lodgings with Miss Havisham's nephew, Herbert Pocket (Alec Guinness, in his screen debut).

A year later, when Pip's education as a gentleman has progressed to the point that he is embarrassed by Joe's country manners when he receives a visit from him in London, he is summoned to Satis House again by Miss Havisham to meet the now grown-up Estella. (Valerie Hobson's stately beauty is as appropriate for Estella at twenty as Jean Simmons' coltish hauteur was for Estella at fourteen; but Hobson's first appearance usually provokes gasps of disbelief from the audience that she is what Simmons has grown into.) Pip hopes that Miss Havisham intends Estella to be his bride, although Estella herself warns him that, thanks to her upbringing, she is incapable of loving him, or anybody. Nevertheless, Pip becomes her constant escort during the London season, where he does his best to shield her from her other admirers, particularly an aristocratic cad named Bentley Drummle (Torin Thatcher).

Pip's hopeful world is dashed to pieces one stormy night when Magwitch knocks on the door of his apartments in the Temple and informs him that he has been his unknown benefactor all along. Jaggers confirms that his having been attorney to both Miss Havisham and the convict was just a coincidence, and that Pip's great expectations are based on the fortune that Magwitch painfully accumulated during years of forced exile in New South Wales. Jaggers further warns Pip that Magwitch was transported under penalty of death if he ever returned to England, and that the old man has enemies who would not hesitate to inform on him if they knew of his presence in London. Pip determines to flee with Magwitch to a place of refuge out of the country, but, before he goes, he takes the coach down to Satis House to say his final goodbye to Miss Havisham and Estella. He finds Estella preparing for her wedding to Bentley Drummle, a circumstance that fills him with horror. He confronts

Miss Havisham with the knowledge of what her transformation of Estella into an instrument of revenge has meant in terms of blighting the young woman's chance for a happy, normal life. Miss Havisham repents of her deed, but it is by now too late; and Pip leaves her staring dumbly into the fire. Suddenly, the old woman's tattered gown catches fire from a spark, and, before Pip can put out the flames, Miss Havisham is burned to death.

When Pip gets back to London, the porter at the Temple hands him a note from Jaggers' clerk, Wemmick (Ivor Barnard), warning him not to go home. Pip goes to Wemmick's house (which, in the film, is just a house, and not the ingenious miniature castle described in the book), where he finds him sitting with his father, the Aged Parent (O. B. Clarence). Wemmick tells Pip that he has learned of an old enemy of Magwitch's who was about to turn him over to the police, and that he and Herbert Pocket have removed Pip's benefactor to a new lodging overlooking the river, where he should be safe. From there, when conditions are right, he can be rowed downstream to meet a packet boat leaving the country. When, a few weeks later, Pip and Herbert attempt to do this, they are intercepted by a government longboat in which Magwitch's enemy is sitting. The old convict, furious at this betrayal, leaps for his enemy and drags him into the water, where the informer is crushed by the side paddle wheel of the approaching packet. In spite of Jaggers' best effort at his trial, Magwitch is sentenced to hang, although he dies in prison from the effects of his struggle in the water before his execution can take place. In the meantime, Jaggers has told Pip the most astonishing coincidence of all: Estella is really Magwitch's daughter, whom Jaggers took to live with Miss Havisham after the old man's first conviction many years before. Worn out by his exertions and the surprises he has had to bear during the last two or three months, Pip falls ill himself and is nursed in his delirium by Joe the blacksmith and his intended bride, Biddy (Eileen Erskine). (Pip's sister had died when Pip was still Joe's apprentice.)

Only when the recovered Pip goes to pay his final visit to Satis House does the screenplay depart significantly from the action of the novel. Dickens had at first written an unhappy ending in which Pip, his great expectations dashed when Magwitch's fortune was claimed by the Crown after the convict's death, went off to the colonies and was never reunited with Estella. Then, on the advice of his friend, novelist Edward Bulwer-Lytton, Dickens scrapped this chapter and wrote a scene describing Pip's visit to the ruins of Satis House years later, where he found the now widowed Estella also silently contemplating the wreck of Miss Havisham's strange domain. It was implied that Pip and Estella were married shortly after this chance encounter. Both endings have been criticized as unsatisfactory: the first because it ends the story too abruptly before Pip and Estella have had time to redeem themselves, the second because nothing in Estella's demeanor suggests that her feeling for Pip has changed in the years since their last meeting, however much she may have softened in other ways.

The ending found for the film improves upon Dickens' two attempts dramatically and psychologically. Pip arrives at Satis House and finds Estella sitting in Miss Havisham's old chair in her darkened boudoir. Estella tells him that she was jilted by Bentley Drummle after he learned the truth about her parentage, but that she is content to repeat the pattern of her guardian's self-immurement. "Then I defy you, Miss Havisham!," cries Pip, and rips down the heavy draperies that have shut off the interior of Satis House from the sun. Estella starts like a woman waking from a trance, and looks wonderingly about her at the squalor and decay in which just a few seconds before she had thought herself willing to live out her life. The film ends with a visual equivalent of Dickens' hopeful final words: "I took her hand in mine, and we went out of the ruined place; . . . and in all the broad expanse of tranquil light . . . I saw the shadow of no parting from her."

Making allowance for the inevitable sins of omission committed while trying to compress a long, rambling novel into a two-hour movie (one who knows the book may wonder about the omission of Miss Skiffins, or Orlick, or those two alarming representatives of youth, the Avenger and Trabb's boy), Lean and his collaborators did a remarkable job of tidying up the action of the story without doing violence to Dickens' basic plot. One may question, of course, whether Dickens tidy is really Dickens at all: the strange career of Mr. Wopsle, for example, who in the book goes from parish clerk to London actor and intersects with Pip's adventures only briefly and at long intervals, afforded Dickens opportunity to write two of his priceless descriptions of second-rate nineteenth century theater. Furthermore, Mr. Wopsle's hopeless ambition to be a second Kean slyly comments upon Pip's own delusion that his benefactor is Miss Havisham, an authentic member of the landed gentry, rather than a convicted felon. One concludes by wondering, with James Agee and Dillys Powell, why Lean and company did not try at least to sketch in more of the minor characters and incidents, given the screen's ability to show in less than a minute what takes pages to describe in a book.

Great Expectations was nominated for Academy Awards for Best Picture of 1947 (although it lost to *Gentleman's Agreement*), for Best Direction, and for Best Screenplay, and won in the categories of Best Black-and-White Cinematography (Guy Green) and Best Art Direction and Set Decoration (John Bryan and Wilfred Shingleton). The film is undeniably beautiful to look at, although, to echo Agee again, perhaps too beautiful for Dickens: something like the dark, crabbed look of the original Phiz illustrations would have been more appropriate.

Charles Hopkins

THE GREAT GATSBY

Released: 1974
Production: David Merrick for Newdon Company; released by Paramount
Direction: Jack Clayton
Screenplay: Francis Ford Coppola; based on the novel of the same name by
  F. Scott Fitzgerald
Cinematography: Douglas Slocombe
Editing: Tom Priestley
Costume design: Theoni V. Aldredge (AA)
Music: Nelson Riddle (AA)
Running time: 146 minutes

Principal characters:
Jay Gatsby	Robert Redford
Daisy Buchanan	Mia Farrow
Tom Buchanan	Bruce Dern
Myrtle Wilson	Karen Black
George Wilson	Scott Wilson
Nick Carraway	Sam Waterston

The mid-1970's experienced a huge wave of nostalgia for the prohibition era that had been captured so well by the "voice of the Jazz Age," F. Scott Fitzgerald. Fitzgerald's short stories and novels have a recurring theme of a quietly pensive man in love with a rich and vivacious young woman. Typically, the man takes his life in hand to better his chances with her. Whether the nostalgia of the 1970's for this not-so-distant past was caused by David Merrick's *The Great Gatsby*, or whether the film was an example of an already existing nostalgia, is problematic; in any case, "Great Gatsby" costumes found their ways into both high fashion and department store racks, and the romanticism bred by the story of patient and undying love became a dominant theme in many phases of entertainment, including music, television, and film.

As in Fitzgerald's novel, the story in Merrick's film is told largely from the point of view of Nick Carraway (Sam Waterston), a cousin of the heroine, Daisy Buchanan (Mia Farrow). Nick has taken a cottage on the lavish estate of Jay Gatsby (Robert Redford), and from this vantage point he watches the old love affair between his cousin and Gatsby rekindle and grow. Gatsby, rebuffed by Daisy years earlier because of his humble and impoverished background, has amassed a large fortune, presumably from a bootlegging business although that fact is never directly revealed. He now creates a luxurious environment for Daisy's romantic and hedonistic delight, hoping thereby to attract her to him. Because of his desire to have his money dance and do tricks before Daisy's eyes, Gatsby gives a series of elaborate parties. Rather than attend them, however, he surveys the crowd from a lofty balcony window in the hope that Daisy might one night attend and that he might watch her reveling with the others below.

More is going on in the story besides Gatsby's wooing. Tom Buchanan (Bruce Dern), Daisy's husband, is having an affair with a woman of lower social origin named Myrtle Wilson (Karen Black). It is this preoccupation that keeps him from recognizing the growing commitment between Gatsby and Daisy until it is well under way. On a climactic, sweltering afternoon, a party, including Gatsby, Daisy, Tom, and Nick, decides to leave the country home for an escape into the city. In this new environment, the impact of the shifts of personal allegiance and love become more apparent, and prototypal jealousies, easily ignored or sublimated in the self-contained society in the country, erupt. The party splits up, returning home in groups of two or three. Daisy and Gatsby return to the country together. Daisy asks to drive Jay's expensive roadster, and, for obscure reasons, momentarily loses control of the car, striking and killing a woman whom we later learn is her husband's lover.

As the situation begins to revert to normal after the guests return to their various homes, the dead woman's crazed husband comes looking for his wife's killer. He first comes to Daisy's home. Daisy's husband, seeing the man through the breakfast room window, redirects him to Gatsby's mansion where the easily identifiable automobile still sits, convincing the man that it was Gatsby rather than Daisy who was responsible for his wife's death. Gatsby, meanwhile, in an effort to make his home more desirable for continuing his affair with Daisy, has dismissed his domestic staff and is living in his mansion alone. There, during a chilling scene as Gatsby waits on a raft in his pool for Daisy, the wronged husband shoots and kills him.

Some time after Gatsby's funeral, we see Daisy again; she is effervescent and involved in other delights, apparently oblivious to the tragedy she has caused. Mia Farrow's portrayal of Daisy contrasts sharply with Fitzgerald's character. Because the film emphasizes Daisy's selfishness as an active force, Gatsby's motivation becomes correspondingly less convincing. Robert Redford's interpretation of Gatsby as a man driven by a consuming passion is more in keeping with Fitzgerald's intent. Redford plays Gatsby as a man who has already reached his material goals, but whose emotional goals are yet unattained. His commitment to winning Daisy is consuming yet not admirable, demanding yet not rewarding; his passions and motivations are difficult for the audience to identify with. The problem is that when Gatsby's character is juxtaposed against Farrow's bold and sharp version of Daisy, his motivations in seeking her seem less mystical, romantic, and compelling, and finally, less satisfying.

The film emphasizes plot and setting more than the relationships between characters. One example of this approach is the camera's periodic focusing on objects—an empty room, an uneaten sandwich, a cottage full of silver and flowers—in a way that equates the characters with the objects that surround them. Another successful visual device is the repeated use of white: white clothing, white automobiles, white rooms, white furniture. The effect is twofold: not only does the white connote imperturbable richness, but it also suggests an irony. Rather than being pure and uncorrupted as their use of white suggests, the characters are far from pure; Gatsby gained his fortune through illegal means, and Daisy becomes a murderer who washes her conscience as easily as she changes gowns. Also ironically, the film's beautiful visual techniques may have been partly responsible for its lack of critical success. After the initial wave of enthusiasm generated by studio publicity, which lasted just beyond the immediate release of the film, the public essentially wrote off Merrick's film as an extravagant showcase for fine clothes and other displays of opulence.

Bonnie Fraser

THE GREAT McGINTY

Released: 1940
Production: Paul Jones for Paramount
Direction: Preston Sturges
Screenplay: Preston Sturges (AA)
Cinematography: William C. Mellor
Editing: Hugh Bennet
Running time: 81 minutes

> *Principal characters:*
> Dan McGinty .... Brian Donlevy
> The Boss .... Akim Tamiroff
> Catherine McGinty .... Muriel Angelus
> The Politician .... William Demarest
> Thompson .... Louis Jean Heydt
> The Dancer .... Steffi Duna
> La Jolla .... Esther Howard

Early in the summer of 1940, there was considerable anxiety at Paramount concerning a soon to be released feature then entitled *Down Went McGinty*. The film was a political satire, a genre which had never been a proven favorite with moviegoers. The hero was Brian Donlevy, whom audiences had passionately hissed as the bestial Sergeant Markoff in the studio's popular remake of *Beau Geste* (1939); and the author-director was Preston Sturges, an eccentric, unorthodox and unheralded talent. Baffled as how to "sell" the picture, Paramount dispatched Donlevy on a three-week, twenty-city promotional tour; circulated endorsements by popular Paramount personalities such as Claudette Colbert, Bob Hope, and Dorothy Lamour ("I'd wear my best sarong for McGinty any day"); and, on the eve of release, they changed the title to *The Great McGinty*, hoping that the more positive title might help at the box office. Such pains were unnecessary, as *The Great McGinty* became one of the most celebrated "sleepers" in Hollywood history. It was a surprise critical and box-office success that survives today as the cinema's most pungent lampoon of politics and, arguably, the purest satire of the highly original, sadly erratic Preston Sturges.

Actually, Paramount had reasonable cause for apprehension regarding *The Great McGinty*. It was solely the brainchild of Sturges, a wealthy playboy, Broadway playwright, and Paramount contract writer whose work on such films as *If I Were King* (1938), the Bob Hope vehicle *Never Say Die* (1939), and *Remember the Night* (1940) were largely rewritten by less talented but more disciplined contractees before going before the cameras. The cynical tone of the piece worried the front office, but Sturges' offer was economically appealing: he would sell his script to the studio for virtually nothing if he were allowed to direct it. Paramount agreed, then handicapped Sturges with a modest $350,000 budget and a three-week shooting schedule. Sturges cast Donlevy after the jaunty actor passed him on the lot and said "Hi 'ya." (He also remembered Donlevy's being fired by an unhappy producer during rehearsals for Sturges' Broadway play *Young Man of Manhattan* in 1930.) The only other "name" in the cast was Paramount's fine Russian character actor Akim Tamiroff, who portrayed the Boss. The part of Mrs. McGinty went to a fresh studio starlet, Muriel Angelus.

The Great McGinty opens in a seedy Banana Republic saloon, where a drunken embezzler named Thompson (Louis Jean Heydt) is pouring his heart out to a hootchie dancer (Steffi Duna). The ex-cashier bemoans the crime that forced him to forsake his family and fortune: "One crazy minute," he laments, just before the bartender (Brian Donlevy) escorts him to the men's room. "Go ahead—heave-ho," grins the bartender—but instead the drunk tries to shoot himself. The bartender dutifully intervenes, but continues to heap scorn on the remorseful man. The hootchie dancer asks what right he has to do that. He replies: "*I* was the governor of a state, baby."

There is a flashback to an election eve scene during the Depression, in which the bartender, then hobo Dan McGinty, is one of many people in a soup line provided as a ploy by the Politician (William Demarest), who is looking for hungry souls willing to vote for his candidate for two dollars apiece. McGinty agrees, and returns late that evening—after voting thirty-seven times. The Politician takes him to the Mayor's headquarters, where McGinty stuffs himself with a hero sandwich, orders a boilermaker, and swaps insults with the Boss. The Boss is impressed, and roars: "He thinks he's *me!*"

McGinty is soon in the Boss's employ. Sporting an outrageous checkered suit and derby hat, he collects protection money from a brothel madame, La Jolla (Esther Howard), and others. With Irish charm and ham fists, he rises fast, quickly becoming an alderman. Soon the Boss asks him to run as a reform candidate for Mayor. "In this town I'm *all* the parties!" bellows the Boss to a questioning McGinty. "You think I'm going to starve every time they change administrations?" McGinty warms to the idea of being Mayor until the Boss demands that he marry ("Women got the vote, and they don't like bachelors"), at which time he stomps out. "I know all about it," he sneers, speaking of matrimony. "My parents was married." However, McGinty's pretty blonde secretary Catherine (Muriel Angelus) is smitten with him, and, wary of wolves, proposes a loveless marriage: "We'd never have to see each other except to be photographed on the steps of the City Hall . . . I could run the house for you and make speeches at the women's clubs." After surveying her legs, McGinty agrees, but does not find out until after the wedding that Catherine has failed to inform him about her little boy and girl.

McGinty becomes Mayor, and for a time the convenient marriage agrees with him—"At least we ain't got nothin' to fight about like people that's in love with each other." However, he soon falls in love with his wife, becomes a doting father to the children, and feels their loving influence tempting him to become an honest, caring politician. Catherine encourages this idealism, and assures him that he will someday be sufficiently strong to escape the corrupt influence of the Boss.

McGinty soon wins the race for Governor and confronts the Boss with a full repertoire of schemes for new dams, buildings, and bridges. He offers to pay back the $400,000 that the Boss spent to get him elected, and announces plans for a child labor bill and a sweatshop and tenement reform. The outraged Boss blames McGinty's idealism on his "cheapskate" wife. McGinty hits him, whereupon the Boss tries to shoot McGinty. The Boss is thrown in jail, and that night, after he reveals the details of McGinty's past deals, McGinty lands in jail with him.

Next, the Politician, disguised as a policeman, frees McGinty and the Boss from prison, and McGinty calls Catherine from a pay phone as he flees to escape the country. He tells her to get a divorce, informs her of a safe deposit box where he has left some securities for just such an emergency, and apologizes: "You can't make a silk purse out of a pig's ear."

Back in the bar, the Governor-turned-bartender concludes his story. The hootchie dancer pronounces him a liar. "O.K., sister," he replies. "Have it your way." McGinty rings up the embezzler's tab, pilfering some of the money, and is caught by the saloon proprietor—who is the Boss. "You cheesy cheapskate!" he roars. "You fat little four-flusher!" replies McGinty, as the two begin another slugfest. "Time out, gents," bemoans the Politician, now a waiter. "Here we go again!"

Released on August 25, 1940, *The Great McGinty* was an instant success. *Time* hailed it as ". . . shrewd, silly, adroit . . . an actor's dream. Brian Donlevy makes the dream come true." The *New York Times* placed the film seventh on its 1940 "Ten Best" list, and an Academy Award went to Preston Sturges for Best Original Screenplay. *The Great McGinty* established Donlevy as a popular leading man of the 1940's, and launched the career of Sturges, who, acclaimed by Paramount as "The Miracle Man," proceeded to create such satirical classics as *Sullivan's Travels* (1941), *The Miracle of Morgan's Creek* (1944), *Hail the Conquering Hero* (1944), and others, before his strange genius burned itself out in the late 1940's.

The Great McGinty remains a marvelous experience. Sturges' blend of subtlety and pratfall humor is perfect. Donlevy's satiric performance as McGinty is a joy, whether he is snarling at the Boss ("Take your finger out of my face!"), reading his children a bedtime story about "Muggily-wump the Tortoise," or warning his wife about the trials of being an honest governor ("There's no money in it, you understand—just a salary"). Akim Tamiroff is a marvelous incarnation of the traditionally greasy, amoral, backroom politician. Muriel Angelus plays Catherine McGinty with style and charm, and the colorful players who would become Sturges' favorites—William Demarest, Frank Moran, and Harry Rosenthal—spark the picture with the atmosphere, spirit, and fireworks of a raucous Tammany parade.

Americans have always been cynical about politics. *The Great McGinty* remains Hollywood's most delightful celebration of that cynicism, an emotion that, in this post-Watergate age, makes *The Great McGinty* all the more enjoyable.

Gregory William Mank

THE GREATEST SHOW ON EARTH

Released: 1952
Production: Cecil B. De Mille for Paramount (AA)
Direction: Cecil B. De Mille
Screenplay: Fredric M. Frank, Barre Lyndon, and Theodore St. John; based on the screen story by Fredric M. Frank, Theodore St. John, and Frank Cavett (AA)
Cinematography: George Barnes, Peverell Marley, and W. Wallace Kelley
Editing: Anne Bauchens
Costume design: Edith Head, Dorothy Jeakins, and Miles White
Music: Victor Young
Running time: 151 minutes

Principal characters:

Holly	Betty Hutton
Sebastian	Cornel Wilde
Brad	Charlton Heston
Angel	Gloria Grahame
Buttons the Clown	James Stewart
Phyllis	Dorothy Lamour
Klaus	Lyle Bettger
Henderson	Lawrence Tierney
Detective	Henry Wilcoxon
John Ringling North	Himself
Emmett Kelly	Himself

Considering producer/director Cecil B. De Mille's fondness of Barnumlike spectacle, his decision to make a movie on the circus would seem to be a particularly apt choice. A long-cherished personal project, the planning of *The Greatest Show on Earth* took some three years prior to the several months of actual shooting. Never one for half measures, instead of the usual "cast of thousands" De Mille hired the entire Ringling Bros.-Barnum & Bailey Circus in addition to his several starring players. Beginning at the circus' winter quarters in Sarasota, Florida, the film chronicles the show's annual cross-country circuit, albeit with a few De Mille plot complications en route.

Reduced to its barest premise, the film's theme is "The show must go on." If circus life is naturally a communal affair, De Mille lets us know in no uncertain terms that it is also a very capitalistic endeavor. Just as the high-wire artists risk life and limb, so the circus is like a tightrope walker, inching toward success, yet always in danger of plummeting to ruin. The person around whom all this drama revolves is the boss, Brad (Charlton Heston). Viewed as a benign dictator, determined, omniscient, always putting the circus ahead of personal satisfaction, he appears to be very similar to De Mille's image of himself.

De Mille seemed to love weaving complicated yarns with a number of subplots, and this film is no exception. There is a professional, and later romantic, rivalry between the two trapeze artists, Holly (Betty Hutton) and Sebastian (Cornel Wilde). Their conflict revolves around who will occupy the center ring, each trying to outdo the other. Their stunts become ever riskier, causing Brad no small amount of trouble, until Sebastian suffers a crippling accident. Another subplot centers on Angel (Gloria Grahame), the elephant girl, and the trainer, Klaus (Lyle Bettger). Insanely jealous, Klaus almost kills Angel when he finds that he is losing her affections to Brad. Dismissed from the circus, he derails the circus train in revenge and is killed in the process. As a result of the wreck, the mysterious past of Buttons the Clown (James Stewart) is revealed. He is really a doctor who is wanted by the FBI for the euthanasia killing of his wife. Seemingly at the end of its tether, the circus is led by Holly, who has learned her lesson, to the nearest town for another performance. In addition to the train wreck, the circus also endures a disastrous fire, sabotage by a rival circus, petty infighting, and the vagaries of the weather. It is a testimonial to De Mille's skill as a storyteller that each of these various incidents and intrigues finds its place without pulling the story apart in many directions.

Whether De Mille's films depict the parting of the Red Sea or the journey of Cleopatra's barge down the Nile, they are usually built around larger-than-life moments. There are two such spectacle sequences in this film. The fire sequence is by far the more vivid of the two. The fire, well paced from the first spark until it gradually becomes a blazing inferno (although using a liberal amount of back-projection), is startlingly real and gripping as both man and beast panic in the flames. If De Mille in one of his epics had chosen to depict Hell, he could not have done better than he has here. The train wreck, similar to an earlier sequence in *Union Pacific* (1939), is done very effectively with miniatures. For the aftermath, elaborate sets were built to depict the wreckage. Unfortunately, the scenes following the wreck do not ring true. Nobody except the villain is killed or seriously hurt, and the animals are quickly and easily put back into their cages.

Although the spectacle is handled with the director's customary flair, it must be admitted that the film as a whole does suffer from serious defects in dramatic credibility which are paralleled in much of De Mille's work. Stern-minded moralist that he was, De Mille never depicted characters beyond a very simple level. And having his roots in the tradition of barnstorming theatricals, De Mille's nineteenth century sensibilities never allowed for much psychological ambiguity in his characters.

Existing alongside De Mille's three-ring circus of a movie is another show-within-a-show, a modest and effective depiction of the real circus. Most people, it seems, never outgrow a fascination for the circus, and fortunately neither did De Mille. Actual circus acts probably have never been more lovingly filmed, portrayed with all the glitter and excitement of the real circus. The finest moments of the film are those events which one usually does not see, such as the massive circus tent being raised in the early hours of the morning, and the tedious rehearsals of the performers. It is here that the film achieves a poetry which transcends its more banal plot.

However one rates De Mille, there can be no doubt that he was wholly responsible for his films. Working independently through Paramount, De Mille went his own way, oblivious to the rest of the cinema world. Although sometimes trite, old-fashioned, and bombastic, there is an innocent charm about several of his films which may well outlast many of the more recent so-called "thinking man's spectaculars." At a certain point, an invigorating vulgarity is preferable to smug pretentiousness. As his Westerns in particular prove, De Mille was squarely in line with another American primitive, novelist James Fenimore Cooper. Like Cooper's characters, De Mille's characters gain in mythic resonance what they lose in dramatic sense. When not lured away by the religious epic, De Mille made films about America, including *The Greatest Show on Earth*, which was awarded the Oscar for Best Picture of the year. Although it is often guilty of reactionary excesses, De Mille's vision remains determinedly optimistic.

Mike Vanderlan

THE GUNS OF NAVARONE

Released: 1961
Production: Carl Foreman for Columbia
Direction: J. Lee Thompson
Screenplay: Carl Foreman; based on the novel of the same name by Alistair
  MacLean
Cinematography: Oswald Morris
Editing: Alan Osbitson
Special effects: Bill Warrington and Wally Veevers (AA)
Music: Dmitri Tiomkin
Running time: 157 minutes

> *Principal characters:*
> Captain Mallory .... Gregory Peck
> Corporal Miller .... David Niven
> Andrea Stavros .... Anthony Quinn
> C.P.O. Brown .... Stanley Baker
> Spyros Pappadimos .... James Darren
> Major Franklin .... Anthony Quayle
> Maria Pappadimos .... Irene Papas
> Anna .... Gia Scala

At its time of production, *The Guns of Navarone* was one of the largest-budgeted war films ever made. Its resounding box-office success established it as a precedent in its genre for many years following. Produced and scripted by Carl Foreman, the widescreen color film, superbly photographed by British cameraman Oswald Morris, details the nearly suicidal attempt of a hand-picked band of saboteurs to rescue a force of two thousand British soldiers beseiged on Kheros, an isolated island in the Aegean Sea off the coast of Turkey.

The movie's prologue, produced by UFA, the cartoon company, sets the stage. The only approach to the island is by sea through a narrow channel near Navarone. At the top of four-hundred-feet-high sheer cliffs set in a deep natural cave impregnable to air attack are a pair of huge 210 mm guns manned by a Nazi force. Allied Intelligence learns that the Germans plan to blitz the trapped soldiers very soon, and the saboteur force, headed by Major Franklin (Anthony Quayle), has six days, later reduced to five, to destroy the guns as the British fleet sets out to evacuate the men. Along with Franklin, the band is composed of Captain Mallory (Gregory Peck), a famous mountaineer; explosives expert Corporal Miller (David Niven); Andrea Stavros (Anthony Quinn), a Greek Resistance fighter who has vowed to kill Mallory after the war because the Captain was indirectly responsible for the wartime deaths of his wife and children by Nazis; and two trained killers, C.P.O. Brown (Stanley Baker), the so-called "Butcher of Barcelona," and Spyros Pappa-dimos (James Darren), an American soldier reared in urban slums but a native of Navarone.

The team sets out in a converted fishing vessel and before long destroys an inquisitive German patrol boat. In a tumultuous storm, the boat is wrecked at the foot of the Navarone cliffs, largely unguarded by the Germans because they are considered impossible to scale. Mallory slowly leads the group up the treacherous face of the cliffs and takes command when Franklin is injured. Traveling across the island, they link up with two Resistance members, Spyros' sister Maria (Irene Papas) and a schoolteacher, Anna (Gia Scala), who was struck dumb by Nazi torture.

In the small village of Mandrakos, the force is captured by Germans, but Stavros engineers a trick whereby the group escapes in Nazi uniforms, leaving Franklin behind with deliberately false information which Mallory knows he will reveal to the enemy in his delirium. On the evening before the assault on the guns, Miller denounces Anna as a traitor who has been revealing their positions to the Germans. Before Mallory can kill her (they had previously shared a romantic interlude), Maria shoots her. The SS uses a truth drug on Franklin, who tells them of an assault landing; and the Germans pull out the Navarone forces to meet the invaders. Mallory and Miller sneak into the fortress and lay the explosives, knowing some of them will be discovered. The others stage diversionary actions, during which both Pappadimos and Brown are killed. The survivors escape to the sea in a boat secured by Maria, who leaves with Stavros to continue fighting in the Resistance. Mallory and Miller watch the British ships make their approach. The huge guns begin to fire, but the two men's horror turns to triumph as the last charge, carefully hidden under an elevator, finally goes off, triggering a massive series of explosions during which the guns fall harmlessly into the sea.

The production of the 5.6-million-dollar film was something of an epic in itself. Foreman had acquired the rights to the novel by Alistair MacLean as early as 1958, but refused even to contemplate production until his screenplay was letter-perfect. He wisely chose to shoot on locations as authentic to the novel's setting as possible and visited nearly every country in Europe looking for a site. He finally settled on Cyprus, where the local government, ranging from Bishop Makarios to Governor-General Sir Hugh Foote, promised lavish aid in the form of troops and military equipment from local British bases, with an eye to the prestige a large movie company filming a major production could provide the tiny island. However, Foreman, nearing production, was soon innocently involved in Cyprus' political problems, which concerned the colony's increasingly urgent desire to leave the Commonwealth. Foreman was accused of being a British agent. Despite assurances to Columbia of the movie company's safety by all three factions in Cyprus vying for power, Foreman pulled out and relocated to Rhodes, where the Greek government assured him of full cooperation, providing troops, destroyers, helicopters, planes, armaments, and military advisers, mainly for the impetus the project would provide to the fledgling Greek film industry.

Production finally began in early 1960. Well into the shooting, director Alexander MacKendrick fell ill and had to be replaced. Foreman himself took over for two weeks until J. Lee Thompson was hired. The shooting dragged on for seven months, which included time spent in London's Shepperton and Elstree Studios (where the harrowing shipwreck and storm sequences were shot in a tank). The film received a series of Royal Premieres in London and opened in June, 1961, in the United States, where it became the top-grossing film of the year for Columbia, which had financed the project (although it was produced by Foreman's British company). According to *Variety*, by the end of 1978, the film had returned rentals to the distributor of over $13 million, earning it a place on the all-time top-grossing films list.

The movie did not do as well critically, with reviewers chiefly finding fault with impassive acting, illogical plotting, and long, dialogue-laden passages containing Foreman's themes of personal *versus* "national" responsibility. Indeed, Foreman and Thompson are best in the wordless stretches of the film: the explosive fishing boat encounter with the German U-boat, the storm and shipwreck, and the agonizing scaling of the rain-swept cliffs. These fine sequences served up an exciting one-two punch that the film does not match until the finale. The thematic elements of the movie, including the Good German/Evil Nazi dichotomy, have since become standard themes for the genre. The film established a continuing vogue of producing films from Alistair MacLean's other war and espionage adventure novels. None, however, has enjoyed the success of *The Guns of Navarone*. Foreman's casting for the film, which had every agent in Hollywood with a candidate scurrying to the telephone, helped immensely to put the film over, catching Peck, Niven, Quinn, and Baker in ascending popularity, and throwing in Papas for a bit of class.

Foreman, Thompson, MacLean, and Columbia announced a sequel to the film as early as 1967. The project shifted hands several times, with Foreman gradually losing interest. MacLean's sequel scenario eventually was published as a novel which became a best seller. The poorly made and received film that finally appeared, from American-International in 1978, *Force 10 From Navarone*, was technically not a sequel although it opened with the original film's rousing finale and involved two of its characters, Mallory and Miller (played by Robert Shaw and Edward Fox, respectively), on a World War II mission to destroy a bridge and dam in Yugoslavia.

The Guns of Navarone won Golden Globe Awards for Best Motion Picture (Drama) and Best Score; it was voted Best Picture in the annual *Film Daily* poll; and it was nominated for seven 1961 Academy Awards, including Best Picture, Direction, Screenplay, Editing, Music, Sound, and Special Effects. It deservedly won in the last category while losing in most of the others to the major Oscar-winner of that year, *West Side Story*. The New York Film

Critics nominated *The Guns of Navarone* for Best Motion Picture and Best Director.

David Bartholomew

HALLELUJAH!

Released: 1929
Production: King Vidor for Metro-Goldwyn-Mayer
Direction: King Vidor
Screenplay: Wanda Tuchock, Ransom Rideout, Richard Schayer; based on
  the story of the same name by King Vidor
Cinematography: Gordon Avil
Editing: Hugh Wynn
Art direction: Cedric Gibbons
Music direction: Eva Jessye
Song: Irving Berlin
Running time: 109 minutes

> *Principal characters:*
> Zeke .... Daniel L. Haynes
> Chick .... Nina Mae McKinney
> Hot Shot .... William Fountaine
> Parson .... Harry Gray
> Mammy .... Fanny Belle de Knight
> Missy Rose .... Victoria Spivey
> Spunk .... Everett McGarrity

Hailed as the first all-Negro musical, *Hallelujah!* has long overshadowed
its immediate predecessor, Paul Sloane's *Hearts in Dixie*, released earlier in
1929 by Fox. Technically, however, *Hallelujah!* really is the first in that category, since there is not a white actor in the entire film, while *Hearts in Dixie*
features Richard Carlyle as a white doctor. Both are dramatic portrayals of
the life of the poor black in the South. However, *Hallelujah!*, a King Vidor
film, concentrates on a continuous flow of music to highlight each scene. The
Texas-born Vidor, who had been directing since the age of twenty-three and
had long wanted to make the movie, was prestigious enough to persuade his
company, M-G-M, to join him in financing the film. Vidor produced the film
from his own original story, which was further polished by several other
writers. He had written the part of Zeke for Paul Robeson but wound up
with Daniel L. Haynes, an understudy in the stage version of *Show Boat*,
when Robeson was unavailable. Similarly, Ethel Waters and Honey Brown
were being considered for the role of Chick before it went to Nina Mae
McKinney, an energetic seventeen-year-old performer who had been appearing onstage in Lew Leslie's *Blackbirds* review in New York. Most members of the cast were making their film debuts, including eighty-six-year-old
ex-slave Harry Gray, cast as the parson-father of Zeke.

Hallelujah!, which was Vidor's only musical, was filmed on location in
Tennessee and Arkansas; interiors were then made at the new Culver City
studios of M-G-M, where the sound on disc was recorded by Western Electric

Sound System for the location sequences. Along with the well-known spirituals and work songs were two original compositions by Irving Berlin, "Waiting at the End of the Road" and "Swanee Shuffle." Music supervision was by Eva Jessye, who also directed the Dixie Jubilee Singers heard throughout. In the shuffle number, McKinney shows enough style and talent to have made her an instant star, if such a thing were possible in the early sound days of Hollywood.

Whether *Hallelujah!* is a true representation of the plight of blacks in the 1920's or is a disguised series of stereotypes reacting to melodramatic situations is certainly debatable. Either allegation can be looked upon as having varying degrees of truth, although the film is full of life and movement and many individual scenes can be enjoyed on a high level. Chick's sexuality is evident in every scene, as are Zeke's baser instincts, which often overcome a strong will. The baptism in the river, ending with Zeke's pawing of the hysterical Chick, and the revival meeting, which almost resembles an orgy, point up the raw energy which Vidor brought to his project. Additionally, they serve to illustrate the struggle between religious and sexual fervor which dominates the film.

Hallelujah! opens with cotton pickers singing "Swanee River" as the Johnson family finishes the day's work. Zeke (Daniel L. Haynes), the eldest son, jokes with his Mammy (Fanny Belle de Knight); he lives happily with her and his father, a parson (Harry Gray), younger brother Spunk (Everett McGarrity), three little brothers (Milton Dickerson, Robert Couch, and Walter Tait), and an adopted sister, Missy Rose (Victoria Spivey), with whom he is in love. The three youngest boys need no excuse to begin dancing. That night, the Parson is called upon to unite Adam and Eve, a couple with eleven children who want to make their union permanent. As Rose plays "Here Comes the Bride" on a shaky-sounding organ, Zeke forces her to kiss him. He apologizes, but it obviously is not necessary. The newlyweds celebrate with a cakewalk.

Mammy sings the youngest boys to sleep and then retires with a "Thank God" for everyone getting through another day safely. The next day, Zeke and a chorus sing about cotton as he and Spunk bring their load to a mill, where it is processed and baled. There, Zeke joins in a rendition of "Waiting at the End of the Road." He sees the cotton loaded onto a riverboat before overhearing a crap game in progress and then encountering Chick (Nina Mae McKinney), a young dancer on the docks. He impulsively stops her and says she is just what he had in mind. She responds, "Get outta here, small change, you don't look like big money to me." Zeke lures her with the money he has just made by selling the cotton while a band blasts away at a saloon, where Chick introduces a song-and-dance number, "Swanee Shuffle." A couple dances to the song and then a huge man shuffles it before Chick and a group of singing waiters bring the proceedings to a rousing conclusion. During a slow dance with Chick, Zeke mentions that he has a hundred dollars with him; she replies that it would be easy to double it. Soon Zeke is gambling away all the money with Hot Shot (William Fountaine), Chick's partner.

Demanding to see the dice Hot Shot used, including the loaded pair in his pocket, Zeke forces the gambler to act. As Hot Shot pulls a gun after Zeke draws his knife, Spunk enters the premises. In a grapple for the gun, Hot Shot fires two shots, which hit Spunk. Grabbing the weapon, Zeke fires wildly three more times and then finds a sobbing Spunk on the floor. His brother is dead by the time Zeke reaches home with his body. The wake is a sorrowful, song-filled affair as Zeke mourns, prostrate in the field. Filled with religious fervor by the Parson, Zeke chants that the Lord is all, while Rose clings to him.

Next, a title proclaims, "And Zekiel became a Preacher." In the next scene, a congregation waiting for Zeke to step down from his gospel train sings "Get on Board." Children in a procession sing as Zeke proceeds on a mule. Heckling from the sidelines are Hot Shot and Chick, who remember Zeke from Greensville. The new preacher roughs up his two critics. At an outdoor meeting, the congregation does "Give Me That Old Time Religion" as Chick continues to jeer "Make me cry." Zeke acts as a conductor on a train, with Repentance the last station for sinners before Hell. He and the congregation sing "Waiting at the End of the Road." A sobbing Chick runs to the platform with the other converts.

The spiritual "Goin' Down to the Water" is sung while Zeke presides at baptisms in the river. A self-proclaimed wicked woman, Chick is filled with emotion as she is immersed. Zeke carries her back to his tent and tries to seduce her until Mammy intervenes, calling her a hypocrite. Troubled, Zeke asks Rose to marry him when they stop at the next station. Chick is singing "Give Me That Old Time Religion" when Hot Shot enters her house, over-riding her objections with the statement that sinning is in her blood. She knocks him down and begins hitting him with a poker, stating that she will do that to anybody who stands in her path to glory. Rushing to a revival meeting where Zeke is preaching, Chick joins in the singing and dancing. Zeke is drawn to her and follows her outside, then he carries her off. Rose then runs out and yells for Zeke. She returns to the church, where her wailing for him is mistaken for praying by the others.

Months later, Zeke is working at a saw mill to provide a modest cottage for Chick. The latter is entertaining Hot Shot, who makes a quick exit before Zeke arrives home. While Chick sings "St. Louis Blues," Zeke asks about the buggy out front. Suspiciously, Zeke pretends to sleep while Chick slips out with Hot Shot. He fires two shots at them, then races furiously after the buggy. It loses a wheel and Chick is thrown into a ditch. She tells Zeke of her fear of the Devil, who is coming for her as she dies. Pursuing Hot Shot through a swamp, Zeke kills him. On a rock pile, Zeke works as others sing.

Probation comes and Zeke strums a banjo while singing "Goin' Home" (on a barge, on top of a train, and in the fields). Once home, he is instantly forgiven, particularly by Rose, who still loves him.

Hallelujah! was not universally well received by the critics. Many confined their reviews to discussions of the film's treatment of blacks without discussing the work as drama, and therefore commented negatively on its impact. Later critics, however, have recognized its merits as a musical and have considered it as an important part of film history both for its sociological and cinematic values.

John Cocchi

HAMLET

Released: 1948
Production: Laurence Olivier for Two Cities Films; released by Universal-
   International (AA)
Direction: Laurence Olivier
Screenplay: Laurence Olivier and Alan Dent; based on the play of the same
   name by William Shakespeare
Cinematography: Desmond Dickinson
Editing: Helga Cranston
Art direction: Roger K. Furse (AA)
Set decoration: Carmen Dillon (AA)
Costume design: Roger K. Furse (AA)
Running time: 153 minutes

> *Principal characters:*
> Hamlet ....Laurence Olivier (AA)
> Claudius .... Basil Sydney
> Gertrude .... Eileen Herlie
> Ophelia .... Jean Simmons
> Polonius ....Felix Aylmer
> Laertes ....Terence Morgan

At the start of 1947 with *Henry V* (1945) an international success, Laurence
Olivier decided on another try at filming Shakespeare. Filippo Del Giudice,
who had been the producer of the stage production of *Hamlet*, had encouraged
him to make another film, and many members of the earlier production team
could be easily assembled. The question was which play to film? Olivier was
too young to do *King Lear*, his most recent stage success, and Hollywood
had already filmed *Romeo and Juliet* (1936) and *A Midsummer Night's Dream*
(1935). Furthermore, Orson Welles had just filmed *Macbeth* (1948) and had
announced plans for *Othello*. Therefore the choice almost necessarily fell to
Hamlet.

This was not an easy decision. At age forty, Olivier was a little old to play
the bedeviled prince of Denmark. Nor did he believe himself temperamentally
inclined to the role, feeling that his acting style was more suited to stronger,
less lyrical and poetic characters (such as Hotspur or Henry V). He briefly
considered casting someone else as Hamlet and only directing the film; but
reconsidered when he realized that financial backing depended on his playing
the role and that no other actor might be willing to submit to his highly
personal ideas about the part.

Thus, the problem became one of dealing with what is one of Shakespeare's
most complex plays, one that includes long philosophical soliloquies, a large
number of subplots and subsidiary characters, and a leading character whose
confusing behavior and often enigmatic reactions have given rise to more

psychological studies than virtually any other character in the theater. Even the basic plot is sometimes confusing and contrary.

Hamlet (Laurence Olivier), the crown prince of Denmark, is still trying to cope with his father's sudden death and the equally sudden remarriage of his mother, Gertrude (Eileen Herlie), to his uncle Claudius (Basil Sydney) when a ghost appears crying foul murder and vengeance. As Hamlet tries to weigh the veracity of the ghost's charge, plots and counterplots are set up involving Polonius (Felix Aylmer), the king's chief counselor, Ophelia (Jean Simmons), his virginal daughter, and Laertes (Terence Morgan), his hot-headed son. There follows a visit by strolling players who perform a melo-drama designed to reveal Claudius' guilt (it does); a heated quarrel in Ger-trude's bedroom that ends with the death of an innocent bystander (Polonius); Ophelia's reaction to Hamlet's seeming madness; an interruption by pirates; and a final confrontation involving poison rapiers, poison drinks, and the death of almost everyone, including Hamlet.

In short, it is a most unwieldly play, running four and a half hours when performed uncut. Olivier's wife, Vivien Leigh, advised him to cut a number of subsidiary characters, including the two fawning courtiers, Rosencrantz and Guildenstern, since these roles never really advance the action of the play, although they do add counterpoint, irony, and further dimension to the principal roles. Olivier himself soon realized that many of Hamlet's famed soliloquies would have to be deleted; in the final film, only the introductory "O, that this too too solid flesh would melt," the famous "To be or not to be," and the Advice to the Players remain largely intact. These are often treated as interior monologues, spoken over the sound track as Hamlet paces, broods, and wonders. Olivier also took time to revise the order of a few scenes to tighten up the story and drastically cut down some of the big set-piece scenes; the ghost is all the more haunting for being much less garrulous, and the play-within-a-play is a simple mime show with no tedious exposition to follow. With the advice of Shakespearean scholar Alan Dent, Olivier even updated a few Elizabethan anachronisms; for example, at one point in the dialogue "persists" was substituted for "perseveres."

In a more controversial decision, Olivier felt that there simply was not time in the final film to display many of the play's multifaceted notions; the meaning and resulting interpretation of the cast would have to be simplified. This simplification led some people to believe that Olivier was only trying to put a part of the total play on film. To impress further upon the audience a sense of the remotely austere miasma in which Hamlet wanders, Olivier and his set designer Roger K. Furse deliberately constructed a Danish castle that is more fortress and keep than living quarters. Its wide rooms, long hallways, and stone stairs are almost bare of furnishings and suggestive of no period. The light is theatrically artificial, almost always coming from above with no windows in sight. All scenes outside Denmark have been eliminated by cutting, and the one or two moments during which the film ventures outside the castle grounds itself are among its weakest: depictions of Ophelia's death by drowning and Hamlet's adventure with the pirates.

Olivier used black-and-white cinematography not only because he considered color too beautiful for tragedy but also because, technically, black-and-white cinematography could keep a character in focus at any distance, thus allowing the cameras to swoop and slide with far greater dexterity. Some scenes are shot with the players as much as 150 feet from the camera. Olivier deliberately means for his camera to have a personality of its own, moving through the castle like a man in a dream, seeing everything, influencing nothing, and then moving on. At the start of the film the camera slowly moves down into the castle, encompassing the first ghost scene on the ramparts, picking up settings and objects (Gertrude's bed, for example) that will ultimately become important, and finally reaching the central action in the main hall, the king's throne room.

At the film's end, with bodies littered about that same room, the camera withdraws as courtiers carry the dead Hamlet up through the castle, past many of the same areas, and up again to the ramparts. Realistically, this last journey of the dead Hamlet seems a bit incongruous, but psychologically, it is a retracing and a resolution of the film's philosophical path. Olivier meant to treat the castle at Elsinore as a mental labyrinth; only by keeping track of the paths can the audience find a way out.

The result, not surprisingly, was the production of a film with an already built-in theatricality; other factors gave it more. Eileen Herlie, signed to play Hamlet's mother, was in fact thirteen years younger than Olivier and rather looks it on film, despite deliberately unattractive cinematography. The rest of the cast were seasoned Shakespearean professionals, with one exception: eighteen-year-old Jean Simmons was such a theatrical newcomer that not only had she never appeared in a Shakesperean play, she had not even seen one. Ophelia's lines, excluding a few of the coarser references regarding the mad scene, were carefully explained to her.

As was often his habit on stage, Olivier delighted in finding at least one place in which to display a breathtaking prowess of athletics. For *Hamlet*, he decided the moment should be in the final duelling sequence when the dying prince finally leaps upon Claudius and kills him. Olivier decided that the leap should be from a balcony down upon the throne, a considerable jump. When Basil Sydney, portraying Claudius, demurred playing the scene and a professional strong man was substituted, it inspired Olivier even further. The leap turned into a swan dive which struck the stand-in with such force that he was knocked to the ground and lost two front teeth. However, it is a tour de force moment in the film, reminiscent of some of the amazing athletic stunts which Buster Keaton used to perform.

The film was widely acclaimed upon release in both England and America and won five Oscars in 1948 including those for Best Picture and Best Actor. But praise was by no means universal. Many a purist pointed out that the considerable time the camera used in prowling the corridors at Elsinore could have been better taken up by restoring cut dialogue. Many a reviewer also found the supporting performances weak, agreeing with James Agee that Jean Simmons was "the only person in the picture who gives every one of her lines the bloom of poetry and the immediacy of everyday life."

In the end, the same theatricality that had added so much to the film adaptation of *Henry V* became something of a detriment to *Hamlet*. No matter how in focus a character is at 150 feet away, the audience is still going to see more set in such a shot than anything else; and while the camera swoops were often fascinating and psychologically indicative (as when the camera flies down at different angles upon a plotting Claudius and Laertes, indicating how each is slowly using and enmeshing the other), Jean Renoir in a criticism candidly asked what that type of cinematography had to do with Shakespeare? The all-important verse is not illuminated by such techniques, yet the verse is the primary consideration of the play. If *Hamlet* is a miasma, then the way out should be through words, not through camera angles.

On the other hand, the play itself is somewhat impossible even with the limits Olivier had put upon it. Subsequent film and television presentations have not improved upon this 1948 version and have frequently been both hazier and duller. The areas in which Olivier excelled are here in good abundance. He brings in humor both when it is expected (as with Osric) and when it is not, and he charts his way through the shoals and reefs of "To be or not to be" with admirable dexterity and vocal manipulation. If prince Hamlet himself still remains an enigma, whether a Freudian one or an Aristotelian one, it is definitely the character and not the actor portraying him that causes him to be one. If the film still remains far from an ideal depiction, it may be because the mind will always find and demand more from *Hamlet* than any one production is able to give.

Lewis Archibald

A HARD DAY'S NIGHT

Released: 1964
Production: Walter Shenson for United Artists
Direction: Richard Lester
Screenplay: Alun Owen
Cinematography: Gilbert Taylor
Editing: John Jympson
Music: John Lennon and Paul McCartney
Running time: 85 minutes

Principal characters:
John Lennon .... Himself
Paul McCartney .... Himself
George Harrison .... Himself
Ringo Starr .... Himself
Grandfather .... Wilfrid Brambell
Norm .... Norman Rossington
Television Director .... Victor Spinetti
Shake .... John Junkin

When it was released in 1964, *A Hard Day's Night* caused general amazement among film critics and audiences alike. If they expected anything from a film starring the Beatles, who were then known mainly for their hairdos, their hysterical fans, and their fairly simple music, critics and audiences expected the standard pop music film—a silly plot serving as an excuse for the performance of a number of songs. The Beatles' film was different, however, because the Beatles were unique, as they were to prove in the ensuing decades. The film was also original because its makers, and especially director Richard Lester, were imaginative and wanted to make a good film rather than merely a showcase for the group. At every level the film is fresh, inventive, and exciting. The script, music, acting, and directing fit together perfectly.

Ostensibly, the film is the story of some twenty-four hours in the life of the Beatles—John, Paul, George, and Ringo—as they take a train, escape from their fans at both ends of the trip, have a press conference, go dancing, and then rehearse for and perform a television show. In between they escape together to play in an empty field, and later a moody Ringo takes a walk by himself. Throughout, they try to cope with Paul's grandfather (Wilfrid Brambell), whom they are taking along because Paul's mother thinks the trip would do him good.

The imaginative use of both music and natural sound is especially notable. The film opens with the Beatles running down a street pursued by fans. The only sound is the title song on the sound track, but when the song ends, we hear the natural sound of the fans screaming as the Beatles board a train and escape from the noise of the mob into the quiet of the train. Soon they go to the baggage car to keep Paul's grandfather out of trouble, and as they begin playing cards, another song, "I Should Have Known Better," is heard on the sound track. As the song continues, their cards are suddenly replaced by instruments, and the boys perform the song. Then, as the song ends, the cards and the natural sounds return.

After the train reaches its destination, the Beatles once again have to escape from their fans; but when they get to their hotel room, they briefly revolt against their managers, Shake (John Junkin) and Norm (Norman Rossington), by going off to a dancing club when they are supposed to answer fan mail. The next day they begin rehearsals for a television show with an extremely tense and worried director. When they are told to wait in a dressing room until they are needed, they instead rush out of the studio before anyone can stop them.

The visual *tour de force* of the film is this sequence in which the four run out of the studio, down a fire escape, and frolic about in a field to the song "Can't Buy Me Love." Perfectly edited to the rhythm of the song, their actions are both playful and visually captivating as they run and jump about. Great variety comes from the high, low, and normal camera angles as well as accelerated, slow, and normal motion. It is a very inventive and energetic sequence which wonderfully expresses the Beatle's joy at being free from all the constraints which they have been under: their fans, their managers, and the television studio. The lyrics of the song have nothing to do with the content of the sequence, but that is not important since the song's mood and rhythm precisely match the sequence's visual and emotional qualities. The scene, which begins with Ringo shouting "We're out," ends suddenly with a man gruffly telling them, "I suppose you know this is private property," as the song ends. "Sorry if we hurt your field, Mister," George responds as they turn to go back. There is nothing for them to do but return to the television studio.

After they come back to rehearse for the television show, they find that they are not the only ones restive because of the claustrophobic lives they are forced to lead. Paul's grandfather complains that he is supposed to be getting a change of scenery, but so far has been in "a train and a room, a car and a room, and a room and a room." After the boys perform "I'm Happy Just to Dance with You," Ringo is told to look after the grandfather, and the two go to the canteen. But mischiefmaker that he is, the old man provokes Ringo into going out "parading the streets," disguised in an old coat. Ringo's wanderings are a quiet counterpoint to the rest of the film as he meets a young boy playing hooky, tries to throw darts in a workingman's pub, and gallantly spreads his coat over some puddles for a young woman. "Parading," however, does not seem to be very rewarding for Ringo. The boy leaves to rejoin his friends; Ringo is asked to leave the pub; and the young woman falls into a manhole he has covered with his coat. To cap it all, he ends up in a police station, picked up for "wandering abroad" and "malicious intent."

In the next sequence Lester proves that the police chase, which has been a staple of film from its earliest days, can still be fresh and exciting. After the other Beatles find Ringo, they go to the police station to rescue him so that he can be at the television studio in time for the show. John, Paul, and George rush into the station and then rush out followed by a large group of policemen, with Ringo himself following along last of all. He walks calmly down the steps and then suddenly joins the chase. The Beatles and all the policemen reach a dead end, reverse, go back into and then out of the police station. Finally the Beatles reach the theater in time for the television show. The sequence has all of the usual appeal of a police chase—the quick action and the escape from authority—as well as such Lester touches as a man stealing a car unnoticed as the Beatles and policemen run past only to have a policeman enlist the help of the surprised thief as he starts to drive away. The basic vitality and rhythm of the sequence comes from its being artfully synchronized with the song "Can't Buy Me Love."

The Beatles then do the television show in front of a theater full of screaming fans and immediately afterward escape to a helicopter which rises into the air as the film ends.

All of the songs in the film were composed by John and Paul. Some are used to underscore the action, as when Ringo is wandering or when all four are cavorting in the field or being chased by their fans or the police. All of the others are performed on stage or in the baggage car of the train. The lyrics, consequently, have no specific connection with the plot. The songs are nonetheless integral to the film, partly because Beatle music naturally fits a story in which the Beatles are playing themselves and partly because many of the scenes were photographed and edited to fit specific songs.

The excellent script by Alun Owen, besides giving overall shape to the visual and musical elements, provides witty and trenchant comedy, often based on the theme of the Beatles' conflict with authority or convention. In their train compartment, for example, a crusty older man insists on closing the window even though they want it open. When he tells them he fought the war for their sort, Ringo replies, "Bet you're sorry you won." And the boys are continually uttering mock serious profundities. Ringo: "That's why I took up the drums. It's me active compensatory factor." George: "Yes, he's filled his head with notions seemingly." John, when told the train station is surging with girls: "Please, can I have one to surge with?"

One of the most pleasant surprises of the film is the performances of all four Beatles. It is dangerous to ask nonactors to play roles even if they are asked to play only themselves. Too frequently the result is that they appear to be bad actors rather than real people. However, all four give convincing performances. Also, they are well-supported by the other actors. Victor Spinetti as the television director and Wilfrid Brambell as the grandfather are especially memorable.

A great measure of the credit for the quality of the film must go to the director, Richard Lester. As well as having worked extensively in live television, both in the United States and Great Britain, he had been a member of the Goons, a group which included the British comedians Peter Sellers and Spike Milligan. With Lester as director, the Goons had made a zany eleven-minute film called *The Running, Jumping and Standing Still Film*, a collection of such gags as a violinist standing so far from his music that he has to read it through a telescope and must bicycle to and from the music stand to turn the pages. Out of these experiences Lester had developed an inventive and seemingly spontaneous visual style which proved to be ideal for the Beatles.

Indeed, the combined talents of the Beatles, Lester, and screenwriter Alun Owen lift *A Hard Day's Night* above the category of the pop music movie to the realm of film art, winning from critic Andrew Sarris the accolade "The *Citizen Kane* of juke-box musicals."

Timothy W. Johnson

HAROLD AND MAUDE

Released: 1971
Production: Colin Higgins and Charles Mulvehill for Mildred Lewis and Colin
  Higgins Productions; released by Paramount
Direction: Hal Ashby
Screenplay: Colin Higgins
Cinematography: John A. Alonzo
Editing: William A. Sawyer and Edward Warschilka
Music: Cat Stevens
Running time: 91 minutes

> *Principal characters:*
> Harold Chasen .... Bud Cort
> Maude .... Ruth Gordon
> Mrs. Chasen .... Vivian Pickles
> Uncle Victor .... Charles Tyner

Harold Chasen is a very rich twenty-year-old obsessed with death and the
staging of faked suicides. Maude is a willingly impoverished seventy-nine-
year-old dedicated to a life-affirming and cheerful approach to her existence.
The relationship that evolves between these two highly divergent characters
is the focus of one of the 1970's most enjoyable comedies.

Harold (Bud Cort), a pale and gangly youth, spends considerable time
trying to gain the attention of his manipulative socialite mother by staging
grisly "suicides." They are both horrendous and hilarious. However, they
usually fail to impress Mrs. Chasen (Vivian Pickles), who instead goes blithely
about her self-appointed task of turning Harold into a man with "responsi-
bilities." One of her ploys is to find a girl friend for Harold, and to this end,
she engages a computer dating service. In one magnificently ridiculous sequence, she corners Harold to fill out the dating service's questionnaire, and
as Harold sits mutely by, Mrs. Chasen directs the questions to Harold but
answers them to her own specifications. Three dates ultimately are sent to
the Chasen mansion over a period of time. Two are driven away by the
suicides that Harold stages to bedevil them; but the third beats Harold at his
own game. She becomes more involved than he in staging a fake *hara-kiri*.

Another of Harold's death-oriented pastimes is his regular attendance at
the funerals of strangers. At one of these he encounters Maude (Ruth Gordon), who also shares his strange passion. At first he is somewhat reluctant
to strike up a friendship with her; but it is not long before Harold is charmed
by the old woman's vitality and unconventional ways.

Harold soon becomes a regular visitor at the renovated railroad car that
Maude calls home. It is during these visits that Maude, by sharing her zest
for living, begins to teach Harold the meaning of life and love. She first

awakens his awareness of the world by getting him to use his five senses. She exposes him to yoga breathing, tactile sculpture, and the tastes of oatstraw tea and ginger pie, and teaches him to play the banjo. In conversations, she shares her philosophy of life with him. She believes in individual freedom and has little patience with the repressive forces in society that seek to impose conformity and spiritual death.

It is quickly apparent that Harold is learning a positive attitude toward life. At the same time, however, his mother, undaunted by the failure of the computer dating approach to make a man of Harold, now decides that a stint in the Army will succeed where she has failed. She turns Harold over to his Uncle Victor (Charles Tyner) for a preinduction pep talk. An earlier reference has characterized Uncle Victor as having been General MacArthur's "right-hand man." When he first appears on the screen, the audience sees that he has lost his right arm—only an empty, starched sleeve that performs a me-chanically controlled salute remains. In one of the more cynically biting scenes, Uncle Victor takes Harold on a visit to an old soldier's home at which he extols the virtues of Army life while decrepit and handicapped inmates falter and collapse on the ground.

Harold and Maude, however, devise a scheme to keep Harold out of the Army. In full view of Uncle Victor, Harold "murders" Maude to convince his uncle that he is too psychopathic even for the Army. The ruse succeeds; Harold's Army career comes to an abrupt end.

By this time, Harold has fallen in love with Maude. She graciously accepts his tokens of affection and they become lovers. In one fleeting, poignant scene, the audience glimpses a number tattooed on Maude's arm. Thus dra-matically we are made to know that Maude has survived a concentration camp and yet remains a lover of life who relishes her freedom and her individuality.

Harold soon produces pandemonium when he announces his intention to marry Maude. In rapid succession the straitlaced and horrified reactions of his mother, his psychiatrist, a minister, and his Uncle Victor are shown. All are so appalled by the unconventional alliance that none bothers to address the fact that Harold has found love and aliveness with Maude.

Over all objections, Harold pursues his plans to marry Maude. He intends to propose to her on the occasion of her eightieth birthday celebration. When he arrives at her home, he finds, to his horror, that Maude has taken an overdose of sleeping pills and is quietly awaiting death. When the frantic Harold demands an explanation, Maude simply explains that she had always planned to be gone by the time she reached eighty. In this way she will avoid lingering illness and incapacity. An ambulance rushes Maude to the hospital. Harold, tears streaming down his face, accompanies her. He tells her that he loves her; she replies that she loves him too and that he should "go out and love some more." Doctors attempt to save her, but they are too late. Maude's death has proven to be her last act of self-determination.

In the final scene, Harold is seen speeding his minihearse through the rainy countryside. The car plummets over a cliff, bursting into flames as it hits the rocky beach below. Enough time elapses to allow the audience to believe that Harold has now committed a real suicide, but the camera pans upward to reveal Harold standing on the cliff, playing the tune on his banjo that Maude had taught him. Having learned the meaning of real living and loving, he walks away performing a little jig as he continues to play his tune.

Hal Ashby's sensitive direction of the film saves it from becoming either an unbelievable farce or a maudlin love story. He balances the two seemingly contradictory but interrelated themes of the film: life is to be lived and enjoyed and yet it will ultimately end in death. The delicacy with which he delineates these themes gives the viewer a sense of the rhythm of life, along with an acknowledgment that death is an integral part of life. Death need not be dreaded if, in fact, life has been lived well and to the fullest.

Harold and Maude was Ashby's second directorial effort, following *The Landlord* (1970). These two films were the seminal beginnings of a distinguished career that has subsequently included such memorable films as *The Last Detail* (1973), *Shampoo* (1975), *Bound for Glory* (1976), and *Coming Home* (1978).

Ashby's direction evokes some impressive acting performances. Bud Cort is appealingly whimsical in his portrayal of Harold. From the ashen and depressive eccentric of the early scenes, he flowers believably into a cheerful and robust young man. Ruth Gordon's performance maintains the credibility of Maude's quirky but delightful character throughout. Another gem is Vivian Pickles' interpretation of Harold's unflappable and self-absorbed mother.

While the film is a comedy, it is also a biting social satire of an era. Its condemnation of the Army, as personified by Uncle Victor, represents the concerns of a generation that was questioning United States involvement in Vietnam. Other previously sacrosanct institutions are also examined in a satirical fashion: the policeman is seen as officious, doltish, and inhuman; the psychiatrist is a shoddy copy of an outmoded Sigmund Freud; and the clergyman is a ridiculous man who attempts to deal with both relationships and sexuality without ever having had, one surmises, the benefit of firsthand experiences. The forces of society that are inclined to straitjacket us are weighed against the value and dignity of human life. In effect, the film encourages the viewer to examine the possibilities of his own life. Rather than accepting the preformulated definitions and answers handed down by traditional authorities, the film urges the viewer to experiment and then savor the results.

Mention should be made of Cat Stevens' musical score. The sprightly and ephemeral quality of his melodies eloquently express the mood of the film.

When *Harold and Maude* opened in December, 1971, reviews were somewhat mixed. Some critics hailed it as a joyously innovative piece of film-making, while others felt that the story line was inconsistent in seeking to glorify life yet ending with Maude's suicide. In the last analysis, the earlier criticisms have proven somewhat superfluous since *Harold and Maude* has developed a life of its own, becoming a minor cult film. From 1971 to mid-1978 it continued to draw such sizable audiences in neighborhood art and revival theaters that a new print of the film was released in mid-1978. Thus, despite the initial lukewarm response of some critics, *Harold and Maude* continues to please the critics that matter most—the paying audience.

Isabel O'Neill

HARVEY

Released: 1950
Production: John Beck for Universal-International
Direction: Henry Koster
Screenplay: Mary C. Chase and Oscar Brodney; based on the play of the
  same name by Mary C. Chase
Cinematography: William Daniels
Editing: Ralph Dawson
Running time: 103 minutes

Principal characters:
Elwood P. Dowd .... James Stewart
Veta Louise Simmons .... Josephine Hull (AA)
Miss Kelly .... Peggy Dow
Dr. Sanderson .... Charles Drake
Dr. Chumley .... Cecil Kellaway
Myrtle Mae Simmons .... Victoria Horne
Marvin Wilson ....Jesse White

Harvey represents a successful film adaptation of the Pulitzer Prize-winning play by Mary C. Chase. After a successful run of five years on Broadway, the screen rights were purchased by Universal Studios for $1,000,000, then a record. To help insure the success of the movie version, the studio made very few changes in the script and retained the talented Josephine Hull and others from the original cast, adding James Stewart, who had also appeared in the stage version in summer stock. He was not, however, the originator of the amiable alcoholic Elwood P. Dowd, as many people believe. The Broadway play actually starred Frank Fay. Hull was primarily a stage actress, but this second screen role (her first was in *Arsenic and Old Lace*, 1944) won her an Oscar for Best Supporting Actress in 1951.

The movie is still a favorite because of the strength of the original play and because of its wonderful cast. Besides Stewart and Hull, most of the other characters were portrayed by well-known character actors playing the roles they knew best: Cecil Kellaway as Dr. Chumley, Jessie White as Wilson, and Charles Drake as Dr. Sanderson. While such a film would probably not be made today, it stands as a classic comedy in which fantasy triumphs over the Victorian repressions of society.

The basic plot concerns the problems caused by Elwood P. Dowd's friendship with a rabbit, six feet, three inches tall, named Harvey. This situation immediately leads the audience to suspect the state of Elwood's mind, but what generates the comedy is the fact that Harvey is more real than is at first suspected, at least within the context of the plot. Harvey is a pooka, a mischievous spirit, who had introduced himself to Elwood on Fairfax Street one night. Harvey represents the forces of fantasy and magic which counter-balance the repressed, straitlaced "normal" world that Elwood has left be-hind. As he later states, he wrestled with reality for forty years, and then, when he met Harvey, he won.

Elwood is a forty-two-year-old Taurus who has inherited money, thus ex-plaining how he can spend his days in leisurely amiability. He lives in the family mansion with his sister Veta (Josephine Hull) and her daughter Myrtle Mae (Victoria Horne). The family is not concerned about Elwood's obvious fondness for martinis, but they are upset because his invisible companion is embarrassing and interferes with Veta's plans to find Myrtle Mae a suitable husband.

As the picture opens, Veta has planned a meeting of the Wednesday Forum to introduce Myrtle Mae to society. For years the two women have been recluses because of Elwood, but Veta has finally decided to risk a party while her brother is out for the afternoon visiting his many friends about town. Elwood and Harvey unexpectedly come home, however, and as they arrive the viewer is treated to a hilarious rendition of a spring song about flowers and rabbits going hop, hop, hop. The ladies are enchanted by this entertain-ment, but they are very upset by Elwood's introduction of Harvey. The juxtaposition of the song lyric with the movie theme illustrates the wry humor that pervades the film. As the women make their hurried exits, the first points are scored in the central conflict over just whose sense of reality and propriety should be questioned. The stage is also set for Veta's reaction. She has "had it," and calls the family lawyer to arrange for her brother's commitment.

By this time it is clear that Elwood, while perhaps a little peculiar, is far from dangerous. In fact, he is a truly gentle man, extremely courteous and likable. What frightens the women and what bothers Veta is his total accep-tance of his fantasy and his insistence on drawing them into it. This is the crux of the movie's theme: the inability or refusal of most people to let down their defenses and admit the extraordinary into their lives. As Elwood, Stew-art is an engagingly whimsical missionary. To filmgoers of today, the role seems perfect for Stewart's easy drawl and shy, boyish mannerisms, although at the time his choice for the role was criticized because of his age and the popularity of his predecessor on the stage, Frank Fay. The charm works wonderfully on film, however, and it is easy to believe that for Elwood, every day is a beautiful day.

Moving to the Chumley Rest Home, the plot takes some rather predictable turns. Responding to Veta's agitated state, Marvin Wilson (Jesse White), a young staff psychiatrist, assumes that she is the new case, and she is taken away by Wilson babbling about rabbits and pookas. During her initial meeting with Dr. Sanderson (Charles Drake) Veta had blurted out an admission that once or twice she had seen Harvey, a fact which explains her great sensitivity to the problems his friendship with Elwood has created. It also explains why she rigidly refuses to put up with Elwood any longer—she fears for her sanity. While she is confined at the Home, several minor romantic plot lines are developed. Wilson is introduced as a possible match for Myrtle Mae, and although it is obvious that he is not "suitable" within the context of the film it is very probable that their attraction will develop into something more serious. Dr. Sanderson and his nurse, Miss Kelly (Peggy Dow) constitute another obvious couple; but he, like so many of the rational characters in the film, takes life too seriously to notice romantic possibilities. One of Elwood's positive accomplishments is helping to bring both of these couples together.

Eventually, the mistaken commitment of Veta is discovered and she returns home ready to sue Chumley (Cecil Kellaway) and have Wilson arrested. Chumley goes in search of Elwood, certain that he can help him back to sanity. Elwood, meanwhile, has been searching for Harvey all over town, and finally runs into him at Charley's, a local bar. When Chumley finds them, it is clear that he should have heeded Veta's warning concerning what he was up against. Even an eminent psychiatrist is no match for a pooka, and after a few drinks Chumley not only argues with Harvey but with the man at the next table as well, and is expelled from the bar. Harvey, it seems, is visible and real to those who are free enough to admit his existence, although there is admittedly a certain danger in letting go of one's normal inhibitions. The effect of Harvey on Dr. Chumley reflects essentially the same appeal that the movie holds for audiences. Harvey's presence epitomizes the desire to escape the reality of our everyday problems and to begin to indulge our fantasies. The comic twist is that a pooka is also mischievous, and makes it difficult to live comfortably in both worlds.

Later, back at the Home, Elwood and Dr. Chumley have quite a discussion about the wonderful things Harvey can do for his friends. Chumley begins to wish that his fantasies would become reality through Harvey's remaining with him, and this appears to be the plan. There is, however, still the matter of Elwood's commitment to deal with, and, despite the doctor's acknowledgment of Harvey's existence, a drug injection is recommended to rid Elwood of his delusions. The always charming Elwood consents because Veta asks him to do so. Fortunately, at a crucial moment a cab driver interrupts the procedure and helps Veta understand that this injection will not only get rid of Harvey, but will make her brother all too normal: he will become miserable, crabby, and mean. She stops the doctors just in time, saving both Elwood and Harvey. She has realized that Elwood's pleasant nature is too valuable to lose.

There is only one major theme in this story about a man and his rabbit, but it takes many forms. Veta, although she is as lovable as her brother, represents a social and sexual repression which is the antithesis of the fantasy and freedom represented by Elwood and Harvey. Her solution to the problem of sexual feelings is to go out for long walks, while Elwood's is to encourage closeness and feeling through pleasant compliments and flowers. Veta is the perfect foil for Elwood's ramblings. As she becomes hysterical, he remains calm and sincere, undermining her attempts to be rational and to take life too seriously. The magic inherent in Elwood is his ability to help people see their problems as small and manageable. Veta strives throughout to maintain her rationality by denying Harvey's existence, although deep inside she knows that he is real. By the end of the film, she must either accept him openly or deny the benefits of his existence by drugging her brother.

A final statement about magic, added to the movie version, constitutes a nice touch. Chumley wants Harvey to stay with him, putting Elwood's pleasant nature to the ultimate test. Of course he agrees, as long as Harvey had no objections. In the stage version, Chumley merely tries to "steal" Harvey by injecting Elwood with his formula, thus preventing Harvey's return to his old friend. Magic, however, as every reader of fairy tales knows, can be used for good or for selfish purposes, the former being preferable. Chumley's desires, as we suspect all along, are too personal and dull, in sharp contrast with Elwood's friendly nature; and as the film ends, Harvey rejoins Elwood. Fortunately, Elwood observes, they may just have time for a nightcap before the bars close.

Christine Gladish

HEAVEN CAN WAIT

Released: 1943
Production: Ernst Lubitsch for Twentieth Century-Fox
Direction: Ernst Lubitsch
Screenplay: Samson Raphaelson; based on the play *Brithday* by Laszlo Bus-Fekete
Cinematography: Edward Cronjager
Editing: Dorothy Spencer
Art direction: James Basevi and Leland Fuller
Interior decoration: Thomas Little and Walter M. Scott
Running time: 112 minutes

Principal characters:
Martha	Gene Tierney
Henry Van Cleve	Don Ameche
Hugo Van Cleve	Charles Coburn
E. F. Strabel	Eugene Pallette
Mrs. Strabel	Marjorie Main
His Excellency	Laird Cregar
Albert Van Cleve	Allyn Joslyn
Bertha Van Cleve	Spring Byington
Randolph Van Cleve	Louis Calhern
Jasper	Clarence Muse
Mademoiselle	Signe Hasso

Heaven Can Wait begins in an anteroom of hell, to which the recently deceased Henry Van Cleve (Don Ameche) reports to accept his assignment to one or another infernal circle. The doorkeeper ("His Excellency") is not convinced, however, that Van Cleve is a good candidate for eternal damnation and demands a review of the facts in the case of Van Cleve's life.

The story that unfolds is that of a spoiled though amiable child of a late nineteenth century New York family of established wealth, who sows as many wild oats as he can within the bounds of discretion imposed by the reigning Victorianism. He elopes with his cousin's betrothed; loses her as a result of his continuing dalliances; recaptures her with his limited though unabated charm; enjoys a thoroughly happy married life; rears a son; plays the field again after his wife's death; and finally himself succumbs under the strain of sudden ministrations from a beautiful nurse—managing all the while to avoid a single day's work or any endeavor which could be even remotely construed as socially useful.

Though Van Cleve may exclude all extraromantic considerations from his life, he does not come across to the viewer as some Dionysian reveler; he has not thrown it all away in some *l'amour fou*; he has not lost his soul in some Faustian compact in which passion has been his reward. The very structure of the film militates against any such perception: for the greater part, Van Cleve is simply the husband in a marriage that endures thirty years. His extramarital affairs are alluded to rather than seen; his transgressions are invariably discreet; his submission to society's standards is such that his life comes to seem rather prosaic, an impression that is deliberately reinforced by the casting. Yet the film stands in judgment of the sins of Henry Van Cleve (Don Ameche). Of what sins could so infinitely mild a hedonist be guilty, or even capable?

However, it is precisely his mildness that is the issue: Van Cleve—and, to a certain extent, the world the film depicts—stands accused of triviality. In a sense, this is not a new development in Lubitsch: the characters in his films frequently are both in and of circumscribed worlds from which he maintains an ironic, if affectionately inconsistent, distance. In *Heaven Can Wait*, however, Lubitsch deals with the most vulnerable players and limited characters of his career, and he is correspondingly gentle with them—his attraction to them is real.

Partly as a matter of self-protection, though, Lubitsch does reverse one career-long pattern. Traditionally, his sophisticated leads are the objects of audience identification, and his bumbling supporting characters the objects of audience derision. In *Heaven Can Wait*, this arrangement is reversed. As Henry's foxy grandpa, Hugo Van Cleve (Charles Coburn) serves as an island of sanity in a sea of fools. While other characters spout clichés among themselves, his undercutting asides are a kind of direct address to the audience— a characteristic function of Lubitsch leading players. Significantly, though, Hugo Van Cleve cannot refrain from indulging his grandson, whose elopement he abets. A similarly mediating role is played by the black manservant Jasper (Clarence Muse) of the Strabels (Eugene Pallette and Marjorie Main), the parents of Martha (Gene Tierney). Jasper serves as an emissary between the cartoonlike, choleric couple, and then between them and their outcast daughter. When we first meet the Strabels at home, they are engaged in mortal breakfast-table combat which culminates when Mrs. Strabel prematurely reveals to her husband, E. F. Strabel, the outcome of that morning's episode of the Katzenjammer Kids. Hugo and Jasper stand fastidiously above such nonsense, but ultimately they are committed to their respective households, thereby serving as refractions of Lubitsch's own critical affection.

Indeed, the tug of war between affection and gentle derision permeates every aspect of the movie. The interplay between Henry Van Cleve and Martha is, as James Agee called it in his near-rave review, a "mosaic of kidded clichés." It is as if Lubitsch were placing quotation marks rather unobtrusively around much of the material. When the angry Martha flashes her eyes or the lovesick Henry coos with fervent emotion, the quotation marks grow suddenly more obvious. A similar commentary is implicit in the sets, which move in ravishing color (*Heaven Can Wait* is the only film whose use of color was known to have excited D. W. Griffith) from the stuffy parlors of the 1890's to the sleek Art Deco living rooms of the 1920's. The modification of dress, speech, and posture as the film moves across the decades is wonderfully handled and encloses the characters deeper within prevailing conventions.

That Lubitsch is touched by the trivial life even as he feels superior to it becomes clearer in the later parts of the picture. Tokens of the past become precious. The dying Van Cleve tells his nurse of a dream he has just had: the boat ferrying him across the River Styx becomes a luxury liner with an orchestra playing the Merry Widow Waltz, so popular when he was young. Without losing any of its seriousness, death itself becomes encased in the prevailing archaic genteel frivolity.

At the moment of Van Cleve's actual death, Lubitsch transforms one of his most famous touches—the closed door that symbolizes sexual encounter, guaranteed in earlier Lubitsch films to produce amusement—into a sign of mortality. A beautiful new nurse walks down the hall to come on duty, enters Van Cleve's room and closes the door behind her, the camera remaining, as always, discreetly outside. After a moment, the Merry Widow Waltz starts up, the camera tracks slowly back from the door, then pans downward as the scene dissolves back to hell. This is not merely Van Cleve meeting death: it is also the sick and aging Lubitsch confronting mortality as directly yet discreetly as he had always encountered life.

This may explain why Lubitsch made a film that sought to redeem a man from the charge of triviality. (Van Cleve is indeed redeemed; the doorkeeper sends him up to heaven.) Lubitsch is so inextricably wedded to this society that he cannot conceive of heaven and hell operating on any other basis. Indeed, Van Cleve is greeted in hell's anteroom by an aged, just-deceased old girl friend who makes the ghastly error of showing him her legs and is dispatched immediately to the infernal fires, thus illustrating that taste still matters. These are not transient trivialities; they are ultimate trivialities.

In a sense, the man whom Lubitsch is redeeming from these charges is himself. *Heaven Can Wait*, in this regard, is to Lubitsch what *Sullivan's Travels* (1941) is to Sturges. At a time when artists were supposed to be concerned with the horrific issues of war and Fascism, Lubitsch and Sturges chose to defend the claims of the comic muse, of frivolity and triviality and style, and, by implication, of the validity of their life's work. *Heaven Can Wait* thus becomes the *apologia*, as if one were needed, for Ernst Lubitsch's career.

Harold Meyerson

HEAVEN CAN WAIT

Released: 1978
Production: Warren Beatty for Paramount
Direction: Warren Beatty and Buck Henry
Screenplay: Elaine May and Warren Beatty; based on the play of the same name by Harry Segall
Cinematography: William A. Fraker
Editing: Robert C. Jones and Don Zimmerman
Art direction: Paul Sylbert and Edwin O'Donovan (AA); set decoration, George Gaines (AA)
Music: Dave Grusin
Running time: 110 minutes

Principal characters:
Joe Pendleton	Warren Beatty
Betty Logan	Julie Christie
Mr. Jordan	James Mason
Max Corkle	Jack Warden
Tony Abbott	Charles Grodin
Julia Farnsworth	Dyan Cannon
The Escort	Buck Henry
Krim	Vincent Gardenia
Sisk	Joseph Maher

At a time when films as diverse as *Invasion of the Body Snatchers* (1956), *A Star Is Born* (1937), and *The Big Sleep* (1946) were being remade, and when sequels such as *Jaws II* (1979) and *Rocky II* (1979) seemed a safe proposition, a remake of *Here Comes Mr. Jordan* (1941) must have appeared to be a sure success. Accordingly, Warren Beatty, hedging his bets, collaborated with Elaine May on the screenplay for the remake and with Buck Henry on the direction, but relied upon himself as the film's star and producer. The film, entitled *Heaven Can Wait*, aided by a very clever poster campaign (anyone writing to Paramount could get one free), became a box-office smash and garnered eight Academy Award nominations. It won only one Oscar, however, for Paul Sylbert's and Edwin O'Donovan's Art Direction with George Gaines' Set Decoration.

The story concerns Joe Pendleton (Warren Beatty), a second-string quarterback for the Los Angeles Rams who has an automobile accident. He is supposed to survive the incident, but an overzealous heavenly Escort (Buck Henry) collects his soul and his body is cremated. When the mistake is discovered, Joe and Mr. Jordan (James Mason), the man in charge of sending souls on to their final reward, scour the world in search of a body in good enough shape for Joe to consider occupying it. They arrive at millionaire Leo Farnsworth's mansion just as his wife Julia (Dyan Cannon) and his confidential secretary Tony Abbott (Charles Grodin) are about to murder Leo. The proceedings are interrupted by the arrival of Betty Logan (Julie Christie) representing an English town about to be displaced by one of Leo's refineries. Joe, who is invisible and watches the scene, is charmed by Betty Logan and by the notion that he can inhabit Leo temporarily and do her a favor. Joe decides to occupy Leo's body until he can straighten things out. Betraying his egalitarian roots, Joe invites the press and Betty to a board meeting of Farnsworth's corporation where he makes a virtual shambles of the millionaire's business empire by agreeing not to dispossess the inhabitants of Pagglesham; further, he agrees to stop snaring dolphins along with the tuna that one of his factories cans, and finally to quit dealing in nuclear energy plants. Joe next decides to get Farnsworth's body in shape in order to try out for the Rams. He summons Max Corkle (Jack Warden), his old trainer from the Rams, and convinces Max that he is Joe by massacring a familiar song on his saxophone. He then embarks on an intensive training program which involves the entire Farnsworth household staff, and ultimately buys the Rams so that he can play in the playoffs and take the Rams to the Super Bowl. He becomes increasingly attracted to Betty and declares his love for her just as Abbott and Julia murder Farnsworth. Joe, once again without a body, enters the body of Tom Jarrett, a Rams player who is about to die during a game. This is Joe's final incarnation; Mr. Jordan makes it clear that he will not remember his previous embodiments, and this is borne out by his refusal to recognize his saxophone when Max tells him that he knows that he is Joe rather than Tom. Outside the stadium, Joe, in Tom's body, finds Betty looking for Max. Without consciously knowing who he is, she senses Joe's presence in the quarterback's body and they leave together.

Heaven Can Wait was treated by reviewers as a comedy, but it is not. Rather, it is a modest little morality tale, the heart of which is Joe's Capraesque speech to Farnsworth's board of directors about saving dolphins and respecting people's rights. The darts it throws in the guise of being a social comedy— at treacherous wives, bumbling functionaries, and suave professionals—are very soft. In fact, *Heaven Can Wait* is so plot-heavy, repeating such gags as Joe's dislike of hats, Farnsworth's love of naval uniforms, and a daily flag-lowering ceremony involving a cannon, that there is precious little room for the message. The statements which the film makes concerning ecology get unintentional reinforcement from the filmmakers during a sequence in which Joe travels by helicopter to downtown Los Angeles. There is so much smog that one can scarcely see the buildings, and we suddenly understand and visualize Betty Logan's concern when she says that Farnsworth's refinery will ruin her home town.

Although Beatty obviously conceived of the film as a starring vehicle for himself and Julie Christie, the film is stolen by its supporting players, notably by Joseph Maher as the butler, Sisk, who remains unflappably courteous whether talking to his employer in a darkened closet (where Joe has taken Mr. Jordon and the Escort for a conference) or grimly joining Joe in calisthenics when he trains to rejoin the Rams. James Mason is equally self-possessed as Mr. Jordan, calmly explaining that other people cannot see or hear him; and Buck Henry is owlishly indignant as the inept supernumerary who eagerly collects Pendleton's body too soon. Charles Grodin as Tony Abbott is a model of sneaky rectitude as he talks to Joe from behind his inamorata's curtains during a midnight rendezvous with Dyan Cannon, or in anticipation of their arrest for murder, tells her to "Pick up *The Fountainhead* and pretend to be reading." Cannon as Julia Farnsworth is deliciously two-faced, screaming in the bushes one minute and frantically guzzling scotch from a decanter the next, her candid blue eyes never once indicating that she is ever telling the truth. Jack Warden as Max Corkle has the most colorful role as the cheerful trainer who is both comedic—talking into thin air in the misguided notion that Mr. Jordan is listening—and sentimental—telling Joe at the end that he can tell who he really is because of that ever-present saxophone.

Oddly enough, Beatty miscast himself. He does not represent that blend of flippant sincerity and blithe chicanery that Cary Grant brought to roles such as *His Girl Friday* (1940) and *The Awful Truth* (1937). Beatty is too frantic and too smart; a man capable of absorbing all the corporate data he ingests in a few hours as Farnsworth would not be a football player in the first place. And as a football player, he appears both too old (at age forty-one) and too underdeveloped physically. Julie Christie is bright, pliant, and attractive as Betty, but she is not necessary to the plot; Joe as Farnsworth would have discovered the error of Farnsworth's ways and delivered his populist manifesto without her prompting.

Heaven Can Wait is benign, genial, and slightly addled. It does not so much contain and present ideas as it does present people who talk about theirs. *Here Comes Mr. Jordan* did not bother with a message; it was an unabashed fantasy, whimsical escapist fare for people who wanted to believe in romance and happy endings. That is what *Heaven Can Wait* should be, but it is that only when Beatty and Henry relax. The film is pleasant nonsense which occasionally becomes preachy and unnecessarily strident.

Judith M. Kass

THE HEIRESS

Released: 1949
Production: William Wyler for Paramount
Direction: William Wyler
Screenplay: Ruth Goetz and Augustus Goetz; based on their stage adaptation
  of the novel *Washington Square* by Henry James
Cinematography: Leo Tover
Editing: William Hornbeck
Art direction: John Meehan, Harry Horner (AA)
Set decoration: Emile Kuri (AA)
Costume design: Edith Head and Gile Steele (AA)
Music: Aaron Copland (AA)
Running time: 115 minutes

> *Principal characters:*
> Catherine Sloper .... Olivia de Havilland (AA)
> Dr. Austin Sloper .... Ralph Richardson
> Morris Townsend .... Montgomery Clift
> Lavinia Penniman .... Miriam Hopkins

The Heiress is the story of Catherine Sloper (Olivia de Havilland), a plain young woman in her mid-twenties who lives in a grand house in Washington Square, New York City, in the 1850's. She lives with her father, the prominent Dr. Austin Sloper (Ralph Richardson), and his sister, Aunt Lavinia (Miriam Hopkins). The film is an adaptation of Henry James's novel, *Washington Square*. First produced in New York and London as a stage play under the novel's original title, it was not a critical success; consequently, it was not made into a film until several years later.

The Heiress is recognized for many things, including its performances and outstanding art direction. The story takes place mainly in one location, the Sloper home—a limited setting ideally suited for the theater; however, in a screen version it becomes a challenge to keep the audience engrossed and the film visually exciting. *The Heiress* succeeds on both counts. Directed by William Wyler, the excellence of the performances and the intricacies of the character development work to create a film which succeeds through the power of its subtlety. *The Heiress* is a period piece in the true sense; not only the costumes and sets are evocative, but every nuance of dialogue and behavior is consistent with the formality and elegance of mid-nineteenth century New York.

The simple plot revolves around Catherine's love affair with Morris Townsend (Montgomery Clift), a young man whom her father considers a fortune hunter interested only in her inheritance. Since the action is very limited, the success of the story depends upon close attention to detail and complex characterizations. It is essential to get a sense of the drives and needs of each character as they interact within the stifling social regimentation of the period. Dr. Sloper and Catherine form the most complex relationship which gradually unfolds, revealing the raw emotions which lie beneath their façade of propriety. Dr. Sloper is a model of respectability and elegance. The unresolved pain he experienced at his wife's death years ago permeates his life. Ralph Richardson's performance succeeds in creating a character who, without straying from accepted behavior, becomes racked by bitterness and hatred. It is necessary to perceive the poisonous effect of that pain in order to understand the doctor's failure as a father in his relationship with Catherine. His suppressed hatred toward the child that caused his wife's death at childbirth reveals itself little by little, and it is the appearance of Morris which finally brings that hatred to a head.

To Catherine, Morris' arrival in her life is a dream come true. He is handsome and charming and professes to love her. The doctor uses his own low opinion of Catherine in judging Morris' motives, and he is determined to keep them from marrying. In view of Dr. Sloper's attitude towards Catherine, it is easy to see how vulnerable she is and how deeply she yearns to be loved. The first third of the story prepares the audience for Catherine's exploitation. Her starvation for affection is seen in her desperate attempts to please her father; but another side of her character is revealed through her relationship with her aunt, who accepts and loves her. With Aunt Lavinia, Catherine is clever and vibrant and reveals an innate charm; yet a story she amusingly tells her aunt becomes an awkward fiasco when she attempts to retell it to her father. The damage of his influence becomes increasingly evident. When Catherine is first introduced, she still has the spark of what she might be away from her father's emotional domination; the remainder of the story traces the extinguishing of that spark.

The first time Catherine appears in the film she is buying fish, an obvious contrast to the first introduction of Dr. Sloper and his elegant home. Thinking the fish will please her father, she is instead reprimanded for not letting the servant carry the fish. This, like all of Catherine's attempts at pleasing him, is met with criticism and with negative comparisons between Catherine and her late mother. Dr. Sloper's memory of his wife as a beautiful, talented, and charming lady pits Catherine against a ghost to whom she can never live up in his eyes. Catherine has never known her mother except as an ever-present reminder of her own inadequacies. For example, when Catherine wears a red dress because she thought her mother wore one like it, her father responds mainly to its expensiveness, quietly adding that her mother, unlike Catherine, was fair and dominated the color.

Morris Townsend is more the embodiment of all Catherine's dreams than a real man, and to stress this point, he is often photographed in such a way that he is faceless. When he first approaches Catherine at a party, he is a finely dressed torso with a voice; and throughout the film, his face is hidden when the two embrace. The audience sees only Catherine's blissful face against Morris' neck and dark shoulder. Morris convinces Catherine that her awkwardness and shortcomings are charming and lovable to him. Even as his mercenary nature surfaces, Catherine's blindness to his motives is understandable. She is not stupid; she simply wants desperately to believe him. Montgomery Clift as Morris combines good looks with a perfect ability to behave appropriately. His charm is inexhaustible as he skillfully maneuvers his way into the hearts of Catherine and her aunt. Clift's is a difficult role, since he must be slightly shady at the same time that he charms the audience (as well as Catherine) into wondering whether it might not be a good idea that he marry Catherine. His words and behavior are convincing as he deftly counteracts every suspicion directed toward him; but his questionable motives become more evident when he is dealing with Dr. Sloper, with whom his compliments sound false, his promises empty. The doctor and Morris are transparent to each other; their mutual hostility results from the similarity of their feelings towards Catherine. Morris, as a mercenary suitor who desires Catherine's wealth more than her, does not seem any worse than a father who hates his daughter for not being her mother.

The Sloper house is extremely important as a living environment to which each character reacts as if playing against another real character. The house is frozen in time and serves as Dr. Sloper's shrine to his wife; the furnishings are all as she left them more than twenty years earlier, the only change being a visible expansion of the doctor's medical practice downstairs. The most conspicuous furnishing is the spinet, which is introduced as a symbol of everything Mrs. Sloper was and Catherine is not. When first seen, it is being tuned—unnecessarily, since it has not been played since it was last tuned six months earlier; it is religiously kept in perfect shape in memory of its last player, Mrs. Sloper.

To Morris, the house is a lure whose elegance and lavishness are more desirable to him than Catherine. Viewed through his eyes, it is a showplace of wealth and taste, as close-ups are utilized to show off its fine craftsmanship. Morris adapts to the house in a way that Catherine never seems to. He is at home amongst the rich furnishings and is able to sit down at the spinet and play and sing. To Catherine, on the other hand, the house represents the embodiment of her mother's memory. Like the presence of the spinet, the house constantly reinforces her inability to fill her mother's place. There is no evidence of Catherine's presence in the main rooms other than her embroidery loom which eventually becomes an overt object of her father's disdain for her. The house represents enclosure to Catherine; and it will eventually become her prison.

When Doctor Sloper takes Catherine to Europe in the hope that she will forget her marriage plans, Morris is extended the honors of the house by

Aunt Lavinia. He eases comfortably into the rich life as he helps himself to the doctor's cigars and brandy, all the time properly yearning for Catherine. Upon returning from Europe, the doctor realizes he has failed in his attempt to keep Catherine from Morris. He threatens disinheritance and unmercifully confronts her with his feelings that she is dull and unattractive, and desirable to Morris only because of her prospect of thirty thousand dollars a year. His climatic bite is that she does, however, embroider neatly.

Catherine's shock at her father's release of hostility makes her need for Morris more desperate. She meets him to plan their elopment and naïvely tells him of her threatened disinheritance; they plan to leave that night. The scene that follows is certainly one of the most torturous of the film. As Catherine waits for Morris at the front window, it becomes increasingly evident that he will not come. Her aunt, knowing the truth, wishes that Catherine had just been a little wiser and not mentioned the disinheritance. Catherine suffers the harsh realization that she has been deceived and manipulated by those who supposedly love her.

In the time that follows, the doctor falls ill. It is a hardened Catherine who refuses to go to his deathbed. De Havilland's performance excels here as she makes the transition from a naïve and hopeful young woman to a bitter and cynical heiress. When the story picks up five years later, Catherine is an icy, hard woman. Sitting in her own home now, the loom has taken a more prominent place. There is some mystery as to her psychological state at this point. Morris has returned from California after five years and with Aunt Lavinia's help comes to see Catherine. He begs understanding for deserting her, claiming it was in her best interest. His current flattery is as charming as always; he proposes again and seems truly delighted when Catherine appears to weaken and agrees. It is soon evident, however, that *she* is now toying with *him*. He leaves to gather his belongings and Catherine sits down to finish her embroidery. When her aunt realizes that Catherine has no intention of marrying Morris, she asks how she can be so cruel. Catherine's response is that she has been taught by masters. The ultimate revenge occurs as Morris arrives at the appointed moment and futilely bangs on the bolted front door. Catherine once again mounts the stairs, her eyes bright with perverse satisfaction.

The Academy recognized de Havilland's performance in *The Heiress* with the Oscar for Best Actress; the art directors, John Meehan and Harry Horner, also received Oscars for their work. Edith Head received the award for costume design, and Aaron Copland for his musical score. The blend of these talents as well as the direction and script make *The Heiress* a beautiful film which brings to life believable characters from a different time.

Dena Roth

HELL'S ANGELS

Released: 1930
Production: Howard Hughes for Caddo Company/United Artists
Direction: Howard Hughes
Screenplay: Joseph Moncure March; based on Howard Estabrook's and Harry
  Behn's adaptation of a story by Marshall Neilan and Joseph Moncure March
Cinematography: Tony Gaudio, Harry Perry, and E. Burton Steene
Editing: Frank Lawrence, Douglass Biggs, and Perry Hollingsworth
Chief of aeronautics: J. B. Alexander
Chief technical engineer: E. Roy Davidson
Running time: 119 minutes

> *Principal characters:*
> Monte Rutledge .... Ben Lyon
> Roy Rutledge .... James Hall
> Helen .... Jean Harlow
> Karl Arnstedt .... John Darrow
> Baron von Kranz .... Lucien Prival

    Hell's Angels was the first major production of the multimillionaire playboy, businessman, and aviator, Howard Hughes. The idea for the film was conceived by Marshall Neilan in 1926, and Hughes acted upon it immediately, acquiring more than fifty World War I planes and hiring a hundred pilots, including America's leading stunt flyers led by Frank Clarke. Hughes even established his own airfield, "Caddo Field," at the site of what is now known as Van Nuys Airport in the San Fernando Valley.

    Filming began on *Hell's Angels* as a silent production in October of 1926 with a cast headed by the Scandinavian actress Greta Nissen. However, with the advent of sound, Hughes scrapped all of the silent footage of the principals and completely reshot those scenes, with Jean Harlow, in her first starring role, replacing the accent-ridden Nissen. Silent footage of the air sequences already shot was retained, with sound effects being added where appropriate. The final climactic air battle was filmed over the San Francisco Bay area, because Hughes found the cloud formations there more suitable. Shooting was eventually completed on December 7, 1929, which meant that *Hell's Angels* had been in production longer than any film up to that time and probably longer than any since. In all, more than twenty thousand people were said to have appeared in the finished film; more than three million feet of film was actually shot; and Hughes advertised *Hell's Angels* as a four-million-dollar spectacle, which it may well have been. Certainly the celebrities who crowded Grauman's Chinese Theater on May 27, 1930, for the premiere were not disappointed.

    Because of Howard Hughes's determination to keep *Hell's Angels* out of general distribution and because of the many stories which have circulated through the years concerning its production, the film has taken on almost legendary proportions. In reality, for all its magnificent flying sequences, the production is a disappointment, badly hampered by early talkie acting techniques and overblown melodramatics.

The highspots in *Hell's Angels* are two lengthy flying sequences. The first features a zeppelin raid on London, with the ship appearing, like a gigantic, silent, black whale of death, through the white clouds. The Germans onboard smile a lot and flash their white teeth, and, with a sophistication lacking in recent films in which everyone speaks English, the Germans speak in their native tongue. Titles, in the manner of silent films rather than the subtitles one has come to expect in foreign-language films, explain the action.

The workings of the zeppelin are shown in intimate detail, from the lowering of the observer's car from which a target can be pinpointed to the bomb placements and the great ship's engines. As the British flyers gain on the zeppelin, the captain orders that any extra weight be jettisoned to allow the ship greater speed and higher altitude. With a cold-blooded belief in God, Kaiser, and country, members of the crew silently jump to their deaths to lighten the ship's load. One lone British flyer also demonstrates suicidal patriotism by flying his plane directly into the zeppelin, causing it to burst into flames. With an almost uncanny similarity to the *Hindenberg* disaster of a few years later, the zeppelin plunges to a fiery grave.

The other flying sequence dominates the latter half of the film and shows the two brothers—Roy and Monte Rutledge (James Hall and Ben Lyon)—flying a captured German bomber over enemy territory to destroy an ammunitions dump, thus allowing the Allies to make a major advance. The aerial shots in this sequence are breathtaking, and one soon forgets the very un-European desert scenery clearly visible below. The two brothers, Roy at the controls and Monte at the machine gun, achieve their objective, and appear about to reach safety when they are shot down by Baron von Richthofen. At all times, there is a sense of reality, with only the ammunitions dump appearing to be a miniature.

Roy and Monte are the heroes of the story. Roy, the elder brother, is honest, dependable, and brave, while the younger Monte is the very opposite—lazy and cowardly. The opening scenes of the film, cut from the Astor Pictures reissue of *Hell's Angels*, show the two boys at Oxford, where they form a friendship with a German youth, Karl Arnstedt (John Darrow). Monte's true character is shown in a sequence in which he becomes involved with the wife (Jane Winton) of Baron von Kranz (Lucien Prival) while the trio are on vacation in Munich. He later pretends not to know the woman when challenged to a duel by her husband.

At the outbreak of the war, Roy immediately enlists in the Royal Flying Corps, while Monte is recruited only after another light amorous adventure.

At a charity ball given by a Lady Randolph, Monte becomes infatuated with Roy's fiancée, Helen. As played by Jean Harlow, Helen shows little evidence of being an English socialite and debutante. Harlow does, however, imbue the character with the right degree of sensual arrogance and easygoing sexuality. Her first appearance has her emerging from the bushes with a young officer, his hair in disarray. Later, she invites Monte back to her rooms, which she describes as "a new toy," a description which fits Monte equally well. "Would you be shocked if I put on something more comfortable?" she asks, as she goes into the bedroom to emerge in a very revealing dressing gown. Later, in France, where Helen is working at Lady Randolph's canteen, she is revealed to Roy as the flirtatious loose woman that, for all her wealth and social position, she really is.

After the brothers are captured by the Germans, Monte's cowardice again comes to the fore. Confronted by Baron von Kranz, he is willing to give the Germans details of the Allies' advance in return for his own life. Lucien Prival as Baron von Kranz gives a marvelous performance, with mannerisms apparently borrowed from Erich von Stroheim. In desperation, Roy pretends to be willing to help the Germans in exchange for a revolver with one bullet with which to silence Monte, who would be a witness to his dishonor. As Roy tries to reason with Monte, Monte screams for the Germans to listen to him, and Roy shoots him in the back. As he lies dying in Roy's arms, he tells his brother, "Don't cry, it was the only thing you could do." As the Baron discusses with an aide what is to be done, Roy is marched away for execution, and through an open window, we hear his final defiant cry: "I'll be with you in just a minute, Monte." No sooner have the shots of his execution been heard than there is the sound of shelling. The final scenes are of the Allies on the march—"Come on, we've got them now," shouts a soldier—indicating that Roy's and Monte's deaths were not in vain.

There are many interesting subplots in an epic such as *Hell's Angels*. One involves Karl, who is on the zeppelin during its raid on London and deliberately steers the ship over the river rather than have his fellow countrymen bomb Trafalgar Square. Karl in the observer's car is the first to go when the captain orders the zeppelin to be lightened. A curious silent sequence begins with a title, "Somebody always gets it on the night patrol," and shows scenes of the British planes in flight, followed by a beautifully composed shot of a crashed plane on the beach.

For its flying sequences, Howard Hughes deserves every credit for a masterly job of direction, but the story and dialogue have dated badly. Perhaps in a way *Hell's Angels* shows Hughes to be a man with more money than sense, a man lacking the cinematic sense necessary if the talkies were to succeed.

Anthony Slide

HERE COMES MR. JORDAN

Released: 1941
Production: Everett Riskin for Columbia
Direction: Alexander Hall
Screenplay: Sidney Buchman and Seton I. Miller (AA); based on the play
  Heaven Can Wait by Harry Segall (AA)
Cinematography: Joseph Walker
Editing: Viola Lawrence
Running time: 93 minutes

Principal characters:

Joe Pendleton/Bruce Farnsworth/ Ralph (K.O.) Murdock	Robert Montgomery
Mr. Jordan	Claude Rains
Max Corkle	James Gleason
Messenger 7013	Edward Everett Horton
Bette Logan	Evelyn Keyes
Julia Farnsworth	Rita Johnson
Tony Abbott	John Emery

Stories which carry an audience to other worlds or realms of experience are enthusiastically received regardless of trends, fads, or the prevailing national mood. This is seen in the enormous popularity of two versions of the same story which have been successfully released almost forty years apart. *Here Comes Mr. Jordan*, a celestial fantasy first released in 1941, was remade thirty-seven years later as *Heaven Can Wait*, and both films garnered more than the usual number of nominations for Academy Awards. The 1941 version received seven nominations, winning two awards, and the 1978 version received nine nominations and one award.

Here Comes Mr. Jordan is a variation of the usual simple motif of a benevolent angel being sent on a mission to earth. The film begins its rather complicated and enjoyable tale by turning the tables and having a human being journey to heaven to rectify an angelic error. Joe Pendleton (Robert Montgomery), a saxophone-playing heavyweight title contender, is prematurely snatched from a plummeting plane by an overzealous heavenly messenger named 7013 (Edward Everett Horton) who has wanted to spare him the pain of the crash. Joe protests that nothing could ever happen to him as long as he has his lucky saxaphone with him; but 7013 insists that Joe is really dead and that confirmation of this fact can be made with Mr. Jordan (Claude Rains), the man in charge of transporting souls to eternity. Mr. Jordan, however, admonishes 7013 for being overzealous in trying to establish a new record and admits that Joe, indeed, should still be among the living. He is not scheduled to join his deceased parents for another fifty years, becoming heavyweight champion in the interim. Naturally, Joe is anxious to return to his body. This would be relatively simple, but Joe's manager, Max Corkle (James Gleason), has already had Joe's body cremated. Mr. Jordan offers to let Joe be reborn but Joe refuses. Thus, the only alternative is to find a new body for Joe, and he agrees to this as long as they can find one that is in the prime condition that his former body was in when 7013 prematurely called it in.

Their search begins, but it is not until the 134th candidate that a body is found which Joe is willing to accept, and then reluctantly. It is the body of unscrupulous millionaire Bruce Farnsworth, who is, at that very moment, being drowned in his bathtub by his wife (Rita Johnson) and her lover, Farnsworth's private secretary, Tony Abbott (John Emery). At first, Joe is not interested in putting himself into such company; he changes his mind, however, upon the arrival at the Farnsworth mansion of Bette Logan (Evelyn Keyes) who has come to plead with the millionaire to reveal the truth about a fraudulent stock scheme that he has orchestrated and which has resulted in her father's imprisonment. Joe sees that if he were to step into the millionaire's body he could help the young woman. Thus, he agrees to take Farnsworth's body only on the condition that it is temporary until he can get the Logans out of trouble. Immediately, a dripping Joe Pendleton in Bruce Farnsworth's body steps out of the tub where the millionaire has died as Mr. Jordan explains why the audience still recognizes Joe, "You still are Joe Pendleton, just doing business from within Farnsworth's body." Julia Farnsworth and Mr. Abbott can barely mask their consternation when the obviously healthy Farnsworth comes down the stairs. Farnsworth directs Abbott to show Miss Logan to him, and then dismisses him with "and stay out of my bathroom."

Joe, as a more kindly version of Farnsworth, promises a very skeptical Bette Logan that he will indeed take care of the terrible mess her father is in, and he does just that, causing no end of protests from the dour-faced executives of Farnsworth Industries. However, just as Joe is beginning to enjoy unraveling Farnsworth's treacheries, he learns of news that could only be important to Joe Pendleton, the boxer. Ralph (K.O.) Murdoch, Joe's rival for the title bout, automatically becomes a contender since Joe is dead. Joe turns to Mr. Jordan to get him another body that can fight Murdoch; however, Jordan reminds Joe that he has agreed to remain Farnsworth for a certain length of time and that the time has not yet expired. Joe, nevertheless, will not be deterred: he sends for his ex-manager, Max Corkle, and in a hilarious scene convinces Max that he is really Joe Pendleton looking at him through Farnsworth's eyes. Corkle agrees to train him in order to get Farnsworth's body in shape to challenge Murdoch.

Meanwhile, Bette Logan purportedly visits Farnsworth to thank him for saving her father; it is obvious, however, that their feelings for each other have not remained neutral. Aware that he will not always be Farnsworth, Joe asks Bette if she can recognize someone by their eyes, a question that will have great meaning for them both later. The heavens, however, have decided that Farnsworth shall not fight the championship match, and Mrs. Farnsworth and Mr. Abbott finally succeed in bringing about his untimely demise. Again Joe must transmigrate and find a body "in the pink" as he calls it on short notice—a body that is at the point of death. Although Joe has missed the chance to fight Murdoch since Murdoch is now in the ring with the defending heavyweight champ, the fates have not deserted him. Murdoch is the target for racketeers who have bet a great deal of money on his losing the fight. Unheard by the noisy crowd, a gunshot is fired and Murdoch falls. The referee begins the count and the gangsters are confident, but then Murdoch slowly gets back on his feet. As the crowd roars its approval, he continues the fight to win the title, but it is not Murdoch. With the help of Mr. Jordan, it is Joe Pendleton doing business from inside Ralph Murdoch's body. Although Joe has won the title, it appears that he lost the girl. However, as he leaves the locker room after the fight, he rounds a corner only to run into Bette Logan who is looking for Max Corkle. At that moment, Mr. Jordan erases Joe's memory of all that has happened, and as their eyes meet, they experience the feeling of having known each other. The heavyweight champion/ex-millionaire/ex-prize fighter and the pretty girl walk away arm in arm to get to know each other better.

Here Comes Mr. Jordan is a story to delight and refresh, but its real strength lies in the performance of Robert Montgomery. His sustaining sense of awe concerning all that is happening neither falters nor becomes overdone, and he never allows the audience to entertain the idea that the film is fantasy. Claude Rains's performance as Mr. Jordan is immaculate, and Edward Everett Horton makes one hope that none of his descendents are still in the heavenly messenger business. James Gleason as feisty Max Corkle comes close to scene-stealing, and all the male characters are solid, well-written roles.

As clever and quick as the male actors' dialogue is, the dialogue is proportionately bland and unimaginative for the women; and one wonders how anyone as special as Joe Pendleton could be sparked by anyone as dull and shallow as Bette Logan. Each male character has his own style of patter which adds dimension to what could have been a silly story; unfortunately, the women are uninteresting.

The story remained essentially the same in the 1978 version entitled *Heaven Can Wait* with appropriate updatings, but the ingredient that was so prominent in the original that seemed to escape the newer one was innocence. Whereas Robert Montgomery's Joe Pendleton is never quite at ease stepping into the role of a millionaire, Warren Beatty's Joe Pendleton fits all too slickly into the role of wealthy playboy, his rough edges disappearing completely under his cashmere clothing. Nevertheless, if *Here Comes Mr. Jordan* is given a new film treatment in another thirty years, assuredly it will be met with the same generous response from audiences of all ages. It is a timeless story.

Juliette Friedgen

HESTER STREET

Released: 1975
Production: Raphael D. Silver for Midwest Films Production, Inc.
Direction: Joan Micklin Silver
Screenplay: Joan Micklin Silver; based on the story "Yekl" by Abraham Cahan
Cinematography: Kenneth Van Sickle
Editing: Katherine Wenning
Running time: 90 minutes

Principal characters:
Jake	Steven Keats
Gitl	Carol Kane
Bernstein	Mel Howard
Mamie	Dorrie Kavanaugh

Hester Street is the painful story of a cultural clash and the painfulness of change. It is an ambitious effort to dissect and scrutinize one central activity in the development of the American character—the assimilation of hundreds of thousands of immigrants into the uniquely American *mélange*. Director Joan Micklin Silver has sharply focused on one street, one neighborhood, and one family of Russian Jews in order to explore the painful process of Americanization and its effect on the lives it devoured. In her first feature film effort, Silver utilizes her considerable experience in educational film-making to present this small, ironic story.

The setting is New York's teeming Lower East Side in 1896. The principal character is Yekl, who, in his eagerness to embrace his adopted culture, has changed his name to Jake (Steven Keats). Jake is a tailor slaving in a sweat shop to make a meager living and to save for the arrival of his wife and young son from the Old Country. He is, however, also experiencing a growing fascination with a very American dancer named Mamie (Dorrie Kavanaugh). She is all brass and boldness, and epitomizes Americanization at its most base as well as its most free. Gitl (Carol Kane), Jake's wife, is as much bound to her tradition and religion as to the confining wig she will not be without and the Yiddish language to which she clings. She epitomizes all that Jake would like to reject. Through their conflict, Silver lays bare the throes of the cultural clash that repeatedly rent the nation during those years of mass influx of Eastern Europeans that came close on the heels of the Industrial Revolution.

To further polarize the issues, a young Yeshiva student, Bernstein (Mel Howard), is introduced as a boarder who lives the old life of religious study and discipline, and who is in sympathy with the bewildered Gitl. Divorce follows the agonizing attempts of Jake and his pious, pitiful mate to recapture whatever definition of marriage they held before the uprooting. Jake goes to the irrepressible Mamie, who, he learns, is not all glitter and fun. Gitl and Bernstein create an asylum for each other in the midst of their rapidly changing environment. The ending is not a typical "happy-ever-after" one, although the viewer does come away with a sense of continuity if not optimism concerning the outcome.

Jake's character embodies the vulgarity of Americans as seen through the eyes of Europeans. Emerging from what one assumes is the controlled paucity of spirit of the Orthodox life-style, he behaves with a recklessness, a brash and transparent cockiness, and a kind of hedonism. His one sympathetic moment comes during a family picnic where his warm, open play with his young son reveals his tender side, his longing for the irresponsibility of youth; but his basic character is one of show without substance, future without past. Jake is so lacking in sympathy that one clearly feels confronted with the director's own biases toward a post-Vietnam America. There is an unmistakable nostalgia for the old ways, a longing to return to the simplicity and order of another time and place, and an aversion to gloss and youthful irreverence. Steven Keats is only adequate in the role of Jake, lacking the depth necessary to reveal the tremendous conflict and momentum of change we anticipate in the character. With the exception of the picnic scene, his acting is generally flat and predictable.

There is considerably more affection invested by the filmmaker in the character of Gitl. Yet behind her wide-eyed passivity and frailty, a subtle contempt undermines the obvious sympathy she would otherwise invoke. She represents the universal resistance to change thrown against the terrible force of American progress and pride. The fact that Silver creates a sympathetic solution for her in the end (if one considers Bernstein a solution) detracts from the emotional potential of *Hester Street*. Yet the character shows small signs of flowering toward the end, of resisting strictures in such a way that she does not seem to give in to the dominant culture as much as to begin taking advantage of it.

Carol Kane as Gitl is appropriately gentle, and her facial expressions are studied and effective; her work earned her an Academy Award nomination, a special distinction considering the unpretentious nature of the film. Yet one wishes for greater irony and power in her acting out of her trauma. It is an exceedingly difficult role, requiring obvious restraint and the kind of covert emotionalism that seizes an audience before it knows it. The difficulty of both of the major characterizations is accentuated by the sparse, documentarylike quality of the film. The black-and-white starkness of the environment and the camera's narrow range demand of its actors a wider range and greater depth. Bernstein is adequately portrayed, wearing his restraint like a dull but serviceable overcoat; Mamie constitutes a convincing foil, forcing us to cringe at our repressed shamelessness. The yenta neighbor is a warm, comic addition who occasionally bridges the extremes.

Generally, the balances and counterbalances in Silver's characters seem to indicate some underlying dislike for the American character, for its excesses and wanton disregard of history and tradition. The direction of *Hester Street* seems largely experimental, which is the result, in part, of Silver's crossing of the usually well-defined line dividing educational from feature film. The film is neither, and it is both. The slightly shaggy homemade movie quality creates an ambivalence that gives a sense of charm and substance on the one hand and of inadequacy on the other. The detail is rich and memorable, and except for the frequent lapses in the camerawork, the film achieves the intimate reality essential to its purpose.

The liberal use of Yiddish, supplemented by subtitled clues to the dialogue, works reasonably well, setting a mood as well as lending authenticity. The dialogue is somewhat strained and sometimes difficult to follow. Several factors contribute; the interspersing of Yiddish is only one of them. The sound itself leaves much to be desired; it is disappointingly flat and often uneven. Another technical failing that mars the final product is the poor lighting; although some may argue that the lighting effects are deliberate, they fail nonetheless to achieve any sustained impact. Likewise, the editing lacks that extra measure of imagination needed to excite and pace the audience through this microcosmic story. Overall, the film moves slowly—the combined result of poor editing and the complexity of Silver's screenplay.

However, *Hester Street* is saved by its faithfulness to detail and its fearless exploration of issues basic to an understanding of Americans as a people; therein lies the importance of the film. As an instrument of self-exploration, predating the mass phenomenon of *Roots*, and as a critical examination of ourselves and our collective psyches, this small film is an affirmation of courage—a small beginning effort to focus on a small but intriguing part of our heritage. It pricks the collective conscience and demands response in an age of increasing individual isolation and declining commitment to any national institution.

Hester Street offers a moment of history suspended and magnified, in which Silver has allowed us a tiny glimpse of how we came to be a country of such confusion and contradiction. We see it in Jake's disdain for the confines of his old life and his ill-disguised fear of it. Gitl's passivity feeds her intransigence and leaves her powerless; yet it rewards her with happiness in the end. Mamie's brash hedonism belies her underlying insecurity and disillusion. The setting's gray yet teeming tone gives them all something to conquer, to rise above, to bloom against. In his or her own way, each does.

Such is the kaleidoscopic nature of the American personality. There is some pretension and obvious hazard in attempting to identify such a collective entity. The merit must lie in the concept of a working model, dynamic and open to continuing analysis. In that way we are able to grapple with our consciences, our values, and the quality of our lives. The process is painful, but that kind of self-criticism is basic to our culture. As the yenta cajoles Gitl into a new corset, she tells her: "If you want to be American, you gotta hurt."

Hester Street's insight demands that those hard questions be examined; and one of the strongest sources of that insight is its authenticity. With more attention to art and more technical facility, Silver's first feature film would have achieved the grace to make it more than memorable. The maturity of her wisdom and perception is still far ahead of her filmmaking. However, the prognosis for her future work, based on this effort, is exciting and positive.

Sally V. Holm

HIGH NOON

Released: 1952
Production: Stanley Kramer for Stanley Kramer Productions; released by
United Artists
Direction: Fred Zinnemann
Screenplay: Carl Foreman; based on the story "The Tin Star" by John W.
Cunningham
Cinematography: Floyd Crosby
Editing: Elmo Williams and Harry Gerstad (AA)
Music: Dmitri Tiomkin (AA)
Song: Dmitri Tiomkin and Ned Washington, "High Noon" (AA)
Running time: 84 minutes

> *Principal characters:*
> Will Kane .... Gary Cooper (AA)
> Jonas Henderson .... Thomas Mitchell
> Harvey Pell .... Lloyd Bridges
> Helen Ramirez .... Katy Jurado
> Amy Kane .... Grace Kelly
> Percy Mettrick .... Otto Kruger
> Frank Miller .... Ian MacDonald

The Western as a genre film is no longer in vogue, although its popularity
has been extremely durable. Until the 1970's it honestly could be said that
almost every top-rated star had appeared in at least one Western at some
time during his career. Perhaps it has been the abundance of Westerns on the
television screen that has decreased their popularity as theatrical films, but
whatever the reason, the Western remains anathema to modern producers.
In 1952, however, the Western was at the height of its popularity, and Stanley
Kramer's production of *High Noon* is deservedly rated as one of the best
Westerns ever filmed. It boasts a beautifully written, tight script by Carl
Foreman; superb direction by Fred Zinnemann; and an Academy Award-
winning performance by Gary Cooper.

High Noon tells a very simple story. Will Kane (Gary Cooper) has been
marshall of Hadleyville, a small Western town, and on a particular Sunday
morning in 1870 he has turned in his badge and is waiting to be replaced
officially by a new and younger marshal. He has married Amy (Grace Kelly),
a Quaker girl he truly loves, and he now wishes to move to a new town, settle
down, open a store, and have a family. In the midst of Kane's wedding party,
however, word comes that Frank Miller (Ian MacDonald), a killer he had
long ago captured and testified against, with the result that Miller was sentenced to the penitentiary, has been pardoned, and is on the train due to
arrive in Hadleyville at noon. It is now 10:40 A.M., and on the otherwise
deserted station platform three of Miller's cohorts are waiting for him to

arrive so that the four can ride into town and avenge themselves by killing Kane.

Amy Kane implores her husband to leave town at once with her because she is a Quaker and deplores violence of any kind. The newly appointed marshal is on his way, and theoretically it is now his responsibility to deal with the situation since Kane has already turned in his badge. Many of the townspeople are leaving temporarily in order to be gone when Miller shows up, including the judge who had sentenced him (Otto Kruger). The young deputy, Harvey Pell (Lloyd Bridges), who has been Kane's friend and helper, deserts the former marshal because he resents having been passed over in favor of an unknown stranger for the vacated post. Even Kane's ex-girl friend, Helen Ramirez (Katy Jurado), urges Kane and his bride to leave before Miller arrives. Kane is tempted, but he is an honest man with a high sense of morality, and he sees this showdown as a challenge he must meet even if he is killed.

The train arrives on time; Miller is met by his gang and they set out for Hadleyville's main street and the office where Kane waits alone. It is one of Cooper's finest performances, as he conveys Kane's fear, tension, and frustration, while the clock ticks off the minutes after twelve. In the dramatic conclusion, Kane's wife is the only person to help him, having put aside her beliefs to raise a rifle in protection of her husband. This denouement is one of the most famous scenes in the Western film and one that has been copied frequently. The final scene of the film shows Kane and his wife leaving town riding off to their new life.

The role of Amy Kane was only Grace Kelly's second screen performance, and, although not long or exacting, it won her an M-G-M contract. Gary Cooper is perfect as Kane, a role similar to that which established his reputation as a Western hero in *The Virginian* (1929). The entire supporting cast of *High Noon* is perfectly chosen; every actor acquits himself honorably, particularly Ian MacDonald as the antagonist, Frank Miller. *High Noon* brought Cooper his second Oscar; he had won his first in 1941 for *Sergeant York*, and had been nominated for *Mr. Deeds Goes to Town* (1936); *The Pride of the Yankees* (1942); and *For Whom the Bell Tolls* (1943).

High Noon is one of the few films to observe the dramatic unities. Interestingly, however, when the screenplay was first written and shot, it had a subplot that periodically took the action away from Hadleyville by cutting to scenes of the newly appointed marshal (James Brown) being delayed on his journey to the town. Zinnemann was quick to see, however, that those scenes lessened the film's tension rather than building it, so the episodes were dropped, thus eliminating Brown's role in the picture altogether. Editors Elmo Williams and Ned Washington were in complete accord; thanks to them and to Zinnemann, the suspense in *High Noon* mounts with every moment until it becomes almost unendurable. Zinnemann was nominated for an Oscar as Best Director, although the award went to John Ford for *The Quiet Man*; but Williams and Washington both won Oscars for Best Film Editing. Dmitri Tiomkin and Ned Washington's original ballad "High Noon," sung throughout the film by Ted Ritter, won the Oscar for Best Song, and Tiomkin also earned an Oscar for his scoring of the film.

If one were to list the all-time best Western films, *High Noon* would merit a high place on the list, in the company of such Western classics as *The Covered Wagon* (1923), *The Iron Horse* (1924), *Stagecoach* (1939), *The Ox-Bow Incident* (1942), *The Gunfighter* (1950), *Cimarron* (1931), *Red River* (1948), *Shane* (1953), *Will Penny* (1967), and *The Virginian* (1929). The West remains an integral part of the American heritage; perhaps the pendulum of popularity will someday swing back to favor the Western again.

DeWitt Bodeen

HIGH SIERRA

Released: 1941
Production: Hal B. Wallis for Warner Bros.
Direction: Raoul Walsh
Screenplay: John Huston and W. R. Burnett; based on the novel of the same name by W. R. Burnett
Cinematography: Tony Gaudio
Editing: Jack Killifer
Music: Adolph Deutsch
Running time: 100 minutes

Principal characters:
Marie .... Ida Lupino
Roy Earle .... Humphrey Bogart
Babe .... Alan Curtis
Red .... Arthur Kennedy
Velma .... Joan Leslie
Doc Banton .... Henry Hull
Pa .... Henry Travers
Louis Mendoza .... Cornel Wilde
Jake Kranmer .... Barton MacLane
Big Mac .... Donald MacBride

By 1941, the possibilities of the gangster film had been fairly well exhausted; at the same time, world events were proving to be far more dramatic and compelling. Warner Bros., generally acknowledged to be the leading purveyor of "socially significant" gangster films, had an impressive roster of hardboiled male stars. The titans were James Cagney, Paul Muni, and Edward G. Robinson as well as George Raft and the newly arrived John Garfield. By contrast, the tried and true heavy, Humphrey Bogart, found himself for the most part relegated to supporting roles in which he invariably played a despicable and doomed character.

The studio found itself running into difficulty when it attempted to cast the leading role in Raoul Walsh's new film, *High Sierra*. The top stars of Warners' *Murderers' Row* (1966), after having established themselves in crime films, had gone on to prove their talent in a wide variety of roles; consequently, none of them was particularly eager to become a public enemy again. Raft complained that he was tired of getting killed in the last reel. Finally, at Walsh's suggestion, the studio settled on Bogart for the role of the Dillinger-type Roy Earle. Ida Lupino received top billing and performed admirably, but the film belonged to Bogart, for whom the role was a major step forward in his career.

The complete film was a fairly faithful adaptation of W. R. Burnett's novel, chronicling the last weeks in the life of Roy Earle, an aging bank robber newly released from prison through the efforts of an old pal, Big Mac (Donald MacBride), who needs him to rob a resort hotel in California. Big Mac is dying, and Roy, out of gratitude for his release and loyalty to his old pal, agrees to this one last "caper." Doubts arise, however, when he meets the other members of the gang composed of Babe (Alan Curtis) and Red (Arthur Kennedy), young hotheads whose prior criminal expertise is limited to filling-station and liquor-store holdups; Marie (Ida Lupino) a dance-hall girl along for the ride; Louis Mendoza (Cornel Wilde), a desk clerk at the hotel and the gang's inside man; and a corrupt policeman named Jake Kranmer (Barton McLane).

On the cross-country drive to California, Roy has met and befriended the Goodhue family and their granddaughter, Velma (Joan Leslie), a beautiful lame girl. They have migrated to California hoping to find a doctor who might perform an operation to correct Velma's handicap. This decent family reminds Roy of his own upbringing. He falls in love with the girl and, without her knowledge, finances the operation. Once the job is over he hopes to marry Velma and settle down to the kind of peaceful, untroubled life which has so long eluded him.

Gradually, as the gang marks time before the robbery, Roy begins to depend on Marie, who is more levelheaded than Red or Babe. Marie has fallen in love with Roy; and a symbol of the bond which is gradually forming between them is the stray dog, Pard, rumored to be jinxed, who loves them both.

The holdup is a success, but during the getaway Red and Babe's car goes off the road and explodes. Mendoza is implicated and soon names Roy as the leader of the gang. Roy heads for Los Angeles to deliver the goods to Big Mac, who is to supply a "fence" for the jewelry taken from the hotel safe; but when he arrives, he finds Big Mac dead of a heart attack. The greedy ex-policeman Kranmer attempts to take the money and jewels from Roy, who is forced to kill him.

Roy, Marie, and Pard are on the run. Still obsessed by his dream of a life with Velma, Roy stops off at the home of the Goodhues intending to propose to Velma, only to find that she has become engaged to the young playboy who had jilted her when she was still a cripple. His hopes shattered, the embittered Roy leaves. For the first time he realizes how Marie feels about him.

However, the net has begun to close around him. Half-acknowledging his love for Marie, he puts her and Pard on a bus, promising that he will come to her when things have cooled off. A well-coordinated manhunt is on for "Mad Dog" Earle, as the press melodramatically labels him. Unable to spend any of the money stolen from the hotel, he attempts a drugstore holdup and is spotted by the police. In the ensuing chase, Roy abandons his car at the foot of Mount Whitney and climbs to a high vantage point from which he holds the police at bay with a machine gun.

Hearing the news of the impending capture, Marie gets off the bus and makes her way to the base camp at the foot of the mountain. Unable to reach the outlaw, the police send a sharpshooter to climb around behind him. At dawn the police once more urge Roy to surrender. His reply is, "Come and get me!" Pard, hearing Roy's voice, jumps from his wicker basket and races toward him. Seeing the little "jinxed" dog and knowing that Marie must be with him, Roy forgets himself, stands up, and calls out to Marie; he is shot down by the sharpshooter's bullets. Alone again, Marie takes consolation in the knowledge that at least Roy's agonizing life of crime is at an end.

Two brilliant filmmakers, Raoul Walsh and John Huston, here combine to make a memorable film. Of the same generation as the more highly lauded Ford and Hawks, Walsh, with his unpretentious, uncluttered style, seemed to lack some of the obsessions which made his two contemporaries stand out and, for a time, overshadow him. Walsh was, however, quite probably the finest action director, in whatever genre, to emerge during the period. His reputation remained secure for the four decades in which he was active as a Hollywood director, and, since the release of his final film in 1961, there has yet to appear any new director to claim Walsh's crown.

For this last in a long line of gangster films, Walsh and Huston created an essentially decent man who, because of the Depression, went wrong. There is nothing of the Big City or organized crime about Roy Earle. He is no little Caesar; instead, in the tradition of Jesse James, he is a farm boy-turned-outlaw who retains some of the humane traits he had before he entered a life of crime. It is to their credit that Walsh and Huston are able to establish the character of Earle with a minimum of dialogue. In one of the initial scenes we walk with the just-paroled ex-convict, enjoying, through his eyes and ears, the sights and sounds of a world without bars or guards. The two shots of the rugged High Sierras behind the opening credits and again at the very end of the film convey a sense of ineluctable fate.

It is doubtful that Walsh, Huston, and Bogart thought they were making a great film; they had simply done their best with another gangster story. That it would prove financially successful there was little doubt; yet it was more than that. Emerging just as America was about to enter World War II, *High Sierra* was a fitting denouement to a decade of gangster films; in future, the antisocial hero would take a back seat. Actors such as Humphrey Bogart (*All Through the Night*, 1942) and Alan Ladd (*Lucky Jordan*, 1942) were soon involved in transitional films in which they abandoned crime in favor of patriotism. Finally, *High Sierra* is notable as the first true "Bogart picture," elevating him to stardom and providing him with the opportunity to prove that he could play highly sensitive roles with skill and even brilliance.

Michael Shepler

HIS GIRL FRIDAY

Released: 1940
Production: Howard Hawks for Columbia
Direction: Howard Hawks
Screenplay: Charles Lederer; based on the play *The Front Page* by Ben Hecht and Charles MacArthur
Cinematography: Joseph Walker
Editing: Gene Havlick
Running time: 92 minutes

> *Principal characters:*
> Walter Burns .... Cary Grant
> Hildy Johnson .... Rosalind Russell
> Bruce Baldwin .... Ralph Bellamy
> Earl Williams .... John Qualen
> Molly Malloy .... Helen Mack

Howard Hawks's *His Girl Friday* is a culmination of the "screwball" comedy tradition of the 1930's. Hawks had a habit of coming last to a genre; but his contribution was never the least; it was always an excellent entry. This film, a reworking of Ben Hecht's and Charles MacArthur's *The Front Page*, is charged with new life through Hawks's masterful direction and major script changes. In this version, he adds a sophisticated battle of the sexes by turning the "male" Hildy Johnson into a Hildegarde, and pitting her against her boss and former husband, Walter Burns. The new love triangle replaces the old plot of political corruption and newsroom nonsense, but the changes cause only minor discomfort. The story, like the original, is all surface and no substance. The dialogue rather than the plot gives the picture its distinction.

Rosalind Russell as Hildy Johnson turns the newsroom upside down as she throws her well-padded shoulders around. Accepted by the newsmen as "one of the boys," she is fast-talking, with a quick retort for every wisecrack. A hard competitor, she is extremely successful in a man's world. Russell's acting is always adequate and at times captivating. Her most dramatic scene, for example, is with the condemned criminal Earl Williams (John Qualen) midway through the film when, as Hildy, she builds a "story" out of Williams' use of a gun to kill, turning it into a philosophical argument about "production for use." The character of Walter Burns is made-to-order for Cary Grant. Unlike the romp through the woods that Hawks gave Grant and Katharine Hepburn in *Bringing Up Baby* (1938), the stunts in *His Girl Friday* are verbal. The insults fly like daggers, and with Hawks, Grant, and Russell throwing them, they are rarely misdirected.

The pace is sometimes frenzied, yet the film does not suffer from its weak thread of a plot. As the story opens, Hildy returns to the *Morning Post* to flash her new engagement ring in her ex-husband's face and to bid him, the newspaper business, and the city farewell. She is marrying Bruce Baldwin (Ralph Bellamy), a bland insurance salesman from Upstate New York; he represents security, stability, and a white picket fence in Albany. Nothing could be duller, unless it is Bruce himself. While Hildy staunchly insists that Bruce is what she wants, Burns and the audience believe that she desperately wants to be convinced otherwise. From the beginning, Bruce is an open challenge for Burns's mischievous mind, and it is obviously no contest.

Although Hildy is ready to leave on the next train for Albany, Burns delays her departure with a plea that she cannot refuse. His star reporter, he claims, is unavailable to cover the imminent death-row story on Earl Williams. Still desperately hoping for a pardon, Williams faces execution at dawn. Hildy, Burns argues, is the only reporter "man" enough to enter the prison and get the story.

Hildy stalls Bruce from one train to the next, promising not to miss the last one. But Burns is determined to get rid of Bruce for good. Through a series of contrived mishaps which he masterminds, Bruce lands in jail twice and is nearly killed in a car accident with his "mother," all in one night.

As the evening wears on, the Governor's pardon of Williams is intercepted and concealed by a corrupt mayor who feels that his reelection depends on the execution. Meanwhile, after an interview with Hildy, the somewhat confused Williams dramatically escapes from death row, then suddenly appears in the prison newsroom where he finds Hildy alone. True to her profession, Hildy hides Williams in a rolltop desk to protect him as well as her scoop. Complications set in when Williams' alleged girl friend, Molly Malloy (Helen Mack), is interrogated for information about Williams' whereabouts. Under the pressure, Molly breaks down and leaves through the second story window, falling to her death on the pavement below.

The film does not skip a beat as, in true Hollywood "screwball" fashion, the mayor, the criminal, the love triangle, and the mother-in-law all converge in the newsroom for the grand finale. Phones ring, guns fire, and everyone shouts at once. The corrupt mayor and his henchmen are exposed and Hildy and Burns team up for another round of marriage.

Hawks's presentation of the battle of the sexes is as old as Shakespeare, and the treatment of Hildy and Burns is typical of the egocentric type of hero that the director enjoyed. However, love and respect get the better of their self-centered interests and ultimately the two join forces against the wooden, lifeless people who, they consider, make up most of the population of the world.

The directorial style of *His Girl Friday* is as straightforward as Hawks's dialogue. His direct cuts and lack of montage keep the film from being dated and keep extraneous movement to a minimum. Time dances frantically by; the comedy is copious and varied; the gags are rapid-fire. The sarcastic banter between Hildy and Burns is the soul of the film, and it is this clever repartee that captures the audience. Representative of Hawks's comedy at its best, *His Girl Friday* is a treat not to be missed if the opportunity arises.

Joanne L. Yeck

HOBSON'S CHOICE

Released: 1954
Production: David Lean for London Films; released by United Artists
Direction: David Lean
Screenplay: David Lean, Norman Spencer, and Wynyard Browne; based on the play of the same name by Harold Brighouse
Cinematography: Jack Hilyard
Editing: Peter Taylor
Running time: 107 minutes

Principal characters:
Henry Horatio Hobson	Charles Laughton
Willie Mossop	John Mills
Maggie Hobson	Brenda De Banzie
Vicky Hobson	Prunella Scales
Alice Hobson	Daphne Anderson
Freddy Beenstock	Derek Blomfield
Albert Prosser	Richard Wattis
Mrs. Hepworth	Helen Haye

The term "Hobson's Choice" describes a situation in which there is no choice at all. While there may appear to be two or more courses of action, all but one are impossible, or totally undesirable. The Hobson of *Hobson's Choice* is Henry Horatio Hobson, bootshop owner, widower, autocratic father, drinker, and miser. During the course of the film, he receives his comeuppance when he is twice confronted with a "Hobson's Choice."

Henry Hobson (Charles Laughton) is a self-indulgent tyrant who, with the help of his daughters, has arranged his life so that he has the minimum amount of work to distract him from the maximum amount of pleasure. His best employee, Willie Mossop (John Mills), is a master at making the high quality boots that keep the well-to-do customers of Salford in Lancashire returning to Hobson's. His eldest daughter, Maggie (Brenda De Banzie), and her younger sisters, Vicky (Prunella Scales) and Alice (Daphne Anderson), run his business and his house with such efficiency that he has little to do with either. That his daughers do this without remuneration does not bother Hobson in the least. Such organization and low overhead allow him to hoard his money and to spend much time at the local pub, the Moonraker Inn, engaged in heavy drinking and "debating" with his cronies. It is a perfect arrangement for Hobson and one that he considers his due.

Nevertheless, Hobson would like to marry off Alice and Vicky since they complain too much. This would suit his daughters very well, as they are not at all satisfied with the situation. Vicky, twenty-one, is in love with Freddy Beenstock (Derek Blomfield), the son of a rich merchant family, and Alice, twenty-three, is in love with Albert Prosser (Richard Wattis), a young lawyer. While both girls want to marry, and Hobson would like to get them out of the house, he refuses to furnish the marriage dowry that both young men expect. The women are even more exasperated when Hobson declares that he will find husbands for them who will not expect dowries. When Maggie, who is thirty years old, asks if he will find a husband for her too, Hobson tells her: "If you want the brutal truth, you're not the sort of wench men marry. You'll make a proper old maid, Maggie, if ever there was one." The real truth is that with her sharp business sense Maggie is simply too valuable an unpaid worker to be let go.

Hobson is oblivious to the fact that Maggie will not be content with spinsterhood. She is smart enough to outwit him, and in doing so will arrange not only her own marriage but those of her sisters as well. She has already chosen her man, Willie Mossop, her father's best bootmaker. He is first seen emerging from his underground workroom, an action which is symbolic not only of his lowly station in English life, but also of his attitude toward himself. When Maggie tells him that with his skill he could certainly find work in a higher class bootshop than Hobson's, he replies that he would be afraid to work in one of the really fine places. He is a seemingly acquiescent man of little education who has a feel for leather and a talent for making well-fitting boots. Not one to be coy, Maggie tells Willie outright that he has the talent to make boots which sell themselves, while she has the talent to sell hard-to-sell boots made by others. She proposes that they form a partnership-in-marriage. The astounded Willie is at first totally against this blunt proposal from a lady above his station, but Maggie is not to be put off. She has been watching him for six months and has seen a potential that everyone, her father included, has missed. Willie begins to change his attitude toward Maggie when she extricates him from an unofficial "understanding" with a woman for whom he cares little. When Maggie tells her father that she intends to marry Willie, he scoffs at the idea and threatens to beat the innocent Willie for trifling with his daughter. Willie rebels against Hobson's threats and, to Maggie's joy, tells him that he is going to leave the shop and establish one of his own with Maggie, who will be his wife. Hobson washes his hands of both of them, and, of course, will not provide a dowry. It is the first time that Willie has shown any backbone, but Maggie is determined that it will not be the last. She immediately begins giving Willie lessons in speaking, reading, and writing.

The night before Maggie and Willie's wedding, Hobson has more than his usual large share of drink at the inn. On his way home he falls into the sidewalk trapdoor to Beenstock's warehouse, slides down the chute, and spends the night sleeping among sacks of corn. When Maggie hears of the incident, she decides to put it to good use. She contacts Alice's fiancé, Albert Prosser, the lawyer, and in the name of the elder Beenstock has him draw up a lawsuit against Hobson. A copy of the suit is placed in Hobson's hands while he sleeps off his drunk, and upon waking he finds himself both hung over and in trouble. As the sisters and their beaus gather at the newly married Mossop's cellar bootshop and home, a dejected Hobson shows up, asking Maggie for advice. He is totally embarrassed by the incident and wants to avoid any publicity that would hurt his business. He is afraid of having his reputation ruined by court battles and adverse publicity. With her husband, sisters, Beenstock, and Prosser in attendance, Maggie works out a settlement for £500 to be paid to the younger Beenstock in return for dismissal of the lawsuit. Hobson is faced with his Hobson's choice, which is no choice at all: if he does not part with his precious £500 he will face ruin. Once he has promised to pay the money, Maggie reveals that it will be evenly divided between the two young couples so that they can be married. Realizing that he has been tricked into promising to pay dowries for his younger daughers, Hobson leaves in anger, declaring himself happy to be free of such ungrateful offspring.

A year passes during which Vicky and Alice marry their young men, leaving Hobson alone to tend his business. Maggie and Willie have put their talents to good use and have prospered; in one year they are able to repay the £100 they had borrowed from a wealthy client of Hobson to start their own boot business. Not only has the business prospered, but Willie has learned well the lessons in speaking and writing that Maggie has been giving him. When Maggie tells them that they can repay their benefactress, Mrs. Hepworth (Helen Haye), Willie tells her with pride that he has already done it. This bit of initiative shocks and then pleases Maggie.

On the other hand, Hobson's business has declined as his customers have switched to Mossop's for their boots. Hobson, who has taken to drinking even more heavily at the Moonraker Inn, becomes ill, and the doctor calls the three daughters to the house to see if one of them will watch over him and nurse him back to health. Vicky and Alice refuse, and the strong-willed Maggie now demurely declares that she will have to speak to her husband to see if he will allow her to live with her father again. When Willie arrives, Hobson tries to lure him back to his old workbench in the cellar so that both he and Maggie will stay. Willie refuses and Maggie quietly agrees to leave with him. When Hobson scoffs at the lowly Mossop shop, Willie truly finds his tongue. With pride he relates his accomplishments of the year and points out that all of Hobson's customers are now coming to Mossop's for their fine boots. He would be a fool to give up his own growing business to return to one with a failing reputation. The only way he will return to Hobson's is as a partner, with Hobson as a silent partner who will not interfere in his running of things. In order to regain his health and his business, Hobson needs to have Maggie and Willie with him; it is his second Hobson's choice. Maggie is pleased at Willie's strength and eloquence as he bargains with her father, and she agrees with him that it is partnership or nothing.

However, Maggie balks at Willie's demand to change the shop name to "William Mossop, late Hobson." Willie's newfound confidence enables him to hold his ground even in the face of Maggie's opposition until a compromise is made: the business will be called Mossop and Hobson. Before Hobson can gather his old bluster, Willie suggests that Maggie take her father to Albert Prosser's to draw up the papers for the partnership. As Hobson leaves to get his hat, Maggie admiringly congratulates her husband on his bargain. Willie, still a bit surprised at himself, acknowledges the credit due her for the change in himself. When Hobson returns, he has regained some of his old confidence and now acts as if the partnership were his idea. As Willie surveys his new shop, and Hobson and Maggie prepare to leave for the lawyer's, it is clear that all three are happy with the outcome.

Hobson's Choice had been a favorite repertory play in England long before David Lean brought it to the screen, and the roles of Hobson, Maggie, and Willie were considered to be choice parts. When the film was released, critics were almost unanimous in their praise of Brenda De Banzie and John Mills, but reaction was mixed toward Charles Laughton, who was criticized for overacting and for having made Hobson much less likable than he might have been. Some critics have considered the film to be one of David Lean's lesser efforts; but it has gained a following of faithful viewers who take great relish in the play, the performance, and the faithful re-creation of an 1879 and early 1880's England. These fans have decided that here even a lesser Lean and an overblown Laughton add up to excellent entertainment.

Ellen J. Snyder

HOLIDAY

Released: 1938
Production: Everett Riskin for Columbia
Direction: George Cukor
Screenplay: Donald Ogden Stewart and Sidney Buchman; based on the play
  of the same name by Philip Barry
Cinematography: Franz Planer
Editing: Otto Meyer and Al Clark
Running time: 94 minutes

Principal characters:
Linda Seton	Katharine Hepburn
Johnny Case	Cary Grant
Julia Seton	Doris Nolan
Ned Seton	Lew Ayres
Nick Potter	Edward Everett Horton
Susan Potter	Jean Dixon
Edward Seton	Henry Kolker

One of the best comedies of the 1930's, *Holiday* sparkles with undiminished radiance even today. Sophisticated and witty, it is a romantic comedy with serious undertones. Underlying the intelligent, urbane banter and the critical view of the rich is the struggle of two kindred spirits to overcome social and psychological obstacles.

Having met and fallen in love with Julia Seton (Doris Nolan) during a vacation at Lake Placid, Johnny Case (Cary Grant) does not know that she is a member of a socially prominent and wealthy family. A charming, clever, free-spirited soul with no social position, Johnny is attracted to Julia at once because she is sweet and intelligent; he assumes that she wants the same kind of life he does although he knows nothing much about her. When, after the vacation, he first visits the Seton house, he is astonished at all he sees as the butler escorts him through the palatial marble-floored hall with its tapestries, paintings, and statuary. When the butler leaves him gingerly perched on the edge of an antique chair, he performs a flip-flop to keep from being over-awed. Once Julia arrives, he finds that their romance is not going to be as simple as he had expected, and the audience begins to see that he and Julia may not be so well-matched after all. Johnny laughingly chides her for not telling him she is rich. "Aren't you funny to talk about it?" she responds. "Is it so sacred?" he asks, and when she tells him quite seriously that she expects him to make millions himself, he responds equally seriously that he will not be doing that. The basic conflict between them is thus established.

The atmosphere is very different, however, when he is introduced to Linda (Katharine Hepburn), Julia's sister. He and Linda like each other immediately, and beneath their light banter we can see that they are kindred spirits, although it takes them a while to recognize it.

Linda Seton is, in fact, the film's central character. As critical of the society in which she lives as Johnny Case is, she is also a product of that society. To it she owes the poise and elegance that a background of money and secure social position can provide, but her sensitivity and intelligence are always at odds with the constricted and pompous circle of family and acquaintances who surround her. Linda has tried painting, acting, and nursing without success. Her problem, as she confides to Johnny, is deciding whether she wants to be Joan of Arc, Florence Nightingale, or John L. Lewis. There are elements of self-pity and theatricality in Linda's character, but she is basically honest and sincere, although puzzled about how to break out of the life she is living. One reason she is instantly attracted to Johnny is that he is a nonconformist.

Significantly, it is to Linda that Johnny explains his philosophy of life. He wants to take a holiday for a few years to find himself and to find out why he is working—surely it is not just to pay bills and pile up more money. There are new, exciting ideas around, he says, and he wants to discover how he fits into the changing world. The catch, as he explains to Linda, is that he wants to retire young and work when he is older. There is an element of pleading in Johnny's voice as he talks to the sympathetic Linda. He almost seems to be reassuring himself at the same time that he asks for her support and confidence.

Linda is not the only Seton who does not fit into the family's marble-pillared world. Her younger brother Ned (Lew Ayres) is also unhappy; but he is less courageous. Having given in to his father's pressure to work in the family bank, he has taken refuge in alcohol to forget that he is a talented musician and wants to pursue music as a career. Their mother, they tell Johnny, "tried to be a Seton for a while and gave up and died."

Representing this nonconformist side of the Setons is a part of the mansion completely different in spirit from the echoing marble halls—the playroom. It is Linda's refuge—a warm, intimate room filled with dreams, childhood mementos, Ned's musical instruments, and a portrait of their mother over the fireplace. Linda invites Johnny up to the playroom, and she and Ned go through an amusing little charade with Johnny to prepare him for the cross-examination he can expect from their father. Julia, however, is not amused and tries to stop them. When Linda says, "Money is our God," Julia is seriously upset and tells Johnny that it is not true. Amused, Johnny responds, "I ask myself what General Motors would do and do the opposite."

Having found out that Johnny has a promising financial future, Mr. Edward Seton, the father (Henry Kolker), decides to overlook his lack of social standing and give his consent to the marriage of Julia and Johnny; but all the conflicts culminate at their engagement party. Linda is so happy that Julia has found such a good man—"Life walked into this house," she says—that she wants to give a small engagement party for them with "no white ties, no formal invitations." As she speaks these words, however, the scene dissolves to a close-up of an engraved invitation and then to a huge formal party— Edward Seton and Julia have not agreed with her idea. Because giving an intimate party was so important to her, Linda stays in the playroom and refuses to come downstairs.

The only people invited who are not connected with the Setons are Johnny's good friends, Nick and Susan Potter (Edward Everett Horton and Jean Dixon). When they appear, they are self-conscious and obviously out of place. Stared at by the butler, they nervously produce their invitations to prove that they have been invited. Seeking to escape, they accidentally end up in the playroom with Linda. An immediate rapport is established among the three, and when Ned wanders in they all begin playing and singing and laughing together.

Soon Johnny, wearing white tie and tails, appears, sent by Julia to persuade Linda to come downstairs. He joins the group after being properly chastised for allowing the marble pillars to overwhelm him. Linda and Johnny attempt an acrobatic trick and end up falling on the floor just as Mr. Seton and Julia enter. Mr. Seton, losing his temper, tells Linda that she has caused enough trouble and orders her downstairs. Turning to Johnny, he tells him how extremely pleased he is with the success of his stock market manipulations and offers him a desk at the Seton bank. Johnny chooses this moment to try to explain his idea of taking a long holiday and to turn down the offer. Neither Julia nor her father can understand him, and Julia has to persuade her father to leave to prevent an open quarrel. After an inconclusive conversation Julia leaves; but Johnny stays to talk to Linda, and they begin waltzing to a music box. It is a very quiet, tender moment in which they are drawn closer together. Then Johnny goes back to the party for the announcement of his engagement to Julia.

Johnny then spends several days vacillating between compromising his principles and leaving Julia for good. Julia will not bend; she insists that he accept her father's position. Finally Johnny tells her, "I love feeling free inside more than I love you"; and he leaves to join the Potters on a trip to Europe. When Julia admits that she does not love Johnny, Linda sees her opportunity to escape and join the man she loves. She arrives at the ship just in time to see Johnny do a flip-flop, and the film ends with their first real kiss.

Johnny's friends, Nick and Susan Potter, are very important to the development of *Holiday*. They are in the very first scene, in which Johnny comes to tell them that he is going to marry Julia; and they are in the last, when Johnny comes to the ship to tell them that he is going to Europe with them. Although they are older than Johnny and are both intellectuals (Susan is a former teacher and Nick a university professor) the film never makes them seem ridiculous. In fact, they are a human, witty, interesting couple. When they look and feel out of place at the formal engagement party, we know that their values are right and that the others' are wrong. When they meet Linda, they immediately side with her against the stuffy side of the Seton family.

Perhaps the only question we might ask is why Johnny does not realize that Linda rather than Julia is right for him long before he does. Indeed, Linda herself does not realize until near the end that Julia is, as Ned tells her, "a very dull girl." Everyone, he says, is taken in by her looks.

Closely following the play by Philip Barry, the script by Donald Ogden Stewart and Sidney Buchman artfully blends wit, feeling, and romance. Although the dialogue always seems natural, it is carefully constructed to have a certain rhythm and to be very revealing of character. Also skillful is the naturalness of the exposition. Most of the characters are just meeting each other, so we learn about them as they learn about one another. There are no scenes in which a character explains something solely for the benefit of the audience. The chief virtue of the script, however, is the creation of four interesting and believable characters: Linda, Johnny, Nick, and Susan.

Brilliantly bringing the script to life is a cast perfectly directed by George Cukor, who wisely realized that the acting had to be slightly stylized but without affectation. Katharine Hepburn as Linda ranges from playful and witty when she first meets Johnny Case and his friends, the Potters, to intense and serious as she finds Johnny a sympathetic person and unbends to him; it is one of her best performances. As Johnny, Cary Grant is also at his best in portraying the charm and spirit of a young man with his own ideas about what is meaningful in life. Edward Everett Horton and Jean Dixon as the Potters and Lew Ayres as Ned excel in crucial supporting roles; indeed there is not a weak performance in the film.

Holiday set box-office records in 1938 and has been recognized ever since as a great achievement of three artists of the cinema, George Cukor, Katharine Hepburn, and Cary Grant.

Timothy W. Johnson

HORROR OF DRACULA

Released: 1958
Production: Anthony Hinds for Hammer Films; released by Universal
Direction: Terence Fisher
Screenplay: Jimmy Sangster; based on the novel *Dracula* by Bram Stoker
Cinematography: Jack Asher
Editing: Bill Lenny
Running time: 82 minutes

Principal characters:
Count Dracula .... Christopher Lee
Dr. Van Helsing .... Peter Cushing
Arthur Holmwood .... Michael Gough
Mina Holmwood .... Melissa Stribling
Lucy .... Carol Marsh
Jonathan Harker .... John Van Eyssen
Vampire Woman .... Valerie Gaunt

In 1958, Count Dracula, the most infamous of vampires, arose from his coffin and stalked across America's cinema screens. *Horror of Dracula*, a Hammer Film Production directed by Terence Fisher, was at first glance just another film about the Count. It all began in 1897 with a novel entitled *Dracula* by the Irish author Bram Stoker. This alchemist's blend of folklore, fantasy, and fact was transmuted into pure gold, a classic that has fired the imaginations of authors and producers ever since it was published.

A historical Dracula did exist; medieval histories record him as a fifteenth century Balkan nobleman whose sadistic cruelties more than justified his name (Dracul means "devil" in Rumanian). Although no mention is made of vampirism in the case history of Dracula, there seems little doubt that he inspired the book that bears his name. When European filmmakers and actors began emigrating to America in the early 1900's, the Count came with them. Bela Lugosi, in his stage presentation of *Dracula*, followed by his portrayal of the Count in the 1931 Universal film of the same name, was the man most responsible for Dracula's rapid rise to fame. Lugosi's portrayal of the bizarre Transylvanian aristocrat remained unchallenged for nearly twenty-seven years, and it was not until 1958, when the British actor Christopher Lee starred in *Horror of Dracula*, that a vampire film lived up to the Lugosi tradition.

Lee, whom Fisher had directed as the monster in *The Curse of Frankenstein* (1957), was perfect for the part of the Count. He was thin and six feet, four inches, tall, satisfying the physical requirements set down by Stoker. In addition, he had a royal background, being a descendant of the Borgias. Makeup artist Phil Leakey, adhering closely to the physical aspects of the traditional

Stoker vampire, outfitted Lee with a gray-streaked wig combed straight back to give the illusion of pointed ears and a pronounced widow's peak, a set of elongated canine teeth (never used in the Universal/Lugosi films), and red contact lenses. He was clothed entirely in black.

Writer Jimmy Sangster altered Stoker's plot line for budgetary reasons. Hammer was a low-budget production house despite its use of lavish sets and attention to detail in portraying particular periods of history. The entire story takes place in Central Europe, the Count never journeying to England as in the original story. In addition, the relationships between some of the characters are changed and a dramatic new ending is concocted. Under the expert production of Michael Carreras and cinematographer Jack Asher, the film is shot in color, thus heightening the effect of the lavish Hammer sets.

Horror of Dracula opens, as in the Stoker novel, with Jonathan Harker (John Van Eyssen) arriving at Castle Dracula on the pretext of indexing the Count's journals and books. Actually, he has been sent by Dr. Van Helsing (Peter Cushing) to investigate the Count in relation to an epidemic of vampirism that has recently swept the area. Harker is shown into the castle and served a solitary repast in the solemn, cavernous dining room. Suddenly a woman is at his side, a raven-haired beauty who exudes a curious aura of pathos and sexuality. She maintains that she is a prisoner of Dracula and begs Harker to rescue her from the evil clutches of the Count, but she disappears as suddenly and silently as she came when a dark, ominous figure comes into view at the top of the staircase. The air fairly crackles with the impact of his announcement: "I am Dracula." The Count shows Harker to his room and explains the duties connected with indexing the rare books in his collection. As he turns to leave Harker's room, the Count's eye is caught by a picture of Lucy, Harker's fiancée.

Harker is hard at work in the Count's library when he is again approached by the beautiful woman in white. Valerie Gaunt is excellent in the part of the vampire mistress, for there is a haunting "otherworld" quality to her beauty. She draws closer to Harker and, unable to resist the temptation any longer, she bites him, drawing blood. Suddenly the screen is filled with the terrifying visage of the Count, his eyes gleaming with satanic fire, his blood-smeared mouth open in a snarl, his fangs caked with the gore of the night's victims. This scene, shot in close-up, accompanied by the rising crescendo of James Bernard's music, has become a classic in horror film history. Harker, who has fainted during the Count's attack, awakens later and finds the telltale punctures on his neck. He knows what he must do. A search of the castle discloses the crypt where Dracula and the vampiress sleep. Opening the coffin, Harker drives a wooden stake through her heart and watches, with a combination of horror and relief, as she shrivels into a toothless old hag. He then hurries to Dracula's coffin, but he is too late; the coffin is empty. He turns, terror-striken, to see the Count watching him silently from the entrance to the crypt.

There is no escape for Harker.

Concerned for the safety of his friend, Dr. Van Helsing (Peter Cushing) arrives at Castle Dracula. As he drives up to the castle, a black hearse bearing a white casket and drawn by two white stallions speeds away. Cautiously entering the castle, Van Helsing finds Harker slumbering in the vampire state and drives a stake into his chest, releasing him from the curse of a living death. Meanwhile, the Count has left the castle, seeking out Lucy (Carol Marsh), Harker's former fiancée, as a replacement for his staked mistress. This is a change from the original story, for Lee, under Fisher's direction, heightens the sexual implications of the vampire myth. Lee's Dracula seduces his victims, then finally sinks his fangs into their necks as they lapse into ecstasy.

Carol Marsh as Lucy is like most of Hammer's heroines, buxom, beautiful, and scantily dressed. As in the Stoker novel, Lucy dies from Dracula's repeated attacks and then returns from the tomb lusting for human blood. There is only one solution; steeling themselves for what they know must be done, Van Helsing and his friend Arthur Holmwood (Michael Gough) find Lucy in the sleeping state and destroy her with a stake.

Mina Holmwood (Melissa Stribling), Arthur's wife, becomes Dracula's next target. Dr. Van Helsing discovers Dracula's coffin hidden in a cellar on the Holmwood estate and tosses a cross into its dirt-filled interior, thus effectively preventing the Count from returning to his daily resting place. Threatened by the approaching dawn, Dracula takes Mina and flees to his castle with Van Helsing and Holmwood in close pursuit. They arrive barely in time to thwart Dracula's attempt to inter the unconscious Mina.

The climax of the film remains one of the most spellbinding sequences in the genre of horror films. There, in the predawn darkness in the depths of Castle Dracula, the Count and Van Helsing battle in mortal combat. With a snarl, Dracula grabs his opponent's throat in a superhuman grip. The audience watches with trepidation as Van Helsing lapses into what appears to be a state of unconsciousness. With fangs bared, the Count bends to inflict the fatal bite. Suddenly, Van Helsing revives, catches the Count unawares, and breaks loose from his viselike grip. Leaping across the room, Van Helsing tears down the lush red draperies, allowing the deadly rays of the sun to fill the room. The Count screams in anguish as the burning rays strike his foot, reducing it to smoldering ashes. Desperately he seeks an escape, but Van Helsing has fashioned a cross from two silver candlesticks and forces him back into the searing sunlight. The good doctor watches as the once-powerful Count turns gray, decays, and crumbles into dust that is blown away by a breeze from an open window. The scene of Dracula's destruction was attacked by English critics as being in questionable taste; consequently, some of the shots were cut. In foreign releases, however, the stages of decomposition were left intact, producing a gruesome but powerful impact.

Under Fisher's expert direction, Lee portrayed the Count as a dynamic, feral creature possessing supernatural strength and supreme cunning. Lee has a commanding screen presence and invests Dracula with a depth of character that immediately captured the imagination of his audience and established Lee's performance as one of the finest portrayals of the king of vampires. Lee's Count has all the nobility, ferocity, and sadness with which Stoker endowed him. Since its release more than twenty years ago, *Horror of Dracula* has maintained a reputation among horror film buffs as one of the best of its kind ever made. There is no question that it is the finest vampire film ever produced and the vehicle that established Christopher Lee as a bona fide star of the horror film.

The number of films Lee has appeared in since *Horror of Dracula* is prolific. He has teamed with Fisher in three additional pictures, *The Two Faces of Dr. Jekyll* (1961), *The Gorgon* (1964), and *Dracula, Prince of Darkness* (1966). In addition to his outstanding performances in such pictures as *The Man Who Cheated Death* (1959) and *City of the Dead* (1960), Lee has portrayed the Count in seven different vampire films. Fisher went on to direct such classic films as *The Hound of the Baskervilles* (1959) and *The Phantom of the Opera* (1962).

D. Gail Huskins

THE HOSPITAL

Released: 1971
Production: Howard Gottfried and Paddy Chayefsky Productions in associ-
ation with Arthur Hiller; released by United Artists
Direction: Arthur Hiller
Screenplay: Paddy Chayefsky (AA)
Cinematography: Victor J. Kemper
Editing: Eric Albertson
Running time: 103 minutes

> *Principal characters:*
> Dr. Herbert Bock .... George C. Scott
> Barbara Drummond .... Diana Rigg
> Drummond .... Barnard Hughes

The Hospital is a crowded, dizzying film, very much in line with Paddy
Chayefsky's other work: an institution is dissected by a hero who is both close
to the heart of its process and yet, in principle, embodies its opposite. In *The
Americanization of Emily* (1964), the hero (James Garner) is a General's
aide who preaches to his widowed girl friend the cult of his own very proud
cowardice (one's real patriotic duty being, he feels, to avoid combat, stay
alive, and perpetuate the species); in *Network* (1976), a formerly rational
newscaster (Peter Finch) undergoes a conversion, or breakdown, and
preaches on the air against the dehumanizing influence of television.

In *The Hospital*, the institution is a sprawling hospital complex, sparkling
amid a section of tenements in New York City. Its hero is the hospital's Chief
Resident, Dr. Herbert Bock (George C. Scott), recently divorced, alienated
from his children, suffering from impotence, and spiritually bottoming out
after having been proclaimed a genius in his early career. The hospital itself
is a mess.

In the film's opening moments, a voice drily narrates as an elderly man,
complaining of simple chest pains, is admitted to the hospital in the early
morning and shuttled from floor to floor, receiving a variety of treatments for
a variety of different diseases, each administered in ignorance of the other,
until by evening he is dead from the conflicting treatments. "I mention all
this," the narrator (Chayefsky himself) tells us, "only to explain how the bed
in room 406 became available."

The story that follows is an account of two days in this medical inferno.
The bed in question is used by one of the more sexually ambitious interns
as a trysting spot to meet one of his girl friends. After they make love, she
leaves him sleeping peacefully, and the next morning, he is found dead. He
was a diabetic, and a night nurse, mistaking him for the bed's previous tenant,
came in while he was still dozing and plugged him into a glucose bottle. Dr.

Bock enters the scene and is given an embarrassed account of all these events. He also hears the story of Drummond (Barnard Hughes), another old man, still alive but comatose, occupying the second bed in room 406: he was brought in for a check-up, in perfect health, and ended up having a kidney needlessly removed in an operation that damaged the other kidney. Bock is, to say the least, flabbergasted. "Where did you train your nurses, Mrs. Christie—Dachau?"

Dr. Bock has been on the verge of suicide, and that night, after a second dead intern has been found, implying murder but having taken place under similarly negligent circumstances, Bock sits in his office getting ready to give himself a fatal injection. He is interrupted by Barbara Drummond (Diana Rigg), the daughter of the old man still alive in 406. She has come to see about taking her father home. Drummond, who was once an eminent doctor himself, underwent a conversion, or breakdown, and now preaches the apocalypse to a tribe of Indians in northern Mexico. Barbara feels he would be better off there, having his kidneys looked after by Medicine Men.

This encounter between Bock and Barbara is the highlight of the film: Barbara, who is very sensual and wears her denim blouse almost totally unbuttoned, talks about her erotic and hallucinogenic experiences with a candor that arouses Dr. Bock in spite of himself; Bock, for his part, makes an impassioned speech, humorously defending his impotence and almost tearfully confessing his helplessness in the face of modern suffering. Barbara is nonplussed by his desire to kill himself. "Well, it's hard for me to take your despair very seriously, Doctor. You obviously enjoy it so much." Bock almost injects himself to prove that he is serious, but ends up smashing the bottle and pouncing on Barbara. The close brush with death seems to have left him potent; by morning he has, as Barbara puts it, "ravished" her three times. They are both very much in love and plan to pack up the old man and go off to Mexico together.

The old man, however, has other plans: he is not in a coma at all, but a self-induced trance, and rises occasionally (Frankensteinlike with his intravenous tubings), unplugging himself in order to prowl the hospital in the uniform of the first dead intern, which has been hanging ignored in his room's closet. It is he who is killing off the hospital staff. By mid-morning he has facilitated the death of a nurse by placing her unconscious on the gurney intended for a fifty-year-old woman: the mistaken identity goes unnoticed by the indifferent staff, and she is given an overdose of anesthesia. When Bock and Barbara catch up with him, he is on his way to dispatch the last physician on his list.

He explains to them that he is doing the Lord's work; he had been a witness to the death of the elderly man so drily narrated at the beginning of the story. The murdered interns and nurse each had a hand in the poor man's demise, and Drummond has been careful in each instance to make himself only the instrument of Divine Will—stopping short of murder but placing his victims in a position where the atmosphere of negligence and incompetence prevailing around the hospital would take its natural course. Bock and Barbara, realizing they have to act fast, get ready to take the old man and flee to Mexico before he attracts any more attention than he already has. However, the patient in the next bed overhears the entire confession.

As it happens, the last victim on Drummond's list, the physician who both removed his kidney and gave the erroneous and fatal diagnosis to the first old man, dies of a heart attack when he hears by telephone that his incorporated Medical Group on Long Island is being investigated by the Security Exchange Commission. The two lovers try to spirit the old man out of the building at this point; in the climactic melee that ensues, a confused staff member puts the name "Drummond" on the death certificate, and Bock, seeing the error, exchanges glances with Barbara but says nothing. Providence seems to have finished the job Drummond started.

They get the old man bundled into a taxi and are about to head for the airport, but Bock stops short of joining them at the last minute. Throughout the story, protesters have been encircling the complex, and now they are swarming into the building itself like a plague of locusts; colleagues of Bock's are abandoning ship, quitting on the spot, and he is pained at the sight. If Bock is married to anything, it is the hospital. "Somebody has got to be responsible, Barbara," he tells her. Although she is not happy about his decision, she nevertheless sees it would be fruitless to object, and leaves with her father. Bock, a healed man, steps back into the center of the chaos.

One of the problems so common to every Chayefsky script that it seems almost a trademark—like the witty dialogue and metaphorical-industrial situation—is that the hero, after tearing the institution apart brilliantly for the entire story, invariably turns around at the last moment and opts for the *status quo*. James Garner, as the General's aide in *The Americanization of Emily*, at his friend Emily's eleventh-hour urging accepts his role as war hero, despite his splendid eloquence of the previous two hours, so as not to let down the boys who are still fighting. Peter Finch as the newscaster in *Network*, after making perfect sense for three-quarters of the picture, does a complete about-face when given the hard sell by an equally witty but far less persuasive character. The backing-off never strikes one as genuine, although Chayefsky is crafty enough that on repeated viewings, the decision seems inevitable. In *The Hospital*, this flaw or idiosyncracy appears in force at the film's conclusion. Chayefsky's script, also a trademark, is for the most part ingeniously written: intricately structured, the dialogue is vivid and believable at the same time that all the characters sound alike. The rest of the ingredients—direction, performance, cinematography, editing—are models of fidelity to the Chayefsky script when they are not simply brilliant.

Arthur Hiller, who also directed *The Americanization of Emily*, does a clean job, is equal to every turn of the story, and keeps the actors moving at a pitch that is both vaudevillian and tragic; this is exactly what the script calls for. There are no obtrusive stylistic flourishes; the overall film has the look and feel of a documentary in its use of seemingly natural light and cuts that impose a tempo on the seemingly "found" workaday environment of a busy hospital. All of this adds to the nightmarish quality of the humor.

George C. Scott is magnificent as Bock. As always, he exudes vitality, even as his character is seemingly disintegrating, and in the manner of any great actor, he makes use of the paradox. His Bock is both coarse and elegant, and Diana Rigg is a sublime counterpart to him. Her role calls for someone who is rather cerebrally sexual, cool even about her appetite, but she brings this quality down to earth with her presence and offsets it with a very physical sensuality. The other performers—Hugh Barnard, the victims, the nurses, and the other doctors—all act with equal ability.

Upon its first release, the critical reaction to *The Hospital* was mixed (Pauline Kael called it "trash" but allowed that it was "funny and lively" and an "entertaining potboiler"), and audiences, either confused about whether to laugh or become depressed about the film's topical plausibility, shied away from it. Still, the film has persisted on late-night television and in rerun houses, entering film history in its own right and taking its place along with the best of Chayefsky's work. The screenplay won an Oscar, and, as with the rest of his films (more obvious here because in *The Hospital* there are more than sixty-seven characters), the script is the star.

F. X. Feeney

THE HOUND OF THE BASKERVILLES

Released: 1939
Production: Darryl F. Zanuck for Twentieth Century-Fox
Direction: Sidney Lanfield
Screenplay: Ernest Pascal; based on the novel of the same name by Sir Arthur Conan Doyle
Cinematography: Peverell Marley
Editing: Robert Simpson
Running time: 78 minutes

Principal characters:
Sherlock Holmes	Basil Rathbone
Dr. Watson	Nigel Bruce
Sir Henry Baskerville	Richard Greene
John Stapleton	Morton Lowry
Barryman	John Carradine
Dr. James Mortimer	Lionel Atwill
Sir Hugo Baskerville	Ralph Forbes

Sherlock Holmes, the violin-playing, drug-addicted, eccentric but brilliant detective of 221B Baker Street, London, is one of the world's most famous fictional characters. His translation into film was inevitable and continues into the 1970's with such recent offerings as *The Seven Percent Solution* (1976), and *The Adventures of Sherlock Holmes' Smarter Brother* (1976). Not inevitable, however, was the tremendous success of the series of Holmes films which started with *The Hound of the Baskervilles*. These films, running from 1939 through the late 1940's, constituted the most successful series of all time until the exploits of James Bond.

This first film in the series is the only one to make even a pretense of following one of Conan Doyle's original stories. This is understandable, for it is the idiosyncratic character of Holmes which led to the popularity of the stories, not the cleverly concocted exploits Doyle created for his hero. Similarly, the success of this film and the subsequent sequels is indisputably due to the incisive portrait of the detective created by British actor Basil Rathbone. According to one source, Rathbone was the highest paid and most steadily employed freelance actor in the Hollywood of his time. His roles were many and often distinguished, including Murdstone in *David Copperfield* (1935) and the arch villain Guy de Gisbourne in *The Adventures of Robin Hood* (1938). Nevertheless, he will be popularly remembered for his fine performances as Sherlock Holmes.

The Hound of the Baskervilles skillfully incorporates every aspect of the legendary detective: his expertise with disguise; his ever-present pipe, hunting cap, and cape; his scratchy violin performances at odd moments; and his secretive ways and boundless nervous energy. His drug habit is also suggested, albeit obliquely, in the film's last line: "The mystery is unraveled and all parties filled with gratitude." Holmes accepts all the parties' profuse thanks, and as he starts to leave, he turns and says: "Oh, Watson, the needle." At Rathbone's suggestion, Nigel Bruce was chosen to play Dr. Watson; this was a masterstroke of casting. Bruce became as apt a Watson as Rathbone was a Holmes. The contrast and unlikely friendship between the lean, quick, hawklike Holmes and the blustering, rotund, well-meaning Watson are a major appeal of the series.

The plot of *The Hound of the Baskervilles* is pure melodrama, resoundingly unrealistic, filled with red herrings, and thoroughly enjoyable. The current Lord Baskerville has just died mysteriously, and attempts are being made on the life of Sir Henry Baskerville (Richard Greene), the new heir to the estate. Rumors are abroad that the ancient curse of the Baskervilles begun in the time of the evil Sir Hugo Baskerville (*circa* 1650) is at work again. According to the legend, a vicious supernatural hound stalks Hugo's descendants to avenge his murder of a young peasant girl, an event which is effectively presented in the film in the form of a flashback.

The setting for the drama is a blasted, fog-enshrouded heath filled with treacherous quicksand pits. Even in daylight, the heath appears murky, and since most of the action takes place at night, the sense of menace is ever present. The sets for the film have a particularly appropriate gothic quality, and the camera work is quietly effective in the many shadowy, often candle-lit scenes.

Through a combination of brilliant deduction and bold action, Holmes at last uncovers the mastermind behind the present happenings at Baskerville Hall. He is John Stapleton (Morton Lowry), ostensibly a resident of the community, who is actually a distant relative of the Baskervilles. He has plotted the death of Sir Henry so that he will gain the Baskerville inheritance. Before this unexpected denouement, however, the audience's suspicions have been alternately directed to two incidental characters, Barryman the butler and Dr. James Mortimer, played admirably by John Carradine and Lionel Atwill. The plot obviously has a traditional gothic appeal, a fact which perhaps explains why the movie has been remade at least twice.

The Hound of the Baskervilles, however, has a significance beyond that of a gothic mystery. It represents a type of motion picture which has all but vanished from the scene: a professionally filmed, moderately budgeted B-movie designed to please a mass audience. As such, it falls between the most prevalent current offerings of American cinema, which are either high-budget and/or superstar vehicles or less professionally produced amateur efforts which appeal to special audiences.

Susan Karnes Passler

HOUSE OF WAX

Released: 1953
Production: Byran Foy for Warner Bros.
Direction: Andre de Toth
Screenplay: Crane Wilbur; based on a screen story by Charles Belden
Cinematography: Bert Glennon
Editing: Rudi Fehr
Running time: 88 minutes

Principal characters:
Professor Henry Jarrod .... Vincent Price
Lieutenant Tom Brennan .... Frank Lovejoy
Sue Allen .... Phyllis Kirk
Cathy Gray .... Carolyn Jones
Scott Andrews .... Paul Picerni
Matthew Burke .... Roy Roberts
Sidney Wallace .... Paul Cavanagh

By the early 1950's in the United States, television presented a threat to the film industry, and cinema producers sought special lures to seduce potential audiences away from their televisions and homemade popcorn and back into the theaters. One of Hollywood's most legendary attempts to recapture its audience was the special effect of three-dimensional cinematography, and the most famous "3-D" film of all is *House of Wax*, a grand and eerie chiller that ironically survives today, on television, as a Grand Guignol classic even bereft of its highly touted 3-D effects.

House of Wax was a remake of Warner Bros.' 1933 *Mystery of the Wax Museum*, an early Technicolor thriller which starred Lionel Atwill as Ivan Igor, victim of a wax museum fire that leaves him with an insane mind and a hideous face. It proved to be one of the 1930's best-remembered horror films, celebrated for the sequence in which ever-screaming Fay Wray attacks Atwill's face, a wax mask, and it cracks, revealing the monstrous effects of the fire. In revamping the film, Warners' gave *House of Wax* a late nineteenth century setting and decided to produce the film in 3-D and stereophonic sound in order to heighten the impact on the audience. Many in Hollywood, including Vincent Price, refused to take the idea of 3-D seriously. Initially, Price took Warners' proposal that he star in *House of Wax* as a joke; a lucrative offer, however, changed his mind. Production began under the direction of Andre de Toth, a one-eyed Hungarian whose handicap prevented him from seeing the final effect of the 3-D shooting. (Toth accepted the situation with rather pretentious stoicism: "Beethoven couldn't hear music either, could he?")

House of Wax tells the grisly saga of Professor Henry Jarrod (Vincent

Price), a sculptor whose entire life is devoted to the historical characters he re-creates in wax. When wealthy Sidney Wallace (Paul Cavanagh) visits him in the museum one evening, Jarrod introduces his characters, all but caressing his masterpiece, Marie Antoinette, to whom he apologizes for betraying her beauty secrets after explaining her construction to Wallace. Wallace is awed by Jarrod's beautiful wax creations and pledges his patronage to continue bigger and better projects; but they never come to pass. Jarrod's partner Matthew Burke (Roy Roberts) is determined to burn the museum and Jarrod's "people" for the insurance. In a thrilling sequence, Jarrod and Burke fight viciously as the museum becomes an inferno and the wax figures, faces, watching the brawl, melt into grotesque forms. While Burke escapes the flames, Jarrod is presumed burned to ashes.

A short time later, a reign of terror begins. Burke, about to wed giggly blonde Cathy Gray (Carolyn Jones in a charmingly comic performance), is murdered by a nightmarish figure with a fire-scarred face, a black cloak, and a broad-brimmed hat, who tosses Burke down an elevator shaft at the end of a rope to suggest suicide. Next, Cathy is slain in her bed and her body is discovered by her roommate, Sue Allen (Phyllis Kirk), who also discovers the black-clad monster in the room. A spine-tingling sequence ensues as the murderer pursues Sue through the fog-shrouded streets, his bestial breathing sounding in the night as the terrified girl seeks refuge at the home of her boyfriend, Scott Andrews (Paul Picerni). Scott has just been engaged as a sculptor to help Henry Jarrod, who reveals that he has escaped the fire, but is now confined to a wheelchair and has lost the use of his hands. Jarrod plans to open a new wax museum with a chamber of horrors which will terrify the patrons.

Jarrod's new museum soon has a gala opening, and Sue attends. There she is deeply upset by the statue of Joan of Arc, which bears a strong resemblance to her dead roommate Cathy. Adding to Sue's uneasiness is the fact that Cathy's body had been stolen from the morgue after her murder. Jarrod, seeing her distressed, glibly thanks her for reacting so deeply to his work, and all the while thinks how much Sue looks like his long-since melted Marie Antoinette. The inevitable soon happens. Sue, searching for Scott, ventures, with the characteristic recklessness of a horror film heroine, into the bowels of the museum, past a swinging devil and guillotine of the shadowy chamber of horrors. As she again passes the statue of Joan of Arc, she is unable to resist and lifts the black wig to reveal Cathy's blonde hair. "You shouldn't have done that, my dear!" says Jarrod, who rises from his wheelchair and begins stalking Sue. Hysterical, she strikes at his face, and the wax cracks, revealing the monster who chased her through the streets on that foggy night.

Meanwhile, police lieutenant Tom Brennan (Frank Lovejoy) has pieced together enough evidence to realize that Jarrod is a maniac who murders his victims and then coats them in wax for display in his new museum. Brennan and his men crash into the museum laboratory just before the crazed Jarrod embalms the naked Sue, who is coyly covered with a coat by Brennan in a touch that greatly amused 1953 audiences. Jarrod is knocked into his own vat of boiling wax and Sue is rescued.

Warner Bros. spared no expense in promoting *House of Wax* at its premiere in the spring of 1953. It was a gala Hollywood event, where the celebrities included Dracula-caped Bela Lugosi holding an ape-suited extra on a leash, and an onslaught of 3-D heralding publicity teasers, such as "SEE Crazed, Lustful Monsters leap from the screen INTO THE AUDIENCE!" In actuality, the special effects that the audience saw through their cardboard glasses were not quite so sensational. Aside from some bric-a-brac thrown into the screen, the most lavish 3-D effects concerned a ball on a paddle and some chorines can-canning their legs into the camera; and, in the final shot, Lovejoy thrusts onto the screen a wax head of Jarrod's assistant Igor, played by 1970's box-office star Charles Bronson. "What hath the Warner Brothers wrought?" demanded an outraged Bosley Crowther of the *New York Times*, lambasting the film for its "savagery," "brutal stimuli," "morbidity," and "idiocies." Yet *House of Wax* proved to be a box-office bonanza, and although not the first of the 3-D films (United Artists' 1953 *Bwana Devil* preceded it by two months), it became the most famous of them all, winning a spot on *Variety*'s Box Office Champions list with a $4.65 million domestic gross ($9.2 million worldwide) and establishing Price as the screen's top purveyor of gothic mayhem.

Despite the success of *House of Wax*, the 3-D craze swiftly extinguished itself. Exhibitors were not enthused about the maintenance of the cardboard glasses, which many patrons tried to sneak out of the theaters, or the need to run both projectors at once, or the dangers of lost picture synchronization, and moviegoers soon became more taken with newly developed Cinema-Scope. Such films as M-G-M's *Kiss Me Kate* (1953) and Hitchcock's *Dial M for Murder* (1954), shot in 3-D, were thus released "flat." In late 1971, *House of Wax* was rereleased in the original 3-D, proving a great curiosity to many film fans.

Even without the 3-D effects and the stereophonic sound, however, *House of Wax* is a sterling chiller, as proven by its perennial popularity on television. It boasts excellent atmosphere, frills of picturesque relief, and most of all, Price's fastidiously wicked performance as the horrific Jarrod. The star is, as *Time* put it, "splendidly clammy" as he lopes and gasps through the foggy streets in pursuit of the heroine, or gleefully informs the bound Sue Allen of her imminent death via boiling wax ("There is a pain beyond pain, an agony so intense, it shocks the mind into instant beauty!"), or suavely offers smelling salts to three young ladies when his Chamber of Horrors proves too much for their corseted stomachs. Price himself has vivid memories of *House of Wax*: "They didn't let us see any of it at Warners' until the entire film had been completed. And when I finally saw it, it scared the hell out of me!" *House of Wax* continues, in the fine tradition of the gothic genre, to frighten audiences as it has ever since its release.

Gregory William Mank

HOW GREEN WAS MY VALLEY

Released: 1941
Production: Darryl F. Zanuck for Twentieth Century-Fox (AA)
Direction: John Ford (AA)
Screenplay: Philip Dunne; based on the novel of the same name by Richard Llewellyn
Cinematography: Arthur Miller (AA)
Editing: James B. Clark
Art direction: Richard Day and Nathan Juran (AA)
Interior decoration: Thomas Little (AA)
Running time: 118 minutes

Principal characters:
Mr. Gruffydd .... Walter Pidgeon
Angharad .... Maureen O'Hara
Mr. Morgan .... Donald Crisp (AA)
Bronwyn .... Anna Lee
Huw .... Roddy McDowall
Mrs. Morgan .... Sara Allgood
Ivor .... Patric Knowles
Dai Bando .... Rhys Williams

How Green Was My Valley was the last in a distinguished group of human dramas directed by John Ford during the late 1930's and early 1940's, including such films as *Stagecoach* (1939), *Young Mr. Lincoln* (1939), and *The Grapes of Wrath* (1940). This new film firmly established Ford's growing reputation as a successful commercial director. The film, like the novel on which it is based, became an instant popular success.

Richard Llewellyn's novel is a nostalgic remembrance of life in a late nineteenth century Welsh mining town. It is a first-person narrative, told by the aging coal miner Huw Morgan (Roddy McDowall) as he prepares to leave the valley that has been his lifelong home. The novel is essentially a collection of loosely related episodes in the lives of young Huw and his family, relying more on characterization and gentle humor than on a dramatically cohesive plot for its appeal.

The opening fifteen minutes of the film preserve the flavor of the novel almost perfectly. As the offscreen narrator (the adult Huw) begins to reminisce about his past, the audience is introduced in quick succession to young Huw, his older brothers and father (Donald Crisp) who work in the coal mine, his sister Angharad (Maureen O'Hara), and his mother (Sara Allgood). The skillfully assembled sequence establishes the peaceful order of this society in the past: the natural beauty of the valley and surrounding mountains, the community of miners who sing their way to and from work, the loving harmony of the Morgan family, the joyous wedding celebration for Huw's older brother Ivor (Patric Knowles) and his bride Bronwyn (Anna Lee). Employing vigorous narrative images with a minimum of dialogue, the sequence exemplifies one of the film's significant strengths.

The vision of this idyllic existence does not last, however. As the story moves forward, we see the gradual erosion and collapse of the Morgans' former way of life. Greedy mine owners begin to cut the wages of the miners, leading to disputes among them and eventually to a strike. Huw's older brothers angrily disagree with their authoritarian father about the strike and the formation of a miners' union and move out of the family home. Against this background of social and domestic upheaval, twelve-year-old Huw enters adolescence. One winter night Huw takes his mother up the mountainside to a secret meeting of the miners. On their return, mother and son become lost in a storm and nearly freeze to death. During his long convalescence, Huw finds a mentor in Mr. Gruffydd (Walter Pidgeon), the village minister who encourages him in his studies, and later, he attends the National School over the mountain in a neighboring valley. Mr. Gruffydd and Angharad fall in love, but because of his extreme poverty Mr. Gruffydd stoically declines to marry her, and Angharad consequently enters into an unhappy marriage with the mine owner's son. As the black slag heap from the mine spreads over the once-green and beautiful valley, we see the disintegration of Huw's world: his sensitive, musical brother Ivor dies in a mine accident, his other brothers emigrate to find work, his friend Mr. Gruffydd is forced from the valley by vicious gossip linking him with Angharad, and finally Huw's beloved father also dies in the mine.

Although considerable condensation and rearrangement were necessary to give the scenario a manageable length, the screenplay by Philip Dunne adheres to the episodic form of Llewellyn's novel. As a result, the film has a rather loose dramatic structure. Apparently as the result of a decision to cast a single young actor as Huw, the screenplay tends to emphasize the early episodes of the novel, which involve Huw at a younger age. The long section about Huw's difficulties at the National School—the taunting older students and his sadistic bully of a teacher—is included virtually intact in the film, and is one of the most satisfying sequences of the film. However, the young age of the actor is a minor disadvantage in a later episode when Huw as an older adolescent moves in with his sister-in-law Bronwyn in an attempt to take the place of his dead brother Ivor. This has considerable poignancy in the novel, but is merely amusing when played onscreen by a twelve-year-old.

The film benefits from very good actors who go a long way toward making the idealized simple folk of Huw's memory credible. Particularly effective are Donald Crisp and Sara Allgood as Huw's parents, the respective "head" and "heart" of the Morgan household; Crisp won an Academy Award for his performance as Gwilym Morgan. Roddy McDowall gives a memorable performance as the shy, sensitive Huw. In a smaller role, Rhys Williams gives a fine, lusty portrayal of Dai Bando, the professional boxer who teaches Huw to fight and who takes exquisite revenge on the teacher who beat Huw so mercilessly. The international nature of the cast, including as it does American, Irish, and Welsh actors, is responsible for a variety of vocal accents; as a result, the lilting Welsh speech is heard rather unevenly.

How Green Was My Valley is particularly distinguished by its richly detailed visual surface. The art direction was done with painstaking care. An entire mining village—stone houses, chapel, and colliery—were constructed at considerable expense for this film in California's Ventura hills. (This huge exterior set also appeared in several other films of the 1940's.) In fact, the memorable long view of the village, with the row of houses sloping uphill toward the mine at the summit, is the film's visual hallmark. Arthur Miller's superb black-and-white cinematography contributes much to this aspect of the film. His scenes are consistently arranged with care and with strong pictorial composition. In this film the camera itself moves only rarely, and then with clear, dramatic purpose: as Ivor's choir prepares to depart for a royal command performance, the camera pans slightly from the proud but troubled Mrs. Morgan in the foreground to capture a glimpse of two other sons who are leaving home to go abroad.

John Ford's direction of *How Green Was My Valley* confirmed his reputation as a master cinematic storyteller. His perfected narrative technique, weaving together a richly textured fabric of individual images and actions, nearly compensates for the rambling dramatic structure of the screenplay. His control seems to falter only in the film's occasional lapses into sentimentality. These can be partially justified, perhaps, as being inherent in the novel, as well as in the fact that overt sentimentality on the screen was then a more acceptable artistic convention than it is today.

How Green Was My Valley was a successful and highly honored film in 1941. It received Academy Awards in six categories, including Best Picture; but in making this last award, the Academy overlooked Orson Welles's innovative classic, *Citizen Kane*, choosing instead this more conventional and commercial motion picture. Nevertheless, *How Green Was My Valley* endures as a film of great visual beauty, nostalgic charm, and warm human feeling.

David Bahnemann

HUD

Released: 1963
Production: Martin Ritt and Irving Ravetch for Paramount
Direction: Martin Ritt
Screenplay: Irving Ravetch and Harriet Frank, Jr.; based on the novel *Horseman, Pass By* by Larry McMurtry
Cinematography: James Wong Howe (AA)
Editing: Frank Bracht
Running time: 112 minutes

Principal characters:
Hud Bannon .... Paul Newman
Homer Bannon .... Melvyn Douglas (AA)
Alma Brown .... Patricia Neal (AA)
Lon Bannon .... Brandon De Wilde

Hud is a Western; but it is a modern Western, examining the manner in which the values of the Old West function in modern society. Essentially a four-character story, the film delineates the conflicts between the values of the nineteenth century and those of the twentieth century, as personified by Homer Bannon (Melvyn Douglas) and his son Hud (Paul Newman). Observing this conflict, and sometimes serving as reluctant participants, are Lon Bannon (Brandon De Wilde), Homer's grandson and Hud's nephew, and Alma (Patricia Neal), the ranch cook.

The film opens in the small town of Thalia, Texas, where Lon is searching for his Uncle Hud. Lon's transistor radio informs the audience that it is 6:00 A.M., and the cafe cook tells Lon that she has seen Hud's pink Cadillac parked down the street. Lon goes to the house and calls for Hud, who comes to the door buttoning his shirt. With a casual farewell to the woman inside, Hud leaves with his nephew just as the woman's husband arrives home. Hud is totally charming, arrogant, and amoral. It is obvious that his seventeen-year-old nephew admires and envies him very much. Hud is everything Lon feels he is not—sexually proficient, mature, capable, and attractive.

At breakfast Homer Bannon explains to Hud why he has sent Lon to find him. The elder Bannon has found a dead heifer and he is concerned. He instructs Hud and Lon to round up the herd while he calls the veterinarian. Homer is a stern, moral man, the exact opposite of his son. Clearly, Homer and Hud are very different role models for Lon, who is torn between the two—the glittering but corrupt uncle, and the cold but principled grandfather.

As they round up the herd and await the vet's diagnosis, Hud argues with his father about the future of the ranch. Hud wants to drill for oil, but Homer believes that oil wells would destroy the ranch and his way of life. The vet announces that the heifer has died of hoof-and-mouth disease, and that the entire herd must be destroyed before others are infected. Hud immediately suggests to his father that he sell the herd in the North before the government finishes the testing. Homer refuses, saying simply that he could not do that to his neighbors. The tensions between the two men intensify as they wait for the final orders to destroy the herd. Lon slowly realizes that Hud is not worthy of his admiration, and he comes to respect his grandfather and the values he represents. Hud tells Lon that he wants to have Homer declared incompetent and take over the ranch himself. Lon is outraged, but incapable of stopping his uncle.

At last the government is ready to destroy the herd. Bulldozers dig huge pits in the ground, and the cattle are herded into them. Cowboys shoot the cattle in the pits, and then the carcasses are limed and buried by the bulldozers. Only the longhorns which Homer has raised as reminders of the Old West remain. Lon tries to persuade his grandfather to save them, at least; but Homer silently walks out with his rifle to kill the steers himself. He returns a broken man, his way of life now only a memory. Meanwhile, Hud, drunk and wild, breaks into Alma's room and attempts to rape her. Lon stops him, but cannot persuade Alma to stay on the ranch. Lon takes her to the bus stop where Hud sees her leaving, and tells her that he will remember her as the one that got away. Alma replies that if he had not been so mean, perhaps she would not have had to leave.

As Lon returns to the ranch, he finds Homer crawling across the road; he has been thrown from his horse. Hud also arrives, and together they try to comfort the old man as he dies. After the funeral, Hud asks Lon to stay on, but Lon is now thoroughly disenchanted with his uncle and walks off the ranch. Hud is briefly shaken by this defection, but then shrugs and opens a can of beer as the film ends.

Homer Bannon is clearly a product of the Old West and of the nineteenth century. A stern, aloof man of principle and morality, he is clearly repelled by his son. Hud has no morals; he is greedy, self-centered, and has no interest in preserving his father's way of life. These might be described as twentieth century attributes, but Larry McMurtry, the author of the novel on which the film is based, has described Hud as a direct descendant of the same era that produced his father. The qualities that Hud exhibits are also qualities that built the great ranches and settled the frontier. Homer represents the best of the pioneer spirit; but Hud is in the pioneer tradition as well. Hud at one point asks his father what he has ever done for him, implying that had Homer been less rigid and more understanding, perhaps Hud would not now be the grasping, egotistical person that Homer finds so disgusting. The two men represent vastly different but equally influential attitudes in the traditions of the West—attitudes which still shape our lives today.

The role of Hud is perhaps Paul Newman's finest characterization. He brings to the part a charisma and a virility that are very attractive. It is difficult to despise the character totally, and it is very easy to understand why both Lon and Alma are so drawn to him. Newman was nominated for but did not receive an Oscar for the role; Patricia Neal did win the Academy Award for Best Actress for her role as Alma. Playing a small part, but one that is very important in softening the pyrotechnics of the male cast, Neal is both dignified and slatternly, motherly and earthy, in a memorable performance. Melvyn Douglas was awarded an Oscar for Best Supporting Actor; James Wong Howe won for Best Cinematography. Howe's camerawork added immeasurably to the film, framing the stark landscape in beautiful images. Martin Ritt, Irving Ravetch, and the art and set decorators were also nominated for awards, but did not win.

Don K Thompson

HUMORESQUE

Released: 1946
Production: Jerry Wald for Warner Bros.
Direction: Jean Negulesco
Screenplay: Clifford Odets and Zachary Gold; based on a story by Fannie
    Hurst
Cinematography: Ernest Haller
Editing: Rudi Fehr
Running time: 125 minutes

>   *Principal characters:*
>   Helen Wright ....Joan Crawford
>   Paul Boray .... John Garfield
>   Sid Jeffers .... Oscar Levant
>   Esther Boray .... Ruth Nelson
>   Rudy Boray ....J. Carrol Naish
>   Gina .... Joan Chandler

After Joan Crawford's remarkable comeback success in *Mildred Pierce* (1945), producer Jerry Wald realized that its very success spelled a real problem: her second comeback vehicle had to provide her with a new kind of role, and the picture had to have as much audience appeal as her first for Warner Bros. That studio did not have a backlog of stories that suited her, and it would have been wrong to put an actress who had just won an Academy Award in a remake of a Bette Davis feature.

However, Wald was planning to produce a remake of Fannie Hurst's story *Humoresque*, which as a silent had been the first picture to win the *Photoplay* magazine Gold Medal. It was to star John Garfield as a poor boy who became a great violinist. The big parts would go to Garfield and to the actress who played his self-sacrificing mother. Then Wald conceived the idea of introducing an entirely new character, a sophisticated woman who would come between mother and son. As Joan Crawford was casually looking over the upcoming projects at Warner Bros., she discovered the new character in *Humoresque* and was interested. Obviously, costarring Crawford with Garfield might mean a box-office bonanza. Screenwriters Clifford Odets and Zachary Gold expanded the new character of Helen Wright, the very rich neurotic who ignores her husband to concentrate on a series of young male protégés. She is nearsighted and wears large-rimmed glasses which she is continually putting on to peer more closely at some man who arouses her interest. She drinks incessantly and has a cutting tongue and a cruel sense of humor.

Crawford was intrigued with the character; she had never had anything like it during her M-G-M days, and playing so self-centered a heroine after all the shopgirls and rich young rebels she had played at M-G-M piqued her interest. There was only one trouble with the part: Helen Wright does not come into the picture until it is nearly a quarter over. The first part of *Humoresque* deals with the boyhood of a young violinist, Paul Boray (John Garfield), who is spurred on to fame in his adolescence through the faith and devotion of his mother. It is not until the boy is grown and becomes a promising young musician that he is summoned to play at a party given by Mrs. Wright (Joan Crawford). She is aware of her guests' interest in his performance, and, putting on her glasses, she moves closer to inspect him. His violin performance is arresting and completely professional, and it draws the plaudits of his audience. Helen tries to cut him down with a belittling remark, but in Paul she has met her match. Ambitious but fiercely independent, he scorns her first words, and they fight a verbal duel. She concedes that the world may soon be divided into two camps: pro-Boray and anti-Boray. "And which side are you on, Mrs. Wright?" he asks.

She has never been so much on the defensive; and she has also never been so attracted. Paul Boray, although considerably younger than she, has a positive belief in himself that fascinates her, and she determines to make herself important in his life. She furthers his career, eventually arranging an audition for him with the conductor of the New York Philharmonic Orchestra. Total opposites, they nevertheless become lovers. Soon she is hopelessly enamored of him; his music comes first in his life, but he does not deny that Helen Wright comes second.

This is not what his mother had planned, however. It was she who first became aware of his interest in music when he was still only a small boy. She had planned, prayed, and "gone without" so that Paul's career as a violinist could advance. She had never dreamed that so hedonistic a force as Helen Wright could come into her son's life. It had now become Mrs. Boray *versus* Helen Wright for the place of honor in Paul's universe.

The introduction of the character of Helen Wright created an entirely new story line in what had been a simple narrative in Fannie Hurst's original story. The wonderful success of the 1920 (silent) *Humoresque* had spawned a whole series of imitative "mother love" pictures, but in this 1946 remake, the character of Paul's mother, Esther Boray, all but disappears as the conflict between Paul and Helen is magnified.

Ironically, what was to have been a starring vehicle for Garfield, and then a costarring feature for Garfield and Crawford, grows into a sympathetic and glamorous starring role for Crawford. She had never been so glamorously gowned by Adrian as she is in this vehicle. Cameraman Ernest Haller photographed her beautifully, and director Jean Negulesco unintentionally favored her in every scene. *Humoresque* becomes Joan Crawford's film, and what had been the struggle of a poor young man to achieve his rightful place in the sun becomes the love story of an aging woman who has every material possession but is obsessed with a great love for a young man who is not in her world and has no need for her except to take what she can offer him toward the advancement of his career.

The picture had begun by adhering faithfully to the narrative Fannie Hurst had written for Frances Marion to adapt to scenario form for the silent screen. Beginning on Paul's birthday, the audience is made acquainted with his humble beginnings. His mother, Esther Boray (Ruth Nelson), sends her husband Rudy (J. Carl Naish) off to buy the boy a suitable present at the novelty story run by Sid Jeffers (Oscar Levant). The father suggests something like a baseball bat, but Paul, whose interest in music has already been aroused by his friendship with a pianist working in his father's store, has eyes only for a violin. Mr. Boray, angered by his son's stubbornness, takes him home with no present. His wife, seeing the disappointed tears of her son, marches downstairs, grabs the day's receipts from the cash register, and undaunted, goes out to buy the violin. That night, when Paul blows out the candles on his cake and opens the gift-wrapped violin, his face is so bright with surprise that his mother knows she has done the right thing. Her satisfaction grows day by day as she sees the intense determination of Paul to master that most difficult of instruments.

So much for the original premise, and, indeed, for Fannie Hurst and the prize-winning scenario of Frances Marion. Once young Paul Boray has grown up to be John Garfield and gone to play as a divertissement for a rich woman's guests, and that woman is Joan Crawford as Helen Wright, it becomes a different kind of *schmaltz*. What had been a story of mother love has turned into an impassioned romance—a love story enacted against a background of beautiful violin music ranging from Dvorak's plaintive "Humoresque" to the "Liebestod" of Tristan and Isolde from Wagner's opera as adapted for the violin by Isaac Stern (who in the film does the actual playing). What had been a drama of the miracle of faith has become a tragedy of a love too impassioned to survive in the modern world.

Paul rises quickly. His promise as a violinist is fulfilled, not because of the sacrifices made by his mother but because Helen Wright directs his life and career. Yet theirs is no happy love story. They argue constantly; he goes on long tours and she cannot accompany him, but must stay with a husband who does not even pretend to love her. Also, she drinks. Her drinking had always been a problem, but now it becomes a vice. Paul has broken with his mother, who is hurt by his open indifference to his family and humble beginnings. Helen's husband, aware of his wife's infatuation for Paul, realizes the truth when her emotion is no longer that of infatuation. She is completely possessed by love, and if not allowed to realize it, will destroy both herself and the man she loves. Helen's husband suggests that she divorce him so that she will be free to marry Paul. Together, they might achieve a mutual happiness; together, she might bring him lasting greatness in his career.

This sets the scene for the finale and Crawford's finest hour. She pays a visit to Paul's mother, who convinces her that marriage with Paul would only ruin him. Paul is soloist that night with the Philharmonic, but Helen does not attend the concert; instead, she goes out to her beach home and listens on the radio. Realizing that there is no hope for the love she had coveted, she takes her last drink, and then, as the "Liebestod" rises in a crescendo of longing, she walks out onto the beach and into the sea, bravely seeking her own resolution to a love that not only cannot be but is destroying the man she loves. This was pure Crawford magic, and the final scene of her trudging against the sea wind in her sequinned gown is one of those moments that is unforgettable. To one who has not seen the picture, it might sound like an imitation of Fredric March's suicide in *A Star Is Born* (1937); but Crawford makes it her own tragic dilemma, resolved with proper Crawford glamour.

Crawford and Garfield were old acquaintances. They had known each other from Group Theatre days, when, as Mrs. Franchot Tone, she had hosted many social gatherings to which Garfield had been invited. They play together effectively, but she often overwhelms him, as many actresses have done with their leading men. This was Garfield's last film for Warner Bros.; it was Crawford's second, leading to *Possessed* (1947) and a second Academy Award nomination.

Still, the role of Helen Wright in *Humoresque* shines as Joan Crawford's best since the brilliant M-G-M days. Oscar Levant maintains that the story of *Humoresque* as Crawford played it was based on a rejected script of *Rhapsody in Blue*, written by Clifford Odets. This may possibly be true, for it indeed reveals little kinship with the Fannie Hurst story or with the Francis Marion scenario for the silent version.

The score of twenty-three classical and seven popular numbers, which brought an Academy Award nomination for Franz Waxman (the score for *The Best Years of Our Lives* won), gives the film a place of honor in the history of film music. Garfield could not play the violin, and extraordinary tricks were employed to make him convincing as a virtuoso. The great Isaac Stern was originally slated to play for Garfield onscreen, wearing a mask of the actor. But this was abandoned after much work, and an even more elaborate device was substituted. In close-ups of Garfield playing, two violinists out of camera range follow the prerecorded Isaac Stern music, one doing the difficult fingering and the other the bowing. The effect is amazingly realistic, at least to the average moviegoer, since Garfield was frequently asked to play the violin at parties after the movie's release.

Larry Lee Holland

THE HUNCHBACK OF NOTRE DAME

Released: 1939
Production: Pandro S. Berman for RKO/Radio
Direction: William Dieterle
Screenplay: Sonya Levien; based on Bruno Frank's adaptation of the novel
  Notre-Dame de Paris by Victor Hugo
Cinematography: Joseph H. August
Editing: William Hamilton and Robert Wise
Art direction: Van Nest Polglase
Interior decoration: Darrell Silvera
Special effects: Vernon L. Walker
Makeup: Perc Westmore
Costume design: Walter Plunkett
Music: Alfred Newman
Running time: 114 minutes

Principal characters:
Quasimodo	Charles Laughton
Esmeralda	Maureen O'Hara
Dom Claude Frollo	Sir Cedric Hardwicke
Clopin	Thomas Mitchell
Pierre Gringoire	Edmond O'Brien
King Louis XI	Harry Davenport
Archbishop	Walter Hampden
Phoebus de Chateaupers	Alan Marshal
Procurator	George Zucco
Beggar	George Tobias
Phillipo	Rod La Rocque
Old Nobleman	Fritz Leiber

There have been three film versions of *The Hunchback of Notre Dame* and one television production. In 1923, a silent version directed by Wallace Worsley starred Lon Chaney as Quasimodo, Patsy Ruth Miller as Esmeralda, Ernest Torrence as Clopin, Tully Marshall as Frollo, and Norman Kerry as Phoebus, and was notable for its lavish sets and for the bravura performance of Chaney in one of his classic roles. A 1957 French version starred Anthony Quinn and Gina Lollobrigida as Quasimodo and Esmeralda. Despite the asset of Technicolor, this version was not as robust as its predecessors and was handicapped by the dubbing in of its English-language release. A British Broadcasting Company television version shown in the United States in 1977, with Warren Clarke in the title role, was well acted but had apparent low-budget production values. Additionally, James Cagney reconstructed a scene from the 1923 version in his film biography of Lon Chaney, *The Man of a Thousand Faces* (1957).

Though some scholars prefer Chaney's version, the critical consensus is that the finest and most memorable film of Victor Hugo's 1831 novel was made in 1939 by RKO, under the direction of William Dieterle, with Charles Laughton playing Quasimodo. Filmed and produced on an epic scale, it was at once an impressive spectacle, a poignant love story, and a masterpiece of the macabre.

The story begins in 1482, during the reign of Louis XI. It is both Epiphany Sunday and the Feast of Fools, and a vast throng of Parisians have turned out for the festivities. There are clowns, tumblers, dancing girls; it is a Brueghelesque carnival of medieval city life. Despite a prohibition against gypsies, a beautiful young gypsy dancing girl, Esmeralda (Maureen O'Hara), has managed to enter the city, hoping to plead with the King for tolerance for her people; in the meantime, she does magic tricks with a trained goat. Nearby, Pierre Gringoire (Edmond O'Brien), a poet and playwright, is trying to produce an allegorical masque of death and retribution, but the mob pays little attention and eventually hoots him down. Instead, the crowd clamors for a contest to elect a Pope of Fools—the person who can make the ugliest face. Numerous contestants are scoffed at, but suddenly the crowd gapes with horror and falls into an awed silence as the grotesque face of Quasimodo (Charles Laughton), the bellringer of Notre Dame cathedral, appears framed through a papier-mâché rose window at the back of the stage. The mob instantly acclaims him the Pope of Fools and crowns him with a jester's cap and bells. Quasimodo, a deformed foundling, has an immense hunchback, a misshapen face with one eye seeming to dangle halfway down one cheek, the other cheek twisted upward with the eye turned outward, a shapeless nose, and a mouth full of ragged teeth. His limbs are twisted and one leg is shorter than the other. Hitherto, he has been a figure of horror in the city, and he is now delighted to be the center of attention and seemingly of admiration. In an imbecilic way, he is enjoying himself immensely until the festivities are interrupted by the stern priest, Dom Claude Frollo (Sir Cedric Hardwicke), who has adopted Quasimodo and who now angrily orders his charge to return to the cathedral. The poor monster is crushed but obeys, holding on to the stirrup of his master's horse and dangling his crown in the other hand as he lurches along.

Though a priest who has taken a vow of chastity, the seemingly ascetic Frollo is a repressed sensualist who has been smitten with lust for Esmeralda. He sends Quasimodo to abduct her, but the hunchback appears as a malevolent apparition to the terrified girl. She flees, but despite his awkwardness, he has a grotesque agility and enormous strength, and he succeeds in intercepting and seizing her. However, the abduction is seen by Captain Phoebus de Chateaupers (Alan Marshal), a handsome gallant, who with his guardsmen succeeds in rescuing Esmeralda and capturing the hunchback.

Meanwhile, Gringoire, the discouraged playwright, having no money and no place to spend the night, accidentally drifts into the Parisian underworld and is suddenly alarmed to find himself in the Court of Miracles, a slum of thieves and beggars, where the lame and blind "miraculously" regain the use of limbs and eyes as they remove the sham deformities they use in their roles as beggars. Gringoire is taken prisoner and led before Clopin (Thomas Mitchell), the king of beggars. Intruders are usually put to death, but Clopin gives Gringoire a chance: if he can successfully pick the pocket of a mannequin spangled with bells and dangling from a rope, he can join them and live. Gringoire tries manfully but loses his balance and grabs the mannequin, which jingles crazily. Clopin is about to pass the sentence of death when Esmeralda, who has entered and observes the scene, takes pity on Gringoire and saves his life by taking him in marriage. Gringoire is enchanted, but she intends the marriage to be in name only, for she has become infatuated with the handsome Captain Phoebus.

Quasimodo, meanwhile, has been taken before a deaf judge. Deafened himself by the tolling of Notre Dame's massive bells, Quasimodo does not understand the judge's questions. Thinking the hunchback is mocking him, the judge sentences him to be bound to a wheel before Notre Dame, flogged, and left in chains at the mercy of the sun and the mob. Frollo refuses to intervene, and Quasimodo is tortured. After the flogging, the mob taunts him and pelts him with debris, but Esmeralda, passing by, takes pity on him. Though he had tried to abduct her only hours before, she braves the hostile crowd and gives him water. In his inarticulate way, he looks at her with adoration.

Frollo continues to burn with lust for Esmeralda, and when he finds her embracing the handsome Phoebus, in jealousy he stabs the captain. Esmeralda is arrested for murder, and because of her magic tricks with the goat, she is tried as a witch. Frollo's frustrated desire has turned to fear and hatred, and he becomes her chief prosecutor. After she confesses under torture, she is sentenced to be hanged in the square before the cathedral, as Gringoire stands by watching in helpless agony. From one of the cathedral towers, however, Quasimodo also watches. His dim brain comprehends the situation, and he begins climbing down the scaffolding of some construction and repair work being done to Notre Dame. Just as the hangman is about to carry out the execution, Quasimodo grabs a rope from the construction, swings down, seizes Esmeralda, and before the startled crowd can stop him, swings back with her into the tower, crying "Sanctuary!"

For the time being, Esmeralda is safe; she finds the misshapen hunchback to be a gentle, sensitive soul who protects her and respects her person. Although deaf, he can speak in a halting fashion, and she comes to sympathize with his loneliness and deformity. He has indeed repaid her for her mercy when he was tortured.

Meanwhile, fearing that the nobles will try to violate sanctuary and carry

Esmeralda off to execution, Clopin assembles an army of beggars and marches to rescue her. Gringoire tries to dissuade him, arguing that the pen is mightier than the sword and that he has written an appeal to the King, but Clopin ignores him. As night falls, his band of vagabonds arrives before the cathedral, but the doors are barred. When they try to force the gates, Quasimodo thinks they have come to kill Esmeralda. In an agony of suspense, he fights them singlehandedly, hurling down upon them a deadly rain of building stones and timbers from the construction. Undaunted, Clopin orders his men to pick up one massive timber and use it as a battering ram. Notre Dame is now under seige, and it looks as if the beggars will win, but Quasimodo lights fires under caldrons of lead intended to repair the roof. When the beggars have almost breached the door, he pours the molten metal into the rain gutters. It runs through the rainspout mouths of gargoyles and drenches the attackers in a deadly downpour, killing Clopin and defeating the beggars. At this point, the King's troops arrive, and Quasimodo realizes to his horror that he has fought the wrong side. Fortunately, however, Gringoire's appeal has reached the King and Louis has granted it, ensuring Esmeralda's safety.

Soon Quasimodo hears the bell that he has told Esmeralda to ring to penetrate his deafness if she is in danger. He clambers towards her eyrie to find that Frollo is pursuing her. Turning against the man who hitherto has been his master, Quasimodo in turn pursues the priest and after a brief struggle lifts him over the battlements and hurls him to his death. In the end, Esmeralda, realizing that she truly loves Gringoire, is carried off with him in triumph, as the forlorn hunchback sits alone among the gargoyles. He embraces one and says, "If only I had been made of stone, like you."

This ending does not follow Hugo's novel, in which Esmeralda is hanged, and her body taken to the charnel house of Montfaucon, where Quasimodo enters the vault and stays with her, embracing her body until he dies of starvation. Only the 1957 French film followed this ending; in the silent version, Esmeralda marries Phoebus, who is not dead after all but only wounded.

Even with some alteration in plot, the success of the story is practically guaranteed, with pageantry, suspense, spectacle, and a virtuoso role for the actor playing Quasimodo. It is, among other things, a variation on the theme of Beauty and the Beast, and part of its magic is a sense of legend. Although there never was a historical Quasimodo, his characterization entered folklore. RKO backed up the story with superlative production values. The sets were immense, and Paris was reconstructed on a vast scale in the San Fernando Valley. To direct, Pandro S. Berman chose William Dieterle, a German expatriate who had worked with Max Reinhardt in Berlin. In Hollywood, Dieterle was Reinhardt's assistant on the 1935 *Midsummer Night's Dream*. He directed a number of outstanding film biographies starring Paul Muni—*The Story of Louis Pasteur* (1936), *The Life of Émile Zola* (1937), and *Juarez*

(1939)—and was later to direct *Dr. Ehrlich's Magic Bullet* (1940), *All That Money Can Buy* (1941), *Tennessee Johnson* (1942), *Kismet* (1944), and *Love Letters* (1945). Leslie Halliwell calls him "all incomparable master of crowd scenes and pictorial composition," qualities particularly notable in his version of *The Hunchback of Notre Dame*.

Cast in the lead was Charles Laughton, who four years earlier had played a memorable Javert in Hugo's *Les Miserables* (1935). As a character, Quasimodo is a living counterpart to the gargoyles adorning the towers of Notre Dame. Lon Chaney had created his own makeup, which, although striking in 1923, now appears crude. RKO turned the job over to Perc Westmore, who covered the left side of Laughton's face with sponge rubber, hid the left eye, and made an artificial socket further down on the cheek. He pulled down one part of the face and pulled up the other. A contact lens gave the relatively normal eye a milky opacity. To make Quasimodo's deafness convincing, Laughton had his ears plugged with wax so that he would not show any reaction to sudden loud sounds. Not only did Laughton wear a hump made of four pounds of foam rubber, but his costume was padded and his torso encased in rubber to project a sense of immense strength. During filming in September, the heat was so great that perspiration sometimes washed away the makeup. Although a stand-in did most of the acrobatic scenes, Laughton's performance was a strenuously physical one: he had to swing on cathedral bells, haul heavy chains, move with a twisted, deformed gait. Although he suffered considerably during filming, he called Quasimodo "Probably one of the greatest parts any actor was ever allowed to play." The role of Quasimodo, having very little dialogue, consists largely of pantomime, with which Laughton managed to convey both terror and pathos. He made no attempt to copy Lon Chaney, observing that "Any actor who understands his stuff always plays to catch the tempo of the moment."

Part of that tempo was the beginning of World War II. The script makes a deliberate parallel between the persecution of the gypsies in the Middle Ages and that of contemporary Jews, and when Laughton was ringing the church bells, he said that he felt he was tolling them for mankind. William Dieterle wrote to Elsa Lanchester in 1968, "When Laughton acted the scene on the wheel, enduring the terrible torture, he was not the poor, crippled creature, expecting compassion from the mob, but rather oppressed and enslaved mankind, suffering injustice . . . ."

Nevertheless, several reviewers complained that the story was an outmoded shocker that, although well put together, should not have been resurrected in 1939. In one sense, *The Hunchback of Notre Dame* is a horror film; yet the monstrous hunchback is actually a kind of gentle person whose exterior ugliness masks his beauty of character. As a human being, he is superior both to the false priest and to the elegant and worldly aristocracy portrayed throughout the film.

The rest of the cast provided Laughton with sterling support. Nineteen-year-old Maureen O'Hara made her American debut as Esmeralda. She had acted with Laughton a year earlier in the British *Jamaica Inn* (1939). The Laughtons had become fond of her, and Charles arranged for her to play in *The Hunchback of Notre Dame*. Later, they made one more film together, Jean Renoir's memorable *This Land Is Mine* (1943). Edmond O'Brien also made his Hollywood debut as Gringoire; his previous work had been on stage with the Mercury Theatre. Although he later became a corpulent actor, O'Brien is almost gaunt as the starving poet, and he projects an idealistic intensity as the romantic hero. Sir Cedric Hardwicke, the saintly Bishop in *Les Miserables*, brings a cold, austere fanaticism to the repressed priest Frollo, while Walter Hampden, renowned for creating Cyrano on the American stage, is quietly effective as his saintly brother. Thomas Mitchell is an energetic, roistering Clopin. Harry Davenport is a curious Louis XI: instead of the traditionally sinister spider king, portrayed brilliantly the year before by Basil Rathbone in *If I Were King*, Davenport's Louis is a kindly, benevolent, grandfatherly monarch. In addition to this excellent supporting cast, thousands of extras swarm all over the film.

It has often been said that 1939 was the greatest year in the history of movies, yet despite its contemporary competition, *The Hunchback of Notre Dame* remains outstanding. John Baxter, in *Hollywood in the Thirties*, calls the film "Dieterle's triumph" and says it "has seldom been bettered as an evocation of medieval life, while Charles Laughton's portrayal of the grotesque Quasimodo makes even that of Lon Chaney seem feeble. The early sequences are of an unbelievable detail and intensity." The Feast of Fools sequence has an immense vitality, but there are equally brilliant sequences throughout. An atmosphere of superstitious fear prevails—from the opening with Gringoire's mystery play on the Dance of Death, through his infernolike descent into the Court of Miracles, and on through the interrogations for witchcraft. Among the unforgettable scenes are the Feast of Fools; the belled mannequin jangling insanely when Gringoire fails his test; Quasimodo on the wheel; the long unbroken shot where he swings from the cathedral to the scaffold and carries Esmeralda back to the church tower, crying "Sanctuary," while Gringoire and Clopin laugh hysterically from joy and the sound track breaks into a hymn of triumph; Quasimodo demonstrating the bells for Esmeralda, first starting them with a kick, then leaping bodily onto the great bell and riding it by its handles, laughing madly while she holds her ears in horror; and the entire episode of the beggars storming Notre Dame. Although Frank S. Nugent, reviewing the film for the *New York Times*, found the cast "expert" but denounced the story as "a freak show" with too many horrors and too much coarseness for his taste, what he calls coarseness is, instead, an energetic vitality. *The Hunchback of Notre Dame* was a huge hit upon release at Radio City Music Hall and subsequently around the country. It currently not only plays on television with some regularity but also has been revived at a number of RKO retrospectives.

Robert E. Morsberger

THE HURRICANE

Released: 1937
Production: Samuel Goldwyn for Goldwyn-United Artists; released by
  United Artists
Direction: John Ford
Screenplay: Dudley Nichols; based on Oliver H. P. Garrett's adaptation of
  the novel of the same name by Charles Nordhoff and James Norman Hall
Cinematography: Bert Glennon
Editing: Lloyd Nossler
Special effects: James Basevi
Sound: Thomas T. Moulton (AA)
Running time: 102 minutes

   Principal characters:
   Marama .... Dorothy Lamour
   Terangi .... Jon Hall
   Mrs. De Laage .... Mary Astor
   Father Paul .... C. Aubrey Smith
   Dr. Kersaint .... Thomas Mitchell
   Governor De Laage .... Raymond Massey
   Warden .... John Carradine

The tensions that create rich and complex characters and relationships between those characters, though internal in the greatest works of narrative, are the external structural determinants of *The Hurricane*. They take the form of a fundamental nature *versus* culture dichotomy, with the natives, sexuality, passion, freedom, and beauty opposed to law, prison, repression, duty, and honor. The film performs essentially the same ideological function as most of the "South Seas" genre in that it extols the natives for their "primitive" virtues and pits them against the corrupt ones of civilization. The interworkings of the forces of nature and culture are thus externalized and romanticized, and the critique of the white presence in the South Seas is emasculated. It is rather at the level of myth or parable that *The Hurricane* finds its expression, and it performs the myth's function of mediation and reintegration with great beauty and emotional satisfaction.

Like all myths, *The Hurricane* has a narrative past inscribed in its structure, as well as a narrator whose relationship to the myth is both privileged because he was there, and distanced because his involvement was primarily as observer and mediator, rather than as an agent of action. The film opens as a ship in the South Seas passes a desolate island upon which the wrath of God seems to have been visited. Dr. Kersaint (Thomas Mitchell) begins his role as narrator, telling the others that it was once the most beautiful island in the Pacific. The essential movement of the film has already been set forth. How did the island become scorched earth? A dissolve into the past immediately sketches the tensions which will come into conflict to produce the answer.

The European governor, De Laage (Raymond Massey), represents "the law" in his white coat and uncompromising posture. He is contrasted with the natives, Marama (Dorothy Lamour) and Terangi (Jon Hall), whose wedding is celebrated. The couple is identified with smooth freedom of movement, passion, and the trees and flowers of nature, as they run out of the church. Terangi is immediately linked with birds, an imagery which continues through the film. In the next of the series of oppositions, De Laage's wife (Mary Astor) arrives by ship. She is kinder and less formal than her husband primarily because, in terms of archetypes, women are always depicted as being aligned with the nature half of the nature/culture dichotomy, regardless of their cultural identification. Likewise, Marama displays a closer affinity to nature than does Terangi. His wish to wear a uniform cap and be "just like a white man" is the seed of their tragedy. The De Lagges' reserve is contrasted with the sensuality of the newly married couple. Further, Governor De Laage inhibits not only the natives but his own wife as well.

Once this is established, Terangi sails off to Tahiti, already nearly entirely corrupted by the influence of the Europeans, and leaves Marama behind. The best in Terangi, not the worst, will destroy him in this corrupt place. His imprisonment (building on his earlier linking with bird imagery) is determined through tensions constructed in the first sequence. Terangi's passionate nature, which cannot be suppressed, leads to a fight with a white man who disparages a present he has bought for Marama. The injustice which makes this a serious crime begins with the relationship of the governor with the native population. The governor as the agent of the law thus becomes Terangi's jailer, and the structural opposition is made concrete.

Terangi, with more libido than logic, cannot be confined. The visual depiction of the jail is dark and confining, with shadows, chains, and a sadistic warden (John Carradine). Terangi attempts to escape repeatedly, each time enduring savage beatings and suffering a lengthening of his sentence. Governor De Laage, who has more of a sense of honor and duty to the law than to his subjects, continues to carry out the cruelly mechanistic increasing of the sentence, in spite of the counsel of both his wife and the narrator. As a doctor, and because he is somewhat morally weak, Kersaint is closer to the European woman and to the natives than to De Laage. The source of Terangi's need becomes clear in the bird imagery and through a montage of dissolves between Marama and Terangi. His life and its sustenance are tied to his sensuality and to nature. He cannot do otherwise than try to escape, even as they systematically beat him down. The level of opposition and of injustice increases until Terangi escapes again, accidentally killing the sadistic guard. Upon hearing of the escape, the governor swears he will lock Terangi up again, but as the exhausted Terangi paddles his canoe to the island, he brings with him not the logic of the law, but the wrath of God. A hurricane hits the island. One of its first effects is to sweep the legal papers off De Laage's desk. The hurricane destroys everything on the island in one of the most impressive storm sequences on film.

At the same time, in a manifestation of the convergence of the forces of nature, a baby is born and Dr. Kersaint's role as mediator is best illustrated. He is able to give aid because he has not been acting on the side of the "antinature" forces. When the storm finally abates, many people are left alive, but no trees or buildings remain standing. Nature has destroyed the site of European cruelty, although the governor still retains the power of the legal system he represents. He has to give some indication of learning before the tension of the established opposition can relax. This is achieved, in accordance with the archetype, through his wife. Thinking her dead, he is so overjoyed when a canoe brings her to him that he runs into the water to greet her, and having been touched by it and by her, he says he will not pursue Marama and Terangi, who have given her back to him.

The romantic notion that Polynesians (like blacks) are closer to nature, simpler, more childlike, more sensual and musical than others is probably the least attractive aspect of *The Hurricane*. The abundance of destructive stereotypes in the film (the governor, the sadistic warden, and the unbelievably evil corruption of Tahiti) points up the archetypal level of the narrative, rendering it perhaps less dangerous, but no less savory. It is still the Europeans who can learn. They can take on some of the characteristics of the natives without losing their sophistication. The natives, who cannot learn and retain their sensuality, are destroyed by the contact with the developed culture, but not *vice versa*. A European has the role of narrator/mediator who can somehow be in touch with both poles. Further, as a doctor he is the agent of the life born of the storm. These are not agreeable aspects of the film, but at the level of myth *The Hurricane* delineates its task and performs it with amazing clarity, satisfaction, and grace. Despite the simplicity of the binary oppositions, Ford fills the space in between with life and emotional color, and the film is richly successful on that level.

A remake of the film by Dino de Laurentiis appeared in 1979, but it was not successful on either a critical or a financial level.

Janey Place

THE HUSTLER

Released: 1961
Production: Robert Rossen for Twentieth Century-Fox
Direction: Robert Rossen
Screenplay: Robert Rossen and Sidney Carroll; based on the novel of the same name by Walter Tevis
Cinematography: Gene Shuftan (AA)
Editing: Dede Allen
Art direction: Harry Horner (AA); set decoration, Gene Callahan (AA)
Running time: 135 minutes

Principal characters:
Eddie Felson	Paul Newman
Sarah Packard	Piper Laurie
Bert Gordon	George C. Scott
Minnesota Fats	Jackie Gleason
Findlay	Murray Hamilton
Charlie Burns	Myron McCormick

With the release of *The Hustler*, director Robert Rossen returned to the kind of institutional corruption which he had studied over a decade earlier in *Body and Soul* (1947) and *All the King's Men* (1949). Similar to those films, *The Hustler* deals with the struggle to reach the top—in this case, the top of the world of pool. Walter Tevis' novel (1959) provided Rossen with the characterization of a skilled, cocky young man, Eddie Felson, whose self-destructiveness changes into a search for value, or "character," as he comes to call it, within that urban sordidness and criminality he can deny but never escape. Rossen, following the example of the European realists, especially uses his decor as the visual extension of the often twisted relationships among the principals. The film's art direction and cinematography both won Academy Awards; and Rossen handles his material with sureness throughout, although at times he lapses into an uncomfortable dreariness or harshness that results from his tight control. *The Hustler* was Rossen's penultimate film (he died in 1966). His last film, *Lilith* (1964), was commercially unsuccessful but has since gained more favor among critics, although *The Hustler*, because of its intensity and naturalistic detail, will probably remain better known.

Fast Eddie Felson (Paul Newman) is a pool hustler, an expert player who, by shooting a mediocre game, traps ordinary players into heavy betting and then wins carefully enough that those opponents fail to see they have been cheated. With his manager Charlie Burns (Myron McCormick) he goes to Chicago to challenge the famous Minnesota Fats (Jackie Gleason), who beats him soundly in a marathon contest. Eddie then meets Sarah Packard (Piper Laurie), a lame, alcoholic tramp attending college, and encounters Bert Gordon (George C. Scott), a gambler who offers to sponsor him; however, he refuses Bert's offer because Bert wants a seventy-five percent share of the winnings. A few days later, Eddie, recognized as a hustler, has his thumbs broken by one of his hustled victims and his friends. Once his thumbs are healed, Eddie and Sarah team up with Bert in Louisville, where Eddie beats millionaire Findlay (Murray Hamilton) at billiards. While there, Sarah, partly because of Bert's control over Eddie, commits suicide at the hotel. Eddie breaks up his association with Bert, then plays Minnesota Fats again, this time winning. When Bert demands his share, Eddie refuses, and, acknowledging Bert's warning that he will never play big-time pool again, walks out on him.

In Rossen's *Body and Soul*, boxer Charlie Davis has to learn to deal with his success; in *The Hustler*, Eddie must learn what he has to do to become truly successful, to graduate from hustler to respected professional. Eddie, as he begins this evolution, has his limitations clearly defined in the thirty-six-hour match with Minnesota Fats. After playing against him for some twenty-four hours, Charlie reports that Eddie had won eighteen thousand dollars, but Fats, although losing the games so far, understands how to win the match psychologically. With Eddie haggard, exhausted, and unsteady from the bourbon he has been drinking straight from the bottle, Fats goes to the men's room, and returns shortly with his hair combed, his face washed, and his clothes straightened, ready to begin anew. The effects of the bourbon and the sight of his now refreshed opponent overwhelm Eddie, who, in the final twelve hours, loses all but a few hundred dollars. Fats victoriously declares the match over.

In time Eddie learns what is necessary to win. Several days after the match with Minnesota Fats, he listens to Bert's carefully worked-out theory on the psychology of winning. Although Bert acknowledges that Fats has "more character in one finger" than Eddie has in his whole body, he still believes Eddie has displayed abundant talent. Fats had simply waited until Eddie lost control. Bert sees Eddie as a compulsive loser, but also a first-rate pool player, one who can learn what he needs to know to become a winner. It remains unclear how Eddie interprets Bert's arrogant rebuff, and not until after he has his thumbs broken does he admit that he needs Bert's help. In the match with Findlay, Eddie plays from a new psychological stance, and the game develops as a slightly modified version of Eddie's match with Fats. For the first part of the night Eddie loses. Findlay plays billiards rather than pool, and the difference between the two games keeps Eddie off balance, especially since his healing thumbs critically affect his shooting ability. Eddie handles himself with caution, however, finding out all he can about Findlay, as well as the game of billiards. Bert thinks he does not know when to quit, but continues to back him reluctantly, finally grasping the importance of Eddie's determination and restored self-esteem. Eddie has seen in Findlay the same carelessness arising from over-confidence that had let Fats beat him, and using it to his advantage, he wins twelve thousand dollars from Findlay.

Much of Eddie's regeneration comes from his relationship with Sarah, who takes him in shortly after his loss to Fats and cares for him while his thumbs are healing. Sarah's lameness from polio becomes an obvious reflection of an inner deformity: she represents an amalgam of various neuroses strengthened by a fully developed sense of self-pity, and has continued to attend college so that her parents will support her and her drinking. Her love for Eddie only manages to break down his devotion to his game while she is still alive; for Eddie, love and its attendant commitments have always meant suffocation. Yet, she communicates to him a notion of probity and of direction, convinced, apparently, that by saving him, she also saves herself. Sarah nonetheless lacks the sanity to integrate into her own life any of the values she attempts to instill in his, particularly the value of loving. She hates Bert for the hold he has over Eddie; it is one that corrupts him further and, to be sure, neutralizes her own influence on him. Eddie must necessarily reject her, for only by playing for Bert can he earn the front money necessary to meet Fats again. As Eddie returns from his match with Findlay, Sarah betrays him, as has Bert, and then slashes her wrists; but before she commits suicide she writes on the mirror in lipstick some of her favorite words—"sick," "perverted," "twisted"—condemning herself along with Eddie and her archenemy Bert.

In his return match with Fats, Eddie plays superbly, the way he did at the beginning of their first encounter, and is thus able to win handily, with Fats finally admitting defeat. The victory over Findlay, the emotional toughening that comes from Sarah's suicide, and the decisive break from Bert exemplify the "character" Eddie has been required to acquire in order to complement his unquestioned talent. Too late he sees the extent and the importance of his love for Sarah. He shoots dispassionately, almost aloofly, lecturing Bert on the necessity of moral awareness. The rematch with Fats becomes more crucial than ever for Eddie because of his newly found motivation and purpose. He must beat Fats, no longer to gain money or glory, but to redeem himself: the game of pool has been translated into a philosophical vehicle for understanding how the drive to win, unchecked by integrity, comes to degrade the human spirit. Bert evinces a wry tolerance for this speech which, after all, serves as Eddie's defense against Bert's earlier criticisms of him as a loser; Bert recognizes, moreover, as he did in the match with Findlay, the advantages brought about by Eddie's will to win, and turns it to his own profit. In time, Fats himself senses that the match is lost.

This film features Paul Newman at the beginning of his stardom, and his characterization of Eddie quietly moves from a brash, rootless hustler to a veteran with some facility for introspection, ever nudging the audience's attention toward the potential under the crude exterior. Yet, the film explores not so much the principal characters themselves as the shifting barriers among them. George C. Scott, who deservedly gained notice three years before in *Anatomy of a Murder* (1959), plays Bert, the entrepreneur who expertly fashions an astuteness born of cynicism and the right percentages. Whatever progress Eddie makes in aligning his goals with his own increasing perception of value, Bert tries to frustrate or destroy; this happens most notably in Findlay's billiard room, where a significant battle develops within the uneasy coalition of Eddie and Bert—a battle for personal identity and control that goes well beyond the money involved. Gleason's characterization of Minnesota Fats is a series of effortlessly posed stills, but the audience never forgets that it is watching Gleason, the comedian, in a dramatic role. The dapper Fats has a muted interaction with Eddie, to whom he remains more a legend than a man, and in the end, he proves to be discreetly sympathetic to Eddie's struggle to free himself from Bert's domination. Sarah's characterization on the other hand, reflects a major flaw in *The Hustler*, as Piper Laurie's self-consciousness with her role makes the power she can muster largely centripetal, even in the best scene outside a pool room, the picnic with Eddie, where he explains to her the elation that comes to him through winning. Most of the fault with Sarah, however, rests in script and direction: she is an obscurely drawn figure, a promising but finally ineffectual blend of a Dostoevskian prostitute and a malformed deranged character of Tennessee Williams. The ponderous middle section of the film suffers from sentimentality, disrupting the carefully executed hardness of the beginning and end. Although Eddie's relationship with Sarah is integral to the plot, it remains awkwardly conceived.

Placing its subject matter of pool aside, although half of the story takes place at a pool table, *The Hustler* works because of the central contest—one in which the young challenger upsets the informally crowned old master whose experience now compensates for his declining power. Rossen's aspirations to convey this contest have on the whole overreached his talents, although his pool room sequences are remarkably expressive. Ably supported by Deedee Allan's editing, Rossen frames a netherworld and its warped inhabitants, drawing out the violence and greed that underlie the competition of the contest. Nonetheless, the film ends with a kind of reconciliation: Eddie is the familiar antihero caught in a menacing, sterile environment; Bert, the confident percentage player who never lets his ego interfere with profits to be taken. Eddie recognizes that Bert, belonging to a gambling syndicate, has the means to destroy him to whatever degree he desires, and that Fats is but one of the stable; but Bert, once again moved by Eddie's determination, permits Eddie to walk away with all the money in his pocket. The fact that Eddie has begun to assume the values of the outside world now saves him, for Bert realizes that Eddie is lost to him forever.

William H. Brown, Jr.

I AM A CAMERA

Released: 1955
Production: Romulus Production; released by Distributors Corporation of
   America
Direction: Henry Cornelius
Screenplay: John Collier; based on the play of the same name by John Van
   Druten, adapted from the *Berlin Stories* by Christopher Isherwood
Cinematography: Guy Green
Editing: Clive Donner
Running time: 99 minutes

> *Principal characters:*
> Sally Bowles ....Julie Harris
> Christopher Isherwood .... Laurence Harvey
> Natalie Landauer .... Shelley Winters
> Clive .... Ron Randell
> Fraulein Schneider ....Lea Seidl
> Fritz Wendel .... Anton Diffring

The film *I Am a Camera* begins with a prologue in the form of a publisher's
cocktail party in honor of Sally Bowles (Julie Harris), whose book of remi-
niscences has just been issued. One of the guests is Christopher Isherwood
(Laurence Harvey), an established writer, and this introduction serves as a
vehicle for Chris's own recollections of the time years before when he had
first known Sally during the early 1930's in Berlin.

During the resulting flashback, Chris is living in Berlin and supporting
himself by giving English-language lessons. He hopes one day to become a
writer and thus justifies his situation of being impoverished in Berlin by
believing that this is giving him an opportunity to observe and experience
life, so that he will eventually be able to use his experiences in his writings.
In one of the initial scenes, Chris explains that his aim as a writer is to be
an impersonal observer. An author must look at life and subsequently be able
to portray it as though he were a camera.

In one of the cabarets typical of the period, Chris and his friend Fritz
(Anton Diffring) meet Sally Bowles, an English girl who is performing there.
It is apparent that Sally does not have great talent as a serious stage performer;
however, she is good-natured and uninhibited. People like her and she enjoys
life. However, Sally is jilted by her lover. When she discovers that he has
gone, in her rage and frustration she goes on a rampage smashing whatever
she can get her hands on. Now stranded in Berlin, Chris befriends Sally and
she subsequently moves into his flat. Both are broke.

Almost at once, however, Sally meets a wealthy American named Clive
(Ron Randell). One of the major sequences in the film occurs at a wild party

thrown by Sally and Clive in the latter's hotel suite. Chris, who has worked himself into a state of exhaustion, has to be dragged from his bed against his will in order to get him to go to the party. As more and more people arrive at the party, Sally is determined to have a good time and forget the preceding weeks of destitution. While the party is going on, several doctors give the semiconscious Chris a series of hydrotherapy treatments. This whole party sequence, composed of the portrayals of unconventional guests and the treatments of the sick Chris, is comparable in incongruity to a Marx brothers' film. When Chris wakes up the next morning, he finds to his surprise that he is feeling fit and cured of what was probably a hangover.

In the weeks that follow, Clive takes Sally and Chris to the races, the theater, the casino, and other entertaining places. He helps them both financially, thus enabling them finally to enjoy themselves. Their newfound life style is in contrast to the situation of the majority of people in depression-ridden Berlin. Clive next proposes to take Sally and Chris on a world tour; Sally starts making preparations and Chris is also willing to go. At this point several scenes are inserted in the film to reveal the extent to which Chris is made more aware of the growing power of the Nazis in his day-to-day business when he discovers that the Nazis are making life difficult for his Jewish student Fritz and his fiancée Natalie (Shelley Winters).

Chris and Sally's life of leisure soon evaporates, however, when a telegram arrives stating that Clive has left Berlin. Although Sally had been counting on Clive's continued help, Chris tells her that she was foolish to expect life to have continued as it recently had. Sally and Chris quarrel, and he orders her to move out. Later, Chris visits Fritz, and, on his way home, becomes involved in a street brawl with some Nazis, an encounter that makes him more aware of the increasing reality of Fascism. When Chris returns to his flat, he finds Sally, who announces that she is pregnant. Chris offers to marry her so that the baby will not be born out of wedlock, but Sally favors an abortion as the best solution. Sally's pregnancy and the couple's lack of money are the stimuli that finally encourage Chris to write an article which is accepted by an editor, who gives him more important assignments. Although Sally now agrees to marry Chris, it is only after Chris gets drunk because of his doubts about the burdens he is assuming, that Sally casually states that she has miscalculated her period and that there is no baby. With their marriage plans dropped, Sally gets an offer to join Clive and become a movie star in Paris. She leaves Berlin and Chris immediately, and the film ends with an epilogue—a return to the same cocktail party with which the film began. Sally is still the same carefree Sally and, of course, broke again. Thus, once more, Chris takes her in.

When British-made *I Am a Camera* was released in the United States in 1955, it was denied the then-important Production Code seal of the Motion Picture Association. A similar fate had happened two years earlier to the film *The Moon Is Blue*. While there is no single daring visual image in *I Am a Camera*, as was the case in the former film, verbal allusions went contrary to the conventions of the time. The dialogue in *I Am a Camera* casually refers to such topics as virginity, sexual intercourse, having a child out of wedlock, abortion, and miscalculated periods of menstruation. However, the characterization of Sally Bowles is so outrageous and Julie Harris' performance so accomplished, that the remarks seem more amusing than shocking. In any case, the film set a precedent by incorporating subjects previously considered taboo into the dialogue of a successful general release film.

   I Am a Camera was intended to be a comedy, and it succeeded. Most of the film's attention is focused on the high-spirited, good-natured, but amoral Sally Bowles. Christopher Isherwood, interpreted by Laurence Harvey, is the cool, impersonal observer who only gets personally involved in life through the efforts of Sally Bowles. However, there is a more serious side to *I Am a Camera*. Since the story takes place in Berlin during the early 1930's, the time and place of the film's action necessarily evoke reflections on the rise of the Nazis, the depression in Germany, and the difficulties increasingly being experienced by the German Jews. While these subjects are peripheral to the main story of Sally and Chris, the intrusion of the real world upon the madcap adventures of Sally Bowles provides contrast and poignancy through its juxtaposition of what we know to be real and that which is make-believe.

   The musical *Cabaret* (1972), starring Liza Minnelli, was a remake in color of *I Am a Camera*. While this later version more explicitly covered the topics merely discussed in *I Am a Camera*, the film's emphasis still centered on Sally Bowles—an extravagant but ingenuous personality functioning in a frantic and depraved environment. Once again, the story served both as a superb vehicle for the actress playing Sally Bowles and as a historical commentary on the time and place of the story.

Mark Merbaum

I AM A FUGITIVE FROM A CHAIN GANG

Released: 1932
Production: Hal B. Wallis for Warner Bros.
Direction: Mervyn LeRoy
Screenplay: Howard J. Green and Brown Holmes; based on the story "I Am a Fugitive from a Georgia Chain Gang" by Robert E. Burns
Cinematography: Sol Polito
Editing: William Holmes
Running time: 85 minutes

> *Principal characters:*
> James Allen .... Paul Muni
> Marie Woods .... Glenda Farrell
> Helen .... Helen Vinson
> Pete .... Preston Foster
> Barney Sykes .... Allen Jenkins

I Am a Fugitive from a Chain Gang was a typical 1930's Warner Bros. product and marked the transition from prison to topical films. Following a series of pictures centering around prison life, such as *The Big House* (1930) and *Twenty Thousand Years in Sing Sing* (1933), this film was an attempt to show not only how brutalizing prison life can be, but also how forces within society can conspire unjustly to imprison a man and trap both his body and his spirit.

Mervyn LeRoy initiated the project in 1931 by bringing to Jack Warner's attention a book he had recently read, the autobiography of a man named Robert Burns who had escaped from a Georgia chain gang and was living quietly in New Jersey, a state which had no extradition agreements with Georgia. The book described the incredible tortures and barbaric practices then prevalent in that state. LeRoy was moved by the book and convinced Warner that it would translate into a great motion picture. With Hal B. Wallis assigned as producer and LeRoy as director, the three men arranged to have Burns secretly smuggled into Hollywood to act as technical adviser. Burns was understandably reluctant to leave New Jersey; his life was at stake, since California and Georgia did have an extradition agreement. LeRoy kept the author's presence a secret, however, and Burns provided invaluable assistance, especially to Paul Muni, who was to play the chain gang victim.

Muni had come to films from the stage and had scored a huge success on the screen in *Scarface: The Shame of the Nation* (1932). He still considered himself a man of the theater, and he approached every film role as he did his stage parts—with total immersion of himself into the subject. Muni read everything he could on the prison system and talked with prison guards and other ex-members of chain gangs. He had several meetings with Robert Burns in Burbank, studying the way the real fugitive walked, talked, and breathed. Muni told Burns, "I don't want to imitate you, I want to *be* you"! A replica of a prison camp was built on the Warner Ranch, and all during the back-breaking, brutal work sequences that took place in the prison and in the yard, Muni refused the use of a double. He and several hundred extras playing convicts broke stones with pickaxes in the blazing sun, bringing an intensified element of realism to the film. But more than merely being realistic, this film, made in 1932 at the height of the Depression, was a scathing attack upon a major American institution and reflected a social awareness that was typical of Warner Bros. during the 1930's. No other studio was dealing with real issues at that time. Most films of the period tried to pull American audiences out of the realities of the Depression, while *I Am a Fugitive from a Chain Gang* confronted them with some harsh truths.

The film opens as James Allen (Paul Muni) returns home after World War I intent on avoiding his old factory job and desirous of going into engineering. He is tired of the routine of soldiering and wants to be creative. But family pressures force him into a job in a shoe factory, which he eventually leaves. Allen packs up and leaves home, traveling about the country looking for work. He soon realizes how little qualified he is, trying to compete for jobs when the country is in the midst of a vast wave of unemployment. As he wanders from city to city, Allen becomes an outcast in the country for which he fought, and this fact becomes an important theme of the film. James Allen is always portrayed as a patriotic man who loves his country but to whom his country can offer nothing. Finally, penniless and desperate, he attempts to pawn his war medals, but is shown a whole case of such medals by the pawnbroker. Joining forces with a hobo companion, he enters a dingy road-house. Allen's friend waves a gun at the counterman and demands hamburgers, for he has no money. The police hear the commotion, enter the restaurant, and arrest Allen, who is sentenced to ten years at hard labor in a chain gang for stealing a hamburger.

In the next section, the imagery is all of confinement—the lock, the fence, the chain. The camera shows the prisoners' faces as those of broken and defeated men devoid of any hope except that of escaping a beating. LeRoy depicts these men as suffering, trapped human beings and the guards as sadistic brutes. Expressionistic camera work is used effectively during the prison scenes, in which the violence is implied rather than directly shown, especially in one sequence in which James Allen is being beaten and only his shadow is shown on the wall, bent over in misery. With the help of a fellow inmate who breaks the chain from his foot on the rock pile, Allen escapes the chain gang with the bloodhounds baying at his heels. He gets away and blends into society. After a fleeting liaison with a rather cheap girl, he goes to work for a Chicago engineering firm.

For five years, Allen works hard and eventually attains a position of prominence, both in the firm and in the community in which he lives. He falls in love with Helen (Helen Vinson), a refined young woman who knows nothing of his past. They are about to be married when Marie (Glenda Farrell), the girl from his past, comes back, having learned of his conviction and escape. Marie threatens to blackmail Allen unless he marries her, which he does. His security is destroyed when Marie later informs on him, in effect wiping out his record of six years as an upstanding citizen. Because of Allen's position in the community, his case becomes a *cause célèbre*, with groups formed to keep him from going back to prison. A deal is made whereby Allen will serve a symbolic ninety days on the chain gang doing easy tasks, and after that, the state will consider his debt to society paid. Allen is suspicious, and justifiably so. No sooner is he back on the chain gang than the brutalization begins anew. Near the breaking point, Allen again escapes, but this time into an America sunk even deeper in the Depression, with no job in sight. He is now a permanent refugee on the fringes of society. At the film's end, he comes back to see Helen, the woman he loves. She sees him outside her house, his face peering out of the black night. As she asks him how he lives, he whispers "I steal!" and disappears back into the darkness.

The ending of the film was almost unbearable for some people in its unremitting despair. LeRoy has written in his autobiography that when Muni's face disappears in the dark, it was because a light had blown out, but that upon seeing the frames, it looked so effective that he retained the take. The film had great emotional impact upon its audiences, and, beyond that, a significant social impact. The nation became collectively offended at the harsh Georgia penal code. Reform committees were formed, letters were written, and editorials composed all over the nation, seeking to force the state of Georgia to change its laws. These efforts were successful, for shortly after the film opened, the Georgia chain gang system was revised. Mervyn LeRoy and Jack Warner, however, were not welcome in the South. They received anonymous letters telling them that if they ever set foot on Georgia soil they would be arrested, or worse. Muni, nominated for an Oscar, was proud of his role in the film, feeling that it was one of his most significant parts.

I Am a Fugitive from a Chain Gang was revised frequently in the 1960's when America was again going through social upheaval. The film now has a new generation of devoted fans, but it is ultimately a product of its time. There has probably never been a bleaker American film. It represents a world devoid of hope and justice, with no relief in sight.

Joan Cohen

I MARRIED A WITCH

Released: 1942
Production: René Clair for Paramount; released by United Artists
Direction: René Clair
Screenplay: Robert Pirosh and Marc Connelly; based on the novel *The Passionate Witch* by Thorne Smith, completed by Norman Matson
Cinematography: Ted Tetzlaff
Editing: Eda Warren
Art direction: Hans Dreier and Ernst Fegte
Special effects: Gordon Jennings
Music: Roy Webb
Running time: 76 minutes

Principal characters:
Wallace Wooley .... Fredric March
Jennifer .... Veronica Lake
Daniel .... Cecil Kellaway
Dr. Dudley White .... Robert Benchley
Estelle Masterson .... Susan Hayward
Margaret .... Elizabeth Patterson
J. B. Masterson .... Robert Warwick

Critical opinion of the films of director René Clair has fallen in recent years. Once numbered among the greats, even his best work from the late 1920's and 1930's appears slight beside the more lasting achievements of Jean Renoir and Jean Vigo. His first two films arose out of the *avant-garde—Paris Qui Dort* (*The Crazy Ray*), 1923, is whimsical science fantasy, and *Entr'Acte* (1924) is a Dadaistic exercise. The early films shift between lightweight comedy (*The Italian Straw Hat*, 1927; *Le Million*, 1931) and fantasy (*Le Voyage Imaginaire*, 1925; and *Under the Roofs of Paris*, 1930). Never far from the satirical, his considered masterpiece, *A Nous la Liberté* (1932), anticipates Chaplin's *Modern Times* (1936) in its depiction of modern industrialized man. It formerly was held that Clair's hiatus in Hollywood was responsible for his later decline, though much the same thing was also said of Jean Renoir, Fritz Lang, and Alfred Hitchcock. A later generation of critics rightly resurrected the works of these men, while Clair continues to be underestimated. Most nearly approaching Clair's experience in America is that of another European expatriate, Ernst Lubitsch. While Lubitsch, however, particularly in his late works, was making the warmly romantic *The Shop Around the Corner* (1940), the black comedy *To Be or Not to Be* (1942), and the nostalgic *Heaven Can Wait* (1943), Clair contented himself with lightweight whimsy. Lubitsch could shift from the sharply witty to the deeply moving very effectively, while Clair lacked this range. There is something a little too neat about Clair that makes most of the films, however entertaining, seem emotionally shallow.

Clair seemed destined for a certain type of film even before he arrived in America. His first film outside France was *The Ghost Goes West* (1936), made in England for Alexander Korda. After *Break the News* (1938), with Maurice Chevalier, and the uncompleted *Air Pur* (1939), he came to Hollywood at the outbreak of World War II to make his most satisfying film, *The Flame of New Orleans* (1941), a romance which benefits considerably from Marlene Dietrich's exotic presence. The next two films found Clair once again in the familiar vein of fantasy with *I Married a Witch* and *It Happened Tomorrow* (1944), the latter starring Dick Powell as a reporter who is able to get the news a day before it occurs. Finally, he made an efficient, if rather mechanical, adaptation of Agatha Christie's *Ten Little Niggers*, with the title changed to the less offensive *And Then There Were None* (1945).

I Married a Witch, adapted from a tale by Thorne Smith (who wrote *Topper*), had originally been a Preston Sturges project. For whatever reason, Sturges dropped out, and Paramount farmed out the film to an independent production company, although it is easy to see how the elements of political satire in the story might have appealed to Sturges in the first place. The film did make use of a number of Paramount technicians such as Hans Dreier, however, and Paramount released the picture in its theaters.

The story begins with a prologue. In seventeenth century Salem, Massachusetts, we find that two witches, Jennifer (Veronica Lake) and her father, Daniel (Cecil Callaway), are being burned at the stake upon evidence given by one Jonathan Wooley. Although they are immolated and their ashes buried beneath a sturdy oak tree, Jennifer puts a curse on all the male members of the Wooley clan: that they shall each marry the wrong woman. There follow a series of scenes in which a succession of Wooleys, played in various disguises by Fredric March, are henpecked by their shrewish spouses. This leads up to the present, and we see gubernatorial candidate Wallace Wooley about to suffer a similar fate with his fiancée.

During a storm, a bolt of lightning strikes a venerable oak, releasing the corporeal spirits of Jennifer and Daniel. Flying through the air, they come to a nearby house where a party is in progress. There Jennifer sees with satisfaction that her curse is still working, but Daniel scoffs at her, saying, "All men marry the wrong woman." In order to make Wooley truly unhappy, he must fall in love with a woman he cannot have. Thus the seed is planted for Jennifer's revenge. Before that, however, the two witches go in search of some cornfields to ruin, Daniel remarking that "'Tis a good way to limber up."

Having lost their bodies through fire, it is necessary that the ghosts should regain them in like manner. They find a fitting site for Jennifer's rebirth by fire in the Pilgrim Hotel. With the hotel slowly and mysteriously burning from the top floor downward, the inhabitants are evacuated, but the fire department is unable to stop the blaze. Having stopped to watch, Wooley hears screams inside and dashes in to investigate. There follows a slightly risqué scene in which Wooley finds the unclad Jennifer in the smoke-filled rooms. Rather stuffy himself, he is embarrassed by her total lack of shame. He lends her his coat and later puts her in a taxi. Reminiscent of the final shot in *The Flame of New Orleans*, the coat is unceremoniously tossed out the window.

On Wooley's return home he finds, to his surprise, that Jennifer is waiting there for him. Jennifer has no trouble in totally bewitching him by morning. Everything is going according to plan until she drinks the love potion intended for him; now she must prevent his marriage to Estelle Masterson (Susan Hayward). It is upon this marriage that Wooley's political ambitions hinge, as Estelle's father owns a powerful newspaper chain. Jennifer enlists the aid of her father, but he is bent on causing other mischief for the Wooleys. After he disrupts the wedding, he causes further grief for the couple by staging his own fake murder and implicating Wooley. Fortunately, Jennifer is able to trick his spirit into entering a bottle of old New Bedford Rum. With Daniel safely ensconced there, Wooley and Jennifer, now married and entering the governor's mansion, are able to live happily ever after, although in an epilogue their daughter seems to have inherited her mother's former penchant for riding a broomstick.

The dialogue by Robert Pirosh and Marc Connelly is both pointed and witty and its delivery effectively understated. Fredric March is ideally suited for his role as Wallace Wooley. Veronica Lake displays her largely neglected flair for comedy, which was exploited elsewhere only by Sturges in *Sullivan's Travels* (1941). In supporting roles, Susan Hayward, using her bossiness to good effect, is properly nasty as Estelle, while Robert Warwick and Elizabeth Patterson lend comic color to their parts. Robert Benchley is as droll as ever. Standing out, however, is Cecil Kellaway as the charmingly malevolent Daniel.

On the technical side, Clair is ably assisted by Gordon Jenning in his work with special effects. The cinematography of Ted Tetzlaff is at times appropriately low-key. The sets, by Hans Dreier and Ernst Fegte, are authentic. Clair's signature is clearly apparent in the proceedings, but the question remains whether he has anything to say. It often seems that Clair, gliding easily over the surface, is unable to delve into any deeper waters. Expert as he is, he fails to make a truly challenging film. Compared to the more substantial work of Renoir, Clair produces lightweight entertainments which, pleasant as they are at the moment, leave one hungering for more. Yet, if Clair is not to be mistaken for an artist of the first rank, we can still be grateful that he possessed buoyancy and charm, qualities in short enough supply at any time.

Mike Vanderlan

I SEE A DARK STRANGER

Released: 1947
Production: Sidney Gilliat and Frank Launder for Eagle-Lion Films
Direction: Frank Launder
Screenplay: Sidney Gilliat and Frank Launder
Cinematography: Wilkie Cooper
Editing: Thelma Myers
Running time: 98 minutes

> *Principal characters:*
> Bridie Quilty .... Deborah Kerr
> David Baynes .... Trevor Howard
> Miller .... Raymond Huntley
> Man in the Straw Hat .... Norman Shelley
> Captain Goodhusband .... Garry Marsh
> Michael Callaghan .... Brefni O'Rorke

The Republic of Ireland was officially neutral during World War II, and one effect of this neutrality was to make the country an especially effective haven for German spies, some of whom were aided and abetted by Irish citizens, although less out of love for the Nazis than out of hatred for the English. Director Frank Launder's *I See a Dark Stranger* (also entitled *The Adventuress* in the United States) is a richly textured, atmospheric psychological drama about one such collaborator, a young Irishwoman named Bridie Quilty. The film is meticulously structured, with a prologue, an epilogue, and three distinct expository sections in between. It features Bridie Quilty (Deborah Kerr) pursuing the chimera of an Irish war against England, getting caught up in, and finally being pursued by, a Nazi spy ring. Although Launder integrates some romance and even a bit of comic relief, the film is most effective when Launder concentrates on the ambivalent emotions of his heroine as she struggles to come to terms with the implications of her bitter hatred of the English.

Launder opens the film with a short prologue. The scene is set in a pub in rural Ireland; the time is 1937. A teenage girl listens raptly as her father and uncle regale their listeners with tales of their heroism against the hated English Black and Tans, tracing the roots of the Anglo-Irish animosity back to the seventeenth century Commonwealth of the much despised Oliver Cromwell. Although the men's tales are largely fabrications (in a telling aside, one of Launder's characters reveals that Daniel Quilty did most of his fighting in pubs), young Bridie accepts them without question, and thereby acquires a bone-deep hatred for everything English.

The scene shifts to 1944. Bridie has come of age, and resolves to follow in what she believes were her late father's footsteps. She travels to Dublin, where she seeks out Michael Callaghan (Brefni O'Rorke), a hero of the Irish rebellion, and asks him to enlist her in the Irish Republican Army. Callaghan, however, has mellowed over the years, and has no use for the IRA. "Forget this notion and go home," he counsels her. Bridie, however, has gone too far to stop here. She has resolved to fight the English, and if she cannot do it as an Irishwoman, she will do it as a spy for the Germans. This proves to be a fateful decision.

Launder walks a tightrope in his development of the character of Bridie Quilty. On the one hand, he makes it clear that Bridie's obsessive hatred for England is irrational and counterproductive; even Callaghan, the hero of the Rebellion, is shocked by her ferocity. On the other hand, however, he must avoid emphasizing Bridie's negative qualities to such an extent that his audience comes to dislike her, and he accomplishes this by continually emphasizing, through her dialogue, that Bridie is basically still a naïve young country girl.

In the next, and best, section of the film, much of Bridie's dialogue is spoken to herself in a stream-of-consciousness voiceover effect. She has gone to work for a German spy named Miller (Raymond Huntley); her primary job is to date English soldiers and extract information about troop movements from them, but recently she has begun to be troubled by her work. Initially, that anxiety manifests itself as a self-consciousness so intense as to border on paranoia: Bridie is forever seeing dark strangers and reading sinister implications into innocent statements and actions. Much of this part of the film is shot in murky bars, dimly lit hotel rooms, and gloomy, rainy nights, effectively heightening the tense, confused atmosphere. Throughout this section of the film, Launder uses repeated close-ups of Bridie's face, which reflects and echoes the inner turmoil that her thoughts, appearing as a voiceover on the soundtrack, also reveal. Indeed, by focusing the audience's attention so completely on Bridie, Launder is able to provide some startling shocks for his audience. Twice, at widely spaced intervals, while Bridie's face fills the screen and her troubled thoughts dominate the sound track, a loud, urgent, and threatening voice seems to signal Bridie's arrest. She, and the viewer, jump in alarm, but in neither case does the jarring interruption actually threaten anything more than Bridie's peace of mind. Her growing paranoia, so successfully transferred to the audience by Launder, is by this point threatened by even the slightest hint of trouble.

Sudden complications end Bridie's career as a spy. One of her "dates," an English Army officer named David Baynes (Trevor Howard), falls in love with her; and Miller, her boss, is shot and killed. Before he dies, he orders her to dispose of his body and sends her to fetch some secret papers that turn out to contain information of the site of the D-Day invasion. All this responsibility is too much for Bridie; she no longer wants the deaths of thousands of Allied soldiers—even if some of them are English—on her conscience.

Getting out of the business of espionage—which occupies the third section of Launder's film—is not easy, however, even after Bridie burns the documents that identify Normandy as the site of the Allied invasion. She has been pursued to the Isle of Man by both her persistent suitor, David Baynes, and also by a mysterious man in a straw hat (Norman Shelley) who turns out to be a German agent. A very unlikely romance blossoms between David and Bridie, only to be threatened when David, ever the proper Englishman, feels obligated to turn his lover in to the British authorities when she reveals herself to be an exspy. Launder also introduces a bit of comic relief into the film in the person of Captain Goodhusband (Garry Marsh), a lecherous and incompetent English soldier who has been put in charge of finding Bridie, by now identified as a German collaborator.

Although things become temporarily tense when the German in the straw hat abducts Bridie and David, all eventually ends well. The two lovers elude their German captors; and when the D-Day invasion is successful, David is no longer adamant about turning Bridie over to the English authorities. The film ends on a humorous note with a postwar epilogue. Bridie and David have married, and they check into a hotel on their honeymoon. Bridie glances out the window of their room, and suddenly storms out in a huff. David, and the audience, are baffled, until the camera comes to rest on a sign that reveals the name of the hotel: "Cromwell Arms." Despite her marriage to an Englishman, Bridie has never forgotten nor forgiven the hated Cromwell.

Despite its obvious merits, *I See a Dark Stranger* is not a perfect film. The script by director Launder and his long-time collaborator, Sidney Gilliat, has flaws. David Baynes's overnight infatuation with Bridie Quilty is without motivation; we might well believe that the young and naïve Bridie would fall in love at first sight, but Baynes is presented as a man of intellect and experience, and thus his relentless pursuit of Bridie lacks credibility. In addition, the last third of the film fails to sustain the intensity it generates earlier. The comic bits at the end are amusing enough, but they do not flow smoothly from the action that precedes them.

The film's basic strengths are Launder's compelling direction, particularly in the middle section, and an outstanding performance by Deborah Kerr in the role of Bridie Quilty. Kerr's role was especially demanding; Bridie is a complicated, often contradictory character, and Launder's decision to rely heavily on close-ups put additional pressure on Kerr's skills as an actress. She is equal to the task in every respect, managing to convey a sense of Bridie's basic sweetness and decency which keeps the audience on her side even when her naïveté and bad judgment repeatedly get the best of her.

In the other significant roles, Trevor Howard is adequate, though a bit "stiff-upper-lippish," as David Baynes. Curiously, Howard gets better as the film gets worse, and is at his best in the film's comic scenes. Raymond Huntley and Norman Shelley are appropriately sinister as Miller and the unnamed man in the straw hat, respectively; and Garry Marsh is a delight as the bumptious Captain Goodhusband.

Frank Launder had a long career as a director of entertaining, but largely undistinguished English potboilers such as *The Belles of St. Trinian's* (1954) and *The Blue Lagoon* (1948). *I See a Dark Stranger* and *The Lady Vanishes* (1938) are by far his finest efforts, and although by no means perfect, *I See a Dark Stranger* merits study as a compelling psychological drama and as a vehicle for one of Deborah Kerr's finest performances.

Robert Mitchell

I WANT TO LIVE!

Released: 1958
Production: Walter Wanger for Figaro, Inc. Production; released by United Artists
Direction: Robert Wise
Screenplay: Nelson Gidding and Don Mankiewicz; based on newspaper articles by Ed Montgomery and letters of Barbara Graham
Cinematography: Lionel Lindon
Editing: William Hornbeck
Sound: Gordon E. Sawyer
Music: John Mandel
Running time: 120 minutes

Principal characters:
Barbara Graham	Susan Hayward (AA)
Ed Montgomery	Simon Oakland
Peg	Virginia Vincent
Henry Graham	Wesley Lau
Emmett Perkins	Philip Coolidge
Jack Santo	Lou Krugman
Bruce King	James Philbrook
District Attorney	Bartlett Robinson

I Want to Live! is a film which defies easy classification. It is both a documentary type of drama about the conviction and subsequent execution of Barbara Graham in the gas chamber at San Quentin on June 3, 1955, and a damning indictment against capital punishment. It is also the story of a woman, a petty thief, prostitute, perjurer, forger, loyal friend, and loving mother, who was, according to a psychiatrist, neither a drug addict nor a person capable of physical violence. Until her execution, she maintained her claim of innocence. The controversy over Barbara Graham's guilt or innocence did not die with her in the San Quentin gas chamber, but will continue as long as the question of what constitutes cruel and unusual punishment remains unanswered.

Figaro, Inc., the company which produced this grim but compelling drama, had previously produced such outstanding films as *The Barefoot Contessa* (1954) and *The Quiet American* (1958) for release by United Artists. *I Want to Live!* was produced by Walter Wanger, whose production credits include *Smash-Up* (1947)—a film for which Hayward received an Academy Award nomination—and directed by Robert Wise, who counts among his credits such films as *Run Silent, Run Deep* (1958) and the film biography, *Somebody Up There Likes Me* (1956). The screenplay by Nelson Gidding and Don Mankiewicz is based on newspaper and magazine articles by the Pulitzer

Prize-winning journalist Edward S. Montgomery, one of the leading criminal investigative reporters in the nation. Additional sources of reference were the actual court transcripts and Barbara Graham's personal letters written during her term of imprisonment. These letters, sent mostly to a friend, Sharon Stone, provide a harrowing account of a condemned person's mental anguish.

Director Robert Wise chose the cast for the film carefully. He selected Susan Hayward to portray Barbara Graham based on her unsettling but totally realistic performances in the films *Smash-Up, My Foolish Heart* (1949), *With a Song in My Heart* (1952), and *I'll Cry Tomorrow* (1955). All of these films dealt with the personal tragedies and ordeals suffered by slightly less than respectable principal characters, and each performance resulted in an Academy Award nomination for Hayward. For his supporting cast, Wise chose proven actors, but none who had the status to overshadow the principal lead or provoke enough recognition to detract from the stark realism and atmosphere of the film.

This drama, filmed in black and white to heighten its overall documentary feeling, is divided into roughly two parts. The staccato tempo through the first half is established by a progressive jazz rhythm which was arranged by John Mandel, one of the foremost composers of jazz, and performed by the well-known Gerry Mulligan combo. This was the first time jazz had ever been used to score an entire film, and the music serves to embellish the film's realism. Using a fast-cut, cinemagraphic style that complements Mandel's beat, Lionel Linden's constantly moving camera pans and captures the changeability and seediness of the San Francisco tenderloin district, an area frequented by Barbara Graham.

Barbara is a contradictory and complex woman who spent much of her childhood in foster homes and reform schools. She speaks with a slangy "jive" vernacular that reinforces her image of being street-wise and tough. Yet, this image does not accurately reflect the total woman, for the letters written to her counsel and friends while she was imprisoned reveal a highly literate, sensitive, philosophic side of her personality.

After serving a prison sentence for perjury, Barbara marries bartender Henry Graham (Wesley Lau) and has a child by him. Graham turns out to be a hopeless drug addict. Pressed by both the responsibility for her child and a lack of excitement in her life, Barbara becomes involved with two petty crooks, Emmet Perkins and Jack Santo, with whom she had worked before. Perkins is played by Broadway actor Philip Coolidge; Santo is played by Lou Krugman, a veteran television actor.

Then, on the night of March 9, 1953, Mrs. Mabel Monahein, an elderly widow, is beaten to death in her Burbank, California, home during an attempted robbery. An underground figure, Bruce King (James Philbrook), claims he was present at the scene of the crime, turns state's evidence, and directs the police dragnet to the hideout of Barbara and her associates. The crime is first revealed to the audience when the police close in on the trio's hideout in Lynwood, California. Although the murder is not depicted in the film, the details of King's testimony are strongly suspect, which Edward Montgomery's investigation later confirms.

The scene depicting the capture of the three suspected murderers reveals much about Barbara Graham's defiance and spirit; it raises the question of her innocence as well. While searchlights bathe the hideout in a pitiless glare, a curious but uneasy crowd gathers; inside, Barbara calmly fixes her makeup. Some long minutes after the surrender of her partners, she emerges from the beleaguered building; a burlesque bump and defiant toss of her head leave little doubt about her contempt and disdain for all concerned. The first half of the film sets the stage for the harrowing second half, for now the march to the gas chamber begins. The tempo becomes solemn, dirgeful, inexorably beating out the seconds, minutes, and hours of Barbara Graham's final days. Under Wise's masterful direction, Susan Hayward vividly portrays the changes that take place in Graham's personality as she draws closer to the horror of the death chamber. She has appeared as the tough, flippant B-girl and the disdainful, suspected murderess. Now, as she languishes in first one jail and then another anxiously awaiting the correction of justice that does not come, tormented by the knowledge that her two-year-old son will soon forget her, we see her plunged into the depths of terror and despair, praying for a death that will finally end her mental anguish.

Only a few voices are raised in Graham's behalf: her staunch and loyal friend, Peg (Virginia Vincent); the psychiatrist who is convinced she was incapable of physical violence; and reporter Ed Montgomery (Simon Oakland). Montgomery, after labeling her "Bloody Babs" during the trial, interviews her numerous times on death row and becomes convinced of her innocence.

Hayward has the power to involve her audience so profoundly that the question of Barbara Graham's guilt or innocence becomes secondary. Stunned by the horror of what is happening, the audience watches helplessly as the state's legal machinery grinds blindly toward the execution of justice. Time and again reprieves are granted, then ground to dust. The execution is set for 10:00 A.M. on June 3, and Barbara is outwardly calm, prepared to face her death. Twice that morning, the execution is postponed as her lawyers desperately maneuver to save her life, one stay coming as she stands at the door to the gas chamber. At 11:12 A.M., after all maneuvers have failed, the final phone call comes, and at 11:34 A.M. the cyanide pellets drop into the solution of sulphuric acid.

Under Wise's taut direction, the suspense and anguish of Barbara Graham's last few days mount to a point of unbearable intensity. The film, which earned Susan Hayward a well-deserved Academy Award as Best Actress, also received Academy Award nominations for Best Director, Best Screenplay, Best Black and White Cinematography, and Best Sound Direction. Following her unforgettable performance in *I Want to Live!*, Susan Hayward, before her untimely death in 1975, went on to appear in a number of other fine films.

D. Gail Huskins

THE IMPORTANCE OF BEING EARNEST

Released: 1952
Production: Teddy Baird for British Film Makers Limited and J. Arthur Rank; released by Universal
Direction: Anthony Asquith
Screenplay: Anthony Asquith; based on the play of the same name by Oscar Wilde
Cinematography: Desmond Dickinson
Editing: John D. Guthridge
Running time: 95 minutes

Principal characters:
Jack Worthing .... Michael Redgrave
Lady Bracknell .... Dame Edith Evans
Gwendolyn Fairfax .... Joan Greenwood
Miss Prism .... Margaret Rutherford
Algernon Moncrieff .... Michael Denison
Cecily Cardew .... Dorothy Tutin
Canon Chasuble .... Miles Malleson

When Oscar Wilde's *The Importance of Being Earnest* was filmed in 1951, Anthony Asquith decided to forget the moviemaker's usual anxiety about "opening up" the action of a play for the screen and instead called on the resources of the studio to keep the comic masterpiece as close to an ideal production as possible. Michael Redgrave—a handsome, virile, and appropriately earnest Jack Worthing—heads a flawlessly chosen cast, whose excellence extends even to the actors playing the servants. Jack Worthing's valet is portrayed by Richard Wattis, a well-known character comedian who later attracted notice in Laurence Olivier's *The Prince and the Showgirl* (1957), and as the bespectacled airport manager in Asquith's *The VIP's* (1961). Dame Edith Evans' performance as Lady Bracknell, a role that she played many times on the stage, is one of the marvels of twentieth century theater. We should be grateful to Asquith for preserving it in his film.

The shooting script, which Asquith prepared himself, was simply the text of the play, with the action of some scenes transposed to give the camera more to record than the drawing room, garden, and library sets called for in the original. Canon Chasuble, for example, was given an ornately carved gothic sitting room for his second act conversation with Jack about the christening; and Asquith broke up the action of the first act by having Algernon's conversation with Jack about the cigarette case take place in Jack's rooms in the Albany, rather than in Algernon's flat in Half-Moon Street. The art director, Carmen Dillon, took full advantage of the screen's superiority at conveying visual detail to flesh out simple stage descriptions. As photographed by Desmond Dickinson's Technicolor camera, no further visual embellishment was necessary. To cover his transpositions, Asquith made a few trifling cuts and added a few lines of his own dialogue; but otherwise the film version of *The Importance of Being Earnest* is the same play that has been delighting theater audiences for more than half a century.

The film opens on the first-night production of Wilde's new comedy in 1895. A couple in full evening dress is sitting in a stage box waiting for the curtain to rise on the first act. The orchestra strikes up the overture; while they play, the lady in the box obligingly turns the pages of her program so that we can read the credits, which are printed inside. The lights dim, the curtain rises, and the lady puts her opera glasses to her eyes to study the action on stage more closely. She finds herself staring at the back and shoulders of a naked man, and the camera pulls back to reveal that Mr. Ernest Worthing (Michael Redgrave) is having his morning bath. While he is dressing, his best friend, a fashionable young man about town named Algernon Moncrieff (Michael Denison), calls to return the cigarette case that Ernest had left behind at a dinner party a week or two before. But the cigarette case has an unexpected inscription: "From little Cecily, with her fondest love to her dear Uncle Jack." When Algernon questions him about this, Ernest confesses that his name is really John Worthing and that the cigarette case was a present from his ward, Cecily Cardew.

Cecily, who lives quietly at Worthing's home in the country, is the eighteen-year-old granddaughter of the late Mr. Thomas Cardew, who adopted "Uncle Jack" as a baby, gave him the name John Worthing, and appointed him Cecily's guardian in his will. Jack, when he is living at home, feels obliged to set Cecily a good example by adopting a high moral tone on all subjects. But, as he tells Algernon, "a high moral tone can hardly be said to conduce very much to either one's health or one's happiness." So, in order to get up to London occasionally, he has invented a scapegrace younger brother named Ernest, who lives in town and is always having to be rescued from some predicament. Algernon, far from being scandalized by Jack's duplicity, is delighted and exclaims that his friend is just what he has always suspected him of being: a confirmed Bunburyist. He goes on to explain that, just as Jack has invented a useful imaginary brother named Ernest, so he has invented an imaginary friend named Bunbury, an invalid who lives in the country and whose frequent illnesses call Algernon down from town whenever he has a social engagement that he does not want to keep.

Algernon and Jack have a tie between them stronger than Bunburying, however: Jack is in love with Algernon's cousin, Gwendolyn Fairfax (Joan Greenwood), and is overjoyed to hear that Gwendolyn and her mother, Lady Bracknell (Dame Edith Evans), have been invited by Algernon to tea in his flat that afternoon. At the appointed hour, Jack turns up and pleads with Algernon for a minute alone with Gwendolyn, which Algernon arranges.

Once they are alone, Jack proposes marriage to Gwendolyn; she accepts his proposal, but discomforts him by saying that one reason she loves him is that she has always dreamed of marrying a man with the name of Ernest. Jack timidly asks if she could not love him if his name were something else—Jack, for instance. She answers no, adding that "the only really safe name is Ernest." Jack secretly resolves to have himself rechristened Ernest at the earliest opportunity.

When Lady Bracknell comes back into the room and discovers that her daughter and Mr. Worthing have become engaged in her absence, she dismisses Gwendolyn and tells Jack that she is willing to add him to her list of prospective sons-in-law if he will answer a few questions. Jack is able to satisfy her about his income and habits; but, when he discloses that instead of having parents of his own, he was found by Mr. Cardew in a handbag that had been abandoned in the cloakroom of Victoria Station, her reaction is one of horror. She advises him, ". . . to try and acquire some relations as soon as possible." Gwendolyn returns a few minutes after her mother has gone to tell Jack that what she has learned of his origin only makes him that much more romantically appealing to her. She gets him to tell her his address in the country, which Algernon, who has been intrigued by Jack's description of his young ward, surreptitiously copies down on his shirt-cuff, grinning all the while.

The action now shifts to Jack's country home. Cecily (Dorothy Tutin) is discovered dreamily watering the roses in the garden by her governess, Miss Prism played by Margaret Rutherford, who brings to this role her own wonderful and inimitable mixture of earnestness and quivering bewilderment. Miss Prism sets Cecily down to her afternoon lessons, then, at Cecily's suggestion, leaves to take a stroll in the park with her devoted admirer, Canon Chasuble (Miles Malleson), the rector. The butler comes in to announce the arrival of Mr. Worthing's brother Ernest, who has driven over from the station with enough luggage for a weekend visit. "Ernest" turns out to be Algernon, who pretends to be disappointed when Cecily tells him that her Uncle Jack is in town and will be unable to receive him. The two young people are immediately smitten with each other. Cecily tells Algernon that she has been fascinated by the thought of her cousin's wicked behavior; and Algernon tells Cecily that he believes he could reform for her sake.

Meanwhile, Canon Chasuble and Miss Prism, returning from their walk, are shocked to see Jack Worthing alight from a carriage in front of the Manor House, dressed in the deepest mourning, with a crepe hatband and black gloves. Jack tearfully tells them that his brother Ernest has died suddenly in Paris; but, before he can proceed further with this invention, Cecily bursts from the house with news that Ernest is staying with them as a guest and has promised to reform that very afternoon. When Jack discovers that "Ernest" is really his friend Algernon, he refuses to shake hands and icily informs him that he will have to leave at once. While Algernon is waiting for the dogcart to be sent around, he steals a few minutes to tell Cecily he loves her; and, before he quite realizes it, he has asked her to marry him and she has accepted. He is taken aback, however, when Cecily tells him, as Gwendolyn told Jack, that she could only really fall in love with a man named Ernest. Algernon runs off to the rectory to arrange to be rechristened, telling Cecily that he will be back in a half hour.

While Cecily is waiting, the butler comes to her in the garden to announce that Miss Gwendolyn Fairfax has arrived from town on important business with Mr. Worthing. Cecily goes to greet Miss Fairfax in her uncle's absence; Jack, too, has gone to the rectory to arrange for his christening. Gwendolyn is a little astonished to discover that her dear Ernest has a pretty eighteen-year-old ward he has never told her about, but believes the mystery cleared up when Cecily tells her that her guardian is Ernest's elder brother Jack. Cecily then shyly volunteers the information that, in fact, she and Ernest have just become engaged. Gwendolyn produces her diary to prove that she and Mr. Ernest Worthing have been engaged since five-thirty yesterday after-noon and that, consequently, she has the prior claim. Prevented from quar-reling openly by the arrival of the butler with tea, the two young women politely volley a few insults at each other. In his one serious lapse from Wildean elegance, Asquith has the butler swivel his head to follow this ex-change like a spectator at a tennis match. When Algernon and Jack return, Jack confesses that he has never had a brother Ernest at all. Cecily and Gwendolyn embrace tearfully and march back into the house, leaving Al-gernon and Jack to finish tea by themselves.

The young women forgive them, however, when they learn that both men have made arrangements to be christened Ernest that afternoon. Their joy is interrupted by the sudden arrival of Lady Bracknell, who reminds Jack that he is not to consider himself engaged to Gwendolyn until he has cleared up the mystery of his parentage, although she readily consents to the marriage between Algernon and Cecily when Jack tells her of the fortune Cecily will inherit when she comes of age. Jack, however, announces that as Cecily's guardian he will not consent to the marriage until Lady Bracknell relents and allows him to marry Gwendolyn.

The impasse is only resolved by the arrival of Canon Chasuble and Miss Prism. To everyone's astonishment, it is revealed that twenty-eight years earlier, Miss Prism, in her capacity as nursemaid, had left Lord Bracknell's house in charge of a perambulator containing a male infant. They never returned; but the perambulator was found a few weeks later containing the manuscript of a three-volume novel inside instead of the baby. Miss Prism admits to being the author of the novel and confesses that she had mistakenly put the baby in her handbag in the cloakroom of Victoria Station. Jack runs up to his room for the handbag in which Mr. Cardew had found him; it has been kept in a bell jar at the foot of Jack's bed. Lady Bracknell tells Jack that he is really the son of her late sister and her husband, General Moncrieff, and consequently Algernon's elder brother. Furthermore, he was named after their father, whose Christian names were Ernest John. The lovers—Jack and Gwendolyn, Algernon and Cecily, and even Canon Chasuble and Miss Prism—fall into each other's arms. "My nephew," Lady Bracknell says to Jack, "you seem to be displaying signs of triviality." "On the contrary. . . . I've now realized for the first time in my life the vital Importance of Being Earnest." As Redgrave speaks Wilde's great curtain line, the camera pulls back to reveal the library set and the actors framed by proscenium and footlights. The comedy is over.

Charles Hopkins

IN NAME ONLY

Released: 1939
Production: George Haight for RKO/Radio
Direction: John Cromwell
Screenplay: Richard Sherman; based on the novel *Memory of Love* by Bessie Breuer
Cinematography: J. Roy Hunt
Editing: William Hamilton
Running time: 94 minutes

Principal characters:
Julie Eden .... Carole Lombard
Alec Walker .... Cary Grant
Maida Walker .... Kay Francis
Mr. Walker .... Charles Coburn
Suzanne .... Helen Vinson
Laura .... Katherine Alexander

The plot of *In Name Only* might appear similar to that of a romantic melodrama, but the film transcends the clichés of soap opera largely because of the thoughtful, restrained performances of the actors and the intelligent direction of John Cromwell.

The story begins when wealthy Alec Walker (Cary Grant) meets Julie Eden (Carole Lombard), an attractive young widow who is living with her young daughter and divorced sister, Laura (Katharine Alexander), in rural Connecticut for the summer. Though Alec falls in love with Julie, she wants to end their relationship when she learns he is married. He explains that his marriage to Maida (Kay Francis) is a marriage in name only—that she married him for wealth and social position and refuses to give him up. Nevertheless, Julie decides to return to New York rather than be the "other woman" in Alec's life; but Alec soon follows her with the news that Maida has agreed to a divorce. Julie and Alec are happy until it becomes obvious that Maida has no intention of getting a divorce and is playing a waiting game.

In the beginning, however, the film leaves the audience in doubt about what the true situation is and where its sympathy should lie. At first Alec and Julie appear to be a perfect couple, but then we learn that Alec is married. Julie is presented as an attractive, straightforward, trusting person, and all of her early scenes with Alec are calm, happy, and touched with humor. Alec's scenes with his wife, Maida, present a sharp contrast. With Maida, Alec seems tense, morose, and rude, even to the point of leaving the room when she enters it. He barely responds to her conversational gambits and seems almost to hate her. On the other hand, Maida seems to be patient and understanding, gracious enough to put up with Alec's foibles and tactful enough to smooth over his rudeness in front of his parents.

We cannot understand Alec's bitterness until a crucial scene between the two reveals Maida's true character and motivations. Having assured Alec that she loves him, that she loved him when she married him, and that she is deeply wounded by his seeing Julie, Maida has to admit that she is lying when Alec produces a letter in which she admits that she married Alec for his money and social position and does not love him.

Maida's character, although presented in the worst possible light, is still an interesting one. She is a study of an obsessive, selfish, greedy, and cunning woman. In contrast to Julie Eden, she has no illusions and is not impulsive. Every word, every action, seems to be carefully calculated for its effect and to be part of her overall design to get not only Alec's money but his father's fortune as well. The chief interest in such an unpleasant personality lies in the restraint with which Kay Francis plays the role. In a character with seemingly few nuances, she gives a modulated, nuanced performance that makes her hard, unscrupulous wife the most fascinating albeit unlikable character in the film.

Julie Eden, on the other hand, is a romantic, a heroine who wants to keep some of her illusions. Although she is attracted to Alec, she is especially sensitive about her position as the other woman in the triangle because her sister Laura's marriage was broken up by another woman. She likes Alec, but when he suggests that they can still continue to see each other and remain friends, she is honest enough to admit that they could not remain merely friends.

Alec Walker is more mercurial. He is easily cast down and just as quickly made ecstatic. After a quarrel with Maida he goes to a roadhouse for dinner where he is seen by Maida's predatory friend Suzanne (Helen Vinson). She is eager to have an affair with Alec, but when he flippantly agrees on the condition that they get married, ignoring the gossip and scandal and sacrificing their positions in society, she quickly retreats. When Maida agrees to give him the divorce, he is jubilant and unable to contain his high spirits. In one of the film's most humorous scenes he arrives at Julie's apartment in New York and pretends to be a census taker. With machine-gun rapidity he fires question after question at her, allowing her no time to respond until she, too, catches his infectious enthusiasm and agrees to marry him. Predictably, he is also the one hardest hit when Maida finally admits she has no intention of getting a divorce and threatens a nasty scandal if Alec tries to get one. He goes on a drunken binge, gets pneumonia, and loses his will to live.

Outside Alec's hospital room, Julie tries to discover from Maida why she will not give him the divorce. Maida lets down her guard for a moment and tells Julie that alimony from Alec is not enough for her—she wants his father's fortune too. She hears a gasp from behind her, turns, and finds that Alec's parents have heard the whole conversation. She stands, frozen and alone, outside the door to Alec's room while Julie and Alec's parents enter it together. Her face is a mask of conflicting emotions, her eyes staring straight ahead, her hand clutching her throat. We see her like this until the door to Alec's room closes.

The final confrontation neatly ties up the story line and paves the way for a happy ending. Although the sequence is handled well, it is the most contrived and melodramatic part of the film. Bathos is avoided through the utter sincerity and conviction of Carole Lombard's portrayal of Julie Eden, by Kay Francis' underplayed Maida, and by director John Cromwell's refusal to dwell on the tears and sentimentality.

Kay Francis is not the only one who gives a fine performance. Cary Grant and Carole Lombard, usually considered good light comedians, demonstrate their ability to handle straight dramatic roles. As Alec Walker, Grant is his usual flippant self but with an aura of charming thoughtfulness and disillusionment that makes him completely believable. Carole Lombard as Julie Eden moves between gaiety and despair convincingly. Her performance is generally disciplined, making her emotional scenes even more effective.

A mature, well-made film, *In Name Only* presents some interesting character studies that come to life with the performances of the actors and the expert touch of the director to create a memorable film.

Julia Johnson

IN OLD CHICAGO

Released: 1938
Production: Darryl F. Zanuck for Twentieth Century-Fox
Direction: Henry King
Assistant direction: Robert Webb (AA)
Screenplay: Lamar Trotti and Sonya Levien; based on the novel *We, The O'Learys* by Niven Busch
Cinematography: Peverell Marley
Editing: Barbara McLean
Special effects: H. Bruce Humberstone, Fred Sersen, Ralph Hammeras, and Louis J. Witte
Running time: 110 minutes

> *Principal characters:*
> Dion O'Leary (older) .... Tyrone Power
> Belle Fawcett .... Alice Faye
> Jack O'Leary (older) .... Don Ameche
> Molly O'Leary .... Alice Brady (AA)
> Gil Warren .... Brian Donlevy
> Bob O'Leary (older) .... Tom Brown
> Dion O'Leary (younger) .... Gene Reynolds
> Jack O'Leary (younger) .... Billy Watson
> Bob O'Leary (younger) .... Bobs Watson

For decades, cinemagoers have delighted in the Hollywood disaster picture. Indeed, for most audiences, the basic ingredients are irresistible—colorful characters, a melodramatic plot spiked with sex and action, and a last-reel catastrophe in which the stars survive or perish amidst elaborate special effects. Such extravaganzas of the 1970's as *Earthquake* (1974), *The Towering Inferno* (1974), and the *Airport* sagas, among others, have made many forget that Hollywood also enjoyed a heyday of prolific destruction and wrath in the mid-1930's. RKO's *The Last Days of Pompeii* (1935) unleashed the horrors of Vesuvius; in M-G-M's *San Francisco* (1936) Clark Gable dodged the carnage of the 1906 earthquake as Jeanette MacDonald sang "Nearer My God to Thee"; and United Artists' *The Hurricane* (1937), directed by John Ford, climaxed with a hellish typhoon. However, the disaster epics of the 1930's peaked on the back lot of Twentieth Century-Fox studios, where Darryl Zanuck produced *In Old Chicago*. Based on the legend of Mrs. O'Leary's cow, which reputedly set Chicago ablaze in October, 1871, by kicking over a barn lantern, the 1938 release has become a classic and the prototype of modern disaster films.

Darryl Zanuck's forte was historical drama, and he saw *In Old Chicago* as a lavish spectacle—so lavish, in fact, that the producer initially thought that none of the young stars at his burgeoning studio were worthy of the top roles.

Fox entered a complex series of negotiations with M-G-M, hoping to sign Clark Gable for the male lead of rogue Dion O'Leary and Jean Harlow for the role of saloon singer Belle Fawcett. Hopes for Gable were soon dashed and Zanuck presented the part to his most promising young star, Tyrone Power. Harlow's role was arranged, but when she died on June 7, 1937, the role of Belle Fawcett passed to Alice Faye, who had won her Fox contract partially because of her Harlowesque quality. Fox's reliable Don Ameche drew the third starring role of Jack O'Leary, Dion's crusading brother, and Zanuck entrusted the project to the studio's master director, Henry King, with a lavish $1,800,000 budget.

In Old Chicago opens on a lonely Midwestern prairie in 1854. It is night, and Patrick O'Leary and his family are concluding their journey to Chicago. When a train appears on the nearby tracks, Patrick cannot resist racing it with his wagon. The horses rip loose, and Patrick is dragged across the prairie land. Molly (Alice Brady) and her three sons, Jack (Billy Watson), Dion (Gene Reynolds), and Bob (Bobs Watson), gather to hear Patrick's dying dream: ". . . everybody speakin' with respect of the O'Learys and how they grew up with the city and put their mark on it!" The family buries him, and Molly inherits the challenge of rearing her family in sprawling Chicago.

Unconquerable Molly soon establishes a thriving laundry in Chicago, and by 1867, the boys are grown. Jack (Don Ameche) is an idealistic lawyer, Bob (Tom Brown) drives the laundry wagon, and Dion (Tyrone Power) is a charming, conniving opportunist. The arrival at the laundry of a tablecloth from "The Hub," an infamous saloon, marked with the scribbled details of the latest corrupt scheme of The Hub's proprietor, gaudy politician Gil Warren (Brian Donlevy), spurs Dion to confront Warren. It is at The Hub that Dion sees Belle Fawcett (Alice Faye) performing on stage. Within a few scenes, Dion has made love to her, lured her away from the smitten Warren, and established his own saloon, The Senate, where Belle is the star performer.

Soon Warren visits The Senate and comments on how easily it could go up in flames. Yet Warren vows he has come to "bury the hatchet"; he is going to run for mayor and he wants Dion to be his campaign manager, clinching the deal by giving Dion a check for $10,000. Dion, however, has other plans. He secretly manages to get Jack nominated as the reform candidate for mayor; then, on election eve he instigates a riot at Warren's campaign headquarters that results in all of his supporters being arrested. The next day, Jack O'Leary is Chicago's new mayor.

Dion becomes the town's real power, and his illegal machinations become the talk of Chicago. Jack, however, wants to clean up the city and promises that he will prosecute his own brother, even if it means summoning Dion's lover Belle to the witness stand. At this point, the smooth-talking Dion proposes to Belle despite his mother's objections, and asks the delighted Jack to marry them. After the ceremony he announces, that, as Mrs. O'Leary,

Belle is no longer legally able to testify against him. Belle, feeling used, becomes angry and storms out. Jack and Dion engage in a brutal fistfight, which Jack wins. Shortly thereafter, Mrs. O'Leary's cow kicks over that lantern and Chicago is soon in flames. The bitter Warren leads a violent mob through the streets, hellbent on vengeance against Dion. Finally realizing their love for each other, Jack and Dion forget their differences, and, with brother Bob, stand against Warren's mob. To reroute the fire, Dion tries to dynamite his own saloon, but Warren stuns him with a brick. When Jack picks up the torch, Warren has him fatally shot in the back, but not before Jack lights the fuses and the building explodes. The explosions cause nearby cattle to stampede. While Dion escapes the horror, Warren is trampled by the rampaging cattle.

Dion looks for his family, all of whom have survived but Jack. At the docks he finds Belle and Molly. His wife has saved his mother from being trampled to death. He tells Molly of his reconciliation with Jack before his death, and she finally approves of his marriage to Belle. She then looks at the burning city and says: ". . . It was a city of wood—and now it's ashes—but out of fire'll be comin' steel. . . We O'Learys are a strange tribe, but there's strength in us, and what we set out to do we'll finish."

Zanuck had many reasons to be proud of *In Old Chicago*. It boasted strong performances by his most prized leading men, Power and Ameche; a star-making effort from Alice Faye, delightful in the grandiose numbers "Carry Me Back to Ol' Virginny" and "In Old Chicago"; colorful villainy by Brian Donlevy; and a superb portrayal from Alice Brady as the matriarch of the O'Leary clan. But, most of all, *In Old Chicago* had the fire; for three days and nights, it raged on Fox's back lot in Beverly Hills, costing $750,000 and filling twenty-five minutes of screen time, five minutes more than the climax of *The Hurricane*.

Though officially shown in early 1938, because of early previews it was a contender in the 1937 Oscar contest. Nominated for Best Picture, it lost to Warner Bros. *The Life of Émile Zola*, but won Academy Awards for Alice Brady (Best Supporting Actress) and Robert Webb (Best Assistant Director— the last year the award was presented). It placed sixth in *Film Daily's* 1938 "Ten Best" list, and was one of the top-grossing pictures of 1937-1938. In 1939, Zanuck tried to outdo his fire with flood in *The Rains Came*, which ended the 1930's disaster melodramas.

The great charm of *In Old Chicago* is that it was not merely a hodgepodge of characters and plot pieced together as a prelude to a crowd-pleasing disaster sequence; it was also a splendid, if historically distorted, story, as witnessed by the fact that on October 9, 1944, Cecil B. De Mille presented a version of *In Old Chicago* on his "Lux Radio Theatre," where only sound effects could suggest the chaotic fire. *In Old Chicago* survives as the disaster film *par excellence*, a classic that has been and should continue to be studied by cinema producers determined to perpetuate the curious, fascinating disaster genre.

Gregory William Mank

IN THE HEAT OF THE NIGHT

Released: 1967
Production: Walter Mirisch for Mirisch Company; released by United Artists (AA)
Direction: Norman Jewison
Screenplay: Stirling Silliphant (AA); based on the novel of the same name by John Ball
Cinematography: Haskell Wexler
Editing: Hal Ashby (AA)
Sound: Walter Goss and the Samuel Goldwyn Studio Sound Department (AA)
Running time: 109 minutes

Principal characters:
Virgil Tibbs .... Sidney Poitier
Bill Gillespie .... Rod Steiger (AA)
Sam Wood .... Warren Oates
Mrs. Leslie Colbert .... Lee Grant
Eric Endicott .... Larry Gates
Delores Purdy .... Quentin Dean
Ralph Henshaw .... Anthony James

In the Heat of the Night was a film whose time had come when it was released. It took the delicate moral and social problem of racism and dealt with it in terms of the established form of the mystery story. Audiences in 1967 and 1968 responded to the issues more intensely than they might have at any earlier time. In fact, considering the climate of those years, Sidney Poitier's fight for justice in a remote backwater may even have evoked a form of nostalgia among whites.

The film opens with the discovery of the murder of the owner of a proposed factory in Sparta, Mississippi. Virgil Tibbs (Sidney Poitier), a black Northerner who is just passing through, is arrested at the train station and charged with the crime. Upon interrogating Tibbs, local police chief Bill Gillespie (Rod Steiger) discovers that he is no mere vagrant but a pathologist with the Philadelphia police force. When a phone call to Philadelphia confirms this, Gillespie is superficially apologetic and embarrassed, while Tibbs wants only to catch the next train out of town. The Philadelphia police, however, decide that since this is Sparta's first murder, they will volunteer Tibbs's services to help solve the case as a friendly gesture. Neither Tibbs nor Gillespie is very pleased by this decision, as each stares at the other in the wake of the phone call.

Beginning with the evidence (the blunt object used to bludgeon the victim) and impressing the rural lawmen with the simple rudiments of autopsy, Tibbs leads the search and makes enemies both for himself and Gillespie as their quest exposes a subculture of fiscal and moral corruption that permeates the town. The murdered man was a wealthy Northerner; the factory he had proposed to build was an issue that had bitterly divided the local people. Thus the town's opposition to Tibbs as an investigating police officer is similarly bitter and intense. There are several attempts to remove him from the case: the first of these, a town council decision, is warded off by the victim's widow, Mrs. Leslie Colbert (Lee Grant), who threatens to take the factory to another town if Tibbs is not retained; a second, a violent confrontation in a garage, is deflected by Gillespie, who has grown to like Tibbs (although this is impossible for him to express, particularly since his own shaky position in the town is not much helped by the black man's presence). The other two attempts, consisting of a threat made by a wealthy landowner and the film's climactic confrontation, are both overcome by Tibbs himself. In the first, when the millionaire slaps Tibbs in the face, Tibbs simply slaps him back; in the second, during which a gathering of armed rednecks encircles him late in the night, Tibbs saves himself by summoning forth the real murderer from among their number.

In the film's course of events, the authorities almost arrest four different people in the resolution of the murder: Tibbs himself, a local delinquent (saved because the murderer had to have been left-handed), the wealthy landowner, and even Sam Wood (Warren Oates), the deputy who arrested Tibbs in the first place. Thus, suspicion and its attendant prejudices come full circle. In the end, the murderer turns out to be the least likely suspect: he is the skinny, spooky counterboy, Ralph Henshaw (Anthony James), at the all-night restaurant who needed money for his girl friend's abortion.

The final suspect, the deputy, is released, and the town seems to have reconciled itself to Chief Gillespie and even Tibbs, though to a lesser extent. Walking with him through the station, the Chief even carries Tibbs's suitcase as he sees him off on the train heading North.

Poitier and Steiger are well cast as antagonists. Their performances are concrete and convey the right touch of naked reality. Steiger, who received an Oscar for his performance, plays against the cliché of the stupid, bullying Southern cop. Gillespie's bigotry, rather than being presented as flagrant, is revealed as deep-seated and primal.

In a very touching scene, Gillespie has Tibbs over to his house for dinner and reveals more than he intends to concerning the lonely life he leads. He is on his fifth round of bourbon when he sums up his existence. He is thirty-seven years old, with no wife and no children, an insomniac scratching for a living in a town that does not want him. "You know something, Virgil? You're the first person who's been around to call. Nobody else has been here . . . nobody comes." Tibbs touches his shoulder in a moment of spontaneous compassion but Gillespie recoils: "Don't treat *me* like the nigger!" Tibbs's face goes blank. Poitier likewise plays his character in this scene against one's expectations. Tibbs's face goes blank, neither obsequious nor outraged, without either retracting his sympathy or at the same time letting Gillespie get away with his indulgence. The characterization is invariably complicated and dignified.

The supporting cast—Warren Oates; Lee Grant; Larry Gates as Endicott, the local landowner; Anthony James as the murderer; and Quentin Dean as Delores Purdy, James's girl friend—are fine. Of the group, Oates and Gates define their characters best and most believably.

The screenplay was written by Stirling Silliphant. Despite the drawbacks that inevitably arise from the use of the mystery format (for example, the inability to develop supporting characters of any depth, a problem of consequence in a plot whose theme pivots on human nature), the film's structure is workable. Apart from the performances of Poitier and Steiger, the subtle unity of *In the Heat of the Night* is its most striking aspect. The murderer, the counterboy at the all-night restaurant, is the first person we meet in the entire film. The film proceeds from there with Sam the Deputy's 3:30 A.M. patrol of the town during which the audience is given everything it needs to know about the circumstances of the murder, though there is no way to recognize this except in retrospect. Delores Purdy's nude strolls have caused Sam to be off his route, making him a suspect later on, and have invited the impregnation which later causes the counterboy to commit the murder. The characters are introduced in reverse order of their importance to the outcome, and the dialogue is vivid and believable.

Norman Jewison, who directed such films as *The Russians Are Coming, the Russians Are Coming* (1966), *Fiddler on the Roof* (1971), and *Rollerball* (1975), is a director who makes a career out of rising to the challenge of a script. His films reflect competence and eclecticism as well as a preference for entertaining plot lines that mask a "serious" and usually humane theme. His direction here is crisp and in tune with the script. The most powerful sequence in the film is the opening, and many credit its excellence to the cinematographer, Haskell Wexler. The heat of the night is rendered in warm blues interrupted by penetrating reds (a flashing train signal, the tail lights on a police car, a Coke machine), a contrast which creates a mood of anxiety climaxed by the blood of the dead man. This tension, however, is not maintained in the subsequent scenes, many of which take place in the daytime in an autumnlike season. This change of mood defeats the powerful effect of the film's beginning, undermining the images of heat and night and thus robbing it of its initial symbolic atmosphere.

Although some critics, including author James Baldwin, questioned the film's accuracy in dealing with the subject of racism, and attacked it for having an anti-South attitude, most reviewers praised the film. It was a box-office hit and swept the Oscars of that year, earning awards for Best Picture, Best Actor (Rod Steiger), Best Screenplay, Best Editing (Hal Ashby), and Best

Sound (Samuel Goldwyn Studio Sound Department). Although it has primarily endured only on late-night television, *In the Heat of the Night* makes a substantial contribution to film history because it deals, honestly if not altogether successfully, with racism, and because its lead performances are exceptional and create an indelible impression.

F. X. Feeney

IN WHICH WE SERVE

Released: 1942
Production: Noel Coward for Two Cities Productions; released by United Artists
Direction: Noel Coward and David Lean
Screenplay: Noel Coward
Cinematography: Ronald Neame
Editing: Thelma Myers and David Lean
Music: Noel Coward
Running time: 115 minutes

Principal characters:
Captain Kinross ....Noel Coward
Chief Petty Officer Walter Hardy .... Bernard Miles
Ordinary Seaman Shorty Blake .... John Mills
Alix (Mrs. Kinross) ....Celia Johnson
Freda Lewis .... Kay Walsh
Mrs. Hardy .... Joyce Carey
"Flags" .... Michael Wilding
Young Sailor .... Richard Attenborough

Noel Coward was, without question, an extraordinarily talented man, and nothing demonstrates his talents better than *In Which We Serve*, a film which Coward scripted, produced, scored, codirected (with David Lean), and in which he also played the leading role. Similar to the 1933 *Cavalcade*, which it resembles in its episodic plot, *In Which We Serve* is a glorious tribute to a nation, both at peace and at war. It stands alongside the documentaries of Humphrey Jennings—*Listen to Britain* (1941), *Words for Battle*, and others— as not only one of the best British wartime films, but also as one of the best films to deal with World War II made by any country.

Noel Coward was determined to do his part for the war effort, but his early attempts at propagandizing, in particular his involvement in the British war relief campaign of Hollywood's English colony, were far from successful. He was photographed enjoying life in California and drinking champagne, which did little for his image in wartorn England, and he was also accused of income tax evasion, which was even more detrimental. Coward realized that he could do most for his country as a filmmaker, and the idea for *In Which We Serve* originated with Lord Louis Mountbatten, a close friend, who told Coward of his experiences onboard the destroyer *H.M.S. Kelly* until its sinking during the Battle of Crete. With the support of the British Admiralty, Coward wrote his story, enlisted naval personnel as actors, and filmed most of the sea sequences in a gigantic water tank at Denham studios. Coward's perseverance and vision of the perfect propaganda film paid off handsomely; *In Which We*

Serve was screened before its release, was hailed by both King George VI of England and President Franklin D. Roosevelt, and was purchased for American release by United Artists for the record sum of $750,000.

In Which We Serve has no story line in the accepted sense. Coward states at the opening of the film, "This is the story of a ship," and the film's heroine is no Hollywood or British starlet but the fictionalized *H.M.S. Torrin*. The ship is the star, and her crew and their families are the secondary players. The film opens with the birth of the ship in the dockyard, a fine piece of documentary filmmaking the style of which is adhered to for much of the rest of the film. As the ship is launched, the camera rests on a headline of the front page of the *Daily Express* which reads "No War This Year." The *Daily Express* had been Coward's most vocal critic, and the filmmaker obviously could not resist this dig at the newspaper's failure to grasp the facts.

Immediately a title announces "Crete, May 21, 1941," and *H.M.S. Torrin* is seen in action, with Coward performing coldly and precisely as her captain. As the dawn rises, the ship is attacked by enemy planes and slowly sinks while her captain and crew swim for the life rafts. In a scene which is almost identical to one in *The Scoundrel* (1935)—Coward's only previous film appearance apart from a brief scene in D. W. Griffith's *Hearts of the World* (1918)—the captain, almost drowning in the ocean, sees two scenes from his past flash before his eyes: his signing for the ship from its builder, and a happy family evening during which he tells his wife Alix (Celia Johnson) that war will soon be a reality.

As the captain and a group of his men cling to a life raft while an enemy plane strafes them with machine-gun fire, the audience comes to know something of their backgrounds. There is Chief Petty Officer Walter Hardy (Bernard Miles), whose wife and mother-in-law are killed during a bombing raid on Plymouth. His niece, Freda Lewis (Kay Walsh), marries Ordinary Seaman Shorty Blake (John Mills). "Flags" (Michael Wilding) also thinks of his marriage. Each man is seen celebrating Christmas with his family, and each man toasts the one object that is as close to him in his affections as his loved one— the *H.M.S. Torrin*. At the Captain's dinner table, his wife makes a halting speech in which she recognizes that the ship is her rival, and always will be, for such is the lot of a sailor's wife. In a brief cameo, Richard Attenborough appears as a young sailor who, in a fit of terror, abandons his position onboard ship, but later gives his own life to drag a fellow sailor to the life raft. As the ship finally sinks beneath the waves, Coward, in true British fashion, asks his men for three cheers for the *H.M.S. Torrin*, while one of the men reminds the Captain of his earlier remark on the day the ship was commissioned, that she had been a happy and efficient ship.

The use of flashbacks was apparently decided upon by Coward after shooting was completed, and it is a method which works admirably. As the film draws to a close, the flashbacks catch up with the present. Shorty Blake's wife and mother receive a telegram announcing that he is safe, the group having been picked up and landed at Alexandria. Captain Kinross' wife also receives a telegram as she sits in front of the fire with her children; and each woman's face, before the telegram is opened, expresses the torment and anguish that a wartime telegram meant to the women left behind.

Captain Kinross gathers his remaining crew (five officers and ninety men) together and shakes hands with each one individually. Over shouts of the men of the British Navy, Coward says, in an epilogue:

> Here ends the story of a ship, but there will always be other ships, for we are an island race. Through all centuries the sea has ruled our destiny. There will always be other ships and men to sail in them. It is those men in peace or war to whom we owe so much. Above all victories, beyond all loss, in spite of changing values in a changing world, they give, to us their countrymen, eternal and indomitable pride. God bless our ships and all who sail in them.

In Which We Serve boasts one of the finest casts of British actors ever assembled for one production. Some, such as John Mills, Bernard Miles, Richard Attenborough, and Michael Wilding, went on to have distinguished careers in film and the theater. Celia Johnson, Kay Walsh, and Joyce Carey were three of a small group of players who became almost a Noel Coward repertory company in British films during the 1940's. As an interesting aside, two children in the cast were later to gain fame: John Mills's daughter in the film is played by his own daughter, Juliet Mills, and Coward's son is portrayed by Daniel Massey, son of Canadian actor Raymond Massey, who later played Coward in the Julie Andrews' vehicle, *Star!* (1968).

In Which We Serve was described as the British answer to Metro-Goldwyn-Mayer's *Mrs. Miniver* (1942), but it was far more than that. It demonstrated a quality of reserve and understatement, a dignity and a peculiarly British charm, that the glossy Hollywood production lacked; and it displayed a restraint and understanding of British patriotism and British strength which *Mrs. Miniver* could not hope to achieve. *Mrs. Miniver* could provide nothing more musically British than "The British Grenadiers," but in its use of "Roll Out the Barrel" and "Run, Rabbit Run," *In Which We Serve* showed what typically British music really was. *Mrs. Miniver* was voted Best Picture of 1942 by the Academy of Motion Picture Arts and Sciences, but *In Which We Serve*, which was not eligible for Academy Award consideration that year, was also honored by the Academy, with Noel Coward receiving a Special Award for "his outstanding production achievement."

Anthony Slide

THE INCREDIBLE SHRINKING MAN

Released: 1957
Production: Albert Zugsmith for Universal
Direction: Jack Arnold
Screenplay: Richard Matheson; based on his novel *The Shrinking Man*
Cinematography: Ellis W. Carter
Special cinematography: Clifford Stine
Editing: Albrecht Joseph
Art direction: Alexander Golitzen and Robert Clatworthy; set decoration, Russell A. Gausman and Ruby R. Levitt
Optical effects: Roswell A. Hoffman and Everett H. Broussard
Running time: 81 minutes

> *Principal characters:*
> Scott Carey .... Grant Williams
> Louise Carey .... Randy Stuart
> Clarice .... April Kent

Traditionally, successful horror films are modest in budget and scale and rich in imagination. *The Incredible Shrinking Man* is no exception. Most of the action takes place on a few interior sets which represent a triumph of art direction, since the design of the sets had to be continually and subtly altered to allow for the protagonist's changing physical relationship to his environment. Special effects, though used to a lesser extent than might be expected, are employed with skill and subtlety. The film is so thoughtfully executed that technique never calls into question the premise which the film asks its audience to accept.

It is important that the premise be taken as an entirely credible one, because *The Incredible Shrinking Man* has a different philosophic rationale than most horror films. This may be explained in terms of its being also a science-fiction film, although it disavows the traditions of that genre by its disdain of elaborate and dazzling effects. The relationship of *The Incredible Shrinking Man* to other horror films is interesting and provocative. Horror films derive from unconscious fears, personified by the monster, vampire, giant ape, or colossal spider, which threaten the normalcy represented by the principal characters. Not only does *The Incredible Shrinking Man* differ in this respect, but it also advances a different attitude toward the universal fear of the unknown. It cannot be said that there are any true monsters in the film; in fact, only the protagonist himself is abnormal in relationship to the world in which he lives. Because of his situation, a house cat and a spider are perceived as monsters, with resulting sequences of horror. Perceiving them objectively, they are harmless. However, the audience identifies so strongly with the protagonist, that such objectivity becomes impossible. The horror for Scott Carey (Grant

Williams) is his perception of his place in the world, which means that his struggle is spiritual as well as physical. To make the film similar to other horror films in which the monster is defeated and harmony restored to the normal world would require that Carey be cured and restored to his normal size. However, that does not occur, and instead the film proposes an unusual happy ending in which Carey accepts and affirms his altered place in the universe. *The Incredible Shrinking Man* does not reject the unknown as something cruel and frightening; it embraces it.

In order to lead the audience to this unconventional resolution, *The Incredible Shrinking Man* first appeals to all of the conventional feelings customarily aroused by horror films. Richard Matheson, the writer of both the film and the book from which it was adapted, and Jack Arnold, the director, both had experience in the genre and knew how to construct the film so that its intensity would mount. As usual, the hero is an ordinary, likable young man, married and living a comfortable, suburban existence. Following the opening sequence, in which Carey is exposed to a strange mist while on his boat, he does not become aware immediately of the shrinking process, allowing his secure and normal existence to be established in the following scenes. When he becomes aware that he is shrinking, fear overtakes him. The end of an effective marriage is intimated when his wedding ring falls off his finger, but hope is restored when science appears to find a cure. Carey befriends a midget, Clarice (April Kent), demonstrating his future ability to adjust to the terms of his existence. The first half of the film concludes as he begins shrinking again, and the second half begins sometime later when he is living in a doll's house. It is this second half which introduces the bizarre and horrifying elements as Carey wanders along through the basement of his house, which has become his world following his escape from the cat upstairs. He alone must prove his existence by surviving. The people in his life, perhaps with a certain gratitude, believe him to be dead. Carey passes every test posed to him, even as he continues to shrink. Ultimately, his victory over the spider for the food they both covet is a hollow one. The normal needs of life no longer apply to him, and he makes his way out of the basement into a new and beautiful world of the infinite.

The Incredible Shrinking Man is a film with the courage of its convictions, and most of the credit for this belongs to Matheson, who correctly understood the hero's situation both as a metaphor for the diminishing of individuality in the nuclear age and as a cautionary fable which examines man's need to adjust to the changes which are being brought about by the events of the twentieth century. That Matheson was able to invent a simple and effective story to present his ideas speaks well for him.

It is Jack Arnold, however, who is the true artistic hero of *The Incredible Shrinking Man*. As director James Whale (*Frankenstein*, 1931) was ideal for Universal's horror films of the 1930's being a master of fanciful imagery and an expressionistic style, Arnold was the ideal director for Universal's 1950's horror films (*Creature from the Black Lagoon*, 1954, *Tarantula*, 1955). Arnold possessed the ability to make everything seem normal. His images are direct and uncluttered. His actors give selfless performances which emphasize their ordinariness and make the horror that much more credible; Grant Williams as Carey is an excellent example.

The visual quality of Arnold's settings is remarkable. In several films, he makes a desert location seem like a modern wasteland. In his realization of *The Incredible Shrinking Man*, Arnold demonstrates his flair for placing his protagonist most effectively in each shot in relation to the other details of the shot, continually inviting our awareness of the growing precariousness of Carey's situation. His handling of the spider sequence is a major example of how to create horror, as he saves until the last moment the most terrifying shot, the low angle from Carey's point of view as he pushes the needle into the spider and blood begins to ooze from the creature. The final shots of the film have a spellbinding beauty. Arnold was a humble craftsman and is taken by only a few to be a significant figure in cinema, but *The Incredible Shrinking Man* is a masterpiece with a feeling all its own.

Blake Lucas

THE INFORMER

Released: 1935
Production: Cliff Reid for RKO/Radio
Direction: John Ford (AA)
Screenplay: Dudley Nichols; based on the novel of the same name by Liam O'Flaherty
Cinematography: Joseph H. August
Editing: George Hively
Music: Max Steiner (AA)
Running time: 91 minutes

Principal characters:
Gypo Nolan .... Victor McLaglen (AA)
Mary McPhillip .... Heather Angel
Dan Gallagher .... Preston Foster
Katie Madden .... Margot Grahame
Frankie McPhillip .... Wallace Ford
Mrs. McPhillip .... Una O'Connor
Terry .... J. M. Kerrigan
Bartly Mulholland .... Joseph Sauers
Tommy Connor .... Neil Fitzgerald
Peter Mulligan .... Donald Meek
The Blind Man .... D'Arcy Corrigan
Dennis Daly .... Gaylord Pendleton

The Informer is one of John Ford's darkest dramas both thematically and visually. He did not allow humor or light moments, which might have diluted the intensity of the story, to intrude on his tapestry. The film takes place in a single night, while shadows and fog surround the characters as they walk the streets. Even when the action moves off the cobblestones, the darkness seems to follow almost as if Gypo Nolan's brooding mind dims the lighting. Ford uses this technique to punctuate Nolan's increasing isolation induced by internal and external forces, both leading to the inevitable dead end.

The film is a single character study focusing on Gypo Nolan, brilliantly interpreted by Victor McLaglen, who was a regular of John Ford's stock company. McLaglen, almost fifty at the time, could alternately be tender and brutish, scheming and confused, running a wide range of mental attitudes. His performance was rewarded with an Academy Award for Best Actor that year.

The film is set in Dublin in 1922. It is a strife-torn city in the throes of the Sinn Fein Rebellion. Gypo Nolan, a simple-minded brute of a man, wanders the fog-shrouded streets and stops to stare at a police poster which proclaims a twenty-pound reward for information leading to the capture of Frankie McPhillip (Wallace Ford), a rebel leader and friend of Nolan. Nolan angrily rips down the notice and throws it into the street, but the poster, seeming to have a life of its own, persistently clings to his leg until he finally frees himself of it.

Later Nolan encounters his streetwalker girl friend, Katie Madden (Margot Grahame), who is being propositioned by a well-dressed man. Nolan, infuriated, throws the man to the ground, only to be condemned by Katie, who is penniless. A nearby window sign advertises passage to America for ten pounds, a sum that appears to be out of reach of both Katie and Nolan. The girl torments Nolan, reminding him that for twenty pounds they both could escape the circle of poverty and go to America. They argue and Katie walks away, exclaiming that she cannot afford his fine principles.

Fugitive Frankie McPhillip, dodging the British street patrols, breaks his six-month forced absence and returns to the city to see his mother (Una O'Connor) and sister, Mary (Heather Angel). Frankie arrives at Dunboy House, a cheap tavern, where he meets Nolan, who tells Frankie that he has been thrown out of the rebel organization. A traitor had to be silenced, he explains, and the members drew straws to determine who would carry out the execution imposed by the rebel court. Nolan had drawn the short straw but did not have the heart to kill the man when the victim pleaded for his life. His release of the condemned man disgraced Nolan with the rebels, and he was mistrusted by the British; consequently, he has been unable to find work and is poverty-stricken.

Frankie promises to try to help his friend. He asks Nolan to check and see if the Black and Tans (British soldiers) are watching his mother's home. Nolan, obsessed with getting the money to pay for passage to America for Katie and himself, sees Frankie's reward as the solution. He tells the wanted man that the route to his mother is clear, but as soon as McPhillip leaves, he goes to police headquarters and betrays his friend. Shortly after Frankie is reunited with his mother and Mary, the soldiers arrive and break down the front door. Frankie, trapped, opens fire on them and is killed in the ensuing gunfight. Nolan, waiting at police headquarters, learns of Frankie's death. He receives his reward and is ushered out the back door. Startled by a stranger, Nolan almost strangles him until he recognizes that the man is blind. As he walks through the swirling fog, Nolan begins to realize the consequences of what he has done.

He wanders into a bar and orders a drink. Katie finds him there and is surprised when the bartender brings Nolan his change. Nolan tells her that he has robbed an American sailor. Katie, who is in love with Nolan, apologizes for their earlier argument and returns to her flat to await him while he goes to the McPhillip home to attend Frankie's wake. The combination of Nolan's conscience and his drinking make him a pathetic figure when he arrives to express his condolences to Mrs. McPhillip. Some coins fall from his pocket and they arouse the suspicion of two members of the organization who are present. Bartly Mulholland (Joseph Sauers) and Tommy Connor (Neil Fitzgerald) approach Nolan and tell him that Dan Gallagher (Preston Foster), the leader of the rebels, wants to talk to him. They escort Nolan to rebel headquarters, where Gallagher asks him for his help in uncovering the identity of the informer responsible for McPhillip's death. He promises Nolan reinstatement in the organization if he will help them. Nolan seizes on the opportunity and accuses the local tailor, Peter Mulligan (Donald Meek), claiming he saw the man enter the Tan headquarters. He concocts a motivating story about McPhillip and the tailor's sister. Gallagher orders a court of inquiry for 1:30 that morning at the ammunition dump and tells Nolan to be present.

Following Nolan's departure, Mulholland and Connor express their belief that he is the informer, but Gallagher does not accept the accusation, knowing that Nolan was Frankie's friend. Mulholland follows Nolan as he goes from bar to bar, trying to erase the guilt of what he has done. A street brawl in which Nolan knocks two men unconscious, one of them a policeman, promotes him as a hero to the crowd. Reveling in this newfound admiration and spurred on by Terry (J. M. Kerrigan), an opportunistic member of the crowd, Nolan treats the assemblage to fish and chips with part of the reward money. Later, Terry and Nolan leave the pub together. Terry, mistakenly believing that Nolan has expended his resources, turns on him. Now drunk, Nolan is confused when Terry tells him that he only accompanied him because of his money and now that it is gone he has no further use for him. Nolan then pulls out his bankroll and Terry quickly changes his attitude once again, becoming Nolan's "good friend." Terry persuades Nolan to enter a high-class after-hours club. The initial reaction to Nolan and his friend evaporates when he shows the owner and guests his money.

Meanwhile, Dan Gallagher, who is in love with Mary McPhillip, visits the girl at her home to offer his sympathy on the death of her brother and to continue the investigation into who was responsible for Frankie's death. He questions her about the events leading up to the police raid and learns that Frankie had spoken only to Nolan before coming home. He then asks Mary to come to the court of inquiry later that night.

In a drunken stupor, Nolan is beginning to lose his grip on reality. He mistakes one of the other guests for Katie and eventually gives the woman part of his reward money so she can return to London. Terry is extolling the virtues of "King Gypo" and encouraging him to buy drinks for the other patrons when Mulholland, who has been following Nolan on his spending spree, arrives at the club with two other men. Mulholland tells Nolan that it is time for the court to convene. The group leaves, but they meet Katie a short distance away. Nolan gives her a five-pound note, the last of his money. Realizing that Nolan is in trouble, she lets the note fall to the gutter.

Gallagher, Mary, and the other members of the court are waiting when Nolan and his fellows arrive at the ammunition dump. Nolan is too drunk

to understand why Mulligan is present and embraces the man he has accused
before he realizes what is happening. Mulligan, a meek, mild-mannered man,
is asked to give an account of his actions from noon that day. The tailor's
story exonerates him while it punctuates Nolan's deception. Gallagher gives
Mulligan some money, apologizes, and sends him home. Mary then tells the
court that Nolan had seen Frankie at the Dunboy House that night. Gallagher
talleys a list of Nolan's expenditures, which total twenty pounds. Confused
and despondent, Nolan confesses that he betrayed his friend. Mulholland is
about to shoot Nolan, but Mary's scream prevents him. Gallagher orders
Nolan locked up while they draw straws for the man who will carry out the
sentence. Mary pleads with Gallagher that the killings should stop, but he
explains that while Nolan lives they are all in danger, because Nolan's own
fears will eventually drive him to the authorities. Young Dennis Daly (Gaylord
Pendleton) loses the draw and opens the door to Nolan's prison. Nolan,
however, through his amazing strength, manages to escape through the ceil-
ing. Gallagher orders the other men to search the city and prevent the fugitive
from reaching the Black and Tan headquarters.

Nolan, however, seeks refuge with Katie at her apartment. He tells her
that he betrayed McPhillip so they could use the reward money to go to
America. The girl is shocked and blames herself for driving the man she loves
to betray a friend. Like a small, frightened child, Nolan falls asleep by Katie's
fireplace.

Katie goes to the McPhillip home where Dan is visiting Mary. She entreats
them to spare Nolan's life, but Gallagher must still refuse since there are
other lives at stake. Katie inadvertently tells them where Nolan is hiding and
is overheard by Mulholland. Daly and two other men arrive at Katie's flat,
guns in hand. They break in, but Nolan manages to fight them off and rushes
out the front door. Mulholland is waiting for him and empties his revolver
into the ill-fated informer. Mortally wounded, Nolan stumbles to a church
where Frankie's mother silently prays. He confesses to her that he betrayed
her son and asks her forgiveness. The old woman, tears running down her
cheeks, forgives the informer, and Nolan dies in front of the altar.

There is very little violent action in *The Informer*, and the film is almost
devoid of villains. The character of Terry, whose chameleonlike loyalties
change with the social or political spectrum of his environment, is the only
character who elicits a negative response. Ford does not even treat the British
as the brazen interlopers he could have, nor do we get to meet them on a
personal basis. The repression against which Dan Gallagher and the other
rebels are fighting is shown only in the presence of the street patrols and the
dark shadows featured in the effective silhouettes of the titles. Consequently,
all attention is centered on Nolan as villain-hero, a loyal traitor.

The trio of women who at first seem to be only peripheral characters are
actually second only to Nolan; they directly or indirectly initiate most of the

action. Two of them try to give Nolan life but gain him death, and the third offers him redemption. Katie unwittingly is the cause of Nolan's crime and, although she begs for his life, she causes his entrapment. The virginal Mary also pleads for Nolan, but only after she has given the evidence which condemns him. Only Mrs. McPhillip redeems Nolan, giving him consolation and spiritual life as he dies at her feet.

The Informer is one of Ford's most award-honored films, although it is not one of his best achievements. The film earned four Academy Awards: Ford for Best Direction, Dudley Nichols for Best Screenplay, Max Steiner for Best Musical Score, and Victor McLaglen for Best Actor. These awards helped to elevate Ford to a position of importance and gained him recognition as a major Hollywood talent.

Dan Scapperotti

INTERIORS

Released: 1978
Production: Jack Rollins and Charles H. Joffe for United Artists
Direction: Woody Allen
Screenplay: Woody Allen
Cinematography: Gordon Willis
Editing: Ralph Rosenblum
Running time: 93 minutes

Principal characters:
Renata	Diane Keaton
Joey	Marybeth Hurt
Flyn	Kristin Griffith
Eve	Geraldine Page
Arthur	E. G. Marshall
Pearl	Maureen Stapleton (AA)
Mike	Sam Waterston
Frederick	Richard Jordan

Unlike many of the comics who came from the old Brooklyn tradition, Woody Allen has never been hateful. At the center of his comic personality is a little guy who wants to rob death of its potency; he is a man who wants to live. Similarly, behind the slapstick and lavish lampoons in his comic films, the Woody Allen character searches for comfort and stability. His comedies have never lacked earnestness, and they tend to make serious statements about the human condition.

In recent years, Woody Allen's films have become increasingly bittersweet, and it seemed only logical that someday he would make a film like *Interiors*. Released in 1978, *Interiors* is not Allen's first serious drama, but it is his first film that does not try to be funny. As the title suggests, the film both distills and nourishes the particulars of our lives. Without the help of background histories or dialogue, the audience is asked to learn about the characters from within their personalities. This is true from the beginning. When Arthur (E. G. Marshall), a rich, successful lawyer, is introduced to the viewer, his back is to the camera as he talks about how his life began to lose meaning after his children had grown. By being denied even a glimpse of Arthur's face, the viewer becomes immediately preoccupied with Arthur's internal condition. Then the audience is introduced to his eldest daughter, Renata (Diane Keaton). From a leather chair, she looks directly into the camera and, as if the audience were her psychoanalyst, she reflects on her mother, her childhood, and her recent creative impotence.

Woody Allen has called *Interiors* a primitive film in the sense that it simplifies the world to get to its human foundations. The story is about a family and, for the most part, concerns only their relationships with one another. Very few outsiders ever appear on the screen. In this way, the family gains a greater significance by encapsulating a much larger living unit, and the viewer's focus is deliberately restricted to the symbolic basis of a much larger structure. The treatment of the family and the individual characters enhances the film's posture; while the audience may participate in the dramatic tension, it is continually reminded of a larger, philosophical perspective, of a larger sense of things.

After the audience is introduced to Arthur and Renata, the film returns to the beginning of the story line. At the family dinner table, Arthur tells his wife and two of his daughters that he wants a separation and plans to move out of the house. Typed as a successful lawyer, Arthur has a mechanical, emotionally remote disposition. Eve (Geraldine Page), his wife, copes with the news as well as she can, though she is incapable of concealing her hurt and anger. Eve is a classic matriarchal figure. She is a woman who has done all the necessary things in the way we are taught to design our lives; she married, reared her family, and made a career for herself as an interior decorator. She suffers immensely when her ideals break apart at the seams.

Arthur and Eve's separation and ensuing divorce create the central tension of the plot, while the subplots concern the stories of their three daughters, Renata, Joey (Marybeth Hurt), and Flyn (Kristin Griffith). Renata is a poet whose work is well received by the critics. She is married to Frederick (Richard Jordan), a writer of novels which are published but apparently do not sell well. Renata is, perhaps, too successful for her husband; they maintain a turbulent, violent marriage. Frederick drinks heavily and is sometimes spiteful; he pities himself for his failings and is only antagonized by Renata's attempts at helpful reinforcement. Renata, though occasionally tormented by self-doubt and prone to solitary, emotional outbursts, is driven to perfection at the expense of understanding others. She devotes very little time to her anguished mother, whom she knows is deluding herself with an unwarranted hope of reconciliation with Arthur, and actually encourages the fantasies.

Unlike Renata, Joey takes every opportunity to remind Eve of the futility of her hopefulness. It is obvious that the two sisters have been extremely competitive, and Joey is referred to as the smartest child, though she is tormented by a lack of focus. She is a failed writer and a failed actress who shifts from one meaningless job to another. Though sensitive, she is also stubborn, bitter, and melodramatic. Joey lives with Mike (Sam Waterston), a political activist filmmaker. Their relationship teeters on Joey's confused self-absorption. When she becomes pregnant, he tries to persuade her to settle down and have the baby. Joey, of course, is not ready to sacrifice her own ambiguous aspirations.

Flyn is strikingly different from her sisters and the most detached from the family unit. She is an actress who lives in California and makes mediocre television movies. Her smile, hair, and supply of cocaine are her greatest concerns.

As the film proceeds, the viewer becomes aware that Arthur has requested a divorce in order to marry another woman. The daughters and sons-in-law are gathered together over dinner to meet Arthur's fiancée; and they assemble once again at their wedding. The woman, Pearl (Maureen Stapleton), stands in contrast to the family members. Although she lacks both intellectual and conversational refinement, she is a giving, loving, and energetic woman. Pearl has decent, uncomplicated ideas of right and wrong, and an unselfish belief in life and happiness. At the wedding, she dances with Arthur, with the young men, and with two of the daughters; Joey rejects her out of bitterness. All along, it is clear that Renata is most happy when she can believe that everyone else is stable, thus allowing herself the freedom to perfect her own life. Consequently, she tries to reinforce Pearl and Arthur, though she too is visibly troubled by the situation. Her brooding husband, Frederick, becomes drunk after the ceremony, flirts with Flyn, and later attempts to rape her. The family's attempts to have a good time during this traditionally happy occasion during these understated wedding scenes constitute the greatest dramatic tension of the film.

After dark, when Arthur and Pearl have gone to bed, the attention focuses on Joey, gazing sullenly into her own private abyss. She begins speaking to her mother, who was not present at the wedding. As if a part of Joey's imagination, a ghostly profile of Eve's face appears from the darkness of the porch. Joey, too withdrawn to recognize her mother's condition, again condemns her for pursuing Arthur. After hearing voices, Pearl comes down the stairs and startles the defeated Eve, who then turns and runs out into the ocean to her death. Ironically, the whole family is finally reunited at Eve's funeral, which ends the film.

Alongside, and in contrast to, the emotional and psychological struggles of the plot, *Interiors* is a visually impressive motion picture. Together, Woody Allen and cinematographer Gordon Willis create serenity through simplicity; each frame's composition complements its predecessor. As in many of Ingmar Bergman's films, there is a tremendous study of the female face and figure. The colors are deliberately selected from a consistent palette. Pearl first appears in a bright red dress, visually shattering the consistency of the otherwise low-keyed composition. True to the title, many of the camera shots are of interiors; an ocean wave or the blank walls of a room. The characters themselves are often observed standing in a room looking out through a window. It is as if this studied serenity is the fulfillment the characters are searching for in their lives, which, like the ocean and the sandy beaches, will clearly remain outside of them.

The film is also successful dramatically. Geraldine Page, well-known for her stage performances, gives a splendid performance as Eve and deserved an Academy Award for her efforts, although she only garnered a nomination for Best Actress. Her Eve is gracefully understated, a sympathetic though pitiful character whose immense trust is betrayed by a greater loneliness. Similarly, Maureen Stapleton gives an outstanding portrayal of Pearl, which earned her an Oscar for Best Supporting Actress. A most memorable scene finds her dancing unabashedly alone at her wedding. Renata is an extremely challenging character to portray, but Diane Keaton succeeds impressively. Also, the performances given by Marybeth Hurt and E. G. Marshall should not be overlooked.

Interiors is remarkably objective; while the audience is sympathetic to aspects of the characters' personalities, Woody Allen does not try to persuade viewers to like his characters with music or typical mechanical techniques. Renata, for example, talks too much to say so little. E. G. Marshall is too emotionally detached and is therefore cruel. Even Eve is unjustly demanding and self-deluding. If there is a depressing aspect of the film, it lies in the characters' apparent destinies; though they all suffer immeasurably, their lives remain unchanged. Given the manner in which the film is fashioned, this results in a rather bleak and saddened perspective.

Ralph Angel

INVASION OF THE BODY SNATCHERS

Released: 1956
Production: Walter Wanger for Allied Artists
Direction: Don Siegel
Screenplay: Daniel Mainwaring; based on the novel *The Body Snatchers* by
   Jack Finney
Cinematography: Ellsworth Fredericks
Editing: Robert S. Eisen
Special effects: Milt Rice
Music: Carmen Dragon
Running time: 80 minutes

   Principal characters:
     Dr. Miles Bennel .... Kevin McCarthy
     Becky Driscoll .... Dana Wynter
     Dr. Dan Kauffman .... Larry Gates
     Jack .... King Donovan
     Theodora .... Carolyn Jones

Invasion of the Body Snatchers, made in 1956, is very much a product of its time. Based on the three-part Jack Finney story, which appeared in *Colliers* magazine in 1954 and was later rendered into a novel of the same name, the film received no significant recognition at the time of its release. Later, when B-films caught the attention of cinema critics and scholars, the picture achieved a modicum of the attention it merited. Interestingly, while *Invasion of the Body Snatchers* appeared to come and go, it left a highly profitable market in its wake for low-budget films dealing with aliens from outer space, creeping creatures, and flying saucers. The spinoffs in the science fiction and science fantasy genre cashed in on the new trend, but few endured to attain a comparable lasting stature.

Invasion of the Body Snatchers is now regarded as a leader in the genre and is acclaimed as a masterpiece of B-filmmaking. It is outstanding for its concise storytelling, precise execution, innovative style, and flexibility of interpretation. Director Don Siegel, who served an apprenticeship editing in the cutting room, has at his best always stripped a film to its essentials, packed it with action, and correctly maintained the story line. *Invasion of the Body Snatchers* is a classic example of the straightforward, uncluttered Siegel: it deals with a deeply disturbing and profound theme with a direct thrust in which there are no vectors or tangents.

Dr. Miles Bennel (Kevin McCarthy) returns to the little town of Santa Mira to find its citizens enmeshed in a growing mass hysteria. The grocer's little boy, Jimmy Grimaldi, claims his mother is not his mother; a middle-aged lady, Wilma, maintains that her uncle is not her uncle; and other examples of alienation are provided. Into this scenario enters Becky Driscoll (Dana Wynter); recently divorced and a former sweetheart of Dr. Bennel, she supplies the romantic interest and rekindled love which sustains the couple through the horrible ordeal to come.

Bennel soon discovers that aliens are invading Santa Mira, duplicating and eliminating their human counterparts by means of transfer from giant pods. The process of duplicating the townspeople happens when an exact copy of the body and detailed features of each citizen is constructed in a pod. Once the people go to sleep, the life force and consciousness of each is replaced in the new physical vehicle, but personality and emotion are altered. As a result, the "Pod people" bear only a physical resemblance to their former selves. The body is no longer a place of human emotion such as anxiety or love, faith, or hope since inside it resides the zombielike consciousness and obedient will of the alien invader.

The invasion goes further than the once-quiet and rather dull little town of Santa Mira and, in the end, begins to extend to all neighboring towns, villages, and cities. Bennel is almost helpless in his efforts to fight it alone. "You're next!" he yells at the audience, his intonation and expression becoming those of a crazed prophet of doom.

Invasion of the Body Snatchers was originally shot without the prologue, extended narration, and epilogue forced upon it by studio distributors. The prologue establishes the film's theme through a series of flashbacks as Dr. Bennel tells his harrowing tale to an incredulous police—if he can get help, and if the police and the FBI believe him, then there is hope that the invasion can be stopped. The narration has worn badly with the passage of time and, to a certain extent, the prologue and epilogue hurt the original force of the theme. Siegel is dealing with complacency and a delirium of mental anguish that are beautifully expressed in the images of the action. The trite appended narration is unnecessary and dated. In the development of hysteria, there is no rational sense—only crushed sensibility and the smashed edges of sanity. A positive epilogue may be satisfying to some but to others, it becomes an unnecessary statement, greatly weakening the bold and self-explanatory motif of the deranged individual lost on the battlefield of breaking worlds.

Given the studio distributor interference, the tight budget, and a short shooting schedule, *Invasion of the Body Snatchers* is a dazzling success in almost every way. The beautiful black-and-white cinematography of Ellsworth Fredericks reflects the dark and light corners of the mind. The play of light intensifies the element of good; the stark black shadows and blinding chiaroscuro effects achieved with car lights cutting through the darkness compel a mood of paranoia and tip the ominous portent of the story.

Milt Rice's special effects are used minimally and contribute the maximum effect: the harmless-looking pods become a terrifying spectacle as we identify them with their abhorrent mission. They are used most effectively in the famous greenhouse scene in which Dr. Bennel and Becky, with friends Jack (King Donovan) and Theodora (Carolyn Jones), discover pulsating, foaming pods that are splitting open to reveal their grotesque duplicates. In the scene, Bennel takes a pitchfork, wields it in a low angle, suggesting that he is stabbing at the audience, and plunges it forward, stabbing at a pod. The pods again are effectively used in the morning sequence in the town square. It is broad daylight and all appears to be normal. At this moment, pedestrians fill the streets and trucks pull in jammed with pods. The townsfolk walk about taking instructions and carrying the pods without question. The audience is stunned into a dread fascination, just as Bennel and Becky watch helplessly from an upstairs window.

It is the specter of the silent menace that frightens us, the deadly adversary spreading like a contagion unchecked in a seemingly normal community. What we are confronting here may be a virulent germ, a harmful ideology, or the potential for an alien takeover. Since the film's fashionable acceptance, various theories have been propounded. In this unpretentious study, Siegel has given us a variety of interpretations that all bear credibility to the degree to which the viewer reacts and identifies. The pods, and the numbed psyches resulting from them, give each of us a focus for our own paranoia, and in view of this, it seems too limiting to analyze the film as an anti-Communist manifesto or a full-scale attack on McCarthyism of the 1950's, as some critics have argued. Though these ideas reasonably may be read into the film, Siegel should be credited with digging deeper into the corners of the universal human consciousness and jabbing at it with a pitchfork pliant with possibilities. Whatever malignancy may lurk, it should be uprooted and contained; similar to the hero Binnel, we should not acquiesce or surrender; we must fight.

The final sequences of the film manifest this viewpoint. They concern the efforts of Bennel and Becky to elude the enemy and escape to get help. As they run and seek shelter in a deserted mine tunnel, they hide beneath the floorboards, perilously close to their pursuers. It is only when the aliens depart the mine to look elsewhere that Bennel leaves the exhausted Becky for a moment. After discovering the control center of the invaders—a farm operation from which the pods are dispatched—Bennel returns to Becky who, almost asleep, lies prostrate with fatigue. Siegel signals her transformation with a discordant note in the score, and as Bennel takes her in his arms, the camera, in a tight shot, pulls in on her sleepy face. Her dark eyes flicker closed for an instant; as they open, they are dilated and show no expression. Becky's consciousness has been invaded, her body snatched.

The horrified Bennel, now completely alone, rushes in panic and shock from the tunnel, clambering over the hills to the busy highway below. Crazed with fear and followed by his pursuers, he rushes headlong into the center of busy freeway traffic, shouting cries of warning to the unheeding traffic jam and finally flinging himself onto the windshield of an oncoming auto. Throughout the scene, he is met with anger and rejection. The cross-flooding lights of the speeding cars lend a nervous intensity to the hero's hysteria. He is the image of the helpless individual fighting alone to save his unknowing cosmos from its insane invasion. The epilogue which follows functions only as a device to demonstrate the credibility of the tale which Bennel begins in the prologue. The picture closes with the comforting assurance that the FBI and police will help.

The staying power of *Invasion of the Body Snatchers* as an entertainment piece and subject of genre study has been amply tried and tested over the years, and it has ascended into a position of cinematic prominence. An effort was made to remake the film in 1978, aided by brief appearances by both Kevin McCarthy and Don Siegel; this effort proved that the modest but commanding original may be imitated, but unlike its characters, it will never be duplicated.

Kevin McCarthy gives an arresting performance as Bennel and Dana Wynter supports him beautifully as the ill-fated Becky Driscoll. Among the supporting actors, Larry Gates stands out as the psychiatrist turned alien, Dr. Dan Kauffman. The film has a strong script written by Daniel Mainwaring, which, although hardly subtle, is steady. The superb lighting and special effects complement each other, providing variants of *film noir*—all resulting in an inspired piece of moviemaking.

With *Invasion of the Body Snatchers*, Siegel ventured into a territory where masters of filmmaking have often feared to tread. Through his direction, the film's startling style and genuine lack of pretention induce the moviegoer to think and ponder. *Invasion of the Body Snatchers* is a landmark film; it raised the scope and quality of its genre, and provided cinematic art and gripping entertainment.

Elizabeth McDermott

IT HAPPENED ONE NIGHT

Released: 1934
Production: Harry Cohn for Columbia (AA)
Direction: Frank Capra (AA)
Screenplay: Robert Riskin (AA) and Frank Capra (uncredited); based on a
  story "Night Bus" by Samuel Hopkins Adams
Cinematography: Joseph Walker
Editing: Gene Havlick
Running time: 105 minutes

> *Principal characters:*
> Peter Warne .... Clark Gable (AA)
> Ellie Andrews .... Claudette Colbert (AA)
> Alexander Andrews .... Walter Connolly
> Mr. Shapeley .... Roscoe Karns
> King Westley .... Jameson Thomas
> Bus Driver .... Ward Bond

Made at a studio regarded as second-rate, with a reluctant star and script
trouble, *It Happened One Night* was an unexpected success. However, it may
have been precisely these conditions which allowed the film to become a
runaway hit at the box office and at the Academy Awards, where it won all
five major honors, a feat unduplicated until *One Flew Over the Cuckoo's Nest*
(1975) forty-one years later.

Later in his career, director Frank Capra was able to sign such stars as
Barbara Stanwyck and Gary Cooper for a film even before they saw a script,
but in 1933, when he was trying to cast a film for which he and Robert Riskin
had written a script (based on a *Cosmopolitan* magazine story by Samuel
Hopkins Adams), all the actors and actresses they contacted turned it down.
Luckily for Capra and for film audiences ever since, M-G-M at that time
wanted to discipline Clark Gable, so they loaned him to Columbia, a studio
which was then held in such low esteem that it was widely known as "Siberia"
or "Poverty Row." Gable did not want to do the film, but under the rigid
studio contracts of the 1930's, he had little choice. Claudette Colbert was
signed to play the heroine, and filming began with nearly everyone involved
thinking that the project was nothing more than a routine picture. Even
Capra, so tired from all his work to get the project started, just wanted to
get it finished. However, this very atmosphere may have, in the end, contributed a natural, unpretentious air to the film in a time when major studios
often spoiled their prestigious films by using a too-reverential approach to
both the subject and the stars.

Capra also gives credit for the quality and appeal of the film to his friend
Myles Connolly, who suggested improvements in an early version of the

script. Connolly's main suggestion was to change the hero from a vagabond painter to a newspaper reporter so that audiences could better identify with him.

The theme of *It Happened One Night* is one that was quite popular in Hollywood romantic films of the 1930's and early 1940's: love triumphing over social and economic differences. At the opening of the film we learn that Ellie Andrews (Claudette Colbert), a rich man's daughter, has just married King Westley (Jameson Thomas), a man of her own social class, but also a ne'er-do-well aviator. Her father, (Walter Connolly), opposes him and wants to have the marriage annulled. Next we meet Peter Warne (Clark Gable), a reporter who has just lost his job for sending a story to his newspaper in free verse. It might seem unlikely that these two would ever meet, much less fall in love, but when Ellie escapes from her father's yacht by diving overboard, determined to make her way from Florida to New York to join King Westley, circumstances bring them together.

They meet quarreling over a seat on the night bus to New York. Ellie has never ridden on a bus before, but is doing so to escape detection by her father; Peter is traveling on the bus because that is the only fare he can afford. Their first "conversation" ends with Peter saying, "Now listen, I'm in a very ugly mood. I put up a stiff battle for that seat. So if it's just the same to you— scram." Ellie, however, does not scram, and the two eventually travel all the way from Florida to Pennsylvania together.

During the trip a romance develops between the two without either of them quite realizing it. After discovering her true identity, Peter regards Ellie as a spoiled brat who thinks her money can get her anything she wants, and she regards him as an uncouth opportunist. However, several times circumstances force them to pretend that they are married: to discourage the amorous attentions of a traveling salesman, to save money on motels (called autocamps in the film), and to fool two detectives her father has sent looking for her.

The first night they spend together in a motel is a justly famous highlight of the film. A washed-out bridge stops the bus and makes it necessary for all the passengers to find accommodations for the night. It is a situation Ellie is completely unequipped to handle on her own. Indeed, this trip is her first attempt at doing things by herself rather than having them done for her; by contrast, Peter is used to living by his wits and quickly realizes that they must register as husband and wife to save money. When Ellie gets indignant and asks what gave him the idea she would stand for such a scheme, Peter explains that he is only interested in her as a headline. He is a newspaper reporter, he tells her, and needs to sell the story of her "mad flight to happiness" to his editor to get his job back. He will, therefore, help her reach King Westley for this reason, but if she rebels, he will turn her over to her father.

Peter then explains that he likes privacy. Stringing a rope between the two beds in their room, he hangs a blanket over it to divide the room into two parts. "The walls of Jericho" he calls it, but Ellie is dubious about the arrangement and refuses to go to her side of the wall. Peter tries to reassure her by telling her that he does not have a trumpet to bring the walls tumbling down as Joshua did in the Bible. When she still does not move, Peter begins taking off his clothes one article at a time while discoursing on the various ways men take off their clothes. When he has removed everything except his trousers, Ellie hurriedly retreats to her side, acquiescing in the arrangement.

Another highlight of the film is the hitchhiking scene. They have had to leave the bus because another passenger has also recognized Ellie, and Peter is becoming quite smug about his ability to take care of the helpless rich girl. He tells her they will have to thumb a ride and explains in great detail the technique of hitchhiking. When he tries to demonstrate his infallible methods, however, he is totally unsuccessful. After watching car after car pass without even slowing down, Ellie finally says she will try, and by lifting her skirt above the knee she stops the first vehicle. The man who picks them up later tries to steal Peter's suitcase, but Peter runs after him and returns with both the suitcase and the car, and he and Ellie continue their journey by automobile.

Finally Ellie realizes that she loves Peter and tells him so (in a conversation conducted over the "walls of Jericho"). They do not immediately get together and live happily ever after, however. When she says she loves him, Peter is taken aback, never having considered the idea. By the time he ponders and accepts the idea, Ellie is asleep. He leaves for New York to obtain some money from his editor because he does not want to be penniless when he proposes to her. After his departure, Ellie is awakened by the owner of the motel, and finding Peter gone, thinks she has been abandoned; she therefore has her father come to get her. Once they return to New York, they prepare for a large formal wedding for her and King Westley, although neither she nor her father is enthusiastic about the idea.

Shortly before the wedding Peter goes to see Ellie's father. Both her father and Ellie assume that Peter wants to collect the ten-thousand-dollar reward that was offered, but he asks for only $39.60, the exact amount of his expenses for the trip. Under the father's questioning he even admits to being in love with Ellie. "But don't hold that against me," he says. "I'm a little screwy myself." The wedding ceremony begins, but on the way to the altar her father explains the situation to Ellie and tells her he has a car waiting for her if she wants to escape. At the moment in the ceremony she is asked to say "I will," Ellie picks up the train of her wedding dress and rushes off to Peter's waiting car.

In the last scene we see the outside of a motel cabin, then we hear the sound of a trumpet and see a blanket fall to the floor as the film ends.

In *It Happened One Night* Clark Gable gives one of his best performances. His Peter Warne is tough, masculine, and cynical on the surface, but has a certain tenderness and romanticism underneath. Gable makes both facets of his personality perfectly credible. In addition, the character Gable plays does some acting of his own. For the benefit of some friends he plays the ultra tough guy, telling off his boss on the telephone, although we know that the boss is no longer on the line. Later he pretends to be a gangster to frighten off the passenger who has also recognized Ellie, and he and Claudette Colbert do a humorous scene as a quarreling married couple so that a pair of detectives will not realize who Ellie is. Capra summed it up best: "I believe it was the only picture in which Gable was ever allowed to play himself: the fun-loving, boyish, attractive, he-man rogue that was the *real* Gable.

As Ellie Andrews, Claudette Colbert perfectly complements Gable in what is arguably the best role of her career. She must show both sides of Ellie, the spoiled rich girl who expects the bus to wait for her while she has a leisurely breakfast, and the spunky woman with whom Peter falls in love almost against his will. It is not easy to make both antagonism and romance credible in one relationship, but Gable and Colbert do it to perfection.

Director Frank Capra later became famous for celebrating the virtues of the common man in such films as *Mr. Smith Goes to Washington* (1939) and *It's a Wonderful Life* (1946). It is a theme which is important in *It Happened One Night* and is particularly underscored in the final scenes in which the down-to-earth reporter can barely tolerate the elaborate and meaningless extravagance of the rich. This theme is not, however, as important as it is in later Capra pictures; instead, the film is chiefly a romantic comedy. Capra proves himself a master of the genre as, with careful pacing, he builds the characterizations upon which the comedy depends, so that *It Happened One Night* is more a comedy of character than of events or surprises. Indeed, the many imitations of the film in the 1930's and the remake *You Can't Run Away from It* (1956) are so inferior to the original that they merely reinforce one's appreciation of the artistry of Frank Capra.

Timothy W. Johnson

IT'S A WONDERFUL LIFE

Released: 1946
Production: Frank Capra for Liberty Films; released by RKO/Radio
Direction: Frank Capra
Screenplay: Frances Goodrich, Albert Hackett, and Frank Capra, with additional scenes by Jo Swerling; based on the story "The Greatest Gift" by Philip Van Doren Stern
Cinematography: Joseph Walker and Joseph Biroc
Editing: William Hornbeck
Sound: Richard Van Hessen, Clem Portman, and John Aalberg
Music: Dmitri Tiomkin
Running time: 129 minutes

Principal characters:

George Bailey	James Stewart
Mary Hatch	Donna Reed
Mr. Potter	Lionel Barrymore
Uncle Billy	Thomas Mitchell
Clarence	Henry Travers
Mrs. Bailey	Beulah Bondi
Violet Bick	Gloria Grahame
Mr. Gower	H. B. Warner
Bert	Ward Bond
Ernie	Frank Faylan
Pa Bailey	Samuel S. Hinds
Cousin Tilly	Mary Treen
Bodyguard	Frank Hagney
Nick	Sheldon Leonard

When Frank Capra returned to Hollywood from his service in the Army during World War II, he was a colonel and had been awarded the Distinguished Service Medal. He had left Hollywood, one of its foremost directors, to make films at home and abroad for the War Department. He worked on all seven pictures in the *Why We Fight* series, including the Oscar-winning *Prelude to War*; another series beginning with *Know Your Ally* and *Know Your Enemy*; the *Army-Navy Screen Magazine*; *The Negro Soldier in World War II*; *The Battle of Britain*; *Two Down and One to Go*; and several other films which he codirected. Now, in the spring of 1945, he was a civilian once again, back in Hollywood looking for a new project. Together with three other colonels who had seen service in the war—William Wyler, George Stevens, and Samuel Briskin—he formed Liberty Films, of which he was President; and the company committed itself to make nine pictures for release through RKO/Radio.

As of yet, Capra had no film in mind to make as his first for Liberty Films.

One day Charles Koerner, head of production at RKO, came to his office to tell him about an original story, "The Greatest Gift," which he had purchased for RKO from Philip Van Doren Stern. It had been written as a Christmas card to be mailed to Stern's friends, but Koerner saw a full feature film in its few paragraphs, bought it, and had already spent a fortune hiring three writers—Dalton Trumbo, Marc Connelly, and Clifford Odets—to make a screenplay of the story. So far none of their efforts had come to fruition, and Koerner wanted Capra to read the story and see what he thought. Capra read it and was overjoyed; it seemed to him to be the story he had been looking for all his life. Liberty bought "The Greatest Gift" for the fifty thousand dollars Koerner had paid for it, and Koerner threw in the three previous screenplays as part of the bargain. Capra, however, wanted a fresh start; he hired Frances Goodrich and Albert Hackett as writers, and later wrote some scenes on his own. The new title for the venture was *It's a Wonderful Life*.

Seldom has a picture been produced with more love. Capra got his old friend James Stewart, who had also been a colonel in the Air Corps, to play the leading role and the rest of the cast fell easily into place. Three actors—Lionel Barrymore, Donna Reed, and Gloria Grahame—were borrowed from M-G-M; the others, for the most part, were enlisted from what Capra has called the Ford-Capra stock company: brilliant character actors such as Thomas Mitchell, H. B. Warner, Beulah Bondi, Ward Bond, Frank Faylen, Samuel S. Hinds, Mary Treen, Frank Hagney, plus two talented additions to the ranks—Sheldon Leonard and Henry Travers.

The hero of *It's a Wonderful Life* is George Bailey (James Stewart), who never planned to be a hometown boy. Born, reared, and educated in the typical small American town of Bedford Falls, George is a victim of circumstances. He had always wanted to travel, to see the world and develop beyond Bedford Falls; but when his father died, George was committed to keeping alive the Bailey Building and Loan Company as the only alternative to allowing Bedford Falls to fall completely under the ownership of greedy and unscrupulous Henry F. Potter (Lionel Barrymore).

George's sacrifices begin at once. He gives up a trip abroad for which his father had paid in order for his brother to go to college, while he himself goes to work for the Bailey Company. He falls in love with and marries Mary Hatch (Donna Reed), but when there is a run on the Bailey Building and Loan Company, fomented by Mr. Potter, George is forced to use his honeymoon money to bolster the dwindling assets. Ending the bank day with only one dollar left, George goes home to the dilapidated old mansion which Mary has taken over to begin their future life together.

George is doomed to stay in Bedford Falls, the best-liked man in town. He and his wife have children, and the machinations of Mr. Potter seem to have come to a halt. Then Mr. Potter, obsessed with the idea of owning the town, again starts trying to gain control of the Bailey Company. When

George's partner Uncle Billy (Thomas Mitchell) loses several thousand dollars, George is tempted to give up. It is the Christmas season, but there is no love and the spirit of giving is gone in George's soul. His town has become the wreck of an American dream, turned sour by one selfish, evil man. All George wants is out—for good.

While standing on the bridge over the river at Bedford Falls, George is thinking about something that Potter had said to him about being worth more dead than alive when a stranger calls out for help from the ice water below. George jumps to his rescue, forgetting for the moment that he had been thinking about killing himself just moments before. They are both pulled from the water by the tollhouse keeper, who takes them into the tollhouse to dry off. The stranger, whose name is Clarence Oddbody (Henry Travers) tells George that he is his guardian angel, but he is an angel who has not earned his wings, which he will get if he can keep George alive. George, however, wishes that he had never been born; so Mr. Oddbody describes how different life would have been in Bedford Falls had George never lived. For example, when George was young and worked in a drugstore, he averted a tragedy when the distracted pharmacist, Mr. Gower (H. B. Warner), accidentally put poison into a prescription he was preparing. George learns, thanks to Mr. Oddbody, that he has unknowingly become the town's most important citizen, and has been involved, directly or indirectly, in the fates of almost all the townspeople.

Later, Bert (Ward Bond) the policeman finds George on the bridge and demands to know where he has been, since the whole town is looking for him. George by now is glad to be alive. Meanwhile, the citizens of Bedford Falls, filled with good will and the Christmas spirit, want to prove their faith in George. They bring him all the cash they can scrape together so that once more George can defeat old Mr. Potter. The miracle of friendship allows him and his town to celebrate. Men who have real friends know the best there is in life. Good deeds, as Everyman learned in the old morality play, are all that follow each man beyond the span of his earthly days.

It's a Wonderful Life was Capra's own favorite film of all the features he directed, and it was James Stewart's favorite as well. It received a goodly share of praise from the critics, although some were unmoved by its moments of fantasy and earnest Americanism. The public, nevertheless, greatly admired the picture, which earned five Academy Award nominations, but no Oscar; the major share of the Oscars went to the superb *The Best Years of Our Lives*, directed by William Wyler for Samuel Goldwyn as Wyler's last film before he joined Liberty Films.

As many times as a filmgoer sees *It's a Wonderful Life*, he cannot fail to be moved by certain sequences, in particular the scenes of the high school dance held in the school gymnasium. The sequence was shot at Beverly Hills High School, and when somebody in the crew mentioned that the dance floor was movable and that underneath it was a swimming pool, Capra could not resist taking advantage of the unique circumstance. Thus was born the gimmick of the Charleston contest: one of George's rivals pulls the switch which moves the floor apart, until George and Mary Hatch, performing a hectic Charleston on the very edge of the separating floor, finally tumble down into the water, followed by nearly everyone present, including the principal.

It's a Wonderful Life is still a much-loved film, with its theme that no man is a failure as long as he has one friend, and that every man's life touches everybody he knows, so that no man ever lives alone. Many fans have made a practice of viewing it on Christmas Eve, just as Capra himself still does in his own home. It is a true holiday film, intended to spread good will and cheer, which it does liberally; it is, in fact, a kind of modern morality movie, not unlike Dickens' *A Christmas Carol*, with James Stewart playing a character similar to Bob Cratchit, a worthy hero whose faith is put to the test, and Lionel Barrymore portraying a modern-day Ebenezer Scrooge.

DeWitt Bodeen

JANE EYRE

Released: 1944
Production: William Goetz for Twentieth Century-Fox
Direction: Robert Stevenson
Screenplay: Aldous Huxley, Robert Stevenson, and John Houseman; based
  on the novel of the same name by Charlotte Brontë
Cinematography: George Barnes
Editing: Walter Thompson
Music: Bernard Herrmann
Running time: 96 minutes

Principal characters:
Jane Eyre .... Joan Fontaine
Edward Rochester .... Orson Welles
Helen Burns .... Elizabeth Taylor
Adele Varens .... Margaret O'Brien
Jane Eyre (younger) .... Peggy Ann Garner
Brocklehurst .... Henry Daniell
Mrs. Reed .... Agnes Moorehead
Dr. Rivers .... John Sutton

Transforming a classic of literature into a film is a risky undertaking. If the filmmaker strays too far from the original, he is attacked by purists for adulterating a classic. If, on the other hand, he remains painstakingly faithful to the original, he is accused of not exploring sufficiently the unique possibilities offered by the medium of film. This confusion has probably contributed to the high failure rate, both artistically and financially, of classics adapted into film from Shakespeare to Hemingway. In adapting Charlotte Brontë's nineteenth century novel *Jane Eyre*, the filmmakers chose a middle course. They chose to remain generally faithful to the events of the novel while altering or, rather, heightening the spirit.

Of the two most famous Brontë sisters (Emily, who wrote *Wuthering Heights*, and Charlotte), Charlotte was clearly the more conventional. The difference is reflected in their novels. *Wuthering Heights* is a tortured, romantic story of two lovers (Catherine and Heathcliff) who through the intensity of their passion drive each other mad. It is a dark, brooding tale with gothic settings: isolated manor houses, windy moors, and desolate heaths. The story is full of torment and death. *Jane Eyre*, while working within the same romantic, gothic tradition, downplays the darker, more Satanic elements of life in order to emphasize an angelic, positive vision. Jane is guided by a strong, self-righteous, religious mentality unlike anything Catherine ever possessed. Her behavior is more determined by her conscience than by any passion. Her pivotal decision not to stay with Rochester because of his earlier indiscretion, only returning to him after he has been purified by fire—his mad wife, the indiscretion, is killed in the same blaze—is her way of demonstrating these moral priorities.

The film version of *Jane Eyre* is a curious blend, an attempt to combine the plot and characters of Charlotte Brontë's novel with the mood and spirit of her sister Emily's story. Very little of the self-righteous moralizing so prevalent in the original novel remains in this version. In the film, the desertion of Edward Rochester (Orson Welles) by Jane (Joan Fontaine) upon discovering the existence of his wife seems more motivated by jealousy than any convention of morality. In the same way, the only major section of the book to be completely eliminated is Jane's stay, after leaving Rochester, with the minister St. John Rivers. It is during this sojourn that Jane grows even closer to God by finding her spiritual bearings. Instead, in the film, she returns to her dying aunt to nurse her. As if in reparation for deleting the more religious content of the book, a character, Dr. Rivers (John Sutton), is introduced into the film; he follows Jane through childhood, school, and into womanhood, acting as the conscience of the film and verbally establishing the guidelines Jane should follow.

As the moralistic character of *Jane Eyre* recedes, the romantic, gothic components come to the fore. The film opens with Jane being brought from the darkness to face a disapproving aunt and a sinister-looking Brocklehurst (Henry Daniell), the headmaster at Lowood Institution where a recalcitrant Jane is to be sent for "reformation." The two adults are shot from a low angle and with a wide lens, subjectifying the experience, forcing the audience to see them from the point of view of a frightened child. Lowood Institution itself is converted, in the film, into a place of unrelenting misery by emphasizing the medieval tortures inflicted on the children: forced marches in circles in the pouring rain, shaved heads because of minor infractions of the rules, severe beatings without justification, and so on. In this place Jane makes her first friend, Helen Burns (played by a young Elizabeth Taylor). But even the solace of friendship is denied her. Helen dies of pneumonia after being forced to parade in the rain. After this incident (Helen dies while sleeping with Jane), Jane's rebelliousness slowly turns to quiet acceptance. She excels at Lowood, hiding whatever bitterness she may have under a cloak of aloofness.

Upon reaching womanhood, Jane decides to venture into the world. She advertises for a position as a governess and receives an offer. Jane's arrival at Thornfield Manor, where her pupil lives, and her subsequent love affair with its troubled master, Edward Rochester, is laden with terror and mystery. Thornfield Manor in the film differs considerably from that of the novel. It is photographed in fogs and shadows, increasing its aura of mystery and doom. It resembles in appearance and mood the gothic castles so prevalent in early romantic literature. Cavernous fireplaces, hidden corridors, moldy dungeons, hidden staircases, and dark towers characterize the manor. As with all literary gothic castles there is a terrible secret at the heart of this mansion. Early during her stay there Jane observes some strange, unexplained phenomena: cackling laughter from behind walls, doors locked and bolted against entry, figures scurrying about in the dark, and fires set by unknown persons (one such fire almost immolates a sleeping Rochester).

The mystery of Thornfield Manor is but an extension of the mystery of its master. Edward Rochester, as played by Orson Welles, is a high Byronic character. Jane's first meeting with him is on a foggy night while walking about the grounds. He emerges from the fog on a black stallion that rears at the sight of Jane and throws its rider. Like his stallion and his mansion, Rochester is a dark-tempered, tortured, fiery figure who has buried some deep wound behind his own walls of cynicism. Jane senses this mystery, this affinity, and falls in love with him. Like the affair between Catherine and Heathcliff, their affair is, although far more subdued, one of twisted intensity. But passion ultimately triumphs and Jane and Rochester are to be married. Calamity strikes during the ceremony as the brother of Rochester's mad wife exposes his secret. Jane is aghast. Deciding to reveal everything and put himself at Jane's mercy, he takes the wedding party back to the manor to show them his wife. As he opens the bolted door leading into the cavernous darkness, the same cackling sound Jane heard earlier reverberates, and two clawlike hands reach out tearing at Rochester, almost dragging him into the pit. Jane, however, is unable to forgive. Emotions of jealousy and betrayal preclude any reasonable actions, so she departs for her hated childhood home.

There she nurses her dying aunt and waits, not knowing for what, until one night during a storm she hears Rochester's voice on the wind calling her. Unable to repress her passion any longer, she returns to Thornfield. There she discovers the charred remains of the manor and hears from a servant how Rochester's wife burned the mansion to the ground, destroying herself and blinding Rochester in the process. The object of her jealousy gone and Rochester now purified by fire, Jane embraces him as they gaze out into the new light.

Orson Welles's presence in the film extends far beyond his role as actor. The look of the film, especially in the scenes with Welles, strikingly resembles that of his own films. Chiaroscuro lighting; deep-focus photography; overlapping dialogue; tracking camera shots; mannerist acting; even the presence of Mercury Theater regulars such as Agnes Moorehead, producer John Houseman (who acted as screenwriter on the film), and composer Bernard Herrmann point to the influence of Welles. In addition, Welles had adapted this novel earlier for his own Mercury Theater company. This, along with his legendary penchant for "taking over" productions with which he is involved no matter how peripherally, would seem to give further credence to this contention.

James Ursini

JAWS

Released: 1975
Production: Richard D. Zanuck and David Brown for Universal
Direction: Steven Spielberg
Screenplay: Peter Benchley and Carl Gottlieb; based on the novel of the same
   name by Peter Benchley
Cinematography: Bill Butler
Editing: Verna Fields (AA)
Sound: Robert L. Hoyt, Roger Herman, Earl Madery, and John Carter (AA)
Music: John Williams (AA)
Running time: 124 minutes

    Principal characters:
       Brody .... Roy Scheider
       Quint .... Robert Shaw
       Hooper .... Richard Dreyfuss
       Ellen Brody .... Lorraine Gary
       Vaughan .... Murray Hamilton

Jaws was the box-office sensation of 1975 and the number-one hit movie of the decade until 1977's *Star Wars*, at a time when the success or failure of a few blockbusters began to determine the course of the entire motion picture industry. Similar to several of the other huge hit movies of the 1970's, *Jaws* began as a novel, which was then sold to a film company prior to its publication. Yet *Jaws* remains solidly a director's film from the first ominous chords of John Williams' moody score. In this, his second directed film, Steven Spielberg demonstrates remarkable ability to develop a standard scary story into a sweeping adventure with the power to capture audiences and hold them in breathless suspense.

The plot of *Jaws* is deceptively simple. A marauding Great White Shark of tremendous size begins attacking bathers in the waters off Amity Township, a New England seaside resort. Local Sheriff Brody (Roy Scheider) believes the warning of young icthyologist Hooper (Richard Dreyfuss) that the killings will continue, but yields to the pressure of Amity mayor Vaughan (Murray Hamilton) not to close the beaches. As the Fourth of July weekend approaches, the mayor fears the loss of Amity's tourist revenue more than the possibility of additional tragedy.

When the monster shark strikes again, the beaches are finally closed. Crusty shark hunter Quint (Robert Shaw) is retained by the Township to pursue and destroy the menace and sets out in his boat *Orca*, accompanied by Hooper and Brody. Guilt-ridden over his earlier decision to allow the beaches to remain open, Brody goes to sea in an effort to regain his self-esteem.

The initial confidence of the hunt is clouded by the uncanny intelligence of the monster shark, which seems to be endowed with supernormal, perhaps diabolical powers. Compounding the peril, Quint turns the hunt into a personal vendetta, restraining Hooper from using "scientific" means to kill the creature and finally wrecking the boat's radio when Brody tries to summon aid. The shark cripples the *Orca*—Hooper disappears, apparently gobbled up like bait in a shark cage, and Quint is eaten alive as the terrified Brody looks on. Just when his prospects for survival seem nil, however, Brody summons his courage in a last-gasp offensive and defeats the seemingly unkillable monster with ingenuity, luck, and force of will. With the *Orca* sunk, Brody is joined by a miraculously unharmed Hooper, and together they paddle to dry land.

As a fright film *Jaws* is without peer. The bulk of the carnage occurs largely offscreen; the touches of gore that are seen are used effectively to increase one's dread of the next shark attack. *Jaws* achieves its thrills by appealing to the viewer's imaginary senses of adventure and danger, unlike, for example, *The Exorcist* (1973), whose offensive images and sound track bludgeon the audience into submission. *Jaws* is humane in that the audience is encouraged to care for every victim, and Spielberg's sympathetic direction ensures the viewer's direct involvement in each attack.

This first portion of the film delineates the simple yet powerful story and moves the action to a more intimate arena: three men in a boat against the unknown. In terms of pacing, logic, and pure suspenseful storytelling skill, this part of *Jaws* is impeccable. Spielberg's ability to manipulate his audience is evident in the ease with which he continually works against viewer expectations. No matter when or where one anticipates the shark's next appearance, it always bursts at the actors from an unexpected direction and at an unexpected moment; yet Spielberg and Academy Award-winning film editor Verna Fields avoid lame devices such as shock cuts or sound track stingers. Humor is used to good advantage as well. The most chilling episode in the film happens while Brody is ladling bait off the *Orca*'s stern. It is a scene in which it seems appropriate for the shark to appear, but Spielberg outlasts the audience's expectations by suspending the action through several lines of dialogue. Just when the punch line of Brody's humor disarms the audience, the shark attacks, and the jolt is twice as strong.

The film's few technical and dramatic rough edges are nullified by the strength of its editing. Even when revealed as an obvious mechanical prop, the monster shark remains terrifying. By the time it is fully viewed, the audience is so rattled that a cardboard fish would probably suffice to frighten. The high state of tension created throughout the film overrides a breach or two of logic (such as the fact that Hooper's shark-killer kit contains sure-fire devices whose uses are never considered). Also audience-accepted are extremes of character actions (for example, only after the fact does Quint's radio-smashing episode seem the result of plot necessity rather than genuine character motivation).

Spielberg draws precise and economic performances from his actors. Roy Scheider is a particularly apt choice for the part of the sea-hating New York cop whose flight from the urban jungle lands him, ironically, in a more basic struggle for survival. When Scheider, who was already familiar as a detective hero of both *The French Connection* (1971), and *The Seven-Ups* (1973), empties his service magnum into the whale, Spielberg seems to dispose of the monster while at the same time ending the cycle of the early 1970's "cop" films whose heroes used the handgun as a viable defense.

Richard Dreyfuss carries most of the comedy yet portrays a character whose professional knowledge as an ichthyologist helps the viewer to participate better in the strategies between man and beast being battled out on the high seas. Lorraine Gary's role is also mostly support, but it is also to the author's credit that the novel's Hooper-Mrs. Brody love affair was dropped for the film version. Robert Shaw's mannered performance as the eccentric Quint spikes the tension of the man-against-shark conflict, as in the scene when he retells the grisly fate of the crew of the ship *Indianapolis*, but his obsession sometimes makes him too closely resemble an inferior Ahab on his own quest.

Although its plot borrows heavily from *Moby Dick*, *Jaws* is not exploitive. It attempts to be no more than a good product of the monster-genre films its director clearly admires. Examples from them abound: the underwater stalking of victims is reminiscent of scenes in *The Creature from the Black Lagoon* (1954); the shot in which Brody sets up his defense communications on the holiday beach is a direct copy of a scene in *Forbidden Planet* (1956); and the subjective smash-zoom shot of Brody's shocked face as he witnesses a shark attack comes from Hitchcock's *Vertigo* (1958). These adaptations of past scenes and devices become creatively new under the direction of Steven Spielberg, and *Jaws* stands independently as a superior adventure-thriller.

Glenn Erickson

THE JAZZ SINGER

Released: 1927
Production: Jack L. Warner for Warner Bros. and the Vitaphone Corporation
(AA Special Award)
Direction: Alan Crosland
Screenplay: Alfred A. Cohn; based on the story "The Day of Atonement"
and the play of the same name by Samson Raphaelson
Cinematography: Hal Mohr
Editing: Harold McCord
Music direction: Louis Silvers
Title design: Jack Jarmuth
Running time: 88 minutes

Principal characters:
Jakie Rabinowitz (Jack Robin) .... Al Jolson
Jakie Rabinowitz (younger) .... Bobby Gordon
Mary Dale .... May McAvoy
Cantor Rabinowitz .... Warner Oland
Sara Rabinowitz .... Eugenie Besserer
Cantor Josef Rosenblatt .... Himself

The Jazz Singer was not the first Vitaphone feature, nor for that matter was it Al Jolson's first screen appearance. Yet through the years, it has taken on mythological proportions as the feature film more responsible than any other for the introduction of sound to the motion picture and as the film which made Al Jolson a legend.

Warner Bros. dubbed the film a "supreme triumph," and certainly, in 1927, it was. In transferring Samson Raphaelson's popular Broadway play to the screen, Warner Bros. spared no effort, shooting on location at New York's Winter Garden Theater and on Orchard Street, and at Chicago's State Theater. Israel's leading cantor, Josef Rosenblatt, who died in Jerusalem in 1933, was engaged to make his screen debut. George Jessel, who had already appeared in a Vitaphone short and was the star of the Broadway production, was announced to play the lead; but for reasons which today are unclear, he was replaced by Al Jolson. For the score, Warner Bros. selected a host of popular songs, from "My Gal Sal" and "Waiting for the Robert E. Lee" to "Dirty Hands, Dirty Face," "Toot, Toot, Tootsie," and, of course, "Mammy." "Blue Skies," written a year earlier by Irving Berlin, became a hit thanks to The Jazz Singer, as did the film's theme song, "Mother O' Mine." Musical director Louis Silvers deserves tremendous credit for the score, which brilliantly intermixes music as varied as works by Tchaikowsky and Debussy with Kol Nidre and popular songs. It was a combined effort by the entire Warner Bros. studio personnel, from production chiefs Jack L. Warner and Darryl F. Zanuck to the Vitaphone engineers; no one man or woman was responsible for the success of *The Jazz Singer*. It had a competent director in Alan Crosland, whose film career began with the Edison Company and who was responsible for many of Warner Bros. early sound films, including the first Vitaphone feature, *Don Juan* (1926). Veteran Hal Mohr was behind the camera. Samson Raphaelson went on to script many of Ernst Lubitsch's most famous productions, including *One Hour with You* (1932), *The Smiling Lieutenant* (1931), *Trouble in Paradise* (1932), and *The Merry Widow* (1934). May McAvoy was one of the most popular of Warner Bros. contract actresses, while Eugenie Besserer had been one of the screen's first stars, with the Selig Company.

Samson Raphaelson claimed to have received the inspiration for his original story, "The Day of Atonement," on which *The Jazz Singer* is based, after seeing Al Jolson perform "Where the Black-Eyed Susans Grow" in *Robinson Crusoe Jr.*, while the young Raphaelson was a junior at the University of Illinois. Warner Bros. publicized *The Jazz Singer* as Jolson's own story; and in that the singer was one of America's favorite jazz singers and that he entered show business against his cantor father's wishes, they were correct.

The story of *The Jazz Singer* opens with the young Jakie Rabinowitz (Bobby Gordon) singing popular songs at Muller's Cafe, where his cantor father finds him and drags him home. Cantor Rabinowitz (Warner Oland) is determined that his son shall continue in the family tradition and also become a cantor. "I will teach him he shall never again use his voice for such low songs," Cantor Rabinowitz tells his homely wife (Eugenie Besserer), whose large bosom seems built for one purpose, that of engulfing her son in warmth and love. Yet despite the mother's love, the boy rebels against his father's wishes and runs away from home. It is this mother love and misguided yet affectionate paternal sternness which are continuing themes throughout the film.

The plot moves forward ten years and three thousand miles from the Jewish ghetto of Jakie's childhood. Jakie is now Jack Robin (Al Jolson), a name which symbolizes his rejection of his Jewish faith, and he is entertaining at a popular restaurant named Coffee Dan's. Here, Al Jolson first speaks the lines that have become some of the most famous in film history: "Wait a minute, wait a minute, you ain't heard nothing yet! Wait a minute, I tell you. You ain't heard nothing yet. Do you want to hear 'Toot, Toot, Tootsie?' " However, these are not the first words heard in the film. Of course, music and sound effects have accompanied the action and subtitles throughout the production. It is Bobby Gordon, playing Jolson as a child, to whom the honor of first being heard goes, as he performs at Muller's Cafe. Later, an unidentified voice, singing offscreen for Warner Oland as Cantor Rabinowitz, performs Kol Nidre. And even before Jolson's plea to wait a minute, the star has been heard singing "Dirty Hands, Dirty Face."

At Coffee Dan's, Jack Robin meets Mary Dale, played by May McAvoy, a leading vaudeville star who tells Robin, "You sing Jazz, but it's different—there's a tear in it." She introduces him to an impressario and is responsible for setting him on the road to New York, described in a title as symbolizing, "New York—Broadway—MOTHER." Just as New York means his mother to Jack Robin, so does Mary Dale symbolize a further rejection of his Jewish heritage for she is a *shiksa*—a Gentile. As a counterpoint to Jack Robin's success, the film cuts to Cantor Rabinowitz listening to a young, would-be cantor sing. In answer to a question as to his own boy, Rabinowitz responds, "I have no boy." His wife, Sara, weeps silently to herself.

Her weeping is shortlived, for her son returns. In perhaps the most sentimental, and by today's standards clichéd, scenes in the film, Al Jolson sits down at the piano and sings "Blue Skies," while apparently improvising dialogue about the plans he has for his mother. As Jolson rambles on about moving up to the Bronx—"Lots of nice green grass up there, and a whole lot of people you know, the Ginsbergs, the Gottenbergs, and the Goldbergs, and, oh, a whole lot of Bergs I don't know at all"—Eugenie Besserer, as the mother, becomes more and more flustered, managing an occasional yes or no in response until Jolson tells her what has already become very apparent to the audience, that she is getting kittenish. What impresses about this dialogue is its natural, unforced, unrehearsed quality. Like Jolson's first words at Coffee Dan's, it has an adlibbed ring to it. It is so natural, so close to reality, that it becomes almost embarrassing to hear. One feels an encroachment on the intimacy of the couple, an intimacy helped by the use of fairly close camerawork. Very few of the early talkies which followed *The Jazz Singer* could boast such unstilted use of dialogue. The end of the dialogue sequence also displays a superb understanding of the use, or rather nonuse, of sound. Cantor Rabinowitz enters the room. He looks at the pair, and shouts, via a title, "Stop!" The orchestral music recommences, and *The Jazz Singer* has become ostensibly a silent film again.

As Jack Robin rehearses for his big show business break, he is visited by his mother who tells him that his father is dying and there is no one to sing Kol Nidre in the synagogue that night. Despite the urgings of the producers of the show that his career will be ruined if he fails to appear on opening night, Jack Robin realizes where his place is. For one night, for one last time, he must become Jakie Rabinowitz; as his father listens from his deathbed, Jolson sings Kol Nidre. "Mamma, we have our son again," are the Cantor's last words.

Despite all the dire warnings as to what will happen to Jack Robin if opening night is cancelled, the show is able to open successfully a day late. Broadway apparently has a heart. As his mother sits in the auditorium, listening and weeping, Al Jolson in black-face sings "I'd Walk a Million Miles for One of Your Smiles, My Mammy." She has come to realize that "He is not my boy anymore. He belongs to the world."

The impact of *The Jazz Singer* should not be underestimated. Through its success, Warner Bros. was assured of financial prosperity; Al Jolson became the biggest box-office attraction of the late 1920's; and the Academy of Motion Picture Arts and Sciences, with its avowed purpose of advancing the arts and sciences of the motion picture, was quick to honor the film, at its first awards ceremony, with a Special Academy Award for "the pioneer talking picture, which has revolutionized the industry."

Anthony Slide

JEZEBEL

Released: 1938
Production: Hal B. Wallis for Warner Bros.
Direction: William Wyler
Screenplay: Clements Ripley, Abem Finkel, and John Huston, with assistance from Robert Bruckner; based on the play of the same name by Owen Davis, Sr.
Cinematography: Ernest Haller
Editing: Warren Low
Costume design: Orry-Kelly
Music: Max Steiner
Running time: 104 minutes

Principal characters:
Julie Marsden	Bette Davis (AA)
Preston Dillard	Henry Fonda
Buck Cantrell	George Brent
Dr. Livingstone	Donald Crisp
Aunt Belle Bogardus	Fay Bainter (AA)
General Bogardus	Henry O'Neill
Amy Bradford Dillard	Margaret Lindsay
Ted Dillard	Richard Cromwell

Jezebel has often been dismissed as Warner Bros.' black-and-white version of *Gone with the Wind*, and Bette Davis' Julie as a pale imitation of Vivien Leigh's Scarlett O'Hara. It is true that Warner Bros. originally bid for the Margaret Mitchell novel, intending to star their studio queen Davis. It is also true that Davis tested for the role of Scarlett when David O. Selznick won the screen rights. Having lost the competition all around, Warner Bros. proceeded with their production of *Jezebel*, a period drama set in antebellum New Orleans, its centerpiece a selfish Southern belle.

Such obvious similarities in period and character invite unfortunate comparisons. *Jezebel* cannot compete with *Gone with the Wind* as a romantic Southern epic—the Warners' production lacks the historical scope of Margaret Mitchell's novel and the Technicolor brilliance of Selznick's beautiful film. But in its portrait of prewar New Orleans, *Jezebel* offers a far more realistic appraisal of "the glorious South" so romanticized in American literature.

New Orleans in 1850 prides itself on being "the Paris of the South." It has the grand manner of Southern tradition mixed with the earthy gaiety of its French and Creole heritage. The city's reigning debutante is Julie Marsden (Bette Davis), beautiful and willful ward of General Bogardus (Henry O'Neill) and his wife Belle (Fay Bainter). Julie is engaged to marry Preston Dillard (Henry Fonda), scion of a wealthy banking family. The engagement is long-standing, owing mainly to Julie's mercurial and demanding nature. Although she can command any young man in town, she wants Preston simply because he will not be bent to her will.

This rather trite state of affairs is played out against a fascinating backdrop. The New Orleans of 1850 has been painstakingly re-created with authentic settings, using genuine antiques and perfect copies of period costume. We are treated to a little vignette depicting Southern manners in a bar scene which introduces Buck Cantrell (George Brent), a young gallant and one of Julie's many admirers. Buck and Preston's brother Ted (Richard Cromwell) are drinking in a replica of the famous Long Bar. Buck is holding forth on his usual topics of hunting and horses when another patron comments about the unconventional Julie Marsden. Forestalling Ted, Buck challenges the unfortunate man to a duel because, "No gentleman mentions a lady's name in a bar." We are given to understand that Buck is a veteran of such affairs. He is much admired by the younger Ted as the quintessential Southern gentleman: interested in horses and dogs, gallant to ladies, and eager to defend them against any real or imagined slight to a strict and exaggerated code of honor. The character of Buck has a double purpose here. He serves as an illustration of Southern chivalry while offering a contrast to Preston Dillard.

Preston is a banker. This puts him at odds with his environment because he does not play at his position or apologize for it. He is an earnest businessman, an innovative as well as diligent citizen constantly urging civic improvement upon his complacent, unheeding fellows.

Julie seems at first the ideal match for Preston. She flaunts her rebellion at conventional behavior, arriving late for her own engagement shower dressed in a riding habit, head high, crop swinging at her side. Her Aunt Belle Bogardus is scandalized; but Julie shrugs her shoulders and boldly explains to the assembled ladies that a fractious horse must be made to know its master. Bette Davis does not have to steal this picture—it was meant to showcase her as Julie Marsden. Every character and event in the film revolves around her, reacting to her behavior, acceding to her demands, competing for her attention. This was Davis' first large scale film, and director William Wyler spared no effort in spotlighting her considerable talents. Davis won the Academy Award for Best Actress for *Jezebel* because the audience, fully aware of Julie's selfish, even vicious, nature, could not help sighing like the young girl at the engagement shower, "I think she's wonderful." Julie is vibrant, exciting, alive.

We see the friction between Julie and Preston when he keeps her waiting in a carriage while he concludes an important business conference. Furious at this slight, she determines to punish him. The highlight of the New Orleans' social season is the Olympus Ball to which all unmarried young women traditionally wear virginal white gowns. Julie obtains a shocking red dress meant for a *demi-mondaine* and, ignoring Preston's ominous objections, wears it to the ball where their engagement is to be officially announced.

In a memorable scene Julie walks into the ballroom and realizes that Preston was right; she has gone too far. The white gowned debutantes and their parents withdraw to the edges of the room, clearing the floor for an agonizing procession as Julie and Preston run the gauntlet of assembled males. Preston stares hard at each man, daring them to comment; Julie stares straight ahead, eyes huge, face frozen. She begs to be taken home; but Preston is adamant that, having ignored his wishes for the last time, she must live with the consequences. He forces her to circle the empty floor with him in a grand waltz.

The waltz for the Olympus Ball is the centerpiece of a beautiful Max Steiner score. In a stiff year of Oscar competition, Steiner lost to *Alexander's Ragtime Band*, and Ernie Haller's cinematography lost to *The Great Waltz*. But the winning combination of Steiner music, Haller cinematography, and Orry-Kelly costume design was established for future Davis pictures at Warner Bros.

The waltz completed, a humiliated and tearful Julie turns to Buck Cantrell who escorts her home. Disgusted, Preston breaks the engagement and leaves to work at the Philadelphia branch of his family's bank. Julie goes into seclusion, retreating from society, certain that Preston will come back to her in spite of Aunt Belle's belief that her ward has driven him away for good this time.

Julie lives on hope for three years. When she learns that Preston has returned, she anticipates that he will marry her and plans a party at Halcyon, her country estate. When Preston arrives Julie greets him in a luminous white gown that appears to be made of spun glass. Kneeling at his feet, she humbly apologizes to him for her behavior. In reply Preston introduces her to Amy (Margaret Lindsay), his wife. Spurned, Julie recovers her old spirit. Assuming a brittle courtesy, she acts the gracious hostess to Preston and his Yankee wife, while encouraging the assembled guests to ridicule Amy's Northern manners.

When Preston repulses Julie's sexual advances, she fabricates an insult and goads Buck into dueling. Preston is called to the city, where a yellow fever epidemic has broken out, and his younger brother, Ted, fights Buck and kills him. As he dies, Buck realizes how he has been used by Julie. The assembled company reviles her, and her aunt and uncle refuse to continue as her guardians. In a telling scene Aunt Belle tells Julie, "I am thinking of a woman who did wrong in the sight of God. Her name was Jezebel." Fay Bainter won an Academy Award as Best Supporting Actress for her portrayal of Aunt Belle. In her faultless characterization of a truly gallant lady, she serves as a perfect foil for Davis' Julie. Her quiet courtesy and grave, gentle manner point up Julie's shallow, selfish nature. When the gracious and staunchly loyal Aunt Belle turns from Julie, so must we all—she is truly a Jezebel.

Quarantined by the epidemic, the uneasy company must remain at Halcyon with Julie, knowing that she is held in contempt by all present, acting as hostess. When word is received that Preston has been struck down by fever, Julie returns to New Orleans, running the blockade by traveling through the swamps. Martial law has been declared in the city. Cannons are fired and torches burned to dispel the swamp air believed to carry fever vapors. Fever victims are heaped onto carts, the living and the dead sent off in boats to Lazerette island, an old leper colony. This is the South's answer to Preston's expressed admiration for the Yankee practice of draining swamps near cities.

Julie nurses Preston day and night. When the militia comes to cart him away she begs Amy to let her accompany him in his wife's place. Speaking the Creole dialect, she argues that she is better able to nurse him, and she swears to send him back to Amy if they survive; in a moving speech she begs Amy for the chance to redeem herself, "to make myself clean again." Julie bumps through the nightmare streets in a wagon, cradling Preston in her lap, traveling with her loved one to probable death.

Besides the astounding artistry of Davis' performance, *Jezebel* is distinguished for its "Yankee viewpoint." John Huston, Abem Finkel, and Clement Ripley fashioned a screenplay that uses the yellow fever epidemic of 1853, which left eight thousand dead, as a symbol of Southern decadence. There are no happy slaves singing on plantations in *Jezebel*; Southern chivalry is portrayed not as a tragic lost ideal but as a senseless nobility that costs a good man his life. Julie Marsden, rather than a charming, self-centered flirt, is a Jezebel who has done wrong and must journey to the hell of Lazarette island to redeem herself. It is this viewpoint that places *Jezebel* outside the category of the standard romantic Southern epic. In this film the perfume of the magnolias is sweetly rotten.

Cheryl Karnes

JOHNNY GUITAR

Released: 1954
Production: Republic
Direction: Nicholas Ray
Screenplay: Philip Yordan; based on the novel of the same name by Roy
  Chanslor
Cinematography: Harry Stradling, Jr.
Editing: Richard L. Van Enger
Running time: 110 minutes

> *Principal characters:*
> Vienna ....Joan Crawford
> Johnny Guitar ....Sterling Hayden
> Emma Small .... Mercedes McCambridge
> Dancin' Kid ....Scott Brady
> Turkey .... Ben Cooper

Johnny Guitar is one of the strangest Westerns ever made. A *film noir* mood, a female protagonist, highly stylized acting, and a lack of narrative action logic resulted in angry reviews when the film was released. *The Hollywood Reporter* on May 5, 1954, called it ". . . One of the most confused and garrulous outdoor films to hit the screen in some time." Even those kinder to director Nicholas Ray were aghast at Joan Crawford's performance as the mannish owner of a gambling saloon whose get-rich plans to sell her property to the railroad take precedence over all else, including her femininity. Yet today *Johnny Guitar* is a cult favorite and is widely regarded as one of the highly acclaimed director's "most personal" pictures, appearing on most lists of the "Ten Best Westerns." It is hailed for its mature love story, its thinly veiled political invective, its brilliant use of color and the CinemaScope frame, and a narrative that moves by the logic of emotion rather than of action.

The story involves Emma (Mercedes McCambridge), the driving force behind a vigilante group of cattle ranchers who do not want the railroad to be built. Emma accuses Vienna (Joan Crawford) of being part of the Dancin' Kid's gang, which claims to have a hidden silver mine. When the gang is suspected of committing a robbery, Vienna is implicated in the crime. Because of Vienna's friendship with the Dancin' Kid (Scott Brady)—guilt by association—and because of sexual conflict, Emma pushes the men to hang Vienna without a trial. Vienna comes under further suspicion when she withdraws her money from the bank as the Kid and his men rob the same bank. Angry at being falsely accused, they may as well become robbers if they are going to be hunted for the crime anyway. Emma finally wins the vigilante group over when a wounded member of the Dancin' Kid's criminal gang comes to

Vienna for help and is discovered hiding in her saloon. Although she is accused of no crime and no trial has been held to determine the gang member's guilt, the townspeople decide to hang them both. When Turkey (Ben Cooper), the teen-aged gang member, is promised freedom if he will implicate Vienna, he despairingly asks her what he should do. "Save yourself," she answers wearily. When he falsely names her, they are both taken out to be hanged.

Emma's accusations break down when Johnny Guitar (Sterling Hayden) rescues Vienna and the vigilante herd chases them to the Dancin' Kid's hidden silver mine, which they find because a member of the Dancin' Kid's gang has betrayed the others. Finally Emma explains her motives: Vienna means the railroad, and she should not have the right to do with her land as she pleases. The economic motive is stated, and the rest of the vigilantes begin to lose interest in the slaughter, leaving Emma to face Vienna alone.

However, there is a further reason for Emma's neurotic hatred of Vienna, and it is sexual. Emma loves the Dancin' Kid, with whom Vienna has been involved. This psychological dimension of the motivation for the action of the film dominates all others. Perhaps it is this emotional feeling rather than narrative logic that so disconcerted reviewers of the time who were expecting a "horse opera" and instead saw a *film noir* melodrama. Johnny and Vienna were lovers five years earlier, and he begs her to tell him she has waited, that there were no other men. There is a strong implication that she bought her land with money earned as a prostitute, but she answers Johnny's pleas with mechanical assurances such as "I waited for you, Johnny," delivered in a flat monotone that points not only to their falsity, but also to his lack of a right to ask. Finally, to his final plea, "Tell me lies," she answers with emotional conviction, "I have waited for you, Johnny."

The shift in levels between stylized acting and the momentary ability of their love to blot out the last five years must have been startling, indeed, for a viewer expecting a typical genre film, but this is exactly what gives a certain veracity to the emotionally expressive use of color, costuming (Vienna wears black men's clothes before Johnny comes, and changes to a flowing white dress just before they try to hang her), and camera movement and angle. Only this preeminence of emotion could fuel Emma's neurotic, hysterical revenge, and it is an indication of the film's achievement that it is so coherent on the psychological level.

As a Western, *Johnny Guitar* is an intriguing example of a strange hybrid: it has the conventions of the Western genre and the brooding, paranoid themes of fear and anger characteristic of *film noir*. *Film noir* produced some of the most psychologically compelling films of the late 1940's and early 1950's. The value systems of their confused, alienated heroes have crumbled, leaving them unsure even of themselves, and in real danger from the spider women who so often replaced the nurturing, ineffectual film heroines of melodrama. In *film noir*, the woman is a strong, ambitious woman, so ambitious that she often uses the man to further her own aims by pretending to love him. Joan Crawford was rarely so conniving a heroine, but her strong, determined, and passionate *persona* was perfect for the many roles in which she portrayed the woman so strong that no man could be worthy of her. Obviously, the strong, mobile heroine and passive hero are not conventional in the Western. Vienna controls the camera in most shots in which Crawford appears, whether we see her from low angle looking down at the vigilantes in her saloon, or center frame playing her piano as they search the room. She determines the action: Johnny saves her from hanging and helps her escape, but the drive behind their actions comes entirely from her, and the final shoot-out is between Emma and Vienna.

There were many unconventional Westerns made in the 1950's as the culture changed and needed different emphases from its myth forms, but the intersection of *film noir* and the Western genre was relatively rare. *Film noir* was much more suited to the detective/gangster film genres, in which the urban environments, the already shifting values, and the lack of stability of fundamental beliefs were given ready expression in already existing forms. The Western tends to work on the level of myth; it is abstract and archetypal, and thus less malleable to the shifts of *film noir*. The tension between these forms is totally rewarding in *Johnny Guitar*.

The high degree of stylization was probably another factor in the consternation of the 1954 reviewers over the film. The first confrontation scene—in which Emma accuses Vienna, Johnny introduces himself as "Johnny Guitar" and offers to play them all a song, the Dancin' Kid grabs the hysterical Emma and twirls her around the floor, and the dialogue between Johnny and Vienna obviously refers to information not yet revealed—must have been difficult to understand in a genre where quick action and clear moral lines are the rule. The characters' names are fanciful and childlike—Turkey, Dancin' Kid, Johnny Guitar, and Vienna—suggesting their vulnerable humanity, their instability, and director Nicholas Ray's affection for them. In this same scene, one of Vienna's men turns to the camera and says, "I never thought I'd end up working for a woman—and liking it!" Certainly this "calling attention" to the audience, a self-conscious device now used with such regularity as to become almost unnoticed and simply another element of film language, was doubly startling in a genre of highly conventionalized, traditional form.

Janey Place

THE JOLSON STORY

Released: 1946
Production: Sidney Skolsky for Columbia
Direction: Alfred E. Green
Screenplay: Stephen Longstreet
Cinematography: Joseph Walker
Editing: William A. Lyon
Choreography: Jack Cole
Music direction: M. W. Stoloff
Production numbers: Joseph H. Lewis
Running time: 128 minutes

Principal characters:
Al Jolson .... Larry Parks
(singing voice, Al Jolson)
Steve Martin .... William Demarest
Julie Benson .... Evelyn Keyes
Cantor Yoelson .... Ludwig Donath
Lew Dockstader .... John Alexander
Tom Baron .... Bill Goodwin
Mrs. Yoelson .... Tamara Shayne
Al Jolson (younger) .... Scotty Beckett
Ann Murray (younger) .... Jo-Carroll Dennison

The Jolson Story is easily one of the two best musical film biographies ever made, the other being *Yankee Doodle Dandy* (1942). In fact, the two films have much in common. Each film is about a musical performer who was half-forgotten by the public when the film was made; each displays first-rate Hollywood production values; and each makes up for lack of conflict in the life of its principal characters by virtue of the actor's bravura performance. In short, each film succeeds as an example of how to make a compelling drama where one does not really exist through sheer cinematic style and star performance.

The similarities end there, however, because James Cagney is remembered for more than his role in *Yankee Doodle Dandy*, while Larry Parks is usually recalled for his capitulation to the House Committee on UnAmerican Activities in 1951. He did make several films besides *The Jolson Story* and its mediocre sequel, *Jolson Sings Again* (1949), though none was as well received by the public as his first Jolson film.

The Jolson Story traces Al Jolson's life and development as a professional entertainer from his beginnings as a child soprano in New York to his comeback in the early 1940's after a few years of self-induced, though strained retirement. Much of the plot is reminiscent of Jolson's first film, *The Jazz Singer* (1927). Like the character of Jack Robins in that celebrated early "talkie," Jolson was reared in an orthodox Jewish household. His father was a cantor who hoped his son would follow in his footsteps. Instead, Asa Yoelson became Al Jolson, a first-rate popular singer with a distinctive voice and electric personality. Unlike Jack Robins, Jolson's father approved (grudgingly at first—at least in the movie) of his son's career, largely because he had a gift he was sharing with the world.

The first half hour of *The Jolson Story* depicts Asa Yoelson's rise as a singer in the world of vaudeville. He is discovered one day by master vaudevillian Steve Martin (William Demarest, who also appeared briefly in *The Jazz Singer* and who, in real life, had been a star performer during the heyday of vaudeville) during the course of Martin's act. It is Martin who prevails upon Cantor Yoelson (Ludwig Donath) to let Asa go on the road with him. The cantor relents because this is obviously what his son wants to do with his life.

A string of successes quickly follow for the team of Martin and Jolson (Martin having decided that Yoelson was not a marquee name) until the day Al's voice changes in the middle of the act. Like a seasoned trooper, he pulls a rabbit out of his hat of many talents and stunningly imitates a bird call. (Whether this really happened is academic; it is a fine moment of cinema.) Martin is duly impressed but refuses to let Jolson sing anymore till his voice has sufficiently matured.

Years later, when Jolson recovers his voice, he and Martin are appearing in a vaudeville show which the great minstrel impresario Lew Dockstader (John Alexander) happens to be watching in his search for new talent. Recognizing an opportunity for his star to rise, Jolson dons blackface, taking the place of a dead-drunk mediocre singer (Bill Goodwin). His flamboyant style captivates Dockstader, who immediately hires Jolson for his show.

Martin realizes that this is Jolson's big chance and unselfishly packs him off on a train by himself. But minstrel shows are no place for a man of Jolson's talent and imagination. He prevails upon Dockstader to let him tamper with the conventional format of the show by introducing a new kind of music known as jazz. Dockstader refuses, so Jolson leaves the show to make a name for himself, which he does, starting with the Ziegfeld Follies.

Outlined in this way, there is nothing inherently compelling about the life of Al Jolson. He is presented as a very talented, generously kind, well-liked, unfailingly sincere human being. That *The Jolson Story* succeeds in making us care about a nice guy is due to Stephen Longstreet's inspired screenplay, Alfred E. Green's energetic direction, and Parks's electrifying performance; Parks had the uninhibited nerve to portray Jolson as the bright, exhibitionistic entertainer he was.

Ironically, because of Parks's good looks, it is difficult to watch the real Jolson in his own movies because he was not at all handsome. Another irony is that Jolson appeared in *The Jolson Story* despite the director's wishes.

Jolson was determined to get into the movie at any cost so he refused to teach Parks his bird call trick, forcing the director to use him. As a result, you can see Jolson in a long-shot when the script calls for Parks to do the bird call on a theater runway. Jolson's own voice is also heard instead of Parks's singing the songs in the film.

The Jolson Story also plays rather freely with the facts of the man's life. Though the film depicts him as a virtuous young man waiting for the right moment to propose to his childhood sweetheart, Jolson was not quite the universally beloved fellow depicted here. He made his share of enemies in show business, including Fannie Brice, who is said to have remarked upon Jolson's death that she was "glad the son-of-a-bitch is dead."

The most obvious toying with facts is also the most puzzling. While one can accept the other white lies in the name of a smooth, uplifting show, it is strange that Ruby Keeler, Jolson's second wife, emerges with a different name, Julie Benson, as Jolson's first wife. It may be that Keeler refused to let her name be used, but it is perplexing all the same because all the other names used are real.

The Keeler episode also paves the way for the film's stickiest moment, when Jolson tries to convince her of his love. The dialogue, direction, and acting in this scene are uncomfortably awkward, partly because they ring false, partly because it is almost all done in one static shot.

While *The Jolson Story* is pretty much Parks's show, the supporting actors are equally memorable. William Demarest is a delight as Steve Martin, expanding his usual grouchy *persona* with smiling warmth; Ludwig Donath is endearing as Cantor Yoelson, a rare instance of a Jew playing a Jew in a Hollywood movie; John Alexander is properly starchy as Dockstader; Bill Goodwin is cheerfully supportive as Tom Baron, the drunk singer; and Evelyn Keyes is radiant as Ruby Keeler by another name.

Also of note are the dazzling production numbers staged by Joseph H. Lewis, with excellent choreography by Jack Cole, as well as Morris Stoloff's impeccable music direction, William Lyon's flawless editing, and Joseph Walker's superbly crisp Technicolor cinematography. Most of these men were house craftsmen at Columbia for many years, particularly Walker, who is best known for having photographed most of Frank Capra's pictures. Their work on *The Jolson Story* is a supreme example of ensemble artistry.

How much of the film's dramatic success is due to Green's direction and how much to Parks's performance is difficult to ascertain. Green was a generally routine director whose only other noteworthy films are *Ella Cinders* (1923) with Colleen Moore, and the early talkie versions of *Disraeli* (1929) and *The Green Goddess* (1930), both with George Arliss. Perhaps the movie succeeds because of Longstreet's script for *The Jolson Story*, or because Green's later attempt to duplicate this success with *The Eddie Cantor Story* (1953) is noteworthy only for its consistently poor quality, proving that the quality of a given movie depends as much on the script as on the director. Whatever the case, *The Jolson Story* remains a superior, though slightly flawed, accomplishment.

Sam Frank

JULIUS CAESAR

Released: 1953
Production: John Houseman for Metro-Goldwyn-Mayer
Direction: Joseph L. Mankiewicz
Screenplay: Joseph L. Mankiewicz; based on the play of the same name by
  William Shakespeare
Cinematography: Joseph Ruttenberg
Editing: John D. Dunning
Art direction: Cedric Gibbons and Edward Carfagno (AA)
Set decoration: Edwin B. Willis and Hugh Hunt (AA)
Music: Miklos Rozsa
Running time: 120 minutes

> *Principal characters:*
> Julius Caesar .... Louis Calhern
> Antony .... Marlon Brando
> Brutus .... James Mason
> Cassius .... John Gielgud
> Calpurnia .... Greer Garson
> Casca .... Edmond O'Brien
> Portia .... Deborah Kerr
> Artemidorus .... Morgan Farley
> Octavius .... Douglas Watson
> Lepidus .... Douglas Dumbrille

Julius Caesar is one of Hollywood's more successful screen adaptations of Shakespeare. Producer John Houseman and screenwriter and director Joseph Mankiewicz wanted to keep Shakespeare's words and the action of the drama from being swamped by either spectacle or irrelevant detail. Thus, the film faithfully preserves the main outline of Shakespeare's action, characters, and themes while adapting the text and Shakespeare's intention to the technical resources and psychological climate of the contemporary audience. *Julius Caesar* is an intense tragedy of direct personal strife which is marked by political, ethical, and psychological ironies of a modern kind. Houseman has explained that one of their first decisions, an aesthetic one, was to do the film in black-and-white, eschewing the grandeur of color in order to capture the intensity of the interplay and conflict of character and personality expressed through the words of individual characters. Thus the film is designed and executed in the monochromes of the documentary. While there is no deliberate exploitation of historic parallels, Houseman was aware of an emotional empathy arising from political events of the immediate past such as the rise of Fascism. Because of the black and white of the newsreel, audiences may perceive echoes of Nazi Germany in the use of spectacle, such as mass rallies, and ritual, such as stiff-armed salutes, to sustain political power. Yet Mankiewicz does not oversimplify or sentimentalize his script; he places emphasis directly and cinematically on the characters.

The film begins with the titles shown against an imperial Roman eagle, followed by a quote from Plutarch describing Caesar as "odious to moderate men through the extravagance of the title and powers that were heaped upon him." The action begins in a square where people are celebrating and a fountain with Caesar's image is decked with flowers. An angry Flavius and Marullus berate the people, strip the bust of flowers, and are arrested by soldiers. The Roman eagle and Caesar's bust will reappear throughout the film to suggest Caesar's dominance and arrogance. After the processional entrance of Caesar (Louis Calhern) into the Colosseum, preceded by eagle-topped staffs, the audience sees his insensitivity to his wife's feelings in his reminder to Antony (Marlon Brando) to touch the barren Calpurnia (Greer Garson) during the race. In one of the great scenes of the film, a crafty Cassius (John Gielgud) follows Brutus (James Mason) upstairs to a gallery to draw him into the conspiracy as shouts are heard in the background. Caesar enters holding onto Antony's arm, and the cynical and sardonic Casca (Edmond O'Brien) relates how Caesar has refused the crown offered by Antony. Wind rises as the scene ends. Next, a frightened Casca braves a storm at night to meet a conspirator; then he meets Cassius, who draws him into the conspiracy.

We see Brutus that same night, standing at his balcony next to a bust of an ancestor. He descends into his garden and walks in a circular pattern around a leaf-filled pool while deciding his course of action. That he is "with himself at war" is cinematically suggested by the irregular shadow lines of a tree branch which cross his body. By the time he finishes his circular walk, he has decided that Caesar must die. The conspirators then arrive and make plans for the assassination. After the conspirators leave, Portia (Deborah Kerr) joins Brutus and, standing in front of the bust of Brutus' ancestor, persuades him to tell her all.

Events then move quickly to climax in Caesar's death. In Caesar's chamber Calpurnia's nightmare moves Caesar to have the priests offer a sacrifice, and he agrees to his wife's plea not to go to the Senate. A conspirator, however, plays on Caesar's vanity until he decides to go. On the Capitol steps, Artemidorus (Morgan Farley) is unsuccessful in warning Caesar, who mocks the soothsayer. Inside the Capitol, Caesar is encircled by the conspirators. Casca strikes the first blow and the others follow. Caesar staggers toward Brutus, who has backed away; he is stabbed by his friend and falls at the feet of Pompey's statue. The conspirators then wash their hands in Caesar's blood. Next, Antony enters cautiously and is allowed by Brutus to live and to speak over Caesar's body. This is one of several tactical errors by Brutus. At the battle of Philippi, for example, he will leave the security of the hills to fight on the plain.

The great Forum scene begins with Brutus explaining to the crowd how Caesar has been killed for the good of Rome. Suddenly Antony appears holding the body of Caesar; the crowd is shocked, and a low-angle camera shot of Antony suggests the visual dominance of a new demogogue. As Antony addresses the crowd, the camera moves from the speaker to the crowd revealing how quickly the multitude can forget Brutus' reasoned explanation and fall prey to Antony's emotional rhetoric. As the riotous mob exits, Antony smiles, and we are aware of how he has used the crowd for his own political ends.

As Caesar's funeral pyre burns, a title overlay tells of the outbreak of civil war. Octavius (Douglas Watson), Antony, and Lepidus (Douglass Dumbrille) decide in Caesar's chamber which Romans must die, and when Lepidus leaves, it is decided by the other two that he must also die. Antony walks to the balcony, stands at Caesar's statue, then sits in Caesar's eagle-crested chair. The imperial eagle and Caesar's bust are now associated with Antony's growing power and tyranny. At Brutus' camp, Cassius enters outraged that Brutus has ignored his plea on behalf of a wronged man. They argue and reconcile, but Cassius is shocked at Brutus' news that Portia is dead. He gives up opposition to Brutus' battle plan to meet the enemy on the plain. That night Caesar's ghost appears to the sleeping Brutus and vows to see him at Philippi, but when Brutus rouses his guards, they see nothing.

The next morning Cassius bids Brutus farewell and denies approving this battle plan. At Philippi, in a scene reminiscent of a Hollywood Western, Antony and his troops observe from above as Cassius' troops march through a pass. Antony smiles after his troops attack and are victorious; on a hillside, the defeated Cassius commands his servant to kill him. On the battlefield Octavius' troops rout Brutus' forces, and a wounded soldier refuses to tell where Brutus has fled. Brutus finds Cassius' body, acknowledges the presence of Caesar's spirit, and has a servant hold his sword as he runs against it. In the final scene, funeral drums are heard as Octavius and Antony enter the tent where Brutus lies. Octavius says Brutus will have rites, and Antony walks to the corpse, declaring that of all the conspirators only Brutus did not strike Caesar out of envy. As the drums get louder, the lamp at Brutus' head goes out.

The Academy Award-winning architectural set designs of the film reinforce the intense clash of political ideas and personalities in the play. Major characters are filmed most often in medium and long shots, and arranged in geometrical patterns—triangles, squares, or rectangles. Director Joseph L. Mankiewicz treats Shakespearean soliloquies as highly charged dramatic speeches and emphasizes character's words by avoiding close-up and reaction shots. The majority of textual cuts omit unnecessary details, and a few scenes are cut entirely.

The cast, recruited from both stage and screen, exhibits a broad spectrum of acting styles, but the individual performances are expert. Louis Calhern is an imposing Caesar, combining intellectual sensibility with arrogance and a royal elegance of demeanor. Veteran Shakespearean actor John Gielgud, in his Hollywood debut, plays Cassius with an appropriately lean and hungry look and the meticulous diction necessary for the leader of the conspirators. James Mason, although appearing somewhat youthful, gives a brooding performance as Brutus that effectively portrays a conscience-stricken man. The most unusual casting, which made many people apprehensive at the time, was the selection of Marlon Brando for the part of Antony. Brando's diction worried the film's producers who were familiar with the slurring speech employed in his characterization of Stanley Kowalski in Tennessee Williams' *A Streetcar Named Desire* (1951). Although his speech is not classically Shakespearean, Brando creates a smoldering, sullen character and brings excitement to a critical role. The end result of the direction and performances is a faithful interpretation of the Shakespearean drama.

Andrew M. McLean

KEY LARGO

Released: 1948
Production: Jerry Wald for Warner Bros.
Direction: John Huston
Screenplay: John Huston and Richard Brooks; based on the play of the same
name by Maxwell Anderson
Cinematography: Karl Freund
Editing: Rudi Fehr
Running time: 101 minutes

> *Principal characters:*
> Frank McCloud .... Humphrey Bogart
> Johnny Rocco .... Edward G. Robinson
> Nora Temple .... Lauren Bacall
> James Temple .... Lionel Barrymore
> Gaye .... Claire Trevor (AA)
> Ziggy .... Marc Lawrence
> Ben Wade .... Monte Blue
> Clyde Sawyer .... John Rodney

After winning two Oscars in 1947 for Best Director and Best Screenplay in *The Treasure of the Sierra Madre*, John Huston was asked by Bogart: "So what do we do for an encore, kid?" Huston encored with *Key Largo*, a project that had no problems, merely lots of hard work and laughs with Bogart. Playwright Maxwell Anderson's plays were produced for stage and screen for almost thirty years, yet today, few perform his plays and many critics consider him overrated. Wedding social commentary to blank verse, he wrote in a style which, although popular at the time, is now found burdensome. He is remembered more for the films which were made from his plays than for the actual plays themselves. Anderson wrote *Key Largo*, a formal pre-World War II drama, in 1939, four years after *Winterset*, his most famous play; but it was not one of his better efforts. The story deals with a Spanish Civil War deserter who tries to rationalize himself into performing a duty that might cost him his life.

John Huston and Richard Brooks completely rewrote Anderson's material making many improvements; their script tones down the pompous verse and adds outdoor action as well as an original ending. Confined mostly to a single, handsome set, the story moves along at a steady pace, and if the script has a problem it is limited to the dialogue. (For example, Bogart sounds unnatural speaking blank-verse lines such as "You don't like it, Rocco, the storm?") *Key Largo* is a director's film, and Huston is in full control of the story and actors. Huston's directing adds a vitality, insight, and continuity within each scene that is inventive and imaginative. His characters, atmosphere, emotions, and ideas evolve exactly as they should. His direction improved upon the script, which was overly preachy. The dialogue about courage and good *versus* evil seems somewhat stilted and dated today, and even in 1945, the gangster theme was becoming obsolete.

Huston was impressed by the problems facing the returning soldiers after World War II. He saw the collision of postwar realities with the expectations of men trying to find themselves again. In *Key Largo* he wanted to touch upon this theme and to say that a man cannot dispel his problems by avoiding them, nor can he find personal freedom without taking a stand. Anderson's original protagonist, a deserter from the Spanish Civil War, was transformed into a disillusioned GI who has difficulties adjusting to postwar life.

The atmosphere is established firmly at the beginning of the film. A bus is seen moving across the bridge leading to the Florida Keys. A sheriff's car overtakes it and brings it to a stop; the sheriff is looking for two Indians who have escaped from jail. This scene introduces the main character of the film, Frank McCloud (Humphrey Bogart), who is one of the passengers. His destination is the Florida Keys. It is the dead of summer when tourists avoid the heat and humidity that settles over the Key Largo Hotel, which is closed for the season. Ex-army major McCloud has come to the island to see James Temple (Lionel Barrrymore) and his daughter-in-law Nora (Lauren Bacall), the father and widow of a wartime buddy.

McCloud finds Key Largo a place where he can establish roots in the home of a dead friend's family and reaffirm who he is and what he believes in. He has been fighting for his country, but the realities of death on the battlefield have changed him. He claims that he will only fight again for himself and what is his, but he has never had to make that distinction before. He had a commitment to World War II, and although he makes passing reference to cowardice, we learn that such references are only a part of his disillusionment with all war.

McCloud finds the hotel inhabited by strange guests: a "Mr. Brown" (Edward G. Robinson), his alcoholic girl friend Gaye (Claire Trevor), and his henchmen. The first shot of Brown is a famous one which shows him sitting in a bathtub, mouthing his cigar in typical Edward G. Robinson style. McCloud recognizes Brown as Johnny Rocco, a notorious racketeer who had been deported from the United States. At Key Largo, Rocco is making an attempt to regain his former power after a long absence from this country. He decides to hold McCloud and the others at the hotel prisoners while he awaits the arrival of another gangster to buy a fortune in counterfeit money. A battle of wits ensues between McCloud and Rocco—a battle that results in death, but at the same time resurrects McCloud's moral commitment.

Temple and Rocco become foils not only for each other but also for McCloud. Here Huston attempts to establish his perception of postwar America. McCloud returns to the States only to find the same delusions despite the war's end. Temple, as a flag-waving patriot, believes in the absolute truth of noble ideals. The limitations of his views are handled well by Huston. Temple is a cripple confined to a wheelchair (as was the case with Barrymore himself); therefore he is incapable of fighting for what he believes in, and must have a champion to do it for him. Rocco, too, has a strict code of ideals, although they differ from those of Temple. Both men have witnessed the passing of an earlier era, a time when there was no conflict between a man's heart and his head. They both live in the past, while McCloud struggles to cope with the present.

Huston utilizes aspects of the gangster film genre to heighten his theme. With a collection of stars who made many of the original gangster films, such as Edward G. Robinson and Bogart, the allusions are all the more evident. In fact, this film becomes a parody of its type, especially as it develops Rocco's character. He is like many of his cinematic predecessors, small and tough, yet he is also a pathetic figure as he tries to regain his former stature. He foresees the return of the glorious days of prohibition, beginning with his venture of running counterfeit money. When McCloud has a chance to kill Rocco, however, he passes up the opportunity because he is too concerned with saving his own life, and because his disillusionment makes him reluctant to fight again for any cause. When the island is swept by a storm, Rocco loses control and refuses to let Temple admit a group of Indians requesting shelter in the hotel. Seeing this injustice renews McCloud's strength.

Just before another gangster, Ziggy (Marc Lawrence), arrives Rocco humiliates Gaye, the star turned alcoholic, by forcing her through a painful attempt to sing her old theme song. The scene ironically parallels that of a nightclub with an audience sitting around and the singer at the center. She has no stage, no spotlight highlighting her painted face, however; instead empty tables and chairs piled on them surround her, and no piano accompanies her almost hysterical voice. Gaye fails miserably, and when Rocco cruelly refuses her a promised drink, McCloud pours it for her, receiving a slap from Rocco for his trouble.

After the storm ends, Rocco receives a visit from Ziggy, who has come to buy a shipment of counterfeit money. Rocco's meeting with Ziggy underscores the pathos of his position. He calls for Gaye when Ziggy appears and treats her as a plaything in order to show her off in much the way that women were used in earlier gangster films. Ziggy is immediately impressed, and before he has a chance to see what a shell she has become, Rocco dismisses her. The two gangsters' meeting seems like a college reunion where they laugh about old times far too loud and too long. They make their deal, but it does not matter, for Prohibition and its accompanying gangsterism is not coming back, because people like McCloud will not let it.

When Ziggy departs, Sheriff Ben Wade (Monte Blue) comes looking for his deputy, Clyde Sawyer (John Rodney), who was after the two Indians who escaped from jail. When Wade finds the body of Sawyer, whom Rocco has killed, Rocco implies that the fugitives are guilty. Wade finds the Indians and, when they try to get away, he kills them both. Sickened by all of this, McCloud realizes finally that there can be no compromise with Rocco, who destroys innocent people. McCloud thus agrees to pilot a boat for Rocco, who is going to Cuba. Before leaving, Rocco tells Gaye that he is leaving her behind, so she takes a gun from his pocket and passes it unseen to McCloud. With the smuggled gun, McCloud plans to get rid of the mob once out at sea.

A cat-and-mouse chase on the small cruiser ensues, with McCloud picking off the henchmen one by one. Finally, when Rocco is the only one left, he bargains with McCloud, while hiding below deck, offering him all the money obtained from Ziggy. McCloud waits patiently for Rocco to show himself, then kills him when he does. Turning the boat around, McCloud heads back to Key Largo and the waiting Nora, who had been attracted to McCloud. The film falters somewhat in this rather melodramatic ending which sends the victorious McCloud cruising back to Nora through a blanket of sunlight; this sentimental conclusion detracts somewhat from the strength in the rest of the film. Beyond this flaw, however, the film reflects Huston's ability to find within another work elements relevant to his own ideas and to transform that work into a unique creation of his own.

Humphrey Bogart, playing more of a human being than many of his previous characterizations, gives a strong performance which lacks overdone heroics; instead, he moves the audience by his subtlety. Edward G. Robinson returns to the familiar role of the gangster who struts, leers, snarls, and gestures. Rocco is a different type of gangster, however; he is deeper, an almost bizarre deviation from the usual "tough guy." Claire Trevor gives a performance that makes one wonder why she was so rarely used to best advantage in films. Her part as a drunk and a moll is superlative, as she captures the pathos of her character, especially in the sequence in which she tries to recapture the days of her singing career. This particular scene has been credited as the reason why she won an Oscar for Best Supporting Actress.

Because most of the action takes place within the confines of the resort, Huston shot much of the picture at Warners' sound stages. He did travel to Florida for some location cinematography, however, and his cameraman, Karl Freund, gave the film its compact, moody sheen.

Lawrence Fargo, Jr.

KIND HEARTS AND CORONETS

Released: 1949
Production: Michael Balcon for Ealing Studios
Direction: Robert Hamer
Screenplay: Robert Hamer and John Dighton; based on the novel *Israel Rank*
   by Roy Horniman
Cinematography: Douglas Slocombe
Editing: Peter Tanner
Running time: 106 minutes

> *Principal characters:*
> Louis Mazzini/
> Mazzini's Father .... Dennis Price
> Sibella .... Joan Greenwood
> Edith .... Valerie Hobson
> Ascoyne d'Ascoyne/Henry
> d'Ascoyne/Canon d'Ascoyne/
> Admiral d'Ascoyne/General
> d'Ascoyne/Lady Agatha d'Ascoyne/
> Lord d'Ascoyne/Ethelbert,
> Duke of Chalfont/the Old Duke .... Alec Guinness
> Mrs. Mazzini .... Audrey Fildes
> Lionel .... John Penrose
> Hangman .... Miles Malleson

As Charles Barr has pointed out in his authoritative study *Ealing Studios*, *Kind Hearts and Coronets* has the distinction of being the only Ealing comedy still frequently revived today that was not either written by T. E. B. Clarke (*Passport to Pimlico*, 1949; *The Lavender Hill Mob*, 1952; *The Titfield Thunderbolt*, 1953) or directed by Alexander Mackendrick (*Whisky Galore*, 1948; *The Man in the White Suit*, 1952). Instead, the screenplay for *Kind Hearts and Coronets* was written by the director, Robert Hamer, whose previous work for Ealing included the mirror sequence in *Dead of Night* (1946) and *It Always Rains on Sunday* (1948), a crime thriller that was a pioneer in the kitchen-sink school of British social realism. Assisting him was John Dighton, whose previous screenplays included two literary adaptations with historical settings, *Nicholas Nickleby* (1947) and *Saraband for Dead Lovers* (1948). The result of their collaboration was a comic murder story with a period setting that seems likely to go on being revived long after even *The Lavender Hill Mob* and *The Man in the White Suit* have been put on the shelf as relics of a distant time. Barr calls *Kind Hearts and Coronets* "quite possibly the most memorable of British films," and notes that Sir Michael Balcon, head of production at Ealing from 1938 until the company was absorbed by the Associated British Picture Corporation in 1959, claims the film as a personal favorite. There is evidence, however, that Balcon quarreled with Hamer while the picture was being shot. Hamer was not allowed to proceed with the film he had planned for his next project, and his only other work for Ealing was a mild political satire, *His Excellency*, released in 1952.

In his chapter on *Kind Hearts and Coronets*, Barr dismisses the widely held assumption that the film both improves upon and considerably alters the story of the novel *Israel Rank* by Roy Horniman (1872-1907), upon which it was based. The truth, says Barr, is that "The book is a Wildean novel of the Edwardian decade . . . [whose] influence is evident in the overall structure and tone of the [film], and in certain happy details." The American reader who goes to the trouble of finding the book will probably agree with Barr's evaluation; but he may conclude that there remain significant differences between novel and film that make Hamer's treatment of the material more satisfying to modern sensibilities.

To begin with, the hero of Horniman's novel is half-Jewish, as, what the British would ironically call his *Christian* name, Israel, proclaims; Louis Mazzini, the hero of Hamer's film, is half-Italian. Since the plot of both novel and film revolves around the hero's cold-blooded murder of the half dozen or so relatives who stand between him and a dukedom, for Hamer to have kept the hero Jewish would have brought the same charge of anti-Semitism that plagued David Lean's very fine film version of *Oliver Twist* the year before. Horniman does not himself appear to have been anti-Semitic. The fictional Israel's anger at the anti-Jewish prejudice he occasionally encounters is presented without irony; and his Jewish commercial traveler father is one of the book's more sympathetic characters.

Hamer's solutions to the problem of finding different ways for Louis to dispatch his victims have an elegance and unexpectedness that is better suited to the hero's aristocratic pretensions than Horniman's sometimes brutal imagination can devise. Throughout the novel, poison, with the attendant death agonies realistically described, remains Israel's favorite murder device. He varies his tactics by having a male cousin beaten to death by a village youth whose sweetheart the cousin had made pregnant, by burning down an elderly relative's house with the old man asleep inside, or giving the infant heir to the Gascoyne earldom a handkerchief to play with that has been used to wipe the brow of a child suffering from scarlet fever. Louis' methods in the film are both more ingenious and funnier since there is no indication that his victims suffer much pain. A female relative who is a suffragette is shot down while she is bombarding London with leaflets from a balloon; a cousin who is an amateur photographer is blown to bits when Louis hides an explosive among the chemicals in his darkroom; another cousin and the girl he has taken to a resort hotel for the weekend are drowned when Louis unties the canoe in which they are making love and they unknowingly drift downstream over a weir.

Hamer's supreme stroke of genius, however, was his decision to cast Alec Guinness, then nearing the peak of his fame as one of the ablest young actors to emerge in England after the war, as each of the nine members of the d'Ascoyne family who stand between Louis and the dukedom. This device takes the edge off any uneasiness we may still feel at Louis' ruthlessness. We know that Guinness will soon be popping up again in another wig and costume, and it hardly seems as if the d'Ascoynes are being killed at all. Furthermore, the d'Ascoynes' resemblance to one another emphasizes the position of the very dissimilar-looking Louis (Dennis Price) as an outsider.

The extreme artificiality of having one actor play nine parts is also an element in the film's heavily stylized evocation of the Edwardian period. It recalls the contrivances and improbable coincidences that are part of the comedy of *The Importance of Being Earnest* (1952). If, as Barr says, *Israel Rank* is a Wildean novel, *Kind Hearts and Coronets* is much more a Wildean movie. Horniman had a satirist's eye for the pretensions of Edwardian society; but, writing in 1907, there was nothing exotic to him in the way his characters dressed or talked, or in the routine of their daily lives. Horniman probably thought of himself as very modern and up-to-date: he is explicit about Israel's love affairs, and introduces a minor character who is unmistakably homosexual. Forty years later, however, in an England that was still digging itself out from the rubble of World War II, the long summer of the Edwardian decade shimmered in memory like a vision of warmth and plenty. Hamer and his art director, William Kellner, created for Douglas Slocombe's camera a world of exquisite and carefully controlled appearances, in which the smallest gesture was calculated and the least article of clothing chosen for its effect as part of an overall costume. Even the background music was by Mozart, and it perfectly complements the mood of Slocombe's elegant, sunny photography.

The film stays closest to the novel in its depiction of Louis' relationships with the three important women in his life: his mother (Audrey Fildes), who married beneath her for love but transmitted her pride in being a d'Ascoyne to her son; his cousin Edith (Valerie Hobson), whom Louis settles on as fittest to share with him the duties of the d'Ascoyne dukedom; and Sibella (Joan Greenwood), the suburban doctor's daughter who was his childhood sweetheart but who rejected his proposal of marriage to become the wife of a prosperous young businessman. Sibella, who later becomes Louis' mistress, represents the principle of sexual anarchy, the wild card in the stacked deck of Edwardian society, that dogs the young outsider's progress toward his goal. There is a tension set up between the claims of eros and the attraction of worldly success that gives both novel and film an intellectual distinction lacking in farcical murder comedies such as *Arsenic and Old Lace* (1944). In the film, the theme is stated in the title, which comes from Tennyson: "Kind hearts are more than coronets/And simple faith than Norman blood."

When Edith quotes these lines to Louis, he nods his assent but seems to disagree with her. Yet his mother, when she eloped from Chalfont Castle with a penniless Italian musician, was acting on just this principle; and when Louis vows vengeance on her grave for the shabby way the d'Ascoynes treated her, it is plain that except for this spark he would probably have made the best of the shopkeeper's existence to which his mother's poverty had condemned him. His passionate father had dropped dead of excitement the day his son was born. Louis himself gives the case for eros its most forceful expression just before he shoots Ethelbert d'Ascoyne, Eighth Duke of Chalfont and his final victim. He explains that he is avenging his mother: "Because she married for love, instead of for rank, or money, or land, they condemned her to a life of poverty and slavery, in a world with which they had not equipped her to deal." This speech is not in the novel, which develops the theme of eros in conflict with money by concentrating on Israel's dual courtship of Edith and Sibella.

The film, like the novel, is cast in the form of a memoir written by Louis, or Israel, while he is in prison waiting to be hanged for murder. In the book, Israel is arrested after he has stupidly poisoned the sitting duke's wine with arsenic, which a police chemist later detects, in his impatience to remove the final obstacle between himself and the dukedom. Hamer and Dighton do not make the mistake of spoiling our appreciation of Louis' cleverness by having him caught for a murder he actually committed. Instead, Louis is tried and convicted for the murder of Sibella's boorish husband, Lionel (John Penrose), with whom he was seen to quarrel openly after refusing to lend him money to keep his business from failing. Lionel later committed suicide, and Sibella, who has long since caught on to the reason for her lover's rapid rise in the world and who resents being thrown over for the aristocratic Edith when the dukedom is within Louis' grasp, keeps her husband's farewell letter a secret until the night before Louis' execution. She then visits him in prison to suggest that if he can only find a way to dispose of Edith afterward as he did the other d'Ascoynes, she in turn might "discover" Lionel's letter in time to secure his pardon. Louis agrees.

When Louis walks out of prison the next morning, he finds both Edith, his wife, and Sibella, his mistress, waiting for him in separate carriages. He is distracted from the necessity of having to choose between them by a reporter who approaches him with an offer to buy his memoirs for newspaper publication. "My memoirs?," Louis asks, and then recollects with horror that he has left his incriminating autobiography behind in his cell. Here the British version of the film ends, leaving the audience to decide for itself whether Louis did, after all, pay the penalty for his crimes. Although, as Barr asks, can there be any doubt that Louis had only to speak to the prison governor to have his memoirs returned to him before they could be read? It was to remove this element of ambiguity that a sequence was added to the original

American prints of the film, showing the disappointed executioner (Miles Malleson) and the prison governor discovering Louis' memoirs before he can ask to have them handed back to him. The theatrical prints in release in this country today are made from the British negative, but the alternative American ending still turns up occasionally when the film is shown on television. In the novel, Israel is cleared of the duke's murder without having to strike a bargain with Sibella. He leaves prison with his memoirs under his arm, and settles down happily in full possession of Edith, Sibella—who continues as his mistress—and the dukedom.

Charles Hopkins

A KIND OF LOVING

Released: 1961
Production: Joseph Janni fo: Vic Films
Direction: John Schlesinger
Screenplay: Willis Hall and Keith Waterhouse; based on the novel of the same
   name by Stan Barstow
Cinematography: Denys Coop
Editing: Roger Cherrill
Running time: 112 minutes

> *Principal characters:*
> Vic .... Alan Bates
> Ingrid .... June Ritchie
> Mrs. Rothwell .... Thora Hird
> Mr. Brown .... Bert Palmer
> Mrs. Brown .... Gwen Nelson
> Christine .... Pat Keen

Between 1959 and 1963, the British film industry underwent a minor revolution. Called the new realism or the "kitchen sink" school of drama, this
movement had its antecedents in the theater, where plays such as John Osborne's *Look Back in Anger* had changed the face of British drama. Here,
working-class life was presented without any frills and without the customary
British politeness. It was natural that the film industry should follow suit, and
in the early 1960's, a young group of film directors came into prominence who
attempted to explore relationships among the working classes and to take
films out of the studios and into the back streets of the small drab towns in
which their characters lived. One of the most talented of the new directors
to emerge in this period was John Schlesinger, who had been employed as
an actor and as a BBC film producer. He had made a short documentary film
for the British Transport Committee called *Terminus* which depicted a day
at Waterloo Station; it attracted enough critical attention to enable him to
direct his first feature film, *A Kind of Loving*. Adapted from a best-selling
novel by provincial writer Stan Barstow, the script was well written by Willis
Hall and Keith Waterhouse, who were also to write the next film Schlesinger
directed, *Billy Liar* (1963).

The story of *A Kind of Loving* is set against the stark, wintry background
of England's industrial North; a number of Lancashire towns were used for
filming. Barstow wrote about the milieu in which he grew up and which he
knew well—the small-town engineering firm, the dance hall, and the local
pub. Both these settings and the use of Lancashire colloquialisms were new
to British films. Here was life as millions of people actually lived it, a far cry
from Noel Coward drawing rooms. Alan Bates, who was known for his roles

in *The Entertainer* (1960) and *Whistle Down the Wind* (1962), was cast as Vic Brown. For Ingrid, twenty-year-old newcomer June Ritchie was chosen. The film was similar to other treatments of the same theme. Audiences had already seen and liked *Saturday Night and Sunday Morning* (1960), and some critics felt that the landmarks were becoming too familiar. But the revolution proved all too short-lived, and in retrospect, *A Kind of Loving* ranks as one of the few films from that period that remains true to its working-class origins and that still represents much that is true about life in industrial England today.

As the film opens, Vic Brown is watching his sister's wedding and is thinking about his own future. Among the crowd of spectators at the church is Ingrid Rothwell, a pretty young secretary whom Vic first noticed at Dawson Whittakers, the engineering firm where they both work. Vic looks at her with new awareness, and in the next few days his attempts to attract her attention make him the butt of blunt humor among his draughtsmen colleagues at the factory. From her studied indifference to him, it is clear that Ingrid is also attracted to Vic. Their romance finally starts when Vic follows her onto a bus and invites her to the pictures with him the following Saturday night. They hold sweaty hands in the cinema and kiss nervously in the park. Between kisses, Ingrid tells Vic that she was named for actress Ingrid Bergman. It is in these early scenes of their courtship that Schlesinger catches so well the awkwardness of those too inarticulate to verbalize their feelings. Ingrid is worried that Vic thinks she is common, and Vic wonders whether she is really all that interesting. Their romance is presented with a notable lack of sentiment. Sometimes Vic thinks he is in love with Ingrid, and sometimes he cannot stand the sight of her. Behind all of this young adult horseplay lurks the specter of stability. What Ingrid wants is what every respectable young woman wants—a man who loves her, who will marry her, and who will provide her with a home and children. Schlesinger sensitively shows the conflict in a man like Vic, who also thinks those things are worth having, but feels that maybe there is more in life.

When Ingrid's mother (Thora Hird) goes away for a few days leaving her daughter alone in the house, Vic and Ingrid begin a full-blown affair. As soon as they make love for the first time, Vic realizes that for him, Ingrid is merely another girl, only a conquest. He stops coming round to see her and weeks pass. When Vic and Ingrid next meet at the firm's annual party, Ingrid breaks the news to him that she is pregnant; with a tone of extreme resignation, he tells her he will marry her.

The next and last section of the film deals with the married life of Vic and Ingrid, and at first glance, the material seems destined for cliché—the vicious mother-in-law, the neglectful husband, and the pregnant wife. But here Schlesinger shows real mastery, for in many ways this is the finest and truest part of the film. Whereas the first part is about youth, horseplay, sex, and confrontation, the section on the couple's marriage is about maturity and real change. Vic and Ingrid are driven further and further apart by Ingrid's mother's constant interference and obvious dislike of Vic. When Vic tries to explain what he is going through to his married sister, she reminds him that he has made his own bed, and now he must lie in it. Vic feels that he and Ingrid would at least have a chance at contentment if they had a place of their own. Things come to a head when Ingrid has a miscarriage and Mrs. Rothwell does not even call Vic to come to the hospital. He sees, ironically enough, that he need not have married Ingrid after all, but his innate decency makes him determined to find a small home for himself and his wife, hoping that they can make a new start and that "a kind of loving" will carry them through.

The honesty and directness of *A Kind of Loving* impressed most critics. The film made an even bigger star of Alan Bates, and John Schlesinger went on to become a major director of both British and American films. By the mid-1960's Britain was going through more changes, and this type of film ceased to be popular. When the impact of the Beatles was felt and Mary Quant and swinging London emerged, audiences were less anxious to see films about working-class people's problems and instead wanted to peek in on the lives of those supposedly enjoying the new prosperity. Two years after *A Kind of Loving*, John Schlesinger forsook the industrial North for the world of fashion models and public relations men in *Darling*; another era in British film was over. Not since that brief flowering in the late 1950's has the British film industry been able to command the writing, directing, and acting talent of so many gifted people and combine those talents to make a group of films so essentially British. *A Kind of Loving* represents British filmmaking at its finest.

Joan Cohen

THE KING AND I

Released: 1956
Production: Charles Brackett for Twentieth Century-Fox
Direction: Walter Lang
Screenplay: Ernest Lehman; based on the novel *Anna and the King of Siam* by Margaret Landon
Cinematography: Leon Shamroy
Editing: Robert Simpson
Art direction: John DeCuir and Lyle R. Wheeler (AA); set decoration, Walter M. Scott and Paul S. Fox (AA)
Costume design: Irene Sharaff
Sound: Twentieth Century-Fox Sound Department (AA)
Music: Alfred Newman and Ken Darby (AA)
Song: Richard Rodgers and Oscar Hammerstein II
Running time: 133 minutes

> *Principal characters:*
> Anna .... Deborah Kerr
> The King .... Yul Brynner (AA)
> Tuptim .... Rita Moreno
> Lady Thiang .... Terry Saunders
> Louis Leonowens .... Rex Thompson

The King and I utilizes one of the most foreign locales of any American film musical. Based on Margaret Landon's book *Anna and the King of Siam*, and with the help of two superlative performances by Deborah Kerr and Yul Brynner, the movie faithfully conveys Rodgers' and Hammerstein's stage musical classic to the screen. The choice of setting for the musical was a fairly daring one to make. In the early years of this century, stage musicals regularly had been set in foreign lands, and it seemed that the more exotic the locale was, the better audiences would like it. Japanese queens, Asian princes, Polynesian romances, all had been topics of musicals which are now hardly remembered, but they had so broadly caricatured their exotic locales that their premises became laughable to later, more sophisticated audiences. For the next few decades, American musicals reflected their composers' caution regarding the use of exotic locales, with the vast majority taking place during various periods of American history, including, of course, contemporary times. If the story line was not about Americans at home, it might represent Americans abroad, but certainly in no place more foreign than England or France.

Rodgers and Hammerstein risked Siam, and unlike the "foreign" musicals of a few decades earlier, their choice of the exotic was not entirely cosmetic. They made every attempt to incorporate what they knew of Siam in the mid-1800's—the time of Landon's governess—including the society of the King's court, slavery, customs, and manners. Whether they succeeded in capturing the actual traditions of another culture more than the *Japanese Princess* had done thirty years earlier, there is no doubt that *The King and I* appeals to modern audiences in a way that the earlier musicals did not. The musical's translation to film was a success with audiences, who must have believed that the film's charm was timely, regardless of whether it was accurate.

The King and I is essentially the story of a woman who brings order and calm to a royal household: the culturally fractured and half-civilized court of Siam. Desiring Western scientific knowledge which his own society lacks, the King of Siam (Yul Brynner) hires an English governess for his many children and wives. Complications arise, however, when the governess assumes that English customs are a necessary part of that education. Anna (Deborah Kerr), the headstrong governess, expects the courtesies and amenities which would be accorded a governess in England, and she clashes with the powerful King, who, above all, must have subjects who are obedient. The King appears amusingly arrogant and determined to have his own way; Anna, a dignified widow, is equally insistent on asserting her will. Anna's young son is her only link to her home and British culture, but she tries to educate her pupils in Siam with similar British values by teaching them Western knowledge and customs. As an arbiter of custom, she initially challenges the King's authority, also based on cultural custom, but eventually comes to respect and love the King, who also learns to admire her.

Anna's and the King's battle of wills reaches a crisis over the question of slavery. Tuptim (Rita Moreno) is a princess from another Eastern kingdom who has been given to the King as a present, and, with Anna's assistance, tries to express her feelings about her slavery to the King by adapting a story of Western slavery, *Uncle Tom's Cabin*; her version, a ballet choreographed by Agnes De Mille, is called "Little Hut of Uncle Thomas" and becomes a charming adaptation of the original, but its presentation does little to change the King's mind. Finally Tuptim tries to run away with a Burmese lover, and when the runaways are caught, Anna helps the King see their side of the story. At last he is able to admit to himself that he has been wrong, and Anna, who during the crisis has had plans to return home, agrees to stay with the King and continue his "education."

A great deal of the charm of the movie depends upon the strengths of its leading characters, Yul Brynner and Deborah Kerr, who provide *tour de force* performances. The King especially is a role which is totally identified with Brynner, and revivals of the stage musical have either suffered from his absence, or been guaranteed success by his presence. The dancing lesson which Kerr gives Brynner in "Shall We Dance?" remains a classic musical number, presenting a deft interplay of light comedy and allusive romance with Marni Nixon dubbing the singing voice of Kerr. Other strong performances include Rita Moreno's Tuptim, especially in the ballet sequence. The directing style of Walter Lang, however, is certainly not equal to the wit and force of his players, who carry the film for him. Of all the directors given the task of bringing a Rodgers and Hammerstein musical to film, Lang is perhaps the weakest, rivaled only by Joshua Logan's direction of *South Pacific* (1958).

Although some scenes in the film seem stodgy and unimaginative, they cannot harm the musical score by Rodgers and Hammerstein, and the big hits of the stage musical remain, including "I Whistle a Happy Tune" and "Getting to Know You." Several songs were dropped in the transition from stage to film, including Tuptim's "My Lord and Master" and Anna's acrid "Shall I Tell You What I Think of You?"

The battle of wills in *The King and I* is presented in cultural metaphors, with Anna and the King arguing over foundations of a society in transition, but the childish King and no-nonsense governess are also involved in a more basic struggle—a classically Western "battle of the sexes." Similar to many domestic comedies filmed in Hollywood during the same period of time as *The King and I*, the problem of defining authority becomes a focal point for the couples involved. Commonly, the assumed authority of the man is comically contrasted with the woman's common sense, with adjustments being made to allow each face-saving dignity. A man's home, which in this case is literally his castle, is humorously examined with an eye on the woman behind the throne. Thus, despite an exotic location, the characters' conflict in *The King and I* is familiarly domestic, both to Hollywood which produced it, and to the audiences who view it. Perhaps this familiarity of theme, along with the superb music of Rodgers and Hammerstein, is responsible for the film's continued popularity with audiences of all ages.

Leslie Donaldson

KING KONG

Released: 1933
Production: Merian C. Cooper and Ernest B. Schoedsack for RKO/Radio
Direction: Merian C. Cooper and Ernest B. Schoedsack
Screenplay: James A. Creelman and Ruth Rose; based on an idea of Merian
   C. Cooper and Edgar Wallace
Cinematography: Edward Linden, Vernon Walker, and J. O. Taylor
Editing: Ted Cheeseman
Chief technician: Willis O'Brien
Running time: 100 minutes

Principal characters:
Ann Redman .... Fay Wray
Carl Denham .... Robert Armstrong
Jack Driscoll .... Bruce Cabot
Captain Englehorn .... Frank Reicher

Almost half a century after its release, *King Kong* remains one of the most beloved of all fantasy films. Time may have taken its toll on some of the film's dialogue, and its performances today seem a bit exaggerated; yet *King Kong* ranks as a great film with many of its animation sequences remaining unequaled today. Its story line and theme have had countless imitators; it has served as a prototype for the industry's "rampaging monster" films. *King Kong* offers a skillful blend of fantasy and romance in its story of a gigantic ape who is fascinated by a beautiful blonde woman. It is a classic retelling of the Beauty and the Beast fable, and Kong himself has become a part of American folklore. The film's final moments, in which Kong meets his death atop the Empire State Building, make for one of the most memorable sequences in cinema history.

Released by RKO/Radio in 1933, *King Kong* was filmed for a then-staggering cost of $500,000. A year in production, it was a major gamble for RKO, which at the time was facing bankruptcy. However, the gamble paid off, as *King Kong*, released in 1933 at the height of the Depression, became one of the most popular films both of the year and of the decade. It broke attendance records at both New York's Radio City Music Hall and Hollywood's Grauman's Chinese Theater. After quickly establishing itself as a film favorite, *King Kong* gave RKO a new lease on life, and for the next twenty years, the studio turned out hundreds of outstanding film titles, including Orson Welles's *Citizen Kane* (1941).

Throughout the succeeding decades, the popularity of *King Kong* has been subjected to much analytical scrutiny. Various critics have suggested that the film is heavily symbolic, some saying that Kong represents the black man and his dilemma in America, while others insist that the film has economic and political connotations. It has even been reported that Kong's climbing of the phallic-shaped Empire State Building lends the film sexual significance. While such analyses offer some diverting and interesting speculations, they also seem far-fetched. A serious analysis of theme and content may pass over the most obvious cause for the film's success: *King Kong* is, quite simply, a masterful piece of pure escapism; it is a richly visual journey into a fantastic world of adventure. Through still-impressive special effects, supervised by Willis O'Brien, *King Kong* makes the impossible (dinosaurs, and Kong himself) seem, for a fleeting moment, possible. Max Steiner's stirring score is also enhancing, and there is no denying that Kong himself leaves an indelible imprint upon the film. Although ferocious and of awesome size (fifty feet in height), he is also a victim. Abducted from his domain and transported to an environment far removed from his own, he resorts to violence because it is all he can do. The film's ending, portraying Kong atop the Empire State Building hopelessly fighting off four attacking Navy biplanes, has an inherent message with which each viewer can identify: life is not fair.

The film's story begins in New York, where movie producer Carl Denham (Robert Armstrong) befriends Ann Redman (Fay Wray), a starring actress. With a promise of "money and adventure and fame and a long sea voyage," she is talked into joining Denham and his all-male crew aboard the *S.S. Venture*. Almost from the beginning, the script makes ominous references about the ship's impending mysterious journey. It is revealed that the crew aboard is three times larger than is usually necessary, and that the ship carries "enough ammunition to blow up the harbor," as well as huge knock-out gas bombs.

As the *Venture* makes her way through foggy seas, the beauty and the beast theme unfolds. Denham, who is brash but likable, has the ship's captain, Englehorn (Frank Reicher), follow a seemingly primitive map which Denham has obtained from an old sea captain. Their destination is Skull Island, and Denham, who has become fascinated with reports of a mysterious god called Kong, plans to shoot film on the island. The journey progresses, with Ann becoming interested in the ship's good-looking but indifferent first mate, Jack Driscoll (Bruce Cabot).

As the *Venture* nears Skull Island, an element of mystery, romance, and fantasy looms over the horizon so that Kong's appearance seems inevitable. The island natives' respect and fear of the "god" is detailed during an extravagant ceremonial sequence. The crew members and Ann have sneaked ashore in order to photograph the ceremony, but they are discovered, and the nighttime ceremony comes to a halt. Intrigued by Ann's blonde beauty, the chief offers six of his native women in exchange for Ann, but the crew is able to scare off the natives and retreat to their moored ship. Driscoll, who has been fighting an attraction to Ann, now becomes protective of her, displacing his anger with Denham for bringing her on the journey and thus placing her life in jeopardy.

When Ann is kidnaped from the ship by the natives, the crew members return to the island and arrive just as Kong carries off his sacrificial bride, Ann. The scenes of Ann, tied to the altar where she will become the "bride of Kong," provide the film with some of its most effective and horrifying moments. Ann's eyes signify terror and complete helplessness as she sees Kong approach. When Kong comes at the altar in a rash of anger and mighty roars, Ann breaks out into shrill screams; when Kong at last reaches for her, she slumps in a faint. However, Kong's hostility subsides as he takes Ann in his hand and carries her off into the jungle.

The crew members, with Driscoll in the lead, pursue Kong, and the chase sequences across the island's eerie landscape of twisted vines, foggy marshes, and tangled undergrowth provide credence to the horror of Skull Island. The crew battles along the way with creatures, including a stegosaur. Kong, who is taking Ann to his mountaintop lair, also does battle with a tyrannosaur, and the scenes of the two improbable creatures coming together are amazingly realistic. Later, as Kong fights a pteranodon, Driscoll is able to reach Ann, and he leads her back to the native village, followed by a much-angered Kong. Denham, always the opportunist, waits with a trap outside the village's great wall, and when Kong bursts through, he is captured by means of the gas bombs. Victoriously, Denham bellows, "Why, the whole world will pay to see this! We're millionaires, boys!"

Through dialogue, Denham details his dream of taking Kong to New York's Broadway. Telling his men to build a raft in order to float Kong out to the ship, Denham declares, "In a few months it'll be up in lights: 'Kong, the Eighth Wonder of the World!'" Then, with much showmanship, the film cuts to a shot of the Broadway marquee touting the arrival of Kong; it is a brilliantly conceived film transition.

Chained and exhibited to an amazed audience at his world premiere, Kong grows furious when a flood of flashbulbs go off. When Kong breaks free of his chains, Driscoll, who now loves Ann and fears for her life, grabs her by the hand, and the two escape. Kong then begins his now-famous assault on New York City; one of the most famous moments in this sequence shows him destroying an elevated train. Perhaps his most cruel and terrifying act takes place when he reaches into a window for a woman he believes to be Ann. Then, after discovering that she is not Ann, Kong opens his fingers, dropping her, and she plummets headlong to her death.

Once Kong has located Ann and taken her from Driscoll, he carries her in his gigantic hand and makes his way for the city's highest point. For Kong, the Empire State Building is reminiscent of his mountaintop home, but, of course, there is no safety for him. After the plane attack, the bleeding giant gently places Ann safely on a ledge and then falls to his death. Denham is among those who rush to examine the massive body, and when a policeman claims, "the airplanes got him," Denham shakes his head, saying, "It was beauty who killed the beast."

King Kong marked the final collaboration of producer-directors Merian C. Cooper and Ernest B. Schoedsack. Cooper, a journalist-turned-explorer-turned-filmmaker, had first teamed with Schoedsack, then a cameraman, for the commercially successful documentary, *Grass* (1925). After *King Kong*, Cooper stayed with producing duties, often in collaboration with John Ford. Schoedsack continued to direct, and in 1949, delivered *Mighty Joe Young*, another giant ape picture marked by a much more lightweight and less effective story line. *King Kong*'s special effects supervisor, Willis O'Brien, was considered to be one of the grand masters of animation, specifically the stop-motion technique. In 1925, O'Brien supervised the effects for *The Last World*, which starred Wallace Beery. Although the film did not captivate audiences at the time of its release, it is noteworthy because O'Brien utilized the then-innovative technique of placing live actors and animated dinosaurs in the same frame. That technique, of course, would be showcased superlatively in *King Kong*.

The Academy Awards of 1933 completely bypassed *King Kong*, with the year's Best Picture honors going to *Cavalcade*, now viewed as a rather dusty relic which details in episodic fashion the trials and tribulations of a British family. Special effects achievements were not yet recognized by the Academy in 1933, and did not constitute an award category until 1939; thus the film's chief merits went unrewarded. Twenty years after the release of *King Kong*, however, Merian C. Cooper received an honorary Oscar for "his many innovations and contributions to the art of motion pictures." Willis O'Brien's special effects work in *Mighty Joe Young* was also honored with an Oscar. After a number of successful theatrical reissues in 1938, 1942, 1952, and 1956, *King Kong* became a television staple, even today commanding impressive television "ratings." During one of its reissues, the film was subjected to censorship cuts; some three minutes were removed with the snipped scenes involving violence, as well as a moment in which Kong rips away Ann's dress. However, most of the missing scenes were eventually restored.

Performers Robert Armstrong, Bruce Cabot, and Fay Wray—all effective in *King Kong*—were always to be identified with their work in the film. Wray, in particular, had a difficult time shedding the image she projected in the film, and for the remainder of her career was offered roles of blondes-in-distress—an ironic note, considering that Wray was a natural brunette who went blonde specifically for the role in *King Kong*. Kong himself remains such a part of American folklore that visitors to the Empire State Building can still buy souvenirs of Kong's "climb," and *King Kong* sequels and imitators abound. Perhaps most noteworthy is *Song of Kong* (1933), directed by Schoedsack and again starring Armstrong. Among the least meritorious of the Kong "sequels" is the Japanese film, *King Kong vs. Godzilla* (1962). In 1976, producer Dino De Laurentiis updated the King Kong story, giving it a somewhat campy approach in a relatively unsuccessful remake of *King Kong*.

Pat H. Broeske

KING OF HEARTS
(LE ROI DU COEUR)

Released: 1967
Production: Philippe de Broca for Fildebroc Productions; released by Lopert Pictures
Direction: Philippe de Broca
Screenplay: Daniel Boulanger
Cinematography: Pierre Lhomme
Editing: Françoise Javet
Running time: 102 minutes

Principal characters:

Private Charles Plumpick	Alan Bates
General Geranium	Pierre Brasseur
The Duke	Jean-Claude Brialy
Coquelicot	Genevieve Bujold
Colonel Alexander MacBibenbrook	Adolfo Celi
The Duchess	Françoise Christophe
Madame Eglantine	Micheline Presle
Colonel Helmut von Krack	Daniel Boulanger

During the 1960's the work of a French film director, Philippe de Broca, was much admired internationally, and particularly in America. The comedies he made, with all their offbeat humor, slapstick action, and impudence, were fresh and innovative. Such intelligent comedy fare as *Playing at Love* (1960), *Time Out for Love* (1961), and *That Man from Rio* (1963) were bright and charming capers; but his film *King of Hearts* is the work which has not only captured audience interest in this country, but also held it. *King of Hearts*, much admired by both public and critics, grew to be a cult favorite, and it still plays often at Saturday "midnight matinees." For all its comic brilliance, it is, nevertheless, a moral fable that is not only funny but also wise and touching in a very gentle way. It is de Broca's most enduring film.

The action takes place during the last days of World War I, in a little French village where the fleeing Germans, in an effort to halt their pursuers, plant an enormously powerful booby trap in the village square which will blow up the entire town. It is triggered to explode when an armored knight on the church steeple clock strikes the midnight hour with his mace. The news leaks out as soon as the German troops have vanished, and the townsfolk flee in terror, forgetting the inmates of their local insane asylum.

In evacuating the town, the villagers encounter a Scottish regiment to whom they impart knowledge of the bomb. A quiet, rather mild-mannered Scotsman, Private Charles Plumpick (Alan Bates), is sent to investigate the predicament. To his astonishment, the town is now populated by a harmless and carefree lot; they have moved into the homes that had been vacated and are assuming the roles of barber, bishop, general, duke and duchess, and madame of the local bordello. Plumpick does not realize the identity of these inhabitants until they name him their King of Hearts and announce to him that he must take Coquelicot (Genevieve Bujold), a young and very pretty onetime acrobat, in marriage as his rightful Queen. Much as Plumpick admires the gentle Coquelicot, he sadly realizes that all these charming people are escaped inmates of the asylum.

Plumpick has not forgotten his reason for having been sent to the village, but it is only a chance remark which leads him to the village clock, and he is able to defuse the bomb a few minutes before midnight, when it is due to explode. The merrymaking goes on until dawn, but now the Scots regiment advances cautiously into the village, only to be met by the German battalion returning to see why the bomb they had set has not exploded. The war resumes, and both sides open fire until every soldier on either side has either run away or been killed. The asylum inmates, witnessing this insane slaughter, immediately seek refuge within the safety of their asylum.

A relief force enters the town, and Plumpick is assigned to another unit. His eyes have been opened, however, and he does not stay long with them, deliberately falling behind to divest himself of his uniform and battle equipment. The nuns who answer the bell at the asylum gate find him standing there, stark naked and carrying a birdcage, waiting to be admitted.

King of Hearts, although whimsical in its comic approach, is the kind of story that was to gain great popularity from the 1960's onward, reaching a peak in 1975 with the release of *One Flew Over the Cuckoo's Nest*. It asks whether the inanities of lunatics are not preferable to the insanities of armies. Life among those who have retreated from sanity is often dark and sad, but it makes more sense than living in the outside world among people gone mad with bloodlust. De Broca has added what the *New York Times* called "a curious and disturbing dimension to his theme," because the inmates of his asylum are not only joyously happy, but they have consciously chosen their "vagrant lunacy" as well.

De Broca is singularly fortunate in having cast Alan Bates as Private Plumpick. It was Bates's first experience away from British filmmaking, although he had left England to go on location several times with British companies, especially to Crete in 1964 for *Zorba the Greek*. Bates is a versatile and very sensitive actor, equally at home in a sympathetic or a nonsympathetic role. He is completely heroic in *King of Hearts*, a puzzled but very sane man who deliberately chooses to desert the world of reality for that of fantasy. He came to France at de Broca's invitation to join a group of international players, and the entire production was shot in the wonderfully attractive little town of Senlis. Bates fit in immediately with the French-Italian company chosen by de Broca. Today, whether on stage or in films, Bates is one of England's most accomplished and winning actors, and has earned an international audience.

The other players are equally at home with de Broca and with their material. The pretty and charming French-Canadian actress Genevieve Bujold is delightful as Coquelicot, Queen to the King of Hearts. The inmates include the consummate Parisian actor Pierre Brasseur, who makes General Geranium as subtly amusing a character as any he played in such celebrated films as *Les Enfants du Paradis* (1944), *Quai des Brumes* (1938), and Sacha Guitry's *Napoleon* (1955). The Duke and his Duchess are played by the accomplished French actors, Jean-Claude Brialy and Françoise Christophe, while the local whorehouse mistress Madame Eglantine is portrayed by the beautiful and seductive Micheline Presle. The eminent Italian comedian, Adolfo Celi, plays the "sane" Scots leader, Colonel Alexander MacBibenbrook; and Daniel Boulanger, who also wrote the screenplay, appears as the German Colonel von Krack.

DeWitt Bodeen

KING OF KINGS

Released: 1961
Production: Samuel Bronston for Metro-Goldwyn-Mayer
Direction: Nicholas Ray
Screenplay: Philip Yordan
Cinematography: Franz Planer
Editing: Harold F. Kress and Renee Lichtig
Music: Miklos Rozsa
Running time: 168 minutes

Principal characters:
Jesus Christ	Jeffrey Hunter
Mary	Siobhan McKenna
John the Baptist	Robert Ryan
Pontius Pilate	Hurd Hatfield
Mary Magdalene	Carmen Sevilla
Barabbas	Harry Guardino
Judas	Rip Torn
Herod Antipas	Frank Thring

While Hollywood producers have never been shy about exalting themselves at the expense of the Bible, they have proven to be relatively timid about presenting Jesus Christ. A voice, a silhouette, or a pair of hands have represented Christ in such religious screen epics as *The Robe* (1953), *The Big Fisherman* (1959), and *Ben-Hur* (1959)—a wise caution, since millions of the faithful are quick to regard as blasphemous anything that does not meet their own personal image of Jesus. In 1927, Cecil B. De Mille accomplished the near-impossible in his favorite film, *King of Kings*, which won universal acceptance and an audience of 500,000,000 because of the director's balance of gaudy spectacle with genuine reverence and the masterful performance of H. B. Warner as Jesus. That silent film played in theaters and on Easter Sunday telecasts for more than three decades before Samuel Bronston announced in 1960 that he would begin filming a new version of *King of Kings*, which became one of the most inspired yet maligned films in the history of the religious genre.

From the beginning, wails of cynicism greeted Bronston's dream. As with many "classics," De Mille's version had become so well-liked that the mere thought of remaking it was itself a blasphemy to many filmgoers. Additionally, the various uncompromising conceptions of Christ and his teachings were at odds with one another in those preecumenical-movement days, so that the challenge of creating a film that would not alienate large segments of the cinema audience seemed even more impossible than it had been in 1927.

Bronston remained firm. Engaging Philip Yordan, author of such varied films as *Broken Lance* (1954), for which he won an Oscar, and *God's Little*

Acre (1958), to write the script and hiring Nicholas Ray (*Rebel Without a Cause*, 1955) to direct, he exhaustively blueprinted his production. Bronston leased two of Europe's largest studios, the Sevilla and the Charmartin in Madrid, and scouted the Spanish countryside, painstakingly selecting his locations. He chose the chinchon hills near Venta de Frascuela to film the Sermon on the Mount, which itself took a month to shoot and employed seven thousand extras. He selected the village of Manzanares to build his conception of Nazareth; Lake Alberche to represent the Sea of Galilee; and a lonely peak above Navacerrada to present the crucifixion on Calvary. The producer contracted Ray Bradbury to write the narration and Orson Welles to speak it, Miklos Rosza (*Quo Vadis*, 1951; *Ben-Hur*, 1959) to create the musical score, and an international cast to play the major parts. The cast boasted Siobhan McKenna of Ireland's Abbey Players as Mary, Hurd Hatfield as Pontius Pilate, Spanish Carmen Sevilla as Mary Magdalene, Robert Ryan as John the Baptist, Harry Guardino as Barabbas, and Rip Torn as Judas. For Jesus, Bronston picked thirty-three-year-old Jeffrey Hunter, who had earned attention in John Ford's *The Searchers* (1956) and *The Last Hurrah* (1958). "I could only approach this role with two guideposts," said Hunter, "absolute humility and a willingness to accept emotional and spiritual guidance."

Hollywood continued to ridicule the new *King of Kings*. The casting of the wholesome Hunter as the Lord soon resulted in the film's being sarcastically referred to as *I Was a Teenage Jesus*. Bronston and company ignored such remarks, and soon such favorable reports reached Hollywood from Spain that M-G-M president Joseph Vogel decided to investigate. M-G-M was swelling with the profits from *Ben-Hur* and Vogel thought *King of Kings* possibly could prove a worthy follow-up. He was hugely impressed, as was M-G-M's head Sol Siegel, and the studio made a hefty investment in Bronston's film and arranged to release it under the Metro-Goldwyn-Mayer name as a major roadshow attraction. As such, *King of Kings* had its premiere in the fall of 1961—in 70 mm Super Technirama—at a cost of $8,000,000.

The reaction in many circles was almost hysterical. *Time*, in an especially caustic review, attacked Hunter for everything from his blue eyes to his shaved armpits, and used such words as "corniest," "phoniest," and "ickiest" to ridicule the film. The clergy severely criticized the film for presenting Barabbas and Judas as kindred Jewish revolutionaries plotting the overthrow of Rome, for ignoring the part the Scribes and Pharisees played in Christ's crucifixion, and for failing to stress the divinity of Jesus. The Roman Catholic Legion of Decency went so far as to place the film in a special category, suggesting strongly that Catholics ignore it entirely. Upon scrutiny, most of these onslaughts were overly cruel, petty, and specious, for *King of Kings*, as noted by many critics, is a visually beautiful and touching film.

Hunter's performance as Jesus is warm, striking, and moving. *Films in*

Review praised his portrayal as ". . . the kind of Christ image that stirs mankind." He is a vital Christ, handsome but never insipid, and although his voice never quite conveys the impression of true divinity, his performance is filled with conviction and compassion. Especially fine in a supporting role is Siobhan McKenna as Mary, who acts with a gentility and grace rarely seen in contemporary cinema. While the villains of the film—Barabbas, Judas, and King Herod—become somewhat broad at times, their excesses somehow work, forming an interesting contrast and adding a special dimension to the simplicity of Hunter's performance. The magnificent cinematography creates a feeling of looking at a famous biblical painting. Ray Bradbury's narration is majestic and moving, and Miklos Rosza's score is triumphant yet sensitive. All these qualities contribute to the total effect of taste, intelligence, and inspiration.

No Oscars were awarded *King of Kings*. While the film fell far short of the expectations M-G-M held for it, it eventually grossed $6,512,000, making it the studio's top moneymaker of the season. The film did not prove an impetus to Jeffrey Hunter's career. His final years were spent in European films and television (including the pilot for "Star Trek"); he died of a brain hemorrhage in 1969 at the age of forty-two.

Although *King of Kings* is flawed, notably in Yordan's departure from the Gospels and the bypassing of Christ's miracles, it is due for reevaluation today. Certainly, in the wake of such quasibiblical films as *Godspell* (1973) and *Jesus Christ Superstar* (1973), it might be welcomed by the clergy who once criticized it with such vehement intolerance.

Gregory William Mank

KING RAT

Released: 1965
Production: James Woolf for Columbia
Direction: Bryan Forbes
Screenplay: Bryan Forbes; based on the novel of the same name by James Clavell
Cinematography: Burnett Guffey
Editing: Walter Thompson
Art direction: Robert Smith; set decoration, Frank Tuttle
Running time: 134 minutes

Principal characters:
Corporal King	George Segal
Lieutenant Grey	Tom Courtenay
Peter Marlowe	James Fox
Max	Patrick O'Neal
Lieutenant Colonel Larkin	Denholm Elliott
Dr. Kennedy	James Donald
Tex	Todd Armstrong
Colonel Smedley-Taylor	John Mills
Colonel Jones	Gerald Sim

King Rat takes place in the Japanese-held Changi Camp for Allied prisoners-of-war in Singapore during the closing days of World War II. Unlike previously released films of World War II POW's such as *The Great Escape* (1963) and *Stalag 17* (1953), there are no heroes, no high codes of honor, and few gallant sacrifices for fellowmen. Nor is this an adventure story of escape and harassment of the enemy; no one wants to escape from Changi as the surrounding jungle is more of a threat than the rather lax Japanese guards. It is a story of survival of the fittest, and the fittest in this case is the American Corporal King (George Segal).

King is the "King Rat" of the title, and he earns his name from his rat-breeding enterprise. There is also a parallel between the conditions in which King and rats thrive. The camp is a filthy wasteland where hunger, disease, boredom, and demoralization have provided a ripe milieu for the opportunistic King to rise to power. Of the thousands of men at Changi, he is the only one who lives a decent life. Through smart black market dealings with the Japanese guards and other prisoners, he has created an empire in which he, the corporal, controls officers and noncommissioned officers alike. While all others have wasted away to skin and bones, Corporal King remains healthy. While officers are reduced to wearing loincloths and going barefoot, Corporal King always wears freshly pressed uniforms and shined shoes. Even top officers are willing to be placed on his payroll in order to receive extra rations from his larder of chickens and eggs.

The camp is a world apart from the heroic war effort of which the men had been a part. These POW's have lost their war and are now trying to survive by any means possible, even if it means cheating their fellow prisoners out of food. To be caught means death, but this threat does not deter the men. Theirs is a world in which traditional moral standards have no place.

While the men serve King, they also loathe him. He is their source of extra food, but he makes officers and enlisted men alike grovel to receive even one egg. No one hates him more than Lieutenant Grey (Tom Courtenay), a British officer who has made his hatred of King his reason for living. Grey is a lower-class martinet who came up through the ranks to officer status. He has risen above his station by hard work, and as camp Provost Marshall he has decided to be a one-man police force to guard the conventional morality. He would like nothing more than to catch King at some of his illegal doings, thereby toppling him from his position of power, but because of King's network of lookouts and informants, Grey can never quite catch him. However, for all his moralizing even Grey has his price. When he catches two other officers stealing rice with a rigged weight scheme, he is bribed out of pursuing the matter with the offer of a promotion to captain. His ambition overcomes him and he accepts, but the knowledge of his own corruption does not weaken his desire to catch King.

Into this pit of degradation comes Flight Lieutenant Peter Marlowe (James Fox). He is handsome, intelligent, and very upper-class British. Because he speaks fluent Malay, King wants to use him in his black market operation. Torn between his sense of honor and his liking for King, Marlowe is slow to join him; but soon he does, and he and King become friends. With this friendship, Grey now has a further reason to catch King; if he succeeds, he will also catch Marlowe, who represents the rich and privileged upper class that Grey hates.

In this atmosphere of weakness and greed, it is King who leads the others in the art of control and degradation. When a prisoner's pet dog is destroyed for having killed a chicken, King secretly serves up the unfortunate animal's carcass in a stew for his favorite acolytes. When he reveals that it is Hawkins' dog, the men are at first repulsed; but one by one they taste it and soon they are laughing and devouring the stew with gusto. King's masterstroke, however, is to breed rats secretly under the American NCO's hut and then sell the rat meat as an "Oriental delicacy" to Japanese guards and senior Allied officers. Not only does he make money from the scheme, but he and his group also get a great deal of enjoyment from watching the unsuspecting officers dine on the rodents.

A real friendship develops between King and Marlowe. They work well together with Marlowe translating during King's black market negotiations with the Japanese. After being given the money to complete a transaction, involving the purchase of a diamond, Marlowe is seriously injured, his arm gashed by a tree stump during a wood hauling detail. Without proper drugs for treatment, the wound festers and gangrene develops. The doctors decide that the only solution is to amputate the arm. Feverish and sick from pain and fear of losing his arm, Marlowe hides the money in the jungle to avoid being caught by Grey with it in his possession. Without the money, King cannot complete the deal. Out of necessity as well as friendship, he pays for the black market drugs with which to treat Marlowe's arm. The treatment is successful, and after his fever clears, Marlowe retrieves the money and gives it to King along with his total devotion and gratitude for having saved his arm.

When the news runs through the camp that Japan has surrendered, the situation begins to change immediately. With hope, self-respect, and order about to be restored to the men of the camp, King's power dies. Men who had polished his shoes and cooked his meals in exchange for an egg or some cigarettes allow their pent-up resentment to surface into rebellion. Max, one of King's favored lackeys, finds the liberation from his degradation too much and has a violent breakdown. King is the only one who is not happy to see the end of his imprisonment, as he knows that it is the end of his influence. With the arrival of British and American supplies all his food stocks will be useless excess, and already his huge bankroll of Japanese money is worthless. No longer will he be able to buy favors and control lives. Like a rat, he cannot survive without the proper conditions. He is a corporal and must once again take commands from the officers and NCO's who only yesterday slavishly did his bidding. Marlowe is the only one to seek him out after the news of peace. Marlowe realizes that he has survived the ordeal with his mind and body intact only because of King, but when he approaches King he is brusquely rebuffed by the sullen corporal who now calls him sir.

King's downfall is underscored when a lone British officer liberates the camp. At the sight of this seeming apparition from the real world all the POW's recoil from fear at the horror they see reflected in the eyes of this officer as he looks as them, fear of what they have become in order to survive. The only one brave enough to talk to the officer is King. At first relieved that someone at least can talk, the officer soon turns suspicious as he notices the difference between King's neat, well-fed appearance and the ragged, emaciated look of the others. He menacingly tells the corporal that he suspects him of illegal activities and that he will remember him later.

When the Americans arrive to take away their men, Marlowe tries one last time to see King, but again he is rebuffed. As the truck pulls away and Marlowe hears some of the officers openly rejoice at King's downfall, he is the only one to realize that whether they liked or disliked King, it was either his favors or hatred of him that kept many of them alive. As the truck bearing King leaves the camp, Marlowe and King silently stare at each other. In the final image of King from the back of the truck, he is seen uncharacteristically sweaty and unshaven.

When released, the film received excellent reviews for its top-notch acting, direction, cinematography, and engrossing story. It was nominated for Academy Awards for its black-and-white cinematography, art direction, and set decoration. But the American public stayed away. In 1965 the theme of moral failure and survival at any cost was a few years ahead of its time. The anti-Vietnam War protests had hardly begun and the American audience was not interested in a totally nonheroic portrayal of Allied POW behavior. It was not until the late 1960's, when the protests were gaining great momentum, that people began to see *King Rat* and make it into a cult film. However, even if historical events had not made its story popular and relevant to contemporary issues, the film would still be a classic because of its story, acting, directing, and cinematography.

Ellen J. Snyder

KLUTE

Released: 1971
Production: Alan J. Pakula for Warner Bros.
Direction: Alan J. Pakula
Screenplay: Andy K. Lewis and Dave Lewis
Cinematography: Gordon Willis
Editing: Carl Lerner
Running time: 114 minutes

Principal characters:
Bree Daniels .... Jane Fonda (AA)
John Klute .... Donald Sutherland
Peter Cable .... Charles Cioffi
Frank Lagourin .... Roy Scheider
Arlyn Page .... Dorothy Tristan

It is soon evident that *Klute* is not about John Klute (Donald Sutherland), a small-town policeman, but rather about Bree Daniels (Jane Fonda), a big-city prostitute. Little more is learned about Klute than is known from the first minutes of the film, but a great deal is discovered about Bree. It is Bree's tape recorded voice that is heard as the credits and titles are being shown. She is talking to a customer, making him relax, telling him to forget his sexual inhibitions, that she will do anything for his enjoyment. The irony of the story revolves around the tape. As Bree tries to get out of prostitution and create a new life, the man she is addressing on the tape comes out of the past to destroy her because of her knowledge of his sick habits. The same tape is heard to good effect several times during the film as the killer uses it for his own perverted enjoyment and as a psychological weapon against Bree.

When Bree is first observed, she is, rather unsuccessfully, trying to make her living as a model and actress. Because she still reverts to her former profession now and then, she is also seeing a psychiatrist. The scenes with the analyst are spaced throughout the film, and it is through them that Bree reveals the most about herself. She gets no enjoyment from sex or from her customers; what she likes is the control she has over the situation. The more nervous the man is the better she likes it, since it makes him easier to manipulate, and for one hour she is the best actress in the world. The polished speech on the tape is part of her act. Bree has built an emotional wall around herself, and nothing breaks through except fear. The fear comes not from the loneliness of her life, but from obscene letters, unknown phone callers, and a feeling that she is being watched.

John Klute has come to New York to find his friend, Tom, who has been missing for six months. He is supported in his search by Tom's wife and by Peter Cable (Charles Cioffi), a friend and business associate of Tom. All three refuse to believe the detectives who say that the home-loving Tom has apparently disappeared to pursue the dark side of a lurid double life and has possibly been sending obscene letters to a New York call girl.

Klute's only clue is the girl, Bree, but she is totally uncooperative. He persistently follows her and watches as she makes a late night call on an old man in his garment factory. When she returns to her apartment, Klute shows her that he has taken a room in her building and has tape recorded her phone calls in the hope that Tom will call. Bree is abrasive at first, but later, in her apartment, she turns seductive in an effort to get the tapes from him. Klute seemingly goes along with her, but then informs her that someone is watching them through the skylight. Thinking the voyeur might be Tom, Klute tries to catch him. He is unsuccessful. When he returns, the shaken Bree tells him about the same things that she told the detectives investigating Tom's disappearance: the receiving of the obscene letters; that Tom might be the man who once tried to beat her to death, but she cannot positively identify him.

The man who beat Bree and who, it is learned later, killed Tom, is revealed to the audience as he listens to the tape of Bree's voice. As his face is seen in distorted reflection on the highly polished surface of a desk, the camera pulls back to reveal Tom's friend and Klute's employer, Peter Cable, to whom Klute has been reporting his information. Cable is shown to be a successful and powerful man, albeit a sick one. He is often seen reflected in or framed by windows, a device Pakula uses to show his isolation.

Bree is frightened into helping in the search for Tom, but she exacts a price. One night, filled with fear, she comes to Klute's room and seduces him. The act of manipulation momentarily restores her confidence, and she is bitchily triumphant as she lets Klute know that he has been duped. Once back in her apartment, however, the fear returns.

Bree takes Klute to Frank Lagourin (Roy Scheider), who used to pimp for Bree and two other women. They find out that Jane McKenna, who was jealous of Frank's attention to Bree, knew a man who liked to beat girls, and set up Bree with him. Since Jane has committed suicide, Klute needs Bree to find the third girl, Arlyn Page (Dorothy Triston), who might also know of the man. Arlyn has become a junkie, and the search takes them lower and lower until they find her in a slum, strung out and anxious for a fix. Arlyn does not remember much about the perverted John, except, when shown a picture, that it was not Tom.

Visiting the scenes of Arlyn's degradation unnerves Bree and sends her running back to Frank and to drugs. She becomes ill and Klute moves in with her to nurse her back to health and to help her get over the shock of the news of Arlyn Page's suicide. Bree responds to his kindness and grows to care for him in spite of herself. In a key scene with the psychiatrist, Bree explains that for once she is not setting up anything with a man, and that feelings flow naturally between them. Klute has seen her mean and ugly but accepts her as she is. She even enjoys sex with him; but she also finds Klute's intrusion on her emotions a threat. She realizes that she is beginning to feel again and it frightens her. She wishes she could go back to the comfort of being numb. She likes her relationship with Klute but is fearful of her urge to destroy it.

Her conflicting emotions are brought into crisis when her apartment is totally vandalized. As Bree and Klute inspect the damage, the phone rings and Bree hears her own tape recorded voice. In panic she turns again to Frank instead of Klute. When Klute physically tries to stop her from going off with Frank, Bree attacks him with a scissors. She succeeds only in cutting his suit, but Klute immediately backs off and allows her to go. Disturbed by her own murderous intentions, Bree runs from her building, alone.

From his investigation, Klute has come to the conclusion that Jane McKenna and Arlyn were not suicides, but murder victims, and whoever killed them possibly also killed Tom. A comparison of typewritten letters of Tom's friends and family reveals that the obscene letters to Bree were written by Peter Cable. Faced with only circumstantial evidence, Klute tells Cable a story about Jane McKenna recording the names of her customers in an address book. Whoever beat up Bree and wrecked her apartment must be in it, and the case can be closed if he, Klute, can buy it. The ruse works as the panicked Cable, thinking that Bree has the book, cancels his travel plans and ends up waiting for her as she storms out of her apartment building after attacking Klute.

In need of someone to talk to, Bree goes to see the old man in the garment factory, whom she wrongly assumes is a friend. He leaves early in order to avoid her, and as the factory closes, Bree remains behind. Cable corners her there and asks for the book, about which Bree knows nothing. He confesses that he had to kill Tom and the women because of their knowledge about him, and makes Bree listen to a tape of one of his murders. Klute arrives, and during their struggle, Cable falls to his death through a window.

The ending is purposely ambiguous. As Bree is seen happily preparing to leave New York with Klute, there is a voice-over of her telling her psychiatrist that she does not know what will happen, but that the doctor will probably be seeing her next week.

The film established Alan J. Pakula as a major director and earned an Academy Award for Best Actress for Jane Fonda. The acting is excellent throughout. Some of the scenes, such as those with the psychiatrist, are improvised and add an almost documentary touch to the film.

Pakula uses several devices to create an atmosphere of menace. In addition to the innovative use of the tape recorder, the tinkling music which often signals the presence of the killer is highly effective. The cinematography adds to the suspense by creating an almost claustrophobic atmosphere. The camera stays in close as it shows New York's seamy side, and the mood achieved is one of imprisonment. There are also the often-used devices of the unknown stalker; the heroine going off alone so there can be a final confrontation with the killer; and the arrival of the hero in the nick of time. However, in *Klute* they work because they are done better, and the result is a first-class thriller.

Ellen J. Snyder

KRAMER VS. KRAMER

Released: 1979
Production: Stanley Jaffe for Columbia (AA)
Direction: Robert Benton (AA)
Screenplay: Robert Benton (AA); based on the novel of the same name by
  Avery Corman
Cinematography: Nestor Almendros
Editing: Jerry Greenberg
Running time: 105 minutes

Principal characters:
Ted Kramer ....Dustin Hoffman (AA)
Joanna Kramer .... Meryl Streep (AA)
Billy Kramer .... Justin Henry
Margaret Phelps .... Jane Alexander
John Shaunessy .... Howard Duff

By the late 1970's, divorce had become an increasingly prevalent social
phenomenon in the United States; and, like all such phenomena, it was fair
game for filmmakers. *An Unmarried Woman* (1978) and *Starting Over* (1979)
were both reasonably sensitive looks at the problems associated with contemporary divorce. These films, however, dealt with the effects of divorce on
the adult marriage partners. Robert Benton's *Kramer vs. Kramer*, while not
neglecting the husband and wife, introduces the couple's young son into the
equation. *Kramer vs. Kramer* is the story of a broken marriage; of a wife's
struggle (mostly offscreen) to find herself; of a failed husband's struggle to
succeed as a father; and of a seven-year-old boy's struggle to comprehend his
parents' actions.

As the film opens, we see Joanna Kramer (Meryl Streep), obviously distressed, saying goodnight to her son Billy (Justin Henry). When her husband
Ted (Dustin Hoffman) arrives home from the office late, we find out why she
is upset: she is leaving her husband. It takes awhile for her quiet announcement to penetrate her husband's preoccupied consciousness. He has just
received a promotion at the advertising agency where he works, and is too
full of his own thoughts to pay attention to his wife. Finally, however, he
understands that something is wrong. "I'm sorry that I was late, but I was
busy trying to make a living, O.K.?" he explains, still refusing to accept his
wife's decision to leave at face value. Joanna remains adamant, however,
even after Ted recognizes the gravity of the situation and pleads with her to
stay. "What about Billy?" he asks. "I'm terrible with him," she replies. "He's
better off with you."

Thus Benton sets the stage for Ted Kramer's eighteen-month lesson in
single parenthood. It is a period during which Ted will achieve significant

personal growth, but this maturity will not come easily. Ted Kramer has difficulty coping with simple household chores. He makes a complete mess of his first attempt to prepare breakfast, and his efforts are hampered by his determination to remain cheerful to avoid worrying Billy. The effect, of course, is precisely the opposite. Billy knows immediately that something is seriously wrong.

Ted's very real—if, in the beginning, often distracted—devotion to his son is one of several pleasant revelations about Ted's character that director Robert Benton reveals early in the film. Although Ted pledges his unswerving loyalty to the advertising agency (twenty-five hours a day, eight days a week, he swears), he rejects his boss's advice to send Billy to live with relatives. At the risk of jeopardizing his career, he intends to be a father to his son (even though at this point he has no real understanding of what being a father involves).

Further evidence of Ted's basic decency comes when, despite the fact that he cannot fathom Joanna's motives for leaving him, he scrupulously defends her in front of Billy and constantly reassures his son that his mother loves him. Even when Joanna sends Billy an awkward letter that reads, in part, "I have gone away because I must find something interesting to do in the world," and which only hurts the boy further, Ted insists that Joanna's love for Billy is undiminished. Thus we see that, despite his undeniable neglect of his wife, Ted Kramer is basically a good person. But Benton is quick to demonstrate that Ted's desire to be a good father does not make him one overnight. Ted has no conception of Billy's emotional needs, especially his seemingly constant need for attention. Preoccupied with the work that he always brings home from the office, Ted often lashes out at Billy for acting like a child—as if a seven-year-old boy could act otherwise.

Gradually, however, the father and son adjust to each other. Their once-frenetic breakfasts turn into quiet affairs. In one scene that is funny and touching at the same time, the two sit silently, reading—Ted his morning newspaper, Billy a comic book. The two have achieved an intimacy that permits them, at least on occasion, to share each other's lives without talking all the time.

An important figure in this transitional period is the Kramers' neighbor, Margaret Phelps (Jane Alexander). Although Ted is initially hostile to her— she was his wife's friend, and he suspects her of encouraging Joanna to leave him—they have much in common. Margaret is herself a divorced parent, and as her children and Billy play in a nearby park, she and Ted have long talks about life and love (both swearing that they have no interest in returning to their respective spouses). They never become lovers, but they do become friends.

Through his talks with Margaret, and also through his own intense self-analysis, Ted finally comes to some understanding of why Joanna felt that she had to leave him. He articulates his insights in the emotional aftermath of a fight with Billy. His son, it seems, had been blaming himself all along for his mother's desertion. Ted assures him that it is not so. "Mommy left because *I* was bad," he says, and he begins, very simply, to explain that he had never taken the time to try to understand his wife's emotional and intellectual needs: "I thought that anytime I was happy, she was happy."

Even as the relationship between Ted and his son deepens, however, trouble looms on the horizon. Ted's boss is clearly growing frustrated with the inevitable decline in Ted's productivity that has resulted from his increasing attention to Billy; and Joanna is back in town. Having spent several months in California in therapy, she has returned to New York to live and work (at a $31,000 a year job designing sportswear), and she is feeling much better about herself. In fact, she now has enough self-esteem to believe that she would be a good mother to Billy, and she wants him back. Ted vows not to give him up, and the legal battle for custody implicit in the film's title begins.

In the meantime, Ted's preoccupation with his family life finally becomes too much for his boss, who fires him three days before Christmas, and just before the custody hearing. Aware that being unemployed would destroy his chances in court, Ted takes another job, but at a significant reduction in salary and responsibility.

The remainder of the film is a very convincing illustration of the dehumanization that can result from the introduction of courts and lawyers into family disputes. Ted's attorney, John Shaunessy (Howard Duff), warns him that things will be rough, but Ted does not realize how rough until the trial begins. The affair is harrowing for everyone involved. Both Ted and Joanna offer emotional and convincing testimony of their love for Billy and their desire to have custody of him. Neither Ted nor Joanna questions the other's ability as a parent; both emphasize their own strengths in their pleas. However, the two attorneys know that custody battles are not won by acknowledging the competence of your opponent as a parent, and they both base their cases on an attempt to impugn the character of their client's ex-spouse.

As John Shaunessy belittles Joanna's efforts to straighten out her life in California, Ted winces at the savagery of his attack. When Shaunessy asserts to a shaken Joanna that "you were a failure at the one most important relationship in your life," Ted catches her eye, gives her a reassuring smile, and shakes his head no, denying his own attorney's allegations. Joanna's attorney concentrates his attack on Ted's recent career setback. Joanna squirms uncomfortably as it becomes clear that Ted neglected his job only to be a better father to Billy; after his testimony is finished, she tearfully apologizes to him.

Their by-now mutual friend Margaret then takes the stand to testify that they are both good parents, and, addressing herself directly to Joanna, says "Ted is not the same man" he was when Joanna left him. She suggests that if Joanna could know Ted as he is now, a reconciliation might be possible. The cumulative effect of the trial scenes is highly emotional—for the viewer as well as for Ted and Joanna. Though our sympathies tend to lie with Ted—the audience has watched him grow throughout the film, whereas Joanna has been offscreen most of the time—Benton has markedly strengthened Joanna's case. No matter which way the judge's decision goes, we know that a good person and loving parent will suffer.

As it happens, the judge rules in favor of Joanna. Ted is utterly stricken at the thought of losing Billy, but declines to appeal the verdict when Shaunessy tells him that in any subsequent trial it would be necessary to force Billy to testify and take sides. Although he is heartbroken, Ted explains the judge's decision to Billy simply and honestly, by reiterating Joanna's love for her son.

Billy, however, is more than a little dubious about living with his mother, and the breakfast on the morning that Joanna is to take custody (french toast—the same as on the morning after Joanna left fifteen months earlier) is a solemn affair. When Joanna arrives, however, she asks to speak to Ted alone. Visibly shaken, she tells Ted that she has had second thoughts about taking Billy from his father. "I came here to take my son home, and I realized he already is home," she says. Ted can keep Billy. The film ends as Joanna, pulling herself together, prepares to tell Billy of her decision. "How do I look?" she asks Ted nervously. "Terrific" is his reply.

Kramer vs. Kramer was an instantaneous hit, both with the critics and at the box office. The critics, almost by acclamation, declared the film the finest of the year, and indeed, among the finest of the decade. It won most of the year's major awards, including the Academy Award for Best Picture of the year.

The acting among the principals in the cast is uniformly outstanding. Dustin Hoffman's Oscar-winning transformation of Ted Kramer from a gung-ho Madison Avenue automaton into a thinking, feeling, loving father is a joy to watch; it is a quiet *tour de force*. In most films, a performance such as Hoffman's would have overshadowed everything else in the film. In *Kramer vs. Kramer*, however, it simply blends naturally with several other top-notch performances.

Meryl Streep, who won the Oscar for Best Supporting Actress as Joanna Kramer, makes her character, offscreen for much of the time, a dominant force in the film. The wonder is that she created this presence almost entirely in one scene: that of her courtroom testimony (which she reportedly wrote herself). Her eloquent apologia for her fifteen-month desertion of her son and her plea for another chance to be Billy's mother leaves few viewers unmoved. Jane Alexander gives a strong performance as the warm, likable Margaret. Young Justin Henry as Billy accomplishes a difficult task that, over the years, has eluded almost every child actor in the history of the cinema:

he gives a convincing portrayal of a normal child. The viewer comes to love him as much as Ted and Joanna Kramer do. Alexander and Henry were both nominated for Oscars for their roles; however, neither won. Alexander lost to Streep, and Henry, the youngest person ever to be nominated for an Oscar, lost to seventy-nine-year-old Melvyn Douglas for his performance in *Being There*.

Apart from the acting, credit for the film's success is due to Robert Benton, who received Oscars both for his screenplay and his direction of *Kramer vs. Kramer*. Any film about something as emotionally charged as a child custody battle runs a high risk of degenerating into soap opera. Yet Benton, although he never loses sight of the emotion inherent in the situation, never lets these emotions slide into mere sentimentality. The film is expertly paced and judiciously balanced. Although basically a serious film, it contains more than a few humorous moments; and none of the characters—save, perhaps, the attorneys—are either too good or too bad to be true. *Kramer vs. Kramer* is, above all, a film about real human beings.

Like *An Unmarried Woman*, *Kramer vs. Kramer* is perhaps open to the charge that its protagonists hardly represent the typical American family, broken or otherwise. An early clue to the Kramers' social status is revealed when one of the things that Joanna gives up when she leaves Ted is her Bloomingdale's credit card. Too much is made of Ted's cut in salary to a "mere" $28,200. And, after a few months of sorting her thoughts out in California, Joanna, a woman with no previous work history, is able to land a job back in New York at $31,000 a year. Still, *Kramer vs. Kramer* is far from being a story about the problems of the rich.

Additionally, some feminists have argued that the film is unfairly slanted towards Ted Kramer's point of view. Taken narrowly, this criticism is perfectly valid; Ted's character is undeniably better developed than Joanna's, although, as we have seen, Joanna is by no means an entirely unsympathetic person, and Margaret, the only major female role, is also an appealing character.

Perhaps the best response to both of these criticisms is that Benton was not trying to make a film of universal applicability (even if such a film were possible); and that, while it would have been interesting to see a version of *Kramer vs. Kramer* told from Joanna's viewpoint (or from the point of view of a blue-collar family, a black family, and so forth), these are not the films that Benton chose to make. Rather, working from Avery Corman's popular novel, he simply made a film about one particular broken marriage.

Many critics have suggested that a reconciliation between Ted and Joanna is implicit in the film's ending, and there are indeed hints that something like this might take place. Their friend Margaret suggests the possibility briefly at the custody hearing—and Margaret herself, by the end of the film, appears to be on her way to getting back together with her ex-husband. Benton has clearly ended *Kramer vs. Kramer* in an atmosphere of reconciliation. Whether

Ted and Joanna will eventually remarry, however, one thing is clear. By the end of the film they have come to understand and respect each other as individuals and as the parents of their son. This is more than they had accomplished when they were married, and reason enough for the viewer to be satisfied with the outcome of the film.

Robert Mitchell

THE L-SHAPED ROOM

Released: 1963
Production: James Woolf and Richard Attenborough for Romulus Productions; released by Columbia
Direction: Bryan Forbes
Screenplay: Bryan Forbes; based on the novel of the same name by Lynne Reid Banks
Cinematography: Douglas Slocombe
Editing: Anthony Harvey
Running time: 124 minutes

> *Principal characters:*
> Jane .... Leslie Caron
> Toby .... Tom Bell
> Johnny .... Brock Peters
> Mavis .... Cicely Courtneidge
> Doris .... Avis Bunnage

The L-Shaped Room is an intensely personal story of loneliness, friendship, love, and strength. It takes its name from the shape of the bug-infested room that Jane (Leslie Caron), the main character, takes in a decaying rooming house in London's Notting Hill section. Jane is a twenty-seven-year-old, unmarried Frenchwoman who is without friends, and who is pregnant as a result of a loveless affair. The plot revolves around the close friendship she finds in the rooming house, her attempt at an abortion, and her decision to have her baby and face the future on her own terms.

Jane's bumpy road to inner peace and strength begins with a visit to a high-priced abortionist-doctor. Although she has come for the purpose of terminating her pregnancy, the doctor's offhand attitude and inane questions about the child's father and her own parents irritate her. Angrily she replies that the baby's father has nothing to do with this, as she chooses not to marry him, and that she expects no help from her parents, as an unwed pregnancy is simply not possible in their closed-minded world. The doctor's casual and mercenary willingness to make an appointment for the abortion without even examining her infuriates Jane. She upbraids him for not asking that she consider keeping her baby, and leaves in disgust.

She returns to the shabby rooming house in which most of the story takes place. Like Jane, the other boarders are down and out, some permanently so; but while their poverty weighs heavily on them at times, the atmosphere of support eventually wins out. It is altogether a motley group. There is Toby (Tom Bell), an unsuccessful writer currently subsisting on his earnings from creating jokes for cracker boxes, who is obviously interested in girls; Mavis (Cicely Courtneidge), a former vaudevillian who lives surrounded by mementos of her good old days, and who, from her first-floor room, keeps track of all the boarders; Johnny (Brock Peters), a black jazz musician whose presence in the room next to Jane's is both a comfort and a source of trauma; Doris (Avis Bunnage), the bitchy and quixotic landlady whose minor evils include taking nasty delight in confusing the French girl with English slang; and two prostitutes in the basement rooms.

Before her encounter with the doctor, Jane's spirits were already low as a result of spending the first night in her new room sleeping in a chair because her mattress was infested with bugs. When she returns home, her neighbor Johnny, who knows about the condition of the mattress, cheers her by making her some tea. This simple gesture relaxes Jane, and soon a spirit of camaraderie develops between Jane, Toby, Johnny, and Mavis as they successfuly plot a way to get a new mattress for Jane from Doris.

Jane responds to Toby the most; their discussions show Toby's frustration over his lack of success as a writer and his depression over a failed love affair in which the girl dropped him for a wealthy man, while Jane expresses her despair over being twenty-seven years old and not yet knowing what love is. She soon learns, however, as their friendship deepens and they become lovers, but her love for Toby confuses her even more and makes her fearful of telling him about the baby. She tells no one that she is pregnant, but both Mavis and Johnny have learned—Mavis by overhearing her phone call to the doctor, and Johnny as a result of hearing her bouts of morning sickness through the thin walls separating their rooms. Johnny is also aware of the growing relationship between Jane and Toby since he has been a silent listener to their conversations in Jane's room.

The fact that Jane has decided to have her baby and be self-sufficient is underscored when she runs into her former lover, the father of her child. When she reveals that she is pregnant, he suggests that she get an abortion so they can start all over again. Jane rejects this suggestion and comments that everyone is willing to help her get rid of it. Since it was a loveless affair, she refuses to make it more than it was. She rejects his offer of money and informs him that she always has known how to get in touch with him; she simply has not wanted to.

The day after Jane and Toby have become lovers, Jane runs home from work to find him, but Toby is conspicuously absent, and she sees only an angry and jealous Johnny. He calls her a whore for sleeping with Toby and a troublemaker since Toby no longer talks to him as he did before she came. When Toby still has not returned later that night, Johnny apologizes and reveals his knowledge of the baby; he explains that Toby went away after he told him about it. Jane, stricken by this news, forgives Johnny because she sees that it is her own fault for not having told Toby first.

As Jane leaves for work the next day, Mavis gives her some pills which are supposed to cause an abortion. Toby's rejection breaks her will as nothing else has, and she takes all of the pills. As they take effect, she collapses on her way home from work and ends up in the hospital. Shocked back into reality, she realizes that she really wants to have her baby. To her relief, the doctor attending her informs her that she is still pregnant.

Jane returns home happy and thankful and ready to face Toby. When he sullenly meets her at the door, she tells him that she loves him but was afraid to tell him about the baby, and sadly admits that it was a mistake. Toby explodes in resentment and jealously because he loves her and the baby is not his. He accuses her of trying to get him to give it his name through marriage. His anger so destroys what pathetically little emotional strength Jane has left that he immediately becomes apologetic and comforting.

As Christmas approaches, the situation between Jane and Toby remains close but tense. Jane, in the final months of pregnancy, is sensitive about her appearance, and they are both sensitive about their poverty. Toby, particularly sensitive over his poverty, becomes most depressed when a joyous Jane brings him a small present on Christmas Day. Resentful that he has nothing to give her, he tells her that the relationship is over between them. Jane accepts this philosophically but sadly, and tells him that she is not his responsibility; since they are not married, they are both quite free.

All of the boarders except Toby gather in Doris' room for a Christmas party. In the midst of the merrymaking Jane goes into labor. Her baby, a healthy girl, is born prematurely on Christmas Day. When Toby finally comes to see her in the hospital, he brings a present for both her and the baby—a story which he has written entitled "The L-Shaped Room" which is their story, and of which he wants to know her opinion. Now dressed in a suit, it is obvious that things are better for Toby; in addition to having completed the story, he has also found a job in a bookstore. He asks if what he has heard from Doris is true—that she intends to return to France and her parents instead of coming back to the rooming house. Jane confirms that she is returning, but at least on her own terms since no one can take the baby away from her. When Toby apologizes, Jane tells him that she is not sorry she met him, nor is she sorry that she has had the baby. As Toby leaves the hospital, a nurse, assuming that he is Jane's husband, tells him that his daughter is as pretty as her mother.

Before returning to France, Jane goes to the rooming house to pick up her things and to leave the manuscript of "The L-Shaped Room" in Toby's room. It is evident from the note she has attached to it that she has come to terms with her life and does not want to close the door on Toby. In it she tells him that it is a wonderful story, but it has no ending. And on that note, the film ends.

The entire cast is well suited to the drama, pathos, and humor that Bryan Forbes put into his script. While there is more tension than humor, it is the humor that keeps the story from becoming maudlin. The film was a critical success. Both Leslie Caron and Tom Bell were praised for the warmth and intensity of their performances, but Caron received the most honors, winning the British Academy Award and the New York Critics Award for Best Actress, and receiving a nomination for an American Academy Award in the same category.

Bryan Forbes had received widespread acclaim for his first directorial effort, *Whistle Down the Wind*, the year before. With *The L-Shaped Room*, his reputation as a director was solidified. Although there were some problems getting the film past British censors because of the abortion issue, the film, in the end, was released intact because of the careful handling of the subject. Only the clothes and hairstyles date the film. The story and performances are timeless, and the excellence of both have made the film a classic.

Ellen J. Snyder

THE LADY EVE

Released: 1941
Production: Paul Jones for Paramount
Direction: Preston Sturges
Screenplay: Preston Sturges; based on a story of the same name by Monckton Hoffe
Cinematography: Victor Milner
Editing: Stuart Gilmore
Running time: 97 minutes

> *Principal characters:*
> Jean Harrington .... Barbara Stanwyck
> Charles Pike .... Henry Fonda
> "Colonel" Harrington .... Charles Coburn
> Mr. Pike .... Eugene Pallette
> Muggsy .... William Demarest
> Sir Alfred McGlennan Keith .... Eric Blore

After writing a number of films in the 1930's, Preston Sturges began directing his own scripts in 1940 and created a series of eight excellent comedies in the next five years. The third of these, *The Lady Eve*, takes the familiar story of a sophisticated woman trying to take advantage of a naïve man and makes it fresh and funny with so many inventive variations that we are continually surprised as Sturges keeps the mood changing between light romance, sophisticated comedy, and outright farce.

The naïve young man is Charles Pike (Henry Fonda), an expert on snakes and the heir to the Pike's Pale Ale fortune. The sophisticated woman is Jean Harrington (Barbara Stanwyck), the daughter of "Colonel" Harrington (Charles Coburn). The latter two are card sharps who make a very nice living by bilking unsuspecting rich people. We first see Charles at the end of a scientific expedition in the Amazon. It is only when he leaves the uncivilized jungle for a civilized voyage home that he has trouble. On board a luxury liner headed for the United States, he hopes to ignore the rest of the passengers and read a book with the unlikely title, *Are Snakes Necessary?* Most of the women on board, however, know how rich he is and try everything they can think of to get him to notice them. Only Jean Harrington understands his scholarly naïveté well enough to devise an effective stratagem; she trips him and then claims that he has broken the heel off her shoe and must take her to her room so that she can change shoes. There she easily manipulates him with casual disdain. She leans against her trunk full of shoes and asks flirtatiously, "See anything you like?," but later when he makes a tentative move to kiss her, she pulls back, exclaiming that he should be kept in a cage.

She then returns him to the dining room for the next step in her scheme.

She and her father play a friendly game of cards with him, allowing him to win a few hundred dollars in order to set him up for the thousands of dollars they hope to win the next day. That night the Colonel is delighted with the progress of events and is anxiously awaiting the next day when they can take advantage of Charles. Jean, however, finds that she has fallen in love with him and does not want him to be cheated. She then has to protect Charles from her father; even though she outsmarts and outtricks the Colonel in a hilarious card game, Charles ends up losing thirty-two thousand dollars afterwards. When Jean finds this out, her father graciously tears up the check and Jean can look forward happily to marrying Charles, who has of course fallen in love with her.

All Jean's plans collapse, however, when Charles's bodyguard and caretaker, Muggsy (William Demarest), who has been suspicious of the Harringtons all along, obtains proof that they are cardsharps. Charles refuses to listen to any explanation from Jean, leaving her with only a desire for revenge and the thirty-two-thousand-dollar check, which the Colonel had only pretended to destroy.

Jean's scheme for revenge is a completely unexpected and ingenious one. When she finds out that an old friend and fellow shyster, now calling himself Sir Alfred McGlennan Keith (Eric Blore), is living near the Pike home, she arranges to have herself introduced at a party given by the Pikes as Keith's niece, Lady Eve Sidwich, using no disguise except an English accent. She immediately captivates all the men at the party, including Charles's father (Eugene Pallette), and when Charles insists he has seen her before, she easily convinces him that he has not, blithely saying she has never been to South America. Even though Muggsy is certain that she is Jean, Charles is persuaded that she is not because she has made no attempt to change her appearance. "They look too much alike to be the same," he tells Muggsy.

After the party she tells Keith her plan, and as she talks, we see it being carried out. Within two or three weeks she has persuaded Charles to propose to her as Eve, and after the wedding we find out how she takes her revenge. Once they are on the train for their honeymoon, she tells him that she eloped with a stable boy when she was sixteen, assuring Charles that the boy was "no one of the slightest importance." As the train continues, we hear bits of her stories about other men until Charles, overwhelmed, finally takes his suitcases and gets off the train, only to fall down ignominiously in the mud.

Jean now has a perfect chance to get a large settlement from the Pikes in exchange for giving Charles a divorce, but once again, she realizes she still loves him and refuses a settlement. Finding that he is taking a ship back to South America, she takes the same ship and once again trips him as he walks through the dining room. This time, however, he embraces her passionately, and the two rush off to her cabin. He thinks he has met Jean Harrington again rather than Lady Eve Sidwich and momentarily tries to protest that he should not be in her cabin since he is married, but as the door closes, Jean silences him by saying, "But so am I, darling, so am I." As the film ends, the door quickly reopens, and Muggsy slips out, saying, "Positively the same dame."

That the viewer can accept as plausible and be entertained by the wildly improbable notion that Charles never realizes that Jean and Eve are the same person testifies to the successful blending of acting, writing, and directing which makes *The Lady Eve* so delightful. As writer and director, Preston Sturges deserves most credit for the film's success. Especially good are his sense of pacing and his imaginative ways of developing and conveying certain points.

Since the first romance of Charles and Jean is the most credible, Sturges develops it rather slowly; we watch Jean toying with her prey so long that she becomes ensnared herself. The less plausible capture of Charles by Lady Eve is covered so quickly and imaginatively that we have no time to ponder its implausibility. After the party at the Pike house, three fairly short scenes sketch the rest of the story: Jean tells her plans to Keith; Charles proposes in a humorous scene in which his horse keeps getting in the way; a wordless montage shows the preparation for the wedding and the ceremony itself. And the third part of the romance, the final reunion of Charles and Jean, is shown in only one short scene.

Particularly imaginative is the way Sturges presents the female competition for Charles's attention during the first scene in the ship's dining room. We see nearly all of it reflected in a compact mirror which Jean uses to watch the futile efforts of the other women to ensnare Charles while she comments on their lack of skill. It is a clever way of cinematically demonstrating her viewpoint. Also imaginative is the presentation of Jean's "confessions" on the train. In a fairly long scene we hear her tell Charles about the stable boy, and then Sturges begins switching back and forth between short exterior shots of the train as it roars through a thunderstorm and short scenes inside the train to hear just enough to realize Jean is talking about yet another man in her life.

Barbara Stanwyck as Jean Harrington has the choicest role in *The Lady Eve*, and she plays it to perfection. She is alternately cynical, tender, vindictive, vulnerable, seductive, and distant, making all these moods credible. We admire Jean's technique in manipulating Charles without feeling that she is truly a villain. Henry Fonda's role as Charles is more limited, but one which is, in its way, much more difficult. He must make us believe that Charles is so naïve that he does not recognize that "The Lady Eve" is really Jean Harrington; but we must never see him as merely stupid or as only an object of fun. Even when he is least in command, we must see him as a sympathetic character and must understand why Jean loves him. Fonda accomplishes all this impressively.

As in all the great Preston Sturges films, *The Lady Eve* boasts a superb supporting cast which contributes especially vivid comic characterizations. Charles Coburn has one of the best roles of his three decades in film as Colonel Harrington, whose creed, he tells his daughter, is "Let us be crooked but never common." Jean agrees at that time, but later when she has fallen in love and refuses to cheat Charles, the Colonel complains, "Children don't respect their parents any more." As Charles's bodyguard Muggsy, William Demarest, who was a Sturges favorite, is appropriately tough and watchful even if Charles does not always appreciate his help. And Eric Blore is memorable as the confidence man who calls himself Sir Alfred McGlennan Keith. When Jean asks if he knows the Pikes, he replies, "I positively swill in their ale."

The comic genius of Preston Sturges was recognized by both the public and the critics. *The Lady Eve* was one of the most popular films of 1941 and was chosen by the *New York Times* as the best picture of the year. *The Lady Eve* was remade in 1956 as *The Birds and the Bees*, but with George Gobel and Mitzi Gaynor in the lead roles, it was doomed to be weaker than the original.

Timothy W. Johnson

THE LADY VANISHES

Released: 1938
Production: Edward Black for Gainsborough Pictures
Direction: Alfred Hitchcock
Screenplay: Sidney Gillatt and Frank Launder; based on Alma Reville's adaptation of the novel *The Wheel Spins* by Ethel Lina White
Cinematography: Jack Cox
Editing: Alfred Roome and R. E. Dearing
Running time: 97 minutes

Principal characters:
Iris Henderson	Margaret Lockwood
Gilbert	Michael Redgrave
Miss Froy	Dame May Whitty
Dr. Hartz	Paul Lukas
Mr. Todhunter	Cecil Parker
Caldicott	Naunton Wayne
Charters	Basil Radford
Margaret	Linden Travers
Madame Kummer	Josephine Wilson

Alfred Hitchcock's last important and most acclaimed British film, *The Lady Vanishes*, in many ways epitomizes his British films, which are simpler and less pretentious than his later American ones. Few Hitchcock films have had such an enthusiastic critical reception as *The Lady Vanishes*, which is arguably the best of his British films and certainly one of his most ingenious and entertaining. The story concerns an elderly English governess whose disappearance from a train sets off a string of mysterious incidents. The pace never slackens as Hitchcock keeps the tension mounting until the final scene. Indeed, *The Lady Vanishes* is quintessential Hitchcock, complete with a beautiful heroine, a perplexed hero, international spies, and a train journey, all set amidst much suspense.

Somewhere in a Central European country, the passengers on a transcontinental train are stranded at a small inn by an avalanche. Unprepared to accommodate such a large number of guests, the innkeeper does not have enough rooms or food for all of the passengers, two of whom are very British and unflappable cricket fans who are hurrying home to see the championship cricket matches. At dinner they are forced to share a table with an elderly British governess, Miss Froy (Dame May Whitty), who is returning home after having spent six years in an unnamed Central European country and who offers to share her cheese with them since the inn's food had run out some time before. Also staying at the inn is an English heiress, Iris Henderson (Margaret Lockwood), who is having a final vacation before returning to England to be married. Upset by the noise in the room above hers, she has its occupant, Gilbert (Michael Redgrave), a music scholar recording the vanishing folk dances of Central Europe, thrown out. When he responds by threatening to occupy her own room, she hurriedly calls the manager to have him restored to his room.

The next morning the railroad track is cleared and the train's passengers prepare to continue their journey. As Iris is waiting to board the train, however, she is struck on the head by a flower pot; and her momentary unconsciousness and dizziness are conveyed on film by multiple images of her friends and the train wheels. Miss Froy kindly assists Iris into a compartment on the train and later takes her to the dining car for tea. As they pass a compartment with an English couple in it, the man quickly pulls down the blind for privacy.

In the dining car Miss Froy asks the waiter to brew her a special packet of herb tea which she takes from her handbag, and later requests the sugar bowl from the two cricket fans who are demonstrating a cricket play with sugar cubes. While they drink their tea she tries to introduce herself to Iris, but her voice is drowned out by the train's whistle, so she writes her name in the steam on the windowpane. Having introduced the principal characters in the confined setting where most of the action will take place, and having established the principal clues, Hitchcock has carefully prepared the film for the next part of the story.

After Miss Froy and Iris return to their compartment, Iris tries to sleep while Miss Froy begins to do a crossword puzzle. Iris drifts off to sleep and later, as she slowly awakens, looks sleepily around the compartment and realizes that Miss Froy is not there. When she asks the other occupants of the compartment where she is, a forbidding gray-haired Baroness assures her that there has not been any English lady besides Iris herself in the compartment and suggests that the blow on her head has made her forgetful.

Iris begins a search through the train for Miss Froy; when she reaches the dining car, the waiter who has served them insists that Iris took tea by herself, producing a bill to prove it. Unconvinced, Iris continues her search, blundering into the third-class compartment where she encounters Gilbert once again. Although their relationship is more antagonistic than romantic at this point, Gilbert sees that she is seriously upset and offers to help her since he speaks the language. In the corridor they meet Dr. Hartz (Paul Lukas), an eminent European brain surgeon who is picking up a patient at the next station. When Iris asks for his help, he suggests that she is having hallucinations caused by the blow to her head.

Not so easily persuaded, however, Iris continues her search, questioning the other English passengers who have seen Miss Froy, but all have personal reasons for not wanting to admit that they have seen her; Todhunter (Cecil Parker), the Englishman who wanted privacy, is traveling with his mistress, Margaret (Linden Travers), and does not want to be involved in any scandal, knowing that it would harm his career. The two cricket fans, Caldicott (Naunton Wayne) and Charters (Basil Radford), are afraid the affair will delay the train, causing them to miss the cricket matches.

At the next stop both Gilbert and Iris keep careful watch for Miss Froy, but she does not leave the train, and the only person boarding the train is Dr. Hartz's patient, who is wheeled aboard on a stretcher completely bandaged and accompanied by a nun.

Iris' story receives some support, however, when Margaret, hoping to force Todhunter into marrying her after she divorces her husband, admits that she has seen Miss Froy. Jubilantly, Iris tells Dr. Hartz that someone else has seen Miss Froy, but when she returns to her compartment a woman dressed in Miss Froy's clothes is occupying Miss Froy's seat. The woman announces that she is Madame Kummer (Josephine Wilson) and has been in the compartment throughout the journey. Her story is corroborated by the other occupants, and Iris, dazed and confused, appears to be convinced after Dr. Hartz explains to her that her subconscious has substituted Miss Froy's face for that of Madame Kummer.

Still beset by doubt, however, Iris asks Gilbert to take her to the dining car for some tea; there, she sees Miss Froy's name still visible on the steamy window. Her discovery is underscored by a startling blast from the train whistle just before the train hurtles through a tunnel, obliterating the name. Hysterically, Iris appeals to the other passengers to stop the train and search it for Miss Froy, but they stare unresponsively at her. Desperate, Iris wrenches free from Gilbert and Dr. Hartz and pulls the emergency cord, stopping the train just before she faints. When she regains consciousness, Dr. Hartz is trying to calm her, but she obstinately holds to her belief that Miss Froy is aboard the train. Just as Gilbert is becoming more skeptical of her story, the cook throws some kitchen garbage out of the train window. For a brief moment, isolated in a close-up, a label from a packet of herbal tea sticks to the window and is seen by Gilbert.

Now fully persuaded of the truth of Iris' story, Gilbert helps her search the train and finds, in the baggage car, Miss Froy's spectacles in the paraphernalia of a magician.

Suddenly the magician appears and tries to take back the spectacles. He and Gilbert struggle until Iris hits the magician over the head with a bottle, knocking him unconscious. Quickly, they bundle the man into a trunk, but just as quickly open it again since the magician still holds the spectacles. However, they find that he has disappeared through the false bottom of the trunk, taking with him the only evidence of Miss Froy's presence on the train.

A fantastic idea now occurs to Gilbert: what if the bandaged patient is really Miss Froy? Iris then recalls noticing that the nun was wearing high heels, and they return to Dr. Hartz's compartment to verify their wild premise. Before they can unwrap the bandages, however, Hartz appears, and Iris tells him of their suspicions. He persuades them to meet him for a drink in the dining car where they can discuss the matter more fully. After they have had their drinks he takes them back to his compartment, informing them that he has had the nun drug their drinks. He then reveals that the "patient" is indeed Miss Froy and that she will soon be removed at the next stop where he will operate on her, unsuccessfully.

Iris and Gilbert feign sleepiness to get Hartz to leave them; then, in a race against time, Gilbert climbs out the window of the locked compartment to reach the next one, where the nun is guarding Miss Froy. After telling Gilbert that she has not drugged their drinks because she could not tolerate the murder of a fellow Englishwoman, the nun helps him unwrap Miss Froy's bandages. Just as they finish, Madame Kummer enters, so they overpower her and substitute her for Miss Froy.

When Hartz discovers the deception after the "patient" has been taken off the train but before it leaves the station, he arranges to have their train car uncoupled and diverted to a branch line. Finally, realizing what has happened, Gilbert and Iris go to the dining car and tell the other English passengers of their discovery. They are not, however, believed until the train stops and an armed officer approaches and offers to escort all of them to the British Embassy. Gilbert hits the officer over the head, takes his gun, and then makes his way to the engine to get the train moving again. Meanwhile, the cricket fans, proving to be unexpectedly competent with firearms, hold off a group of armed soldiers led by Dr. Hartz. Todhunter, a pacifist, wants to surrender, but when he leaves the train waving a white flag, he is shot.

Miss Froy, who up to now has refused to reveal what is happening, confides to Gilbert and Iris that she is a British spy. Before escaping from the besieged train, she imparts the secret information she is carrying—the vital clauses of a secret treaty between two European nations—to Gilbert so that the information will have two chances of reaching the British Foreign Office. The information is coded in the form of a tune which Gilbert memorizes.

Unable to tell whether Miss Froy has escaped safely or not, Gilbert manages to get the train started just as Hartz and the soldiers prepare to board it, and they all escape across the border. Gilbert and Iris reach London safely, but when they arrive at the foreign office Gilbert finds that he has forgotten the tune. Suddenly they hear it being played on a piano in the next room and discover Miss Froy, alive and well. Needless to say, the course of events has caused Iris to forget her fiancé, and she now plans to marry Gilbert.

The tension and the chilling, undefined menace of international intrigue are masterfully maintained by Hitchock and delightfully counterpointed by the film's wit and humor. Indeed, much of the charm of *The Lady Vanishes* is due to its witty script and amusing characters. The humor is principally centered in the characters of the two British cricket fans, although Gilbert also has some funny exchanges with Iris. Perfect caricatures of the unflappable and insular Englishman, the cricket fans are disdainful of the "third-rate country" in which they find themselves temporarily stranded, and of Iris and her friends, whom they suspect of being rich Americans because of the manager's obsequious treatment of them. Their sense of decorum is offended when they are relegated to the maid's room at the inn, but even in this predicament, they insist on changing into evening clothes for dinner. They are then forced, because of the overcrowded conditions, to share a table and even cheese with Miss Froy, whom they characterize as a "queer old bird" after politely informing her that they "never judge any country by its politics." Their overriding concern throughout the film is to return to England in time to see the championship cricket matches. Reduced to reading an American newspaper, the only newspaper available, they murmur disgustedly that "Americans have no sense of proportion" since the sports section "has nothing but baseball and not a word about cricket." Later, in the midst of the gunfight, their main concern is whether they will get to the cricket matches on time; however, true to their unflappable British tradition, they remain cool and imperturbable during the crisis. Having both survived the gun battle and helped Gilbert get the train started so that they can all escape, they are dismayed to find when they arrive in London that the cricket matches have been cancelled because of floods. Indeed, the news of the cancellation is the only time they show very much emotion during the entire film. The roles, perfectly played by Naunton Wayne and Basil Radford, proved to be so popular that these actors frequently played similar roles in later films.

Margaret Lockwood as Iris and Michael Redgrave as Gilbert are particularly good in providing the romantic comedy aspect of the film with their antagonism for each other turning to love; they are equally adept at conveying the bewilderment of ordinary people caught up in extraordinary circumstances. Dame May Whitty is convincing as the little old lady spy, Miss Froy.

As usual in an Alfred Hitchcock film, *The Lady Vanishes* has tension and a good sense of pace as well as several ingenious touches. Particularly noteworthy is the manner in which the film starts out rather ordinarily with the characters having nothing more serious to worry about than finding a room in a crowded hotel. Although the opening section does not reveal the main plot of the film, it does introduce the characters to one another and to the audience without wasting one scene. Also clever is the manner in which Hitchcock manipulates the evidence of Miss Froy's disappearance. Each time Iris thinks she has definite proof, it seems to vanish; and likewise, each time she gets so discouraged that she begins to doubt her own memory, new evidence appears. To this carefully controlled confusion, Hitchcock adds the further dimension that Iris can never be quite sure who is with her and who is against her. For example, she keeps telling Dr. Hartz what she discovers only to find out, nearly too late, that he is one of the conspirators who have caused the disappearance of Miss Froy. *The Lady Vanishes* is vintage Hitchcock, with the imprint of this master filmmaker evident from the overall conception of plot to the slightest detail of filming.

Julia Johnson

THE LADYKILLERS

Released: 1956
Production: Michael Balcon for Ealing Studios
Direction: Alexander Mackendrick
Screenplay: William Rose; based on his story of the same name
Cinematography: Otto Heller
Editing: Jack Harris
Running time: 95 minutes

Principal characters:
Professor Marcus .... Alec Guinness
Major Courteney .... Cecil Parker
Louis Harvey .... Herbert Lom
Harry Robinson .... Peter Sellers
One-Round Lawson .... Danny Green
Mrs. Louisa Alexandra Wilberforce ... Katie Johnson
Police Superintendent .... Jack Warner

Despite their immense reputation, many of the Ealing comedies have not stood the test of time too well. The years have not always been kind to them, and what once appeared funny can often seem dated today. One problem many of these comedies share is that they rely too heavily on their scripts or upon the acting of their principals, while the direction is usually routine. Such is not the case with *The Ladykillers*, however, which combines a clever script with some excellent acting and vivid direction by Alexander Mackendrick, who left England for a new career in the United States shortly after the film's completion.

Just as Margaret Rutherford is the scene stealer in *Passport to Pimlico* (1949), it is another slightly eccentric lady, Katie Johnson as Mrs. Louisa Alexandra Wilberforce, who not only steals every scene but, despite her diminutive size, completely dominates *The Ladykillers*. Mrs. Wilberforce is one of those little old ladies who are a delight to behold and listen to when one is not directly involved in their problems, but who, face to face, can drive one insane. She lives in an old house at the end of a cul-de-sac near St. Pancras Station in the heart of London, a house which has suffered during the Blitz and in which, because of subsidence, pictures cannot hang straight and water only runs from the tap after the pipe is beaten with a wrench. Sharing this overcrowded haven for Victorian bric-a-brac are three parrots which belonged to her late husband. When his ship sank during a typhoon, he saw to it that they were placed in the last lifeboat, before he, nobly as befits a captain in the mercantile marine, went down with his ship.

Mrs. Wilberforce pays regular visits to the local police station, where we meet her as the film opens, explaining to the kindly superintendent (Jack

Warner) that her friend, Amelia, had not really been visited by a spaceship, as she told the police on a previous visit to the station, but had merely fallen asleep while listening to a program on radio's Children's House about men from Mars and dreamed the whole thing. The superintendent leads her gently to the door, as Mrs. Wilberforce rambles on as to why visitors from outer space would want to visit such an overcrowded place as earth, and that she does not really care too much about her umbrella, perhaps indicating why she keeps forgetting it.

When she played in *The Ladykillers*, Katie Johnson (1878-1957) was no newcomer to films; she had been a character actress in British productions since the silent era and had also enjoyed a lengthy stage career. There was perhaps something of Mrs. Wilberforce in her character, for when she was asked if she had enjoyed appearing in *The Ladykillers*, she commented that the strong studio lights had helped ease her rheumatism.

Into Mrs. Wilberforce's fragile, gentle, and sadly decaying world come Professor Marcus (Alec Guinness), with his strangely evil face and slit for a mouth; Major Courteney (Cecil Parker), the perennial British military type, courteous and bumbling; Louis Harvey (Herbert Lom), an American-style gangster; One-Round Lawson (Danny Green), a bulky, stupid criminal, and yet basically kind human being; and Harry Robinson (Peter Sellers), a small-time London "spiv." Professor Marcus has rented two of Mrs. Wilberforce's rooms ostensibly so that he and his colleagues may practice their music, but in reality to plan the hold-up of a security van full of money. While they plot, with a gramophone record of Boccherini's minuet playing, Mrs. Wilberforce persistently asks if they would like tea. She tells them of her twenty-first birthday dance which was interrupted by the announcement of the death of Queen Victoria. One of the parrots, General Gordon, escapes while she and One-Round attempt to give it its medicine, and the group becomes involved in trying to recapture it.

The robbery takes place as planned, and it is as well-conceived directorally as it is criminally. Mrs. Wilberforce becomes an unwitting accomplice, picking up the trunk containing the stolen money from Kings Cross Station, and almost driving the crooks to nervous collapse by returning to the station with the trunk to collect her forgotten umbrella, becoming involved in a fracas with a barrow boy over the way he is treating his horse, and, eventually, having the police carry the trunk into the house for her. The performances of Kenneth Connor as the taxi-driver and Frankie Howard as the barrow boy are particularly interesting, since both of the two men were to become major British comedians in later years, well-known for their appearances in the *Carry On* series of films.

All goes well with the robbery plan until the gang is about to leave; a strap from One-Round's cello case, which is stuffed with money, gets caught in Mrs. Wilberforce's door and opens to reveal the loot. While Mrs. Wilberforce "scolds" the men for their crime and orders them to take the money back, the gang tries to frighten her by telling her she is their accomplice and will end her days sewing mail bags in prison. At this point, Mrs. Wilberforce's friends, all of whom are as dotty and as full of chatter as she, arrive for tea. The gang is forced to take tea with them and join in singing "Silver Threads Among the Gold" around the harmonium.

The gang decides that Mrs. Wilberforce must die since she knows too much, but in the end it is the gang members who all die, killed off by their own greed and, indirectly, by Mrs. Wilberforce, who holds such power over them— a combination of mother and child nurse—that most of them cannot pluck up courage to murder her. Major Courteney has the first try, very unwillingly it should be mentioned; but as he tries to escape with the money, he is killed by Louis. Harry is next, and he is killed by One-Round, who cannot bear the thought of any harm coming to Mrs. Wilberforce. One-Round is determined to protect the old lady, but he, in turn, is killed by Louis. Louis and the professor are the only two left, and they fight a vicious battle of wits, which Louis, not surprisingly, loses. As each victim dies, he is dumped into a convenient passing train. The professor is killed by the outstretched signal of a passing train, surely the final irony in view of the deadly use to which the gang had put British Railways, and falls into yet another passing train.

The scene fades to Mrs. Wilberforce once more at her friendly neighborhood police station. She tries to explain her problem to the superintendent but he is too busy, and when she tells the sergeant about all the money, he smiles benignly at the old lady, thinking her crazy but harmless, and tells her to keep it. Remembering how Professor Marcus had explained the crime to her, saying that no one would want the money back because the victims would be reimbursed by the insurance companies and the insurance companies would be reimbursed by adding a farthing to everyone's policy, Mrs. Wilberforce decides that perhaps the sergeant is right. After all, it is only a farthing for every policyholder. Once more she leaves the police station, but when one of the men runs after her with her umbrella, she tells him to keep it; "Now I can buy a dozen new ones."

As the barrel organ plays "The Last Rose of Summer," Louisa Alexandra Wilberforce, a symbol of good in a world that will soon change forever, returns to her home at the end of the cul-de-sac. Whatever she decides to do with the money, one knows it will be for the best.

Anthony Slide

THE LAST DETAIL

Released: 1973
Production: Gerald Ayres for Columbia
Direction: Hal Ashby
Screenplay: Robert Towne; based on the novel of the same name by Darryl
  Ponicsan
Cinematography: Michael Chapman
Editing: Robert C. Jones
Running time: 100 minutes

> *Principal characters:*
> Budduskey .... Jack Nicholson
> Mulhall .... Otis Young
> Seaman Meadows .... Randy Quaid
> Chief Master-at-arms .... Clifton James
> Marine Duty Officer .... Michael Moriarty
> Prostitute .... Carol Kane

The Last Detail is one of those rare films that manages to be tightly controlled while appearing spontaneous and to say a great deal while seeming only to entertain. A raunchy, unpretentious "service comedy," it achieves surprising levels of humanity and passion.

A pair of petty officers at a Norfolk naval base are assigned to take a prisoner to jail in Portsmouth. What should be a two-day "detail" stretches to almost five as the result of some unplanned stopovers and excursions. On the journey, the young prisoner does a great deal of growing up, and the petty officers come to see themselves with a forgiving, naked clarity. For all three men, the trip is a winding detour that becomes a road to self-discovery.

The prisoner, Seaman Meadows (Randy Quaid), is an eighteen-year-old victim, awkward, mumbling, and shy. He possesses neither charm nor self-assurance. He now faces eight years in a military prison and a dishonorable discharge for stealing forty dollars from his commanding officer's favorite charity. But Meadows has hardly been born yet. His chaperones say he does not know enough to be angry, and his freedom is wasted because he does not know how to have a good time. The two men who become his friends and teachers are Navy "lifers," men who will stay in the service until they retire. "Mule" Mulhall (Otis Young) is a black with no illusions. He lives without choice. "The man says go and you go"—Vietnam, Portsmouth, it doesn't matter where. His Navy pay supports his mother and gives him the best he thinks he can get out of life; and he wants to protect it.

The chief "honcho" of the detail, "Bad-ass" Budduskey (Jack Nicholson), is much wilder and less resigned. He seethes with fury at the system—at arrogant officers, foolish work, and sadistic Marine prison guards. Over and over he describes things and people with a single crude word that is part of a litany for his barracks, his base, his job, his future. Budduskey has an instinctive sympathy for this prisoner who is about to be robbed of his youth. Step by step he nurtures a relationship with Meadows, starting with a few drinks in Washington, and continuing through a missed train, a side trip to Camden to let the boy see his mother (who is not home), winning some money in a New York tavern, chanting with some Buddhists in a Greenwich Village basement, and an encounter with some girls. In a Boston brothel he buys the boy a night of "love" that will have to last him eight years. Mulhall is at first reluctant to show any kindness lest the boy try to escape, but he gradually comes to share Budduskey's feelings, until a beautiful, unspoken moment on the Boston Common where the two men are almost ready to let the boy go free. Suddenly he tries to escape; they catch him and beat him into submission, yet at the prison they say nothing of his attempted flight and take the blame for "abusing" a prisoner. Ironically, their only victory over the system is to save the boy more punishment by claiming to be sadists themselves.

The Robert Towne screenplay, based on Darryl Ponicsan's novel, richly details the growing ties between the men. Their feelings pivot around an astonishing scene when a bartender will not serve the underage Meadows and threatens to call the Shore Patrol. Budduskey pulls out his own gun and shouts that he himself is the Shore Patrol. The act releases some of his anger and manic energy; he has shown the others that he really is a "bad-ass." Having now stood up for the boy, he feels even more responsible for him.

The men are drawn further together as they reveal more of themselves. Details are mentioned, dropped, and picked up again. The feeling is random, but cumulative, until the stunning revelation of Meadows' home. We already know that his father left when he was a baby, and Meadows is clearly not anxious to see his mother. When Budduskey opens the door to the house, the look on his face explains everything. The interior is a mess, with empty whiskey bottles everywhere. In that one view, and in Budduskey's embarrassed reaction, we know that no one has ever stood up for Meadows, so these men will have to stand up for him now.

The bonding of the sailors emphasizes a pervasive loneliness in their lives. They never discuss it, but it is there in references to women, to being once "sort-of" married, to paying for love, to moving around from one base to another. It is especially clear in a sad-funny moment when the boy tells a woman that his two keepers, whom he has known so briefly, are his "best friends." The texture of service life rings true to anyone who has ever served. The aimless anger and scatology, the futility of being ruled by fools, the long waiting, all add up to the toughest view of peacetime service since *From Here to Eternity* (1953).

Nicholson, Quaid, and Young form a seamless ensemble. Under a stoic exterior, Young suggests a bewildered man doing the best he can with his life and knowing it is not enough. Quaid at first is all doughy cheeks and narrow eyes, a miserable fellow cringing in a body five sizes too large for him; and his growth through the film is deeply satisfying. Watching him learn to smile is a bit like seeing a baby react. The audience feels proud and paternal. As for Jack Nicholson, he proves again that he is one of the three or four best actors in American movies. Explosive, mocking, full of hollow barracks-wisdom and lewd clichés, bitter and lonely within, he invents layers of astonishing reality for Budduskey. Acting students may note, among dozens of details, the way he smokes a cigar or chews gum. He is a man gnawing on a lifeline, at once reassuring himself and cutting himself dangerously loose.

From this film through *Bound for Glory* (1978) and *Coming Home* (1978), Hal Ashby established himself as perhaps the best director of actors of his generation in the United States. His gift is to show eccentric characters as they reveal the humanity they have in common with us all. And his work is largely invisible. There are no stunning visual "effects" of bombardment of "production value." Ashby concentrates on individuals—not good or bad guys but the good-bad mixture in everyone. Coming from a former film editor, it is a surprisingly humanistic approach, and it is likely to prove enduring, for it gives us more than moments or shocks. It gives us people to remember and experiences to share.

Ted Gershuny

THE LAST HURRAH

Released: 1958
Production: John Ford for Columbia
Direction: John Ford
Screenplay: Frank S. Nugent; based on the novel of the same name by Edwin O'Connor
Cinematography: Charles Lawton, Jr.
Editing: Jack Murray
Running time: 121 minutes

Principal characters:
Frank Skeffington	Spencer Tracy
Adam Caulfield	Jeffrey Hunter
Mave Caulfield	Dianne Foster
John Gorman	Pat O'Brien
Norman Cass, Sr.	Basil Rathbone
The Cardinal	Donald Crisp
Cuke Gillen	James Gleason
Ditto Boland	Edward Brophy
Amos Force	John Carradine
Sam Weinberg	Ricardo Cortez
Gert Minihan	Anna Lee
Delia Boylan	Jane Darwell

At the end of his career, John Ford directed a series of films that are similar in mood. Each film is a reexamination of plots and themes that Ford had considered in films throughout his career. For example, *Two Rode Together* (1961) and *Sergeant Rutledge* (1960) deal directly with racial prejudice, a subject Ford had touched obliquely earlier in his career, while *The Man Who Shot Liberty Valance* (1962) is Ford's final statement on the settling of the West. *Cheyenne Autumn* (1964) looks at the price of that settlement from the Indians' point of view. *The Last Hurrah*, like those films, also deals with the end of an era in which machine politics dominated by Irish-American ward bosses are supplanted by more modern politicians campaigning on television. It is an era Ford had known as a child in Portland, Maine, where his father had been a ward leader. *The Last Hurrah* is Ford's fond farewell to a past of better days.

Frank Skeffington (Spencer Tracy) is the four-term mayor of a "large, Northeastern city" (surely Boston) who is about to embark on the campaign for a fifth term. Knowing that it will certainly be his last campaign, Skeffington invites his nephew, Adam Caulfield (Jeffrey Hunter), to accompany him on his rounds and to observe the workings of the campaign. Adam is a newspaper reporter who works for one of his uncle's staunchest opponents, Amos Force (John Carradine) while Adam's father-in-law is another enemy of the Mayor. But in spite of these handicaps, Skeffington is closer to Adam than to his only son, who is a dilettante oblivious to his father's need for filial respect and affection. Skeffington is a widower who mourns his wife deeply and pays homage to her memory by placing each morning a single rose before her portrait, which dominates the grand staircase in the Mayor's residence. Although he is a sportswriter, not a political reporter, Adam accepts his uncle's offer.

Along with Adam we meet Skeffington's cronies and syncophants and learn of some of the more dubious practices of ward politics. Each time Adam expresses doubts about the deals and the chicanery, Skeffington's campaign manager John Gorman (Pat O'Brien) blithely reassures him with the most favorable interpretation of these practices. It is obvious that Skeffington is sincerely concerned for the welfare of his constituents, but the means by which he assists the voters are somewhat less than ethical in every case.

In a key scene in the film, Skeffington and Adam attend the wake of Knocko Minihan. The deceased was not a popular figure in the ward, but the Mayor's presence draws a large crowd of mourners. The Mayor congratulates the widow (Anna Lee) on the large number of people paying tribute to her husband and he also gives Mrs. Minihan one thousand dollars with the transparent explanation that his wife had left it to Mrs. Minihan in her will. Skeffington then gathers his henchmen in a back room to discuss campaign strategy, an action that discomforts Adam, but which Gorman explains with a comment that politics are a lot more cheerful than death.

Skeffington next invades the staid Plymouth Club to confront his strongest enemies, Norman Cass (Basil Rathbone) and Amos Force, in order to persuade them to lend money to the city for low-cost housing for the poor. When they refuse, Skeffington devises a plot involving Cass's idiot son. In order to avoid the embarrassment of Skeffington's plans for his son, Cass agrees to lend the money but also promises to support Skeffington's opponent, Kevin McCluskey, in the election.

With Cass's support, the effective use of television, and Skeffington's clinging to outmoded methods of campaigning, McCluskey defeats the Mayor, much to the surprise and horror of his loyal supporters. As a McCluskey victory parade passes in the background, Skeffington walks home alone through a darkened park, his last hurrah at an end. As he climbs the stairs past the portrait of his wife, the Mayor suffers a heart attack. Now confined to bed, Skeffington receives a stream of old friends and a few enemies who come to pay their last respects. He greets them all with humor and affection. His son is overcome with the imminent loss of his father, and once again is not there when his father needs him. Only Adam and his wife (Dianne Foster) are with Skeffington at the end. On their way out, Adam pauses to place a rose in front of the portrait as the old politicians file by to say farewell to their friend and leader.

The Last Hurrah is a film infused with nostalgia and affection. The sense of the past is palpable as Skeffington moves through his last campaign saying farewell to old friends, having one last fight with old enemies, and revisiting the scenes of happier days. There is affection in Ford's portrait of men who are motivated by their sense of duty to the voters and by their need to stay in office even if their methods are slightly illegal. The Protestant Bishop says that he prefers the engaging scoundrel (Skeffington) to the fool (McCluskey), and so does Ford. Ford clearly prefers the morally ambivalent men of the past with their concern for people to media manipulators unaware that the voters are people like Mrs. Minihan and not numbers on a tote board.

In addition to mourning the passing of an era, Ford touches on darker themes that intensify the conflict between Skeffington and Cass. Adam learns that his employer's grandfather had once fired Skeffington's grandmother for stealing two bananas from the kitchen where she worked as Force's maid. This evidence of racial and religious prejudice adds weight to the conflict between Irish Catholic immigrants and entrenched Puritan wealth. Ford had encountered that prejudice as a boy in Maine. He reminds us that while his politicians are not saints, they are preferable to a rigid establishment that cares little for the people Skeffington represents.

As Frank Skeffington, Spencer Tracy is the center of the film. In his portrait of the mayor we recognize a man worthy of the respect and affection the other characters have for him. Tracy is able to portray subtly a man who is aware of the coming defeat, a man drawn to the past and slowly disengaging himself from the present. His slow walk through the park is the walk of a man both defeated and relieved. In the part of Ditto Boland, Edward Brophy stands out as well-meaning but inept duplicate of the Mayor, so devoted to Skeffington that he apes his every move. But it is John Ford who is the controlling presence in the film. Like most of his films in this period, *The Last Hurrah* is infused with a sense of endings and summations. Like Skeffington, Ford was more interested in the past than the new, plastic present. The men of the past were worthy of respect even though they were all too human.

Don K Thompson

LAURA

Released: 1944
Production: Otto Preminger for Twentieth Century-Fox
Direction: Otto Preminger
Screenplay: Jay Dratler, Samuel Hoffenstein, and Betty Reinhardt; based on the play and novel of the same name by Vera Caspary
Cinematography: Joseph LaShelle (AA)
Editing: Louis R. Loeffler
Costume design: Bonnie Cashin
Music: David Raksin
Running time: 88 minutes

Principal characters:
Laura Hunt	Gene Tierney
Mark McPherson	Dana Andrews
Waldo Lydecker	Clifton Webb
Shelby Carpenter	Vincent Price
Anne Treadwell	Judith Anderson
Bessie Clary	Dorothy Adams

It comes as a surprise to find that *Laura* was described in film trade papers of the 1940's as a "detective thriller." It is a sharply written, literate, and beautifully adapted film, made at a time when Hollywood was turning out some of the best entertainment films ever made. Although contemporary reviewers compared it favorably to *The Maltese Falcon* (1941) and *Double Indemnity* (1944), it does not actually fit into that genre.

Laura is set in the sophisticated world of cafe society, ornate Park Avenue apartments, and expensive restaurants. As the film opens, the audience learns that the body of a young woman has been found in an expensive New York apartment, and, although identification is impossible, it is assumed to be that of Laura Hunt (Gene Tierney), who lives there. Police Detective Mark McPherson (Dana Andrews) is called in to find the murderer. He is a rather taciturn young man who at first treats the case as routine, remarking that "some two-timing dame" gets murdered in her apartment every day.

Laura Hunt's closest friend has been Waldo Lydecker, played superbly by Clifton Webb. Lydecker is a middle-aged columnist and critic, witty and sophisticated but also a waspish, vain egotist. Lydecker is obviously a suspect, but, far from finding this an intrusion into his private life, he seems strangely flattered by the accusation: "To have overlooked me would have been a pointed insult," he says, and he insists on accompanying McPherson on his investigation. It is difficult to imagine any actor who could have played this role better than Clifton Webb, with the possible exception of George Sanders, who appeared in a remake.

The other major suspects are Laura's aunt, Anne Treadwell (Judith Anderson), and Shelby Carpenter. Shelby is being kept by Anne but has recently become engaged to Laura. They were to have been married that week. Shelby has his own strange moral code and claims he has not borrowed any money from Anne since becoming engaged to Laura. But it is clear that Anne is not going to give Shelby up, although she knows he is quite worthless. They have no illusions about each other and are well-suited. Vincent Price plays Shelby as a Southerner, making his weakness just charming enough to convince us that two women could want him.

Some of the film is in flashback, and it is Waldo Lydecker's voice that is used to narrate these sequences; through him we learn of his first meeting with Laura. She approaches him in the dining room of the Algonquin Hotel. Laura is in advertising, working on a campaign for fountain pens, and wants Lydecker to endorse one of the advertisements. He refuses sharply, saying "I don't use a pen, I write with a goose quill dipped in venom," but afterwards realizes that there is something very appealing about Laura. She is young, beautiful, and obviously at the beginning of her career, and the jaded Lydecker wants to see her again. He seeks her out at the agency and endorses her advertisement with an imperious flourish; and the two become close friends. Lydecker introduces Laura to his circle of acquaintances and is a great influence on her cultural development.

McPherson finds himself drawn back again and again to Laura's empty apartment, and he is haunted by the portrait of her which hangs in the living room. It is a picture of an exquisite young woman, exotic and desirable but very refined. McPherson is a stolid, unemotional man.

Lydecker, always alert for signs that men are attracted to his protégée, maliciously points out to McPherson that he is behaving strangely, more like a suitor than a homicide investigator. The detective has fallen in love with the murder victim, but somehow it is not distasteful as Preminger has handled the situation with great delicacy. McPherson is in love with a woman out of his class: not a "dame" but a lovely and successful young woman, unattainable, not only because she is from a different world, but because she is dead. Ironically he has been admitted to her circle only to solve the murder.

Dana Andrews is perfect in the role of the detective, underplaying to the extent that he hardly appears to be acting. McPherson should be out of place with Laura's friends, but he moves among them, saying little and manages to make them appear shallow and brittle.

The plot grows more complicated when McPherson is half-sleeping at Laura's apartment, and Laura herself enters suddenly and demands to know what he is doing there. She has been at her country cottage, without newspapers or radio, and knows nothing of the murder. She went away to think things over, presumably having serious doubts about her marriage to Shelby Carpenter, and is horrified to find herself in the midst of a murder case.

The real victim is model Diane Redfern, who has been using Laura's apartment for a liaison with Shelby. This discovery is treated in a rather detached way; the audience never knows the model and is not expected to feel her loss. It is enough that Laura is alive.

As the film progresses, the audience is drawn deeper into the mystery. Was the victim murdered because she was mistaken for Laura, or was it Laura herself who killed Diane Redfern out of jealousy? McPherson, who constantly plays with puzzles during the investigation, falls deeper in love with Laura, while, at the same time, he suspects that she may be the murderer. At one point he actually arrests Laura, but then lets her go when she tells him that she is breaking her engagement to Shelby. McPherson and Laura realize their mutual attraction, although few words are spoken about it; they share only one good-night kiss.

Lydecker senses that Laura has begun to return McPherson's love, and in the final scene, he is shot by the police after attempting to kill her. He explains that he could not allow his adored Laura to be "pawed" by McPherson, just as he could not allow her to marry Shelby. He had attempted to kill her before, but had mistakenly shot Diane Redfern instead.

In a sophisticated, eerie last moment in the film, Lydecker's radio broadcast ends with the words "good night," and an announcer informs the audience that the broadcast has been prerecorded.

One of the difficulties encountered in filming *Laura* was that the leading actress is missing for a considerable part of the screen time, and, apart from the occasional flashbacks, her presence has to be felt, not seen. A great deal of credit for the success of this technique must go to David Raksin, who composed the title song. It is an excellent example, perhaps the best ever, of a piece of theme music not merely tacked on to publicize the title, but used as a vital part of the characterization. Raksin was at that time a virtually unknown composer at Twentieth Century-Fox, and the score had been offered first to Alfred Newman and then to Bernard Herrman, both of whom had declined. Otto Preminger had wanted to use the song "Summertime" from George Gershwin's *Porgy and Bess*, and when this proved impossible, he had wanted Duke Ellington's "Sophisticated Lady." Raksin had some difficulty with the score, but at the eleventh hour came up with one of film's most enduring musical themes.

Gene Tierney is very convincing, but her portrayal of the screen "Laura" is quite different from Vera Caspary's original "Laura." Why the character was altered is not known; perhaps Gene Tierney seemed too "nice" to play the amoral young woman that the character was originally described as.

The stage origins of *Laura* are apparent, and since there are virtually no exterior shots, cinematographer Joseph LaShelle was confined mainly to studio sets. It is unfortunate that little use was made of the city of New York as a location site, but despite this drawback, the film did receive an Academy

Award for Best Cinematography.

Laura has been remade twice, the first time in 1953 with Dana Wynter as Laura, George Sanders as Waldo Lydecker, and Robert Stack as the detective. This version was a television production, directed by John Brahm, and ran for only forty-three minutes; it was shown in the United States as *Portrait of Murder* (sometimes called *Portrait of a Murder*). A television production in 1968 starred Lee Radziwill in the title role, but this version was not well received and does not appear to have been screened again. Thus, the original *Laura* has taken its place as one of the best black-and-white films of the 1940's and has remained a viewing favorite for decades.

Elizabeth Leese

THE LAVENDER HILL MOB

Released: 1952
Production: Michael Balcon for Ealing Films; released by Universal-International
Direction: Charles Crichton
Screenplay: T. E. B. Clarke (AA); based on his story of the same name
Cinematography: Douglas Slocombe
Editing: Seth Holt
Running time: 80 minutes

Principal characters:
Henry Holland .... Alec Guinness
Pendlebury .... Stanley Holloway
Lackery .... Sidney James
Shorty .... Alfie Bass
Mrs. Chalk .... Marjorie Fielding
Miss Evesham .... Edie Martin

After promising early appearances as Herbert Pocket and as Fagin in David Lean's screen adaptations of *Great Expectations* (1947) and *Oliver Twist* (1951), Alec Guinness achieved international stardom playing all eight members of an aristocratic British family who stood between a penniless upstart and a dukedom in Ealing Studios' brilliant 1949 comedy, *Kind Hearts and Coronets.* The next year, he tested his newfound popularity in more serious roles: as the young salesman doomed by an incurable illness in J. B. Priestley's *Last Holiday* and as Disraeli in Twentieth Century-Fox's *The Mudlark,* his first American film. He also appeared, unsuccessfully, as Hamlet on the stage. *Last Holiday* has its defenders (Pauline Kael, for one), but *The Mudlark,* in which Guinness fought a losing battle for the audience's attention with Irene Dunne's distracting makeup as Queen Victoria, was an unqualified disaster. In 1951 he wisely returned to Ealing Studios and to comedy, the medium in which he had first demonstrated his mastery. Guinness made two films for Ealing that year in which he found two of his best roles: as an obsessed young scientist in *The Man in the White Suit* and as a timid, "fubsy" (Guinness's word), middle-aged bank clerk who becomes a criminal mastermind in *The Lavender Hill Mob.*

Screenwriter T. E. B. Clarke has said that the idea for *The Lavender Hill Mob* came to him while he was supposed to be working on *Pool of London* (1951), a crime thriller about a large-scale robbery organized by a gang of working-class Londoners. In Clarke's comic variation on this theme, Guinness plays Henry Holland, a bank messenger whose job it has been for many years to accompany shipments of gold bullion across London in an armored van. Holland's maddening insistence on always following every step of the security procedure is the despair of his driver and guards, who do not realize that the mind behind his rimless glasses and weak eyes has been busily at work planning the perfect robbery. Just as Holland is about to put his plan into execution, however, he receives a setback when one of his superiors at the bank offers him a slightly less menial position. Holland protests that he is happy in his work as a messenger. "The trouble with you, Holland," the man tells him, "is that you haven't enough ambition. When a good opportunity comes along, grab it with both hands—it may not occur again." Holland considers how he might use the new job to bring off his plan better. "Very good, sir: I'll follow your advice."

Holland lives in the suburb of Lavender Hill, in the Balmoral Private Hotel, a rigidly genteel establishment ruled over by a tiny relic of the Victorian age, Miss Evesham (Edie Martin, who also played Guinness' landlady in *The Man in the White Suite*). Holland approaches a fellow lodger in the Balmoral, a sculptor and paperweight manufacturer named Pendlebury (Stanley Holloway, who had played a character with the very similar name of Pemberton in Clarke's *Passport to Pimlico*, 1949), and asks to be shown his forge and casting machinery. Pendlebury finally catches on to Holland's hints about the use to which this apparatus might be put, and agrees to go in with him on a scheme to smuggle the gold bullion out of England melted down into one of his regular consignments of souvenir paperweights. The other members of Hollands "mob," a singularly inept pair of professional criminals named Lackery (Sidney James) and Shorty (Alfie Bass), prove to be more interested in the results of the Test Match and in catching the last bus home from the greyhound stadium where Holland and Pendlebury recruit them (a greyhound stadium had figured prominently as a location in Clarke's "straight" police thriller, *The Blue Lamp*, 1950), but Holland needs them to knock over the bank van during its regular run. With Holland's help, Lackery and Shorty are just able to manage the robbery, and the bullion is soon on its way to Paris as part of a shipment of paperweight replicas of the Eiffel Tower. A government official is on the air confidently announcing that there is no way the gold can be gotten out of Britain as a customs man approves Pendlebury's shipment for export without even looking inside.

In Paris, Pendlebury and Holland discover that six of the solid gold paperweights have been sold by accident to members of a party of visiting English schoolgirls. Home again in London, they manage to recover, by bribery, five of the weights; but the owner of the sixth insists on taking hers as a gift to her friend, the local policeman. When she goes to his usual corner, however, the different policeman on duty tells her that her friend has been assigned to man a booth at a police methods exhibition. Holland and Pendlebury tail the little girl to the exhibition, where, with true British pluck, they grab the paperweight out of her hands in the middle of a hall swarming with hundreds of cops.

What follows is a wild parody of the famous multicar chase sequence at the end of *The Blue Lamp*: in a stolen police car, Holland and Pendlebury race across London, all the while broadcasting a stream of conflicting orders over the car radio. Finally, after they have caused a massive pile-up of police cars all blaring out "Old MacDonald Had a Farm" from their loudspeakers as the result of crossed wires, the two criminals escape on foot. Pendlebury is soon caught (a true art lover, he had stopped too long to admire a nineteenth century French painting on a peddlar's barrow), but Holland makes good his getaway in one of Clarke's funniest strokes: it is just five o'clock, and the streets are suddenly filled with homeward-bound office workers, all dressed exactly like Holland in sack coats and striped pants, with bowler hats on their heads and each carrying an umbrella. Swept along in this stream, Holland disappears into the London Underground, to emerge months later in South America, where he has been regaling another Englishman with the story we have just seen. The two men are sitting in a cafe. Holland finishes his story, they both rise to leave, and only now do we see that Holland is, in fact, handcuffed to the other man: the last member of the Lavender Hill Mob will soon get the penalty he deserves.

When the Ealing Studio's plant was sold to the Rank Organization in 1955, Sir Michael Balcon, who had headed the operation since 1931, wrote the following inscription for a plaque that was erected there: "Here during a quarter of a century were made many films projecting Britain and the British character." It was Ealing's policy to make films that could earn their cost back in the British market alone, even during the period of the British cinema's international popularity after World War II. For Balcon and his associates, "projecting Britain" usually meant projecting a well-intentioned, middle-class socialist view of the problems the country faced in an era when it was throwing off the twin shackles of imperialism and the class structure. (Charles Barr's book *Ealing Studios* is largely a detailed analysis of Ealing's output as a product of middle-class liberalism.) Even the famous Ealing comedies had their pinprick of social purpose, although the humor in the best and most durable of them—*Kind Hearts and Coronets* (1949), *Whisky Galore* (1948), *The Man in the White Suit*, and *The Lavender Hill Mob*—transcended the merely topical. (Clarke's *Passport to Pimlico*, on the other hand, with its jokes about rationing and nostalgic references to wartime solidarity, has faded badly in recent years.) But if projecting Britain had for Ealing the limited, and limiting, connotation described above, projecting the British character was a duty that gave free play to the talent for observation of actors such as Guinness and Holloway and of writers like Clarke in an insular society where class distinctions still ran deep. Working together, these men created memorable additions to the gallery of English types previously limned by Chaucer, Shakespeare, and Dickens.

The fubsy Holland, with his bowler and furled umbrella carried like a shield proclaiming his respectability, is a representative member of that vast tribe which Bernard Shaw (a former tribesman who realized how lucky he had been to escape) called "younger sons of younger sons." These propertyless offshoots of the genteel middle class—clergymen's grandsons and the children of provincial schoolmasters—accounted for the great majority of city clerks and lower-level civil servants in 1951. Establishments like the Balmoral Hotel, where Miss Evesham strictly enforced such rules as "wipe your feet, no business occupations may be performed on these premises" (quoted from Barr), were a sort of middle ground where men like Holland rubbed elbows with men like Pendlebury, whose genuine culture could not hide the Cockney accent that betrayed his working-class origins. On a lighter note, Clarke's invention of a fellow lodger of Holland called Mrs. Chalk (Marjorie Fielding), with whom he likes to read murder mysteries in the evening, pokes fun at the strange fascination that violent crime has for the essentially gentle and law-abiding British people. Mrs. Chalk would, of course, be horrified to discover that her fellow murder addict had perpetrated an actual bank robbery.

There was nothing in *The Lavender Hill Mob* so terribly British that the film could not be appreciated when it opened in the United States, however. Although the film never played much beyond the art house circuit in this country, Alec Guinness received his first Academy Award nomination for his performance as Holland; and Clarke was nominated for and won the Oscar for Best Original Story and Screenplay. And a young actress who had just one line of dialogue in the South American section of the story was spotted by Hollywood and went on to become one of the brightest American stars of the 1950's. Her name was Audrey Hepburn.

Charles Crichton's direction is usually mentioned almost as an afterthought in discussions of *The Lavender Hill Mob*, a tradition that will not be broken here. He had a talent for fast-moving comedy, as he also demonstrated in *The Titfield Thunderbolt* (1953) and *The Battle of the Sexes* (1960), but Clarke's script, and Guinness and Holloway, could probably have directed themselves.

Charles Hopkins

THE LAWLESS BREED

Released: 1953
Production: William Alland for Raoul Walsh Productions; released by Universal-International
Direction: Raoul Walsh
Screenplay: Bernard Gordon; based on a screen story by William Alland
Cinematography: Irving Glassberg
Editing: Frank Gross
Art direction: Bernard Herzbrun and Richard Ridel
Running time: 83 minutes

> *Principal characters:*
> John Wesley Hardin .... Rock Hudson
> Rosie .... Julie Adams
> J. G. Hardin/John Clements .... John McIntire
> Jane Brown .... Mary Castle
> John Hardin .... Race Gentry
> Ike Hanley .... Hugh O'Brian
> Dirk Hanley .... Lee Van Cleef

Director Raoul Walsh ranks with John Ford, Howard Hawks, and Anthony Mann among the supreme masters of the Western. This is not surprising since he has also created outstanding efforts in every popular film genre; unfortunately, however, since three of Walsh's Westerns, all made during the 1940's, are invariably singled out as outstanding, his other Westerns have not received the attention they deserve. The famous three are his romantic biography of Custer, *They Died with Their Boots On* (1941); his Greek tragedy on the range, *Pursued* (1947); and his remake of his own *High Sierra* as a Western myth, *Colorado Territory* (1949). While these three works are certainly not overrated, such later films as *Along the Great Divide* (1951), *The Lawless Breed*, and *A Distant Trumpet* (1964) are also worthy of sustained attention. They are perhaps more mellow and less vigorous, but it is common for artists to become more reflective in their later works, and Walsh lost none of his psychological or historical insight in these films. *A Distant Trumpet* movingly renews and deepens the theme of the Indian tragically giving up his way of life which the director had treated in *They Died with Their Boots On*; and in the same way, the psychological forces which drive the heroes of *Pursued* and *Colorado Territory* return to motivate the protagonists of *Along the Great Divide* and *The Lawless Breed*.

The Lawless Breed is a key Walsh film. In this fanciful retelling of the story of notorious gunfighter John Wesley Hardin, the director presents a little saga of the West, which begins with the Civil War, moves on to describe a lawless frontier, and finally outlines the arrival of a civilization which will see the gunfighter softened and ready to live in peace with his family on a ranch. The film runs only eighty-three minutes, and, while it is not surprising to find Walsh covering a considerable number of years in this short a time, the quiet and unhurried pace of the film seems paradoxical. There are no underdeveloped scenes, and the emotional interaction of the principal characters is permitted to dominate. The subject of the film is not Hardin's gunfights: although these shootouts are exciting and staged with the director's characteristic flair, they are over quickly and always have a narrative purpose. Although Walsh is justifiably celebrated as an action director, he is more, as *The Lawless Breed* forcefully demonstrates once again. It is at the same time an adventure story and a love story; Walsh enjoys directing adventure stories to call attention to the fact that, for him, love is the richest adventure.

As is often the case with a Walsh hero, Hardin (Rock Hudson) is presented as a man with alternatives, explicitly represented by the two women in the story. The woman he initially believes he desires, Jane Brown (Mary Castle), is respectable, and the audience identifies her with Hardin's father (John McIntire), a severe minister who approves of her. Rosie (Julia Adams), the actual heroine of the story and the woman whom Hardin will come to love, is a saloon hostess and is initially identified with outlaw elements of society. She witnesses his first gunfight, and later, he supports both of them by gambling. Invariably, the prim and proper heroine in a Walsh film is revealed to be selfish and unsympathetic, while the tough and independent rival becomes ideal for the hero, who ultimately turns to her for love. In *The Lawless Breed*, the situation is uncommonly interesting because Jane dies in the same gunfight in which Hardin is trying to avoid capture. Although he has already perceived her lack of loyalty, Hardin feels guilty about Jane's death, and this may be the reason why he initially accepts Rosie only as a mistress after she has protected him and nursed his wounds. Then, when he finally begins to understand how she feels for him, he marries her. The couple ultimately must undergo a long separation when Hardin finally goes to prison, but this situation only strengthens their love.

Hardin's path to maturity is marked by the irony that, although Rosie is identified with his outlaw life, she is not responsible for it, and his love for her ultimately motivates him to turn away from gambling and gunfighting. On the other hand, his father's repressiveness, attested to by an ill-deserved whipping early in the film, creates in Hardin the impulse to violence which leads him to become a gunfighter. Although he convinces himself that he only shoots those who try to kill him, and that the Hanleys, brothers of the first man he kills, are forcing him to defend himself, it seems that he is working through the neurosis resulting from his hostile feelings toward his father. Each time he kills, Hardin reacts ambiguously, his impassiveness concealing emotions perhaps too bewildering for him to understand. This same psychological wound manifests itself and is almost passed on to Hardin's son (Race Gentry) after Hardin has left prison. Finding the young man practicing his draw, Hardin strikes out with the same severity his father had used toward him. However, he is wise enough to see his responsibility, and he prevents the son from repeating his own pattern of life by interfering in his first potentially deadly gunfight.

Most of the story is told in a long flashback, with the departure from prison and the reunion of Hardin, his wife, and son serving as a framing story to resolve the conflict within him, identify his psychological wound, and finally heal it through resolve and action. The scene in which he sees his son with a gun is memorably presented: a close-up of the twirling gun shocks Hardin into memories of his violent adventures, which are superimposed in black-and-white over the color footage. Equally striking is the preceding scene in which Hardin is reconciled with Rosie after his long absence. For a few moments, they stand apart, echoing the sensitivity that allows the audience to feel the tenderness in the relationship before the couple has touched; and as they move together, the camera cuts to a very close shot, beautifully capturing their happiness in this most intimate moment of the film.

Although modest in scope, this film is a fully realized artistic statement in all aspects. With the exception of the brief black-and-white memory flash-back, the film demonstrates the highly specialized use of Technicolor which still prevailed during this period and resulted in soft and subtle colors chosen with great discernment to convey both the masculine and feminine aspects of the director's interpretation. The stars of the film, Rock Hudson and Julia Adams, had not previously been called upon to assume roles as challenging as those of Hardin and Rosie. Under Walsh's direction, they both rise to the challenge, winning sympathy throughout, reflecting all of the changes in the characters and their relationship, and aging convincingly. The fine character actor John McIntire is cleverly cast in two contrasting roles, the righteous father and Hardin's more benevolent uncle. Both visually and dramatically, Walsh's skill in being alternately delicate and forceful distinguishes his handling of a story which would be unmemorable in the hands of others. At the same time, *The Lawless Breed* shows that this director of a number of accepted classics had ceased to court critical favor. His faithfulness to personal subjects not always considered modern by his contemporaries, and the transition to a style characterized more by gracefulness and charm than by insistent virtuosity, are evidence of a maturity rarely attained in cinema.

Blake Lucas

LAWRENCE OF ARABIA

Released: 1962
Production: Sam Spiegel and David Lean for Horizon Pictures; released by Columbia (AA)
Direction: David Lean (AA)
Screenplay: Robert Bolt
Cinematography: Freddie A. Young (AA)
Editing: Anne V. Coates (AA)
Art direction: John Stoll and John Box (AA); set decoration, Dario Simoni (AA)
Sound: John Cox and Shepperton Studio Sound Department (AA)
Music: Maurice Jarre (AA)
Running time: 220 minutes

Principal characters:

T. E. Lawrence	Peter O'Toole
Prince Faisal	Alec Guinness
Auda abu Tayi	Anthony Quinn
General Allenby	Jack Hawkins
Turkish Bey	José Ferrer
Colonel Harry Brighton	Anthony Quayle
Mr. Dryden	Claude Rains
Jackson Bentley	Arthur Kennedy
Sherif Ali ibn el Kharish	Omar Sharif

Lawrence of Arabia, based on one of the classics of modern literature, the writings of T. E. Lawrence, entitled *Seven Pillars of Wisdom* (originally published as *Revolt in the Desert*), is both an adventure story and an intimate biography. Nearly four hours in length, which usually necessitates an intermission, the massive historical epic covers the life of the enigmatic Englishman from the time he was a mapmaker for British Intelligence in Cairo in January, 1917, to the time he brought about the capture of Damascus in October, 1918.

Though Lawrence's exploits are seen as spectacular, there is a pervading fatalistic mood throughout *Lawrence of Arabia*. The film actually begins with its own epilogue, as the first scene shows the hero's death in a motorcycle accident in 1935. From this point we go into a flashback of his earlier years. As the audience first sees the young T. E. Lawrence (Peter O'Toole), he is a twenty-nine-year-old. Scholarly but undisciplined, he is an obscure cartographer who accepts the opportunity to investigate the Arab revolt against Constantinople and to assess the strength of the Arab tribes for the British Political Bureau.

With great enthusiasm, Lawrence undertakes the job. After persuading the rebel leader Prince Faisal (Alec Guinness) to give him a small force of men, he befriends the Sherif Ali ibn el Kharish (Omar Sharif), and attains the cooperation of Sheik Auda abu Tayi (Anthony Quinn). With men, money, arms, and an amazing military prowess, Lawrence leads the attack on Damascus.

With the surrender of the Turkish garrison in this era of World War I, Lawrence receives such titles as Sheikh Dinamit, the Hero of Aqaba, the Liberator of Damascus, and the Uncrowned King of Arabia. At the moment of victory, however, Lawrence discovers that all his work has been in vain. Despite his efforts to unite the Arab people, the British and French have made plans to divide Arabia in half. A disillusioned man, Lawrence seeks obscurity as an airman in the Royal Air Force. Then, in 1935, while attempting to satisfy his appetite for speed and excitement, Lawrence, who is living under an assumed name, is killed while riding his motorcycle.

As T. E. Lawrence, Peter O'Toole is magnificent. Although at the time a relatively unknown, twenty-seven-year-old Irish actor with a background in Shakespeare on the London stage and at Stratford-upon-Avon, O'Toole made an impressive entry into stardom. He is masterful as the enigmatic, larger-than-life, legendary character. Since the actual T. E. Lawrence was a complex man with irreconcilable contradictions in his personality, O'Toole, who was nominated for Best Actor that year, plays the man with many facets and depths. We see Lawrence as a romantic hero, as a brave warrior, and as a modest and thoughtful man. At the same time, we see the British officer as an affected homosexual, a humorless knave, a self-aggrandizer, an admitted sadomasochist, and a charlatan. At one point, the journalist Bentley (Arthur Kennedy) asks, "What is it, Major Lawrence, that attracts you personally to the desert?" Pausing a moment, Lawrence replies, utterly serious, "It's clean."

Perhaps as a counterbalance to the then almost unknown O'Toole in the title role, director David Lean surrounded him with an eminently famous international roster of players. The veteran character actor Claude Rains, in the last significant role of his career, played Mr. Dryden, the British civilian agent who launched Lawrence on his Arabian adventures. As the leader of the Arab Bureau of British Intelligence in Cairo, Rains is intelligent and cagey. Anthony Quinn, who plays the Arab Chief of the Howeitat clan, Auda abu Toyi, with a false hooked nose, portrays his character as animalistic, venal, and violent. This was the type of role which he went on to repeat in some of his later potboiler films.

Alec Guinness as Prince Faisal gives his character dimensions of dignity; Anthony Quayle plays the ingratiating Colonel Harry Brighton, Lawrence's ranking officer in the desert; and Jack Hawkins portrays British General Allenby with typical pomp and authority. Arthur Kennedy as Jackson Bentley, the opportunistic and crass American journalist, gives a solid performance as the man whose reports of the raids helped to gain international recognition for Lawrence; his character here was quite similar to the reporter whom he played in the film *Elmer Gantry* (1960). José Ferrer portrays the Turkish Bey, the governor of Deraa. Malificent and venomous, he orders the captured Lawrence to be flogged, tortured, and left unconscious. Finally, rounding out the cast, is Omar Sharif as Ali ibn el Kharish, the fierce young warrior who becomes Lawrence's best friend. An actor of note only in his native Egypt before *Lawrence of Arabia*, the swarthily handsome Sharif was propelled into international stardom as a result of this role.

Technically, *Lawrence of Arabia* is brilliant. With its vistas, sets, and tableaux, it is a stunning spectacular from an era when film spectaculars were in their prime. Costing $12,000,000, the titanic production, which took fifteen months to complete, was shot on location in Spain, Morocco, and Jordan (where the original exploits took place). Filmed in the Super Panavision 70mm process, the picture effectively captures the ambushes and battles, the rampaging horses and camels, the thousands of Bedouin wanderers, and the Turkish train explosions from Medina to Damascus. We see a panorama of oases and marketplaces, mountains and cliffs, as well as the awesome Arabian deserts and the frightening grandeur of their beautiful, white hot, shimmering sands.

The film's Academy Award-nominated screenplay was written by Robert Bolt, who wrote the play *A Man for All Seasons*. (Michael Wilson also worked on the script, but did not receive screen credit.) The film's director was David Lean, the distinguished British director of such diverse films as *Brief Encounter* (1946), *Great Expectations* (1947), and *Dr. Zhivago* (1965). He and *Lawrence of Arabia*'s producer, Sam Spiegel, were also both responsible for the highly acclaimed *The Bridge on the River Kwai* (1957).

A film of undeniable power, *Lawrence of Arabia* nevertheless has its detractors. Some critics feel that the film suffers from elephantine production values, overexploitation of the Arabian locations, and grandiose visions. Others question the casting of Peter O'Toole as Lawrence. The handsome, six-foot, blond and blue-eyed actor hardly resembles the relatively mousy-looking five-foot-five T. E. Lawrence. Still others question lapses in the script, which does not explain why Lawrence was chosen for the Arab expeditions in the first place. The film assumes either a great background knowledge on the part of the audience, or a suspension of disbelief.

If the measure of a film's success is in either box-office receipts or Academy Awards, however, then *Lawrence of Arabia* was a triumph. It was one of the top box-office films of 1962-1963 and won a total of seven Oscars, including Best Picture and Best Direction. Although 1962 was not, perhaps, an outstanding year (the other nominations for Best Picture went to *Mutiny on the Bounty*, *The Music Man*, *The Longest Day*, and *To Kill a Mockingbird*), the awards which *Lawrence of Arabia* won reflected an overall production effort which still stands up well today.

The blending of magnificent cinematography and music are especially effective. In one of the film's best scenes, a panoramic view of the burning white sands, shown with Maurice Jarre's beautiful and haunting theme music in the background, becomes almost explosive when Freddie A. Young's camera pans in on the tanned, blue-eyed face of Peter O'Toole dressed in Lawrence's white Arabian garb. Both Jarre and Young won Oscars for their work in the film, as did John Box, who designed the production; John Stoll, the art director; and Dario Simoni, the set decorator. The work of these men, coupled with a solid international cast and the expert direction of David Lean, has enabled the film to stand up well over the years. In the final analysis, *Lawrence of Arabia* remains a superlative effort.

Leslie Taubman

LEAVE HER TO HEAVEN

Released: 1945
Production: William A. Bacher for Twentieth Century-Fox
Direction: John M. Stahl
Screenplay: Jo Swerling; based on the novel of the same name by Ben Ames
 Williams
Cinematography: Leon Shamroy (AA)
Editing: James B. Clark
Running time: 111 minutes

> *Principal characters:*
> Ellen Berent .... Gene Tierney
> Richard Harland .... Cornel Wilde
> Ruth Berent .... Jeanne Crain
> Russell Quinton .... Vincent Price
> Danny Harland .... Darryl Hickman
> Glen Robie .... Ray Collins

Leave Her to Heaven is a film whose reputation has grown over the years. One of the beautiful Technicolor products of Twentieth Century-Fox, it was dismissed by contemporary critics as mere soap opera; but in actuality it is a strange love story about an obsessive and cruel woman. In 1945, when all of the evil people in the world of films seemed to be German, no one could quite believe that any studio would make a film about an American woman who was so unredeemably wicked. This film does not present the familiar American wife and mother, doing her part in a munitions factory or staying at home, keeping family values intact while her husband is away at war: the heroine of *Leave Her to Heaven* is mean-spirited, deceitful, and determined to get her own way. She loves with a passion that is powerful enough to drive her to kill. In 1945, such a heroine was fascinating to millions of Americans who perhaps were tired of the standard virtuous character types.

When Ben Ames Williams' novel *Leave Her to Heaven* was published in 1944, it was chosen as a Literary Guild Selection and was read by more than one million people. The American public was obviously captivated by the story of this psychopathic young wife. Seeing the books disappear from the shops, several film studios bid for the rights to Williams' novel, but Twentieth Century-Fox won, reportedly paying a six-figure price. John Stahl, whose credits include such romantic films as *Back Street* (1941) and *Imitation of Life* (1959), was hired to direct. For the important role of Ellen Berent, the murderous heroine, Gene Tierney was selected. Tierney, who had played many half-caste Oriental girls before achieving stardom with *Laura* (1944), was imbued with an attractive face whose expression was at once erotic and impassive—a combination that worked very well in *Leave Her to Heaven*.

Cornel Wilde, who had just scored a huge success as Frederick Chopin in *A Song to Remember* (1945) played her novelist husband Richard Harland; and the all-American Jeanne Crain was chosen as Ruth, the "good" sister.

As the film opens, Richard Harland is returning to his lakeside mountain home "Back of the Moon," after a three years' absence. In an initial flashback to three years earlier, Harland's friend Glen Robie (Ray Collins), watching Harland rowing across the lake in a canoe, tells a neighbor his strange story.

Richard Harland, happy over the excellent reviews for his latest novel, is on his way to visit Robie in New Mexico. On the train he sits across from an attractive woman who is reading his novel. It is Ellen Berent, who is also to be a guest at Robie's home. The two arrive at the lodge, and Ellen loses no time in letting Richard know she is interested in him. Robie, however, tries to discourage his friend from returning that interest by hinting that Ellen's love for her recently deceased father had been abnormally possessive. She had even gone so far as to become engaged to a lawyer, Russell Quinton (Vincent Price), in order to make her father jealous. Ellen's half-sister, Ruth, a perky, wholesome girl, also appears to be interested in Richard, but he cannot resist Ellen. During a very strange encounter in which they go riding together and Richard watches Ellen scatter her father's ashes to the winds, he realizes that he is hopelessly in love with her, and he is glad when she breaks off her engagement to Russell. Richard and Ellen soon marry and go to Richard's home in the Maine woods.

Ellen's mother and sister, Ruth, visit them for a while, but Ellen lets them know that she resents the attention Richard pays her family, so they leave. Ellen cannot so easily get rid of Richard's brother, Danny (Darryl Hickman), however. Danny, a boy of fifteen, is a cripple who comes to live with them after treatment in Hot Springs, Georgia. Richard is devoted to Danny and the realization of their affection for each other begins to drive Ellen mad. One day, while Danny is swimming in the lake as Ellen rows behind him in a boat, she sees a way out. When the boy tires and asks to be let into the boat, Ellen does nothing; she merely sits impassively and lets him drown. Richard goes into a deep depression after Danny's death and tries to lose himself in his writing. Later, when Ellen confides in Ruth that she is losing Richard, Ruth suggests that a child of his own might ease Richard's pain. Ellen becomes pregnant, but after a short-lived reconciliation with Richard, she notices that he is taking long walks with Ruth and seems to prefer Ruth's company to anyone else's.

It is at this point that the film utilizes a very strange scene to reach a new height of perversity. Ellen, perfectly composed and beautiful, carefully dresses in a chiffon peignoir with matching slippers, slowly applies her makeup, and then deliberately falls down the stairs, killing her unborn child. Richard now becomes more withdrawn than ever. Finally, in a kind of desperate hysteria, Ellen reveals to Richard both that she let Danny drown and that she killed their child. Recoiling from her in horror, Richard leaves Ellen. Realizing at last that she has lost him for good, Ellen writes a letter to the district attorney and then takes poison. Ruth is indicted for murder based on the circumstantial evidence that Ellen so carefully planted before her death. At the trial, Richard Harland insists that his wife killed herself and is striking back at Ruth from beyond the grave. He proceeds to cite examples of Ellen's treachery, and the jury finds Ruth not guilty. For withholding evidence of Ellen's crimes, however, Richard is sentenced to three years in the state prison.

Robie concludes his story and peers at the canoe on the lake. The boat reaches the other shore where a woman waits for Richard on the beach. It is Ruth.

There is no way to make *Leave Her to Heaven* sound less melodramatic than it is, but the film constantly rises above its somewhat trite material. Visually, it is stunning. The settings—Bass Lake in the High Sierra and the Sedona Basin near Flagstaff, Arizona—include some of the most beautiful natural scenery in America; and Leon Shamroy won a well-deserved Academy Award for his color cinematography.

The film boasts a dramatic score by Alfred Newman that was written while the film was in production rather than after, as is usually the case. Newman felt that the music would provide a great deal of the atmosphere for this moody film, and it is atmosphere more than anything else that is memorable about *Leave Her to Heaven*. From the use of the brilliant reds on Gene Tierney's lips and nails to the shooting of the mountain ride she takes while scattering her father's ashes, a strange, uneasy feeling is established from the very beginning of the film that continues throughout. Part of this strangeness comes from watching Gene Tierney play a woman completely beyond redemption, but one who is so beautiful that it is almost difficult to hate her. Ellen is portrayed as a "bad" woman, and no attempt is made to explain her wild passions with the psychological interpretations so fashionable during the 1940's; there is no salvation, no kind doctor to remind her of a miserable childhood. On the contrary, she was loved and pampered by her father as a child and can never forget it. Ellen fascinated contemporary audiences, and has continued to intrigue present-day admirers of the film. Rarely has a woman in a film been so bad and looked so good.

Joan Cohen

LETTER FROM AN UNKNOWN WOMAN

Released: 1948
Production: John Houseman for Universal-International
Direction: Max Ophuls
Screenplay: Howard Koch; based on the short story of the same name by
  Stefan Zweig
Cinematography: Franz Planer
Editing: Ted Kent
Art direction: Alexander Golitzen
Music: Daniele Amfitheatrof
Running time: 87 minutes

Principal characters:

Lisa Berndle	Joan Fontaine
Stefan Brand	Louis Jourdan
Frau Berndle	Mady Christians
Johann Stauffer	Marcel Journet
John	Art Smith
Marie	Carol Yorke

Among the later *émigrés* to seek the comparative safety of Hollywood after escaping the onslaughts of Fascism was a bald, cigar-smoking romanticist named Max Ophuls. He had been in transit in Europe for eight years, his various directorial careers curtailed each time Hitler planned a new invasion. Behind him were films made in Germany, France, Italy, Holland, and even Switzerland; but his real roots were in the city of Vienna. Ophuls was of the pre-Freud era which had produced the lilting airs of Strauss and Lehar and the somewhat darker humors of Schnitzler and Wedekind. If his previous films contained one thing in common, it was a bittersweet but very potent sense of romance.

In Hollywood, Ophuls flourished even less than abroad; from 1941 to 1945 America gave him little but a deep sense of frustration. He transcended an unproductive period working for Howard Hughes, who took to calling him "The Oaf," and an attempt by Preston Sturges to work up industry interest in him; finally, in 1946, he was afforded a chance to direct a Universal swashbuckler, *The Exile*, with Douglas Fairbanks, Jr. A year later, a better opportunity arose. Joan Fontaine and her husband William Dozier, an executive producer at Universal, had decided on the first project for their new company, Rampart Productions. They would adapt a Stefan Zweig short story whose title was changed to *Letter from an Unknown Woman*. It was an intensely unhappy romance set in turn-of-the-century Vienna, and they were looking for a foreign director who would provide the right atmosphere and period flavor. Although Hollywood was then crowded with reasonably romantic

Europeans, all of them with better reputations, Ophuls was chosen.

The choice was most appropriate because, in addition to his love of Vienna, Ophuls definitely had more experience directing women than George Cukor ever did, and his past films had been most often related from a woman's point of view, stressing their gallant acceptance of unfortunate romance and lost love. Ophuls brought to his stories a gliding style, a lingering sense of grace under fire, and a slightly mocking sophistication that recalled nothing so much as a *valse triste*. *Letter from an Unknown Woman*, descending upon him in the alien atmosphere of Southern California, must have seemed a godsend to Ophuls.

Determinedly amorous and with its subsidiary characters scarcely developed, *Letter from an Unknown Woman* would have to succeed or fail on its theme of love from afar. The plot tells of the unquenchable passion of a shy young teenager, Lisa Berndle (Joan Fontaine), for the dashing pianist, Stefan Brand (Louis Jourdan), who has moved in upstairs. She cultivates his manservant, sneaks in awe through his rooms, but is completely tongue-tied in the presence of the man himself. When her widowed mother Frau Berndle (Mady Christians) remarries and moves to a small town, the girl, aglow with romance, decides to remain behind and declare her affections. She changes her mind, however, when she sees the pianist with his latest lady love, and leaves Vienna.

Nevertheless, her adoration does not cool, and she finally rejects an officer's attentions to return to Vienna. Working as a dressmaker's mannequin and haunting the pianist's residence, she is eventually rewarded by a night of passion, a sudden emotional farewell, and a pregnancy. Years later, happily married to a wealthy man Johann Stauffer (Marcel Journet) who accepts her illegitimate son, she again encounters the pianist, who is now aging and embittered. Once again he is successful at seducing her, but when she realizes that he has no memory of their past meeting, she leaves him. Later, dying of typhoid, she writes him the letter of the title, in explanation.

Even Dozier and Fontaine must have realized that this was not the sort of film to which postwar audiences were accustomed. Some irony was introduced by placing the whole episode in flashback, with the pianist reading the letter while waiting to fight a duel; only at the end does he realize that his opponent is his lost love's husband, an excellent duelist. Careful attempts were also made to instill some quiet humor into the subject whenever possible with bit roles and "color" parts being turned into jolly and sometimes surprising caricatures: a stiffly uniformed band at a dance pavilion turns out to be all-girl as well; and the pianist's dialogue runs to jests such as, "Champagne tastes much better after midnight, don't you think?" and "I don't mind so much being killed but you know how hard it is for me to get up in the morning." There are also syrupy lines of the sort that later caused Pauline Kael to write, "there are moments when one wants to clobber the poor wronged suffering creature." Clearly it was up to Ophuls to create an authentic atmosphere and style that would support and bejewel the story.

He was not altogether alone in his effort. Cameraman Franz Planer and the great character actress Mady Christians, who played Lisa's mother, had worked together on a number of actual Austrian films. Louis Jourdan, however, in his second leading role as the pianist, was French and inexperienced; and Fontaine had made her reputation as a very English woman, graduating from the shy roles in *Rebecca* (1940) and *Suspicion* (1941) to more serenely glamorous ones in *Frenchman's Creek* (1944) and *Ivy* (1947). She reports in her autobiography, however, that she and Ophuls got along beautifully.

If the film offered Ophuls a chance to work with a particularly receptive actress, it also gave him a chance to exercise his favorite obsession, that of tracking shots. He was a master of the gliding camera providing subtle, controlled, and continual movement throughout a scene. In this film, the camera swoops down, swirls around, and penetrates into the Vienna of everyone's dreams. Elegantly curled staircases are shown in the apartment; confectioners in parkside booths stand so high off the ground that they pass their wares down to their customers in little shuttle boxes; restaurants, walkways, and so forth never exist on one level; nothing is ever still. The result is a city that breathes, a city where something quite literally is always happening. Even when the film moves momentarily to a small provincial town, Ophuls keeps it all alive. Bells fill the sound track, villagers in their Sunday best bow and scrape before their superiors, parasols swirl in unison, and another military band marches throughout—all during a conversation that itself neatly suggests the stultifying politeness of small-town life.

Ophuls, however, uses his camera for more than just atmosphere. When the pianist finally gets around to escorting the lovelorn heroine up that delicately winding staircase to his lair, the scene is filmed with the same slightly slanting movement that has been used for the pianist's other lady friends, neatly implying that, romantic atmosphere or not, Lisa Berndle is nothing special in his eyes.

Nevertheless, despite all of Ophuls' careful attention, the film was not a significant success upon its release. Critics and audiences alike relegated it to the "woman's picture" category, a stigma from which it has taken the film considerable time to escape. Perhaps this is because Ophuls was too faithful to his Viennese ideals. European and particularly Austrian romances had been grounded in a tragic inevitability which could not be fought, such as the sad lovers of Mayerling who had been the subject of one of Ophuls' earlier films, or the bittersweet romances of *The Student Prince* (1954) and *Maytime* (1937), where duty, parental objections, or some other issue always caused frustration and unhappiness. This was the world Ophuls knew and presented.

However, by the 1940's, the American audience wanted their heroes, their fighters, and even their lovers to be of stronger stuff. "Tempestuous" was a favorite adjective of the advertisements of the day, and that is what audiences wanted. Ophuls did not think of love as a battleground. He thought of romance as fragile and tender, easily broken but never forgotten; and for this one time, he tried to convey that view to American audiences. It did not work commercially, and Ophuls' last two Hollywood films, *Caught* (1949) and *The Reckless Moment* (1949), were much more American in tone, setting, and subject. *Letter from an Unknown Woman*, however, still stands as one of the few authentically European films undertaken by a major studio since the days of silent films. Although many foreign directors have either been lured by or have fled to Hollywood, Ophuls is the only one who succeeded, this once, in bringing Europe with him.

Lewis Archibald

THE LIFE OF ÉMILE ZOLA

Released: 1937
Production: Henry Blanke for Warner Bros. (AA)
Direction: William Dieterle
Screenplay: Norman Reilly Raine, Heinz Herald, and Geza Herczeg (AA);
  based on a screen story by Heinz Herald and Geza Herczeg
Cinematography: Tony Gaudio
Editing: Warren Low
Running time: 116 minutes

> *Principal characters:*
> Émile Zola .... Paul Muni
> Captain Alfred Dreyfus .... Joseph Schildkraut (AA)
> Lucie Dreyfus .... Gale Sondergaard
> Maître Labori .... Donald Crisp
> Colonel Picquart .... Henry O'Neill
> Paul Cézanne .... Vladimir Sokoloff
> Major Walsin Esterhazy .... Robert Barrat

One of the most ambitious and successful prestige films of Warner Bros., a studio noted for its screen biographies, was *The Life of Émile Zola*. As the studio's successor to *The Story of Louis Pasteur*, released the previous year, it was the most highly acclaimed film of 1937, winning the Academy Award for Best Picture.

In the manner of most Hollywood biographies, the film rearranges some facts, but at least it admits this in an onscreen disclaimer. It presents the details of the life of Émile Zola (1840-1902), as portrayed by Paul Muni, from his days as a struggling writer living in a Paris garret with his friend, the painter Paul Cézanne (Vladimir Sokoloff), through his success as a novelist and eventual recognition as the social conscience of France. His first big success is the story of a prostitute he has befriended, *Nana*. The years pass and many other successful novels follow, each exposing social injustice and hypocrisy, until Zola is recognized as one of France's greatest novelists.

After the successes of his middle years, Zola has become a complacent, wealthy man who lives in a luxurious house filled with sculpture, paintings, and other art objects. In a revealing sequence we see him dining with his friend Cézanne, who is still struggling and poor. Cézanne is troubled rather than impressed by the luxury in which Zola lives and announces that he is leaving Paris. An artist, he believes, should remain poor, "Otherwise his talent, like his stomach, gets fat and stuffy." Zola asks him not to leave because he needs someone to remind him of the old life. "You can never go back to it," Cézanne replies, "and I've never left it." He does, however, leave Zola his self-portrait. This rich, dignified life is in sharp contrast to his early struggling days and shows how much Zola has to lose should he become involved in any controversial issues.

The second half of the film focuses on the notorious Dreyfus case, and for a time the emphasis shifts from Zola's life to that of Dreyfus as we are shown how the scandal developed. A list of secret documents that could only have been available to someone on the French General Staff is delivered to the German Ambassador, then stolen by a French secret agent and returned to the General Staff. As the members of the staff look at the list of officers, seeking the possible traitor, the camera closes in on the name "Captain Alfred Dreyfus" with the word "Jew" below it. A finger comes into the frame and a voice says: "I wonder how he ever became a member of the General Staff," and another voice says, "That's our man." The word "Jew" is never spoken during the entire film.

The frame-up of Dreyfus (Joseph Schildkraut) continues; he is tried, dishonorably discharged, and sentenced to the infamous French prison on Devil's Island for thirty years. Even when the new Chief of Intelligence, Colonel Picquart (Henry O'Neill), denounces the real traitor—Major Walsin Esterhazy (Robert Barrat), whose guilt the audience has realized from the first— the Army Generals refuse to exonerate Dreyfus. The Army cannot admit it made a mistake, the Chief of the General Staff says, ordering Colonel Picquart to remain silent.

At this point, the fate of Dreyfus becomes intermingled with that of Zola. Madame Lucie Dreyfus (Gale Sondergaard) calls upon Zola to beg his help for her husband, saying she has proof of Dreyfus' innocence. Zola is not very interested and is, indeed, extremely reluctant to disturb his comfortable way of life. Though he tells Madame Dreyfus that nothing can be done, she leaves the folder of evidence behind on his desk. Zola does his best to ignore the folder; he thinks about his election to the French Academy and his happy, contented life; but then he looks at Cézanne's portrait and begins to read the evidence.

The next scene is one of the high points of the film. Both in this scene and the famous courtroom sequence, the film must present events that are not basically cinematic in such a way as to hold the audience's attention. Indeed, this is a problem the film must deal with throughout since it is basically about ideas—abstract concepts of truth, justice, and honor that are difficult to present on film. In the office of the newspaper *L'Aurore*, Zola reads his famous denunciation, "I Accuse." It is an emotional letter, and although there is little action in the scene, the power of Muni's delivery holds the viewer's attention. Zola's "I Accuse" letter arouses indignation all over France, and he is vilified, burned in effigy, chased by angry mobs, and charged with libel by the state.

Zola is tried for libel in a courtroom packed with hostile Army officers. None of the witnesses called in Zola's defense by his lawyer is allowed to testify, and the judge and the jury are intimidated by Army officers who denounce Zola for undermining the safety and glory of France and her Army. In a fine cinematic touch, the huge crowd waiting for news is seen only as a sea of wet umbrellas surrounding the front of the building. Then the camera returns to the crowded courtroom where Zola is preparing to speak in his own defense. His speech is the dramatic high point of the film and one of the finest moments in the distinguished acting career of Paul Muni.

Muni, as usual, had immersed himself in the role, reading the transcripts of the Dreyfus trials and everything he could find about Zola, including many of his books. He studied portraits of Zola and discovered in his research some famous Zola mannerisms: the stoop-shouldered walk, eccentric laugh, and the way he held his hands. Muni was able to use these personal eccentricities which he had discovered to lend dramatic emphasis and diversity to his courtroom speech to the jury. He purses his lips, perches his spectacles on the end of his nose, puts them on and then takes them off, clasps and unclasps his hands, sometimes waving them about to emphasize a point, raises his eyebrows, and sticks out his bushy beard at the jury and the camera. It is an imaginative performance and one which captures the attention of the audience during what is essentially a long monologue. Muni alone provides all the action, not only with his gestures and mannerisms, but also with the inflections and rhythms of his voice.

Despite his impassioned speech, Zola is found guilty; his appeal is denied and he is sentenced to prison. His friends urge him to flee to London so that he will be free to continue writing on behalf of Dreyfus. "At times it is more courageous to be cowardly," they advise him. He leaves his comfortable home and goes to London, where his continuing attacks help to force a new inquiry into the Dreyfus case and cause the nerve of Esterhazy and his coconspirator on the General Staff to crack.

Eventually Dreyfus (whose hair has now turned white) is released from prison, reinstated in the Army, and promoted, but Zola is not there to share his triumph. While working on a new book, *Justice* ("What matters the individual if the idea survives"), which he hopes will help prevent a world war, he dies from carbon monoxide poisoning caused by a faulty stove pipe. At his funeral, Zola is eulogized by French author Anatole France as a "moment in the conscience of man."

Although the film glides over some of the more controversial issues in the Dreyfus case (anti-Semitism is never mentioned) and touches only lightly on its political implications, it is, nevertheless, a memorable and finely crafted film. If it tended to simplify the complex issues and ideas that drove Zola and inspired him to defend Dreyfus, it presented both Zola and Dreyfus as vivid, stirring figures.

Still considered one of the finest film biographies ever made, *The Life of Emile Zola* received Academy Awards for Best Picture and Best Screenplay, and Joseph Schildkraut was named Best Supporting Actor for his moving portrayal of Dreyfus.

Julia Johnson

LIFEBOAT

Released: 1944
Production: Kenneth Macgowan for Twentieth Century-Fox
Direction: Alfred Hitchcock
Screenplay: Jo Swerling; based on a story by John Steinbeck
Cinematography: Glen MacWilliams
Editing: Dorothy Spencer
Running time: 96 minutes

Principal characters:
Constance Porter	Tallulah Bankhead
Gus	William Bendix
Willy, the German	Walter Slezak
Alice MacKenzie	Mary Anderson
John Kovac	John Hodiak
Charles "Ritt" Rittenhouse	Henry Hull
Mrs. Higgins	Heather Angel
Stanley Garrett	Hume Cronyn
George "Joe" Spencer	Canada Lee

Lifeboat, Alfred Hitchcock's seventh American film, marked a considerable departure from the kind of suspense thriller on which his reputation is based. This nine-character story is remarkable in that it takes place entirely in only one setting, a lifeboat—about as small and claustrophobic a space as ever challenged a film director facing a full-length production. The physical and dramatic limitations of the script present obvious difficulties but it is as if Hitchcock deliberately created this restrictive project to prove that he could overcome its inherent problems.

Hitchcock has always taken chances with his films, and *Lifeboat* is one of his most challenging undertakings. For the most part, it is a successful one. The story developed from an idea Hitchcock himself conceived and for which he enlisted the literary help of John Steinbeck to develop dramatically. Steinbeck came up with the overall plot and character development in a twenty-page screen treatment, after which Hitchcock hired MacKinlay Kantor (later author of *The Best Years of Our Lives*) to flesh out a final screenplay. Hitchcock did not like Kantor's treatment, however, and turned the project over to Hollywood veteran Jo Swerling (*A Man's Castle*, 1933; *The Westerner*, 1940; *Blood and Sand*, 1942), who collaborated with both Hitchcock and Steinbeck on the final draft.

The result is a tense drama of characterizations and allegory of the world at war in 1943. Many contemporary critics defined the film by its obvious moral message: "Judge not." However, years later, Hitchcock, who has always been loathe to define the meanings of his films, explained to French director/

critic François Truffaut, what indeed, to him, was *Lifeboat*'s theme:

> "We wanted to show that at that moment there were two world forces confronting each other, the democracies and the Nazis, and while the democracies were completely disorganized, all of the Germans were clearly headed in the same direction. So here was a statement telling the democracies to put their difference aside temporarily and to gather their forces to concentrate on the common enemy, whose strength was precisely derived from a spirit of unity and of determination."

Lifeboat's nine characters represent a microcosm of the world during World War II: Constance Porter (Tallulah Bankhead), a parasitic, luxury-laden journalist; John Kovac (John Hodiak), a crewman from a Marxist freighter; Willy (Walter Slezak), a surgeon and Nazi submarine captain; Gus (William Bendix), the seaman; Stanley Garrett (Hume Cronyn), a naval radio officer; Alice MacKenzie (Mary Anderson), an army nurse; Charles Rittenhouse (Henry Hull), a business tycoon and quintessential capitalist; Mrs. Higgins (Heather Angel), an Englishwoman who is carrying her dead baby; and George "Joe" Spencer (Canada Lee), the ship's steward.

The opening credits move across the screen in front of a sinking ship—a freighter which has been torpedoed by a German submarine—and as the camera moves across floating debris, we see eight survivors climb aboard a lifeboat. The ninth survivor to come aboard is Willy, the only survivor of the U-boat which has sunk the freighter. As his hand comes over the side of the lifeboat, the other passengers help him aboard, to which he responds, *"Danke schön."* As the Allied passengers realize this man is their enemy, the dramatic tension of the picture is set into force. Willy, the Nazi, is the catalyst for all of the film's action.

It is soon apparent that Willy is the only one aboard who has any knowledge of seamanship; when the lifeboat almost capsizes, he is the only one to act. After several days, the survivors reluctantly concede to his taking charge. Kovac, the Communist from South Chicago, is most adamantly against Willy, but group survival overrules his objections. As the film progresses, we see that Kovac's political prejudices are as singleminded as those of Willy. Furthermore, tycoon Rittenhouse is a determined Fascist.

The interaction of these diverse characters creates what dramatic intensity there is in *Lifeboat*, and Hitchcock's orchestration of their actions and reactions prevents them from being merely stock stereotypes. Joe Spencer is presented as a Christian man rather than the usual clichéd black, and Willy, while cunning and singleminded, is not without charm and courage.

The day-by-day ordeal of surviving on the lifeboat with little food and water and fighting the elements causes the survivors to strike out against one another; yet the experience demands that they pull together to keep alive. Willy is the only passenger who remains calm throughout. Unbeknownst to his fellow passengers he has extra water and a compass. They discover that instead of heading for Bermuda as they had thought, Willy is steering them toward the safety of a German supply ship. Proving Hitchcock's thesis that they must, but will not, forget their differences and pull together, the eight passengers accept their fate in the hands of the Nazi, as if to admit that survival in a concentration camp would be better than death at sea.

Despite the single setting, the somewhat stereotypical characters, and the absence of a musical score (Hitchcock used only the sounds of the sea in the film), the realities with which the passengers are forced to deal prevent cinematic stasis. The passengers comfort Mrs. Higgins by wrapping her in Connie's fur coat, and when she is asleep they throw the dead child into the sea. Later, out of despair over her loss, Mrs. Higgins commits suicide by jumping into the sea still wearing Connie's prized possession.

Gus, the Brooklyn seaman whose leg has been seriously injured when the freighter was torpedoed, is diagnosed by Willy as having gangrene. Again the passengers are unable to pull together and amputate Gus's leg, and Willy is left to perform the primitive and gruesome operation. In one of the screen's most terrifying scenes, we see Willy give Gus some whiskey, the only thing aboard approaching medicine, and sterilize the jackknife to perform the necessary surgery.

Following the operation, with the passengers asleep and Willy at the helm, Gus, in his postoperative hallucinations, sees Willy drink from his hidden canteen; Willy, now forced to maintain his cover if any of them are to survive, pushes Gus overboard. When the truth is discovered, the American passengers turn on Willy, in Hitchcock's words, "like a pack of dogs" and beat him to death. Only Joe refuses to participate in the brutal murder.

The passengers are saved through no plan of their own when an Allied ship destroys the approaching German supply ship and rescues them, but not before a young injured German swims to the lifeboat for safety. When he pulls a pistol on the lifeboat occupants, they disarm him and then, ironically, pull him aboard. Once again Hitchcock's message is driven home. In order to overpower and destroy the enemy, people must forget their personal differences and join forces.

While Willy, the German, is the catalyst for the action in *Lifeboat*, it is the superb, offbeat casting of Tallulah Bankhead as Constance Porter that makes the film memorable. Bankhead's unique brand of theatrical acting was never used better on the screen. In the microcosm of Hitchcock's allegory, Connie represents the cynical, materialistic American. As we see her stripped of her possessions—her camera, her typewriter, her fur coat, and finally her prized diamond bracelet, which is used unsuccessfully as bait to catch a fish, she is revealed as a woman of substance and humanity. The script also incorporates the sensual attraction between Connie and Kovac. While drawn to him physically, she reviles his coarseness and his tattooed body by saying, "I never could understand the necessity of making a billboard out of the torso." Later, she mellows and tattooes her initials on his chest with her lipstick.

Bankhead's character also provides the only levity among the characters. At the end when they are about to be rescued, she exclaims, "Twenty minutes! Good heavens! My nails, my hair, my face. I'm a mess." Then seeing Kovac's dismay, she adds, "Yes, darling, one of my best friends is in the navy!" Although this was Bankhead's finest screen performance, the Motion Picture Academy overlooked her entirely for a Best Actress nomination. The New York Film Critics, however, did name her Best Actress of 1944.

Lifeboat provided Hitchcock with the problem of how to make his own brief appearance in the film (his well-known "trademark"), since the script called for only one closely integrated set. His solution, his favorite, he says, was to use "before" and "after" photos of himself advertising a diet drug called *Reduco*. The ad is seen on the back of a newspaper which William Bendix holds at one point in the film, and Hitchcock said he received hundreds of letters asking where to buy the wonder diet drug. He also appears quite briefly as a dead body floating face down in the water at the beginning of the film.

Ronald Bowers

LIMELIGHT

Released: 1952
Production: Charles Chaplin for United Artists
Direction: Charles Chaplin
Screenplay: Charles Chaplin
Cinematography: Karl Struss
Editing: Joe Inge
Music: Charles Chaplin (AA 1972)
Running time: 138 minutes

Principal characters:
Calvero	Charles Chaplin
Terry	Claire Bloom
Neville	Sydney Chaplin
Piano Accompanist	Buster Keaton
Harlequin	Andre Eglevsky
Columbine	Melissa Hayden

One of the recurring trademarks in the films of Charlie Chaplin is the presence of serious themes in many of his best-loved comedies. He examines greed in *The Gold Rush* (1925), the Depression in *Modern Times* (1936), Facism in *The Great Dictator* (1940), and poverty in nearly all of his films. In *Limelight*, made when Chaplin was sixty-three years old, he explores the problems of old age and its effect on entertainers. As the aging music hall clown, Calvero, Chaplin presents a portrait of a man whose fame has faded, and whose humor has turned to sadness.

The film's story centers around the friendship between Calvero (Charles Chaplin) and Terry (Claire Bloom), a young ballerina whom he saves from a suicide attempt. Terry suffers from ill health and paralysis, brought on by her lack of self-confidence. Calvero nurses her back to health and restores her belief in herself, while she, in turn, provides him with the motivation which has been missing from his life since the decline of his career. He attempts to revive his old music hall act, but the results are disastrous and he accepts Terry's help in securing a small part as a clown in the ballet in which she is to star. Terry recognizes the ballet's composer, Neville (Sydney Chaplin), as a struggling music student she had known while working in a music store. Her attempts then to aid him financially had resulted in the loss of her job. The two fall in love during the rehearsals for the ballet, but Terry's gratitude to Calvero prevents her from leaving him to marry Neville. Learning of this, and of the producer's intention of firing him from the ballet, Calvero leaves, fearing that Terry's loyalty to him will stand in the way of her own happiness. He is discovered months later, by Neville, performing for handouts with a band of street musicians. Neville informs Terry, who asks Calvero to perform at a tribute to be given in his honor. Calvero agrees, and does several comedy routines, including one with an old friend (Buster Keaton). The audience responds enthusiastically, and Calvero realizes he has recaptured the comic skill of his earlier years. But his triumph is short-lived, as he suffers a heart attack onstage and must be carried back for his final bow. He asks to be placed on a couch in the wings while Terry performs, and he dies there while watching her dance.

The plot of *Limelight* is serious in nature, yet it is laced throughout with Chaplin's characteristic contrasts between joy and sorrow. Indeed, Calvero's heart attack occurs at the close of his act with Buster Keaton, a comedy sketch involving two musicians which ranks with the best of Chaplin's work in silent films. *Limelight*, however, relies more heavily on dialogue to tell its story than any of Chaplin's previous films, a fact which drew some unfavorable criticism at the time. *Monsieur Verdoux*, made five years earlier, had also been criticized for this reason, and *Monsieur Verdoux* contains far more visual humor than *Limelight*.

Chaplin uses the dialogue in the film primarily to express his philosophy of living, and the film becomes a very personal statement by an artist who had gained fame through silence. The scenes in which Calvero argues with Terry over the value of life present Chaplin with an opportunity to express verbally the determination and optimism which the Tramp had symbolized in his silent films.

And just as the Tramp had grown out of aspects of Chaplin's own personality and childhood, so Calvero represents elements of his later years. Although Chaplin was not destitute and forgotten like Calvero, he had been harshly criticized on both professional and personal levels in the years preceding *Limelight*, and the film's story of a once-loved clown whose public has turned away from him is clearly close to Chaplin's own experience. His performance as Calvero is excellent, ranging from drunken clowning to deep humiliation and despair. In one memorable scene, he sits backstage, ignored by the others, as the lights of the theater go out one by one, leaving him alone in the darkness. The moment stands as an example of both Chaplin's skill as an actor, and his brilliance at capturing human emotions on film.

Claire Bloom brings a touching combination of sweetness and melancholy to the role of Terry. Her devotion to Calvero, despite the difference in their ages and her love for Neville, remains believable throughout the film. Sydney Chaplin is also effective as Neville, although his part is not a large one and leaves him little to work with. Buster Keaton, in his brief scenes with Chaplin, is truly remarkable. It is a rare treat to watch these two great comedians perform together.

Chaplin's influence is felt in every area of the film. Not only did he produce, direct, and star in *Limelight*, he wrote the screenplay, composed the music, and choreographed the ballet sequences as well. The film is also somewhat of a family gathering for Chaplin. In addition to the performance by his son Sydney as Neville, the film contains appearances by Sydney's brother, Charles, Jr., as a clown in the ballet; Chaplin's half-brother, Wheeler Dryden, as the doctor who treats Terry; and Geraldine, Michael, and Josephine Chaplin, the oldest of Chaplin's eight children by Oona O'Neill, as street urchins in the film's opening scene. The film's theme of youth and old age drawing strength from each other is also a direct reflection of Chaplin's own happy marriage to Oona.

Limelight was made during a very difficult period in Chaplin's career. He had been accused of having Communist sympathies during the McCarthy period in the late 1940's, and he left the United States to live in Switzerland several months after the film's release. The American Legion called for a boycott of *Limelight* when the film opened, and as a result, it was never seen in several parts of the country, although the film's theme song became quite popular. The film was not shown in Los Angeles, which prevented it from qualifying for Academy Award nominations. In 1972, when Chaplin returned to Hollywood after twenty years in exile to receive a special Oscar, the film was finally released and Chaplin's music was nominated for, and won, the Academy Award for Best Original Motion Picture Score. The film's story of Calvero's return to the limelight had ended happily for Chaplin himself.

Janet E. Lorenz

LITTLE BIG MAN

Released: 1970
Production: Stuart Millar for National General
Direction: Arthur Penn
Screenplay: Calder Willingham; based on the novel of the same name by Thomas Berger
Cinematography: Harry Stradling, Jr.
Editing: Dede Allen
Running time: 150 minutes

Principal characters:

Jack Crabb	Dustin Hoffman
Mrs. Pendrake	Faye Dunaway
Allardyce T. Merriwhether	Martin Balsam
General Custer	Richard Mulligan
Old Lodge Skins	Chief Dan George
Wild Bill Hickok	Jeff Corey
Sunshine	Amy Eccles
Caroline	Carole Androsky
Historian	William Hickey
Reverend Silas Pendrake	Thayer David

Heroes are important to Americans, and their legends are sacred. However, Americans have sometimes made heroes out of men and women who did not deserve it. *Little Big Man* is a revisionist Western in that it attempts to correct the legend surrounding George Armstrong Custer and his defeat at the hands of Indians at the Little Bighorn. The man chosen to provide the truth is Jack Crabb (Dustin Hoffman), the only remaining survivor of Custer's last stand. As the film begins, a writer has come in search of the "inside story" from Jack. Jack is very old, but his memory is clear and sharp. Warning the man that what he is about to tell might surprise him, Jack recounts the following story.

As children, he and his sister, Caroline (Carole Androsky), are left orphans by an Indian attack upon the wagon train in which they are traveling. Discovered by a party of Cheyenne Indians, they are brought to their village to await the doom they believe is coming. However, nothing happens, and in fact they are treated quite well. Nevertheless, Jack's sister is convinced that she will be raped, and seeing an opportunity to escape, she leaves Jack to face the consequences. Jack is adopted by a warrior and reared as a son. He is schooled in Indian customs and learns the Indian way of thinking. As he grows to manhood, he becomes a warrior and is given the name "Little Big Man" because, although small of stature, he is strong of heart. Nevertheless, when confronted by a soldier during a small skirmish, Jack disavows his Indian upbringing, pleads his case as a white man, and leaves the tribe.

Although returned to white society, he is considered contaminated and sent to live with a strict religious man (Thayer David) and his wife (Faye Dunaway). Once there, he is taught to be God-fearing and encouraged to adopt the values of white society. However, he quickly learns that a white man seldom does what he says.

Jack leaves his new family after the wife attempts to seduce him and takes up with a traveling medicine man (Martin Balsam), only to be tarred and feathered by some irate citizens who have discovered the true ingedients of their medicine. He discovers that the leader of the citizens' group is his sister, and he goes to live with her. Through her tutelage, Jack discovers that he has an uncanny ability with guns. Thus, he dresses as a gunfighter and sets out to live the life of one. In the process, he meets Wild Bill Hickok (Jeff Corey), who demonstrates the more unpleasant aspects of being a gunman.

Next, Jack becomes a businessman and marries, only to go bankrupt and have his wife carried away by Indians. Eventually, Jack returns to the Indian way of life and seems to find his niche. He marries again, has a son, and takes up with his wife's sisters. All goes well until one day the 7th Cavalry under General Custer (Richard Mulligan) comes and slaughters much of the village including Jack's wife and child. Few survive, but Jack and his grandfather (Chief Dan George) escape.

Surprisingly, Jack once again returns to the world of the white man. He becomes a drunk and is about to commit suicide when he sees the 7th Cavalry pass by. Knowing what he must do, Jack gets a job as a mule skinner with the cavalry in order that he might kill Custer. However, when the opportunity arises, Jack discovers that he cannot murder a man in cold blood—not even one like Custer; but for his attempted act, he is sentenced to death. Custer decides instead to use Jack as a barometer in dealing with the Indians. He assumes that he can depend on Jack to provide him with bad advice, so determines to do the opposite of what Jack says. Thus, when Jack tells him the Indians are waiting for him in the valley, Custer believes they are somewhere else, and proceeds into the valley of the Little Big Horn. Going into the valley, he discovers that Jack was telling the truth, and he is defeated. Jack, who has also been dragged into the valley with the 7th Cavalry, is spared by an Indian whose life he once saved.

Discovering the truth to be a little too harmful, the writer decides not to write the story, thus preserving the legend of Custer as a hero.

Jack Crabb is never really characterized as a hero. He is more a spectator than a protagonist, but really not much of either. He does not cause things to happen—events occur around him. He tries various Western life-styles but none suit him. The only peace he really finds is with the Indians, but they are destroyed, leaving him an orphan again. He is ultimately a loner. Everyone who comes in touch with him is destroyed.

While not a hero, however, he is not a very perceptive spectator either. He is lied to, cheated, and fooled time and again. When the reality of his gullibility finally dawns on him, it is too late; cynicism leads to despair, and it is only through revenge that his life takes on meaning.

Nevertheless, Jack remains a likable character because of Dustin Hoffman's performance. He instills in his character a boyish vulnerability exposed to an adult world; he seems out of place wherever he goes. His presence serves as a catalyst, seeming to cause any corruptive element in his vicinity to become active. Evil, cruelty, hypocrisy, and every other negative aspect of humanity seem to thrive when he is around.

The only sympathetic characters are the Indians, who are characterized as rather childlike creatures. Through Jack's grandfather, we learn Indian philosophy and Indian ways; and after Jack's experience with the white man's ways, they appear very attractive. The film is ultimately pro-Indian. Indians are presented as possessing many desirable qualities unknown to most white men; they are more tolerant and understanding (as seen in their acceptance of a homosexual member of the tribe) and less jealous (as demonstrated by Jack's Indian wife, who shares him with her sisters). In many ways the Indians are like Jack. At the beginning of the film they are naïve, fighting soldiers' guns with sticks. However, by the end of the film, they have learned to protect themselves.

General Custer, who is portrayed to be nothing more than a pompous buffoon out to secure his political fortunes, is developed as little more than a caricature. His inevitable defeat is greeted by the cheers of audiences who have been worked into a frenzy by the depiction of atrocities performed by the 7th Cavalry. Unlike earlier film characterizations of George Armstrong Custer, notably by Erroll Flynn in *They Died with Their Boots On* (1941) and Philip Carey in *The Great Sioux Massacre* (1965), Mulligan's interpretation is not heroic by any stretch of the imagination. The film's director, Arthur Penn, has taken great care to leave us with a cold, harsh look at a man formerly thought of as a great American hero.

Some have viewed *Little Big Man* as simply another liberal lament for the Indian. However, the film is more than merely an exercise in "bleeding heart" cinema; it provides an alternate view of the traditional Western hero. Furthermore, it suggests that we need to reevaluate many of the Western myths with which we have grown up, and open our minds to other interpretations of the history of the West.

James J. Desmarais

THE LITTLE FOXES

Released: 1941
Production: Samuel Goldwyn for RKO/Radio
Direction: William Wyler
Screenplay: Lillian Hellman, with additional scenes and dialogue by Dorothy Parker, Alan Campbell, and Arthur Kober; based on the play of the same name by Lillian Hellman
Cinematography: Gregg Toland
Editing: Daniel Mandell
Running time: 115 minutes

> *Principal characters:*
> Regina Giddens .... Bette Davis
> Horace Giddens .... Herbert Marshall
> Alexandra Giddens .... Teresa Wright
> David Hewitt .... Richard Carlson
> Ben Hubbard .... Charles Dingle
> Oscar Hubbard .... Carl Benton Reid
> Leo Hubbard .... Dan Duryea
> Birdie Hubbard .... Patricia Collinge

Lillian Hellman's *The Little Foxes* concerns the Hubbard clan, a ruthless, upwardly mobile family who play out their drama against a backdrop of the South in transition. Crushed by the terrors of reconstruction, the romanticism of the old South gave way to the vitality of industrialism, bringing with it the foxes: the scrappers, the moneymakers. They have nothing but contempt for the old Southern aristocracy whose land and position they covet but whose values they ridicule. The Hubbards have married into this aristocracy because it suits their purposes, but they do not pretend to membership. They revel in their middle-class status.

The leader of the family is the eldest brother Ben. Charles Dingle repeats his stage role, full of joviality, openly proclaiming himself "a plain man, and plain spoken," while hatching devious plots to increase the wealth of the family business and maintain his position as leader. Carl Benton Reid is brilliant as Oscar, the younger brother who has married into the landed gentry at Ben's direction and still follows his lead, vainly attempting to match his ruthlessness and secure a position for his son, Leo. Dan Duryea's performance as Leo is masterful. In his high-pitched whine, he fawns on his uncle Ben's every pronouncement; currying favor on all sides he still manages to put his foot in his mouth every time he opens it. He is constantly curbed by his uncle, whose barbs are explained and softened by his nervous father.

Regina Giddens represents the female of this species. Handsome and clever, she is a match for Ben, fully as ruthless and yet more shrewd. Bette Davis plays her with a reptilian grace that both fascinates and repels. Davis' Academy Award nomination was well deserved, and only the popularity of Alfred Hitchcock's *Suspicion* secured the Best Actress award for Joan Fontaine. Regina's daughter Alexandra seems a role tailor-made for Teresa Wright. She is young and innocent, apparently having no part of the Hubbards in her. We see her with her alcoholic Aunt Birdie (Patricia Collinge), who is gay and charming when she is away from the deliberate cruelties of her husband, Oscar. In the nervous gestures and breathless conversation of her aunt, Alexandra begins to see what might become of her if she remains under the sway of her mother.

The family gathers to entertain Mr. Marshall, a prominent Chicago businessman who plans to build a local cotton gin in partnership with the Hubbards. In an after-dinner scene we observe the Hubbard character. As Birdie and Alexandra play a piano duet Oscar watches his possession perform, Leo surreptitiously catches flies, and Ben tries to interrupt the recital, relentlessly pursuing Marshall with business conversation as the visitor tries to follow the music. Regina silences Ben, stares Leo into dutiful attention, and the recital concludes. She then turns her sexual charms on a receptive Marshall. Marshall asks her to Chicago in an invitation that has obvious sexual overtones. As he leaves, Regina exults to Birdie, "There'll be millions, Birdie, millions." Middle-class riches are not enough for Regina; she craves great wealth and Chicago society.

But Ben puts a damper on her excitement by reminding her that while he and Oscar have put up their third of the money for partnership, Regina's absent banker husband has not made a final commitment. If she does not come up with the cash, she will be cut out of the profits. The Hubbards cannot allow family sentiment to interfere with business.

Regina's husband, Horace (Herbert Marshall), is a heart patient in Johns Hopkins Hospital. Regina determines to send her daughter to fetch him home whether he is well or not, and Alexandra leaves for Baltimore. In the scene at the train station we see that *The Little Foxes* is more successful than most plays in moving offstage. While still relying principally on the playwright's fabrication of character and dialogue, the film manages to re-create the flavor of New Orleans at the turn of the century.

Horace returns home, an ill man, only to be badgered by his wife. In their exchanges we see that he cannot win. Not only his illness but also his character prevent him from besting Regina. He has the wistful despair of the weak aristocrat. He knows what he hates, but lacks the strength of will necessary to fight it. Even his love for his daughter has no vitality; it is genuine but so tinged with his tragic sense of life that it is she who protects and cares for him.

Hellman and her screenplay collaborators, Dorothy Parker and Alan Campbell, made an invaluable addition to the film when they added a character not in the play, David Hewitt (Richard Carlson), a crusading reporter who loves Alexandra. His character provides welcome and necessary relief from the unrelenting despair of Birdie and Horace while competing with the Hubbards in vitality and zest for life. However, in contrast to the Hubbards, David Hewitt's attitude is joyful and energetic, his nature generous. Without Hewitt, Alexandra's character is faced with a choice between the futility of Horace and Birdie and the grasping nature of the Hubbards.

It is in conversation rather than in action that the natures of these characters are revealed. Possibly no American writer can equal Hellman's gift for dialogue. Her speeches are not epigrammatic yet the dialogue of her characters dances along in brilliant counterpoint while remaining grittily realistic. She has a clarity and coherence unsurpassed in American theater.

Horace refuses to invest in the ginning mill. He knows that, like all the Hubbard enterprises, it will become a sweatshop exploiting black labor. The investment deadline approaches and Ben, not wanting any interest in the venture to fall outside the family, convinces Leo, an employee at Horace's bank, to steal negotiable bonds from Horace's strongbox to insure financing for the mill. Regina discovers the theft and plans to blackmail Ben and Oscar into giving her a share of the business. But Horace thwarts her plan by telling Regina that he gave the securities to Leo in order to prevent her from sharing in the mill profits. In a controlled fury Regina turns on him, "I don't hate you. I have only contempt for you. I've always had." She taunts him into a heart attack, and when his shaking hands drop his heart medicine, she watches in silence as he begs her to get the bottle. Horrified at her expression, he tries to rise from his wheelchair and reaches the stairs, gasping. Fascinated, lips compressed in furious concentration, Regina wills him to die. When he collapses she waits a moment and then springs into action calling for help.

Horace on his deathbed uses his last breath to comfort his daughter and urge her to leave with David Hewitt, while downstairs Regina confronts her brothers with Leo's theft and demands seventy-five percent of the mill. They bitterly agree, but Ben suggests that Regina might well be charged with murder. She smiles and defies him to prove it. Alexandra overhears this exchange and in spirited defiance damns them all and vows to leave. She tells her mother,

> Addie said there were people who ate the earth and other people who stood around and watched them do it. And just now Uncle Ben said the same thing. . . . Well, tell him from me, Mama, I'm not going to stand around and watch you do it. I'll be fighting as hard as he'll be fighting, someplace else.

Alexandra leaves, crossing the square in the rain to meet David, while Regina watches from an upstairs window, coldly composed, expressionless, satisfied to remain in the web of her own device.

Although *The Little Foxes* received eight Academy Award nominations, it failed to win in any category. However, Teresa Wright did win the Oscar for Best Supporting Actress for her performance that year in *Mrs. Miniver*. Admittedly, it was a very stiff year in Oscar competition. *Sergeant York*, *How Green Was My Valley*, *Citizen Kane*, *The Maltese Falcon*, and *Suspicion* were only a few of the films in contention. However, more importantly, *The Little Foxes* presented a view of the middle class that was popular with only a minority of the artistic establishment. If Ben, Oscar, and Regina had been peculiar only to their story, the film might have been more successful. But Ben proclaims, "There are hundreds of Hubbards sitting in rooms like this, throughout the country. All their names aren't Hubbard, but they are all Hubbards and they will own this country someday." It is this ugly, unrelieved view of the much maligned merchant class that makes *The Little Foxes* so coldly admired.

Cheryl Karnes

LITTLE WOMEN

Released: 1933
Production: Merian C. Cooper for RKO/Radio
Direction: George Cukor
Screenplay: Sarah Y. Mason and Victor Heerman (AA); based on the novel of the same name by Louisa May Alcott
Cinematography: Henry W. Gerrard
Editing: Jack Kitchin
Running time: 115 minutes

Principal characters:
Jo	Katharine Hepburn
Amy	Joan Bennett
Professor Fritz Bhaor	Paul Lukas
Meg	Frances Dee
Beth	Jean Parker
Laurie	Douglass Montgomery
Marmee	Spring Byington
Aunt March	Edna May Oliver
Brooke	John Davis Lodge
Mr. Laurence	Henry Stephenson

The fifty-year association of Katharine Hepburn and director George Cukor has produced an elegant and impressive body of work. Their ten films together extend from Hepburn's cinematic debut in *A Bill of Divorcement* (1932) to her latest *The Corn Is Green* (1979). Cukor has been able to catch this great star at crucial junctures of her career—her comeback in *The Philadelphia Story* (1940), maturity in *Adam's Rib* (1949), and old age in *Love Among the Ruins* (1975). In the same manner, *Little Women* is for both Hepburn and Cukor a masterpiece of their youth; its high spirits are the projection of filmmakers just reaching the height of their powers.

Little Women fully captures the joy and feeling of the classic 1868 novel by Louisa May Alcott, which parallel's Alcott's own family experiences on the home front during the Civil War. The story's episodic structure follows the development of the March family of Marmee (Spring Byington) and her four daughters, who are always cheerful and quick to help those less fortunate than themselves. The idyllic innocence of youth supplies much of the film's warmth, but sadly, this charm seems to slip away as the girls mature. These idealized glimpses of a cheerful family life surviving amid severe external hardships held a special significance to filmgoers of the Depression, just as they had for post-Civil War readers.

Katharine Hepburn plays Jo March, the imaginative and independent daughter who is the center of the film. In her fourth film role, Hepburn projects a vibrancy that is no doubt derived in part from the closeness of her character's situation to Hepburn's own New England upbringing. Cukor said that she was born to play the role, and in it, Hepburn captures Jo's tomboy qualities and also delicately projects the beauty and intellect of Jo as a woman and budding writer. Following directly upon her Academy Award-Winning performance in *Morning Glory* (1933), *Little Women* won Hepburn the Cannes Film Festival best actress award.

The plot of *Little Women* chronicles the maturation of the four March sisters in Massachusetts during the Civil War. While their father is at war, their mother, Marmee, holds the family together through her inspirational example of doing good deeds. The spirited Jo entertains her sisters with her imagination, helping them to weather the hardships of genteel poverty; but as the girls mature, they go their separate ways to find romance. Bemoaning this loss of innocence, Jo flees to New York, where she meets kindly but provincial Professor Bhaor (Paul Lukas), who tries to settle her down. Sisters Amy (Joan Bennett) and Meg (Frances Dee) find husbands, but Beth (Jean Parker) dies, and Jo, transformed by this event, comes to accept her new life and decides finally to marry the professor.

Little Women presents a gallery of female characters: Jo's boisterousness is complemented by Meg's straight romanticism, Amy's humorous concern with status, and Beth's quiet goodness. Supervising the little women is Marmee, even-tempered through all adversity, and crotchety Aunt March (Edna Mae Oliver), whose complaints conceal an inner strength that makes her a spiritual partner to Jo. Although the March household appears to be a matriarchy, it is the spirit of the absent father that is evoked as the basis for all activity. The men live next door, notably the playful Laurie (Douglass Montgomery), who is a match for Jo in physical exuberance and love of life, and the handsome Brooke (John Davis Lodge). In New York, Professor Bhaor appears sober, shy, and very much a man of the old world and older generation. It is ironic that the energetic Jo should end up with the demure Bhaor, while her pretentious sister Amy marries the boy next door, Laurie.

The performances in *Little Women* are felicitous matches of talent to role. A very young Joan Bennett is superb as Amy, ever scheming for the good life; Douglass Montgomery has the boundless youthful energy necessary for Laurie; and Frances Dee's beauty complements John Lodge's handsomeness. Edna May Oliver, like Hepburn, was born to play the role of the gruff but lovable Aunt March, while Paul Lukas portrays well the difficult role of Professor Bhaor.

Director George Cukor has had a long career in Hollywood. Imported from the Broadway stage by Paramount during the rush to enlist talent to make talking pictures, he began as a dialogue director, quickly advancing to full director status with *Tarnished Lady* (1931), starring Tallulah Bankhead. At RKO, Cukor worked with David O. Selznick on several projects, an association which reached its apogee with *Little Women*, and which later fell apart over the epic problems posed by *Gone with the Wind* (1939). In 1932 and 1933 at RKO, Cukor directed three vehicles for Constance Bennett and Hepburn's first film, *A Bill of Divorcement*, while completing the all-star film version of *Dinner at Eight* at M-G-M. Cukor followed *Little Women* with a series of literary adaptations at M-G-M, beginning with *David Copperfield* (1935).

The struggle of an independent, imaginative woman against the social roles and structures imposed on a female has been a central theme in other Cukor films, such as *Holiday* (1938), *Adam's Rib*, and *Bhowani Junction* (1956). An oft-mentioned Cukorian "touch" is the use of the theater and of theatricality. For example, a climactic moment during the youth of the little women is the performance of Jo's play, "The Witch's Curse," with her in both male roles, hero and villain. This exploration of the male side of the character portrayed by Hepburn prefigures the role of transvestism in *Sylvia Scarlett* (1935), as well as the Hepburn characters who take on male roles in *Adam's Rib* and *Pat and Mike* (1952).

Little Women focuses some attention on the social functions of an earlier age which are depicted in terms of their effects upon the private Jo. Jo's play, with siblings as cast and relatives for audience, places her as the star playing all of the male roles—Roderigo and Black Hugo—as well as both playwright and director. The camera captures it all with a long take of the backstage transformation of Hepburn as Jo, putting on the voice, manner, and goatee of Black Hugo with obvious glee. Later, at a social dance at the Laurence's, we again glimpse Jo in a private moment as she dances by herself in the hall, nervously refusing to mix with ordinary boys. Finally, at the marriage of Meg and Brooke, Jo is isolated from the wedding festivities, poignantly framed by the fence, a nostalgic image of a lost world of innocence frozen for a moment before slipping away.

The adult identity that each girl assumes is distinctly tamer in nature than that which each manifests earlier. Desire has been channeled into romance and legitimized through marriage. The film ends with Jo accepting the marriage proposal of Professor Bhaor; but this is not the unambiguously happy final embrace of many Hollywood romances. The earlier Jo, though headstrong, still had a radiant life force; by comparison, her proposed new life as the wife of this shy older man appears distinctly dull.

Little Women boasts a line-up of creative producers impressive even amid the richness of Hollywood's golden age. The executive producer was Merian C. Cooper, who also in 1933 produced and directed *King Kong*. He later produced a striking series of films with John Ford, including *The Quiet Man* (1952) and *The Searchers* (1956). Although only his associate, Kenneth MacGowan, gets screen credit, the legendary David O. Selznick prepared the film as producer, and his influence is felt throughout, particularly in the film's attention to period atmosphere and detail. Cukor has said that he felt *Little Women* was one of Selznick's forerunners to *Gone with the Wind*, which Cukor himself began as director. The meticulous production accounted in part for the film's great success in 1933, which included Academy Award nominations for Best Picture, Best Direction, and Best Screenplay Adaptation, winning in the latter category.

The award-winning script by the wife and husband team of Sarah Y. Mason and Victor Heerman is an unconventional narrative. Highly episodic, the film focuses on the characters without slavishly following a plot. Dialogue is expressively employed for characterization—from Jo's expletives ("Christopher Columbus!") to Amy's mispronunciations. The maturation of the girls is presented within a seasonal motif that adds richness to every scene. The story of *Little Women* is a classic for young readers, and has provided material for several film versions, including a 1919 silent with Dorothy Bernard and a 1949 M-G-M production, as well as a recent television series.

Jonathan Kuntz

THE LITTLEST REBEL

Released: 1935
Production: Darryl F. Zanuck for Twentieth Century-Fox
Direction: David Butler
Screenplay: Edwin Burke; based on the play of the same name by Edward Peple
Cinematography: John F. Seitz
Editing: Irene Morra
Running time: 73 minutes

> *Principal characters:*
> Virgie Cary .... Shirley Temple
> Captain Herbert Cary ....John Boles
> Colonel Morrison .... Jack Holt
> Mrs. Cary .... Karen Morley
> Uncle Billy .... Bill Robinson

During her childhood career, Shirley Temple starred in a string of feature films which made her contract studio, Twentieth Century-Fox, some thirty million dollars in box-office receipts. When awarded a miniature Oscar statuette during the 1934 Academy Awards ceremony, Shirley was told that she was the loveliest Christmas present that Santa Claus had ever given to the world; and such shameless sentimentality was the stuff of which her films were made. Yet, despite their many clichéd moments, the films boast an undeniable quality that owes everything to Shirley Temple's very presence. Her considerable dancing talents and her ability to dominate scenes allowed her to steal the spotlight away from costars such as Lionel Barrymore, Alice Faye, Victor McLaglen, Carole Lombard, Randolph Scott, and Robert Young. However, of all her many directors, only John Ford went on to be known as an *auteur*. In the light of this, and the fact that she turned out a large number of films in a relatively short period—some twenty-four titles during a six-year span—the overall quality of Shirley Temple's film work is amazingly good.

Shirley Temple's trademarks were dimples, curls—according to press reports of the day there were fifty-five of them—and song and dance. While she performed many famous musical moments (notably, "On the Good Ship Lollipop" from 1934's *Bright Eyes* and "Animal Crackers in My Soup" from 1935's *Curly Top*), it was in the Civil War tale, *The Littlest Rebel*, that she best exhibited her range of abilities.

Perhaps Hollywood's most famous child star, she first garnered industry attention when she literally stole the show in the grandstanding *Stand Up and Cheer*, released in 1934 as a tonic to lift Depression-era spirits. The film was a thinly disguised revue show, a series of flag-waving musical and comedy routines brought together by a flimsy story line which detailed the appointment of a Secretary of Amusement so that laughter and self-confidence could be restored in America. When viewed today, the film appears to be an enjoyable bit of celluloid kitsch amplified by a grand finale in which American workers from all walks of life come together in song and unity. However, it was the diminutive six-year-old Shirley, wearing a white baby-doll dress with red polka-dots, who captivated audiences with her performance of "Baby Take a Bow," and that onscreen moment helped to set the Shirley Temple phenomenon in motion.

The phenomenon was propelled by her screen image: usually that of a sweet, saucy tot who enjoyed assuming the role of a little homemaker and who expertly crooned heart-warming lyrics. In many ways, the love affair spawned in the 1930's continues today, for Shirley Temple, the child star, retains a sturdy position within popular American culture. Early merchandising efforts—ranging from dolls, paper dolls, and glassware to bars of soap shaped like Shirley—have become valued collector's pieces, and reissues of the Shirley Temple doll are available for each new generation. More important, however, are the Shirley Temple films, which have become television staples, serving to introduce legions of young viewers to Shirley and thus keeping her eternally young in the eyes of each generation. Characteristically, the Shirley Temple film story line, loosely entwined around a particular time and setting, proceeds similarly: Shirley, cast as either an orphan or the child of a single and troubled parent, faces a slender string of obstacles; and after managing to bring happiness into the lives of those around her, usually by singing and dancing, she is reunited with her home and family.

In keeping with such a formula, *The Littlest Rebel* finds Shirley with a sick, dying mother and a father who must go off to war. Aside from Shirley's obligatory near-orphan status and a saccharine ending, however, *The Littlest Rebel* probably ranks as her most effective film, succeeding as a dramatic Civil War tale in addition to serving as a vehicle for her talents. Unlike many of her films, in which a backdrop conveniently showcased Shirley's talents, the Civil War setting is inherent to the story line and dramatic theme of *The Littlest Rebel*. (In contrast, the film *Stowaway* (1936) utilizes a Chinese backdrop—Shirley is the orphaned daughter of murdered missionaries—thus allowing Shirley to speak some Chinese, and even to perform on various Chinese musical instruments.)

As a film for young viewers, *The Littlest Rebel* is particularly engrossing because its story line depicts a child's frustration and confusion over war. In addition to its dramatic though thin plot, the film includes several musical numbers which are appropriate accompaniments for the particular period detailed. Singing to John Boles, cast as her father, Shirley croons a lilting "Believe Me, If All Those Endearing Young Charms." And with dancer Bill Robinson, she teams for a lively "Polly-Wolly-Doodle"; their song-and-dance routines also provided highlights for several other Shirley Temple films. (Perhaps ranking as their best song-and-dance number is the enchanting "I Love to Walk in the Rain," featured in the film *Just Around the Corner*, 1938.)

In the opening scenes of *The Littlest Rebel*, the butler, Uncle Billy (Bill Robinson) performs an energetic tap dance for the youngsters attending an extravagant birthday party for Virgie Cary (Shirley Temple). The production immediately establishes the aura of an engaging period piece aimed at young audiences. The assembled youngsters are all dressed formally and are stern-faced as they perform a serious minuet; they are all mimicking the adults in their lives. It is also the adults who burst their daydreams, for war has been declared, and the party is quickly broken up by anxious parents who usher their children out. Virgie's excited protests cannot halt them. In tears, she seeks consolation from her father, Captain Herbert Cary (John Bolls). Telling her of the war, he urges her to be a "brave soldier" and also asks her to care for her ill mother (Karen Morley). The announcement of war, however, cannot completely crush a child's world and with her father off fighting, Virgie returns to her interest and playmates. She merges her playtime with the issues of the day by commanding her own "troops," a rag-tag group of black youngsters at the plantation; these scenes, peppered by supposed black dialect and early black stereotypes, definitely dates the film.

For the most part, however, *The Littlest Rebel* is an effective blend of story line, suspense, and setting. In one of Shirley's most famous scenes, she dons blackface and bandana in order to hide her curls, hoping to elude marauding Union soldiers. Attempting to hide inside a wall panel, she is discovered when one of the soldiers spies a bit of her skirt as it protrudes from the wall. He opens the panel, finding an at first terrified, and later spunky, Virgie. The encounter between the two is interrupted by a kindly Union colonel (Jack Holt), who is charmed by the captivating child. Virgie, who goes on to enchant the regiment, has overcome her fears, so much that when her father becomes a prisoner of war, she journeys to President Lincoln to plead her case. Seated on Lincoln's lap, she brushes away tears while munching on apple slices handed to her by the President. Not surprisingly, by film's end, Virgie is reunited with her father.

Although *The Littlest Rebel* resorts to tampering with history during its final moments, it nevertheless remains a concise drama. Woven especially for children, it is rich in atmosphere, particularly in such scenes as the dramatic nighttime chase by Union soldiers. Shirley's performance stands as her most sincere dramatic outing. It has also been noted that *The Littlest Rebel* contains Shirley's only blackface scene. Director David Butler had previously worked with Shirley in *The Little Colonel* (1935). Because of their titles and Southern flavors, the two projects are frequently confused, but *The Little Colonel* is first and foremost a vehicle for Shirley; in fact, its story line goes no further than a domestic squabble.

Critically, *The Littlest Rebel* ranks as one of Shirley Temple's best productions. It should be pointed out however, that she has had countless popular film moments. *Heidi* (1937) is a particularly delightful experience for children. Loosely based on the Johanna Spyri novel, it is a sentimental tearjerker in which Heidi melts the heart of her angry and misunderstood grandfather (Jean Hersholt, in a memorable performance) and even encourages a crippled girl to try to walk (of course, the girl succeeds). The film includes a Dutch dance dream sequence, "In Our Little Wooden Shoes."

Captain January (1936, also directed by David Butler), in which Shirley, orphaned in a shipwreck, is adopted by a lighthouse keeper, also contains an exceptional song-and-dance sequence. "At the Codfish Ball" pairs Shirley and lanky Buddy Ebsen; the two sashay in a marvel of dance steps down a country village street, as Shirely sings the nautical tune. *Wee Willie Winkie* (1937), based on Rudyard Kipling's classic, placed Shirley in the prestigious directorial company of John Ford, and the result was a fine adventure picture for children. Ford later directed a more grown-up Shirley Temple in *Fort Apache* (1948).

Although Shirley Temple retired from show business following work in television—including *The Shirley Temple Storybook*—during the 1950's, she still frequently garners the public spotlight as Shirley Temple Black, politician and former United States ambassador.

Pat H. Broeske

THE LONELINESS OF THE LONG DISTANCE RUNNER

Released: 1962
Production: Tony Richardson for Woodfall Films and Bryanston-Seven Arts
  Productions; released by Continental
Direction: Tony Richardson
Screenplay: Alan Sillitoe; based on his short story of the same name
Cinematography: Walter Lassally
Editing: Antony Gibbs
Running time: 104 minutes

Principal characters:
Colin Smith	Tom Courtenay
Mrs. Smith	Avis Bunnage
The Governor	Michael Redgrave
Mike	James Bolam
Dr. Brown	Alec McCowen
Audrey	Topsy Jane
Gladys	Julia Foster
Ronalds	John Bull

The Loneliness of the Long Distance Runner is part of the short renaissance of British cinema lasting from 1959 through 1963, when new breeds of directors and actors were working on new kinds of films. The emphasis on their films was on the lives of the working class in England, and doors were opened into rooms that had never before been shown on the screen. In Tony Richardson's stark, unrelenting look at a boy on the bottom of the social heap, the hero is not a victim of his society as are other young men in similar films. He is instead a true rebel, and his choices are all his own.

Colin Smith (Tom Courtenay), a Borstal boy when the film begins, grew up in a world that offered him nothing from his point of view. Instead of trying to better his chances to get ahead, he waged a personal war against the entire middle class. Colin turns to a life of crime not so much out of necessity, for he could get a job, but out of a deep distrust of and revulsion against the system. The film's fascination lies in Tom Courtenay's performance as Colin Smith. Tight-lipped and taut-faced, he seldom smiles, but when he does it is like a gift to the audience. His portrayal is so strong that he emerges a hero in spite of the fact that he is playing a very unlikable character. Director Tony Richardson chose mostly unknown actors for his film except for the commanding presence of Michael Redgrave as the Borstal governor; yet the cast seems to step out of the pages of Alan Sillitoe's story.

Sillitoe, well-known at the time for both the novel and the film *Saturday Night and Sunday Morning* (1961), adapted his own short story to the screen for Richardson. What emerged was one of the strongest English films ever made about the poor. The Establishment is drawn with a cold and relentless eye; nothing positive is said in its favor. Establishment members are either pompous fools or unfeeling brutes. Sillitoe's target is the entire English system, including prisons, penal reform, the police, public school education, and modern psychiatry. The heroes of the film are the next generation's criminals, and their answer to injustice is theft and rebellion. Colin Smith is representative of this kind of boy but he has one advantage over them. He can run. Running has always been a major part of Colin's life, and he tells the governor at one point that "Running's always been a big thing in our family, especially running from the police." Running is one of the film's central motifs; it is Colin's only way of getting back at society.

The film is a series of cross-cuts and flashbacks but the main action centers around Colin's life in Borstal. Caught breaking into a bakery with his friend Mike (James Bolam), he is sentenced to several years in Borstal, a correctional institution for young offenders. The governor of the institution is an ambitious and confident product of an English public school who is very anxious to move up the social ladder and win himself advancement. One sure way to do this is through athletics, so every year he schedules a series of games with a public school. He immediately spots Colin's enormous talent for running and grants him special privileges for running in the competition. Colin's work load is lightened so that he can train, and much of the film takes place on the running fields in the sharp, cold mornings as Colin works out. As he runs, he lets his thoughts wander, and the audience learns the circumstances that led him to Borstal.

Colin reflects on his life in the shabby prefabricated house where his father recently died of cancer after a life of sweat and squalor for nine pounds a week. His mother (Avis Bunnage) tried to escape her desperate life by going out with her "fancy man." The family receives a check for five hundred pounds in compensation for Colin's father's death, but it is quickly spent on cheap furniture, some toys for the younger children, a color television, and a bed for Mrs. Smith and her lover. Colin takes enough of the sudden windfall to pay for a quick weekend at Skegness with his girl friend Audrey (Topsy Jane), complete with a first-class hotel and a third-class train ride home. That weekend stands out in Colin's mind as his only real period of happiness. There he forgot his bitterness long enough to soften and relax. Soon the money is spent, however, and Colin turns to theft. Some stolen pound notes from the bakery robbery are spotted by a detective who sees them falling from the drain pipe in which they were hidden. As he runs, Colin's thoughts turn back to his life in Borstal, and he decides he must not let his enemies get the best of him, even in his present position.

The governor places all his hopes for the big race in Colin, and, when the day of the sports event arrives, he is confident that the boy will win. The runners start, and soon Colin is well in the lead, having already passed the public school favorite. Then, within earshot of the cheers of victory, Colin remembers the life that brought him here: the tough smugness of the governor, his father's hard life, and the brutality of the system which is trying to mold him into its pattern. He suddenly stops running and lets the public school boy win the race, savoring the governor's fury. By losing, he has taken his revenge on them all.

Tom Courtenay makes it clear by his performance that Colin's decision to lose the race was arrived at while he was running and was not one of pre-meditation. This gives the Borstal boy an added element of heroism by showing that for a time he *was* tempted by the glory promised by the governor. By losing the race, Colin exercises free choice and retains some control of his own life, even in so dwarfed an environment as a prison.

Besides Courtenay's top-notch performance, the film contains several other first-rate players. Comedienne Avis Bunnage plays Colin's slutty mother, and sturdy British character actors James Bolam and Alec McCowen play in smaller parts. The cinematography of Walter Lassally is lyrical and moody in its treatment of early morning runs through lonely woods. The critics admired the film for its originality and compassion although some detected a note of pretentiousness in Richardson's direction.

After this film, Courtenay went on to a successful career in British film and theater. Richardson, one of the leading figures of the British "new wave," changed direction after *The Loneliness of the Long Distance Runner*. After making a series of films dealing with the working class, including *Look Back in Anger* (1959) and *A Taste of Honey* (1962), in 1963 he made *Tom Jones*, one of the runaway British hits of the 1960's. This farcical, costumed historical work was far removed from the contemporary provincial scene of his earlier pictures.

Joan Cohen